Evenings

with

the

Orchestra

Evenings with the Orchestra

———❧———

A Norton Companion
for Concertgoers

———❧———

D. Kern Holoman

W · W · Norton & Company
New York London

Printed in the United States of America.
The text of this book is composed in Garamond #3
with the display set in Lucian and Bernhard Modern.
Composition and manufacturing by The Maple-Vail Book
Manufacturing Group.
Book design by Guenet Abraham.
Drawings by Mark Oehlschlager

First Edition.

Library of Congress Cataloging in Publication Data

Holoman, D. Kern, 1947–
    Evenings with the orchestra : a Norton companion for con-
certgoers / D. Kern Holoman.
        p.   cm.
    Includes bibliographical references and index.
    1. Orchestral music—Analysis, appreciation. I. Title
MT125.H62   1992
784.2—dc20   91–3441

ISBN 0-393-02936-0
W. W. Norton & Company, Inc.
500 Fifth Avenue, New York, N.Y. 10110
W. W. Norton & Company, Ltd.
10 Coptic Street, London WC1A 1PU

1 2 3 4 5 6 7 8 9 0

Contents

PART III: SOME GREAT ORCHESTRAS AND THEIR CONDUCTORS

Foreword

Evenings with the Orchestra: A Norton Companion for Concertgoers began its life as a pamphlet for subscribers to the Sacramento Symphony Orchestra, the professional orchestra of the region where I live and work. My colleagues at the University of California, Davis, and I had for some time been writing the program notes as a service to the Symphony. We began in this deceptively difficult trade as rank neophytes and learned as we went along, growing more fluent month by month at saying what we meant in not-too-technical terms.

In conjunction with this project, and because I am a conductor as well as a writer, I found myself addressing countless preconcert assemblages of good people intent on learning more about composers and their works. Their questions about concertgoing were remarkably similar from group to group. One morning in the shower, after something of a confrontation the night before over how difficult music was to listen to and how inaccessible our annotations were, I conceived what seemed at the time the brilliant notion of packing everything you need to know about going to concerts into a short booklet.

The first *Handy-Guide,* as it was commonly known in 1983, proved to be seventy-six pages long, and people seemed to like it, especially the segment of the audience who still found themselves at the beginning of each new concert season uncomfortable about this or that aspect of the practice of concertgoing—uncomfortable, or possibly just bashful. Shamelessly, I mailed a copy to the "Transom of Claire Brook," at W. W. Norton, for Mrs. Brook had once written an engaging piece about how books get published, in the course of which she had described the "over-the-transom" method with little enthusiasm. Together we added to and subtracted from the original booklet to produce what you see before you, and we enjoyed our share of laughs along the way.

That, in one sense, is the point. Going to concerts is, after all, something to enjoy, not to be bashful, wary, or misinformed about. If a book helps, so much the better.

The list of pieces we elected to treat was assembled after a good deal of thought and following conversations with quite a number of music lovers. We checked the recent repertoires of several orchestras, consulted the annual list of works most often recorded in the now-defunct *Schwann Catalogue,* and kept our eyes on newspaper reviews and a variety of other indicators. We tried to target one hundred works for scrutiny here. I came up with 78, an associate provided 135, and then Mrs. Brook came along with a still meatier list. We settled on about 275 works, including clutches of concertos and overtures grouped together for some composers (Bach, Corelli, Handel, Mozart, and Rossini).

The original *Handy-Guide* was also an experiment in producing a book on a shoestring by relying on volunteer labor of all sorts. My students and friends, especially the members of the UC–Davis Symphony, earned, long ago, first place in the list of those I must now acknowledge: Cynthia Bates, Donna M. Di Grazia, and Scott Pfau; Helen Nutter, who prepared the graphics for that edition; and Daniel Stowe, who first drafted the glossary. The staff of the Sacramento Symphony welcomed my harebrained scheme from the first, and I thank them: David Wax, General Manager (now manager of the

Houston Symphony); Carter Nice, Music Director; and Alzada Forbes, Marketing Director (now proprietor of a bookshop called The Avid Reader). Nor would there have been a booklet at all without the subscribers and the members of the Sacramento Symphony Association and its allied support groups, who invited me to give all those preconcert lectures.

Jonathan Elkus, Joseph Kerman, Michael Steinberg, and Richard Swift read various versions of the manuscript and offered useful corrections of fact, editorial suggestions, and appropriate grumblings. Kevin Argys helped us think carefully about the repertoire we selected; Kristi Brown, an assistant editor of *19th-Century Music,* corrected the original pamphlet in preparation for the Norton edition; and Carlo Scibelli and Tracey Rudnick did much of the leg-work for the additions and revisions, while Paul Christopolus prepared the first drafts of some of the added material. Mrs. Brook kept me at it, in one wily way or another, whenever the spirit began to flag.

Any number of my students began their writing careers with Sacramento Symphony program notes that I have approvingly absorbed here, after disapprovingly overediting their original texts of years ago. To my colleagues on the UC–Davis music faculty, program annotators above and beyond the call of duty for five years, on whose work I have relied to prepare this volume, and, more significantly, on whose intellectual capacities I always rely, go my lasting and deep expressions of gratitude: Robert Bloch, Susan Erickson, David Nutter, Jerome Rosen, Richard Swift, and William Valente.

During the last year or so of the project, it was a particular pleasure to welcome two new associates, Darin Wilson and Brian Salter. Their appearance at my door with facts, figures, and prose, their bracing commitment to the goals of the book, and their mystical tendency to nudge and prod at the really critical junctures actually brought the final manuscript to fruition. For that I am as grateful as an author can ever be.

There were some interesting lessons to be learned from all this. *Evenings with the Orchestra* proved a fine opportunity to go back and learn a great deal of music we should already have known. Lots of music, even a great masterpiece or two, slips by even the most avid of listeners. We tend to be satisfied if we know some Beethoven and Mozart and Brahms, and, what is worse, we can be a shade snobbish about the also-rans. These works didn't make it into the repertoire for as long as most of them have been there without reason. Every warhorse, as it turns out, had some merit. To my surprise, I found that I liked nearly all the music you will read about here; being faced with the necessity of looking at each piece anew as I wrote about it rekindled my enthusiasm.

Evenings, and the writing that led up to it, has been for everybody involved a labor of love. It is fondly dedicated to the most important musicians of all, the paying public, without whom none of us would have jobs to begin with.

D.K.H.
PARIS

The

Paying

Public

People naturally congregate around live music-making and must have been doing so since, metaphorically speaking, Jubal and his lyre. Concerts of the repertoire that occupies us here have been going on for about three hundred years, from the early eighteenth century forward. Even within these relatively recent boundaries, however, there has always been a dazzling array of kinds of concerts and venues of performance, from solemnities at the local cathedral to ribaldries at the burlesque house. The important thing was to be able to afford a ticket, or, if you were a member of the aristocracy, to have a high enough standing at court to be invited.

Eighteenth-century court concerts were often formal, precious, and staid. One of Haydn's contractual duties was to assure that when his orchestra was summoned to play "before company, he and all the members of his orchestra . . . appear in white stockings, white linen, powdered, and with either a pigtail or a tiewig." Theater audiences of the next century, on the other hand, often included a rowdy *parterre* of unattached young gentlemen, organized into Jockey Clubs and the like, who prided themselves on late arrival and noisy deportment. And there was all manner of behavior in between.

In metropolitan capitals, at least, the paying public has usually enjoyed selecting from a broad spectrum of pleasures. In London today, one can choose from half a dozen or more first-line concerts any night of the week, and it has been like that for some time. The Viennese critic Eduard Hanslick, for example, wrote at the end of the nineteenth century of the London season by citing a newspaper article from more than a century before:

> The Vienna season is small compared to Paris and nothing at all compared to London. The password is "the season," and once it is spoken London becomes a mecca for everyone in England who plays, fiddles, or sings and for everyone on the Continent who has achieved musical fame. In the summer of 1701 the *Morning Chronicle* noted: "We are threatened with a flood of music so disturbing that it will be difficult to yield to its effects." It advised its readers to "stop up their ears and hold on to their wallets." What could this Philistine say today if he were to look into his paper and see ten or twelve concerts announced every day of the week, not counting the Italian and English opera, various operettas, church performances, etc.?

Then there were the private and semiprivate gatherings to hear concerted music: lunchtime diversions of the nobility, weekly salons of men and women of letters, readings by the faculty and students of the local university. I cite from the "Out-and-About" column in a Leipzig newspaper of the 1720s:

> Both the public musical Concerts or Assemblies that are held here weekly are still flourishing steadily. The one is conducted by Mr. Johann Sebastian Bach, Kapellmeister to the court of Weissenfels and music director at the Thomas-Kirche and Nicolai-Kirche in this city, and is held, except during the Fair, once a week in Zimmermann's coffee house in the Cather-Strasse, on Friday evenings from 8 to 10 o'clock; during the Fair, however, twice a week, on Tuesday and Fridays at the same hour. . . .
> The participants in these musical concerts are chiefly students here, and there are always good musicians among them, so that sometimes they become, as is known, famous virtuosos. Any musician is permitted to

make himself publicly heard at these musical concerts, and most often, too, there are such listeners as know how to judge the qualities of an able musician.

The paying public is sometimes boisterous and always unpredictable. But without a good audience, concerts invariably lose their flavor. Pleasing the audience is always an issue to be reckoned with. The audience, in fact, has often attracted the attention of good writers. Consider the remarks on Italian opera of the eighteenth century by a surgeon named Samuel Sharp:

> It is so much the fashion at Naples, and indeed, through all Italy, to consider the Opera as a place of rendezvous and visiting, that they do not seem in the least to attend to the musick, but laugh and talk through the whole performance, without any restraint; and it may be imagined, that an assembly of so many hundreds conversing together so loudly, must entirely cover the voices of the singers. . . . It is customary for Gentlemen to run about from box to box, betwixt the acts, and even in the midst of the performance; but the Ladies after they are seated, never quit their box the whole evening. It is the fashion to make appointments for such and such nights. A Lady receives visitors in her box one night, and they remain with her the whole Opera; another night she returns the visit in the same manner. In the intervals of the acts, principally betwixt the first and second, the proprietor of the box regales her company with iced fruits and sweet meats. Beside the indulgences of a loud conversation, they sometimes form themselves into card parties.

Or Mozart, writing of a 1778 Paris performance of one of his symphonies:

> I prayed God that it might go well—it is all for his greater honor and glory—and lo and behold, the Symphony began. Raaff stood next to me. Just in the middle of the first Allegro there was a Passage I was sure would please. All the listeners went into raptures over it—applauded heartily. But as, when I wrote it, I was quite aware of its Effect, I introduced it once more towards the end—and it was applauded all over again. The Andante pleased them too, but the last Allegro even better. I had heard that final Allegros, here, must begin in the same way as the first ones, all the instruments playing together, mostly in unisons. I began mine with nothing but the 1st and 2nd violins playing softly for 8 bars—then there is a sudden *forte*. Consequently the listeners (just as I had anticipated) all went "Sh!" in the soft passage—then came the sudden *forte* and no sooner did they hear the *forte* than they all clapped their hands. I was so glad that, the minute the Symphony was finished, I went to the Palais Royal,

ordered a good ice cream, said my Rosary as I had vowed to do, and went home.

Berlioz's huge concert of November 1840 was beset with difficulties, among them an unusual (though, as it happens, by no means unique) situation where

> A moment later another incident . . . set the house in greater commotion. Cries of "Murder! It's monstrous! Arrest him!" were heard coming from the balcony, and the whole audience rose in confusion. Madame de Girardin, looking dishevelled, was waving her arms about in her box and calling for help. Her husband had just had his face slapped by Bergeron, one of the editors of the *Charivari* [a satirical newspaper], a notorious lampooner of [King] Louis-Philippe, and the man popularly supposed to have fired the pistol shot at the King from the Pont Royal a few years before.

The audience was quelled with some effort; the troublesome Bergeron was ultimately sent to jail for three months.

George Bernard Shaw, describing a performance of Tchaikovsky's Second Piano Concerto in 1890, was more intrigued with the audience than the repertoire:

> Although Mr. Manns was inconsiderate enough to select the very wettest day he could find for his benefit the audience was of the largest; and as they all had umbrellas to thump with, the applause was exceptionally effective. Not so the program.

The French novelist Colette, in her newspaper reviews, tended to enjoy the audience more than the music (and left it to Debussy, her colleague on the same paper, to talk seriously about art). Concerning a 1903 Paris visit by Richard Strauss, she writes:

> Richard Strauss drew a small but select audience at the Nouveau-Théâtre. I arrived early and was preceded by Mme Raunay, whose fair-complexioned neck shone out from under black crepe, and Mme Chausson, also fair and also pretty in her beautiful Louis XIII sleeves. Yes, girls, it's the latest fashion. . . .
> And then the Schola [Cantorum of Paris] arrived, trooping in: Séverac, the two Castéras (since one has shaved his beard I can't tell them apart), Doire, and Guilmant—all dressed in silver gray. . . .
> I could go on listing them and listing them in the hope of filling my

column without mentioning Richard Strauss, who embarrasses me and whom I don't like.

To conclude this quick tour of concert audiences through the ages, I cite the articulate London critic David Cairns, writing in 1958 of von Karajan:

> Karajan, master of half Europe, has conquered London. At the Berlin Philharmonic concerts last week he drove his glittering war chariot over the outstretched necks of the multitude and they loved it. After the Brahms C minor Symphony at the second concert such a deep-throated roar went up as can rarely have been heard in a concert hall. You felt that anyone daring to dissent would be thrown to the horns. Through the tumult the heavy brass and percussion moved up and the conqueror, who smiled with his lips while his level gaze took us in dispassionately, celebrated his triumph with a performance of the *Tannhäuser* overture so ruthlessly insensitive that, as I stared at those spidery arms feeling at the controls and the faceless trombones, their yelling bells raised to the roof, images of Attila and Frankenstein went feverishly through my brain. It was superb, irresistible, and terrifying. I was glad to get out into the air.

Of these several observers only Mr. Cairns ever heard a decent phonograph record. Now we have compact discs, the Walkman, cable television, and public radio. One need never leave one's Home Entertainment Center. To be sure, not going out is an attractive response to the gaudy hoopla prepared by marketing strategists to lure us from the comfort of our living rooms—junk English where musical masterpieces are described in the language of ads for designer jeans and Names are paraded before us like brands of canned soup in the grocery store.

But live performance of great art music remains one of the most rewarding experiences in what we think of as The Good Life. Live performance still requires a live audience: audiences continue to share, in roughly equal measure with the composer and the performers, the responsibility for the success of public concerts.

So going to concerts is more than entertainment, and certainly more than Home Entertainment. Works of art are recreated on the spot, ever new and ever fresh. And members of the audience can have the thrill of direct participation in these festivities, as they engage their senses and intelligence in behalf of the composers and works to be performed. Concerts can be enjoyed, or not, from many perspectives: the Jockey Club and Wagner loathed a particular performance of *Tannhäuser,* but from very different perspectives. The more one is prepared to involve oneself in the perception of the structural aspects of music as it passes by, however, the deeper and richer the enjoyment will inevitably be.

PART ONE

Background for the concertgoer

1

Practical

Tips

Preparing for the Concert

It is a maxim among performing musicians that their overriding responsibility to an ensemble is to be in the right place, at the right time, and with the right music and instrument in hand. Trivial as it may seem, the audience's first responsibility is similar: to be in the right place, at the right time, with the right ticket in hand. It's sometimes more difficult than it sounds.

Tickets for musical events are most often available both as subscriptions (tickets for all events in a series) and individually, with subscription holders given priority in seating. Most performing groups make tickets available by mail and telephone through a certain date, and afterwards at the box office. Box offices sell tickets to a variety of events at one time; though mistakes are rare, ticket-holders should check their tickets at the time of purchase for date, seat, and price.

Tickets remaining for the performance may be bought at the door. Discounted student rush tickets are usually available just before starting time, upon presentation of proper identification. Those wishing to attend an event that is sold out can often purchase unused tickets being offered outside the hall. In my experience, you can nearly always get into a concert if you try hard enough, have enough cash, and aren't too fussy about where you sit or stand.

Not to use one's tickets, to be a "no-show," is a cardinal sin. If you cannot sell them, find out if you can turn them back to the producers (who will resell "turnbacks") and claim a tax deduction. Otherwise give them to a grateful music student, or telephone your local high school orchestra or college music department with such an offer.

It is advisable to watch the press for last-minute changes in starting times, repertoire, and for possible traffic and parking advice.

Then there is the matter of preparing the mind for the intellectual experience of the concert. Here you must take your own initiative, and this book is designed to help you do precisely that. The press makes rather less than it should of, in critic Michael Steinberg's words, "the opportunity to help people find a way" into a musical experience. Except in the very best newspapers, advance publicity for a concert generally consists of hype for the artists, and though sometimes entertaining, particularly the ubiquitous feature story of the trials and tribulations of thus-and-such a glamorous soloist, it is useful only to ascertain facts about time and place.

The concertgoer should look elsewhere, then, to discover something about the pieces to be offered. One can always buy a recording and read about the work on the jacket- or liner-notes. (And then listen to it. "Pre-listening" opens the mind, excites the senses, and trains the ear.) Several inexpensive reference works give useful biographical sketches of composers and definitions of musical terms; some of these are listed at the end of this book. The public library or the library of a local academic institution will have further reference books, including the expensive dictionaries like *The New Grove Dictionary of Music and Musicians* (1980) and single-volume works like *The Norton / Grove Concise Encyclopedia of Music* (1988). University departments and schools of music and some public libraries also have large collections of phonograph records. And the better good-music radio stations preview works programed for upcoming concerts.

The performing group itself probably sponsors educational programs designed to aid listeners: cocktail-lectures, dinner-lectures before the concert, intermission features for the broadcast, and so forth. There are clubs and affinity groups that meet regularly to discuss issues of concern to a specific performing group. Bookclubs, church groups, and societies devoted to intellectual pursuits often offer opportunities to meet the artists and discuss programs. A good conductor, in my view, should make at least one or two educational appearances before nearly every concert.

Colleges and universities offer introductory courses in the type of classical music one hears at live public concerts. The nonmatriculated student can usually participate in such a course through an extension program. Academic institutions often sponsor evening and summer courses related to musical events in the geographic area. Investigate these possibilities: what better investment of your time can you make?

Come to the concert prepared, in short, with some advance knowledge, and with the expectation of engaging all your senses in what is about to happen.

Annotated programs are distributed at concerts and sometimes are available in advance from the producers. These can (and should) be mines of information. The avid concertgoer can always arrive early enough to study the program before curtain time. The program will give titles of works with their constituent movements and, where appropriate, the *opus number* assigned the piece by the composer or his publisher as a way of identifying the work; other numeration schemes are explained below. Programs should also give the texts and English translation of any songs or choral works. Listeners should follow the text during the performance, taking care to turn the pages silently.

By the way, performers, scholars, and composers are surprisingly open to questions about their craft. It is silly not to ask because one is afraid to reveal one's ignorance. That there is no limit to the ignorance of humankind is a truth of life, and professional musicians are comfortable with that notion. I, for example, would not know my rock from my roll, but am not afraid to have my memory refreshed about the difference.

Protocol of Concerts

Arrive with time to spare. There may be problems of parking or seating, and if not, one can always study the program and check out the scene. It is inevitable that sooner or later one will be a late-comer, but to be a habitual late-comer is another cardinal sin. The concert will probably start on time; broadcast schedules and overtime provisions in union contracts guarantee that. For free concerts and events with general admission and unreserved seating it is well to arrive a full half-hour early.

Use of cameras and recording equipment is always forbidden and is usually illegal. Leave your cassette machine at home: if you must cheat, record the radio broadcast in the privacy of your own home. There are a number of persuasive reasons for this interdiction, the most obvious of which is the disturbance that the inevitable pops and clicks of this machinery causes.

Glance around you for microphones and microphone cables. Be careful not to jostle them, and be particularly quiet if you are in the vicinity of either a microphone or the performing group. If you have a cough, arm yourself with cough suppressant, taking care to unwrap a lozenge or two in advance. Foot tapping is out. As, of course, is humming along.

What to wear. Most large theaters are unpredictable as to temperature control. Body heat and heat from the lighting promptly warms up houses that seem cold before the concert starts. Theaters try to comply with governmental energy-conservation measures, especially in the summer. It is more likely, then, that you will be hot than cold. Wear jackets and sweaters that can be quietly removed if necessity demands. Artists and management are more interested in the committed presence of the listener than in his or her wardrobe.

What not to wear. Anything that makes a noise: jewelry, buckles, metal-heeled shoes; strong scents of any kind (alcohol-induced ones included); or anything that might block the vision of those seated behind you. Above all, leave your alarm-wristwatch at home. Wear grandpa's pocket watch instead. Nobody will hear the ticking, and it is a refreshing reminder of the way things were in a simpler time. (On second thought, perhaps it would be better to close yourself in a quiet room and listen carefully to exactly what grandpa's pocket watch is doing these days.)

Physicians and others with paging devices may check them with a sympathetic employee of the house.

Applause. Applause is always appropriate to salute a job well done. Convention and a good sense of priorities dictate that applause for works in several movements be held until the end of the complete work, and this is generally a good rule of thumb. (In snooty circles, the thing that distinguishes the "educated listener" from the hoi-polloi is that the latter applaud after the first movement of a symphony, and are roundly shushed by the former.)

What could be more appropriate, however, than to applaud an individual movement that has been exceptionally well rendered?

Heartfelt cries of *bravo!* (*brava!* for a female; *bravi!* for a group) are appropriate at the conclusion of a performance. Cries of *encore!* or *bis!* are sometimes rewarded, though less frequently nowadays than in times past.

At theatrical performances, the situation is more confusing. Swells of applause often greet the unveiling of a particularly striking set or technical effect, and people sometimes clap as the curtain descends, before the music is quite finished. Andrew Porter, the *New Yorker* critic, often tells us that a set is a failure if it provokes applause: music is always better off without interruption. It is customary to applaud the soloist at the end of an aria, but even here, one had best be on solid footing, particularly in works where the music does not stop for long between movements. You might follow the lead of some clearly addicted opera-lover who knows the ropes from years of experience. Just make sure that the ropes do not serve to perpetuate bad habits, bad manners, or stupidities.

My point in all of this is that American audiences tend to be tamer than they need be. A concert is an event, and the talent you hear is the result of years of discipline and struggle. Don't be timid about showing your approval.

It is customary to recall the performers for a least one extra bow at the conclusion of a concert. More bows are the audience's prerogative, as is the standing ovation. The standing ovation is best reserved for something splendid; otherwise it becomes meaningless.

When to leave a concert. One is invited to leave a concert without delay whenever one becomes a distraction to the proceedings (rumbling stomach, cough, and what-not). Excuse yourself quietly, and exit with dignity.

Otherwise it is only permissible to leave after a complete work. In case of utter duress—one's car about to be towed, threat of losing a loved babysitter, and so on—one might leave between movements. But go quickly, and excuse yourself with a brief "pardon me," or some other message without sibilants.

Be careful of the door behind you: help it to close without making noise.

One may gracefully leave the complete concert before any encores; once the encores have begun, it is polite to hear them out. Even if the event proves to be an abomination, wait until the piece concludes to go home; the woman in the next seat may be the soloist's mother. (I once heard, in an elevator, a blistering attack on the staging of the previous night's opera; the two discussants were blissfully unaware that they were sharing the car with the stage director.)

Children. Artists and management welcome children at concerts, for they are the paying public of tomorrow. Infants and very young people typically begin their concert lives at young people's concerts. Older children will enjoy matinee performances. Squirmy teenagers should be advised by their hosts (in advance, that is) to stick it out at least until the intermission.

Concert going should be a positive experience for youngsters. Too few of them are likely to have the opportunity to develop a taste for art music otherwise. Welcome them.

What to Listen For

Art music is the craftsmanlike ordering of sounds. Good music is almost automatically attractive to the ear: attractive because it is somehow deeply moving, or gloriously triumphant, or profoundly melancholy. Sometimes it participates in the telling of a story, so that our experience of the tale becomes somehow sharper and more intense. Music's capacity to affect one's feelings was clear to the earliest philosophers and theorists, and the affective power of music is now so well understood by those who manipulate our minds that tunes are carefully chosen to hurry us through the grocery store or soothe our fears at the dentist's office.

So music can be fulfilling and even powerful without much expenditure of mental effort, just as, for example, the French language can seem richly harmonious even if we do not know what a word of it means. But for most of us, that sort of enjoyment is not enough. Sooner or later our natural curiosity about how things work erupts in a healthy desire to know what's really going on at a concert. It no longer seems good enough just to watch the cymbal player or even to imagine some idyllic but unstated scene the music might be attempting to evoke. We sense that there is a more abstract drama to be perceived in the music. That is true. Great music consists of an infinite number of relationships to be perceived in a nearly infinite number of ways. Each individual listener, by participating in the unfolding of musical events, creates the work anew for himself or herself, just as surely as if he or she were on stage with instrument in hand.

It makes some sense to begin committed listening by glancing around and assessing the situation. What is there to look forward to? What are the possibilities? What is about to happen? After all, a live concert is seen—shiny timpani, glamorous singers, and all—as well as heard, and there is something magical about the sheer number of people who collaborate to make an orchestra concert. You have a single chance to hear the music, and the musicians have a single chance to play it. There is no rewinding the cassette nor going back to correct a mistake. So collect yourself, and be prepared to listen aggressively, to join in the fray.

It all seems very chancy and expensive when compared to the certainty of a stereo recording. And yet listening to a well-honed performance, even if the performers are students and the room a gymnasium, can be as great a thrill as a cliff-hanging football game. It's the very chance of it all that most excites—especially the chance that the composer, the performers, and the audience will strike some unique rapport, have a special night. Everything might click.

So give a willing ear, and listen positively. Listening negatively means that one is waiting to find mistakes and weaknesses; the listener is predisposed to have adverse reactions. This is contrary to one of the basic rules of good criticism: an informal assumption that what we are hearing is likely to be good, because it is the work of serious artists endeavoring to do their best. Besides that, one hears precious few significant errors these days, and in most cases of live performance, the ear can never quite be certain exactly what it just heard. That, indeed, is why composers are careful to repeat musical material and to reconfirm it with recapitulations of various sorts.

One listens, then, to the *performance* with an intent to discover what the performers bring to the composition, from a fine rip by a clarinet soloist to unusually rich tone quality in the lower strings. You listen and watch for things like pacing, registration—can you hear the important instruments at the right time?—and evidence of sympathetic cooperation of the players with each other and with their leaders and soloists. It is singularly rewarding to recognize the technical virtuosity of the players—for example, the bow-work of violins I and II in Glinka's *Ruslan and Ludmila* overture.

But the performers are the intermediaries: high-priced middlemen standing between the composer and the public. Ultimately, one must replace the notion of listening to the *performers,* and even to the *performance,* with *hearing the music.*

For music gains its real power from the host of evocations and inferences I mentioned above. The effort of mastering a few facts and concepts about the art soon rewards the listener with substantially richer powers of perception. The process is simple enough, consisting of knowledge of some of the basic organizational procedures of Western art music, the rudiments of musical grammar, fearlessness in the face of foreign languages (for most Americans, an acquired taste; for nearly everyone else in the world, a way of life), and a little elementary history.

2

The

Orchestra

———————•◦∞◦•———————

The *modern orchestra,* at its usual strength, consists of eighty to a hundred or more instruments. These are arranged in families of woodwinds, brass, percussion, and strings. While the string players are greatest in number, orchestral music is most often notated in scores that start at the top with the flute line and finish at the bottom with the double basses. I will treat the instruments in the order in which they are arranged in an orchestral score.

Woodwinds

Flutes. Two to four players playing two separate parts (though see the remarks on "Doublings," below). Often there is a separate and quite distinctive part for the *piccolo,* a half-sized flute with a range a full

Flute

Oboe

octave above that of its bigger sibling. Unlike modern flutes, which are usually made of metal, the best piccolos are still fashioned of wood. During this century a larger instrument called the alto flute has been favored by both orchestral composers and jazz artists for its sultry, often melancholy, tone.

Oboes. Two to four players playing two separate parts. One of the players may be required to play the *English horn (cor anglais),* a sort of alto oboe with a darker and still more exotic tone quality than the oboe. The English horn is not English; the best guess is that its name is a corruption of French words meaning "angelic horn" or maybe "angled horn."

Clarinets. Two to four players playing two separate parts. Certain works require a higher clarinet, called the *E♭ clarinet;* others ask for a *bass clarinet,* whose range is roughly that of the bassoon. Clarinet players, incidentally, usually have two instruments at hand, one in A (for keys with sharps) and one in B♭ (for keys with flats); they are among the many players in an orchestra who travel with more than one instrument. If there is a *saxophone* part, it is generally played by one of the clarinetists.

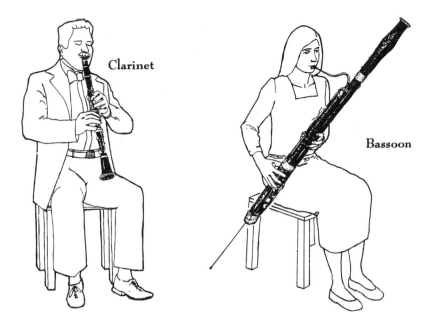

Clarinet

Bassoon

Bassoons. Two to four players playing two (or occasionally more) separate parts. This is the lowest of the standard woodwind instruments. Beethoven, in his Fifth and Ninth Symphonies, calls for a *contrabassoon,* or double bassoon, as well. Twice the size of the ordinary bassoon, this instrument became common in orchestral works of the later nineteenth and twentieth centuries.

Brass

Horns. (Commonly, and not quite accurately, called French horns; the French horn is no more French than the English horn is English.) Four players, playing two or four separate parts. For the rich and luscious works of Mahler and his contemporaries, additional horn players are often required.

Trumpets. Two, three, or sometimes four players playing separate parts. For reasons having to do with tone quality, trumpet players, like clarinetists, use instruments pitched to different keys, typically B♭, C, or D. Many Baroque works call for a trio of trumpets, invariably in conjunction with a pair of timpani; two of these parts are nowadays played on a smaller instrument called the *piccolo trumpet.*

Horn

Trumpet

Some nineteenth-century composers were fond of the mellower and more refined sound of the *cornet,* and many works of that period call for the mix of two trumpets and two *cornets à pistons.* The cornet is also an important member of the military band.

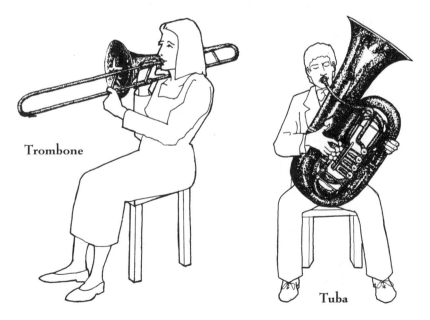

Trombone

Tuba

Trombones. Three players playing three parts. These parts were originally for three separate instruments: the alto, tenor, and bass trombone, though today all three lines are usually played on super trombones
capable of an extensive range. The slide mechanism is a product of
the Renaissance; woodcuts of an instrument closely resembling the
modern trombone first appeared in mid-sixteenth century.

Tuba. Usually a single player, and a single part, though from time to
time the choir of lower brass requires two tubas. This is the lowest
instrument in the brass family. The tuba player also covers parts written by Berlioz, Mendelssohn, and others for an obsolete instrument
called the *ophicléide.* The so-called "bass tuba" is a relative newcomer
to the orchestra, having been introduced to polite society in the 1830s.
Because composers of the nineteenth century were still feeling their
way through the issue of the lowest brass, the repertoire implies the
use of a variety of tubas: tenor, bass, and contrabass.

Percussion

Timpani. Usually one timpanist playing a pair of drums. Timpanists
are surrounded by as many as five kettledrums of different sizes in
order to have more options for tone quality and tuning.

Timpani

Others. The battery of percussion players and instruments varies widely from epoch to epoch. The standard instruments in orchestral music are the *bass drum, cymbals,* and *triangle. Snare drum, tambourine, castanets,* and the mallet instruments (*xylophone* and the like) appear with growing frequency in music of the nineteenth century.

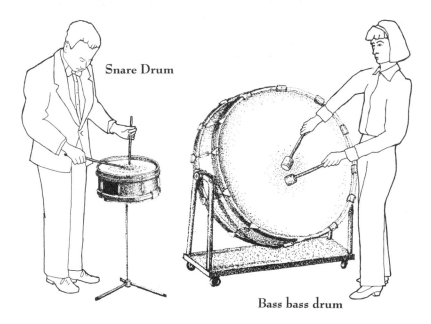

Snare Drum

Bass bass drum

Strings

Violins. Approximately two dozen players playing two separate parts. The specifications of the modern violin—with its metal strings, long fingerboard, chin rest, and taut bow—come from the nineteenth century, when nearly every existing instrument was altered to give it greater resonance and a more ringing tone.

Violas. Approximately a dozen players. The viola is virtually identical to the violin except that it is a little larger and can thus be tuned several pitches lower.

Cellos (more correctly, *violoncelli*). Approximately a dozen players. The cello is the tenor member of the violin family, tuned an octave lower than the viola.

Violin   Viola   Cello

Double basses (contrabasses). Half a dozen or more players. The lowest-pitched instrument of the violin family. They often play along an octave below the cellos. Many fancy orchestral basses are equipped with an outrigging device attached over the scrollwork called a "low-C extension" which allows the bass to sound two tones lower than its normal range.

Orchestras keep dozens of other musicians on call for unusual demands: more percussionists, harpists, pianists, organists, and of course a chorus, chorus master, and accompanist. Details of their contractual arrangements vary, but most of the retainers have agreed to give first priority to the demands of a particular performing group, and thus are considered full-fledged members of the orchestra.

Double Bass

Each *section* is led by a *principal player* responsible for deciding (along with the conductor) matters of phrasing, assigning divided parts, and the like. The principal first violinist is called the *concertmaster* (in England, the *leader*). He or she coordinates the efforts of the section principals, consults with the conductor on certain matters of interpretation, and in general acts as the orchestra's liaison with the conductors and soloists. The concertmaster also supervises the tuning of the orchestra, asking the oboe player to sound an A just as the festivities get underway.

The *conductor,* of course, dictates the tempo, keeps the ensemble together, and reminds it of the interpretations they have worked out together in rehearsal. He stands, for better eye contact with the back rows of players, on a *podium;* he conducts with a *baton,* a descendant of the cane with which eighteenth-century conductors beat on the floor. Whether or not a conductor uses a baton, and whether or not he or she conducts from memory, is musically irrelevant. The conductor's skill is measured in the choices of tempi, in the tone quality of the orchestra, in pacing and dynamic control, and above all in the intellectual mastery of the works being performed.

It was fairly late in the history of orchestral playing that the conductor and the concertmaster were different people. Some of the greatest conductors of the early nineteenth century led performances with a violin bow and played along when they could; later in the century Johann Strauss, Jr. was among the several good composer-conductors who made a career of conducting "from the violin."

Of course, every assemblage of one hundred or more people requires technical assistance, and orchestras have a variety of managers and support staff, from the stagehands and librarians to the personnel manager and the general manager.

The score. Music for this aggregation is notated by the composer in a *score,* which contains a line of music for each instrumental part. After the composer has completed the score, a copyist prepares individual parts for the orchestral players. Later both score and parts for successful works may be printed and sold by a music publisher. The conductor works from the score, and in difficult compositions and often for new music the players may play from score as well. A typical published score is about 10″ × 13″, manuscript scores much larger, and theater works often in multiple volumes. (See also Chapter 7.)

Authenticity. The last several decades have witnessed exceptional growth in interest, by both scholars and the public, in what is often called "authentic" performance practice: the way things were played at the time they were composed. On many university campuses you can hear Baroque music played on Baroque violins, with Baroque bows and Baroque fingerings, ornamentation, and phrasing. Any number of ensembles are playing and recording Mozart, Haydn, and Beethoven today with unreconstructed string instruments, natural trumpets and horns, and all the rest. (Roger Norrington's recent CDs of the Beethoven symphonies have become the focus of very serious attention in the music world.) Sometimes you can hear Berlioz's *Symphonie fantastique* with the ophicléide part played on a true ophicléide (and not a tuba), and performances using the handsome cornet part Berlioz added to the second movement are almost commonplace today. The early-instrument movement, which has become known to a wide audience through commercial recordings, is beginning to have some salutary effect on live performance in the concert hall. And this kind of performance is more than a curiosity: it is a right-minded effort to experiment with the conditions of performance and to discover the way things were in times gone by.

True authenticity, though, is a frame of mind; one should do the best one can with what one has. While the major orchestras will play Haydn and Mozart with reduced forces and appropriately crisp phrasing, they are no more likely to offer their concerts in a Viennese drawing room than they are to find a piano with no steel in it for a Mozart concerto. (It must be acknowledged, however, and with special pleasure, that artists like Malcolm Bilson, who plays on just such a piano, have discovered a wide public following, both in concerts and on record.) Nor does it hurt to take into account later developments in performance tradition. Always, the most rewarding performance is one that has joined genuine commitment to historical principles with a reasoned understanding of the present, one that does not merely replay a work, but actually recreates it.

To draw an analogy with theater: you may well insist (and I think you should) that your Shakespeare be played straight, with Elizabethan dress and all the lines in place. But you would not deny the theater company its luxury of synthetic fabrics for the costumes nor its electric lights. Nor even its laundry facilities and industrial-strength antiperspirants.

COMPARATIVE TABLE OF ORCHESTRAL MAKEUP

	J. S. Bach: Orchestral Suite No. 3 BMV 1068 (c. 1730)	Mozart: Symphony No. 40 in G Minor K. 550 (1788)	Beethoven: Symphony No. 9 (1824)	Berlioz: Symphonie fantastique (1830)	Mahler: Symphony No. 1 (1889)	Stravinsky: Rite of Spring (1913)
Woodwinds						
Flutes	I	I	I-II + piccolo	I-II + piccolo	I-IV + piccolos I-II	I-III + picc. I-II, alto fl.
Oboes	I-II	I-II	I-II	I-II + English horn	I-IV + English horn	I-IV + English horns I-II
Clarinets		I-II	I-II	I-II + E♭ clarinet	I-III + E♭, bass clar.	I-III + E♭, bass cl. I-II
Bassoons	(2) doubling bass line	I-II	I-II + contrabassoon	I-IV	I-III + contrabassoon	I-IV + contrabassoons I-II
Brass						
Horns		I-II	I-IV	I-IV	I-VII	I-VIII
Trumpets	I-III		I-II	I-II + cornets I-II	I-IV	I-IV + piccolo, bass trpt.
Trombones			I-III	I-III	I-III	I-III
Tuba				I-II (ophicléides)	I	I-II + extras
Percussion						
Timpani	I	I	I	I-IV	I-II	I
Battery			bass drum, cymbals, triangle	snare dr., bass dr., cymbals, bells	bass drum, cymbals, triangle, tam-tam	bass dr., cymb., triangle, tambourine, tam-tam, guiro, ant. cymbals
Strings (approx.)						
Violins I	2–3	6	12	15	17	18
Violins II	2–3	6	12	15	16	16
Violas	4	4	10	10	11	12
Cellos	2	3	6	11	10	12
Double Basses	1 (violone)	3	6	9	10	10
Other	Keyboard		soloists (S,A,T,B) chorus (S,A,T,B)	harps I-II (at least 4)	harp	

Orchestra size. For purposes of comparison, I present the makeup of some orchestras of the past from Bach to Stravinsky summarized in the table on page 26. (The figures for Bach are those he said he wanted, not those he could get; composers are always having to compromise about such matters.) The inexorable growth of performing force seems to have subsided somewhat after the late Romantic period. Modern ensembles, however, have to be able to cover all kinds of orchestral music, from Bach to Bartók, and so they tend to keep a great number of players on tap. The Cleveland Orchestra presently comprises 34 violins, 11 violas, 12 cellos, 9 contrabasses, 3 flutes and 1 piccolo, 3 oboes and 1 English horn, 3 clarinets and 1 bass clarinet, 3 bassoons and 1 contrabassoon, 6 horns, 4 trumpets, 3 trombones and 1 bass trombone, 1 tuba, 1 timpanist, 4 percussionists, 2 harpists, and 1 pianist—a total of 105 players: 85 men and 20 women. Vienna remains a bastion of the all-male orchestra. In San Francisco and St. Louis approximately a third of the orchestra membership is female; it is common in the regional symphonies for fifty percent or more of the orchestra members to be women. Ethnic mix depends on the climate of the time: fifty years ago American orchestral ranks were heavy with European names, while today, Asian players are more usual, particularly in the string section.

3

Musical

Form

———————

All composers try to achieve a coherence of structure and materials that they hope will be at least sensed, and if possible understood, by a good proportion of their listeners. Music is an art that exists within the passage of time: you, the listener, react as events pass before you from left to right, so to speak. An analogy with drama is apt, for in both art forms a certain series of events is more or less expected of a work from a certain time and place, and the excitement lies in how the composer or playwright goes about it. Works of art have beginnings, middles, and ends; they begin from points of repose, develop tension and aim for climax, and return to a sense of fulfillment and renewed repose, with problems resolved one way or another. They have, in short, form.

Many of the traditional forms are simple indeed. One common

method is to set forth some musical material, do something that contrasts with it, and then return to the original statement (A B A). Think of the song *Twinkle, Twinkle, Little Star,* a masterpiece of Western music known in Europe as *Ah vous dirai-je maman.* Whoever dreamed up this little composition presented the musical material for "Twinkle, twinkle, little star / How I wonder what you are," then offered a contrasting tune for "Up above the world so high" and so on. The work closes with a return to both the tune and the text of the opening pair of lines. This is a typical kind of rounded form.

Composers inherit musical traditions; they learn from the past, and they begin their careers by imitating their predecessors, teachers, and masters. Thus they develop more or less standard ways of doing things, and these procedures come to have names: *sonata, fugue, rondo, scherzo,* and the like. Composers do *not* write pieces "according to the rules"; rather, they compose music according to dictates uniquely their own, trying to achieve solutions to musical problems that they have posed for themselves.

The majority of music performed by modern orchestras comes from a relatively short period of time, the repertoire circumscribed by the music of Johann Sebastian Bach and his contemporaries at one end and the works of, say, Stravinsky at the other. Large orchestral compositions from these periods consist of a series of free-standing segments called *movements,* arranged to form a dramatic musical discourse. (Symphonies usually have four movements, solo concertos, three.) Good news: virtually every movement in the symphonic literature is cast in a form that can be recognized by the committed concertgoer. For the devotee of symphonic music, by far the most important of these procedures is called:

The sonata. First we must confront a definitional problem, for the word sonata means a host of different things. Initially, it was a general term for a multimovement instrumental work; then, of course, it came to describe a piece for solo recitalist, as, for example, the "Moonlight" Sonata of Beethoven or the same composer's Sonata, opus 69, for cello and piano. A symphony, in that respect, is a sonata for orchestra.

What I am describing here, however, is a way of thinking about large-scale design, a form seen most conspicuously in first movements of pieces and therefore sometimes called "sonata-allegro" or "sonata-first movement" form. Sonata was actually a frame of mind: a feeling for proportion and symmetry that came to the fore in the works of Haydn and Mozart and dominated compositional thought for well over a century.

The three sections in a sonata movement are called *exposition, development,* and *recapitulation.* Their relationship to each other is quite easy to grasp: in the exposition, the composer presents the governing themes, accompaniments, and textures. In the development (called "working-out" in German), he expands on their implications, and in the recapitulation returns to the opening material. In one sense, the operation is much like our *Twinkle, Twinkle* example above, but on a grander scale.

Some sonata movements are preceded by a *slow introduction,* designed to set the musical stage, as it were, and many conclude with a sign-off section, a grand, confirming musical event called *coda* (tail), the longer equivalent of the "stinger" with which a march by John Philip Sousa often concludes.

Within the exposition, there occur two main events: the first group of musical ideas, the first theme—but it's much more than just a theme—and the second. Haydn and Mozart had the notion that the first and second groups would contrast in various ways: in character, instrumentation, and most of all in key (see Chapter 5, Tonality). The second group is *always* in a contrasting key. The process of departing from the home key and arriving at another is called *modulation,* and it, along with the confirmation of the new key at the close of the exposition, is one of the fundamental generators of discourse in the sonata.

Expositions have in fact more than just the two themes to attract your attention. What links the first theme group to the second is called a *transition,* or *bridge,* which encompasses the modulation to the key of the second group. After the second main theme often comes a musical rounding-off and reinforcement of the new key, called *closing material* (or *codetta*). Mozart, for example, goes out of his way to write fetching closing themes.

The score usually calls for a repeat of the exposition. Whether or not to observe this instruction is a decision the performers tend to make based on program time constraints. That is a mistake: there is ample evidence that most composers really meant for the repeats to be observed, and you often compromise the architecture by skipping them.

In the development, the composer has the opportunity to reveal new ways in which his musical ideas can be presented, and here they can come in any horizontal or vertical relationship. Thus the composer may, for example, juxtapose themes from the two groups against each other. He may manipulate and transform them. He may exert other organizational procedures on his material, as for example making a fugue (see p. 35) out of one of the themes. The purpose is to delight the ear and the mind with devices unsuggested by the opening gambits.

The recapitulation is identical to the exposition, with one important difference: the second group remains in the home key, that is, both groups will be in C major if the work began there. The reason is elementary: the work must end in the key in which it began. Having to stay in the home key means that the bridge must be changed from a dynamic and striking move away from the home key to a sort of musical marking of time. The second group will sound modestly different, for the reason that the same tunes will be heard in different tonal position: in general, they have a deeper and rather less striking quality.

Anything goes in the coda, from the routine signing-off of much of Haydn's work to the flamboyant, extended closings of Beethoven and his followers.

Sonata is a recognizable procedure in the vast majority of compositions performed by symphony orchestras, string quartets, solo pianists, and the like. The notions of departure and return, of statement and contrast, and especially of recapitulation indeed permeate nearly every kind of musical procedure one commonly hears.

Now I said above that the great composers, on the one hand, develop standard ways of doing things and, on the other, that they scarcely ever "follow the rules." The challenge in listening to a sonata movement is not, then, to check off exposition and development and recapitulation like laps in a footrace, but rather to see and hear what is new and exciting about a particular musical adventure. When, in the last movement of the "Jupiter" Symphony, Mozart sallies forth into his sonata form, he takes the usual components of the structure and harnesses them in a hair-raising fugal style of writing that takes wing heavenward and stuns the listener with its skill. Beethoven, in general, broadens the form to include far-flung developments and codas, embracing some of the procedures once found only in the exposition. In so doing, he gives himself the opportunity to introduce new thematic material in the development (in violation of the "rules"), thereby establishing an entirely new dynamic for the procedure. He moves the halfway point, or fulcrum of the balance beam, from the close of the exposition to the moment of recapitulation; as much comes after the recapitulation begins as came before. The mid-Romantics, following a couple of leads by Beethoven, work into their sonata movements all sorts of extramusical implications. Brahms writes exceptionally long expositions, with any number of melodies in addition to the two main themes.

And so it goes, with each composer taking the lead from established norms, examining the state of thought about the art of composition, and contributing something unique to the sonata process.

Sonata form controls all sorts of other big movements, including the opera overture and *concert overture.* The latter is a self-contained sonata of descriptive intent, like Tchaikovsky's *1812 Overture,* without a play or opera at the other end. Its very close relative, as cultivated by the Romantic composers, is the *symphonic poem.* Some, like Mussorgsky's *Night on Bald Mountain,* are formally indistinguishible from concert overtures; others, like the symphonic poems of Richard Strauss, contain sub-movements of varying character and intent joined together into a long, uninterrupted orchestral narrative. But sonata form, or at least its vestiges, is usually to be found controlling the plot.

In concertos, the first movement is a sonata hybridized to account for the added responsibility of having a soloist present. Concerto first movements open with an orchestral exposition (or *ritornello*); instead of a repeat of the exposition, though, the soloist enters and proceeds to "lead" the orchestra through a second round of expository material. There is a very important difference from conventional sonata form: the orchestral exposition does not leave the home key, and to the soloist is given the significant role of modulating to the key of the second group.

Departures from these established norms are striking. When Schumann opens his Piano Concerto with a dazzling passage for the soloist, or Beethoven begins his Fourth Concerto with a quiet homophonic passage for piano, they are breaking with tradition in a big way.

Second movements generally provide contrast and some measure of relaxation by being slow. They are sometimes in a sonata form or an abbreviated sonata lacking a development, sometimes simple *rounded forms* (A B A, for example), sometimes a *theme and variations.* In the last-mentioned, a given musical statement is decorated and transformed in a series of well-defined episodes, and the composer invariably reveals the theme to have had more potential than we would have imagined possible. (Mozart and others, composed keyboard variations on the *Twinkle, Twinkle* tune.) In the second movement of his Fifth Symphony, Beethoven begins each variation with increasing elaboration of the theme (see example on p. 34). But he goes on to mix in sonata elements and associations with fate and victory quite at odds with white-wigged tradition.

Most symphonic third movements are either a *minuet and trio* or one of its descendants. The minuet and trio is invariably cast in $\frac{3}{4}$ time, because of its origins in dance. A minuet of two strains, each repeated, is followed by a trio in reduced texture along the same lines. (This middle pair of sections is called a trio because in Baroque dance, two treble instruments and a bass instrument—say, two flutes and a bassoon—would play for a while to give the other performers a chance to relax.) Then the minuet recurs, but without the inner repeats. The composer does not write out the minuet again, but merely instructs

MOZART: Variations on *Ah vous dirai-je, maman,* K. 265

BEETHOVEN: Symphony No.5 in C Minor, op. 67, mvt. II

the performers to go back to the beginning, *da capo,* and play it again.

Beethoven's more lively *scherzos* are spiritual stepchildren of the minuet, and later composers felt free to substitute other dance-based forms: a *waltz,* for example, or a *march.* These forms, too, envelope sonata-based ideas; the first strain will depart to a new key, and the second will develop its implications briefly and then recapitulate the first idea.

The symphonic finale is usually either another sonata or a *rondo.* This term can describe any one of a number of schemes in which a main theme returns repeatedly during the course of the movement. Rondo as a way of thinking about musical form is a descendant of Baroque *ritornello* procedures, described below.

These schemes are outgrowths of the ferment in musical ideas that took place in the late eighteenth century in Viennese circles of which Haydn and Mozart were a part; nearly all of them are influenced in one way or another by sonata form.

Another class of musical procedures you are likely to hear in the concert hall are several that flowered in the Baroque period. These include:

Ritornello forms. These are forms wherein a recurring musical passage or part of it serves as a sort of musical home base from which new sections depart and to which they always return. The most common ritornello form is found in the outer movements of the *concerto grosso.* In a concerto grosso, a soloist or small group of soloists is drawn from and counterbalances the rest of the orchestra. The orchestra (or *ripieno*) plays the ritornello, the soloists *(concertino)* play a solo passage, the ritornello returns, a second solo passage occurs, and so on, to the end of the work. Think of Bach's Second *Brandenburg Concerto:* each of the soloists (violin, flute, oboe, trumpet) states the solo theme, but each of these subsections is framed by an orchestral ritornello.

Fugue. A *subject,* or melodic idea, introduced in one voice, is followed by an *answer* in the next voice; the answer is the same (or nearly the same) musical idea beginning on another level of the scale. While the second voice is answering, the first voice is continuing along with a countermelody that fits with the answer. The countermelodies often achieve enough musical identity to become true *countersubjects.* This subject-answer relationship, and the countermelodies, continues for as many entries as there are voices in the fugue. A four-voice fugue, for example, will have statements consisting of subject-answer-subject-answer. These statements alternate with *episodes* of freer design. Toward the end of fugues, things tend to work themselves into a frenzy of overlapping ideas and mounting tension.

Fugues are technically difficult to compose and are thought, therefore, to represent musical learning at its most rigorous. Though complete fugues are rather less common in works after Bach and Handel, fugal passages occur with great frequency. They are usually the composer's way of drawing attention both to the grandeur of the past and to his own technical mastery of his craft. The trio of the third movement in Beethoven's Fifth, for example, is in fugal style. So is the overture to Mendelssohn's *Elijah.*

Passacaglia (or **Chaconne**). Here, a constantly repeated bass line—a *ground bass*—forms a continuous ritornello. The bass line is generally some sort of descending chromatic figure ending in a cadence (see p. 49). Over it, the composer reveals the marvelous possibilities lurking within the implied harmonic progression. The great composers of passacaglias seem to have had their imaginations set free for flights of fancy by the very constraints of the idea. Some famous passacaglias include Bach's Passacaglia and Fugue for pipe organ in C Minor, the "Crucifixus" from the B-Minor Mass, and the concluding aria from Purcell's *Dido and Aeneas,* "When I am laid in earth" (often called "Dido's Lament"). Brahms, paying homage to the past, composed the last movement of his Fourth Symphony as a modern version of the passacaglia.

Suite of Dances. In the Baroque suite, a first-movement ritornello form is followed by a sequence of two-part dances with every section repeated. The first movement is often a *French overture,* which always begins with a slow section followed by a fast, fugal section, with either a full-fledged return of the opening material or else a few bars of Adagio that allude to the opening concluding the movement.

Among the best-known Baroque orchestral suites are those of J. S. Bach (see pp. 65–69) and the *Water Music* and *Music for the Royal Fireworks* of Handel (see pp. 262–65). In the nineteenth century and later the term suite more frequently describes a series of three or four orchestral movements extracted from a dramatic work. This amounts to an efficient and often profitable way of preserving the essence of an opera, ballet, or the incidental music for a stage play. Some examples of this later style include the *L'Arlésienne* suites of Bizet, the *Peer Gynt* suites of Grieg, and the *Lieutenant Kijé* suite of Prokofiev.

The roots of **sacred music** for orchestra and chorus go back to the earliest monks, its practice so conditioned by the counterpoint of centuries and by the noble edifices where it was heard that no composer could be entirely immune to its traditions. The forms are born of the ancient texts which have their own poetic schemes and points of climax. In a *mass* you will usually find those choral texts common to every service, no matter what the feast day (the *Ordinary*): Kyrie eleison, Gloria in excelsis Deo, Credo, Sanctus, and Agnus Dei. The Gloria and Credo are long prose texts that lend themselves to subdivision, the Gloria typically jubilant, and the Credo more solemn, tending to focus on the mystery of crucifixion and the promise of resurrection. Likewise composers generally put the strongly tripartite organization of the Kyrie, Sanctus, and Agnus texts to musical advantage. The Requiem Mass for the dead incorporates the Kyrie, Sanctus, and Agnus as well, but has as its centerpiece the terrifying medieval poem *Dies irae, dies illa* (Day of Wrath, Day of Mourning).

To such texts Bach will compose his ritornello forms, Haydn and Mozart their sonatas, and so forth. In the age of picture-music, Berlioz will use all the brass and percussion players of Paris for his music of judgment day, and Verdi will terrify you with the lashings of a bass drum. But sooner or later, they will all demonstrate the best counterpoint they can muster.

The *oratorio,* with its characters and story line, is a closer kin of the opera. Handel was progenitor of the big oratorio destined for the concert hall; his successors were Haydn and Mendelssohn. All three had the English middle-class public in mind as they composed.

Contemporary music. Composers of this century make use of a wide array of compositional techniques, wider perhaps than for any other period in the history of music. Many, many twentieth-century works rely in some measure on the forms I have described, for the reason that all of those have afforded pleasing results for a long time. But our century has been equally concerned with going beyond the boundaries of all previous endeavors, and from this point of view it has been difficult for composers not to see the traditional forms as mined out, the tonal system they inherited exhausted.

Thus some composers have abandoned the old forms and have introduced some perplexing new ones. Yet music still starts at the beginning as it always did, goes somewhere, and then finds its end. The forms and structures we discover by coming back for more. ("Never forget," a wise conductor remarked, "the ear is sometimes very slow, the mind is slower, and the heart is sometimes slower still.")

Besides, accusing a composer of formlessness is nothing new. Wagner's *Tristan und Isolde,* once considered in many quarters an aberration, is now well understood and deeply loved by all who have cared to master it. Stravinsky's *Rite of Spring* was at first thought impenetrable. Now it is performed with the clarity of a Chopin mazurka: people can hum it and retain it, and *Le Sacre,* as it is usually called, no longer seems particularly "modern" at all. It is as wrong to dismiss a new composition by calling it nonmusic as it was to hiss, as some did, Beethoven's Seventh Symphony. Creations of the human mind deserve a better chance.

4

The

Periods

of

Music

History

Historians and the literate public are fond of using a set of more-or-less standard terms to describe the various periods in the development of musical style. The terms are used mostly for convenience: everyone understands that the chronological boundaries they describe are approximate. Bach, for example, was the best of the high Baroque composers, but his sons were writing significantly post-Baroque music long before he died.

The orchestra as a recognizable entity postdates the first two periods discussed below. But it is in the Middle Ages and the Renaissance that the roots of the orchestra are to be found, and nowadays it is easy to hear live performances of groups specializing in that literature. Moreover, any number of the works you will encounter at symphony concerts allude in one way or another to the music of those bygone years.

The Middle Ages. Musical culture, like the rest of civilized learning, was kept alive during the Dark Ages by monks dwelling in the monasteries scattered across Latin Europe. It seems to have been in the monasteries where the principles of modern musical notation developed. By the reign of Charlemagne (742–814), King of France (from 768) and Holy Roman Emperor (from 800), a well-defined corpus of so-called "Gregorian" chant—single-voiced music for the celebrations of the Christian liturgy—had developed. Gregorian chant was to undergo constant evolution for several centuries. The basic identity of the tunes, however, comes from very long ago, indeed, and many of those tunes are still in use today. The most notable development toward the end of the Middle Ages was the composition of polyphonic, or multivoiced, music and experiments with ways to notate it.

There was lively secular and popular music in the Middle Ages, but it was written down less often. Music of the troubadours and trouvères in France achieved great refinement and artistry, as did the music for mystery plays and other forms of theater. To us the most famous composition of popular medieval polyphony (partly because it is in English) is the double round *Sumer is icumen in.*

The best of the late medieval composers were the Italian Francesco Landini (1325–97) and the French composer Guillaume de Machaut (c. 1300–77).

The Renaissance. The humanistic attitudes that signal the dawn of the Renaissance were reflected in music as in the other arts: the great composers were admired for their exceptional technical craft, fluency in secular as well as sacred forms, political concern, and general worldliness. Art music was still dominated by sacred composition— the Latin mass and motet—in complex imitative polyphony. There is nevertheless a growing interest by nearly all composers in secular genres like the madrigal and the instrumental dance.

The best of the Renaissance composers were John Dunstable (c. 1385–1453), Guillaume Dufay (c. 1400–74), Johannes Ockeghem (c. 1430–95), Josquin des Prez (c. 1440–1521), and, in the later Renaissance, Pierluigi da Palestrina (c. 1525–94) and William Byrd (1543–1623). The works of these composers constitute a body of masterpieces that is every bit the equal of the works of Haydn, Mozart, and Beethoven.

Renaissance music sounds unusual to many concertgoers, for the reason that the underlying grammatical principles are still relatively far removed from the familiar tonal practice of the high Baroque and later. The Renaissance scales, called modes, are different from the later major and minor scales, and Renaissance vocal techniques and instrumental sonorities have a quality all their own. Nevertheless the basic rules of good composition, above all of good counterpoint, come from the Renaissance.

An epochal development of the sixteenth century was the perfection of music printing, accomplished by master artisans in Venice, Paris, and the Netherlands.

The Baroque. Baroque was originally a term used to describe a certain style of art, particularly architecture characterized by extravagant use of curves and ornaments. The key historical figure of the Baroque is surely Louis XIV of France (reigned 1643–1715), a monarch whose ornate lifestyle, from mode of dress to daily agenda, is the very epitome of the period. Baroque music extends from approximately 1600, the birth of opera, to about 1750, the death of Bach.

The early Baroque saw the practice of music revolutionized in a number of ways. Tonality, where well-defined major and minor keys control musical rhetoric, replaced the modes of medieval and Renaissance practice. Composers began to think more in terms of progression of chords (that is, vertically or *homophonically*) than in the continuous polyphony of the past. New families of instruments appeared, and with them a sizeable body of music for instruments alone. The harpsichord achieved prominence, as did the fabulous Baroque pipe organ, for which J. S. Bach wrote some of his best compositions. It was the era, too, of the famous violin makers of northern Italy: Amati, Stradivari, and Guarneri, working in Cremona south of Milan, made instruments of such striking agility, sweetness, and power that they sounded the death knell for the clumsier Renaissance viols. Composers, beginning with Gabrieli and Monteverdi in Venice, started to call for specific aggregations of instrumentalists in their performing groups, and gradually the modern orchestra assumed a recognizable configuration. Most of the orchestral instruments, by the end of the Baroque, look and sound like primitive versions of modern instruments.

Another prodigious child of the time was *opera,* born of the encounter of the lavish entertainments enjoyed by princely courts with academic experiments aimed at recreating the essence of Greek tragedy.

Early operas, based on antique or mythical subject matter, have such titles as *Orfeo* (Orpheus), *Dido and Aeneas,* and (later) *Giulio Cesare.*

So the significant genres of the era are opera, the instrumental music of keyboard and orchestra and, as before, sacred music. The musical structures are built over a prominent bass line, or *basso continuo.* (Much Renaissance music, by contrast, was built around a tenor voice or constructed of pairs of voices in counterpoint with one another.) This Baroque continuo part is embellished or ornamented by a keyboard player who improvises above the notated bass line. Baroque composers developed a code of numbers to go below the bass line which would help the keyboard player know what harmonies to use. This is called "figured bass."

Presiding regally over the early Baroque was Claudio Monteverdi (c. 1567–1643), a composer equally successful in sacred music and in opera. Other great composers of the Italian Baroque included Giovanni Gabrieli (c. 1555–1612), noted for his majestic brass music for the Cathedral of St. Mark in Venice, and Girolamo Frescobaldi (1583–1643), a pioneer in music for the keyboard. The mid-Baroque, a time of ceaseless civil unrest brought about by the Protestant Reformation, was dominated by the Dresden composer Heinrich Schütz (1585–1672), composer of hundreds of smaller church works—small for the simple reason that his musicians had been decimated by the Protestant wars and by the plague. The mid-Baroque is also the time of Henry Purcell (1659–95) of London, and of Jean-Baptiste Lully (1632–87) in France.

With the late, or high, Baroque we have reached a historical period familiar to many concertgoers. There are dozens of important composers, but the most significant are probably Arcangelo Corelli (1653–1713) of Rome, Antonio Vivaldi (1678–1741) of Venice, Johann Sebastian Bach (1685–1750) of Leipzig, George Frideric Handel (1685–1759) of London, and Jean-Phillipe Rameau (1683–1764) of Paris.

The Classical style. Of all the stylistic developments being summarized here, the emergence of the so-called Classical style took the shortest time, was the most geographically localized (around Vienna), and yet is far and away of greatest significance to the modern concertgoer. For it was during this era that there emerged most of the kinds of music that we hear today in the concert hall: solo sonatas, string quartets and related kinds of chamber music, symphonies and concertos, and the modern opera. It appears that the Austrian composer Franz Joseph Haydn (1732–1809) did much to advance the tenets of the style; indeed, he seems virtually to have invented the modern string quartet and symphony. His example was at first emulated and then extended by Wolfgang Amadeus Mozart (1756–91), on whose heels thundered perhaps the most extraordinary of all composers, Ludwig van Beethoven (1770–1827).

The dominant intellectual issues of the day were the Enlightenment ideals of the worth of every individual, the corresponding obligations of progressive governments, and the power of reason as an empirical method—ideals familiar to us from our own Revolution and that of the French a few years later, and promoted by such brilliant philosophers as Voltaire, Rousseau, and Jefferson, by the playwright Beaumarchais, and by the sculptor Houdon. In music, Enlightenment ideals are reflected in many ways, as for example in the dominance of carefully constructed eight-bar phrases arranged in balanced and proportional groups.

The following hundred years would see the Classical syle expanded, mutated, and sometimes altered beyond immediate recognition, but the advances of those short years at the close of the eighteenth century quite rendered Baroque ideals things of the antique past.

Clearly the most important step forward in instrument building was the advent of the piano, the instrument on which both Mozart and Beethoven achieved international acclaim. Invented in the early 1700s, primarily in Italy, the fortepiano had advantages over the harpsichord that were obvious to everyone. (Bach himself seems to have owned a piano.) The piano concertos of Mozart and Beethoven, along with their solo sonatas for the instrument, assured it a permanent place in concert hall and salon alike.

Public concerts, open to anyone who could afford a ticket, became a way of life. Among these were the Viennese "academy concert" devoted to the music of a single composer. It was in venues such as these that Mozart and Beethoven often presented their works to the public for the first time.

Romanticism. In its narrowest usage, the term Romanticism describes a relatively short-lived literary climate in Germany (Goethe was perhaps the source of it all; Heine's poems are important for musical

Romanticism as well, though literary specialists count him a post-Romantic), England (Keats, Shelley, Byron), and Paris (Hugo, Lamartine, Vigny, etc.). Yet it is customary to call much of the music of the nineteenth century—vivid and sometimes sentimental, and nearly always constructed to tap our emotions and sensibilities—Romantic. Because of the many overlapping artistic currents, of the extensive geographic and cultural embrace of the style—because of the very intensity of this exceptionally fertile period—we now talk more of "the nineteenth century" than we do of "the romantic era." But we mean more than the nineteenth century: we really wish to delimit all those things that happened after the French Revolution and up to the start of World War I.

Composers active after Beethoven had made his mark on the symphony—even Franz Schubert (1797–1828), who died only one year after Beethoven—had to cope with the likelihood that they would never be able to outdo the master at his own strategies. This situation accounts in part for the rise of such miniature forms as the solo song, of which Schubert wrote six hundred or so, and the short descriptive work for piano solo, whose masters were Fryderyk Chopin (1810–49), Robert Schumann (1810–56), and Felix Mendelssohn (1809–47). The opposite current was the rise of the colossalist composers, those who wished to expand on the ideas behind Beethoven's heroic works, notably Hector Berlioz (1803–69), Richard Wagner (1813–83), and their followers. Dominating the generation between the death of Beethoven and the death of Wagner, in personal magnetism if not in compositional accomplishment, was Franz Liszt (1811–86), who one way or another fostered many of the most substantial intellectual achievements of the era. All these composers were interested in the fundamental issues of Romanticism: the relationship between art and nature, the relationship of the artist to his art, and the connections to be found among the several arts.

With *Tristan und Isolde* (1859) and the four operas of *The Ring of the Nibelungs* (composed from about 1851 to 1874; first performed in 1876), Wagner managed to shatter many of the tenets of Beethovenism and of Romanticism itself. Sonata forms played little part in his works; the progress of musical time was immeasurably slowed by his grand forms and stolid motion; and the premises of tonal control were challenged by the very ease with which Wagner was able to move from key to key. Composers after Wagner had to contend with these issues just as surely as Berlioz, Schumann, and the others had dealt with Beethoven.

It was fashionable in the not so distant past to contrast Wagner and Johannes Brahms (1833–97) as two completely different composers doing radically different things: Dionysus and Apollo, radical versus old-fashioned, uninhibited abandon versus cool logic. Now it is easy to see their work as different threads of the same fabric. Common issues of musical time and space are at the root of their use of themes, rich harmonic pallet, and concept of orchestral color. The contemporaries and followers of Brahms and Wagner include Anton Bruckner (1824–96), Piotr Tchaikovsky (1840–93), Gustav Mahler (1860–1911), and Richard Strauss (1864–1949). And the greatest of the Italian composers, Giuseppe Verdi (1813–1901), needs mentioning here, for the simple reason that the combination of Wagner and Verdi opera so far overshadows the competition as to make the rest of the operatic repertoire seem tame.

Meanwhile, throughout Europe, another spirit manifested itself in serious art music, that of nationalism, particularly among composers from the less powerful European nations and those dominated by foreign rule. Nationalist composers peppered their work with melodic and harmonic formulas derived from their folk musics, with rhythmic patterns based on native dance, and with the tone colors of village bands. Nationalism is a clear element in the best works of Chopin (a Pole), Liszt (a Hungarian), and Wagner; it is clearer still with the Czechs Bedřich Smetana (1824–84), Antonín Dvořák (1841–1904), and Leoš Janáček (1854–1928); the Russians Mikhail Glinka (1804–57), Nikolay Rimsky-Korsakov (1844–1908) and Igor Stravinsky (1882–1971); and the Englishman Edward Elgar (1857–1934), the Norwegian Edvard Grieg (1843–1907), and the Finn Jean Sibelius (1865–1957).

I could not possibly abandon a discussion of my favorite century without at least passing reference to its industrial and technological advances. Foremost among these was the railroad, which profoundly altered perceptions of space and time, followed closely by the telegraph. It is the period of steamships, photography (there are photographs of Berlioz, the Schumanns, and Liszt, and even a decent daguerreotype of Chopin), and cheap printing. Theaters began to rely on improved lighting effects from gas and eventually electricity. Most significant of all, from our point of view, were the technological advances which made highly chromatic music accessible to the entire orchestra: valved brass instruments, fully keyed woodwinds, the pedal harp, and so forth.

The Twentieth Century. All these issues came into question as the Western world plunged headlong toward general conflict. The primary challenge to Wagner's notion of beauty came from France, with the music of Claude Debussy (1862–1918). Debussy's use of delicate, sometimes abstract musical textures, of exotic scales and dense but shimmering harmonies, not to mention his disinclination to go on for long, seemed as anti-Wagnerian at the time as they do today. ("Hoyotoho," he wrote of Wagner's *Ring,* "how intolerable these men in helmets and animal skins become by the fourth night.") Much of Debussy's best work is for the piano, but he and his compatriots were also successful in orchestral composition. Their ballets and theater music in particular—Gabriel Fauré's music for *Pelléas et Mélisande,* Debussy's *Jeux,* Maurice Ravel's *Daphnis et Chloé* and *Boléro*—have earned a significant place in the concert repertoire.

Another school of twentieth-century music was centered in Vienna around the composers Arnold Schoenberg (1874–1951), Alban Berg (1885–1935), and Anton Webern (1883–1945). They developed a manner of composing which guaranteed the technical equality of the twelve pitches. By using a fixed series of intervals (hence the term serialism), they could assure that no pitch would achieve tonal domin-ion over the others. Berg's opera *Wozzeck,* his Violin Concerto, and several of Schoenberg's orchestral works have a wide public following. But the delicate miniatures of Webern are in certain respects the most profound, distilling the essence of the style.

Igor Stravinsky is arguably the giant of the century. He lived until 1971, and within months before his death was still turning out works of youthful vitality. An eclectic composer, he was able to assimilate compositional tactics of other kinds of contemporary music into his own highly individual style. The listener whose attention is limited to the three pre-World War I ballets will be deprived of a host of impressive works from later periods: the *Symphony of Psalms* and *The Soldier's Tale,* for example, or later the ballet *Agon,* the cantata *Threni,* and the *Requiem Canticles* written shortly before the composer's death.

Dozens of other composers active before midcentury wrote fine orchestral music of progressive bent: Béla Bartók (1881–1945), Paul Hindemith (1895–1963), Darius Milhaud (1892–1974), Sergei Prokofiev (1891–1953), Dmitri Shostakovich (1906–75), Roger Sessions (1896–1985), and Aaron Copland (1900–90), to mention a few.

In the 1950s, Pierre Boulez (b. 1925), Elliott Carter (b. 1908), and Michael Tippett (b. 1905) came to the forefront of the contemporary scene, where they have remained firmly entrenched. Today we also listen with interest to new works for the orchestra hall by such composers as Ellen Taaffe Zwilich (b. 1939), for example, whose First Symphony won the 1983 Pultizer Prize; David del Tredici (b. 1937) with his works for soprano and orchestra based on *Alice in Wonderland;* and, of course, the minimalist Philip Glass (b. 1937) and post-minimalist John Adams (b. 1947).

Some things are changing, however. The symphony orchestra, expensive and conservative, risks becoming a museum. Most new art music today is composed for much smaller forces and venues, in which the expense is not so great and—I fear—the listeners not so hostile. Whether this state of things portends decay or metamorphosis will be the responsibility of us all: composer, performer, and audience alike.

5

Tonality

Music written by composers from Bach to about the time of Mahler and Richard Strauss exists within the framework of rules and practices called *tonality*. Tonality presupposes a hierarchy of functions for pitches in a horizontal line (a *melody*) and for the chords *(harmony)* that support them. It is because of tonality that certain spots in a composition seem particularly reposeful, while others seem to have great tension built in. This is a natural result of the composer's manipulation of the pitches such that one pitch (or one chord) is more important than another, which is in turn more important than another, and so on.

The building blocks for this system are the *major and minor scales*. The terms "major" and "minor" denote two different organizations of the series of eight pitches in a scale. Major is the brighter mode; minor, the more colorful, sometimes the deeper and more sinister.

Within the major and minor scales, the first note (C, in C major)

MIDDLE C

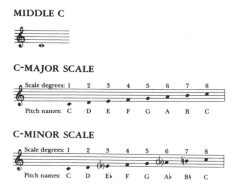

C-MAJOR SCALE

C-MINOR SCALE

is the strongest; it is the home pitch, or the *tonic.* The fifth note (G, in C major) is called the *dominant:* of all the pitches it has one of the strongest pulls back to tonic, especially when it occurs in the bass line. (Each of the other pitches in the scale has a name that describes its function as well: the fourth pitch is the *subdominant,* the seventh, the *leading tone,* and so forth.)

The term *interval* describes the distance between two pitches—either horizontal (melodic) or vertical (harmonic). You simply count pitches: thus C to D is a second, C to E a third, C to F a fourth, and so on. Two identical pitches are said to be in *unison;* an *octave* is the distance between one C and the next C above on the keyboard, for example.

The most frequent references to intervals you will encounter are such formulations as "parallel thirds and sixths," "chains of interlocking thirds," or "hammering octaves in the solo piano." Here is what they look like:

a. Parallel thirds: a traditional way to join pairs of wind instruments; often it is used for a countrified effect.

DVOŘÁK: "New World" Symphony, I

b. Parallel sixths:

BEETHOVEN: Symphony No. 9, IV

c. A rising sequence of interlocking thirds:
MOZART: **Concerto for Flute, K. 313, I**

d. An onslaught of octaves:
TCHAIKOVSKY: **Piano Concerto No. 1, III**

Chords can be built on any note of a scale. Most often a chord consists of three simultaneous pitches arranged in thirds (C–E–G, D–F–A, and so on). These chords are called *triads,* the basic building blocks of tonal harmony. They, too, are called tonic if built on the first scale degree (C–E–G in C major), dominant if built on the fifth (G–B–D in C major), and so on. It is the progression of dominant pull to tonic resolution—a *cadence*—that establishes a key.

Keys, then, are identified by their tonic pitch and by the fact that their mode is major or minor; thus the designation "Symphony in C Major," or "D Minor," or "E♭ Major." Once established, the home key can be left for a time through the process called *modulation* (see p. 30). But, at least until the drastic tonal practices of the early twentieth century, the original tonic key will always return.

So it is not just that musical grammar consists of chords—nearly every concertgoer has some sense of that. What is important is that the chords have distinct functions and operate in hierarchies, that they have a decidedly directional pull and drive. Composers used tonality as a main propellant of musical drama. It is true, for example, that the second theme-group of a sonata form contrasts in melodic quality, texture, and orchestration from the first group; but the overriding difference is the key change. The ear registers this move, to a greater or lesser degree depending on the experience of the listener, as a fundamental component of the structure. It *requires* a return to tonic.

I wrote above that a work most often starts from a position of musical repose, progresses to maximum tension, and returns to musical repose. Tonality plays a role in all this. When Beethoven, in the first movements of his Third and Fifth Symphonies, creates an almost unbearable tension before the recapitulation, he does so by insisting more and more on the dominant. The musical need for resolution to tonic becomes more and more intense, and the wait for resolution, which we all know will come at the point of recapitulation, becomes nerve-wracking indeed. Likewise, the dreamy floating sensation in some of Schubert's music is caused by his careful choice of passive keys that blur the impetuousness of musical dominance. The thick soup of Wagner's orchestral idiom is created in part from his ability to move effortlessly to very distant keys, confusing our sense of direction and spinning things out over extended periods of time.

The beginning concertgoer may not grasp much of this at the start; it may take some directed listening to begin to get the gist of it. Nevertheless, a lifetime of concert attendance affords a substantial opportunity to grapple with the tenets of tonality and all of the other musical procedures described here. The great program annotator and professor Sir Donald Francis Tovey (1875–1940), believed in the ability of every civilized, literate citizen to grasp the essentials of musical process. It makes good sense, if you believe him, to try to hear something new at each concert you attend.

6

Rhythm

and

Meter

—————————❦—————————

Many people are confused by the difference between rhythm and meter. It is simple. Rhythm is concerned with the duration of pitches; quarter notes, half notes, and sixteenth notes are all rhythmic values. Meter is concerned with organizing those rhythms within a regularly recurring pattern of stressed and unstressed beats. Each recurrence of the pattern constitutes a *measure* or *bar*.

Meter is indicated by such signatures as $\frac{3}{4}$, $\frac{4}{4}$, and $\frac{6}{8}$: $\frac{3}{4}$ means that there are three quarter notes in a measure of music; $\frac{6}{8}$ means that a measure contains six eighth notes.

The pattern associated with *William Tell* (and/or The Lone Ranger, depending on your taste) is memorable in its *rhythmic* construction. Waltzes, on the other hand, are characterized by their *metric* pattern of $\frac{3}{4}$, marches by $\frac{2}{4}$ or $\frac{6}{8}$, and minuets by their courtly $\frac{3}{4}$.

ROSSINI: Overture to *William Tell* (theme)

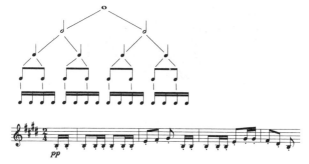

The Orchestral Score and How to Follow One

———————⟡———————

After that naughty question "What does a conductor *do?*," the question music directors most frequently hear is "How do you learn to read an orchestral score?" The answer is that, like every other skill, it comes with diligent practice. Even inveterate score readers register a few more details on each re-reading. And the conductor is lucky: the players nearly always cover his or her mistakes.

Many concertgoers enjoy perusing a score from time to time, for the experience never fails to be illuminating. The easiest way is to begin by following the melody line—the most prominent tune at any given moment as it moves around from instrument to instrument. If, and only if, you own your own copy of the score, mark it with reminders, notes, and cues: nearly everybody does. (Use a colored pencil.) First you have to follow closely enough not to get lost. Soon you will be able to see what's coming next, and eventually the eye and the ear will learn to coordinate to the satisfaction of the brain.

Consider the two examples provided: the first page of Mozart's G-Minor Symphony and the beginning of the Russian Dance at the end of the first scene of Stravinsky's *Petrushka*. Each consists of lines assigned to the various instruments, grouped in systems (or braces) of score. Mozart's orchestra is small enough so that two systems of score can be accommodated on one printed page; note the measure number 6 in the upper left corner of the second system. On the other hand, the Stravinsky orchestra is so large that a conventional printed page barely accommodates all the parts. (These pages are considerably reduced from the size a conductor ordinarily uses.)

The *instruments* ① are listed down the left-hand margin of the first system, usually in Italian but often in the composer's native language. Some scores give abbreviations of the instruments on every page; others, like the Mozart, leave it to the reader to remember which line is which after the first page of a movement. *Fagotti* (Italian for "bundle of sticks") means bassoons; *corno* (plural *corni*) means horn. In the Stravinsky you see *corno inglese* for English horn, and *pistoni* for piston cornets (that is, cornets with ordinary piston valve mechanisms). Names of the other instruments are pretty self-evident.

Both pages are headed with a *tempo indication* ②: *Molto Allegro,* or "very fast" for the Mozart; *Allegro giusto,* "precise" or "strict" Allegro in the Stravinsky. The tempo indication in the Stravinsky is followed by a metronome marking, which indicates that the right speed will allow 118 quarter-note beats in one minute.

First in each line come the *clefs* ⑤, the treble clef (upper winds, violins, etc.) indicating that the second line up is G, the bass clef (all the lower instruments) indicating that the fourth line up is F, and the C-clefs (violas, and the bassoons in *Petrushka*) showing which line is middle C.

The *key signature* ③ comes just after the clef: two flats, for G minor in the Mozart, and no sharps or flats in the Stravinsky example. The nonmatching key signatures have to do with a complication I will describe just below; go for the moment with the majority.

The *meter signature* ④ comes next. The *alla breve* or "cut-C" indication in the Mozart is shorthand for $\frac{2}{2}$, or two half-notes to the bar. In Stravinsky, the signature is $\frac{2}{4}$, or two quarter notes to the bar.

Dynamic markings ⑥ are found at the entry of each instrument

MOZART: Symphony No. 40 in G Minor, K. 550, I

and whenever the dynamic level changes. The Mozart begins *piano* (soft); the Stravinsky begins *forte* (loud).

(The indications "in Si♭" and "in Sol" and "in F" show the keys in which those instruments—called transposing instruments—are pitched, a matter largely having to do with the history of instrument manufacture. What you have to do, if you really care to know *exactly* which pitch is sounding, is to remember that if the clarinet in B♭ plays a

STRAVINSKY: *Petrushka,* First Tableau, Russian Dance

written C, the pitch B♭ comes out. If you are a beginner, content yourself for the moment with watching the contours and textures and don't worry about the transpositions.)

Now allow your memory of Mozart's celebrated G-Minor Symphony to be jogged by the page of score. You can see the repetitive, busy churning figuration in the viola accompaniment that, along with the "G-minor-ness" you recently noted in the title and key signature, gives the movement its quality of restlessness. Now note the contour of the two violin parts, which give the same tune in octaves, and hum along. At the end of the page, where you see the F♯s and the sustained note in the cello, you are at a point of maximum tension, and I hope you are now wishing I had given you two pages, so you could remember how it comes out. (The answer is that the winds, so conspicuous in their absence thus far, are about to enter.)

In *Petrushka* all those terraced-out sixteenth notes suggest the big, merry dance that follows. You can imagine what the big chords in the piano, requiring eight of the ten fingers and a lot of wrist, must sound like. Hear for yourself the *pizzicato* (plucking) in the strings. (It is indicated in the score by the marking *"pizz."* In the flute parts the indication *a 2* means both players play the one line. The word *ouvert* in the French horn III-IV line means "open" as opposed to muted or stopped with the hand in the bell.)

By now you have deciphered enough to keep going. Don't worry if you get lost from time to time; everybody does. The important thing is to discover how much more of the music you can grasp when you *see* what is actually happening in the sounds you hear.

PART TWO

Some great composers and their works

A
Word
from
the
Author

My purpose in the biographical and critical notes note that follow is not so much to account for every major event in a life or work as it is to whet your appetite and suggest a few things to keep in mind during a live performance. You are invited to pick and choose, though I hope you will follow your nose from, say, the Mozart Requiem to those of Berlioz, Verdi, and Brahms, the better to grasp how individual masterpieces fit into the overall picture.

What makes a composer or a composition great? Survival is one criterion; so is the ability to express everything that needs to be said about a style (as is the case with Bach's B-Minor Mass) or to redefine it altogether (as Beethoven's *Eroica* does). Another criterion is to capture a sentiment so persuasively that once heard, the music can never be forgotten: such is the case, I think with the Schumann Piano Concerto and Tchaikovsky's "Pathétique" Symphony.

In short, it all depends—and sometimes the call is arbitrary. In a few cases (Chabrier, Holst, Respighi), a not-quite-superlative composer has left a work or two so well entrenched in the repertoire that you have to call it great, if only on the basis of durability. From time to time I plug for a composer or work not heard in the concert hall as often as quality merits (Sessions). On occasion, a very popular composer or work has been omitted out of sheer orneriness (Orff) and some (like Albéniz) I have left out because I think the vogue for them is done. For Bach and Mozart and Stravinsky and their peers, no amount of summary will do, and those entries, even though they are long, are not long enough. Compromise is demanded.

You will find, in the course of the biographies, references to several great impresarios: J.-P. Salomon, for example, who brought Haydn to England and saw that he came with new symphonies in hand; and Sergei Diaghilev, who managed to acquire immortal ballet scores from Debussy, Ravel, Stravinsky, Falla, and many more. But admire, above all, the great patrons who supported the art for the pleasure it gave, without a thought of financial return: Tchaikovsky's patroness, Madame von Meck, for example; the conductor Serge Koussevitzky, who commissioned the Bartók Concerto for Orchestra, Stravinsky's *Symphony of Psalms,* and a dozen other equally significant orchestral works; Elizabeth Sprague Coolidge, whose foundation brought works from Copland's *Appalachian Spring* through Elliott Carter's Double Concerto and beyond to the tiny theater at the Library of Congress. One could do worse than to acquire one's immortality through the love of art.

In the heading that precedes each work are the sorts of things you will want to know before a performance: title and its translation; details of scoring, and circumstances of the work's composition; first performance; and date of publication. Where an inexpensive score is available, this is indicated. One other comforting thing to know in advance is the approximate duration of the work.

Specifying the performing force is trickier than it looks. Some works, for example, call for two oboes, with the second player expected to double on English horn; others, for two full-time oboists and an English horn player. Both cases I list as "oboes I-II, English horn," without particular attention to who's playing what. That, in any case, is often determined by the established practice of the performing ensemble.

Solo vocal parts are designated with abbreviations common in the profession: SATB means soprano-alto-tenor-bass; Ms. is mezzo-soprano, and Bar. is baritone.

With regard to percussion instruments, the situation is complicated by the absence of standard nomenclature. Following the orchestration treatise by Walter Piston, I use the terms snare drum (the equivalent of the English side drum), tenor drum (a military field drum without snares), and bass drum. The French sometimes distinguish between the shallow snared *caisse claire* and the snareless *tambour, tambour militaire,* and *caisse roulante;* sometime they don't. The word *tambourin* when it appears in a score, is confusing: often it means tambourine (the French *tambour de basque*), but sometime it means a tabor, which is a tiny skin-headed drum whose ancestry goes back to the Middle Ages. I call the case full of tuned metal bars a glockenspiel (rather than simply "bells"); tubular bells I term chimes. The word "bells," it seems to me, should be reserved for instruments cast of heavy metal in the true bell shape.

When several works by a single composer are treated, I give symphonies first, then concertos, overtures, and other one-movement compositions.

Johann Sebastian Bach

Born 21 March 1685 in Eisenach
Died 28 July 1750 in Leipzig

One of a large family of professional musicians active in North Germany for more than two centuries, Johann Sebastian Bach achieved eminence first as keyboard virtuoso and later as a prolific master composer in nearly all the genres of the high Baroque. Each of the several posts he held required its own sort of music from his pen: early cantatas and keyboard work for Arnstadt and Mühlhausen (appointed 1703, 1707), great organ works and another round of cantatas for Weimar (from 1708), secular works including the *Brandenburg Concertos* for Cöthen (from 1717), and religious works in all forms for his long tenure in Leipzig (1723–50). As cantor of St. Thomas church in Leipzig, Bach wrote several years' worth of weekly church cantatas, the St. John and St. Matthew Passions (1724, 1727), and dozens of other compositions to serve the array of church and civic occasions for which the cantor was expected to provide the music. In some respects his most sweeping work is the B-Minor Mass (1733–49), the convoluted genesis of which is summarized below. At the end of his life he composed two collections which summed up his compositional knowledge: *A Musical Offering* (1747) and *The Art of Fugue* (1745–50).

Bach was a happy family man, sire of twenty children, four of whom—Wilhelm Friedemann, Carl Philipp Emanuel, Johann Christoph, and Johann Christian—became excellent composers themselves.

He wrote about a thousand compositions, including the two hundred cantatas, several dozen secular cantatas, masses and Magnificats, passions, orchestral concertos and suites, and keyboard music. His works are arranged by BWV numbers which refer to a catalogue by Wolfgang Schmieder, the *Bach-Werke-Verzeichnis*.

The *Brandenburg Concertos*

No. 1 in F Major, BWV 1046
For solo violin, oboes I-III, bassoon, horns I-II; strings; continuo
Duration: about 25 minutes

No. 2 in F Major, BWV 1047
For solo violin, recorder, oboe, trumpet; strings; continuo
Duration: about 20 minutes

No. 3 in G Major, BWV 1048
For violins I-III, violas I-III, cellos I-III, double bass (violone), and continuo
Duration: about 12 minutes

No. 4 in G Major, BWV 1049
For solo violin, recorders I-II; strings; continuo
Duration: about 20 minutes

No. 5 in D Major, BWV 1050
For solo transverse flute, violin, harpsichord; strings; continuo
Duration: about 25 minutes

No. 6 in B Major, BWV 1051
For violas I-II, viols da gamba I-II, cellos I-II, double bass; continuo
Duration: about 20 minutes

Assembled 1721–22 in Cöthen from works composed there and
in Weimar

First performed in concerts under Bach's direction at the time of
composition; later (April 1729 and afterward) performed in the
Leipzig *collegium musicum* concerts; never performed in
Brandenburg

Unpublished during Bach's lifetime; the standard publications are
found in the old and new Bach editions (Leipzig, 1871; Kassel,
1956). *Inexpensive scores:* Johann Sebastian Bach: *The Six
Brandenburg Concertos and the Four Orchestral Suites in Full Score*
(New York: Dover, 1976)

The six *Brandenburg Concertos* are preserved in a fair manuscript in
Bach's own hand, titled, in flowery French, "Six concertos for several
instruments, dedicated to His Royal Highness Christian Louis, Margrave of Brandenburg and so forth, by his very humble and most
obedient servant, Jean Sebastien Bach, chapelmaster to His Royal
Highness, the Prince Regent of Anhalt-Cöthen." The letter of dedication goes on to remind the margrave that some years earlier, he had
done Bach the honor of asking for some new pieces. Here they are,
says the composer, and he only hopes that the prince will not judge
them too harshly, his "delicate and refined taste" being a matter of
common knowledge. This is the sort of presentation composers made
when seeking employment.

It is because the *Brandenburg Concertos* are so diverse of instrumentation and structure, so daring when considered alongside the hundreds
of commonplace concertos of the time, that they still seem the apogee
of Baroque orchestral practice. The Sixth Concerto is the most unusual
in sonority, by virtue of the unparalleled, rich tone quality of its pairs
of violas and gambas over cellos with double bass. (The *gamba* is a
fretted Renaissance instrument of six strings.) In the Third *Brandenburg* Bach distributes his musical material among three choirs—violins, violas, cellos each divided into three parts—a tactic that yields
multiple possibilities for musical permutation. The First Concerto,
with a minuet and a *polacca* tacked on at the end, calls for winds and
a solo *violino piccolo.*

The Fourth and Fifth *Brandenburgs* emphasize less the collective
efforts of the ensemble than the work of the soloists. The two recorders
in the Fourth Concerto act, in effect, as a tame accompaniment to the

virtuoso violin part, while the Fifth is probably the most splendid of all concertos for harpsichord, whose role quite dwarfs the flute and violin parts. This particular work was apparently written for a specific instrument Bach bought in Berlin in 1719, during the very visit where he played for the Margrave of Brandenburg. It also marks Bach's first use of the transverse flute.

The Second *Brandenburg* is the favorite of modern audiences, largely on account of its brilliant high trumpet part. The choice of solo instruments is unique in the concerto literature.

Each concerto consists of the basic three movements traditional to the genre, fast–slow–fast, though at the center of the Third *Brandenburg* there is merely a pair of chords, *Adagio,* over which improvisation by the keyboard player is doubtless intended. The slow movements invite particular attention, for they are less impetuous than the *Allegros* and afford the listener a more relaxed forum to ponder the interchange of the solo lines and Bach's legendary skill at contrapuntal imitation.

It appears that Bach composed three of the concertos (I, III, and VI) when he was a chamber musician in Weimar (1708–13), and greatly interested in the Italian orchestral repertoire. The Second and Fourth seem to come from early in the Cöthen period, and the Fifth was probably the last composed. The set was assembled and copied in 1720, with the letter of dedication dated 24 March 1721. The composer had probably performed all six of his concertos in Cöthen, but the Margrave of Brandenburg lacked the necessary resources to produce them, and Bach's priceless gift thus went unacknowledged. In short, the margrave earned his immortality from works he never heard by a composer he did not employ.

The Orchestral Suites

No. 1 in C major, BWV 1066
For oboes I-II, bassoon; strings; continuo
Composed between 1717 and 1723 in Cöthen
Duration: about 30 minutes

No. 2 in B Minor, BWV 1067
For transverse flute; strings; continuo
Composed in the late 1730s in Leipzig
Duration: about 25 minutes

No. 3 in D Major, BWV 1068
For oboes I-II; trumpets I-III; timpani; strings; continuo
Composed about 1730 in Leipzig
Duration: about 25 minutes

No. 4 in D Major, BWV 1069
For oboes I-III; bassoon; trumpets I-III; timpani; strings; continuo
Composed between 1717 and 1723 in Cöthen
Duration: about 25 minutes

First performed in concerts under Bach's direction at the time of composition; later (April 1729 and afterward) performed in the Leipzig *collegium musicum* concerts
Unpublished during Bach's lifetime; the standard publications are found in the old and new Bach editions (Leipzig, 1885; Kassel, 1967). *Inexpensive scores:* Johann Sebastian Bach: *The Six Brandenburg Concertos and the Four Orchestral Suites in Full Score* (New York: Dover, 1976)

These four works, called by Bach *ouvertures,* are in fact French suites for orchestra, descended from ballet music of the seventeenth century. French suites were popular in those European courts—most of them, in fact—that enjoyed imitating the manner of Versailles. The dignity of character and the gravity of the Bach suites result in large measure from the brilliant movements with which they open. Each of these is a French overture—hence Bach's titles—with slow, regal outer sections framing the fast, imitative material in the middle. The overture makes up about half the length of each suite.

The works continue with French dances: gavottes, courantes, bourrées, and minuets, with an occasional forlane, passepied, polonaise, or réjouissance. The dance movements are each in two repeated sections. Where there is a second dance with reduced texture, called a *double,* it is conventional practice to go back after the second and play the first without repeats, as in the later minuet and trio form. In a good performance, however, these repeats never seem mechanical or routine. Listen for the differences in nuance and ornamentation the second time around.

Like the *Brandenburg Concertos,* the Bach suites vary in instrumentation. The Second Suite is virtually a concerto for the solo flute; in the Fourth, the choirs of trumpets and timpani, oboes and bassoon, and strings are deployed in tripartite fashion very much as in the Third *Brandenburg*. My own favorite is the great Third Suite, with the "Air for the G String," so-called because a solo version of the movement was a favorite showpiece of nineteenth-century violin virtuosi. Elsewhere its festive band of trumpets and timpani is deployed with such sophistication and restraint that it outdoes in majesty the French courtly trumpet and drum fanfares (known to modern listeners from *Masterpiece Theatre*) that doubtless inspired it. The real competition comes from Handel's very similar French suite, the *Music for the Royal Fireworks* (see pp. 264–65).

Concerto for Two Violins and Orchestra in D Minor, BWV 1043

Vivace
Largo ma non tanto
Allegro

For solo violins I-II; strings; continuo
Composed between 1717 and 1723 in Cöthen
First performed shortly after composition under the composer's direction
Unpublished during Bach's lifetime; the standard is the old Bach edition (Leipzig, 1872). *Inexpensive score:* Johann Sebastian Bach: *The Three Violin Concerti in Full Score* (New York: Dover, 1990)
Duration: about 20 minutes

The Bach "Double," like the Hallelujah Chorus and the "Moonlight" Sonata, is somehow able to withstand the fierce assaults upon it by beginners—it's a Suzuki favorite—on the one hand, and by wizened, overbearing dignitaries on the other—the latter often paired in a televised concert for which there has been too little rehearsal. Every violinist imagines that he or she knows the secret of the piece.

Indeed it is a timeless work of pleasing sentiment. This is due in part to the clarity of the opening orchestral ritornello: a simple rising scalar figure, some outlining of the main chords, and a quick cadence after four bars. Partly it has to do with Bach's skill at weaving the two-in-one effects of the pair of solo instruments into the two-plus-one textures of the solo parts with the basso continuo. Generally speaking the work proceeds along the lines of the typical Baroque concerto (see p. 34), though in the first movement the orchestral passages act like statements of a fugue and the solo breaks as fugal episodes (see, again, p. 35).

The second movement is a relaxed *siciliano* in the relative major key. The last movement, though not quite a gigue, is cast in triple meter with frequent triplet subdivisions of the beat. Its melodies, by contrast with those of the first movement, drive downward, but there are more than a few hints of the syncopations and melodic suspensions that peppered the *Vivace*. Bach takes care to write solo parts of equal importance, to the extent that where, in the first movement, the second violinist was the leader and the first the follower, here the roles are reversed.

Bach was an avid student of the Italian concerto, both solo and grosso. He often transcribed favorite concertos by his contemporaries and forerunners, and he was quick to revise and reset his own works for other solo instruments. For example, the Double is transcribed for two harpsichords (BWV 1062, in C Minor); likewise he reworked the Concerto for Violin and Oboe in D Minor into a double harpsichord concerto in C Minor, BWV 1060. This Double Concerto, like the suites and the *Brandenburgs,* is a product of the Cöthen period, where it was surely played by Bach and his band of eighteen musicians.

St. Matthew Passion, BWV 244

Part I: Passover
Part II: Christ's Trial and Crucifixion

For soloists (Evangelist, tenor; Jesus, bass; Judas, bass; Peter, bass; Pontius Pilate, bass; and several lesser roles); aria soloists (SATB); chorus and orchestra I (flutes I-II, oboes I-IV, bassoon, strings, continuo); chorus and orchestra II (flutes I-II, oboes I-II, strings, continuo)

Text from the Gospel According to St. Matthew, chapters 26–27, with traditional Lutheran chorales and new texts by the poet known as Picander (i.e., Christian Friedrich Henrici, 1700–64)

Composed 1727 or 1729 in Leipzig

First performed Good Friday (15 April) 1729 by the musical forces of the St. Thomas church in Leipzig, Bach conducting; possibly performed two years earlier, Good Friday (11 April) 1727; Bach revised the work substantially for a performance in

1736. The so-called Bach revival traces its roots to the first "modern performance" of the *St. Matthew Passion* on 11 March 1829 by the Berlin Singakademie, Mendelssohn conducting.
Unpublished during Bach's life; the standards are the old and new Bach editions (Leipzig, 1855; Kassel, 1972). *Inexpensive score:* Johann Sebastian Bach: *St. Matthew Passion in Full Score* (New York: Dover, 1989)
Duration: about three hours

The *passion* as a musical genre achieved prominence in North Germany during the mid-Baroque, though its history extends well back into the Middle Ages, from which time there are examples in plainchant. Bach's masterpieces are among the last. The passion sets the story of the suffering of Christ between the Last Supper and His death, following the text of one of the four gospels. Individual singers take the roles of the characters in the story (Jesus, Judas, Simon Peter, Pontius Pilate), and there is always an angry crowd, the *turba judaorum,* urging crucifixion. The evangelist narrates the story. For the Bach passions, eighteenth-century librettists provided texts for arias and choruses that comment on the narrative contained in the Bible.

In the Bach passions, the story is told largely in recitative with short interjections by the chorus. The arias reflect on the events that have transpired; the chorales are affirmations of faith from the congregation. What is exceptional about the many chorales is the way Bach harmonizes them to cast each text in an atmosphere appropriate to the surrounding drama. The big opening and closing choruses are of such majesty and sorrow that they seem to epitomize the meaning of Good Friday in a way that few other composers have ever matched.

Bach wrote these works knowing that he would be able to engage virtuoso instrumentalists for his Easter week performances, such that there is important solo work for gamba, lute, woodwinds, and individual strings players. The somber nature of the commemoration precluded use of trumpets and timpani (these would be heard on Easter morning), but otherwise the Bach passions contain the most varied and unusual instrumental textures in the late Baroque repertoire.

The *Matthew Passion* is longer than Bach's other work in this genre, the *St. John Passion,* because of its much more extensive text, and larger, because of its scoring for two orchestras and choruses. Also unique to the *Matthew Passion* are the consistent setting of Christ's words over sustained chords in the strings and the strong reliance on orchestrally accompanied recitative before the bigger arias. The narrative shifts rapidly from incident to incident. Part I includes the episodes of the annointment of Christ at the house of Simon the leper, Judas Iscariot and the thirty pieces of silver, the Last Supper, and Christ in the garden of Gethsemane; part II treats Christ before Caiaphas and the elders, Peter's denial, Judas's suicide, Christ before Pilate, the scarlet robe and crown of thorns, the way of the Cross, the Crucifixion and last words, and the burial of Christ.

If you never make it past the opening chorus you will nevertheless have heard one of the majestic triumphs of Baroque art. Over a restless orchestral ritornello, the daughters of Jerusalem mourn the Bridegroom Christ, the spotless lamb, bearing His own cross. Who? what? where? asks the second chorus, antiphonally, while a third chorus, made up of boy sopranos, sings the chorale tune *O Lamm Gottes unschuldig* (O Innocent Lamb of God).

Musical symbolism and word painting are deployed often and with great sophistication. Note for example, in the second part, Peter's bitter weeping after he has thrice denied his Lord; the increasingly complex harmonizations of the Passion Chorale, *O Haupt voll Blut und Wunden* (O Bloody Head Now Wounded), culminating at the moment of Christ's death in a setting of splendidly mysterious chromaticism; and, just afterward, the rending of the veil of the Temple as reflected in the continuo part.

A comment of this brevity can do little justice to a work of this magnitude, and you must discover the rest of it for yourself. It's worth a journey of many miles or minutes to make the discovery.

Mass in B Minor, BWV 232

Missa (Mass, i. e., *Kyrie* and *Gloria*)
   Kyrie (3 movements)
   Gloria (9 movements)
Symbolum Nicenum (Nicene Creed, 9 movements)
Sanctus, Osanna, Benedictus, Agnus Dei, Dona nobis pacem (5 movements)

For soloists (SSATB), chorus; flutes I-II, oboes I-III, bassoons I-II; horn, trumpets I-III; timpani; strings; continuo
Text traditional Latin

Fashioned in the late 1740s (c. 1747–49) from works dating back to 1714

Unperformed as a complete work during Bach's life; the full Mass first performed 30 September 1813 by the Berlin Singakademie, Carl Friedrich Zelter conducting

Unpublished during Bach's life; the standards are the old and new Bach editions (Leipzig, 1857; Kassel, 1954). *Inexpensive score:* Johann Sebastian Bach: *Mass in B Minor in Full Score* (New York: Dover, 1989)

Duration: about two and a quarter hours

On 27 July 1733, along with the usual deferential letter, Bach presented the Elector Friedrich August II a set of manuscript parts for a *missa,* that is, a *Kyrie* and a *Gloria,* intended for the Saxon court at Dresden—a traditional gesture of application for employment. Bach was vexed with the conditions of his post in Leipzig, and he imagined that an appointment as titular "church composer" to the historic, though Catholic, Dresden chapel would improve his lot at home. This mostly honorific title eventually materialized in 1736, but the work went unplayed in Dresden, and it appears that the manuscript parts were never used there.

Bach returned to his mass in the early 1740s when he borrowed portions of the *Gloria* for a Christmas cantata, *Gloria in excelsis Deo,* BWV 191. Then, apparently in the late 1740s, he returned to it again, this time to complete a setting of the entire Mass Ordinary (see p. 36). For the most part, this process consisted in identifying earlier compositions for reuse, casting preexisting choruses in five parts rather than the more common four, rewriting texts, and reassigning instrumental parts. (Bach, a Lutheran by faith and conditions of employment, had virtually no prior experience in setting the *Credo* of the Roman Mass; the majestic result has little to do with the demands of either liturgy.) The contents of this huge manuscript, having no comprehensive title page, were eventually dubbed the B-Minor Mass. But for Bach's proofreading work on the *Art of Fugue,* constructing the Mass appears to have been his last major compositional activity.

The so-called B-Minor Mass was thus never a work particularly intended by its composer for consecutive performance; like the *Musical Offering* and *Art of Fugue,* it is rather a cyclopedic and masterly summary of the compositional manners of the Baroque. It may therefore be that a complete performance is "inauthentic." On the other hand, and for those very reasons, the Mass lends itself to successful performance in a wide variety of fashions. (The scholar and performer Joshua Rifkin, for example, presented a highly controversial but elegant performance a few years ago, with only one singer or instrumentalist per line of score—approximately two dozen performers in all. A recording was subsequently issued on the Nonesuch Digital label.)

The B-Minor Mass commences with three powerful cries of "Kyrie," then continues with the greatest of all Bach's slow five-voice fugues, first for orchestra alone, then for chorus and orchestra. Much of what comes afterward consists of big concerted movements for the orchestra and chorus in concerto grosso style, strongly permeated with fugue. Trumpets and timpani do not enter until the *Gloria,* at which point the work turns abruptly from B minor to focus on D major as tonic center, the traditionally jubilant key for trumpets and drums. The solos and duets are usually *da capo* forms of one sort or another; these feature fine work, as well, for the instrumental soloists, as in the florid accompaniment for two bassoons and horn of the *Quoniam.* The movements that constitute the *Credo,* part II, are arranged in a keystoned arch: the old-style *colla parte* fugues at the beginning and end frame the magnificent *Crucifixus* in the middle. This celebrated passacaglia (see p. 35) is built on the sort of descending chromatic bass pattern often associated in the Baroque period with lamentation for the dead.

One has the impression, in some of the vast choruses with orchestra—the *Cum Sancto Spiritu,* for example, or the *Et resurrexit*—that some pent-up passion has been loosed in Bach's magisterial intelligence, a large spring has sprung that must be allowed its full rebound. And the repetition of the soaring *Gratias agimus tibi* for the last movement, *Dona nobis pacem,* especially on the heels of the tragic *Agnus Dei* just before it, is a stroke of genius. Indeed the B-Minor Mass is to the Baroque what the stonework of Chartres cathedral is to the Gothic: one of the most formidable demonstrations of art in the service of religious faith that has been left to us.

Samuel Barber

Born 9 March 1910 in West Chester, Pennsylvania
Died 23 January 1981 in New York

Barber was an early product of the Curtis Institute of Music in Philadelphia, which he entered at age 14 as a member of the first matriculating class; later he taught there. Following his formation at Curtis, Barber won a series of fellowships and prizes, including the American *prix de Rome,* which allowed him to travel extensively in Europe, make the acquaintance of the great musicians there, and compose without the interference of other obligations. He earned acclaim and a Pulitzer Prize for his first opera, *Vanessa* (1957), produced by the Metropolitan Opera. It was natural, then, that he be selected to compose the opera with which the Met opened when it moved to Lincoln Center in 1966: *Antony and Cleopatra,* to an adaption by Franco Zeffirelli of Shakespeare's tragedy. This second opera, by contrast, was a failure with both critics and public.

Barber was by and large a conservative in regard to the compositional issues of his generation, pretty well disinterested in the vocabularies of dissonance and rhythmic experiment then making the rounds. His passion was for the voice and his principal affinity for vocal composition.

His most successful orchestral works include an overture called *The School for Scandal* (1933), two symphonies and four concertos, two *Essays for Orchestra* (1937, 1942), the Adagio for Strings, and *Medea's Meditation and Dance of Vengeance* (1955) from a ballet for Martha Graham's dance company (1946). With the Piano Concerto (1962), Barber won a second Pulitzer Prize.

Adagio for Strings (arranged from the String Quartet in B Minor, OP. 11, mvt. II)

For violins I-II, violas I-II, cellos I-II, double basses
Composed 1936 in and around Salzburg
First performed 5 November 1938, by the NBC Orchestra, New York, Arturo Toscanini conducting
Published by G. Schirmer, Inc. (New York, 1939); dedicated to the composer's aunt and uncle, Louise and Sidney Homer, the former a singer and the latter a composer of songs
Duration: about 7 minutes

In the Adagio for Strings, a work popularized and recorded by Toscanini, Barber's gift for sweeping lyricism finds memorable venue. He crafts this beautiful cameo from the simplest of means: a single meandering (and very familiar) melody that wends its way in quarter notes along conjoining pitches of the scale, a chordal accompaniment, forthright tonality, and a performing force made up of that portion of the orchestra having the greatest homogeneity of tone quality. You first hear this melody in the violins; then it fades downward into the violas and cellos until each instrumental voice has had an appropriate share of the action.

The gesture is one of quiet spiritual reflection, the kind that takes over when you are falling asleep or lost in a reverie. There is a searching quality to the architecture, with every tendency toward upward rise met by a subsequent fall; in the center section the double basses rest as all the voices lift to a shrill treble climax. That is dissipated by the sequence of cadences when the basses return, and what begins as a true recapitulation merely reverses course, settles firmly in the home key, and dies away.

Béla Bartók

Born *25 March 1881* in
Nagyszentmiklós, Transylvania
[then in Hungary; now in Romania]
Died *26 September 1945* in New York

Bartók was not only a master composer but a noted scholar, a collector of Hungarian folk music, and a fine pianist as well. After nearly two decades of training in piano and composition, he was appointed professor of piano at the Budapest Academy of Music in 1907, a position he held until 1934. But his piano teaching was half-hearted at best; his first love was the scientific study of the folk music, not just of the Magyars, but of Romanians, Slovaks, and other nationalities as well. This pioneering work in ethnomusicology was encouraged by his friend and conational, Zoltán Kodály; Bartók would take his Edison Talking Machine on annual travels through the countryside, then notate and codify what he had collected. In 1934 he was engaged by the Hungarian Academy of Sciences to complete his monumental edition of Hungarian popular music. All the while, he toured widely as a concert pianist and lecturer on new music, composing sporadically, and with more than his share of false starts, but in the end enjoying a well-earned celebrity as composer. The series of foreign commissions he received in the mid and late 1930s, for example, is a good indicator of the international esteem in which he was held; these resulted in the *Music for Strings, Percussion, and Celesta,* the Fifth Quartet, and a half-dozen other works of equal merit.

By the end of the decade Bartók's public hostility to fascist rule made it impossible for him to remain in Hungary, and in October 1940 he and his second wife emigrated to the United States. Though he was given a warm welcome, including offers of academic jobs, concert appearances, major commissions, and an honorary degree from Columbia University, he was miserable here and at times virtually destitute. The onset of leukemia dashed his hopes of returning to Hungary, and he died in New York, embittered at his lot.

His musical heritage was that of his countryman Liszt, nurtured by his predilection for the works of Debussy and Richard Strauss and profiting at every turn from his ethnic studies. His works are propelled by a rhythmic and metric practice unlike that of any other composer, freely mingling speech rhythms and vocal fluctuations with the unyielding pulses of dance-based folk music; the result is forward motion at once dominated by the downbeat and at the same time curiously free of it. Harmonically the music is loosely tonal, dwelling heavily on ethnic vertical and horizontal structures and quick to make use of scales with migrating centers. Many of his 120 or so published opuses are groups of shorter dances or descriptive movements, including dozens of songs and piano works. His didactic series for the piano, *Mikrokosmos* (six volumes progressing in difficulty, 1926–37), is widely used for instruction and bears close philosophical affinities with Kodály's theories of choral training. The six string quartets (1908, 1917, 1927, 1928, 1934, and 1939) are the most powerful in the genre after Beethoven. Bartók's most admired orchestral works are his three piano concertos (1926, 1931, 1945), the *Music for Strings, Percussion, and Celesta* (1936), a Violin Concerto, and the Concerto for Orchestra. Suites from his two ballets, *The Wooden Prince* (1917) and *The Miraculous Mandarin* (1919), are often heard as well.

Concerto for Orchestra

Introduzione
Giuoco delle coppie (Game of Pairs)
Elegia
Intermezzo interrotto (Interrupted Intermezzo)
Finale

For piccolo, flutes I-III, oboes I-III, English horn, clarinets I-III, bass clarinet, bassoons I-III, contrabassoon; horns I-IV, trumpets I-III, trombones I-III, tuba; timpani, snare drum, bass drum, cymbals, triangle, tam-tam; harps I-II; strings
Composed summer 1943, mostly at Saranac Lake, New York to a commission from the Koussevitzky Music Foundation; revised February 1945; dedicated to the memory of Natalie Koussevitzky
First performed 1 December 1944 by the Boston Symphony Orchestra, Serge Koussevitzky conducting
Published by Boosey and Hawkes (London, 1946)
Duration: about 40 minutes

Bartók's Concerto for Orchestra—the only work he completed in the United States; his check from the Koussevitzky Foundation was for $1,000—offers a pointed reminder of how varied the currents of contemporary music were at midcentury. Here, in the mid-1940s, three decades after the Stravinsky ballets and only a few dozen months before successful experiments in panserialism and sound synthesis, a compositional giant offered the American public as his valedictory a work based on classical models, embodying almost continuous reference to Hungarian folk melodies and metric patterns, and both tonal and cyclic in the old-fashioned manner. In the 1940s this would surely have been dismissed as passé had not Bartók pulled off his conception of an orchestral concerto so powerfully. Instead, the Concerto for Orchestra is recognized almost universally as his masterpiece. It is about as troubling as music comes; even the bright, humorous movements operate in nocturnal surroundings with a sense of underlying, rather sinister, urgency about them.

Out of the dark motive stated in the first five bars by the cello and double bass grow many of the melodic contours to follow. Soon there are clear indications that this slow introduction is serving as a big crescendo upbeat; the languid flute is echoed first by three trumpets, then by a burst of strings, *tutta forza*. Gradually, too, we become aware that the nonstop eighth-note motion in the bass instruments is gaining momentum. The figure they reach provides the transition to the Allegro vivace and, in turn, material for the first half of the main theme. The rest of the movement is organized as a sonata, with a vigorous first theme in $\frac{3}{8}$ jarred by unpredictable lurches into $\frac{2}{8}$; an undulating second theme is stated by the solo oboe over open fifths in the strings with echoes in the French horn. Throughout this movement (and indeed the rest of the concerto), Bartók's command of technical device is both cool and dazzling: imitation abounds, themes are effortlessly doubled or halved in value, inverted and otherwise transformed. Great canons ring out from the brass to introduce the recapitulation.

The *Game of Pairs* is played by the wind instruments, each section marked off by a cadence from the snare drum. The vertical distance separating members of the pairs mutate as the instruments change; starting with the chorale in the middle, there begin to be pairs of pairs. The nose-thumbing figure of the trumpets brings the movement to its end, with the snare drum having the last word.

The *Elegy* is drawn from the slow introduction to the first movement, Bartókian night music at its best, the textures dominated by glissandos in the harps and long modal arabesques in the woodwinds with hints of a birdcall in the piccolo. Bartók's jolly intermezzo is a sort of one-legged waltz with a lyric interlude for the tenor instruments. The interruption occurs at the midpoint, when a travelogueish theme is stated by the clarinet and razzed forthwith by gross interjections from the brass and giggles in the woodwind. The intermezzo resumes and, after a flute cadenza, reaches its end without further ado.

The finale is a riot of rapid passagework in shifting meters over a taut rhythmic ostinato in the bass. Melodies break forth from the frenzied texture and seem to take flight. What is clearly a fugue subject is announced by the trumpet, and statements of this motive, now in inversion, now in augmentation and diminution, growing closer and closer together, come to dominate the proceedings. For a moment it all subsides into a mysterious *tranquillo* with chromatics that wedge toward a moment of last repose; then there is a race to one of the two different endings Bartók has supplied in the score. You will probably hear the longer and less abrupt of the two, which Bartók fashioned after the first performance.

Concerto for Violin and Orchestra ("No. 2")

Allegro non troppo
Andante tranquillo
Allegro molto

For violin solo; piccolo, flutes I-II, oboes I-II, English horn, clarinets I-II, bass clarinet, bassoons I-II, contrabassoon; horns I-IV, trumpets I-II, trombones I-III; timpani, snare drums I-II, cymbals I-II, triangle, tam-tam, celesta; harp; strings

Composed August 1937–31 December 1938 in Budapest; dedicated to Zoltán Székely, the violinist

First performed 23 April 1939 by the Concertgebouw Orchestra of Amsterdam, Zoltán Székely, violin; Willem Mengelberg conducting

Published by Boosey and Hawkes (London, 1946)

Duration: about 35 minutes

Bartók composed the Violin Concerto (called no. 2, over his objection, because there is a very early forerunner) during his last months in Hungary, a time of pessimism over his personal future and that of his native land. His fears were well-founded: the first performance of the concerto was at the end of April 1939; that September Hitler invaded Poland. Bartók and his wife left Hungary for the last time in October.

The Violin Concerto is a large work, brimming over with technical craft, and of legendary difficulty for soloist, conductor, and orchestral players. Of particular interest and treachery is the way Bartók organizes the passage of time: no tempo holds sway for more than a couple of dozen bars. The music seems always in the process of winding up to or down from something.

Listen well to the notes played pizzicato by the cellos in the first six bars, for these outline the main theme, both for this first movement and for the last. (Note how many of the melodic twists grow from or return to the pitch B-below-middle-C, the first note you hear in the strings and French horn, and the point of departure for the violin soloist.) The violinist's sweeping first melody is but a fleshed-out version of these pizzicato notes. A traditional concerto first movement follows, though with unusually long statements from the orchestra. Quintuplets in solo and orchestra converge on the second group, which begins in a spirited *tutti* with shrieking piccolo. Equally obnoxious trills and flutters from the trumpets and trombones herald the long development, notable for its quiet interlude of soloist over the celesta and harp. In the recapitulation, one of the episodes transforms itself into a majestic, boldly imitative brass choir, after which come a cadenza and a concluding dialogue of multiple stops on the violin with "snapped" pizzicato in the orchestral strings.

The second movement is made up of a modal theme and six variations, each of which reworks the original lyric idea into something radically different. The third variation, for example, is for double stops and played at the frog of the bow; the fourth has very rapid passagework around the pitches of the theme. The fifth is a scherzetto for the high woodwinds, while the sixth deals with rebounds of the bow, echoes, and (again) snapped pizzicato. The movement closes with a simple restatement of the theme.

The form and principal melodies of the concluding movement are closely related to those of the first, though this movement is in triple meter, while the first was prevailingly duple. The thematic groups develop and recapitulate in the usual manner; the more interesting formal aspect is the way Bartók repeatedly thrusts toward, then retreats from, the issue of bringing the work to a close. When he finally does get to the end, it seems almost abrupt simply because you've been expecting it for so long. The work originally concluded in cascading trombone glissandos, but the soloist demanded a more traditional display ending and Bartók provided one. Both endings appear in the published score.

This is a work of dazzling color and texture, brimming over with unusual instrumental effects: the purposefully narrowed half-steps in the solo part, for example, may give you some momentary gastric discomfort. It is fine Bartók, and I think it the equal of the Concerto for Orchestra.

Ludwig van Beethoven

Born *probably 16 December 1770*
in Bonn
Died *26 March 1827 in Vienna*

Beethoven's profound genius, wizardry of imagination, and vice-like grip of sonata-based formal procedures thrust him, even during his lifetime, to the pinnacle of international celebrity. Widely acknowledged as the successor to Mozart, he set the ground rules for the nascent Romantic movement in music. No composer has more greatly affected his age nor more profoundly disturbed and challenged his followers. Beethoven's sad personal life and tragic physiological decline epitomize Romantic heroism: he is, incontestibly, the Napoleon of music.

Beethoven's father, an alcoholic musician, hoped that his son's gifts could be channeled into the same sort of financial success the Mozart family had once enjoyed. In 1787 the young Beethoven made his first visit to Vienna, where he met and played for Mozart. In 1792, already an accomplished composer, he moved permanently to Vienna in order to study with Haydn. His relationship with Haydn never flowered, but he had instruction from two other formidable teachers, Antonio Salieri and J. G. Albrechtsberger. His connections with princely patrons gave him access to the Viennese aristocracy, and for a time he moved successfully in those circles. By the end of the eighteenth century, he had settled into a comfortable routine of composition and public appearances as a piano virtuoso—punctuated by episodes of eccentric, sometimes violent behavior toward friends and employers alike. The works of his early period, including the first two symphonies (opp. 21 and 36, 1800 and 1802) and the First Piano Concerto (op. 15, c. 1800), are well-crafted, often brilliant works that alone would have guaranteed Beethoven a good reputation.

But it was the onset of what we now call Beethoven's "heroic period," announced by the "Eroica" Symphony of 1803, that revolutionized the new century's ways of thinking about music. This middle period, represented by a host of brilliant works of precedent-shattering length, intensity, drive, and formal freedom, is in effect bounded by Beethoven's realization of the seriousness of his hearing problem (1802) and its conclusion in more or less complete deafness (1814 or so). It includes the six symphonies from the "Eroica" to the Eighth, the Fourth and Fifth Piano Concertos, the Violin Concerto, and some of the best piano and chamber works. Beethoven wrote a single opera, *Fidelio,* begun in 1803 and reaching its revised form in 1814; concerning the four overtures asssociated with *Fidelio,* see below under *Leonore* Overture No. 3.

The music of the last period is noted for its introspection, experiments with variation and fugue as organizational procedures, and adventuresome tonality. It includes the Ninth Symphony, the *Missa solemnis* for chorus and orchestra, opus 123 (1823), and the last string quartets, the works commonly summarized by the term "late Beethoven."

Owing to the magnitude of the conceptual problems he set for himself, Beethoven found composition difficult and tedious. He left many hundreds of pages of sketches for his works, documents which can sometimes testify to the genesis of his compositional thought in great detail and which scholars have delighted in interpreting. Beethoven's best-known works are identified by 138 opus numbers attached to them during his lifetime and summarized in a modern catalogue by Georg Kinsky and Hans Halm. Occasionally you will see something called a WoO number, which refers to an index of the many less significant works Beethoven left without opus number (*Werke ohne Opuszahl*).

Symphony No. 3 in E♭ Major, OP. 55 ("Eroica")

Allegro con brio
Marcia funebre: Adagio assai
Scherzo: Allegro vivace
Finale: Allegro molto

For flutes I-II, oboes I-II, clarinets I-II, bassoons I-II; horns I-III, trumpets I-II; timpani; strings

Composed 1803 in and around Vienna; dedicated to Prince Franz Joseph von Lobkowitz, a patron of Beethoven

First performed 7 April 1805, at an Academy Concert of the violinist Franz Clement at the Theater an der Wien, Vienna, Beethoven, conducting

Published by the Contor delle arti e d'industria (Vienna, 1806; parts only). *Inexpensive score:* Ludwig van Beethoven *First, Second and Third Symphonies in Full Orchestral Score* (New York: Dover, 1976)

Duration: about 55 minutes

Its duration alone—nearly twice the length of Mozart's "Jupiter" Symphony—would earn the "Eroica" a prominent spot in the history of ideas. That combined with Beethoven's keen sense of the implications pent up in his themes, the daring harmonic practices, the novel movement structures, and the extramusical connection with Napoleon and his legend, make the impact of the "Eroica" virtually unmatched in the literature. Beethoven went on to cultivate, notably in the Fifth and Ninth Symphonies, many of the notions he first proffered in the "Eroica," but nowhere is their shock value so great as here at the very beginning of the Romantic century. Each of the four movements had its own particular influence on the symphonic repertoire to come.

The landmarks of the first movement are the "extra" theme in the development—one not directly implied by the exposition—and the moment at the end of that section when the French horn, *pianissimo,* foreshadows the recapitulation an instant before it is unleashed. With its panoramic development and extended coda, the movement takes on proportions appropriate to its heroic intent. What seem passing details when they are first heard get "composed out" in the fullness of time: the foreboding C♯ you hear at the end of the very first theme (in cellos) occasions an episode in the recapitulation (D♭). And so on, as the movement gets bigger and bigger.

The *Marcia funebre,* in its evocation of a passing funeral cortege, served the Romantics as a persuasive model of musical space and imagery. At first, it seems little more than a gloomy dead march with an affirmative second strain, rebounding triplets in the strings suggesting the tattoo of muffled drums. (Beethoven is known to have had French military marches in mind.) But then there are interjections of sterner stuff, and all sorts of digressions, as though the witness were perplexed by exactly what the hero's life has stood for. In the trio are mighty fanfares from the brass and drums. But it is the dissolution of all this into fragments that left the Romantics trembling, where Berlioz (for example) saw "shreds of the lugubrious melody, alone, naked, broken, crushed," the wind instruments "shouting a cry, a last farewell of the warriors to their companion at arms." We don't often write about music that way anymore, but his observations make good sense.

Beethoven calls his third movement a scherzo, and with it pretty well sets the precedent for replacing the old-fashioned minuet and trio of the eighteenth century with a movement of much faster triple meter, wherein the composer plays clever games with the listener's perception of downbeat and phrase grouping. It's by no means Beethoven's first scherzo, and he learned the term and some of its concepts from Haydn; nevertheless this movement is the one that sent minuets packing for good. Note, at the beginning of the second strain, how the composer throws in an extra quarter note here and there, so that for a while you're not quite sure how the phrases fall out. The horn calls of the trio, too, set a precedent for movements of this sort.

In the finale, a theme and its variations bloom from the bass progression stated by the strings in unison pizzicato just after the opening spasm. It takes two more variations before a true melody is heard (in the woodwinds, a theme Beethoven had used three times before), and soon afterward it becomes clear that he is really more interested in the fugal possibilities of his progression and with the three loud exclamation points that seem to be there for the purpose of making you pay attention.

One of Beethoven's early biographers first told the story of seeing a manuscript on the master's worktable titled "Buonaparte"; on hearing the news that Napoleon had proclaimed himself emperor, the composer tore the page in half and threw it on the floor. "Is he, too," Beethoven is said to have remarked, "nothing but an ordinary human being?" What is certain is that Beethoven for a time saw cash value in dedicating the work to Napoleon. On the title page of the autograph manuscript score, the words *"intitulata Bonaparte"* are simply scratched out, and the subtitle "Eroica" appeared with the published parts in 1806.

Symphony No. 5 in C Minor, OP. 67

Allegro con brio
Andante con moto
Allegro
Allegro
[No pause between movements III and IV]

For piccolo, flutes I-II, oboes I-II, clarinets I-II, bassoons I-II, contrabassoon; horns I-II, trumpets I-II, trombones I-III; timpani; strings
Composed 1807–8 in and around Vienna; sketches from 1804; dedicated to Prince Franz Joseph von Lobkowitz and Count Andreas Razumovsky, Beethoven's patrons
First performed 22 December 1808, at Beethoven's academy concert at the Theater an der Wien, the composer conducting
Published by Breitkopf & Härtel (Leipzig, 1809; parts only). *Inexpensive scores:* Ludwig van Beethoven: *Fourth and Fifth Symphonies in Full Orchestral Score* (New York: Dover, 1976); Ludwig van Beethoven: *Symphony No. 5 in C Minor,* ed. Elliot Forbes, A Norton Critical Score (New York: Norton, 1971)
Duration: about 35 minutes

The Fifth is shorter than the Third and correspondingly terser. Beethoven's revelation here is how surely the *process* of sonata can flavor the affective thrust of a symphony, in this case from the struggle with which the work opens to the victory in which it concludes. Beethoven is said to have remarked of the famous motive at the beginning, "Thus knocks Fate at the door," and suggestions of the knocking of Fate are heard again in each of the succeeding movements, though transformed according to the surroundings. (The motive's rhythm matches the Morse code pattern for the letter V, so that during World War II it became a musical reference to "V for Victory," a little like Verdi's name being pressed into service on behalf of the unification of Italy—see p. 621.)

The first two statements of the Fate motive end in the dramatic pauses of measures 2 and 5 and thus serve not as a first theme but an introduction. The full thematic statement is then built from the Fate motive, which goes on to govern much of what follows. The horn fanfare that serves as a bridge to the second theme, for example, is built on it. And while the second theme seems in its major key and lyric melody a complete contrast to all that has come before, lurking underneath in the cellos and basses are insistent references to the opening motive, still knocking at the door. In the development listen for the systematic fragmentation of the bridge material into a dreamy progression of dark chords that migrate chromatically; later, as the recapitulation gets underway, a lazy cadenza in the solo oboe fills in the most dramatic of the pauses.

The second movement is a theme and variations in the gentle key of A♭ major, to my way of thinking one of Beethoven's suavest accomplishments in formal organization. For while the viola-and-cello melody is subjected to relatively traditional decorative procedures (see p. 33), the passages that follow it in each variation—the lingerings over the A♭ cadence, the hints of a second theme in the clarinets and bassoons, moving on to fanfares of brass and timpani in C major, the eerie falls back into A♭—undergo much subtler, more organic manipulations. The very last lingering over the cadence, for example, is made exquisitely poignant by the addition of two extra bars, and I cannot help hearing this as the first of the great sobbing figures so common to Romantic music.

The third movement, not identified by the composer as to form, begins as though a melancholy minuet; when the trio is reached—a fugal section that begins in scrambling double basses and cellos—it becomes clear that we are dealing with a kind of scherzo. Note the similarity of the opening theme to that of the last movement of Mozart's G-Minor Symphony, No. 40 (see p. 383); then listen for how the next tune, stated *fortissimo* in the horns, embodies the rhythm of the

Fate motive. At the end, in one of Beethoven's most inspired formal strokes, the timpani and strings settle onto a prolonged C, *pianissimo,* with an A♭ in the bass voices; the violin pokes tentatively upward, the A♭ falls dramatically to the dominant pitch G, woodwinds and brass enter, and the crescendo shows us how this passage has become a long introduction to the fourth movement, which begins without pause.

The orchestra bursts forth in the victorious finale theme built around a simple C-major triad. That the struggle of the earlier movements has ended in victory is reinforced by the stirring sounds of the piccolo, contrabassoon, and three trombones, here making their very welcome debut in the symphonic literature. The movement is broad in scale, with a powerful transition theme and an important passage of closing material, one that embodies the Fate motive so caressively you might not at first recognize it for what it is. What seems at the start a pro-forma development proves to encompass a shocking ploy, for suddenly we find ourselves back in the triple meter of the third movement. The Fate motive reasserts itself as it had been heard in the scherzo, but softly, tentatively, with the clear suggestion that its energy has been spent: victory, not fate, is the dominating spirit. This dramatic turn of events is, moreover, balanced at the end of the recapitulation, where a rousing coda is built from the closing theme of the exposition, now heard twice as fast as before.

Symphony No. 6 in F Major, OP. 68 ("Pastoral")

Erwachen heiterer Empfindungen bei der Ankunft auf dem Lande: Allegro ma non troppo (Awakening of Happy Feelings on Arriving in the Countryside)

Szene am Bach: Andante molto moto (Scene by the Brook)

Lustiges Zusammensein der Landleute: Allegro (Merry Gathering of Countryfolk)

Gewitter, Sturm: Allegro (Thunder, Storm)

Hirtengesang; Frohe und dankbare Gefühle nach dem Sturm: Allegretto (Shepherd Song; Happy and Thankful Feelings After the Storm)

[The third, fourth, and fifth movements are played without pause]

For   piccolo, flutes I-II, oboes I-II, clarinets I-II, bassoons I-II; French horns I-II, trumpets I-II, trombones I-II; timpani; strings

Composed 1807–8 in and around Vienna; dedicated to Prince
Franz Joseph von Lobkowitz and Count Andreas Razumovsky,
Beethoven's patrons
First performed 22 December 1808 at Beethoven's academy
concert at the Theater an der Wien, the composer conducting
Published by Breitkopf & Härtel (Leipzig, 1809; parts only).
Inexpensive score: Ludwig van Beethoven: *Sixth and Seventh
Symphonies in Full Orchestral Score* (New York: Dover, 1976)
Duration: about 40 minutes

What happiness Beethoven enjoyed he discovered during his long
daily walk and frequent holidays in the country. The "Pastoral" Symphony speaks of these rustic delights: the simple joys of countryfolk,
first the beauty and then the untamed fury of Nature. Beethoven's
use of descriptive titles and an extra movement—the storm—that
describes a manifestation of Nature are two novel strokes in their own
way as epoch-making as the idea of the funeral cortege was in the
"Eroica." Not that other periods in the history of musical style are
without water and weather music; on the contrary, there is plenty of
it (see, for example, my remarks on Vivaldi's *Le Quattro Stagioni,* p.
626). It's simply that the best orchestral music of Mozart and Haydn
was for all intents and purposes utterly abstract, and Beethoven here
introduces a new spectrum of possibilities for the pictorially minded.
Nonetheless his effort at picture music was cautious: the manuscript
materials remind us that his conception is "more an expression of
feeling than a painting" and that "painting carried too far in instrumental music loses its effect."

From the beginning, the Sixth is dominated by bright, airy keys
and textures appropriate to its programmatic intent. The tunes are
coupled in simple thirds and sixths, as folksong often is, and the
predominance of drones and other village-band-like orchestration is
meant to be suggestive of rusticity. In the "Scene by the Brook,"
Beethoven uses the $\frac{12}{8}$ meter long in vogue for pastoral imagery in a
sonata movement that relies on gentle rolling figures and prominent
trills to suggest the play of sun, breeze, and water. At the end, the
calls of nightingale, quail, and cuckoo are heard (and are so identified
in the score).

The third movement is a countrified scherzo and trio. The merry
horn and bassoon calls that end the first strain are adopted by the
violins as accompaniment for a strongly syncopated and rather prim-

itive tune stated first by the oboe. For a trio Beethoven suggests a contradanse; the scherzo returns and picks up speed, only to be interrupted by the blowing up of a thunderstorm from the distance. It begins gently, then works into a full-scale, pelting tempest with lightning and thunder, and finally spends itself as summer storms will do. And, likewise inevitably, the country life resumes again, here with a song of thanksgiving built from an open-intervalled melody some shepherd's horn might manage and sounding very much like the Alpine cow-herders' tunes, called *ranz des vaches,* popular with composers a generation later. It is a tune, moreover, whose structure encourages echo effects and allows for the swelling up of expansive, soulful accompanying figures.

Symphony No. 7 in A Major, OP. 92

Poco sostenuto; Vivace
Allegretto
Presto
Allegro con brio

For flutes I-II, oboes I-II, clarinets I-II, bassoons I-II; horns I-II, trumpets I-II; timpani; strings
Composed 1811–12 in and around Vienna; final work begun 13 May 1812; dedicated to Prince Moritz von Fries
First performed 8 December 1813 at a Beethoven concert in the Hall of the University of Vienna, Beethoven conducting
Published by S. A. Steiner & Comp. (Vienna, 1816). *Inexpensive score:* Ludwig van Beethoven: *Sixth and Seventh Symphonies in Full Orchestral Score* (New York: Dover, 1976)
Duration: about 40 minutes

The Seventh Symphony comes about four years after the Fifth and Sixth Symphonies and is roughly contemporaneous with the Eighth. Each of the movements is built over by a pervasive rhythmic ostinato pattern, such that the symphony taken as a whole becomes an essay in musical propulsion. Today we tend to sneer at Wagner's summary of the work as the "apotheosis of the dance," but to me there seems an underlying, if old-fashioned, aptness to the remark.

The movement structures are traditional sonata or sonata-imbued forms, free-wheeling and extended in the style of Beethoven's middle period, with heroic gestures, long developments and codas, and all the rest. I find the orchestration, with its strong emphasis on solo woodwind, notably flute and oboe, to be exceptionally rich in color.

The long slow introduction to the first movement is unusual for Beethoven, probably a nod backward to the style of Haydn. The half-note melody at the beginning interacts with the rising scales in sixteenth notes; a gracious subject with ornamental turn is heard in the woodwind, and these two gambits are repeated as the passage moves harmonically back toward the tonic. The repeated sixteenth notes, first heard as a kind of countersubject, achieve prominence; Beethoven slips in a hint of the rhythm that dominates the Vivace, thereby setting up a transition to the main portion of the movement. The dotted-rhythm ostinato begins gallantly, but as the sonata gains momentum it becomes hammering and valkyresque to such an extent that the empty bars at the end of the exposition and the beginning of the development draw one up quite short. As in the first movement of the Fifth Symphony, the recapitulation expands a fermata first heard in the exposition by adding a brief oboe cadenza.

The great *Allegretto,* with its sea of slow-moving bows and its languid woodwind-dominated trios was easily the most popular symphonic movement in the nineteenth-century repertoire, offered by tea-garden bands and in promenade concerts and often substituted for less successful movements in other symphonies. What Berlioz called a "profound sigh" begins the movement, then a twenty-four-bar theme that dwells largely on reiterated Es is played successively by the various sections of the orchestra over seductive counterpoints. Out of the first trio grows a glorious fugue built on the main theme; after the second, the movement dissolves into the sigh with which it commenced.

In the scherzo, of bright spirit, you should remark the extra bars thrown in from time to time to catch you off guard. The trios begin as though suspended beneath the high note in the violins, then grow majestic with the introduction of trumpets and timpani. The scherzo passages plow toward this turning point with such conviction that, at the last recapitulation, it seems impossible to stop the cycle: but here five summary chords simply shear it off. For the finale Beethoven summons up a theme charged with sixteenth-note passagework, introduced by an abrupt tattoo. A second theme introduces some possibilities for variety by dotted figurations whose halting character daunts, a little, the driving forward motion. But the urgency of the sixteenths cannot be subdued for long, and they always end up in control.

It is the too-common practice nowadays to omit some of the repeats Beethoven calls for in three of the four movements. Without them, however, you miss some splendid details, and you lose in particular the full impact of the double scherzo and trio. Insist on the repeats, if you can, for they give the Seventh Symphony its special measure of heroism.

Symphony No. 8 in F Major, OP. 93

Allegro vivace e con brio
Allegretto scherzando
Tempo di Menuetto
Allegro vivace

For flutes I-II, oboes I-II, clarinets I-II, bassoons I-II; horns I-II, trumpets I-II; timpani; strings
Composed 1811–12; sketched in Vienna and completed in Linz
First performed 27 February 1814 at Beethoven's academy concert in the great Redoutensaal, Vienna, the composer conducting
Published by S. A. Steiner & Comp. (Vienna, 1817). *Inexpensive score:* Ludwig van Beethoven: *Eighth and Ninth Symphonies in Full Orchestral Score* (New York: Dover, 1976)
Duration: about 30 minutes

Mature composers, having mastered their craft and proved their most pressing points, often revert to a certain classicism and restraint, as if to show that cool logic can be as convincing as the whitest of passions. That seems to be the case with the Eighth Symphony, "my little symphony in F," as Beethoven fondly put it. Like the Sixth Symphony, it is in F major, which Beethoven considers a bright, untroubled key. Rhythmic ostinatos are nearly as ubiquitous as in the Seventh, but here have a more restful effect.

The symphony opens in $\frac{3}{4}$, with a main theme of such assurance that, when Beethoven simply abandons it with a couple of chordal exclamation points and an empty bar, you have no idea what he has in mind to do next. The second group then begins in the passive and quite "wrong" key of A major, then lifts into the more appropriate key of C. But by now the pauses and rubatos have begun regularly to throw the simple F and C major into pensive distant harmonies, and whatever conservative elements there may have been to the movement recede from our attention.

The second movement is an *Allegretto scherzando* in B♭, with a scampering theme in the strings accompanied by staccato chords in the winds. Beethoven works through a catalogue of playful devices over the course of three strophes, and thus one never has much sense of being in a slow movement. Doubtless for that reason, he next chooses not to offer a scherzo but rather to cast the third movement in a *Tempo di menuetto*. Its effect, however, is more like a Rhineland waltz than a Viennese minuet and trio. At the cadences the position of the downbeat is obscured by the brass and timpani to comical effect; the trio consists of duo work in the horns and woodwinds over music-box triplets in the cellos.

The big movement here is the last, *Allegro vivace,* a spirited romp where triplet accompanying figures, both in eighth notes and in quarters, consistently challenge the duple structures for precedence. The second theme, *dolce* and legato, touches on the distant key of A♭ before arriving in C major; the first subject returns as though we were dealing with a rondo, only to settle into a brief development. Out of the waddling octaves in bassoon and timpani emerges a recapitulation that seems not quite certain it should be there, nor, when it finishes, where next to go. Beethoven then charges into an extensive coda, as long as everything that has come before, with an important new thematic figure, and far more complex harmonically than the true development was—it has a statement of the main theme in F♯ minor, requiring a change of key signature. Brass and timpani insist that the E♯ of the minor key is actually the tonic F, and succeed in redirecting this digression to its proper though still merry end.

Take a moment to look back on Beethoven's symphonic oeuvre before the valedictory you know to be coming up next: how systematically he has progressed through the opportunities of the genre, how cleverly he has paired his last four works in it, with what variety he has explored the implications of key and meter and form. Now he takes ten years off to mull things over and to experiment with other genres; when he returns to symphonic composition, whatever is left of his Classical urge will be gone forever.

Symphony No. 9 in D Minor, OP. 125 (with a closing chorus on Schiller's Ode *An die Freude* [To Joy])

Allegro non troppo, un poco maestoso
Molto vivace
Adagio molto e cantabile
Presto; Allegro assai; Presto; Recitative; Allegro assai; Allegro assai vivace; Andante maestoso; Allegro energico; Allegro ma non tanto.

For soloists (SATB); chorus; piccolo, flutes I-II, oboes I-II, clarinets I-II, bassoons I-II, contrabassoon; horns I-IV, trumpets I-II, trombones I-III; timpani, bass drum, cymbals, triangle; strings

Text by Friedrich von Schiller (1759–1805), the German poet and playwright; the opening recitative in movement IV is by Beethoven

Composed 1822–February 1824 (sketched 1817–18); dedicated to Friedrich Wilhelm III, King of Prussia

First performed 7 May 1824, at Beethoven's academy concert at the Kärtnertor Theater, Vienna, the composer conducting as best he could

Published by B. Schotts Söhne (Mainz and Paris, 1826).
Inexpensive score: Ludwig van Beethoven: *Eighth and Ninth Symphonies in Full Orchestral Score* (New York: Dover, 1976)

Duration: about 70 minutes.

Beethoven returned to symphonic composition after a decade of intellectual crisis and challenge ending in the creative outburst of 1822–23 that produced the *Diabelli Variations* and the *Missa solemnis* as well as the Ninth. The hiatus meant that he would need to reconcile the evolution of his compositional technique with the certain public expectation of yet another in what had been a series of triumphs. In the years since the Eighth Symphony he had achieved a new lyricism and simplicity, even a certain intimacy of discourse. But with the Ninth there is a sense of return to the heroism of the past, to what Joseph Kerman and Alan Tyson (in *The New Grove*) have called the "symphonic ideal"—that is, those notions of process and working out, of struggle and resolution that characterize the Third and Fifth Symphonies. The turf seems familiar as Beethoven confronts matters of size, cyclicity, progress, and the articulation of his personal vision of universal brotherhood. The Ninth was far the longest symphony thus far composed, and it calls for one of the largest performing forces in the Viennese repertoire.

Beethoven has written three great and lengthy symphonic movements—a fierce sonata, a driving scherzo, and a pair of pastoral themes and their variations—cast in more or less conventional forms, then balanced them with an extraordinary finale in which sonata, variation, and fugual styles all intermingle. The main thematic material of the first movement erupts, volcano-like, from the almost primordial perfection of the open fifths in the strings and horn. There is some contrastive, lyrical material here, but by and large the turbulent elements hold sway. Beethoven's vacillation between the keys of the first and second theme (D minor and B♭ major) is such that what you sense most is the tension between them; when the climax is reached at the point of recapitulation, the tonic chord is an astonishing D *major,* with its F♯ strongly emphasized.

The scherzo, opening with a superb flourish in the timpani, is vast of dimension, with an extravagant inner repeat scheme and tense phrase groupings that shift into triple pulses just as you are beginning to be comfortable with the quadruple. The B♭ tonality pulls at the prevailing D minor here, too, but the trio is in a D major of welcome passivity and in equally welcome duple meter. The scherzo returns with all its repeats intact, and in view of the way things have gone there is some reason to expect a second full statement of the equally massive trio, Seventh Symphony-fashion. But there is only a reminiscence of the trio, cut short by the final pounding cadence.

The importance of the tonal duplicities Beethoven has nourished thus far becomes clearest of all in the *Adagio,* where two different passages are successively varied, one in B♭, the other in D major, this second major mode seeming to demonstrate that the turmoil of the first two movements has begun to recede. Note the solo work for fourth horn in the B♭ sections, decorating each swell to climax.

The explosion at the beginning of the fourth movement—there should be little, if any, pause—leads to recitative-like material in the cellos and basses; these recitatives introduce recollections of the main material from the other movements and finally the main themes of this movement. The explosion recurs, this time to introduce the baritone soloist with the recitative: he banishes the "stressful sounds" that have come before and introduces the more joyful strains of Schiller's apostrophe. The chorus enters at last, and to the singers is given the first substantial modulation thus far. The new section turns out to be a Turkish march in $\frac{6}{8}$, complete with bass drum, cymbals, and triangle. Gradually this evolves into an orchestral scherzo, developmental in character, and another statement of the hymn tune.

Suddenly the forward motion stops, and the men's voices join in hymnodic unison. Here is the central text, from Beethoven's point of view: *Seid umschlungen, Millionen!* Humanity, argue Beethoven and Schiller, must see in the heavens the promise of brotherhood for all mankind. The musical allusions become more complex, for the last section combines the chorale tune and the ode to joy, revealing that they are counterpoints one of the other. To the orchestra alone is left the distinction of bringing the colossal movement to its end—a movement, moreover, for which no single explanation of structure will quite suffice.

Concerto No. 4 for Piano and Orchestra in G Major, OP. 58

Allegro moderato
Andante con moto
Rondo: Vivace
[No pause between movements II-III]

For piano solo; flute, oboes I-II, clarinets I-II, bassoons I-II; horns I-II, trumpets I-II; timpani; strings

Composed 1805–6; dedicated to Archduke Rudolph of Austria; cadenzas by Beethoven

First performed 6 March 1807 in a subscription concert dedicated to Beethoven's works at Prince Lobkowitz's palace, Vienna, the composer conducting from the keyboard; first public performance 22 December 1808 at the Theater an der Wien, with the Fifth and Sixth Symphonies

Published by the Kunst u. Industrie Comptoirs (Vienna and Pesth, 1808; parts only). *Inexpensive score:* Ludwig van Beethoven: *Complete Piano Concertos in Full Score* (New York: Dover, 1983)

Duration: about 35 minutes

The Fourth Piano Concerto is the most transparent of Beethoven's five, with the most intimate relationship between soloist and orchestra. What it lacks in bravura it compensates for with introspection and warmth, and it thus offers symphonic listeners a good look at the mellower tendencies of the middle period. It is the last keyboard work to have been given its public premiere by Beethoven himself.

The opening measures of the concerto afford a particular surprise when the piano alone has the first statement of the chordal pattern that constitutes the main motive and is the germ of the principal theme. There follows a long orchestral ritornello that embraces most of the thematic material to be treated later on. When the solo part returns, it seems largely improvisational and linear, contrasting markedly with the chords at the beginning; these, it proves, are reserved to articulate the main sections. Integration of solo part and orchestra, more than their alternation, seems the rule, and together they cruise in and out of keys theoretically distant from G major yet by other tonal associations convincing. There is a certain serenity here that makes the movement a favorite of performers and audiences alike.

Yet it is the second movement which lingers in our minds after the work is done. There is no true form to be heard, but rather a dialogue between the orchestra and piano: each gruff observation by the orchestra, in unisons and octaves, is countered by the piano with chordal tenderness. Gradually the orchestral surges subside in favor of the plaintive phrases of the piano. There is a moment of cadenza, interrupted by reminiscence of the orchestral figure, now subdued. A longing cadence in the piano leaves the movement open-ended, ready for the next. Liszt suggested that all this portrays Orpheus playing his lyre for the Furies in order to gain entry to hell, and that interpretation has held sway in some quarters ever since.

The *Andante* merges into a sonata-rondo finale that seems for a moment to be in the wrong key. The returns of the main theme are introduced by long scalar flourishes of the piano, semi-cadenzas. After the main cadenza near the end comes a long canonic coda, where piano and clarinet share the same musical material a measure apart, though the orchestra returns, *presto,* to insist on the rondo theme.

Beethoven left a number of different cadenzas for the Fourth Concerto and, inasmuch as they are preserved, it seems to me obligatory for soloists to choose from among them.

Concerto No. 5 for Piano and Orchestra in E♭ Major,
OP. 73 ("Emperor")

Allegro
Adagio un poco mosso
Rondo: Allegro
[No pause between movements II-III]

For piano solo; flutes I-II, oboes I-II, clarinets I-II, bassoons I-II;
horns I-II, trumpets I-II; timpani; strings
Composed February–October 1809 in Vienna; dedicated to
Archduke Rudolph of Austria
First performed 28 November 1811 by the Leipzig Gewandhaus
Orchestra, Friedrich Schneider, soloist; Johann P. C. Schulz
conducting
Published by Clementi & Co. (London, 1810; parts only) and
Breitkopf & Härtel (Leipzig, 1811; parts only). *Inexpensive score:*
Ludwig van Beethoven: *Complete Piano Concertos in Full Score*
(New York: Dover, 1983)
Duration: about 40 minutes

What is most striking about the "Emperor" is its size. A good deal
longer than the Fifth Symphony, it approaches in breadth of form and
proportion the manner of the "Eroica" and is surely to be placed
alongside that symphony and the Fifth as a member of the triumvirate
that virtually defines the period. As in the Fourth Concerto, the work
begins with the soloist, but here with much more flamboyance, a
tactic repeated at the recapitulation and to which Beethoven makes
reference again at the point of cadenza. The orchestral ritornello consists of a succession of some five attractive thematic ideas, among
which the loveliest may be the cascading eighths in the winds, answered
by a staccato mirror image in the strings, just before the ritornello's
end. The pianist, despite having little new thematic material, is given
strokes of great drama: the chromatic scale and long trill that overlap
the final cadence of the ritornello, for example, and passage through
the distant key areas. The cadenza is modest, as if to compensate for
the long improvisations before, and is written out; the orchestra responds
with the horn calls from the ritornello. But there is no struggle in
this movement, as there is in the Fifth Symphony: "the battle," one
authority remarks, "seems to be won even before the forces have been
drawn up."

The second movement is in the distant key of B major. It is a reflective movement, willing to delay forward progress to linger over details of voicing and motive. The orchestral chorale is succeeded by new material in triplets in the piano, leading to a brief excursion into D major. But the chorale predominates, and in two successive statements, the soloist and ensemble (especially the solo winds) weave into its fabric rich textures and hues. A long pedal point begins in French horns when the bassoons sink a half-step. The soloist appears to experiment rather aimlessly with material for a rondo. Suddenly, as though having found the solution, the pianist lights out in the theme of the third movement—not so much a hunt rondo, this, as the stuff of bejewelled *noblesse* at play in the drawing rooms of old Vienna. The persistence of the dotted rhythmic figure propels the movement ever forward, through an expansive episode at the center. It begins to conclude by a winding down in the timpani and piano; then the fancy rolling passagework in the solo part—heard once before—introduces a last exclamation by the orchestra.

You are wondering why it is called the "Emperor Concerto." Nobody knows for sure.

Concerto for Violin and Orchestra in D Major, OP. 61

Allegro ma non troppo
Larghetto
Rondo: Allegro
[No pause between movements II and III]

For violin solo; flute, oboes I-II, clarinets I-II, bassoons I-II; horns I-II, trumpets I-II; timpani; strings
Composed 1806 in Vienna; dedicated to Stephan von Breuning, a close friend of the composer and secretary to the Emperor of Austria
First performed 23 December 1806 at an academy concert of the violinist Franz Clement (1781–1842) at the Theater an der Wien, Vienna, with Clement, soloist; Beethoven conducting
Published by the Bureau des Arts et d'Industrie (Vienna and Pesth, 1808; parts only). *Inexpensive score: Great Romantic Violin Concertos in Full Score* (New York: Dover, 1985)
Duration: about 45 minutes

Beethoven was so late delivering his Violin Concerto, according to well-entrenched legend, that Franz Clement had to sight-read the solo part at the premiere. The concerto is nearly contemporaneous with the Fifth and Sixth Symphonies, the Fourth Piano Concerto, and the Razumovsky String Quartets opus 59, and like those works it is expansive of form and rich in the interrelationship of its melodies. A timpani solo presents the main motive of the first movement: five repeated quarter notes—almost as simple a motto as it is possible to imagine—that goes on to achieve a more significant identity than any of the themes. (It is reminiscent, too, of both the Fate motive in the Fifth Symphony and the soloist's motive at the beginning of the Fourth Piano Concerto.) The wind choir presents the true first theme, and there follows a conventional concerto exposition. Many of the significant orchestral figures are fashioned from rising scales, and their prevalence lends the movement its gently soaring qualities.

The second movement, a *romanza* in the style of the Mozart concertos, presents successive versions of a lyrical ten-bar melody. The role of the violin is limited to decoration at first, though gradually it carves out its own interlude and finally its own statement of the theme, followed by a return of the interlude. All this has remained pretty squarely in G major, ever tranquil and *cantabile,* but just as the movement seems to be lulling itself to sleep, the strings wrench the harmony back toward D major, and the soloist uses the cadenza to effect the transition to the finale without further pause.

This is a rondo in $\frac{6}{8}$, likewise Mozartian, with evocations of the hunt and a correspondingly important role of the horn and horn-like figurations. It is the soloist's movement, however, the orchestra's role limited for the most part to supporting the display work and to nudging things back to speed with tutti statements of the full rondo theme whenever the episodes end in fermatas. Yet on the whole the solo part is soft-spoken and discreet: you sense yourself not so much in the presence of a vehicle as a masterpiece.

Leonore Overture No. 3, OP. 72B

For flutes I-II, oboes I-II, clarinets I-II, bassoons I-II; horns I-IV, trumpets I-II, trombones I-III; timpani; strings
Composed in March 1806 in Vienna
First performed 29 March 1806 with the revised opera at the Theater an der Wien, Vienna, Ignaz von Seyfried conducting
Published by Breitkopf & Härtel (Leipzig, 1810; parts only).

Inexpensive score: Ludwig van Beethoven: *Six Great Overtures in Full Score* (New York: Dover, 1985)

Duration: about 14 minutes

Leonora is the heroine of Beethoven's only opera, *Fidelio*; she disguises herself as the boy Fidelio (a neat trick for girthy sopranos) in order to rescue her husband Florestan from an underground dungeon. There are three Leonora overtures: *Leonore* No. 1, op. 138, *Leonore* No. 2, op. 72a, and *Leonore* No. 3, op. 72b; then, too, there is the overture that goes with the last version of *Fidelio*. This state of things has to do with the protracted genesis of Beethoven's opera, first produced in 1804–5 with the title *Leonore* and the overture now called *Leonore* No. 2. A revised version of the opera with *Leonore* No. 3 was given in 1806. Beethoven, still dissatisfied, spruced up his opera and wrote *Leonore* No. 1 for a production planned for 1806–7, but which never materialized. In 1814 *Fidelio* as we now know it took shape, with the overture that bears its name.

Though not quite a story overture, it helps when you hear *Leonore* No. 3 to recall the basics of the plot, for the offstage trumpet at the end of the development promises certain rescue, and the Presto coda is obviously to be associated with lovers joyfully reunited and galloping off to future bliss. It's a sprawling work with a slow introduction whose metric and tonal intent is anything but clear at first, and with digressive, rambling themes built mainly of arpeggiated triads over long static harmonies. The second theme group, introduced by a pair of horns playing a motive Beethoven associated with the absence of a loved one, has greater promise, but frantic searching seems more the business at hand.

Leonore No. 3 is sometimes trotted out in productions of *Fidelio* to serve as an entr'acte between the two scenes of act II. This is not a particularly good idea, for the music merely repeats the thrust of the dungeon scene that has just taken place.

Egmont Overture, OP. 84 (from the incidental music for Goethe's tragedy)

For piccolo, flutes I-II, oboes I-II, clarinets I-II, bassoons I-II; horns I-IV, trumpets I-II; timpani; strings

Composed 1809–10 in Vienna
First performed 15 June 1810 in the Court Theatre in the
   Hofburg, Vienna; this was the fourth performance of the play;
   Beethoven's score was not ready for the premiere
Published by Breitkopf & Härtel (Leipzig, 1810; parts only).
   Inexpensive score: Ludwig van Beethoven: *Six Great Overtures in
   Full Score* (New York: Dover, 1985)
Duration: about 10 minutes

Lamoral, count Egmont (1522–68), was a historical figure immortalized in Goethe's tragedy of 1788, the play for which Beethoven later provided incidental music. Egmont, a Dutch nobleman, was on the one hand a loyal subject of Philip II of Spain—he pled Philip's troth before Mary I of England—and on the other a fervent opponent of the repressive measures visited on the Netherlands by the Spanish regime. He could neither support the governor-general nor bring himself to join a military insurrection against this Duke of Alba, and was at length captured and beheaded as a traitor for having entertained such high moral scruples.

Beethoven's overture is altogether appropriate to the swashbuckling tale. It begins with a terrifying unison F and then a fateful, sinister progression in F minor. The melodic undulations in woodwinds and first violins are picked up by the cellos, which work the material into the restless theme of the Allegro, still in minor. The second theme is a major-mode version of the mysterious chords heard in the opening bars. A taut sonata makes it way routinely on through to recapitulation, at which point the insistent chords of the second theme are interrupted by a delicate modulation in the woodwinds. From these there breaks forth a coda in F major of rousing military triumph, with piccolos and heroic brass—quite the equal of the memorable coda that concludes the Fifth Symphony.

Alban Berg

Born 9 February 1885 in Vienna
Died 24 December 1935 in Vienna

Berg was a student and intimate friend of Arnold Schoenberg and a member of what has come to be called the "second Viennese school," probably this century's most fertile compositional movement. Though often in poor health, Berg nevertheless served in the Austrian Army during World War I. After the war, he managed the Viennese contemporary music society founded by Schoenberg. (These were called private performances for members only, in order to exclude a hostile press.) His salary for this work, the income from his composition students, and rent from some family real estate afforded Berg long periods of uninterrupted time to work through the complexities of the rigorous compositional problems he had set for himself.

His powerful opera *Wozzeck* (1922), sharply criticized when performed in Berlin and Prague, was welcomed in America and has since become easily the most admired of modern operas. *Wozzeck* was followed by *Lulu*, which he never finished. He wrote few other works: for orchestra there are the aphoristic *Altenberg Lieder*, op. 4 (1913), the Three Pieces for Orchestra, op. 6 (1914–15), a Chamber Concerto for piano and small ensemble, mostly winds (1923–25), and the two works discussed below. Berg composed in a personal style noted for its free atonality, lyricism, and stark dramatic expression. His tonal language is dissonant, but the formal structures supporting it are often traditional: the symphonic music from *Wozzeck*, for example, includes a passacaglia and a suite of dances, and part of the Violin Concerto is based on a Bach chorale.

Concerto for Violin and Orchestra

  I. *Andante (Prelude); Allegretto (Scherzo)*
  II. *Allegro (Cadenza); Adagio (Chorale Variations)*

For piccolos I-II, flutes I-II, oboes I-II, English horn, clarinets I-II, bass clarinet, alto saxophone, bassoons I-II, contrabassoon; horns I-IV, trumpets I-II, trombones I-II, tuba; timpani, snare drum, bass drum, cymbals, triangle, gong (high tam-tam), (low) tam-tam; harp; strings

Composed: April 11–August 1935, to a commission from Louis Krasner; dedicated "to the memory of an angel" (see below)

First performed (posthumously) 19 April 1936 by the International Society for Contemporary Music (ISCM) Festival Orchestra in Barcelona, Louis Krasner, soloist, Hermann Scherchen conducting

Published by Universal Edition (Vienna, 1936)

Duration: about 25 minutes

The American violinist Louis Krasner tendered Berg his commission for a concerto in January 1935, but it was the death that April of the young woman named Manon Gropius that prompted him to compose the concerto in the late summer of that year. "Berg loved my daughter as if she were his own," wrote her mother, Alma Gropius, who was Mahler's widow and a close friend of Mrs. Berg; according to her the dedication "to the memory of an angel" had to do with a role the beautiful eighteen-year-old was to have played in a Salzburg theatrical production. Instead she fell ill with polio and died the following Easter.

In Alma's sentimental words, "She did not play the angel, but in fact became one."

The concerto has close associations, as well, with two other objects of the composer's affection. Number symbolism identifies parts of the work with Hanna Fuchs-Robettin, a woman Berg loved profoundly, though at a distance, for most of his life. (Berg—and more ominously his wife, Helene—almost managed to deprive posterity of any hint of this romance, the ripest fruit of which was the *Lyric Suite* for string quartet of 1927.) Moreover, in the *Allegretto* of the first movement Berg cites a song identified in the score only as "in the Carinthian folk-style," but which we know to be called *Ein Vogel auf'm Zwetschgenbaum* (A Bird in the Plum-Tree). This is a folk tune from the picturesque rural province of southern Austria where Berg's family had a summer house; here Berg makes reference to his teenaged idyll with the servant-girl Marie, by whom he fathered a child. (The Bergs censored this incident, too.) In short, the Violin Concerto is a valedictory of farewell to the forbidden loves of the composer's life, and, as it turned out, Berg's own farewell to life.

His style can seem harsh and difficult at first, especially in a forlorn work like this one, and the concerto may take some getting used to. But the number of brilliant ideas he brings to his composition makes this and his other great works wondrous aural adventures indeed. His is a music of sharp contrasts: diaphanous, transparent textures and such poignant details as the low throb of a contrabassoon are apt to be shattered in percussive diabolical violence at any turn.

The form of the Violin Concerto is symmetrical, with a total of four movements combined in a mirrored pair of pairs: slow–fast, fast–slow. These are organized traditionally, with a sonata-like first movement, a scherzo and trio, a cadenza-dominated movement, and finally a set of variations on a chorale. There are memorial associations to be noted, of course: the first two movements are a portrait of the angel, the third is a movement of catastrophe, and the last seems to treat death and transfiguration.

Serial and tonal organizations coexist and intermingle. At the beginning a bar of arpeggiated intervals in the harp and clarinets sets the stage for the entry of the solo violin, up and back down its open strings, as though tuning, then with a straightforward statement of the row. Note through this first movement the striking instrumental combinations: the saxophone and contrabassoon, the distant gong and triangle, the thump in the double bass of bow-wood on strings (a technique called *col legno*). The *Allegretto* is a scherzo in close harmony in pairs of winds and double-stops for the violin. Berg marks the various melodies "rustic" and "Viennese." Two trios and a return of trio I are heard, then the scherzo again, this time marked "as though a waltz." Toward the end Berg introduces the song of the bird and the plum-tree, announced most prominently in the horn and trumpet and marked there to be played "like a pastorale."

The violinist dominates the *Allegro* with cadenzas, vicious multiple stops, and fiery passagework; at the end comes a glorious passage in two voices, melody and accompaniment, on the single instrument. A long glissando in the harp and solo passages in triple stops announce the climax. Immediately after this "high point" (so Berg marks the score), the movement recedes as the violinist cites the melody of the Protestant chorale tune *Es ist genug!* The text, an utterance of the prophet Elijah, appears in the score: "It is enough! Lord, when it pleases Thee, do Thou unshackle me." Clarinets, succeeded by horns and the other winds, then state Bach's setting of the chorale as found in Cantata 60. Later we hear in the strings and solo violin a distant reminiscence of the Carinthian folk-tune against the chorale as scored for full wind. In the dissolution, the now-familiar intervals of the row are heard once more, and they rise to the celestial register as the brass articulate a calm "amen."

Symphonic Pieces from *Lulu* ("Lulu Suite")

Rondo: Andante (Introduzione; Hymne)
Ostinato: Allegro
Lied der Lulu: Comodo
Variationen: Moderato (I. Grandioso; II. Grazioso; III. Funèbre;
   IV. Affettuoso; Thema)
Adagio: Sostenuto; Lento; Grave

For high soprano solo (in *Lulu's Song* and at the end of the last movement); piccolos I-III, flutes I-III, oboes I-III, English horn, E♭ clarinets I-II, clarinets I-III, bass clarinet, alto saxophone, bassoons I-III, contrabassoon; horns I-IV, trumpets I-III, trombones I-III, tuba; timpani, snare drum, bass drum, cymbals, triangle, gong (high tam-tam), (low) tam-tam, vibraphone; piano, harp; strings

Composed 1934; dedicated to Arnold Schoenberg on his sixtieth
birthday; *Lulu's Song* dedicated to Anton von Webern on his
fiftieth birthday; short score of the opera completed in April
1934
First performed 30 November 1934, by the Berlin State Opera
Orchestra, Erich Kleiber conducting
Published by Universal Edition (Vienna, 1935)
Duration: about 35 minutes

The opera *Lulu,* about the rise and fall of a courtesan, was based on
two tragedies by Frank Wedekind (1864–1918), *Erdgeist* (Earth Spirit,
1895) and *Die Büchse der Pandor* (Pandora's Box, 1903), which Berg
had read during his most impressionable years. Berg was at his best
dealing with human foibles and wickedness: lurid stuff that bemoans
how easily our essential dignities can be compromised. Lulu, a great
tragic heroine, is like the benighted soldier Wozzeck in her power-
lessness to control the world around her.

The opera, and this suite drawn from the unfinished short score as
a sort of "*Lulu* Temptation," is so complex in technical device, so
rigorous in structural control, so extravagant of orchestral costume,
that I can treat only a tiny fraction of the reasons it creates its wondrous effect.

Lulu is in three acts divided between the two scenes of Act II into
the heroine's ascendant and descendant phases. The long *Rondo* that
opens the suite, likewise, is in two halves, preceded by an eight-bar
introduction, drawn note-for-note from the two scenes of act II but
for the omitted vocal parts and the skipping here and there of a few
structurally insignificant bars. Both passages in the opera are duets
between Lulu and Alwa, the son of her most recent husband and a
young man as smitten with Lulu as his father was. The prominent
recurring melody—the main thing that makes this a rondo—is what
you hear in the violins just after an introduction: an open-intervalled
melody, sweeping and expressive, of quite recognizable design. Try
to hear this a pair of repeated wide intervals (of a sixth), then a slightly
narrower interlocking interval (of a fourth), then a downward plunge
and finishing off. Note as well the prominent part for alto saxophone,
the interplay of the solo lines, the way the brass choirs thicken the
textures at the fateful moments. The percussion often plays the thudding pattern associated through the opera with Fate. Part I ends with

a prominent cadence in the strings and vibraphone, with the new section commencing forcefully in the full orchestra and, a little later, an obvious fugue; the Hymn does not begin until later, articulated by imitative entries in the strings, pizzicato, and in piano and harp, legato.

The *Ostinato* starts with a scramble of figures which imitate each other in a frenzy of multiple relationships. It charges forward in speed and volume, then relents slightly into a very prominent *pianissimo* chord of the vibraphone and its arpeggiation in the piano. At this point the music reverses itself palindromically and charges back crabwise to the scramble at the beginning—now, of course, going in the other direction. This comes at the exact mid-point of *Lulu,* and was written to accompany a film projected between the scenes of act II that summarizes the heroine's fortunes in the interim. There follows *Lulu's Lied,* with its birthday dedication to Webern. In five sentences she summarizes her proud remorselessness: men kill for her and give her their old age, but she in return has given them the flower of her youth, and she has never pretended to be anything other than what she is. The *Variations* treat the chorale associated with Lulu's pimp in act III; at the end the theme is stated barrel-organ style, followed by a restatement of the chorale.

Lulu ends in London, when she takes Jack the Ripper as a client. He murders her in a room offstage, then enters and kills the Countess Geschwitz, Lulu's besotted confidante, as the curtain falls. The *Adagio* from the Suite opens with the music of the countess and motivic allusions to the other characters. Then you hear Lulu's shattering death-cry in the orchestra and, at the end, the Countess's dying words: "Lulu! My angel! I am near you for eternity!"

Berg interrupted work on *Lulu* to write his mournful Violin Concerto and died before completing the orchestration of act III. His widow—fearing, as widows do, that her late husband's reputation might somehow be compromised by it—successfully prevented the publication of the final act from the manuscript materials Berg had left behind. She died in 1976 and the entire vocal score was published in 1979; that year, the definitive *Lulu* (with orchestration completed by Friedrich Cerha) was produced in Paris, Hamburg, and Santa Fe.

Hector Berlioz

Born *11 December 1803 in*
La Côte-St.-André, near Grenoble
Died *8 March 1869 in Paris*

Son of a prosperous small-town physician, Berlioz had an excellent though provincial elementary education at the hands of his father and the local bandmasters. He set out for Paris in 1821 to become a doctor, a plan hastily abandoned when he saw, in short succession, a series of grand operas and the dissecting room of the Paris morgue. He became a student of Jean-François Le Sueur, the Conservatoire's excellent teacher of composition, and by 1830 had written his first and most influential symphony, the *Symphonie fantastique*. In the same year he won the *prix de Rome* and left France for his Italian sojourn, an experience from which he drew musical inspiration for the rest of his life.

The decade from 1830 resulted in one remarkable new composition after another: the symphony with solo viola called *Harold en Italie*

(1834), the Requiem (1837), the vibrant opera *Benvenuto Cellini* (1838), the dramatic symphony *Roméo et Juliette* (1839); the lovely songs to Théophile Gautier's poems, called *Les Nuits d'été* (1840); and a ceremonial symphony for band, the *Grande Symphonie funèbre et triomphale* (1840), much admired by Wagner.

Berlioz spent the next two decades traveling throughout Europe to conduct concerts of his own music and, among many others, the works of Gluck, Spontini, Weber, and Beethoven. Over the course of his travels, he befriended Schumann, Mendelssohn, and Wagner; in Paris, he had already formed an intimate friendship with Liszt and a passing acquaintance with Chopin. In 1846 Berlioz composed, performed, and very nearly lost his shirt producing the dramatic legend, *La Damnation de Faust,* and in 1854 enjoyed his greatest popular success with the oratorio *L'Enfance du Christ.* Toward the end of his career, he looked back to the style of his distinguished predecessors Christoph Willibald Gluck and Gaspare Spontini as a model for his grand opera, *Les Troyens* (1858).

Berlioz was one of the most influential musicians of the nineteenth century, excelling in each of this three careers; composing, conducting, and writing music criticism. His *Mémoires,* posthumously published in 1870, are among the best prose left to us by any composer. His compositions were strongly influenced by the simultaneous discovery in the late 1820s of the symphonies of Beethoven and the tragedies of Shakespeare; he imagined his experiments with dramatic music, lavish performing force, and eccentric melodic and phrase structures as natural outgrowths of Beethoven's advances. Among his signal contributions to modern orchestral practice were his advocacy of sectional rehearsal, an international standard pitch for tuning, and conducting with a baton and full score.

Berlioz's personal life was altogether gloomy, particulary after he had outlived both wives, all his brothers and sisters, his beloved son, and most of his closest friends. At the end, he felt his career to have been a failure. He was always confident, however, that a century later his works would be recognized for the masterpieces that they are.

Symphonie fantastique: Episode de la vie d'un artiste (Episode in the Life of an Artist)

Revêries; Passions
Un Bal
Scène aux champs (Scene in the Country)
Marche au supplice (March to the Scaffold)
Songe d'une nuit du sabbat (Dream of a Sabbath Night)

For piccolo, flutes I-II, oboes I-II, English horn, E♭ clarinet, clarinets I-II, bassoons I-IV; horns I-IV, trumpets I-II, cornets *à pistons* I-II, trombones I- III, ophicléides I-II (see p. 21); timpani I-IV, snare drum, bass drum, cymbals, bells in C and G; harps I-II; strings

Composed January–April 1830 in Paris; dedicated (1845) to Czar Nicholas I of Russia

First performed 5 December 1830, at a concert produced by Berlioz in the Salle du Conservatoire, Paris, François-Antoine Habeneck conducting

Published by Maurice Schlesinger (Paris, 1845) as op. 14.

Inexpensive scores: Hector Berlioz: *Symphonie fantastique and Harold in Italy in Full Score* (New York: Dover, 1984); Berlioz: *Fantastic Symphony,* ed. Edward T. Cone, A Norton Critical Score (New York: Norton, 1971)

Duration: about 55 minutes

The *Symphonie fantastique,* probably the most sensational First Symphony ever to be composed, is made cyclic by the use of a recurring motive, called by Berlioz an *idée fixe* and associated with the character of the protagonist's beloved. (The work was conceived in passion for the English actress Harriet Smithson, whom he later married.) The *idée* appears in each movement: as the main theme of the first, across a crowded ballroom in the second, in the distant meadows in the third, as a last vision during the execution scene, and as a mockery during the Witches' Sabbath. The *Fantastique* is packed with pictorial images: heartbeats underpin the first statement of the *idée fixe,* shepherds' pipes and thunder are heard in the scene in the country, and at the end of the march to the scaffold there is the chop of the guillotine, the head-falling-into-basket, and the hurrahs of the crowd. Listen, too, for the juxtaposition of the Gregorian chant for the dead *(Dies irae)* and the witches' round dance in the last movement, an example of one of Berlioz's favorite textural devices, the *grande réunion des thèmes*. This is evocative music of decided originality, suggesting to the next generations of the century's best composers a plethora of novel tactics.

The story is explained by Berlioz in an accompanying narrative, the text of which should appear in your printed program. The cornet solo sometimes heard in the second movement was added by Berlioz for the virtuoso J.-J.-B. Arban, known to countless brass players as the author of *Arban's Famous Trumpet Method*.

Berlioz calls for churchbells, and not chimes, in the last movement of the *Fantastique*. Tubular chimes or large metal plates are usually made to suffice.

Harold en Italie, Symphony in Four Parts with Solo Viola

Harold aux montagnes: Scènes de mélancolie, de bonheur et de joie (Harold in the mountains: Scenes of melancholy, happiness, and joy)
Marche de pélerins chantant la prière du soir (March of the Pilgrims, chanting the evening prayer)
Sérénade d'un montagnard des Abruzzes à sa maîtresse (Serenade of an Abruzzi mountaineer to his mistress)
Orgie de brigands; Souvenirs des scènes précédentes (Brigands' orgy; Reminiscences of earlier scenes)

For viola solo; piccolo, flutes I-II, oboes I-II, English horn, clarinets I-II, bassoons I-IV; horns I-IV, trumpets I-II, cornets *à pistons* I-II, trombones I-III, ophicléide; timpani, cymbals, triangle, tambourines; harp; strings
Composed: January–June 1834 in Paris; dedicated to Humbert Ferrand, a close friend of the composer
First performed 23 November 1834 at the Salle du Conservatoire, Paris, Chrétien Urhan, viola soloist, Narcisse Girard conducting
Published by Brandus & Cie. (Paris, 1848) as op. 26. *Inexpensive score:* Hector Berlioz: *Symphonie fantastique and Harold in Italy in Full Score* (New York: Dover 1984)
Duration: about 50 minutes

The central character of the work purports to be Byron's Childe Harold, a figure greatly admired by the Romantics. The true hero is, of course, Berlioz himself, who had sojourned in Italy a few years earlier.

In *Harold,* Berlioz recreates vignettes from one of the happiest times of his life: his vagabondage in the Abruzzi mountains near Rome. The part of Harold is played by the viola soloist, who is directed to stand, in a splendid example of French Romantic symbolism, away from the orchestral force, a distant hero lost in his musings.

The first movement commmences with a chromatic fugue, then the short, square melody in the viola that proves to be Harold's recurring theme. A relatively traditional sonata-allegro follows. The second movement suggests the approach and passing of a column of pilgrims; each phrase of the quiet marching song ends with a figure in the winds evocative of monks chanting their vespers. The dissonant harp part is to be heard as the distant ringing of a monastery bell. For the contrastive center section, Berlioz provides a little chorale, over which he sets arpeggios in the viola, *sul ponticello* (an eerie, hollow sound, produced by drawing the bow across the strings very near the instrument's bridge). The procession disappears.

The Abruzzi mountaineer of the third movement was a brigand named Crispino, and his nocturnal wooings and dubious musical prowess are affectionately described in the composer's priceless *Mémoires.* Armed with mountain pipes, guitar, and musette, he sallies forth to place himself beneath his beloved's window, where he sings the plaintive melody stated by the English horn. Against this, the viola soloist and strings restate Harold's main theme, spread out over four octaves. At the end, the three themes—musette song, love song, and *idée fixe*—recur together, very much like the *Dies irae* and the witches' round dance do in the *Symphonie fantastique.*

The beginning of the last movement is meant to remind us of Beethoven's Ninth: explosive tuttis are interrupted with reminiscences of each of the preceding movements. The orgy is diabolical, but Berlioz insists, too, on a victorious march theme. A last reminder of the pilgrims's procession is heard from offstage strings, and a wild chase concludes the work.

Berlioz wrote *Harold en Italie* during a period of domestic tranquility, even bliss. (He and the actress Harriet Smithson had been married in October 1833, and they were expecting the birth of their child.) It was begun to answer the need for a piece to show off Paganini's new Stradivarius viola; the virtuoso declined, however, to play so simple a solo part. When ultimately he heard *Harold,* in December

1838, he was overcome with emotion and fell in homage at Berlioz's feet. The next day he sent the composer a check for 20,000 francs in token of his admiration. This money offered Berlioz the opportunity to compose his third and perhaps most significant dramatic symphony, *Roméo et Juliette.*

Le Carnaval romain (The Roman Carnival), Ouverture caractéristique

> For piccolo, flutes I-II, oboes I-II, English horn, clarinets I-II, bassoons I-II; horns I-IV, trumpets I-II, cornets *à pistons* I-II, trombones I-III; timpani, cymbals, triangle, tambourines; strings
>
> **Composed** June 1843–January 1844 in Paris; dedicated to the Prince Hohenzollern-Hechingen, music lover and patron of the composer
>
> **First performed** 3 February 1844, at a concert produced and conducted by Berlioz in the Salle Herz, Paris
>
> **Published by** Maurice Schlesinger (Paris, 1844) as op. 9
>
> **Duration:** about 7 minutes

Berlioz fashioned the *Roman Carnival Overture* for an upcoming concert season for which little of his major work in progress was quite ready. It was meant to convey (or "be characteristic of," as the subtitle suggests) the excitement of the Roman Mardi Gras. Both main themes are borrowed from the opera *Benvenuto Cellini,* which despite its great artistic merit had failed in 1837. The action of the opera takes place on Shrove Monday, Mardi Gras, and Ash Wednesday.

The rapid theme in $\frac{6}{8}$ at the beginning is from the whirling saltarello in *Cellini,* during which the people of Rome make their way to a puppet show in the Piazza Navona. (A similar scene opens Stravinsky's *Petruskha.*) The great English horn solo comes from Cellini's act I love song, *O Teresa, vous que j'aime plus que ma vie* (O Teresa, I adore you more than my own life). But the clever joining together of the two themes in a single movement is new, as is most of the metric jolting caused by throwing the $\frac{6}{8}$ into $\frac{1}{4}$ now and then. The work breathes with a vivacity of color and motion that show the composer at his best, an *élan* of which he was especially proud.

The concert that featured the first performance of *Le Carnaval romain* is interesting for another reason as well. That same afternoon Berlioz presented an early song in an arrangement for six new instruments built by the famous maker Adophe Sax. It appears to have been the public début of the saxophone.

Leonard Bernstein

Born 25 *August* 1918 *in*
Lawrence, Massachusetts
Died 14 *October* 1990 *in New York City*

A prodigious, multitalented American musician, Bernstein was trained at Harvard and the Curtis Institute of Music, where he studied with the best American teachers of the late 1930s, notably Walter Piston and Fritz Reiner. His conducting was perfected under Dimitri Mitropoulos and Serge Koussevitzky. In 1943 he became assistant conductor under Artur Rodzinski of the New York Philharmonic, making a spectacular debut with that orchestra on November 14th of that year, when he took over the podium for the ailing Bruno Walter. At Koussevitzky's death in 1951, Bernstein became head of the conducting department at the Berkshire Music Center at Tanglewood. From 1958 to 1969 he was music director of the New York Philharmonic; he had strong connections, as well, with the Israel Philharmonic, the Vienna Philharmonic, the Concertgebouw Orchestra of

Amsterdam, and the Orchestre National of France. At the time of his death, he was conductor laureate of the New York Philharmonic and a frequent guest with the major orchestras of the world.

Bernstein was an omniscient presence on the American musical scene. He pioneered in educational telecasts of orchestral music (at first on Alistair Cooke's mighty series *Omnibus,* then in his own Young People's Concerts, where he lectured engagingly from the podium). He wrote and spoke tirelessly on music wherever he found himself. His 1973 Charles Eliot Norton Lectures at Harvard University were published as *The Unanswered Question.*

Bernstein's best compositions are for that most American of theatrical institutions, the Broadway stage. They include the ballet for Jerome Robbins called *Fancy Free* (1944), about three sailors on shore-leave, so successful it was expanded into a musical called *On the Town* (1944); the Broadway show *Wonderful Town* (1952), based on *My Sister Eileen;* music for the Marlon Brando film *On The Waterfront* (1954); his operetta to Voltaire's *Candide* (1955–56); and of course the American classic, *West Side Story* (1957), based on Shakespeare's *Romeo and Juliet. West Side Story* has already earned a place alongside Gershwin's *Porgy and Bess* as central to the history of the American lyric stage.

Bernstein's work for the concert hall is often theatrical as well, unfailingly American but with strong religious overtones that have much to do with the composer's Jewish heritage. Among his concert works are the First Symphony ("Jeremiah," 1943), Second Symphony ("The Age of Anxiety," 1949), and Third Symphony ("Kaddish," for narrator, men's chorus, and orchestra, 1961–63); the *Chichester Psalms* (1965), commissioned by the Chichester Cathedral in England; and the multimedia *Mass* (1971), composed, following a suggestion of Jacqueline Kennedy Onassis, for the opening of the John F. Kennedy Center for the Performing Arts in Washington, D.C.

Though not especially prolific—an understandable state of things for a person of his varied obligations—Bernstein was arguably the most successful composer-conductor since Mahler. He was able to bridge, with uncanny vision, the traditional chasm between the appeal of popular music and the rigor of classical idioms.

Bernstein has been regarded in some circles as an aesthetic failure, too fluent and quick for his own good, a victim of his too-easy control of too many parameters of professional music making. I believe, however, that his accomplishments made him an intellectual giant and a model to be emulated. The truth is that few enough American musicians ever enjoyed his artistic stature or matched his breadth of genius, and the American musical scene is the healthier for his efforts.

Overture to the comic operetta *Candide*

For piccolo, flutes I-II, oboes I-II, E♭ clarinet, clarinets I-II, bass
  clarinet, bassoons I-II, contrabassoon; horns I-IV, trumpets I-II,
  trombones I-III, tuba; timpani, snare drum, tenor drum, bass
  drum, cymbals, triangle, glockenspiel, xylophone; harp; strings
Composed 1955–56 in New York
First performed with the operetta 1 December 1956 at the Martin
  Beck Theatre, New York, Samuel Krachmalnick conducting;
  first performed as a concert overture 26 January 1957 by the
  New York Philharmonic, Bernstein conducting
Published by G. Schirmer (New York, 1957)
Duration: about 4 minutes

Voltaire's satire *Candide* (1759) tells of the misadventures of a naive young optimist, hoodwinked by one Dr. Pangloss into believing that "this is the best of all possible worlds." Having mastered this lesson, poor Candide is beset by war, the Inquisition, the Lisbon earthquake, black plague, enslavement, a shipwreck, and sharks. Undaunted, he and his beloved Cunegonde agree at the end to "cultivate their garden" (in Voltaire's words), or, as Bernstein's librettists have it, "We'll do the best we know: we'll build our house, and chop our wood, and make our garden grow."

The episodes of the operetta sprawl from continent to continent, disaster falling on the heels of disaster, in a marvel of modern theatrics. Bernstein's score has survived nearly as many vicissitudes as the title character: cuts, recomposings, rescorings, and retextings all designed to accommodate the tastes and sometimes whims of successive directors and audiences. Although it has never enjoyed the immense popularity of *West Side Story*, *Candide* has its share of memorable songs and, in each of its versions, a healthy dose of literary and musical genius.

The overture is a potpourri of tunes and passages from the show, though not all of these survived the revisions for the 1973–74 production. The splashy fanfare and much of the rest of the rollicking first section allude to the wedding of Candide and Cunegonde and its interruption by war in Westphalia. The lyric second theme is from the duet of the lovers, "Oh, Happy We," where the joys of horticulture and tending livestock become their ultimate goal. It then appears that the work is sonata-like, and both sections recur in order in a kind of recapitulation of the first half. The love song winds down, and there is a bar of silence. The Rossini-style crescendo and dashing coda over an insistent pulse of bass and percussion is from the conclusion of Cunegonde's jewel song, "Glitter and Be Gay." A reprise of the themes rounds the overture off, with, at the very end, the wink of a sparkling eye.

Symphonic Dances from *West Side Story*

> For piccolo, flutes I-II, oboes I-II, English horn, E♭ clarinet, clarinets I-II, bass clarinet, alto saxophone, bassoons I-II, contrabassoon; horns I-IV, trumpets I-III, trombones I-III, tuba; 4 pitched drums, jazz set, 2 snare drums, bass drum, cymbals and suspended cymbal, triangle, timbales, tom-toms, bongos, conga drum, finger cymbals, tambourine, gourds, maracas large and small, cowbells, woodblock, police whistle, tam-tam, xylophone, vibraphone, glockenspiel, chime; harp, celesta, piano; strings
>
> Drawn from *West Side Story* (1957) in 1960 by the composer with Sid Ramin and Irwin Kostel; dedicated "to Sid Ramin, in friendship"
>
> First performed 13 February 1961 by the New York Philharmonic, Lukas Foss conducting
>
> Published by Amberson / G. Schirmer, Inc. (New York, 1967)
>
> Duration: about 20 minutes

Look elsewhere for a medley of the pretty songs from *West Side Story*. This is the jeans-and-sneakers ballet music, in which the studied nocturnal cool of the Manhattan gangs ends in a hot rumble, disaster, and apotheosis. You'll recognize the sinister deserted street-music from the beginning of the show and the extended references to "Cool" and "Somewhere."

The principal sections of this work can be identified as *Prologue* (Allegro moderato), the growing rivalry between the Jets and the Sharks; *"Somewhere"* (Adagio), a visionary dance sequence in which the two gangs unite in friendship; *Scherzo* (Vivace leggiero), the gangs break out of the city into open space, fresh air, and sunshine; *Mambo* (Presto), reality returns as the gangs compete in dance; *Cha-Cha* (Andantino con grazia), the lovers' first meeting based on "Maria"; *Meeting Scene* (Meno mosso), they speak; *"Cool" Fugue* (Allegretto), during which the Jets try to control their hostility; *Rumble* (Molto allegro), a fight ending in the death of the gang leaders; and *Finale* (Adagio), the love music again, the procession accepting "the tragic reality, the vision of 'Somewhere'." The idea is that the dance sequence distills the essence of the drama, as dance so often does so admirably.

The symphonic orchestration is in part the work of the composer's associates, a common practice on Broadway. What results is a good deal richer in sonority than theater-pit scoring, and, at the same time, offers a smorgasbord of sounds not ordinarily heard at symphony concerts: most notably, the finger-clicking and the raft of percussion (keyboards, battery, tuned drums, and traps, not to mention the police whistle). Thought "classical" composers from Gershwin to Milhaud to the present have assiduously pursued the ideal of symphonic jazz, the end product is too often an uncomfortable mélange. (A hundred-piece ensemble reading precise notation feels inauthentic to begin with; so do the evening dress and sumptuous venue.) Here, however, the solution is seductive, for the combined allure of Broadway stage and Philharmonic Hall is precisely what defined so much of Bernstein's career.

You will hear a virtual encyclopedia of popular jazz and dance rhythms (swing, mambo, cha-cha) and just about every kind of syncopation in the book. Eventually, the ear begins to make the connection between the Jets' whistled salute (the first thing you hear) and the "Maria" motive. It is said that the composer found these and many other of his thematic ideas in the symphonic repertoire he regularly conducted.

Georges Bizet

Born 25 October 1838 *in Paris*
Died 3 June 1875 *in Bougival, near Paris*

Bizet, the offspring of professional musicians, was enrolled at the Paris Conservatoire at the age of ten. He literally sailed through its difficult program of study, garnering in the course of his tenure there first prizes in solfège (i.e., singing at sight), piano, organ, and fugue, and finally (1857) the coveted *prix de Rome* in composition. On his return from Italy, he established himself in Montmartre and sought and won the hand in marriage of Geneviève Halévy, daughter of the opera composer Fromental Halévy.

His considerable energies and technical fluidity were directed, as was considered fitting for a *prix de Rome* laureate, to the lyric stage, beginning with *Les Pêcheurs de perles* (The Pearl Fishers, 1863), *La Jolie Fille de Perth* (The Fair Maid of Perth, 1867), and *Djamileh* (1872). Neither his incidental music for *L'Arlésienne* nor his vivid masterpiece

Carmen (1875) gained their subsequent popularity during his lifetime: *Carmen,* with its salacious heroine and denoument in murder, was simply too controversial; *L'Arlésienne,* merely unnoticed. Bizet died at the age of thirty-six from quinsy (a form of tonsilitis), rheumatism, and a pair of heart attacks, his end doubtless hastened by the public outcry against *Carmen.*

Among Bizet's other works for orchestra are a Symphony in C, composed when he was seventeen and bearing the strong influence of Gounod, and a loosely programmatic symphony called *Roma* (1869; revised by Bizet in 1871 and somewhat bastardized for the posthumous publication in 1880). Bizet's music is characterized by supple orchestration, innate ability to cast dramatic characterizations in musical terms, and a corresponding flair for evoking local color. For all that, he never visited Spain, saying it would be "too much trouble."

L'Arlésienne (The Maid of Arles), Suites No. 1 and 2 from music for the drama by Alphonse Daudet

> **Suite 1**
> *Prélude: Allegro deciso (Tempo di marcia); Andantino; Andante molto*
> *Minuetto: Allegro giocoso*
> *Adagietto: Adagio*
> *Carillon: Allegretto moderato; Andantino*
>
> **Suite 2** (extracted and arranged by Ernest Guiraud)
> *Pastorale: Andante sostenuto assai*
> *Intermezzo: Andante moderato ma con moto*
> *Menuet: Andantino quasi allegretto*
> *Farandole: Allegro decisio (Tempo di marcia)*
>
> **For** flutes I-II, oboes I-II, English horn, clarinets I-II, alto saxophone, bassoons I-II; horns I-IV, trumpets I-II, cornets *à pistons* I-II, trombones I-III; timpani, snare drum, tabor, bass drum, cymbals; harp or piano; strings
> **Composed** 1872; Suite 2, prepared by Guiraud, 1879
> **First performed** with the play, 1 October 1872 at the Théâtre du Vaudeville, Paris; Suite 1 first performed 10 November 1872 at a Pasdeloup Concert in the Cirque d'Hiver, Paris, Jules Pasdeloup conducting
> **Published by** Choudens (Paris, 187[6], 1885)
> **Duration:** about 20 minutes each

Bizet was invited to compose incidental music for Alphonse Daudet's drama *L'Arlésienne* by the impresario Léon Carvalho, who had produced Berlioz's *Les Troyens*, Gounod's *Faust* and *Roméo et Juliette*, and Bizet's own *Les Pêcheurs de perles* during his illustrious career with the Paris Théâtre-Lyrique. Carvalho had since become director of the Théâtre du Vaudeville, where he hoped to revitalize the melodrama, which in its original meaning was a practice of accompanying the most significant of the spoken texts with music, usually of the symbolic sort. Carvalho's budget was small, and Bizet was constrained to compose his music for an orchestra of twenty-six.

Bizet wrote more than two dozen individual passages of music for the three-act play, most of them melodramas of a dozen bars or less based on one of the five or six motives that describe the critical situations in the play. Between the acts and for scene changes he provided fully developed movements, and of course there was an orchestral overture. There was music, as well, for on-stage dancing and an off-stage chorus.

The story is of a young man, Frédéri, who has lost his heart to a woman—who is only spoken of, never seen—of suspect virtue. She is from Arles, that picturesque walled city in the region of Provence immortalized in the paintings of Van Gogh. (Daudet was born in nearby Nîmes.) The music adopts provençal tunes, like the "March of the Three Kings" you hear at the beginning, and supplies an occasion for the *farandole,* a festive street dance where lines of dancers in traditional costume, each linked to the next by a shared handkerchief, wend their way through the streets behind a player of the pipe and tabor. It's the sort of dance they enjoy doing on the bridge at Avignon, just up the river from Arles.

Bizet drew his own suite from *L'Arlésienne,* rescoring it for full orchestra, shortly after the play opened. The *Prélude* is identical to the overture of the play: five statements of the "March of the Three Kings," the three tutti variations offset by two quieter ones; then, in the saxophone, the bittersweet theme of the Innocent, the half-witted but insightful younger brother of the hero; and finally, in the strings, Frédéri's motive, often transmogrified during the play into a sort of Fate motive. The minuet precedes wedding festivities in act III— these end in tragedy—as does the carillon movement. The *Adagietto* is heard at the moment when the venerable Mère Renaud, having arrived for the wedding, encounters for the first time in perhaps fifty years the family retainer Balthazar, her former lover. The lovely pastoral duct for flutes in the middle of the carillon is the music of Mère Renaud's entry.

Arranging the second suite was the work of the composer's long-time friend and associate Ernest Guiraud, who also saw as best he could to the preservation of *Carmen*. The *Pastorale* is the morning music before act II, which begins at dawn on the Vaccarès salt marsh in the Camargue, southern Provence; its middle section, with tabor, is in the play a tra-la chorus of offstage merrymakers. The *Intermezzo* is the entr'acte between the two scenes of act II, based on another Provençal folk melody; the minuet is not from *L'Arlésienne* at all, but rather from *La Jolie Fille de Perth,* Bizet's opera of 1867. The *pièce de résistance* is the justly celebrated *Farandole,* and it was Guiraud's most satisfactory idea to introduce it with the "March of the Three Kings" and then to superpose the two.

Ernst Bloch

Born 24 *July* 1880 *in* Geneva
Died 15 *July* 1959 *in Portland, Oregon*

Born in Geneva, educated there and in Brussels, Frankfurt, Munich, and Paris, Bloch was by training and personal inclination an internationalist, as fond, for example, of Richard Strauss's music as of Debussy's and Mussorgsky's. He conducted in Switzerland and lectured for a time at the Geneva Conservatory, then, following a 1916 concert tour of the United States as musical director for a dance company, elected to immigrate; he became an American citizen in 1924. In New York he taught at the Mannes School (1917–20), then was named director of the Cleveland Institute of Music (1920–25) and the San Francisco Conservatory (1925–30). After a period of residence in Switzerland in the 1930s, he returned to the Pacific coast and taught summer courses at the University of California, Berkeley. The long list of his composition students who made good includes the

American composers George Antheil, Roger Sessions, and Leon Kirchner. Through his work as a teacher he thus had a strong influence on American music in the second third of the twentieth century.

As a composer, Bloch is remembered primarily for a series of works on Jewish subject matter that he composed during the second decade of this century. These include the *Trois Poèmes juifs* (1913), *Schelomo,* and a symphony called *Israel* (1912–16); in 1951 he wrote a *Suite hébraïque* for viola and orchestra.

Subsequent to what is called his "Jewish cycle" Bloch composed two concerti grossi for orchestra (1924–25; 1953), two other symphonies including his last major composition, the Symphony in E♭ (1954–55), various works for soloist and orchestra, and two curious nationalist symphonic poems, *America* (1926, an "epic rhapsody") and *Helvetia* (1928, called a "symphonic fresco"). It is in his compositions for orchestra that Bloch is most comfortable and technically assured; he was able to adopt with equal ease, as he progressed, such features of post-Romanticism, neoclassicism, and atonality as were useful to his expressive purposes.

Schelomo (Solomon), Hebraic Rhapsody for Cello and Orchestra

For cello solo; piccolo, flutes I-III, oboes I-II, English horn, clarinets I-II, bass clarinet, bassoons I-II, contrabassoon; horns I-IV, trumpets I-III, trombones I-III, tuba; timpani, snare drum, bass drum, cymbals, tambourine, tam-tam, celesta; harps I-II; strings

Composed 1915–16 in Geneva; score dated January–February 1916; dedicated to the cellist Alexander Barjansky (1883–1961) and his wife, Catherine

First performed 3 May 1917 in Carnegie Hall, New York, at a concert produced by the Society of the Friends of Music, Hans Kindler, soloist, Bloch conducting

Published by G. Schirmer, Inc. (New York, 1918)

Duration: about 25 minutes

The work Bloch first envisaged as a setting for voice and orchestra of passages from Ecclesiastes evolved into this rhapsody for solo cello and orchestra after a visit to Geneva, in late 1915, of the Russian cellist Alexander Barjansky and his wife. With this purely instrumental ensemble, they reasoned, the issue of which language to use could be avoided altogether, and the composer would enjoy more freedom to dwell on his keen feeling for Solomonic lore. *Schelomo,* in fact, comes at the apex of Bloch's interest in "the Jewish soul," as he put it, "the emotion of the race." The perplexities and puzzlements of the solo part, restrained and not a little tragic, are clearly to be heard as the voice of the lone and lonely Solomon, pondering the lessons of life and overwhelmed by the unpredictable, sometimes violent forces that surround our experience. Bloch's fatalistic conception of the Old Testament focused on despair, wrath, and the certain justice of destiny. Solomon, the Preacher of Jerusalem, begins Ecclesiastes with the cosmic resignation of "Vanity of vanities! All is vanity." Bloch wrote, "All this is in us. All this is in me."

That pessimism of attitude, however close it is to the heart of the work, is less apparent to my ear than the vivid, masterly technique Bloch brings to his scoring for the bold post-Romantic orchestra. The cello's motives are woven into the orchestral fabric, gently at first, over such delicate textures as that of the two harps and celesta, and with soft articulations from the deceptively large battery of percussion instruments. Brass and full strings are unleashed in due course, yet such extravagance is always balanced by subtle and often fleeting detail: the hint of a royal march here, the odd quarter-tone there. The themes are few enough and the motives closely enough related—many of them retain their identities throughout the work—that the melodic framework is easily retained by the listener.

Likewise the three-part formal structure is easy to grasp, clearly delineated by the tutti statements with which each section concludes and by the solo cadenzas afterward that effect the transitions. After the opening solo, the cellist and orchestra offer a gentle dance-based section in prevailing triple meter, with strong emphasis on the sixteenth-plus-eighth rhythm commonly called the "Scotch snap." Great scales begin to surge forth and recede back into the depths of the accompaniment: the dance becomes pompous and military, and soon the broad, fateful main theme is given its grandest statement by the full orchestra. This unravels into a terrifying orchestral dispersion, marked in the score *quasi una cadenza*. Dominating the second section are figurations, both thematic and accompanimental, of rapidly reiterated pitches surely meant to suggest a cantor's intonations; the melody in the oboe here is a traditional Jewish tune. Again a full orchestral statement blossoms and concludes with another conspicuous downward tumble; the last section opens with reminiscences of the chant motive in the timpani and a sharp dissonance in the clarinets and violas. Note, in the closing bars, the subdued, restless interplay of the solo part and contrabassoon.

There is strong reliance here on such "oriental" devices as the constantly shifting chromatic inflection of the various motives, and on intervals and contours that derive from traditional Jewish music. But Bloch's spiritual affinity with French impressionism is equally clear—notably in the interplay of the motives and the rich textures and colors. *Schelomo* is thus as western European a work as it is Jewish, and in that respect bears comparison to the descriptive works of Falla, Ravel, and even Respighi.

Alexander Borodin

Born *12 November 1833 in St. Petersburg*
Died *27 February 1887 in St. Petersburg*

Borodin, the illegimate offspring of a Russian prince and an otherwise respectable married woman, was given a suitably patrician education that included good training in music; he first tried his hand at composition during his early teens. His formal studies in St. Petersburg were in the fields of chemistry and medicine, and within a few years of earning his doctorate in chemistry he had become a noted research chemist and author of numerous learned papers. His professional expertise afforded him the opportunity for extensive travels in Europe (1859–62), during which time he developed a keen interest in Wagner and his followers. On his return to Russia in 1862, Borodin was befriended and encouraged in his composition by Mily Balakirev and Modest Mussorgsky, two of the major figures attempting to establish a Russian nationalist school; by 1867, these composers along with Nicolai Rimsky-Korsakov and Cesar Cui, were dubbed the "mighty handful" (*moguchaya kuchka*), or simply "the Five." For the rest of his career Borodin managed, with remarkable success, the simultaneous careers of scientist, composer, and government administrator. He numbered among his intimate friends the chemist Dmitri Mendeleev, who formulated the Periodic Table of the Elements.

He had little enough time to compose, with the result that his musical output, though of great significance to the nationalist movement, is small. His masterpiece was the opera *Prince Igor,* on which he worked for nearly two decades from 1869, leaving it far from done at his death. The young Alexander Glazunov (1865–1936) completed the third act from the sketches and notated the overture from memory—he had heard the composer play it at the piano on several occasions; Rimsky-Korsakov finished the orchestration.

Borodin composed three symphonies (E♭ major, 1862–67; B minor, 1869–76; A minor, 1885—this last also left unfinished and completed by Glazunov); Liszt in his later years took special interest in the second, and it still survives in the orchestral repertoire. Borodin's other major orchestral composition is the "symphonic picture" *In Central Asia,* sometimes called *On the Steppes of Central Asia* (1880), dedicated to Liszt and intended for a series of twelve *tableaux vivants* by various composers on the occasion of the twenty-fifth anniversary of czar Alexander II's reign. As these titles show, it was not merely Russian nationalism that intrigued Borodin, but the intersection of Russian culture with tribal Asia. Two string quartets, No. 1 in A Major (1874–79) and No. 2 in D major (1881), are important as well; of these the nocturne in the second has achieved popularity in an orchestration by Sir Malcolm Sargeant.

Borodin was a strikingly handsome man, affable and well-spoken, with a good-natured optimism; he was moreover fastidious and gentle in deportment, at ease in the major European languages, and of course financially secure. This array of attractions, not to mention the passionately Romantic character of his music, appears to have been what prompted any number of young women to fall madly in love with him. He resisted these temptations, however, and remained happily married to Mrs. Borodin, a pianist.

The music for the Broadway show *Kismet* of 1953 was arranged from tunes found in *Prince Igor, In Central Asia,* the Quartet in D Major, and other Borodin works.

Polovtsian Dances, from the opera *Prince Igor*

Andantino (Dance of Seductive Girls)—Allegro vivo (Dance of Men: Savage)—Allegro (General Dance)—Presto (Dance of Boys)—Moderato alla breve—Presto—Allegro con spirito

For piccolo, flutes I-II, oboes I-II, English horn, clarinets I-II, bassoons I-II; horns I-IV, trumpets I-II, trombones I-III, tuba; timpani, snare drum, bass drum, cymbals, triangle, tambourine, glockenspiel; harp; strings (in the opera, the ballet includes the full chorus and a few lines for Kontchak Kahn)

Composed summer of 1875 in St. Petersburg

First performed 11 March 1879 in St. Petersburg; the opera first performed, posthumously, 4 November 1890 at the Maryinsky Theatre, St. Petersburg

Published by M. P. Belaieff (Moscow, 1889)

Duration: about 15 minutes

Prince Igor is based on a thirteenth-century epic called *The Saga of Igor's Army*. The Polovtsi, a mongol-like nomadic tribe headed by the khan Kontchak, lay siege to Igor's city, Putivl, in the year 1185. Prince Igor leads his troops against them and, by the end of act I, is himself captured. Much of act II, in the encampment of the Polovtsi, is given over to the glamorous ballets presented by the male and female slaves of the Polovtsi to entertain Igor, Kontchak, and their retinues. Four separate dances are presented in succession, then combined into a grand finale. This is a tried-and-true formula for the big ballet in a grand opera, but Borodin makes it exceptionally attractive by virtue of the brilliant rhythmic character of the dances and their wonderful melodies.

After a lazy introduction in the high woodwind over pizzicato cellos and harp, the "young women of undulating movements" offer their dance, singing of the sweet breezes that will float their songs to their distant homeland, a place of nightingales, verdant landscape, and blue sea. The memorable "Stranger in Paradise" tune is first heard in the oboe, then to increasingly rich accompaniment in the English horn and finally in a strophe for violins and flutes. It has a fine countermelody, heard most prominently in the cellos.

The melody of the second dance, that of the savage male slaves, is stated by clarinet, then by flute and piccolo; again there is an important countermelody, heard at first in the lower woodwinds. The dance grows in momentum through the entry of tambourine and trombones, then fades suddenly away, as though spent. The splendid movement in $\frac{3}{4}$ which follows, introduced by an excited crescendo in the percussion, is a chorus of praise to the wisdom and power of the khan, with vigorous downbeats, great upward surges, and shimmering chromatic falls. In the twinkling center section—note the glockenspiel and the flute / piccolo arabesques—Kontchak invites Igor to take "the blonde sea-creature, the brunette rogue of the devil," or any slave he fancies.

Boys, playful and carefree, make their entry in a $\frac{6}{8}$ *Presto,* based on an exchange of motives in the winds; the loud passages are for the grown men, still hailing the khan. This merges into the recapitulatory finale, with at the end, *più animato,* a general pandemonium in praise of the pleasures of dance.

The Polovtsian Dances established Borodin's reputation outside Russia, when, from 1909, Sergei Diaghilev's ballet troupe began offering them to the Paris public. That the dances are called variously "Polovetsian," "Polovtsian," and "of the Polovtsi" is merely a matter of translation.

Pierre Boulez

**Born 26 March 1925 in
Montbrison, Loire valley**

A student of the progressive French composers Olivier Messiaen and René Leibowitz, Boulez emerged during the 1950s as the *enfant terrible* of the contemporary music scene. To the avant-garde his music seemed, from the first, fluent and assured and of almost surreal delicacy, but it was his caustic dismissal of any but the most forward-looking cerebral works in the twelve-tone language that earned him his notoriety. He was not above hissing the great Stravinsky if he thought it warranted, and a few weeks after Schoenberg's death wrote an inflammatory polemic, "Schönberg est mort," in which he reminded the moderns that theirs was merely nascent technique. From 1954 he organized and led an important series of new music concerts in Paris, called the Domaine Musical; by this time *Le Marteau sans maître* had earned him a wide following, and he was invited to lecture and teach composition in Darmstadt and Basel. In 1959 he left France to establish himself in Baden-Baden; in 1963 he was a visiting professor at Harvard.

His expertise as a conductor, gained through his work in the 1940s and '50s with a progressive Paris theater company, gained him further international prestige. In his concerts and recordings of such works as Debussy's *Pelléas et Mélisande* and the Stravinsky ballets, he introduced a clarity and lucidity of interpretation theretofore undreamed of, though his detractors held that his conducting was bloodless. He conducted abroad increasingly, and simultaneously became Bernstein's successor at the New York Philharmonic and music director of the BBC Symphony (1971–75). In 1976 Boulez conducted the centennial performances of Wagner's *Ring* at Bayreuth, with a controversial Marxist staging by his countryman Patrice Chéreau.

It became a goal of the domestic policy of Georges Pompidou, president of France (1969–74), to bring Boulez home. Accordingly what is now the Centre Georges Pompidou in the heart of Paris was planned to include an advanced underground center for new and electronic music, called, following the French passion for acronyms, IRCAM (Institut de Recherche et de Coordination Acoustique / Musique). Boulez did in fact return to Paris, where he remains active as composer, conductor of new music, and politically engaged administrator.

Boulez, like his American counterpart Milton Babbitt a mathematician as well as a musician, is at the forefront of the movement that celebrates scientific, highly rational ordering of musical materials as the only viable premise of composition. He was an early pioneer in using magnetic tape and sound synthesizers and one of the first to employ computers in the composition of new music. At the same time, he is a spiritual descendent of Varèse in his search for transparency of tonal image; with a fiendishly difficult rhythmic and metric vocabulary, his structures cycle ever inward on themselves, resulting in a sensuous formal stasis. Boulez has come to favor a kind of continuing preoccupation with the compositional ideas proposed by previous works, sometimes called open-ended form: the *Improvisations sur Mallarmé* and other works to texts of that poet were adopted into the important composition *Pli selon pli* (Fold by Fold): *Portrait de Mallarmé* for soprano and orchestra (1962); and *Doubles* for Orchestra (1958) was expanded as *Figures–Doubles–Prismes* of 1964. Among his other works for orchestra are *Rituel in memoriam* [Bruno] *Maderna* (1974) and *Eclat* (1980).

Le Marteau sans maître (The Hammer Without Master)

1. *Avant "L'Artisanat furieux"*
2. *Commentaire I de "Bourreaux de solitude"*
3. *"L'Artisanat furieux"*
4. *Commentaire II de "'Bourreaux de solitude"*
5. *"Bel édifice et les pressentiments," version première*
6. *"Bourreaux de solitude"*
7. *Après "L'Artisanat furieux"*
8. *Commentaire III de "Bourreaux de solitude"*
9. *"Bel édifice et les pressentiments," double*

For alto soloist and six instrumentalists: alto flute, guitar, vibraphone, xylorimba, percussion (drum set, 2 pairs bongos, maracas, claves, large bell, triangle, high tam-tam, low gong, deep tam-tam, very large suspended cymbal, 2 miniature cymbals, small cymbals), and viola. The xylorimba (marimba-xylophone) is an instrument encompassing both the low range of the marimba and the high range of the xylophone.

Text by René Char (b. 1907)

Composed 1953–55; revised 1957; dedicated to Hans Rosbaud (1895–1962), an Austrian conductor noted for his performances of new music

First performed 18 June 1955 by the Southwest German Radio Orchestra at the International Society for Contemporary Music (ISCM) Festival in Baden-Baden, Hans Rosbaud conducting

Published by Universal Edition (London, 1954; revised ed., 1957)

Duration: about 35 minutes

All the plinking and plunking in this substantial work may at first hearing get on your nerves and strike you as self-indulgent. But *Le Marteau sans maître* is critical to the modern repertoire, in some respects the starting point for several of the most interesting compositional ideas of this half-century. Listen to a recorded performance before hearing it live, just to get the lay of the land; then, in the concert, try to recall to amazing scope of the whole as its constituent parts go by, each of them foreshadowing, or reflecting, or somehow commenting on what goes before and after.

Le Marteau sans maître is not a true orchestral work, but rather a chamber composition for singer and six instruments. I include it here because of its importance to recent music history, and because orchestral percussion players have a field day with the piece. Watch for it on one of the chamber programs of your local symphony orchestra.

For the texts of *Le Marteau sans maître,* Boulez selected three short poems from the collection of that title by René Char, a surrealist provençal poet admired for his terse, aphoristic verses and vivid imagery. The poems are declaimed by the singer in movements 3, 5, and 6. "Furious Artisans" deals in images of a forced-labor camp: a caravan, a corpse, the workhorses, a knife, dreams. "Beautiful Building and Premonitions": the hollow sound of waves, a pier, child, man, tearful eyes searching for a skull to dwell in. "Hangmen of Solitude": footsteps receding, a sundial, a pendulum, a tombstone. You're supposed to know the text before hearing the work: the composition consists of dreamy reflections on dreamy poems, and one perceives the meaning as through a glass, darkly. The poems are nothing more (nor less) than the source of the work, writes Boulez, both "at the center, and absent."

"L'Artisanat furieux" (no. 3) comes with a prelude (no. 1) and a postlude (no. 7). The song is a brief, rather quiet duet of singer and flute; the prelude a brisk, vivacious quartet; the postlude a trio of the same general structure but terser still. The percussion player is silent in all three of these movements. The two settings of *"Bel édifice et pressentiments"* (nos. 5 and 9) share such figurations as the wide leaps with grace notes and long trills and flutter tonguing, not to mention certain chordal similarities. In the *double* much of the singing is wordless and the accompaniment quite percussive. But it is *"Bourreaux de solitude"* and its three commentaries (nos. 2, 4, 6, and 8) that lie at the heart of the work. Number 6—the deepest, most intense, and longest movement—is slow and dark with constant reminders, in the drums, of the footsteps and the ticking of the clock.

Other principles of order dictate the arrangment of the movements, allowing the work to cycle and interpenetrate itself with cross references of all sorts. But for the relatively inexperienced listener, the first interest of *Le Marteau sans maître* will be in the composer's choice and deployment of performing force. In conscious imitation of Schoenberg's *Pierrot lunaire,* no two of the instrumental movements is for the same combination of players. The tone qualities of the instruments and voice are radically different, yet all but the percussion battery are prevailingly in the alto range. The warm sultriness of the viola and flute (and sometimes the singer), contrast strikingly with the sharper modes of attack of the others. Note, especially, the hypnotic percussion patterns, which come and go in waves, the Indonesian effect of the gongs, bells, and tam-tams. Enjoy this austere yet strangely luxuriant world, with its abrupt changes of direction, wispy melodies, spasmodic and sometimes vicious rhythms. The sheer sound of it is quite unlike any other piece I discuss in this book.

Johannes Brahms

Born 7 May 1833 *in Hamburg*
Died 3 April 1897 *in Vienna*

Brahms's first teacher was his father, a double bass player in the Hamburg orchestras. In his teens, he could claim expertise in composition, violin, and piano, the piano playing nourished by long nights of work in the bar-rooms of the Hamburg docks. During an 1853 concert tour with the Hungarian violinist Ede Reményi, Brahms befriended the virtuoso Joseph Joachim, who urged him to make the acquaintance of Liszt and Schumann. Unlike Liszt, Schumann received him warmly: his famous notice in the *Neue Zeitschrift für Musik* declared Brahms the true successor to Beethoven. Brahms and the Schumanns became lifelong friends—and the attachment between Brahms and Clara Schumann was of the most exquisite complexity (see p. 509).

After Schumann's death, Brahms moved to Vienna, where, with a few interruptions, he spent the rest of his life composing and conducting concerts for a living, with appearances now and then as concert pianist.

It was, indeed, widely held that Beethoven's mantle had fallen to Brahms, and this notion weighed heavily on him. Not until 1876, when he was in his mid-forties, did the First Symphony appear, its way carefully prepared by the Serenades, opp. 11 and 16 (1857; 1860), the First Piano Concerto, op. 15 (1858), and the Haydn Variations, op. 56a (1873). Three superb symphonies followed the First, and all his later multimovement orchestral works are symphonic in scope. These are the Violin Concerto, op. 77 (1878), the Second Piano Concerto, op. 83 (1881), and the Double Concerto for Violin and Cello, op. 102 (1887). Additionally there are the two overtures, *Academic Festival* and *Tragic,* opp. 80 and 81 (1880; 1881) and the most substantial of Brahms's many sacred compositions, *Ein deutsches Requiem* (A German Requiem, op. 45, 1857–68). He was also a prolific composer of chamber music, song, and music for solo piano. There are 122 published opuses.

Brahms was a musical conservative for whom the evocative subject matter so sought after by most composers in the late nineteenth century held little sway. Rather he was interested in adapting the forms and procedures of the past for the purposes of the late nineteenth century, certain that absolute music in the lineage of Mozart still had much to offer. His orchestral writing is lush and sensual: wind players look forward to the solo work in Brahms as much as to anything in the repertoire, and nothing can beat the radiance of the string ensemble when he works himself into a passion. He is a master contrapuntist and rhythmist and a true genius of melody.

Symphony No. 1 in C Minor, OP. 68

Un poco sostenuto; Allegro
Andante sostenuto
Un poco Allegretto e grazioso
Adagio; Più Andante; Allegro non troppo, ma con brio

For flutes I-II, oboes I-II, clarinets I-II, bassoons I-II, contrabassoon; horns I-IV, trumpets I-II, trombones I-III; timpani; strings
Composed 1862–September 1876; finished summer 1876 in Lichtenthal near Baden-Baden

First performed 4 November 1876 by the orchestra of the Grand-
Ducal Theatre, Karlsruhe, Otto Dessoff conducting
Published by N. Simrock (Berlin, 1877). *Inexpensive score:*
Johannes Brahms: *Complete Symphonies in Full Orchestral Score*
(New York: Dover, 1974)
Duration: about 45 minutes

The First Symphony was born in the aftermath of Schumann's decline
and tempered by the certainty of comparison with Beethoven. The
worst thing Brahms could possibly have done, under the circumstances, would have been to propose something overtly derivative, for
the mere testimonial of a disciple would scarcely have passed muster.
What he announced, in fact, was a bold personal statement of new
ideals, a symphony of epic lyricism, and what amounts to an altogether new orchestral sonority. Comparisons with the Viennese Classical symphony, then, hardly seem worth making at all.

Yet in choice of key and the grim heroism of the first movement,
there is undeniable precedent in Beethoven's Fifth, and the themes of
the finales of Beethoven's Ninth and Brahms's First have affinities
that, as Brahms put it, "any donkey can see." Subtler nuances bring
Beethoven to mind as well: Brahms, for example, withholds the
trombones until the last movement, as Beethoven had done in the
Fifth.

Both outer movements of Brahms's First have slow introductions.
The prominent rising pitches you hear in the violins in the very first
bar, C–C♯–D, will go on to color quite a number of other events as
the symphony unfolds. The unsettled and urgent *Allegro,* though it
has the proper constituent parts, seems almost monothematic in the
insistent rising and falling arches prompted by the main theme.
Whenever the tensions begin to subside, a petulant little motive of
three falling eighths reasserts its sinister nuance. The old Beethovenian struggle with Fate is clearly in the air. As is the promise of resolution: at the end of the movement, *Meno allegro,* multiple
reharmonizations of the C–C♯–D motto soon achieve major mode
and placid resolution.

The breathtaking lift from the C-major closing bars of the first
movement into the E major of the *Andante* unveils a reticent orchestral aria that returns again and again to the nodding gesture of the
violins in the third and fourth bars. The second subject consists of

liquid solo work for oboe and clarinet, with recapitulation for the full orchestra, theme in the woodwind. Brahms leaves a most unusual coda for solo horn and violin obbligato, leading to a tender restatement of the big chromatic wedge that opened the symphony. But where in the first movement the effect was to unsettle, here the outcome is serene.

Again we go to a higher key, A♭ major, for the *Allegretto*. The clarinet melody is quite similar in shape and character to the second subject of the second movement, where the clarinet was likewise prominent. Brahms solves the ongoing issue of what to do for a third movement—minuets were dead, and scherzos weren't funny anymore—quite nicely: the simple graciousness of gesture, which it shares with the third movements of the next two symphonies, properly accommodates the needs for repose from first-movement rigors and to establish a prelude for the finale. The form is that of the traditional dance and trio, but with the first section in duple meter. The trio is in ⁶⁄₈; at the *da capo,* the metric shift back to duple and the harmonic shove back to the original key is a moment of special delight.

Serious brooding opens the fourth movement, as though Brahms is returning to some interrupted thought. The tune is a foreshadowing in the minor mode of the famous marching song that follows as the principal theme. (There's a very similar lost-in-thought passage in *Pictures at an Exhibition* [see p. 407], where the viewer seems to be musing on death.) Everything we hear in this long introduction, indeed, comes back in the later material: the wedge, the chase of violins, the French horn solo, and the majestic entry of the trombone trio. The major mode is at length established, and the affirmative *Allegro,* part march and part hymn, gets underway. The second stanza turns quickly into a process of developing, then synthesizing, all that has come before. The movement ends with a fine acceleration (or *stretto)* and heroic tutti treatment of the trombone chorale from the introduction. A more fitting tribute to the Beethovenian ideal of the symphony as struggle and resolution is difficult to imagine.

Symphony No. 2 in D Major, OP. 73

Allegro non troppo
Adagio non troppo
Allegretto grazioso (quasi Andantino)
Allegro con spirito

For flutes I-II, oboes I-II, clarinets I-II, bassoons I-II; horns I-IV,
   trumpets I-II, trombones I III, tuba; timpani; strings
Composed summer 1877 at Pörtschach, Carinthia
First performed 30 December 1877 by the Vienna Philharmonic
   Orchestra, Hans Richter conducting
Published by N. Simrock (Berlin, 1878). *Inexpensive score:*
   Johannes Brahms: *Complete Symphonies in Full Orchestral Score*
   (New York: Dover, 1974)
Duration: about 45 minutes

The wonderful melodies, matchless solo work in woodwind and brass—
consider, for example, the glorious horn solo at the end of the first
movement—and such persuasive architecture as pairing the sprawled,
mysterious second movement with a brief and gentle third: all these
things help make Brahms's Second Symphony perfect. It is the largest
of his four essays in the genre and, to my way of thinking, easily the
loveliest.

The first three notes we hear in the low strings, D–C♯–D, say
much of what follows: the curve of the motive a caress, the C♯ an
injection of darkness. This is one of those big Brahms sonata movements with all sorts of melodies beyond the two main themes. French
horns introduce the first group with a theme based on a real German
lullaby; as this is drawing to conclusion, a solo timpani roll introduces the poignant cadence for the three trombones and tuba—a sonic
event redolent with suggestions of old Vienna. The second group
begins with more lullaby, *cantando* and *dolce,* in the violas and cellos.
The tranquility of this great theme is shattered by an orchestral fanfare and literally pages of semi-development of the thematic material
over a difficult pattern of syncopated eighths and sixteenths in the
clarinet, horns, and violas. (It's one of those close-your-eyes-and-don't-
worry-about-it figures that would drive you crazy if you stopped to
think about it.) Only after these digressions is the closing material
reached.

Conductors too frequently omit the repeat of this particular exposition—an understandable expedient in the days of vinyl discs, where
it was tough to fit the first two movements on side one; but the repeat
ought to be taken, not just to allow us to savor these glories once
more but because there are some interesting things to be heard in the
first ending. A stormy development emphasizes the metric tensions
pent up in the themes; as Brahms begins his retreat into recapitula-

tion, the D–C♯–D quarter notes of the first bar can be heard as three half notes spread out over two bars, notably in the trombone. The coda is richly Romantic: a throbbing horn solo, dallying with the opening theme as though unwilling to be done, is at length nudged aside by the final animato, where for a few moments the beat seems to slip to the right by an eighth note.

So dense is the opening gesture of the *Adagio,* so compelling the rise of the bassoon countermelody, that one's attention isn't drawn into the big cello theme until after it is well underway. The winds linger on this material in dialogue, then turn to a gracious, syncopated *siciliana* in $\frac{12}{8}$. The churning developmental episode lasts but a few bars; a freshly orchestrated restatement never reaches the *siciliana,* but instead veers away to resolve the implications of the unfinished development. Brahms dispels those gravities in a trice when he begins the *Allegretto* as a minuet. Instead of a conventional trio there is a *galop,* not courtly at all but a presto in $\frac{2}{4}$. The return of the minuet is broader and quite dense at its peak, yielding then to a scherzando in $\frac{3}{8}$ as second trio. The minuet now recapitulates fully, with a fine late-century sigh in the coda.

The restless initial theme of the finale clearly bodes larger things to come. In fact it is exploded by the transition. This eventually settles back into the second theme, a broad hymn stated low in the violins and violas, one of Brahms's best. The long exposition begins to conclude at the empty beats and syncopated tutti chords; the short, misty development retreats into a *tranquillo,* with bell-tones on intervals from the main theme. At the point of recapitulation the theme is supposed to be even softer than before, the better to set off the long crescendo to peroration and coda. Here the brass have a field day, especially with the layers of trombone scales that lead to the final jubilant peals of trumpet and horn.

Symphony No. 3 in F Major, OP. 90

Allegro con brio
Andante
Poco Allegretto
Allegro

For flutes I-II, oboes I-II, clarinets I-II, bassoons I-II, contrabassoon; horns I-IV, trumpets I-II, trombones I-III; timpani; strings

Composed summer 1883 in Wiesbaden
First performed 2 December 1883, by the Vienna Philharmonic
  Orchestra, Hans Richter conducting
Published by N. Simrock (Berlin, 1884). *Inexpensive score:*
  Johannes Brahms: *Complete Symphonies in Full Orchestral Score*
  (New York: Dover, 1974)
Duration: about 40 minutes

Brahms composed the bulk of the Third Symphony in the summer months of 1883, though perhaps he made use of sketches from an earlier time; thus it falls between the Second Piano Concerto (completed in 1881) and the Fourth Symphony (1884–85). The orchestral works of the 1880s reflect Hans von Bülow's offer to have his orchestra at Meiningen—one of Europe's most accomplished—read Brahms's new compositions in informal surroundings. Brahms profited greatly from this unusual opportunity to work privately with a fine ensemble, both for work in progress and with ideas for the future.

Commentators enjoy interpreting the Third Symphony as a massive statement of a private emblem, *Frei aber froh* (free but joyful), reflected in the melodic motive with which the symphony in fact opens (F-A-F). (This was Brahms's reply to his friend Joachim's more sullen monogram *Frei aber einsam,* free but alone). However that may be—and Brahms appears to have embedded symbols of all sorts in his music—there is much more to be said of the Third. For one thing, it is the briefest and most compact of the four symphonies. There is, as in the First Symphony, a heroic streak, still Beethovenian. Cyclic thematic recall establishes certain unities of structure, and there are, moreover, some direct allusions to the first movement of Schumann's Third.

The opening motto introduces a big sonata in $\frac{6}{4}$, a meter Brahms manipulates with great imagination, especially when he allows his penchant for watery figurations full play. The second group begins in $\frac{9}{4}$ in a passive key (A major) with the long theme for clarinet and bassoon, reaching closure in great rolling swells of the woodwind choir. Developmental agitations settle out in favor of the expansive horn solo based on the motto intervals; the recapitulation is reached through a twinkling *sostenuto* that ebbs rather than plows into the moment of return.

The *Andante* begins as a chorale for woodwinds. Take careful note of the next theme, the questioning melody for clarinet and bassoon, as this is reused in the last movement to magnificent effect. Once the formal demands have been met, the movement becomes increasingly memorable: the coda starts at the great welling up of sentiment in the strings, goes on to recall fragments of the second theme, and concludes with a wonderful and warmly paternal cadence in the low brass. The third movement is a melancholy waltz in C minor, with a curious center section of leanings-across-the-bar in lieu of true downbeats. Winds have the melodies in the recapitulation: where the horn solo passes to oboe, an ardent countermelody is introduced in the bassoon. Suggestions of the center section lead to the final cadence.

During both the *Andante* and the *Allegretto* a certain tension has built up, since the epic sweep of the first movement has been met so far only by the serenity of the second movement and bittersweet resignation of the third. Questions, in short, have been left unanswered, and the minor-mode restlessness at the beginning of the finale is manifestly driving toward a transfiguration of some kind. One early assurance that this process is under way is the mysterious low-registered recall in wooodwinds and strings of the clarinet and bassoon theme from the second movement. Only at the end of the recapitulation does the major mode finally blossom; shortly afterward the woodwinds and brass give the recycled theme its uplifted, hallowing treatment. But Brahms's master stroke is saved for the very end: a subdued reference in the violins, *sempre pianissimo,* to the majestic opening bars of the first movement.

Symphony No. 4 in E Minor, OP. 98

Allegro non troppo
Andante moderato
Allegro giocoso
Allegro energico e passionato

For piccolo, flutes I-II, oboes I-II, clarinets I-II, bassoons I-II, contrabassoon; horns I-IV, trumpets I-II, trombones I-III; timpani, triangle; strings
Composed summers of 1884 and 1885 in Mürzzuschlag
First performed 25 October 1885 by the orchestra of the Meiningen Ducal Chapel, Brahms conducting
Published by N. Simrock (Berlin, 1886). *Inexpensive score:* Johannes Brahms: *Complete Symphonies in Full Orchestral Score* (New York: Dover, 1974).
Duration: about 45 minutes

The Fourth is a restless, pulsating work, less tragic than epic. (The uncharitable of Brahms's day found it long-winded.) Certainly it is more cerebral than the Second and Third; like the First it has some interesting formal turns and investigates the implications of a minor key.

The pensive falls and rises of the violin theme, as though floating on the billowy surface of something very dense below, introduce the most episodic of Brahms's orchestral sonata movements. Every melodic assertion is met by its upward reflection, and the way it all fits together seems conditioned by a strong sense of pianistic right- and left-handedness. A plethora of thematic material is literally squeezed onto the sonata scaffolding—with which, moreover, one has the sense that Brahms is becoming increasingly impatient. The woodwind fanfare with triplets, for example, is merely part of an extended transition to the second group, but is a vital participant in much that follows; the great soar of violins that introduces the true second theme sounds like a structural pillar, but has no real formal purpose. Note, too, how the development begins with what seems a false recapitulation, and in the imitative pursuit how profoundly you lose your sense of the beat. There's no relief from the tension, either: the movement simply plunges to its close without a hint of taming influence.

In the *Andante*, the horn, soon joined by the other winds, presents a discursive melody centered closely on its opening pitch and meant to sound modal and antique. A lyric phrase in the violins clarifies the E-major key area; a triplet figure, not so different from the wind fanfares in the first movement, serves to make the transition to second theme, here in the tenor range of the cello. It is this theme that returns at the moment of recapitulation; the remainder comes back more or less in reverse order, with the horn at the very end.

If what had come before the halfway point seems commanding of expanse, what comes afterward is positively majestic. The *Allegro giocoso* is in a way, I suppose, jocular and capricious as the title implies. But the overall atmosphere—march-like of meter and tempo, in a C major flavored with jubilant fanfares in E♭, and with good triangling—is one of triumph. Formally, a sonata-rondo procedure is at work, with a big central statement of the march.

Even this excitement is outdone by the stern beginning of the finale, where the trombones, so far unheard, unleash their eight-bar theme. From these measures Brahms constructs a passacaglia (see p. 35); the theme is based on the chaconne at the end of Bach's Cantata 150,

Nach dir, Herr, verlanget mich. The melody, if you wish to call it that, could not be simpler: a rise of the E minor scale to the dominant pitch B, octave fall, and cadence back on E, where the cycle recommences. It is the A-A♯-B of measures 4, 5, and 6 that give the passage its urgency of ascent. Brahms arranges his three dozen or so variations into a near-sonata. The second group is introduced by the flute and clarinet solo, leading to the noble statements of brass and woodwind choir at the center. The return of a statement quite similar to the first actually begins the development; the true recapitulation is louder still, with rolls of timpani and lots of triplet hammering. It can get no louder, so to conclude it gets faster and metrically dense. Here again there is no tendency to resolve stress: both the minor mode and the fury retain their grip to the last bar.

So conclusively do the four symphonies seem to frame his creative universe, that one has the feeling Brahms would have had difficulty sustaining the level of his symphonic achievement without fundamentally rethinking it. Indeed after the Fourth, in the belief that he had said his piece, he turned his attention to other things.

Concerto for Piano and Orchestra No. 2 in B♭ Major, OP. 83

Allegro non troppo
Allegro appassionato
Andante
Allegretto grazioso

For piano solo; piccolo, flutes I-II, oboes I-II, clarinets I-II, bassoons I-II; horns I-IV, trumpets I-II; timpani; strings

Composed in the summer of 1881 in Pressbaum near Vienna, completed on 11 July; dedicated to the composer's "dear friend and teacher, Eduard Marxsen"; drafted in 1879 after a trip to Italy, and finished after a second journey there

First performed 9 November 1881 in the Redoutensaal, Budapest, by the Budapest Philharmonic Society, Brahms, soloist, Alexander Erkel conducting; there had been a private reading with von Bülow and the Meiningen orchestra the previous October

Published by N. Simrock (Berlin, 1882). *Inexpensive score:* Johannes Brahms: *Complete Concerti in Full Score* (New York: Dover, 1981)

Duration: about 50 minutes

The Second Piano Concerto was written a year after the *Academic Festival Overture,* opus 80, and the *Tragic Overture,* opus 81 (both of summer 1880), and a full twenty-two years after the First Concerto. He had begun the work in 1878, but apparently the sketches were laid aside when he began to compose the Violin Concerto. Brahms's last three symphonic works were still to come: the Third and Fourth Symphonies and the Double Concerto.

The colossal size of the Second Concerto stems from the fact that what he had actually composed during his summer holiday was a pair of works for piano and orchestra: "a little concerto" and "a tiny wisp of a scherzo." In October he revised the scherzo and added it as a second movement to the little concerto, having feared the first movement too obvious and requiring something deeper before the equally simple Andante. But this solution, too, gave him some pause, and on at least one occasion he wondered if it would be better to leave the scherzo out, after all. Ultimately all four movements were retained— a workout for all concerned, yet an accomplishment of genuinely symphonic dimension. For the soloist it is among the most difficult pieces in the concerto literature.

The distant and rather lazy horn call at the beginning and the soloist's placid response are taken up for a moment by the woodwinds and then the strings, only to ebb away and be succeeded by the soloist's vehement entry. (The effortlessness of this incursion of solo material into what is traditionally the orchestra's turf owes much to precedent tactics of Beethoven, Mendelssohn, and Schumann. There is no formal cadenza.) The true orchestral exposition commences at the martial statement with brass and timpani. It goes on in a many-themed and harmonically extravagant structure—a sonata, in fact, but in Brahms's best rhapsodic mode and with the materials transforming themselves as they go. Note, for example, how the opening horn motto dominates the structural turning points, though never in its original simplicity.

The second movement is a scherzo that tosses and turns in a D minor of great metrical ambiguities. The wistful fade, just before the repeat and just after the Schumannesque turn in the solo part is an excellent example of the Romantic tendency to reminisce over things once sinister, now tamed. The second strain amounts to a development and climax of the given material. Suddenly the mode shifts to major, and the tempo relents slightly; this trio is in the manner of a bumptious, syncopated country dance. The scherzo returns, with a syncopated coda.

The theme of the third movement is closely related to the opening gestures of Brahms's song *Immer leiser wird mein Schlummer,* no. 2 of the Five Lieder, opus 105. The melody is presented in an eloquent setting for solo cello and strings, later joined by the solo oboe. The key is B♭ major. The piano waxes rhapsodic on the given material, with a violent, harmonically unstable eruption at one point that serves to underscore the passions pent up in the tender theme. At the center is a lovely Più Adagio for the two clarinets and piano. Now we have reached the remarkable key of F♯ major, and the ooze back to B♭ is a process of exceptional harmonic magic. The return once accomplished, there is a gentle improvisatory ending for the cello and piano soloists. It's a movement, in short, of matchless beauty, and well worth the wait.

The last movement is an airy rondo with strong hints, in the scoring for winds, of the Hungarian dance. Nor should you fail to note, knowing of the affinities that existed between Brahms and Dvořák, the strong allusions to the latter's Slavonic manner, particularly in the interludes with flute. The carefree spirit of the movement seems the perfect release from the various passions of the first three. And Brahms was right to have left the scherzo where it was, for what results seems to me a shrewd and abundantly satisfying progress.

Concerto for Violin, Cello, and Orchestra in A Minor, OP. 102

Allegro
Andante
Vivace non troppo

For violin and cello solo; flutes I-II, oboes I-II, clarinets I-II, bassoons I-II; horns I-IV, trumpets I-II; timpani; strings

Composed during the summer of 1887, to a commission from the cellist Robert Hausmann, in the lake town of Thun, Switzerland; dedicated to Joseph Joachim

First performed 23 September 1887 at a private concert in Baden-Baden; first offered to the public 18 October 1887, by the Gürzenich Orchestra of Cologne, Joachim and Robert Hausmann, soloists, Brahms conducting

Published by N. Simrock (Berlin, 1888). *Inexpensive score:*

Johannes Brahms: *Complete Concerti in Full Score* (New York: Dover, 1981)
Duration: about 35 minutes

Getting Brahms to write what became his last orchestral composition was engineered by the cellist of the Joachim Quartet, Robert Hausmann, in an attempt to reconcile the composer with his old friend Joachim. Their rupture had been occasioned by Joachim's divorce, during the course of which a letter by Brahms had been entered as evidence. The mission succeeded, and the Double Concerto was rehearsed and presented to friends under the watchful eye of Clara Schumann at her home in Baden-Baden.

Brahms professed to be uncomfortable with the idea of composing for the two solo stringed instruments, but you wouldn't know it from the result. He manages the two-in-one situation splendidly, with duos, solos, pursuits, extremes of high violin and low cello, and, more interestingly, intersections of the high range of the cello with the low of the violin. There's a particular color to the Brahms "Double," a certain play of light and shadow, resulting in part from the A-minor key but mostly from the unique choice of solo instruments. It profits, to, from a new concision he had carefully nourished since the Fourth Symphony.

The *Allegro* opens with a four-bar tutti. A recitative for the solo cello is extended by the winds into the entry of the solo violin, and together the soloists work through what is in fact the only serious cadenza in the concerto. The full orchestral exposition of the themes follows, commencing from the material with which the work opened and strong on triplet gestures. Once the soloists return they very much dominate the movement. Their first statement simply peters out; after an empty bar the secondary key is reached and the cello states the new theme, rich with peaks and musings. The violin turns this material to more conclusive purpose, and the exposition ends in great wedgings in and out of the soloists: first a strongly marked tumble with violin double-stops, then the two soloists alighting on the same pitch and stretching outward in long, smooth syncopation. Much is made of this figure, especially at the end of the development. The recapitulation slides into the major mode, and the coda thrusts it back into minor.

The D-major *Andante* opens with a horn call and its echo, mostly to establish the new key area. Throughout the long, continuously evolving theme the soloists double each other at the octave. The second section lifts in key and in register, and is primarily a passage for woodwinds ornamented by the soloists. A brief cadenza by the soloists leads to the restatements. The *Vivace* is a strong rondo with a range of sonorities that fluctuates from skeletal (at the beginning) to the familiar Brahmsian abundance (as in the glorious second theme, begun in the solo cello). After the first big section winds down chromatically, new material reminiscent of one of the *Academic Festival* melodies is heard from the soloists, with dotted rhythms and forward-thrusting parallel motion in a major key; this is succeeded by an episode for clarinets and bassoons in a long chain of syncopations. The way is thus cleared for the return of the opening material and a deliberate, twinkly reflection on things before the inevitable vigor of the closing bars.

Academic Festival Overture, OP. 80

For piccolo, flutes I-II, oboes I-II, clarinets I-II, bassoons I-II, contrabassoon; horns I-IV, trumpets I-III, trombones I-III, tuba; timpani, bass drum, cymbals, triangle; strings

Composed summer 1880 in Ischl

First performed 4 January 1881 by the Breslau Orchestral Society, Brahms conducting

Published by N. Simrock (Berlin, 1881). *Inexpensive score:* Johannes Brahms: *Three Orchestral Works in Full Score* (New York: Dover, 1984).

Duration: about 12 minutes

Most distinguished composers are sooner or later awarded the degree of doctor of music, *honoris causa,* for their work: Haydn had one from Oxford, Dvořák from Cambridge, and so on. Brahms was awarded his honorary degree by the University of Breslau (now Wrocław, in Poland) on 11 May 1879. At the ceremony, which he was unable to attend, he was praised as a prince of *"artis musicae severioris."* Two years later he offered his *Academic Festival Overture* for performance in Breslau as a mark of gratitude for the honor. The degree, the convocation, and the festive composition are all in the hallowed traditions of ancient and honorable academic institutions.

Just as ancient though perhaps not quite so honorable is carousing in the local Rathskeller, where students gather to dissipate the pressure of their academic pursuits. They hoist their steins and sing lustily of their aspirations, their loves, and their youth. Berlioz composed a fine scene for *La Damnation de Faust* (in Breslau, as a matter of fact) in which students and soldiers cross paths as they return home from their revels, the students singing their Latin drinking song. You know similar traditions from the Yale Whiffenpoofs and the West Point Glee Club. It was Brahms's very clever notion for his celebration of things academic to concoct a potpourri of German drinking songs.

The *Academic Festival Overture* thus has many themes that amble along in a rather loose sonata. Boisterousness is at the fore, but always in a context of that almost religious depth of conviction that characterizes the wee hours in a drinking parlor. Ominous driving eighth notes pave the way for several of the faster themes; a timpani roll introduces the stirring brass chorale, based on a traditional song about building stately mansions. This passage has effected transition to the noble key of C major, and now in $\frac{4}{4}$ we hear the Allegro proper as it consolidates the material from the long opening. The ringing transitional theme which follows is a hymn to the fatherland; the true second group, a fox song, commences with the animato in the two bassoons and continues with mock-fugal devices meant to suggest the archest form of learned display. After a brief development and straight recapitulation comes the great *Gaudeamus igitur*, through fountains of string passagework. "Let us live, then," students of the thirteenth century had written, "and be glad while youth is still before us."

Variations on a Theme of Joseph Haydn, OP. 56A

Theme: *Chorale St. Antoni (Andante)*—I. *Poco più animato*—II. *Più vivace*—III. *Con moto*—IV. *Andante con moto*—V. *Vivace*—VI. *Vivace*—VII. *Grazioso*—VIII. *Presto non troppo*—Finale: *Andante*
[No true pauses between variations.]

For piccolo, flutes I-II, oboes I-II, clarinets I-II, bassoons I-II, contrabassoon; horns I-IV, trumpets I-II; timpani, triangle; strings
Composed summer 1873 in Tutzing

First performed 2 November 1873 by the Vienna Philharmonic
Orchestra, Brahms conducting

Published by N. Simrock (Berlin, 1874). *Inexpensive scores:*
Johannes Brahms: *Three Orchestral Works in Full Score* (New
York: Dover, 1984); Brahms: *Variations on a Theme of Haydn,*
ed. Donald M. McCorkle, A Norton Critical Score (New York:
Norton, 1976)

Duration: about 20 minutes

Brahms found the "St. Anthony Chorale" in a pleasant eighteenth-
century divertimento for winds, though the attribution to Haydn is
altogether dubious. Forget about this dead issue, paying attention
rather to the characteristics of the theme that govern what follows:
the unusual five-bar phrase lengths in the first of the two phrases, the
departure and return in the second phrase, and the reiterated bell
tones at the end.

Eight variations and a finale then take their course, most of them
following the repeat scheme of the theme. The first three variations
are all rapid, presenting the material according to various relatively
conventional schemes: the second variation, for example, is in the
minor key. Beginning with the fourth variation, like a slow movement, the relationship to the original is less easy to track, and probably not worth the effort. Variation V is a scherzo, with all sorts of
syncopations and false recapitulations; variation VI is a *galop* featuring
the winds and brass; variation VII, a *siciliana,* marked *grazioso,* with
flute solo; variation VIII, a *tour de force* of learned contrapuntal device.

The finale is built over a five-bar passacaglia bass drawn from the
bass line of the chorale. Seventeen variations follow, some contrapuntal with diminution and inversion, some homophonic, like the chorale. The turn to the minor mode foreshadows conclusion, and the
broad coda features the bell peals of the beginning.

This is one of several works that served Brahms as a testing ground
for his First Symphony, which was at length completed in 1876. The
variation form essayed so well here has a number of notable successors,
notably in the Serenades, and in the fourth movement of the Fourth
Symphony Brahms returns, masterfully, to the passacaglia form. The
two-piano version of the Haydn Variations is also worth hearing.

A German Requiem, OP. 45

> *Selig sind, die da Leid tragen* (Blessed are they that mourn)
> *Denn alles Fleisch, es ist wie Gras* (For all flesh is like grass)
> *Herr, lehre doch mich* (Lord, make me to know mine end)
> *Wie lieblich sind deine Wohnungen, Herr Zebaoth!* (How lovely
>   is Thy dwelling-place, O Lord of Hosts)
> *Ihr habt nun Traurigkeit* (And ye now, therefore, have sorrow)
> *Denn wir haben hie keine bleibende Statt* (For here have we no
>   continuing city)
> *Selig sind die Toten* (Blessed are the dead)

For soloists (S., Bar.), chorus; piccolo, flutes I-II, oboes I-II, clarinets I-II, bassoons I-II; horns I-IV, trumpets I-II, trombones I-
   III, tuba; timpani; harps I II; organ and contrabassoon *ad libitum;* strings

Text (in German) from the Lutheran Bible

Composed January 1865–summer 1866 in Vienna, Zurich, and
   Baden-Baden, using material that dates back to 1857; revised
   1868 by the addition of movement V

First performed 18 February 1869 by the Leipzig Gewandhaus
   orchestra, Carl Reinecke conducting. The first three movements
   had been given 1 December 1867 by the Vienna Gesellschaft
   der Musikfreunde in the great Redoutensaal, Johann Herbeck
   conducting; a version of the work lacking movement V had
   been given on Good Friday, 10 April 1868, at the Bremen
   Cathedral, Brahms conducting.

Published by J. Rieter-Biedermann (Leipzig, 1868). *Inexpensive
   score:* Johannes Brahms: *German Requiem in Full Score* (New York:
   Dover, 1987)

Duration: about 1 hour and 15 minutes

Brahms's notion of death is in the Protestant Christian mold: an occasion for comfort to the bereaved and for rejoicing in the certainty of
Paradise. There is no place for a Catholic *Dies irae:* rather the texts
come from the Lutheran Bible, both Old and New Testaments (Psalms,
Isaiah; Matthew, John, James, 1 Peter) and Apocrypha (Wisdom of
Solomon). *A German Requiem,* which he composed and revised over a
five-year period, may be a tribute to his beloved mentor Schumann.
Certainly it is meant as a bow to his German heritage, so rich is it in
severe fugal device and hints of continuo practice. Equally certain
from the evidence of the title and text is Brahms's consciousness of

the *Musikalische Exequien* by the great mid-Baroque composer Heinrich Schütz.

In its mastery of instrumental and choral textures, clarity of declamation, pacing, and dense harmonic language, the *German Requiem* achieves a richness of sound and a tautness of organization without parallel in the literature for chorus and orchestra. It is nevertheless a work of bold contrasts, prone to emerge from its generally assuring tranquility with solemn pronouncements. You are comforted in the harmonic language and splendid orchestration of late century, but the bitter truths of the human experience are established too, and with almost Gothic severity.

The matchless opening, with violas and cellos divided into four parts over throbbing Fs in bass and French horns, introduces one of the Beatitudes of Christ ("Blessed are they that mourn, for they shall be comforted") sung at first by unaccompanied chorus. The harps enter just before the end, and note well the very last words, *getröstet werden,* reiterated *pianissimo* by the chorus, as though nodding an affirmation of universal truth. This is a strategy Brahms will use several more times during the *German Requiem.* The dead march which follows ranks with his most outstanding accomplishments: haunting of key, with violins and violas subdivided into three parts each, and over a relentless distant tattoo in the timpani. The chorus has the theme in unison, "Behold all flesh is as the grass": softly the first two times, the third as the culmination of a magnificent, thunderous crescendo. The terror of the funeral march is offset at the center in major mode; then it recapitulates before Brahms turns to a stentorian reminder that the Lord's voice endures forever and an affirmative concluding fugue.

The baritone solo, too, is taken with the brevity of our time on earth and is also a march in the minor key, this time in duple meter. All is vanity; one's hope is in the Lord, and, the great choral fugue at the end proclaims, the souls of the righteous are in the hand of the Lord. Eighteen pages, at the end, are played over the single pitch D in the bass instruments, a musical symbol of steadfastness in the protection of God.

For most music lovers the fourth movement, "How Lovely is Thy Dwelling Place," is among the most perfect (and most familiar) miniatures in the repertoire. Despite the harp-like figurations, the harps remain silent; indeed Brahms seems to go out of his way to assure us that his evocation of the heavenly apartments is innocent, joyous, and above all dignified. He is said to have composed the fifth movement on the occasion of the death of his mother in 1865, and this was added to the work between the Bremen performance of 1867 and the definitive first performance in Leipzig the following year.

The huge movement that follows almost outweighs the second movement, with which it is paired in the overall structure. It is yet another cortege of minor key. Here the baritone soloist recalls the mystery of resurrection ("all changed in a moment, in the twinkling of an eye") and the trumpet of judgment, and a diabolical dance ensues. The concluding fugue is in slow note values, reminiscent of the white-note fugues of Bach and Handel.

By now you should be aware of the careful balance and symmetry the composer has given his work. The added soprano aria balances the first baritone solo and puts "How Lovely is Thy Dwelling Place" at the center of a structural arch; the two biggest movements come just after the first and just before the last. Now, to balance the first movement, Brahms leaves another beatitude: "Blessed are the dead: they rest from their labors, and their work follows after them." It brings the Requiem to close in F major, where more than an hour before it had begun.

A good performance of the Brahms Requiem uses two harps, following the composer's indication for doubling, as well as organ and contrabassoon to reinforce the bass line.

Benjamin Britten

Born *22 November 1913* *in Lowestoft*
Died *4 December 1976* *in Aldeburgh*

Not since Purcell's *Dido and Aeneas* of 1689 had there been much by way of English opera until Benjamin Britten leapt onstage. A dozen operas later, he could rightly be said to have established the national repertoire.

He composed spontaneously from early childhood, then from age thirteen studied with the eminent composer Frank Bridge, and at seventeen matriculated at the Royal College of Music. Abandoning the notion of going to Vienna to study with Alban Berg, he took work as a composer of film music for documentaries produced by the British Post Office. One of his co-workers there was W. H. Auden, soon a mentor and close friend (and, latterly, librettist for both Stravinsky and Hans Werner Henze). Citing his distaste for the prevailing cultural milieu, Britten emigrated in 1939 to the United States, accompanied by his lifelong companion, the tenor Peter Pears. In New York they were welcomed into the circle of Auden and Christopher Isherwood, who had elected to settle in New York some months previous. But what Britten discovered in America, once the novelty had worn off, was his fundamental attachment to home—above all to the Suffolk coast of his ancestry. In 1942 he sailed home to an England at war, established his status as a conscientious objector, and soon made a home in the seaside village of Aldeburgh. By the end of the war he was completing his tragic opera on the sea and the people whose lives are controlled by the sea.

This was *Peter Grimes* (1944–45), Britten's first stage triumph. There followed many more, and we understand all the rest of his work in terms of that progress: *Billy Budd,* after Melville (1951); *The Turn of the Screw,* after Henry James (1954); *A Midsummer Night's Dream,* after Shakespeare (1960); and *Death in Venice,* after Thomas Mann (1973). His investigations of venue and ritual in the 1960s led him to compose *Curlew River* (1964), after *Samutzen,* a Japanese *Nō* drama; and two other "church parables," *The Burning Fiery Furnace* (1966) and *The Prodigal Son* (1968).

Another masterpiece is the *War Requiem,* composed for the consecration of the rebuilt Coventry Cathedral in 1962. The text is fashioned by joining to the traditional Requiem text nine poems of Wilfrid Owen, the soldier-poet killed in action a week before the Armistice of 1918. "[My] subject is war and the pity of war," he wrote: "All a poet can do is warn." This shattering Requiem is Britten's ultimate statement of conscientious objection.

Britten was an active proponent of all sorts of good causes in English musical life, beginning with the film documentaries and continuing through his particular interest in works accessible to children and amateurs. One of his major legacies was the establishment in 1948 of the Aldeburgh Festival; in the mid-1960s he oversaw the construction of an excellent concert hall for the festival. This has the enchanting name The Maltings at Snape.

Among his works often heard in the concert hall are the two described below; the *Simple Symphony* for string orchestra, drawn in part from compositions of his twelfth year (1933–34); *Variations on a Theme by Frank Bridge,* also for strings (1937); the Serenade for Tenor, Horn, and Strings (1943), and the *Cello Symphony* for Rostropovich (1964). The *Ceremony of Carols* (1942) for boy soprano, chorus, and harp, has become a Christmas tradition in England and the United States alike.

Britten died, too young, six months after Queen Elizabeth granted him a life peerage. He was the first English composer to become a lord.

Four Sea Interludes from *Peter Grimes*, OP. 33A

Dawn
Sunday Morning
Moonlight
Storm

For piccolo, flutes I-II, oboes I-II, English horn, E♭ clarinet, clarinets I-II, bass clarinet, bassoons I-II, contrabassoon; horns I-IV, trumpets I-III, trombones I-III, tuba; timpani, snare drum, bass drum, cymbals, tambourine, tam-tam, church bells, glockenspiel, xylophone; harp, organ; strings

The opera composed January 1944–February 1945 to a commission from the Koussevitzky Memorial Foundation, dedicated to Natalie Koussevitzky; libretto by Montagu Slater, after a poem by George Crabbe, *The Borough* (1810)

First performed in the opera, Sadler's Wells, London, on 7 June 1945, Reginald Goodall conducting; the interludes first performed in concert 13 June 1945 by the London Philharmonic Orchestra at the Cheltenham Festival, Britten conducting

Published by Boosey and Hawkes (London, 1945)

Duration: about 15 minutes

Peter Grimes takes place in about 1830 in The Borough, a fishing village on the East Anglian coast pretty obviously equivalent to Aldeburgh. It is a bleak tale of intolerance, gossip mongering, and community hysteria, summarizing what Britten calls "the perpetual struggle of men and women whose livelihood depends upon the sea." Grimes is a solitary fisherman, half-crazed with violent urges, thus a misfit and outcast. An inquest on the death at sea of Grimes's young apprentice yields a verdict of accidental death, but the villagers clearly believe otherwise. As the opera progresses a new boy is found for Grimes; after the boy has been seen in town with torn clothes and bruises, the men set angrily out to confront Grimes at his hut. In Grimes's scramble to get the boy and his tackle out the cliff door before the men come in the front, the boy loses his footing and plunges to his death.

Later his sweater washes up, a manhunt is organized, and Grimes is found wandering in the fog, now quite mad. One of the men tells him to take his boat beyond the horizon and scuttle it. Dawn comes up, the village returns to work; the Coast Guard observes an accident at sea, too far out to warrant response. No one seems to care.

Six orchestral interludes connect the acts and scenes of *Peter Grimes,* four of which the composer published as the *Sea Interludes,* op. 33a. (A fifth is published as the *Passacaglia,* op. 33b; this is the theme and variations that connects the two scenes of act II). The sea is, of course, the overriding presence in *Peter Grimes*—always there, often of great beauty, yet capable of far greater havoc than Grimes could ever wreak. The interludes are atmosphere and texture pieces, minimal of structure in some respects but thoroughly imaginative in their treatment of color and light.

Dawn connects the prologue and the first act. The figure in high strings and flute is joined by middle register arpeggios, the glint of sunlight on water. Slow-moving chords in the brass, soft but commanding, have to do with the mystic dominion of the sea. The form is simple: alternating statements of the two ideas, with the last of the brass motives reaching a *fortissimo* climax. *Sunday Morning* precedes act II. The French horn ostinato and syncopated merriment in the high winds (demanding, later on, some excellent trumpet playing) evoke the church bells, and eventually real bells begin to peal. The contrastive Mahlerian lyric in violas and cellos is that of the arioso that opens the act, "Glitter of waves and glitter of sunlight," sung by Ellen Orford, the local school teacher and Grimes's one friend.

Moonlight, the prelude to act III, describes the nocturnal equivalent of the glitter of waves and sunlight. It's an exercise in stasis: the sea merely pulsates in gentle orchestral homophony, punctuated by twinkles of flute, harp, and xylophone. *The Storm* may sound to you, with its jazzy ritornello and metric character, more like a rumble in the Bronx. The refrain begins as a fugue, though this loses its identity as the frenzy builds; in the brass episode, Britten cites the brass melody from the first interlude, *Dawn.* For a moment we are in the eye of the tempest, but then the backside of the storm swirls in. The movement ends in a chromatic tumble at maximum volume.

The Young Person's Guide to the Orchestra, OP. 34,
Variations and Fugue on a Theme of Purcell

> *Themes A-F (Tutti; Woodwinds; Brasses; Strings; Percussion;*
> *Tutti)—Variation A (Flutes, Piccolo)—Variation B*
> *(Oboes)—Variation C (Clarinets)—Variation D (Bassoons)—*
> *Variation E (Violins I-II)—Variation F (Violas)—Variation G*
> *(Cellos)—Variation H (Double basses)—Variation I (Harp)—*
> *Variation J (Horns)—Variation K (Trumpets)—Variation L*
> *(Trombones, Tuba)—Variation M (Percussion)—Fugue*

For speaker *ad libitum;* piccolo, flutes I-II, oboes I-II, clarinets I-II, bassoons I-II; horns I-IV, trumpets I-II, trombones I-III, tuba; timpani, snare drum, bass drum, cymbals, triangle, tambourine, castanets, tam-tam, wood block, whip, xylophone; harp; strings

Composed late 1945–early 1946 for a film, *The Instruments of the Orchestra,* produced by the British Ministry of Education; dedicated to "the children of John and Jean Maud: Humphrey, Pamela, Caroline, and Virginia, for their edification and entertainment"

First performed 15 October 1946 by the Liverpool Philharmonic Orchestra, Malcolm Sargent conducting; the film premiere was in London on 29 November 1946; the orchestra in the film is the London Symphony Orchestra, Sargent conducting

Published by Boosey and Hawkes (London, 1947); there is an excellent performance available on video cassette from Phoenix / BFA Films, New York

Duration: about 20 minutes

Britten's invitation to write music for a film on the orchestral instruments coincided with his interest in commemorating in various fashions the 250th anniversary of Purcell's death. Thus he chose to build his film score around a dance found in Purcell's incidental music for a play called *Abdelazar, or The Moor's Revenge.*

The plan is simple enough: a setting of Purcell's theme for full orchestra is followed by strophes for each of the constituent ensembles: woodwinds, brass, strings, percussion. Thirteen variations follow, one for each of the orchestral sections. Britten makes allowances in the score for the conductor to turn around and deliver the narration; the orchestra goes along on its own, with pauses and *ad libitum* repeats to make the seams work out. The text—"The WOODWIND

are superior varieties of the penny-whistle; they are made of wood.
. . . I suspect you all know the sound of the TRUMPETS"—is too
much to bear. (This is by Eric Crozier; it replaces the film narration,
which was by Montagu Sláter, librettist of *Peter Grimes*.)

But, like *Peter and the Wolf*, with which it is often paired on recordings, *The Young Person's Guide* has a beguiling effect on listeners of all
ages. Britten's skill at variation procedures is substantial (there was
good precedent in Elgar), and his flair for clever orchestral effects—
from the arabesques of the clarinet variation to the imaginative percussion writing—is engaging from start to finish. The particular sublimity is the splendid fugue at the end, during which the subjects
and answers are presented by each section in the order of the variations. At the end, Purcell's theme, stated grandly by the brass choir
in long note values and a contrasting meter, settles over everything
else.

Anton Bruckner

Born *4 September 1824 in*
Ansfelden, near Linz, Austria
Died *11 October 1896 in Vienna*

At the age of thirteen, on the death of his father, Bruckner became a choirboy at the monastery of St. Florian, near Linz. There, intent on a career as a schoolmaster, he continued as a teaching assistant, and it was during this period that his powers as a virtuoso organist emerged. In 1851 he was named head organist at St. Florian; in 1855, organist of Linz cathedral. Anxious to compose seriously but well aware of the limitations of his training, he undertook in 1855 a long course of study in harmony and counterpoint with Simon Sechter in Vienna and thereafter had some lessons in orchestration.

It was at this juncture, as he neared his fortieth birthday, that he began to compose his symphonies and masses: three of each in the years from 1863 to 1869. Intellectually and artistically he was ready for a thunderstroke, and that happened when he heard the first performance of *Tristan und Isolde* and met Wagner in Munich in 1865. Bruckner was there, along with a good cross section of the European musical aristocracy, for the first performances of the *Ring* in 1876 and *Parsifal* in 1882; but even among the most idolatrous Wagnerites, Bruckner's veneration of Wagner was out of the ordinary. It is not that he imitated the specifics of Wagnerian technique, for the genres in which they worked were contrary and the particulars of Wagnerian harmony inappropriate to Bruckner's purpose. Where they are similar is in their attitude toward the passage of time, their ability to colossalize. In all other respects, the better pairing is with Mahler, whose symphonies were beginning to appear at about the same time as Bruckner's.

In 1868 he began teaching at the Vienna Conservatory. Performances of his Seventh Symphony, by Nikisch in 1884 and Levi in 1885, launched his international celebrity, and the Te Deum became greatly popular. Financial security and his fair share of honorific recognitions came Bruckner's way. Nothing can diminish the splendor of his symphonic achievement, the polyphonic expertise, the control of leisurely, even sprawling forms that Schubert had begun to experiment with in the Ninth. For all that Bruckner remained a peasant, a social boor, and now and again an intellectual simpleton. He was particularly low on self-esteem. This led him to accept the advice of well-meaning but uncomprehending associates to rewrite his works, often by senseless deletion—advice he might better have ignored.

The result was that at his death his creative enterprise was left in a state of chaos. Piecing it back together again, with the goal of establishing Bruckner's original intent, has been the work of the International Bruckner Society, led first by Robert Haas and later by Leopold Nowak. Nowak's versions of Bruckner's works are the ones most commonly performed today.

In all, Bruckner composed nine numbered symphonies (1866–96, the last unfinished) and early symphonies in F and D minor (1863–64); the second of these Bruckner called his Symphony No. 0. Additionally there are the three masses (No. 2, in E minor, with band) and the Te Deum for chorus and orchestra (1884). The Te Deum and last three symphonies represent the summit of his achievement.

Symphony No. 7 in E Major

Allegro moderato
Adagio: Sehr feierlich und langsam
Scherzo: Sehr schnell
Finale: Bewegt, doch nicht zu schnell

For flutes I-II, oboes I-II, clarinets I-II, bassoons I-II; horns I-IV,
trumpets I-III, trombones I-III, tenor tubas I-II, bass tubas I-II,
contrabass tuba; timpani, cymbals, triangle; strings
Composed: 23 September 1881–5 September 1883 in Vienna and
at St. Florian; dedicated to Ludwig II, king of Bavaria and
Wagner's patron
First performed 30 December 1884, by the Leipzig Opera
Orchestra at the Municipal Theater, Artur Nikisch conducting
Published by Albert J. Gutmann (Vienna, 1885). *Inexpensive score:*
Anton Bruckner: *Symphonies Nos. 4 and 7 in Full Score* [the Hass
edns.] (New York: Dover, 1989)
Duration: about 1 hour

Bruckner's most famous works are his Seventh Symphony and Te Deum,
of simultaneous genesis—one theme, in fact, appears in both compositions—and equivalent popularity. The Seventh is Bruckner's personal memorial to Wagner, composed in the aftermath and aura of
Parsifal and finished in the months following Wagner's death in February 1883. Bruckner always called the coda to the *Adagio* his "funeral
music for the Master." The sonority of the quintet of tubas has, for
everybody, strong Wagnerian associations.

The *Allegro* is a sonata movement quite dominated by the long,
wide-intervalled cello theme at the beginning. The second subject,
for woodwind choir with a prominent Wagner ornamental turn, occurs
where the tempo relents, and there's a faster, dance-like closing theme
a few minutes later. The overall progress is toward the vast crescendo
and accelerando of the closing pages, all played over a static tonic
chord in low strings, timpani, and low brass. It's a huge and on the
whole bright movement, a good place to contemplate the character
and thick brushstroke of Bruckner's orchestral practice.

He told his friends that the theme of the great *Adagio* represented
his reflection of the certainty of Wagner's death. The two thematic
ideas are the lament first stated by the lugubrious instruments and
the more lilting and Viennese material at the shift from slow duple

to a faster triple meter. The ensuing double-variation procedure is similar to that of the slow movement of Beethoven's Ninth. At the big C-major climax near the end, you will probably hear a pair of cymbal crashes and the roll of triangle. Now you are in a musicological minefield: it was Bruckner's conductor and publisher who convinced him to go with the extra percussion, of that we are certain. The remaining evidence, including the word "invalid" in the autograph score but in somebody else's handwriting, can be argued either way. I would probably leave them in. (The Seventh is, incidentally, the *only* symphony of Bruckner published from his own manuscript score.)

In the *Scherzo,* a rapid ostinato figure supports the trumpet call and its rebounding response, at first in the clarinet. Not until a full A-B-A structure has played out over the ongoing ostinato is there a trio. This is quieter, slower, and smoother. You may spot, however, that one of the motives is essentially an inversion of the trumpet theme from the scherzo proper. At the end of the trio, after the last empty bars, comes the old-fashioned sort of *da capo:* the musicians just go back to the top and play the scherzo again. The last movement is a kind of rondo, held together by the dotted figure first stated by the violins, where each stanza reaches a sort of apocalypse for the full orchestra. The conclusion, a crescendo with fanfares over static tonic harmony, is quite similar to that of the first movement, and indeed focuses squarely on their strong thematic similarities.

Bruckner is not for everybody. His style is undeniably longwinded, and if concision is your pleasure, Bruckner will not be. But it's hard not to be thrilled when he really gets going, and the cumulative effect of all that brass is seldom equalled in the concert hall, even by Mahler.

Symphony No. 9 in D Minor (unfinished)

Feierlich, Misterioso
Scherzo: Bewegt, lebhaft
Adagio: Langsam, feierlich

For flutes I-III, oboes I-III, clarinets I-III, bassoons I-III; horns I-VIII, trumpets I-III, trombones I-III, tenor tubas I-II, bass tubas I-II, contrabass tuba; timpani; strings
Composed February 1891–30 November 1894 in Vienna

(movements I-III), with sketches going back to the summer of
1887; movement IV in sketch only at Bruckner's death
First performed 11 February 1903 by the Vienna Philharmonic,
Ferdinand Löwe conducting, performing his own completion
and Bruckner's Te Deum for a finale; first performed in the
Bruckner's original version 2 April 1932 by the Munich
Philharmonic Orchestra, Siegmund von Hausseger conducting.
Hausseger presented both versions of the work, Löwe's widely
accepted edition and Bruckner's original, at the concert.
Published by Universal Edition (Vienna, 1903) in Löwe's edition
Duration: about 1 hour

We can assume that Ferdinand Löwe's motives were good. He was
Bruckner's pupil and most trusted disciple and, I'm sorry to say, one
of the advisors who kept him rewriting old pieces when he could have
been finishing the Ninth. Löwe deserves the bad press he gets for
having cut and redone the unfinished Ninth and for having published
it in that fashion. But he did, after all, see to the performance of the
Ninth and get some version of a score published. The important thing
was to have it circulated; afterward the processes of scholarship and
editorial ethic could, and did, enter into play.

All three movements are profound, despairing in thematic and harmonic character, and epic in scope. Three highly contrastive thematic
elements can be identified early in the first movement: the growling
brass at the beginning, over nearly two dozen bars of unchanging
tonic harmony in the strings; the violent unison explosion and collapse; and finally a true lyric melody in the strings, where the tempo
slows. From these is developed a repertoire of motives whose conflict
and eventual reassimilation into a closing D minor of cosmic expanse
is more important than sonata form. The *Scherzo* is of industrial clatter
in its emphasis of the hammering unisons (and watch for the visual
delight of the sea of repeated downbows); like the scherzo of the Seventh there is a full A-B-A before the trio—in this case a fast, eerie $\frac{3}{8}$
—and a traditional *da capo* afterward.

The *Adagio* favors disjunct thematic structures (as is abundantly
clear from the first two bars, a dramatic case of tonal nondirection)
and a daring harmonic fabric. It is, moreover, peppered with citations
from Bruckner's masses and previous symphonies: the second theme,
for the quartet of Wagner tubas, is drawn, for example, from a motive

in the Mass in D Minor by inverting it. An inexorable crescendo and dissonant climax sink away into a nocturnal E-major close.

You must, through all of this, pay particular attention to the brass work, which is of an expanse you will find nowhere else. But then again, I suppose you don't have any choice: you'll be paying attention to the brass whether you like it or not.

Te Deum

Te Deum —Te ergo—Aeterna fac—Salvum fac—In te Domine speravi
[No pause between submovements]

For soloists (SATB), chorus; flutes I-II, oboes I-II, clarinets I-II, bassoons I-II; horns I-IV, trumpets I-III, trombones I-III, tuba; timpani; organ; strings
Composed 1881–84 in Vienna
First performed 10 January 1886 by the Vienna Gesellschaft der Musikfreunde, Hans Richter conducting. A performance with piano had been given in the Musikvereinsaal on 2 May 1885, Bruckner conducting.
Published by Theodor Rättig (Vienna, 1885)
Duration: about 25 minutes

A *Te Deum* is a hymn of praise to God, to be sung at the dedication of a church, after a great military victory, for the coronation of monarchs, and at similar festivities. The text originated in the fifth century and is traditionally attributed to St. Ambrose. Since they are often wedged into windy affairs of state, Te Deums are usually brief, and Bruckner's is, by Brucknerian standards, positively compact. Nevertheless it was summarily dismissed by the stodgy court conductor Joseph Hellmesberger, who had suggested the idea to begin with, as too long for the use of the Imperial Chapel.

Bruckner's Te Deum is in the regal key of C major and consists of five short movements played without pause. Much of the chorus material is in unison or counterpoint of childlike simplicity. There is a good deal of cross-referencing, especially in the many bright arpeggios and great tonic pedal points; moreover the *Te ergo* and *Salvum fac* are, but for the text and distribution among the soloists, exactly the same. With that, indeed, the organization of this quite minimal work is summarized: huge Gothic washes of chorus, brass, organ, and pealing eighth notes merely alternate with the gentler *Te ergo* and its mirror.

Only in the last movement is there serious polyphony, and then it happens in a big way. In the simple introduction the text is declaimed for all to understand: "In Thee, O Lord, have I trusted that I shall not forever be confounded." Afterward a big double fugue breaks forth —two subjects at once, that is; here things are a little more complicated, but the point is that pairs of voices are answered by other pairs of voices. Church organists of the time were supposed to be able to write such things on demand, but Bruckner's is an especially learned display. Everything seems to move at once, all the time. After the fugue dissipates, a homophonic version of the material prepares the way for return of the tremendous C-major effects from the very beginning.

The Te Deum is a work of Bruckner's steadfast faith, carrying his typical dedication "to the dear Lord." Mahler scribbled in his own score his assessment of the performing force: "angelic tongues, God-seekers, tormented hearts and souls purified by flame." Bruckner was more sanguine, suggesting that on the day he was to meet his maker, "I will show him the score of my Te Deum, and he may judge me accordingly."

Elliot Carter

Born 11 December 1908 in New York City

Carter took degrees at Harvard in order, he said, to be around the Boston Symphony of the Koussevitzky years—and that was surely where to be if you wanted to know what was happening in the orchestral world. His primary teacher was Walter Piston; another was Gustav Holst, who visited Harvard at the time. And he took full advantage of Harvard's offerings and his own innate brilliance, becoming over the years well versed in literature, modern languages, mathematics, Latin, and Greek. From Boston he went to France to study with Nadia Boulanger, 1932–35. On his return to the United States, he was fortunate to find a string of interesting appointments: as music director of Ballet Caravan, the company that produced Copland's *Billy the Kid;* instructor at St. John's College in Annapolis—the "Great Books" college, for whose faculty Carter was by accomplishment and intellectual leaning perfectly qualified; then at the Peabody Conservatory, Columbia, and Yale, among others. He has been elected to all the major academies and granted a host of honorary doctoral degrees. Most of all, he has sought solitude, for that is the composer's truest glory.

Carter's early works are relatively conventional of design and tonally oriented, often on American texts or subject matter (as in the *Pocahontas* Suite, 1938–39). With the Piano Sonata of 1946 and most especially the Sonata for Cello and Piano of 1948, he began to create work in a much more individual, uncompromising rhetoric, where different musical entities move independently of each other even as they coexist in the same movement: one melodic cell growing slower over the long haul, for example, while another grows faster. (Here the debt is to Charles Ives, who had given Carter some early encouragement.) One outgrowth of such an orientation is the technique of *metric modulation,* whereby an overall tempo change is established by allowing the pulse of an internal voice to come to prominence and take control as a leading voice retreats. Another technique identifies an interval or array of pitches with a particular instrument, register, and rhythm and then subjects the resulting cell to its own scheme of variation and development. These kinds of procedures result in music of ceaseless motion and great textural intricacy—and, given the lack of unifying downbeats, immense difficulty. The accomplishment is unquestionably dazzling.

Both the Second and Third String Quartets (1959, 1971) won the Pulitzer Prize. With the Variations for Orchestra, 1954–55, Carter returned to larger ensembles; the concerto, in particular, what with its innate duality of roles, was an ideal forum for his ideas. The Double Concerto for harpsichord, piano, and two chamber-sized orchestras was composed for performance in September 1961 during a congress of the International Musicological Society, meeting for the first time in New York; Stravinsky put this work at the forefront of the American repertoire. There followed a Piano Concerto (1964–65), a Concerto for Orchestra (1969) composed for the 125th anniversary season of the New York Philharmonic, and a Symphony of Three Orchestras (1976–77). In 1987, Carter completed an oboe concerto for Heinz Holliger to a commission from the Sacher Foundation; it was given its premiere in 1988 in conjunction with celebrations of the composer's eightieth birthday. This body of work is about as influential as repertoires come; nearly every serious composer today uses principles Carter first demonstrated.

Variations for Orchestra

Introduction: Allegro—Theme: Andante—I. Vivace leggero—II. Pesante—III. Moderato—IV. Ritardando molto—V. Allegro misterioso—VI. Accelerando molto—VII. Andante—VIII. Allegro giocoso—IX. Andante—Finale: Allegro molto

For piccolo, flutes I-II, oboes I-II, clarinets I-II, bassoons I-II; horns I-IV, trumpets I-II, trombones I-III, tuba; timpani, snare drum without snares, snare drum, bass drum, cymbals, suspended cymbal, triangle, tambourine, wood block, whip, claves or castanets, tam-tam; harp; strings

Composed 1954–55, largely in Rome, to a commission for the Louisville Philharmonic Society; sketches from 1953; dedicated to the Louisville Orchestra and its conductor, Robert Whitney

First performed 21 April 1956, by the Louisville Orchestra, Robert Whitney conducting

Published by Associated Music Publishers, Inc. (New York, 1957; rev. and corrected, 1966)

Duration: about 25 minutes

The Louisville Orchestra (see p. 658) commissioned this work as part of the Louisville Orchestra Commissioning Project in the 1950s. "I was eager," writes Carter, "to put into concrete musical terms a number of ideas I had had about the old form of the variation, . . . [a procedure which] gives expression to the classical attitude toward the problem of 'unity in diversity.'"

To follow the process (or even to begin to follow it) you need to identify the three building blocks: two ritornellos and the main theme. The first ritornello is the orchestral scamper in the introduction, its wide individual intervals defining an overall rapid ascent. This you will hear again in variations I, III, VIII, and the finale, becoming progressively *slower* with each statement. The second ritornello is that of the two solo violins, very high and in slow chromatic descent. It comes back in variations II, VII, and the finale, growing *faster* as it goes.

Beneath the second ritornello occurs the first statement of the theme, beginning in the violins, a slow and expressive rise of quarter notes, passed from choir to choir. It's an easy shape to recognize in the variations to follow. From here you must remember the pluralisms involved. Generally speaking the materials are given in their most diverse states in the first variation and progress toward the equivalencies of the fifth, a process the composer calls "neutralizing" the contrasts of character. From the sixth variation, a fugal treatment of the quarter-note clarinet figure, the process reverses, now investigating the conflicting attributes of the materials. Thus the finale, with many different structures moving in many different fashions all at once, is indeed something of post-Ivesian orgy. The bravura timpani work announces the last climax and fade.

This will probably be a difficult listen the first times around, but you should be able to distinguish the variations without too much difficulty and probably will be aware of some of the intricacies of temporal flow. And the taxonomy is much easier to follow in live performance than on a record.

Emmanuel Chabrier

Born 18 January 1841 in Ambert,
Puy-de-Dôme
Died 13 September 1894 in Paris

Chabrier took his degree in law and entered the civil service to please his father. In the provinces he had been thought a musical prodigy and had thus never lacked for serious, if somewhat disorganized, instruction in violin, piano, and composition. He published his first work, a polka-mazurka for piano, at the age of fourteen.

For the two decades from 1861 his musical passions were nourished after business hours as a member of formal and informal affinity groups of the sort the French of those days were so fond, where he kept company with Vincent d'Indy, Henri Duparc, Ernest Chausson, Gabriel Fauré, and others. Duparc was of messianic zeal in his championing of Wagner, and in March 1880, just after Chabrier had himself begun seriously to compose for the stage, they went off together to hear *Tristan* in Munich. This was a pivotal experience in Chabrier's life: a few months later he tendered his resignation to the Ministry of the Interior and the following year, 1881, was appointed assistant conductor of a new concert-giving society by Charles Lamoureux. He could no longer be considered an amateur.

Chabrier's holiday in Spain in the later half of 1882 inspired the *España* Rhapsody, his one work to remain in the repertoire. Now he was moving in the most glamorous of circles, numbering among his friends and admirers Camille Saint-Saëns, Catulle Mendès (his principal librettist), Villiers de L'Isle-Adam, Paul Verlaine (with whom he had begun to compose two operettas), and Édouard Manet, who twice painted his portrait and of whose work Chabrier was a noted collector. (The famous painting *Bar aux Folies-Bergère* hung over his piano.) His two mature operas, *Gwendoline* (1886) and *Le Roi malgré lui* (1887), enjoyed a certain degree of success. But Chabrier's most influential compositions were works for piano, which Ravel at one point declared to be his primary formative guide. Chabrier is also the perpetrator of *Souvenirs de Munich,* a quadrille for piano four-hands, on themes from *Tristan und Isolde.*

España, Rhapsody for Orchestra

> For piccolo, flutes I-II, oboes I-II, clarinets I-II, bassoons I-IV; horns I-IV, trumpets I-II, cornets *à pistons* I-II, trombones I-III, tuba; timpani, bass drum, cymbals, triangle, tambourine; harps I-II; strings
> **Composed** 1883 in Paris
> **First performed** 4 November 1883 at a concert of the Société des Nouveaux Concerts (Concerts Lamoureux), Charles Lamoureux conducting
> **Published** by Enoch frères & Costallat (Paris, 1883)
> **Duration:** about 7 minutes

Unlike Bizet, who was too busy, Chabrier not only sojourned in Spain but kept sketches of what he heard during his six months there—complaining at one point of the impossibility of notating the true rhythms of a malagueña. He also wrote wide-eyed letters home, describing for instance the "admirable Sevillan derrière, turning in every direction while the rest of the body stays immobile—all to cries of *Olé, olé, anda la Maria! anda la Chiquita! Eso es! Baille la Carmen, anda! anda!"* Chabrier's high spirits were his strong suit, and he had an inbred sense of how to create brilliance of musical texture. Since he had grown up in the French Auvergne, moreover, the operative principles of folk dance and song were second nature to him.

Two themes and their offshoots are easily distinguished, the staccato melody of uncertain metric implication near the beginning, and the broad tenor lyric subsequently introduced in the French horns, bassoons, and cellos. Chabrier meant them to suggest specific Spanish dances, the jota Aragonesa and the malagueña, but these are so gathered into the overall sweep of things that they sound less like two different dances than the familiar first and second themes. Both are catchy tunes—so catchy, in fact, that during the 1950s a Perry Como song based on *España* spent many weeks on the Hit Parade. (It would not do, in a work of this gravity, to give its title.)

What makes for the particular vigor of *España* is the way the meter is kept energetic and unpredictable by routine displacements of the downbeat, often implying a conflict of duple and triple elements. (Actually it's all in $\frac{3}{8}$.) Also enjoy the evocative orchestration, in particular the ever greater intensity of the strumming figures. Toward the end, for example, there are superb guitarish passages for the harps, percussion, and strings. Of the half dozen or so melodic motives in *España,* all but one are based on music Chabrier had heard in Spain. The trombone theme at the midpoint is composed, as it were, from scratch; this injects a new element just where things seem momentarily to have petered out, and asserts yet another metrical eccentricity.

Long on effect and short on demands of the listener, *España* was a popular success from the day it was first offered to the public. It went on, in fact, to become a mainstay of the Lamoureux Orchestra's repertoire.

Ernest Chausson

Born *20 January 1855 in Paris*
Died *10 June 1899 in Limay, near Mantes*

Chausson spent his childhood in the world of books, concerts, and galleries, and his adolescence frequenting the elegant Paris salons where the prominent persons of arts and letters gathered. In his midtwenties, after he had completed his degree in law, Chausson studied orchestration with Jules Massenet at the Conservatoire and composition privately with César Franck. All told it was a highly sophisticated education in the artistic currents of the time, for which the Wagner operas, which he heard during the course of frequent travels to Germany from 1879, served as his finishing school. Of independent though not extravagant means, he never practiced law, preferring instead to pursue composition at his leisure. However attractive that may seem as a life-style, in Chausson's case it led to a rather self-indulgent perfectionism and, in turn, a limited output. He saw the issues clearly, however: the need to "de-Wagnerize," as he put it, the French repertoire by dismissing unnecessary extravagance in favor of clarity and precision of thought. His companion in this intellectual journey was the young Debussy, who went on to accomplish that very thing.

Chausson's career was too short. At the age of 44, just as he was discovering a viable musical language for himself, he was killed in a bicycle accident.

His works with orchestra include the famous *Poème* for Violin and Orchestra, discussed below; a good Symphony in B♭, opus 20 (1889–90); and two works for solo voice and orchestra, the *Poème de l'amour et de la mer,* op. 19 (1882–93), and a *Chanson perpetuelle,* op. 37 (1898). His opera, *Le Roi Arthus,* op. 23 (1886–95), was not produced until 1903.

Poème for Violin and Orchestra, OP. 25

> For violin solo; piccolo, flutes I-II, oboes I-II, clarinets I-II, bassoons I-II; horns I-IV, trumpets I-II, trombones I-III, tuba; timpani; harp; strings
>
> Composed 1896 in Paris for Eugène Ysaÿe, the Belgian violinist, and dedicated to him; originally entitled *Le Chant de l'amour triomphant: poème symphonique pour violon et orchestre*
>
> First performed 4 April 1897 at a Concert Colonne, Paris, Ysaÿe soloist, Édouard Colonne conducting
>
> Published by Breitkopf & Härtel (Leipzig, 1898)
>
> Duration: about 15 minutes

Chausson was outwardly a happy man, who enjoyed his domesticity—with a handsome wife, Jeanne, and five children—his travels, and his work. By the mid-1890s, however, he had acknowledged his negative streak, called variously pessimism, despondency, and defeatism. This coincided, not always comfortably, with the beginnings of his urge to trim away the Romantic fat. It was also the period of his maximum interest in the Symbolist poets of his own nation and the great Russian writers. Responses to all this can be felt in the *Poème,* said to have taken wing from a short story of Ivan Turgenev (1818–83, an intimate of the great mezzo-soprano Pauline Viardot).

The orchestral introduction unveils a world of mutating chromatic harmony and slow forward motion. The main theme, a memorable melody by any measure, comes at the first entry of the soloist: symmetric of phrase structure, poignant of effect, open-ended in direction. It is the successive statements of this refrain, building to the version with full brass at the end, by which the progress of the poem is actually measured. Simultaneously there operates something of a sonata form: after a short cadenza comes a long improvisation and transition that eventually gains in speed and, for the soloist, dextral demands; then a climactic arrival of the new key (C major from E♭, at the *fortissimo* with trumpets and trombones); and finally an almost immediate deflection into the refrain, stated by woodwinds and strings in the distant and rather glamorous key of F♯. The violin seems never to intrude on this organic process but rather to be an intimate part of it.

Eugène Ysaÿe (1858–1931), who gave the premiere, was associated with the Franck / d'Indy circle in Paris, later a professor of violin at the Brussels Conservatory, and after that a conductor—of the Cincinnati Symphony, among others. He was also dedicatee of Franck's Violin Sonata and Debussy's String Quartet.

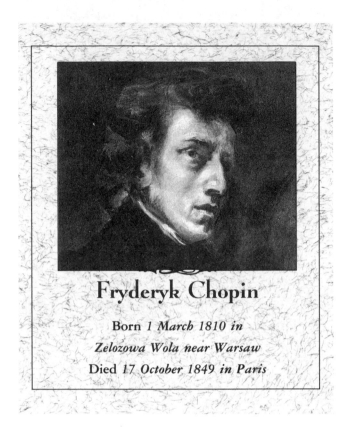

Fryderyk Chopin

Born *1 March 1810 in*
Zelozowa Wola near Warsaw
Died *17 October 1849 in Paris*

Chopin's genius at the keyboard was clear almost from the beginning: at the age of eight he played a concerto of the Bohemian composer Adalbert Gyrowetz and was composing Polish dances for piano. His advanced piano studies were at the Warsaw Conservatory, toward the end of which he was strongly influenced by visits to Warsaw of Johann Nepomuk Hummel, who had been a student of Mozart, and of Paganini. (Not much of Beethoven's music had yet been heard in Poland.) Later the works of John Field, the Irish pianist-composer, also helped form Chopin's musical views. In August 1829, not yet 20, he made a successful Vienna debut with, among other things, his *Krakowiak,* a concert rondo for piano and orchestra that retains a place in the repertoire. There, too, he arranged for his first publications.

In March and October of 1830 he played his two piano concertos before the Warsaw public, then, buoyed by his Viennese success, left Poland to begin what he thought was to be a concert tour of Germany and Italy. But Chopin was never to return home. He made a slow and not especially successful progress through Dresden and to Prague on his way to Vienna, but finding the political unrest in Italy uninviting, set out for Paris and London. News of the Russian occupation of Warsaw reached him in Stuttgart at the end of the summer. On 21 September 1831 he arrived in Paris, then basking in the glow of Romanticism.

There, with few interruptions, he spent the rest of his career, teaching for princely fees, occasionally appearing in public, and in time becoming the darling of the Paris salons. He counted in his inner circle Liszt, Meyerbeer, Berlioz, Hugo, Balzac, Delacroix, and Heine and among those who worshipped him, practically the whole patrician class. Nor was his list of erotic attachments to exceptionally elegant women a brief one. In late 1836 he met the novelist George Sand (who was by no means elegant); by 1838 they had become cohabitants in a relationship that had peaks but many valleys. In 1847, having just written unflatteringly of him in her novel *Lucrezia Floriani,* she summarily dismissed Chopin from her life. He had long shown symptoms of lung disease and by the time of his last concert in Paris, on 16 February 1848, was dying of consumption. Within days the 1848 Revolution broke out in Paris and Chopin fled to England (as did hundreds of artists), taking refuge as teacher of the wealthy Miss Jane Stirling. He overextended himself in England, partly because he needed the fees, partly because the nobility demanded his presence. He was reestablished in Paris by the autumn of 1849 and died there on 17 October. His funeral was extravagant, even for Paris: the Mozart Requiem was played during the ceremony at the Madeleine before a crowd of thousands, with Habeneck himself conducting the Société des Concerts. The body was taken to Père Lachaise and laid to rest between Cherubini and Bellini. His heart, however, was conveyed to Warsaw for enshrinement.

Chopin was probably the best of the early Romantic piano composers, and the one of whom even Schumann (who was almost exactly his age) was moved to remark, "Hats off, gentlemen! A genius!" The piano was at the center of his universe, and no composer has had a greater gift for putting it to work, nor a more natural sense of keyboard melody and its accompaniment. Virtually all his work, however, is for solo piano: the polonaises, waltzes, mazurkas, nocturnes, and etudes you know so well—forms he legitimized, in fact. For orchestra, the *Krakowiak* and two concertos were written before he left Warsaw, as were the Variations on *Là ci darem la mano* of 1827 and the Fantasia on Polish airs of 1828. That leaves only the Grande Polonaise in E♭, op. 22, composed on the road between Warsaw and Paris. Chopin's most interesting work postdates all these.

The score of the *Les Sylphides*, Fokine's ballet of 1909, was arranged from Chopin's piano works by Alexander Glazunov and others (among them the young Stravinsky).

Concerto No. 2 in F Minor for Piano and Orchestra, OP. 21

Maestoso
Larghetto
Finale: Allegro vivace

For piano solo; flutes I-II, oboes I-II, clarinets I-II, bassoons I-II; horns I-II, trumpets I-II, trombone; timpani; strings

Composed autumn 1829–early 1830 in Warsaw; dedicated to Mme la Comtesse Delphine Potocka, *née* Komar, also dedicatee of the "Minute Waltz," notorious Polish / Parisian beauty

First performed 17 March 1830 at the National Theatre, Warsaw, Chopin, soloist, Karol Kurpinski conducting. (A *divertissement* for French horn was heard between the first and second movements.) A quiet reading had been given by Chopin and Kurpinski on 3 March 1830 in the composer's home.

Published by Breitkopf & Härtel (Leipzig, 1836). *Inexpensive score:* Frédéric Chopin: *The Piano Concertos in Full Score* (New York: Dover, 1988)

Duration: about 30 minutes

The greatness of Chopin lies in his all-encompassing, almost mono-maniacal command of the piano as solo instrument, not merely its technical capabilities but its poetic promise as well. It was a single-mindedness of purpose that helps explain his distaste for the concert hall and corresponding fondness for the salon: he was clearly happiest alone with his piano. By the same token he had difficulty finding parallel poetry in the orchestra, whose possibilities he did not really understand, and little affection for the inherited forms of orchestral composition. But that must not mar too much your admiration of the F-Minor Concerto, which is, after all, one of the very few works of Chopin you can hear at an orchestra concert. You forgive the inconsistency of stance—the all-new and completely gripping concept of the soloist's role, standing so uneasily alongside some positively antique ideas about concerto-ness—in your admiration for the great melodies and fabulous elaboration, the rubato and other freedoms of motion, and the shimmering chromaticism that so often gives you the sense of wandering in a garden of delights.

The first movement seems to suggest Mozartian concerto form in its drawn-out orchestral ritornello before the soloist first enters. The offhand dotted figures at the opening are a little deceptive: vigorous tutti exclamations soon suggest the sinister side of F minor. A lovely second theme, in the relative major key, is stated by the oboe; later treatments of this theme afford the pianist some of the fanciest passages in the movement. Once the soloist enters, it is largely his or her show, though with an internal tutti to conclude the exposition and some fine interplay of the woodwind soloists and piano in the development. The recapitulation amounts to a long crescendo, beginning (as the exposition had) quietly, then gathering in virtuosity, speed, and volume to the flourish of trumpets and timpani that introduces the coda.

The stunning *Larghetto,* in A♭ major, opens with a short introductory dialogue of winds and strings mostly to establish the key. At this point the soloist, as though unaware of the orchestral backup, undertakes an extravagant improvisation on the given theme, a theme closely related to the second subject of the first movement. The orchestra participates more directly in the wrenching passage at the center. This subsides in favor of a short cadenza, and in the last statement a little exchange with the bassoon. The movement closes as it began, with the progressions for winds and strings, this time rounded off by an arpeggio from the soloist. This was the first movement of the concerto to be composed: done, said Chopin, out of passion for Konstancia Gładkowska, a voice student at the Warsaw Conservatory.

The soloist states the theme of the last movement, a sort of mazurka / rondo in F minor; the composer has marked the solo part "simple, yet graciously." The orchestra responds tartly, the piano carries on with great assurance, and the tutti brings the first subject to its close. In the long episode that follows, a triplet *perpetuum mobile* breaks out in the piano beneath dialogues of winds; a scherzando follows with *col legno* in the strings, then pauses for a moment at a short remark from the bassoon. The perpetual motion resumes and eventually reaches a recapitulation of the opening materal. But the triplets have gained control: at the end a horn call and its echo signal the beginning of the coda, now veritably racing forward.

Chopin's concertos were published in reverse order; this Second Concerto is actually the first of the pair he composed. The E-Minor Concerto was finished a few months later and performed at the National Theater of Warsaw on 11 October 1830, the composer's last concert, as it turned out, in Poland.

Aaron Copland

Born 14 November 1900 in Brooklyn, New York

Died 2 December 1990 in Westchester

Copland was a first generation American born of Russian emigré parents, by then well-established merchants of Brooklyn. His first serious study of composition, during and after high school, was with Rubin Goldmark. (For some interesting parallels, read about Gershwin on p. 242–49.) On his own initiative and with his own money Copland went in 1921 to become, along with Virgil Thomson, one of Nadia Boulanger's first American students. (Others soon followed, owing in part to Copland's enthusiastic reports home. Eventually there were Walter Piston, Roy Harris, and Elliott Carter, to name but a few.) In Europe he dutifully absorbed his Stravinsky and dabbled in jazz, but the crux of his education there was to recognize from live performances the almost bewildering spectrum of modernism, in the hands of such diverse young composers as Darius Milhaud, Paul Hindemith, and Anton Webern. He returned to New York in 1924.

His Paris contacts helped launch his American career. Boulanger asked him to compose a Symphony for Organ and Orchestra for her American debut, and this was in due course given its first performance by Walter Damrosch and the New York Symphony Society in 1925. Koussevitzky, morever, had just come to Boston from Paris and was quick to extend Copland his patronage: he conducted *Music for the Theatre* in 1925 and a year later Copland's Piano Concerto with the composer as soloist. By now his musical individuality, which favored the spacious gesture, an indigenous Americanism ("plain music," he said), and an overall simplicity of means, was beginning to emerge.

Copland strongly promoted new American music at a time when it was important to the nation to establish its cultural presence in world affairs. He convinced Roger Sessions to join him in producing the Copland-Sessions concerts of new music (1928–31); in 1937 he organized the American Composers Alliance. As a polemicist he lectured often, travelled the North American continent on missions of goodwill, and wrote copiously and well.

Copland's trilogy of ballets, like Stravinsky's, secured his fame. These were *Billy the Kid* (1938), *Rodeo* (1942), and *Appalachian Spring* (1944), representing a continuous technical progress from *El Salón México,* his famous dance-hall piece of 1936. He also composed, in those years, excellent music for the films *Of Mice and Men* (1939), *Our Town* (1940), and *The Red Pony* (1948).

In 1942, as the United States went to war, he wrote his patriotic works *Fanfare for the Common Man* and *A Lincoln Portrait.* The latter, for narrator and orchestra to texts from Lincoln's speeches and writings, was one of a series commissioned by André Kostelanetz from leading American composers. Carl Sandburg was the first of the narrators; among the most interesting of his successors have been Adlai Stevenson, Eleanor Roosevelt, and more recently the bass William Warfield, a black American. Both *Fanfare* and *Portrait* have become part of the American lore, in many communities as much a tradition on July 4th as fireworks and *The Stars and Stripes Forever.*

Gradually Copland devoted more and more of his time to conducting and teaching. For twenty-five summers, from 1940, he taught composition at Tanglewood (the Berkshire Music Center in Lenox, Massachusetts). He gave courses in New York and, during Piston's leaves of absence, at Harvard; in the academic year 1951–52 he offered the Charles Eliot Norton lectures at Harvard, published as *Music and Imagination* (Cambridge, Mass., 1952). His postwar compositions include a Third Symphony (1944–46; the other two are a rewriting of the organ symphony for Boulanger, 1928; and the Short Symphony, 1932–33) and a Clarinet Concerto for Benny Goodman (1947–48). His much-anticipated opera of 1954, *The Tender Land,* was not a success. *Connotations* (1962), a twelve-tone work for the opening of Philharmonic Hall at Lincoln Center, fared rather better. His last major orchestral works were *Music for a Great City* (i.e., New York; 1963) and *Inscape* (1967). Copland did not succeed, as Stravinsky had done, in staying at the vanguard of composition as he grew older. Yet few composers have treated the American experience as successfully as he, and on that front none has outdone him.

El Salón México

> For piccolo, flutes I-II, oboes I-II, English horn, E♭ clarinet, clarinets I-II, bass clarinet, bassoons I-II, contrabassoon; horns I-IV, trumpets I-III, trombones I-III, tuba; timpani, snare drum, bass drum, cymbals, suspended cymbal and brushes, tambourine, wood block, Chinese temple blocks, guiro, xylophone; piano; strings
>
> Composed 1933–36 in New York; dedicated to Victor Kraft, a noted photographer, who had accompanied Copland to Mexico in 1932
>
> First performed 27 August 1937 by the Orquésta Sinfónica de México, Mexico City, Carlos Chávez conducting
>
> Published by Hawkes & Son (London), Ltd. (London and New York, 1939)
>
> Duration: about 10 minutes

"Any composer who goes outside his native land," writes Copland of his trip to Mexico in 1932, "wants to return bearing musical souvenirs. From the very beginning, the idea of writing a work based on popular Mexican melodies was connected in my mind with a popular dance hall in Mexico City called Salón México.'" Copland's Mexican souvenir is a tourist's recollection, loud and splashy: do not expect allusions to ancient civilizations and monuments. But he did read up on Mexican folklore and traditional song, and the little melodic cells sound familiar because they are. His moral support in this venture came from the Mexican conductor and composer Carlos Chávez (1899–

1978), founder of the National Orchestra of Mexico and himself a committed modernist.

El Salón México amounts to a collage of South-of-the-Border sentiments: somnolent night, the mariachi band, dances with sombreros and serapes, and clapping all round. Only one of the melodies, what I suppose could be called the hat-dance-tune, has real thematic significance. The rest is rhapsodic darting hither and yon: lazy bassoon chords from which the mariachi trumpet and clarinet retort are born, a passage for strings "carefree with a naive and pure expression," the big clarinet solo with guiro. Dominating everything is the urgent and persistent metric displacement, so that you get impressions of the dances rather than authentic or pristine dance patterns proper. It's the rhythmic craziness, well summarized by the overwrought bass drum at the end, that gives the work its thrill.

This sort of temporal freedom, along with a performing force heavy with the battery, piano, and xylophone, goes on to flavor any number of "exotic" compositions of the 1940s and '50s. (And there are pronounced affinities here with Milhaud's Brazilian rhapsody of 1919, *Le Boeuf sur le toit*.)

Ballet Suite from *Billy the Kid*

Introduction: The Open Prairie—Street in a Frontier Town—Card Game at Night—Gun Battle—Celebration After Billy's Capture—The Open Prairie Again

For piccolo, flutes I-II, oboes I-II, clarinets I-II, bassoons I-II; horns I-IV, trumpets I-III, trombones I-III, tuba; timpani, snare drum, bass drum, triangle, cymbals, wood block, slapstick, guiro, sleigh-bells, glockenspiel, xylophone; harp, piano; strings with solo violin

Composed 1938 in New York to a commission from Lincoln Kirstein, noted producer of American ballet

First performed as a ballet 16 October 1938 by Ballet Caravan at the Chicago Opera House (scenario by Lincoln Kirstein; choreography by Eugene Loring); first performance of the suite 9 November 1940 by the NBC Symphony, Radio City Music Hall, New York, William Steinberg conducting

Published by Hawkes and Son (London), Ltd. (London and New York, 1941)

Duration: about 20 minutes

It's well within reason to describe *Billy the Kid* as the first all-American ballet, and as a prime example of the flowering of dance in this country during the golden age of George Balanchine, Martha Graham, and Agnes DeMille. About two-thirds of the original ballet score is to be heard in the orchestral suite.

The cattle-rustling Billy the Kid (not to be confused with the train-robbing Jesse James) was born William Bonney in New York in 1859. His family started west, but Billy's father died in Kansas; he and his mother reached Santa Fe in 1865 and Silver City, New Mexico, three years later. It was the county sheriff, Pat Garrett, who brought the twenty-two-year-old Billy to justice, then killed him in a gunfight after he had escaped from jail.

Here the principal characters are Billy; his mother and his Mexican sweetheart, danced by the same woman; rivals all named Alias, danced by the same man; and Billy's best friend and poker buddy, Sheriff Garrett. The ensemble is made up of cowboys and cowgirls, townspeople, and Mexicans. Framing the ballet at the beginning and end are scenes of the pioneers on the open prairie, relentlessly pushing the American frontier westward.

The prairie music at the beginning grows from the open intervals and parallel motion that give Copland's music its characteristic aura of homespun modesty. Over the trudging ostinato of the long journey west a ballad is heard, beginning in the flute; the brass affirm the nobility of the panorama. The scene changes. On the main street of a frontier town, the bowlegged figures of the American West amble by, whistling. We recognize some of the melodies, for example "As I Was A-Walkin' One Mornin' for Pleasure" and later "Good-bye Old Paint." Some Mexican girls do a native *jarabe* in a triple meter settled rather uncomfortably over the prevailing duple; a big cowboy dance ensues, hoedown-style, with woodblock and a little later the jingle of spurs. After a long section in $\frac{5}{8}$ and $\frac{4}{8}$ the atmosphere clears and variations on "Good-bye Old Paint" begin: Billy and his mother have appeared. At the peak of this section, with xylophone and glockenspiel, Billy steps in to separate a fistfight between two drunks. Shots (the slapstick) aimed at Billy kill his mother instead. In white fury he stabs Alias, the perpetrator.

Card Game at Night is an innocent nocturne, with another generic Western melody in the violins and violas, atmospheric throbbing in the woodwinds, and a recitative for solo trumpet at the end. The gunfight erupts in the percussion with rapid-fire figures in the trumpets and snare drums that will sound to you more like Gatling-guns than revolvers. The gunfire subsides: Billy has been captured. Townspeople celebrate in the street, sneering and cocky, the music working itself into a soft-shoe idiom now and then. The distant prairie again, with the gurgling of night creatures: the pioneer music from the beginning returns, inexorable of westward plod and certain of heroic cadence.

Four Dance Episodes from *Rodeo*

Buckaroo Holiday
Corral Nocturne
Saturday Night Waltz
Hoe–Down

For piccolos I-II, flutes I-III, oboes I-II, English horn, clarinets I-II, bass clarinet, bassoons I-II; horns I-IV, trumpets I-III, trombones I-III, tuba; timpani, snare drum, bass drum, cymbals, wood block, xylophone, glockenspiel; harp, celesta, piano; strings with solo violin

Composed 1942 in New York to a commission from the Ballet Russe de Monte Carlo

First performed as a ballet by the Ballet Russe de Monte Carlo 16 October 1942, at the Metropolitan Opera House, New York, Franz Allers conducting (book and choreography by Agnes de Mille, who danced the leading female role of the tomboy cowgirl); three of the episodes first performed in concert 28 May 1943 by the Boston Pops Orchestra, Arthur Fiedler conducting; entire suite first performed by the New York Philharmonic Society, 22 June 1943 at a Lewisohn Stadium Concert, Alexander Smallens conducting

Published by Hawkes & Son, Ltd. (London and New York, 1946)

Duration: about 20 minutes

Billy the Kid assured Copland his limelight and a barrage of invitations to do more of the same. The most appealing of these was a commission from one of the several successors to Sergei Diaghilev's company, this one calling itself the Ballet Russe de Monte Carlo (and despite the name, permanently resident in the United States). Copland and the dancer / choreographer Agnes de Mille proposed another

Western theme, "The Courting at Burnt Ranch," again to feature cowpokes and horsey dances but also to have a prominent Saturday night hoe-down at the ranch. *Rodeo,* more sophisticated of style and structure than was *Billy the Kid,* became even more popular. The four dance episodes—two ensemble numbers and two *pas de deux*—were extracted for the usual reasons.

Miss De Mille writes that the theme of the ballet is "one that has confronted all American women, from earliest pioneer times: how to get a suitable man." The dancers are buckaroos, ranch-hands, and womenfolk. A tomboy rancher's daughter vies for the attentions of the head wrangler by hanging out with the guys and, unsuccessfully, showing off on a bronco. She is left without a date for the dance that night at the ranch house. At the dance, under a starlit sky, couples waltz. At first the cowgirl and the wrangler find nothing in common, but everything changes when she reappears in a bright red dress and bows in her hair (though she is still wearing boots). The hoe-down continues with the new couple at the center of attention.

Buckaroo Holiday opens exuberantly with a plunging scalar theme and prominent syncopations, with a liquescent, perhaps yearning motive alternating among the ensembles. Bowlegged music returns, leading to a hammering figure in a typical Copland scoring of piano, xylophone, and rimshots on the drum; this is based on the traditional Western tune "Sis Joe." A teetering bassoon finally manages to introduce the song "If He'd Be a Buckaroo by His Trade," first heard in the trombone. Here, after a presenting of materials that has much to do with traditional sonata form, comes an extravagant restatement and reorganization of the themes, heavy on the contrapuntal device. The peal of French horns toward the end is part of the process of drawing things to close.

The melodic essence of the *Corral Nocturne,* closely related to things we had heard in the soft pages of *Buckaroo Holiday,* is largely in the winds, the strings underscoring the phrase endings with warm cadences. The prevailing meter is a leisurely $\frac{5}{4}$, frequently altered. In the next episode, *Saturday Night Waltz,* the orchestra seems for a moment to tune up for a square dance; what it actually plays is a winsome waltz, again led by the solo winds.

The *Hoe-Down,* with its fine fiddling, returns us to the high spirits of the buckaroos and their gals; here the principal theme is an old dance tune called "Bonyparte." After the sassy trumpet and rimshot episode, the hoe-down, running low on energy, collapses. It requires only a momentary taking of breath for the dance to fly away again one last time, recapitulating both main themes.

Miss de Mille's Western choreography was widely admired, and she was engaged forthwith by Rodgers and Hammerstein to do the dances for *Oklahoma*.

Appalachian Spring

> For flutes I-II, oboes I-II, clarinets I-II, bassoons I-II; horns I-II, trumpets I-II, trombones I-II; timpani, snare drum, bass drum, cymbals, triangle, tabor, woodblock, claves, glockenspiel, xylophone; harp, piano; strings
>
> Composed 1943–44 in New York to a commission from the Elizabeth Sprague Coolidge Foundation for the Martha Graham Dance Company; dedicated to Elizabeth Sprague Coolidge (see p. 62); orchestra suite prepared spring 1945
>
> First performed as a ballet by Miss Graham and company 30 October 1944, at the Library of Congress in conjunction with the Coolidge Festival; first performed as a suite 4 October 1945 by the New York Philharmonic, Artur Rodzinsky conducting
>
> Published by Boosey and Hawkes (London, 1945)
>
> Duration: about 25 minutes

Copland's great "Ballet for Martha [Graham]", which won the 1945 Pulitzer Prize for music, may be heard in any one of three versions: the original work, scored, because the auditorium at the Library of Congress is so small, for thirteen instruments; a setting for full orchestra, slightly condensed by deleting elements the composer describes as "of purely choreographic interest"; and the condensed version reduced back to the original force of thirteen players.

Martha Graham (1900–91), the bewitching doyenne of American dance, discovered a title for her pioneer ballet in a pair of words buried in *The Bridge,* an epic poem by Harte Crane (1899–1932). *Appalachian Spring* was her 108th ballet.

Copland writes:

The action of the ballet concerns a pioneer celebration in spring around a newly-built farmhouse in the Pennsylvania hills in the early part of the last century. The bride-to-be and the young farmer-husband enact the emotions, joyful and apprehensive, their new domestic partnership invites. An older neighbor suggests now and then the rocky confidence of experience. A revivalist and his followers remind the new householder of the strange and terrible aspects of human fate. At the end the couple are left quiet and strong in their new house.

The music is tuneful, simple, dignified; its contours strongly—almost relentlessly—governed by the rising intervals stated so frequently in the introduction. (If you know the tune of *Simple Gifts,* you can hear these motives as suggestions of what is to come.) This quiet introduction is the first of some eight sections. The next is an excited allegro that begins at the burst of piano, xylophone, and strings; the motives from the introduction are soon woven in. Bride- and husband-to-be have a quiet *pas de deux* where the music begins as a waltz-like transformation of the motto material and becomes, in the middle, chordally complex and a little threatening. Visitors arrive: the faster tempo resumes, a spirited interplay of oboe, piccolo, and clarinet begins the long middle scene, fascinating of rhythmic character. At the center come some ponderous bars, then a brash presto that may well remind you of passages from Stravinsky's *Petrushka.* The last slow interlude, with the high violin solo, is the bride's solo dance. There is a full, gentle cadence.

At this juncture, the clarinet begins the famous variations on the Shaker tune *Simple Gifts* (" 'Tis a gift to be simple, 'tis a gift to be free"). They gather in speed, size of performing force, and contrapuntal sophistication toward the tutti statement in the middle; the familiar trumpet and trombone variation, with its strong sense of mirroring, begins the drive to the concluding statement in long note values. The coda is "very calm," and "like a prayer"—a music to leave the couple quiet and strong in their new house. And that is, of course, the central theme of all three ballets: the courage of the American pioneers: their inexhaustible strength, character, and determination.

Arcangelo Corelli

Born 17 February 1653 in Fusignano,
between Bologna and Ravenna
Died 8 January 1713 in Rome

This singularly successful composer of the generation just preceding Vivaldi, Handel, and Bach—a mild-mannered individual, noted for his courteous behavior and unfailing gentility—enjoyed a quiet career characterized mostly by the consistent, inexorable growth of his powers and prestige. By the end of his life, Corelli was generally recognized as the preeminent instrumental composer of his time.

From 1666 he studied violin and composition in Bologna, a musical capital vibrant with innovations in composition and performance, especially for the violin family. In 1670, at the age of 17, he was elected into the Accademia Filarmonica, a prestigious society of singers, instrumentalists, and composers that met several times a week to study and perform new music. Some five years later he was to be found in Rome, where he spent most of the remaining four decades of his career as violinist and composer. He enjoyed the patronage (and the palatial living quarters) of princes secular and ecclesiastical, of Queen Christina of Sweden, and lastly of the celebrated patron of music Cardinal Pietro Ottoboni. Until his retirement in 1708, Corelli led regular Monday evening concerts in the Ottoboni palace, often appearing in trio sonatas or concerti grossi with his protégé in violin, Matteo Fornari, and the noted Spanish cellist, G. B. Lulier. In 1700 he was made master of the instrumentalists of the Academy of St. Cecilia, and thus found himself, by virtue of that title, at the pinnacle of his profession. He retired a few years later to order, revise, and oversee publication of his diverse works. His remains were laid to rest in the Roman Pantheon, Santa Maria della Rotunda, and there for many years, on the anniversary of his death, memorial concerts of his music were given. For the dedication of the opus 6 concertos, the Elector Palantine granted Corelli, posthumously, the honorific title Marquis of Landenburg.

It is customary to comment at this juncture that the size of Corelli's published work is unusually small for a composer of his stature: six opuses consisting exclusively of solo sonatas, trio sonatas, and concerti grossi, all of them for strings and continuo alone. A few other preserved works can be attributed to him with certainty, including a good trumpet sonata with violins and continuo. What is important, however, is the utter perfection of the six dozen works he did publish. Their formal construction, harmonic vocabulary, and agile, assured command of idiomatic string technique were universally studied and imitated, not least of all in the dozens and dozens of reprints of his works that were soon to be had from music sellers in every corner of Europe. His orchestral compositions demand what he had demonstrated as performer and teacher: mutiple stops, florid ornamentation, and uniform bowings.

It was not simply through his publications that Corelli had such a profound influence on the high Baroque, however, for among his students he numbered such of the great violinist-composers of the next age as Francesco Geminiani and Pietro Locatelli. And during his impressionable years in Italy, Handel met Corelli, absorbed his teachings, and drew on them heavily for his own substantial contributions to the idiom.

Twelve Concerti Grossi, OP. 6

No. 1 in D Major
Largo; Allegro—Largo; Allegro—Largo; Allegro—Allegro

No. 2 in F Major
Vivace; Allegro—Allegro—Grave; Andante largo; Allegro

No. 3 in C Minor
Largo; Allegro—Grave; Vivace—Allegro

No. 4 in D Major
Adagio; Allegro—Adagio; Vivace—Allegro

No. 5 in B Major
Adagio; Allegro; Adagio—Allegro—Largo; Allegro

No. 6 in F Major
Adagio; Allegro—Largo; Vivace—Allegro

No. 7 in D Major
*Vivace; Allegro; Adagio—Allegro—Andante largo; Allegro—
Vivace*

No. 8 in G Minor, *fatto per la notte di natale* ("Christmas
Concerto")
*Vivace; Grave—Allegro—Adagio; Allegro; Adagio—Vivace—
Allegro; Largo; Pastorale ad libitum*

No. 9 in F Major
Preludio—Allemanda—Corrente—Gavotta—Minuetto

No. 10 in C Major
Preludio—Allemanda—Corrente—Allegro—Minuetto

No. 11 in B Major
Preludio—Allemanda—Sarabanda—Giga

No. 12 in F Major
Preludio—Allegro—Sarabanda—Giga

For   violins I-II solo, cello solo; strings; continuo
Composed   in all probability, over the last two decades of Corelli's
    life; revised and assembled for publication from 1708 in Rome;
    the preface was dated 3 December 1712
First performed   c. 1700, during the course of the composer's
    weekly concerts in Rome

Published by Estienne Roger (Amsterdam, 1714 [posthumous]);
dedicated (by Corelli's disciple Matteo Fornari) to the Elector
Palatine Johann Wilhelm, a patron and admirer of the
composer. *Inexpensive score:* Arcangelo Corelli: *Complete Concerti
Grossi in Full Score* (New York: Dover, 1989)
Duration: about 15 minutes each.

Corelli's contribution to the concerto grosso is as Haydn's to the symphony: though there were precursors hither and yon and simultaneous work of significance by any number of others, each has a rightful claim to be considered father of the genre. It was, that is, to Corelli that disciples and imitators looked first of all.

The first eight of these twelve concerti (Corelli's *parte prima*) are in the style of the sonatas *da chiesa:* churchly works, subdued in manner and made up of a series of untitled movements of contrasting meter and tempo. The last four are concerti *da camera* (or, as Corelli puts it, *parte seconda per camera*), theoretically sprightlier than the first eight, each a suite with a prelude followed by three or four named dances. The dance forms are defined in the glossary on pages 683–92; their sequence here, now correntes and minuets, now sarabandes and gigues, is dictated less by precedent that by the general principle of varying character. Lest the purported contrast of church and chamber styles cause you undue alarm, let it be said that in these works the distinction is neither especially clear nor particularly important. The grave eight are sometimes just as spirited as the bright four, nor do these latter lack for rigorous material of their own.

The solo group, or *concertino,* for all twelve consists of a pair of violins, cello, and keyboard, the usual Baroque trio force. In the orchestral *ripieno,* however, is to be found the progressive texture of two violins, viola, and bass parts, at once precursing the standard quartet arrangement to come and replacing earlier preference for divided viola parts.

Corelli's compositional procedures are, likewise, remarkably free. It is the later composers, especially Vivaldi, who make of the genre something formulaic and seemingly predictable and correspondingly less engrossing. Here there is little, at least by way of formal structure, that could be considered paradigmatic. Corelli delights in sudden shifts of character, often interrupting statements of his fast movements with Adagios, and introducing and concluding movements with sections of sharp contrast. The first movement of the Second Concerto, to take but a single example, consists fundamentally of two statements of an *Allegro,* the first departing from the tonic, the second returning to it. But at the beginning is a fanfare with trills, very like Handel in his royal idiom, and between the two halves of the *Allegro* comes an Adagio that wrenches the movement off course, then wends its way chromatically into a reminiscence of the opening. Nor does the movement end with a flourish, but rather in another Adagio interruption and a slow concluding phrase. Such movements as these have, on paper, a choppy look, but the lurches and meanderings are critical to their musical interest and to building a sense of inevitable return from an otherwise tame grammar of motion from tonic to dominant and back. Common to all the concertos is the tight interweaving of the violin solo parts, the steady underpinning of the solo cello, and the crisp, energetic responses from the orchestra. The melodic imitation is all-pervasive, though it is seldom very strict.

The popular favorite among these concertos is No. 8, "composed for Christmas Night," with a shepherd's pastorale and possibly some angel references as well. (But don't ignore the other eleven, wherein there are some equally beautiful things.) The two *Allegros* are exemplary of Corelli's style, each with a pair of repeated phrases where the solo cello outlines the harmonic framework while over it the second violin responds, resolutely, to each new motive of the first. The orchestral interjections are mostly doublings, brief at first, then growingly emphatic as the sections conclude. There is an arioso for the soloists interrupted by a vigorous Allegro for the full ensemble, a dance in minuet fashion, then a merging into the second *Allegro* movement and famous pastorale. Like all such movements this one is cast in a $\frac{12}{8}$ with drones supporting a liquid melody and set in the major mode. It doesn't really conclude—you are meant to believe it could go on forever—but rather simply fades away.

These works, once great favorites, are nowadays heard in the concert hall less often than they should be. You will most likely hear them played by groups that specialize in authentic Baroque performance practice (which is good), and there are some splendid performances of this sort on cassette and CD. A proper rendering might be offered by solo trio, perhaps a dozen in the *ripieno* orchestra, and small organ. There should probably be two continuo players, one for the soloists and one for the *ripieno;* for the former, an archlute (specifically called for by Corelli in other works) is an attractive alternative to the ubiquitous harpsichord.

Claude Debussy

**Born *22 August 1862 in*
*St.-Germain-en-Laye, near Paris***
Died *25 March 1918 in Paris*

To assert that Debussy was the most significant composer between Wagner and Stravinsky is subtly to understate the case, for it fails to account for the extent to which his imagination unveiled the musical future just as the new century dawned. The list of works he completed is on the whole rather short for a composer of his stature, and the list of what he left undone—including an opera on Poe's *The Fall of the House of Usher*—easily as long. But what he finished to his own satisfaction went on to touch and eventually to change virtually every corner of the trade: the piano repertoire, song, opera, and symphonic works.

Debussy was a student (of Franck and Massenet, among others) at the Paris Conservatoire for over a decade, completing his studies when he won the *prix de Rome* for his charming cantata, *L'Enfant prodigue*

(The Prodigal Son, 1884). For a time he taught the children of Tchaikovsky's patroness, Nadezhda von Meck, and twice travelled with her family to Moscow. Subsequently he enjoyed the patronage and eventually the romantic devotion of Mme Vasnier, an amateur singer for whom he wrote some excellent songs. This was interrupted by his prize-winner's trip to Rome, where he composed little but was able to make the acquaintance of Liszt and Verdi. The end of his period of artistic formation was marked by a pair of intellectual thunderbolts: the Bayreuth Festivals of 1888 and 1889, where he was both fascinated and profoundly repelled, and the 1889 Centennial Exhibition in Paris, where, for the first time, he heard the Javanese gamalan and other exotic wonders.

By the early 1890s, Debussy had settled into a quiet life in Paris as a professional composer and sometime newspaper essayist. Though uncomfortable as a public figure he much enjoyed the company of intellectuals such as Claude Monet, Stéphane Mallarmé, and the eccentric Erik Satie. It took him some time, however, to establish a workable domestic arrangement. His long-term mistress Gabrielle Dupont attempted suicide in 1897; the first Mme Debussy did likewise in 1904, when Debussy moved away to take lodging with Emma Bardac, another singer and another man's wife. Their daughter Claude-Emma, Debussy's beloved Chou-Chou, was born in 1905. This last was a loving household, where he was content for the rest of his life. Debussy and Emma Bardac were finally married in 1908; Chou-Chou survived her father by just over a year.

Debussy's first orchestral masterpiece was the *Prélude à "L'Après-midi d'un faune"* (Prelude to "The Afternoon of a Faun," 1892–94). This was followed by his ravishing opera on Maurice Maeterlinck's *Pelléas et Mélisande* (produced 1902), and by three descriptive orchestral works: *Nocturnes* (1897–99), *La Mer* (1903–5), and the *Images pour orchestre* (1905–12: *Gigues, Ibéria, Rondes de Printemps*). The ballet *Jeux* (1912–13) was written for the Ballets Russes and choreographed by Vaclav Nijinsky. Debussy also wrote several dozen songs for voice and piano, a string quartet, solo piano music, and rhapsodies and sonatas for the orchestral instruments. He had suffered from cancer for some years and succumbed to it in Paris during the closing weeks of World War I.

Debussy's greatness lies in his having discovered and pursued new avenues for musical expression at the very peak of the Wagner vogue, especially in France. He welcomed a much expanded array of sonorities: whole-tone, pentatonic, and non-Western scales; parallel movement of all sorts, including sequences of chords of unresolved dissonance; chords with added notes; layers of sound, to name but a few. His orchestral works are delicate, pointillistic affairs of exquisite orchestration and what he called a halo of sound (and what others called Impressionism, in the manner of painting). It was a repertoire of typically French refinement and consistency which, in tandem with the music of Ravel, returned the eyes of the musical world to Paris.

Prélude à "L'Après-midi d'un faune"

For flutes I-III, oboes I-II, English horn, clarinets I-II, bassoons I-II; horns I-IV; antique cymbals in E and B; harps I-II; strings
Based on a text of Stéphane Mallarmé (1842–98)
Composed 1892–94 in Paris; dedicated to Raymond Bonheur
First performed 23 December 1894 by the Paris Société Nationale, Gustave Doret conducting
Published by Eugène Fromont (Paris, 1895). *Inexpensive scores:* Claude Debussy: *Three Great Orchestral Works in Full Score* (New York: Dover, 1983); Debussy: *Prelude to "The Afternoon of a Faun,"* ed. William W. Austin, A Norton Critical Score (New York: Norton, 1970)
Duration: about 10 minutes

Debussy's delicate miniature for orchestra is meant as a sort of reflection on Mallarmé's eclogue, or pastoral poem, *"The Afternoon of a Faun."* It doesn't especially matter whether the poem is printed in your program, because the imagery is practically impossible to understand unless you ponder it for a much longer time that the music lasts. This dream of Classical antiquity concerns a faun, drugged in half-sleep, half-wakefulness, who spots the nymphs of his dreams playing before him, pursues them rather aimlessly, and, in the end, falls back into the revery of slumber.

The solo flute states the lazy, undulant theme, evocative of the play of pan-pipes. (The key is E major, strongly colored by the prominent C# with which the melody begins.) Atmosphere gathers in the harp glissandos, gentle vibration of the horns, tremolandos in the strings, and finally the shimmering revolutions of the motive overtaken by

first violins. At the clarinet entry the structure gathers in anima-
tion—hints, doubtless, of the chase. The oboe solo leads the orchestra
to a climax and fall. Here the key slides into a warm, secure major
(that of D♭) for the middle episode, sustained and expressive in its
outpourings of the full orchestra. The flute solo returns, its phrases
now separated by staccato figures in the winds; the entry of the antique
cymbal signals the final strophe for the flute, surrounded by memories
of what has been, and fading away with echoes in the horns.

Debussy achieves the incomparable dreaminess that pervades his
music of fawn and nymph by letting suggestion suffice and by tight
control of the details of individual sonority that go to make up the
performing force. Then he adds a little mist: the tremolandos and
glissandos and wind arabesques.

The 1912 ballet, *Afternoon of a Faun,* became a mainstay of the
Diaghilev's Ballets Russes, where it was in repertoire with Ravel's
Daphnis and Chloe and Falla's *The Three-Cornered Hat.* A marvelous
watercolor rendering of Nijinsky as The Faun is preserved, and there
are some good photographs of the production.

Nocturnes

Nuages (Clouds)
Fêtes
Sirènes

For "wordless chorus of women's voices" (*Sirènes*); flutes I-III,
oboes I-II, English horn, clarinets I-II, bassoons I-III; horns I-
IV, trumpets I-III, trombones I-III, tuba; timpani, distant
snare drum, cymbals; harps I-II; strings

Composed December 1897–December 1899 in Paris; dedicated to
Rosalie Texier, the first Mme Debussy, in the autograph
manuscript; the printed edition is dedicated to Georges
Hartmann, Debussy's publisher

First performed (*Nuages* and *Fêtes*) 9 December 1900 at a
Lamoureux Concert, Paris, Camille Chevillard conducting;
Sirènes first performed 27 October 1901 by the same orchestra

Published by Eugène Fromont (Paris, 1900). *Inexpensive score:*
Claude Debussy: *Three Great Orchestral Works in Full Score* (New
York: Dover, 1983)

Duration: about 30 minutes

Debussy's *Nocturnes* have a somewhat more specific descriptive purpose than the half-reality of the *Prélude à "L'Après-midi d'un faun."* He
appears to have chosen his title in imitation of James MacNeill Whistler,
who called some of his paintings nocturnes; the two had met shortly
before at the artist's studio in London.

The clouds, said Debussy, are a study in "gray vagueness, tinted
with white." The clarinets and bassoons circle gently but ceaselessly;
the throaty motive always given to the English horn was suggested to
the composer by the horn of a barge on the Seine. There lies in the $\frac{6}{4}$
meter an uneasy coexistence of triple and duple subdivisions, and this
tension is a major constituent in the uninterrupted mutation of the
clouds. Very near the end the tempo accelerates slightly and a true
theme is heard in the harp and flute (quite similar, in fact, to motives
from *L'Après-midi*). Only suggestions of the earlier music are to be
heard thereafter: the clouds have parted.

The *Fêtes* take place in the Bois de Boulogne by night: one perceives, faintly at first, a torch procession under the trees and distant
music by the band of the Garde Républicaine. From the beginning,
it is a movement feverish with activity. The allusions are to farandole
and gigue, both street dances, and to the fanfares of the military
band. In the middle the dance step shifts for a time to a strict duple
meter, and at the climax there is an allusion to a motive from *Nuages*.
The triplets come again to the fore: the procession, it seems, passes
close by before disappearing.

The Sirens were bewitching temptresses of Greek legend whose
singing lured unsuspecting sailors to wreck their ships. Here their
voices are heard from a group of sixteen women with untexted vocalise
on the syllable "ah." The orchestral textures are primarily watery,
with magnificent use of the harp and string glissandos. The sailors
approach ever closer, and with inevitable result. Within moments of
the ecstatic peak, the movement is dissolving away. Virtually the
entire structure is generated from the temptresses' two-note oscillations.

La Mer (The Sea), Three Symphonic Sketches

De l'aube à midi sur la mer (From dawn until noon on the sea)
Jeux de vagues (Play of the waves)
Dialogue du vent et de la mer (Dialogue of the wind and sea)

For piccolo, flutes I-II, oboes I-II, English horn, clarinets I-II,
bassoons I-III, contrabassoon; horns I-IV, trumpets I-III, cornets *à pistons* I-II, trombones I-III, tuba; timpani, bass drum,
cymbals, triangle, tam-tam, glockenspiel (or celesta); harps I-II;
strings

Composed August 1903–5 March 1905 in Paris, Burgundy, and
Eastbourne, England; dedicated to Jacques Durand (1865–
1928), his publisher

First performed 15 October 1905 at a Lamoureux Concert in
Paris, Camille Chevillard conducting

Published by A. Durand et fils (Paris, 1905; rev. 1909).
Inexpensive score: Claude Debussy: *Three Great Orchestral Works in
Full Score* (New York: Dover, 1983)

Duration: about 25 minutes.

Debussy's big orchestral works merit both individual and joint scrutiny, not just to evaluate the growth of the style, but because they
have a notable consistency of purpose and share many structural details.
La Mer, the last of Debussy's large-scale symphonic works, is his most
assured, but everywhere you hear allusions to the music that has led
up to it.

We know his conception to have been considerably influenced by
The Wave, an illustration by the great Japanese color print maker,
Hokusai (1760–1849), whose works were then much in vogue.

Motives of melody, rhythm, color, and texture interplay in spacious forms, much as do the light, sea, and air of the out-of-doors.
Everywhere, of course, there are waves, and each of the three essays
accumulates toward a monster wave at the end. The first movement
grows almost entirely from the short-long rising motive you hear in
the cellos at the start and the woodwind figure that succeeds it. After
suggestions of sunrise comes the sudden glisten of sunlight on water
in pairs of flute and clarinet. All the brilliance and shimmering are
primarily the result of intricate partwriting. A strong lyric phrase
from cellos divided into four separate parts, and golden of hue, suggests a new aspect of the sea. The movement begins to conclude with
the English horn solo, a version in long notes of one of the principal
motives. There's a majestic final climax with brass.

The *Jeux de vagues* is a quiet, enigmatic scherzo with willowy passagework for the solo winds. In section after section Debussy reveals
different facets of the same basic material. At the halfway point, the

movement builds into a determined accelerando, only to subside in waves of harp glissando. The *Dialogue du vent et de la mer* begins in the low strings over a roll of timpani and bass drum and stroke of the tam-tam. As it goes along, the movement cites motives from both preceding sketches. The first of the important themes is announced by the trumpet; shortly thereafter comes the first statement, in the woodwinds, of the immense and palpitating phrase that will seize control of the movement and then quite obviously lead the entire work to its climax. All the urging forward and settling back again is the conductor's job, and you may well pay particular attention to what's happening on the podium as *La Mer* comes to its close. The last wave breaks just before the frenzied close.

The waggish Satie said that he particularly liked the part at quarter past eleven.

Antonín Dvořák

Born 8 September 1841 in
Nelabozeves, north of Prague.
Died 1 May 1904 in Prague.

Along with his older compatriot Bedřich Smetana (1824–84), Dvořák was head of the circle of composers who contributed so formidably to the Czech nationalistic movement. He studied at the Organ School in Prague, then supported himself in bands and theater orchestras and as a church organist. Attracted to the same aesthetic and political ideas that motivated Smetana, Dvořák began to compose music in which he consciously strove to incorporate dance rhythms, instrumental combinations, harmonies, and melodies of traditional Bohemian folkmusic into the genres of classical art music. In the 1870s he was befriended by Brahms, who encouraged his ambitions and recommended his work to the distinguished music publishing firm N. Simrock of Berlin. His fame spread quickly, owing largely to the popularity of the Slavonic Dances, op. 46 (1878). He made several international journeys, among them some trips to England and a long sojourn in the United States (1892–95) as director of the National Conservatory of Music in New York. He spent his summer vacations with the Czech colony in Spillville, Iowa, there absorbing into his works in progress not a few Americanisms. Those years produced some masterpieces, including both the Cello Concerto and the E-Minor Symphony ("From the New World"), first performed by the New York Philharmonic in 1893. On his return to Bohemia, he became director of the Prague Conservatory, a position he retained until his death.

Dvořák's major orchestral works are his last three symphonies, variously numbered and now called Symphony No. 7 in D Minor (1883), Symphony No. 8 in G Major (1889), and the "New World" Symphony No. 9 in E Minor (1893). In addition, for orchestra there are the Slavonic Dances, opp. 46 and 72 (1878, 1887), a *Scherzo Capriccioso,* op. 66 (1883), a cycle of three overtures, opp. 91–93 that includes *Carnival* (1891), and the great Cello Concerto in B Minor, op. 104 (1894). To these should be added two perennial favorites for reduced orchestral forces, the Serenades for Strings (op. 22, 1875) and for Winds (op. 44, 1878). Dvořák, a prolific composer, also wrote operas, religious music, tone poems, songs, piano works, and fine chamber music. There are 115 published opuses.

Symphony No. 8 in G Major, OP. 88

Allegro con brio
Adagio
Allegretto grazioso
Allegro ma non troppo

For piccolo, flutes I-II, oboes I-II, clarinets I-II, bassoons I-II; horns I-IV, trumpets I-II, trombones I-III, tuba; timpani; strings

Composed 26 August–8 November 1889 in Prague; offered in 1890 "for my installation as a member of the Czech Academy of the Emperor Franz Joseph for Sciences, Literature, and Arts"

First performed 2 February 1890 by the National Theater Orchestra, Prague, Dvořák conducting

Published by Novello, Ewer & Co. (London, 1892). *Inexpensive score:* Antonín Dvořák: *Symphonies Nos. 8 and 9 in Full Score* (New York: Dover, 1984)

Duration: about 40 minutes

The leisurely cello melody that begins the G-major Symphony does much to establish the bucolic character we associate with the work. (A similar sort of opening is found in Mendelssohn's A-minor Symphony, the "Scottish," see p. 351.) Some momentum is established with the cheery flute solo; timpani and tuba begin an orchestral crescendo that leads first to another tenor phrase—this one for violas as well as cellos—and then to a brief tutti climax. But that is immediately deflected, and by the arrival of the second group the sonority has been transformed into the minor mode and an orchestration dominated by flutes and clarinets in close harmony. This section is an excellent example of the Bohemian idiom: of pensive but not quite melancholy theme, airy orchestration, a touch of mystery suggested in the low brass, and easy shift into the major mode for affirmative climax and then out into minor again. A double bar at this point in the score confirms that the exposition is done, but Dvořák clouds the issue by beginning the development with a quotation of the cello and flute themes from the beginning: it seems for a time there's been a repeat back to the beginning. What follows is not so much true development, anyway, as a sort of rhapsody on the given material—Dvořák's most natural and assured tactic of composition—with his idiomatic "Three Blind Mice" figure very much in evidence. The thematic recapitulation overlaps the end of the development in a blare of trumpets; only when it subsides do we reach the proper key area. None of these novelties is especially earth-shattering for their time or place, but Dvořák accomplishes it all so smoothly you cannot help being enchanted.

The second movement's opening gambit is uncertain, searching, and largely in minor. For every optimistic flutter of the high woodwind, there is a frowning riposte in the throbbish register of the clarinets. In view of this discourse, the arrival in C major—falling scales in the violins, staccato and pizzicato elsewhere, with a lyrical melody in flute and oboe—sounds naive. The brass entry with sudden *forte* shows the heroic side of the key, but the unsettling dialogue of flutes and clarinets soon reasserts itself. When the French horn soars forth with its soulful version of the clarinet ripostes, we encounter one of Dvořák's great eruptions of Slavic passion. The major-mode material recapitulates as well, climaxes with a hint of minor, and fades in a sparkle of distant trumpet calls.

But for its unmistakable nationality, the third movement might be dubbed Brahmsian, as much a waltz as a scherzo, and rather similar to the minor-mode waltz in Brahms's Third. The theme of the lovely trio, in the parallel major, is presented by flute and oboe in unison; a repeat of the opening section is followed by the brisk duple coda—with yet another incarnation of the Three Blind Mice motive.

A trumpet fanfare introduces the finale. Again the cellos have a suave melody, not so different from that of the first movement: tame of forward motion, relaxed of attitude, rich of sonority. When the full orchestra shatters this atmosphere with a faster and much more excited version of the same melody, we realize we are in the midst of a fiery Bohemian dance, combining attributes of sonata, rondo, and variation practice. The tempo picks up still further with the flute episode; at the shift into minor mode there is a hollow march for the wind band. The opening cello phrases recapitulate, and there follows a long winding down. This of course only makes the release of the last tutti all the more sensational.

Symphony No. 9 in E Minor, OP. 95 ("From the New World")

Adagio; Allegro molto
Largo
Scherzo: Molto vivace
Allegro con fuoco

For piccolo, flutes I-II, oboes I-II, English horn, clarinets I-II, bassoons I-II; horns I-IV, trumpets I-II, trombones I-III, tuba; timpani, cymbals, triangle; strings

Composed 10 January–24 May 1893 in New York City and Iowa, finished later in the summer

First performed 16 December 1893 by the New York Philharmonic Society, Anton Seidl conducting

Published by N. Simrock (Berlin, 1894). *Inexpensive score:* Antonín Dvořák: *Symphonies Nos. 8 and 9 in Full Score* (New York: Dover, 1984)

Duration: about 35 minutes

Within a few weeks of arriving in this country in the autumn of 1892, Dvořák was at work on a new symphony of "impressions and greetings from the New World"; it had been sketched by late spring

1893 and was completed during the Dvořáks' summer holiday that year in Spillville. It is true that Dvořák had by that time heard and enjoyed various American folk musics, including that of black Americans, and that the second and third movements grew, according to the composer, from his ruminations on *Hiawatha*—the *Largo* possibly inspired by Minehaha's funeral and the scherzo on an Indian dance described in the poem. But likewise by his own account, Dvořák remained what he always was, a "simple Czech musician." What seems American about the "New World" Symphony—the cakewalk rhythms, the "primitive" instrumental colors, the folkish melodies—all of these, in truth, are just as typical of the composer's own native style. The spiritual *Goin' Home* was fashioned after Dvořák, not the other way around. And the apparent reference to *Swing Low, Sweet Chariot* in the second theme of the first movement is probably coincidental.

Whatever the ethnicity of the "New World" Symphony, its unmistakable preoccupation is with the out-of-doors. The Adagio introduction, for example, establishes a certain pastorality with the little cakewalk motive first heard in the cellos, then threatens it with ominous thrusts of the strings and parries in the winds and timpani. A horn call arching over more than an octave opens the exposition, answered by dancing figures in the woodwinds. The transitional passage lingers over a jiggish figure drawn from the opening. A hush settles for the second theme from the solo flute, virtually an inversion of the opening horn call. The development treats this relationship extensively, on occasion stormily; the recapitulation is conventional until the transition material is reached, at which point Dvořák embarks on a hair-raising tonal excursion, with the second theme stated in A♭, by any measure a distant key.

The famous *Largo* is introduced by a solemn chord-progression in low brass and woodwind. Following the familiar English horn solo and its developments, there is a pensive soliloquy that begins in the flute and oboe and carries on in the violins; the retransition pointedly mingles the themes of the first and second movements. The English horn melody returns, and the movement closes with the chord progression that had begun it, but less thickly scored, a little subdued. The scherzo (with triangle), Beethovenian of speed and metric cleverness, focuses on the three-note rhythm stated so prominently in the introduction and which goes on to become a constituent of nearly all the themes. The scherzo itself has a contrastive center section, *soste-*

nuto, with a broad melody first stated by flute and oboe; this should not be confused with the trio, which begins with a still gentle but rather livelier dance pattern for the woodwind choir and French horns. In the coda, the horn motive from the first movement is introduced in dialogue with the primary theme of the scherzo.

By now it's been well established that the symphony has cyclic elements, and we can confidently expect more action along these lines in the finale. A sinister introduction builds into the powerful French horn theme in E minor. Momentum gathers with the triplets, and the distant, yearning second theme expands into a second group of themes with a long, dancing digression on a "Three Blind Mice" motive. Moreover, the seam between the exposition and development is imperceptible, a point you grasp for certain when recollections of the *Largo* and scherzo creep into the fray. Next Dvořák demonstrates the close affinities between the finale theme and that of the *Largo,* and finally the theme of the first movement begins to reassert itself. This process of thematic integration takes priority over the recapitulating, and the arrival in the tonic E minor is long delayed. All this serves to release the last *stringendo:* horn calls, amalgamation of the first- and last-movement themes, galloping figures, and a titanic statement of the big chord progression from the *Largo*—now fully fleshed out, as though to make up for implications left unresolved earlier. There's a last fade and recall of the scherzo, and a last tutti on the main themes. The twelve-bar closing, *Allegro con fuoco,* ends in one of the very difficult final bars in the literature: a long-held chord diminishing in volume to *pianissimo.*

Concerto for Cello and Orchestra in B Minor, OP. 104

Allegro
Adagio ma non troppo
Finale: Allegro moderato

For cello solo; flutes I-II, oboes I-II, clarinets I-II, bassoons I-II; horns I-III, trumpets I-II, trombones I-III, tuba; timpani, triangle; strings

Composed 8 November 1894–9 February 1895, primarily in New York; revised through 11 July 1895; dedicated to Hanus Wihan (1855–1920), the cellist for whom it was composed

First performed 19 March 1896, by the London Philharmonic
Society, Leo Stern, soloist; Dvořák conducting
Published by N. Simrock (Berlin, 1896). *Inexpensive score: Great
Romantic Cello Concertos in Full Score* (New York: Dover, 1983)
Duration: about 45 minutes

Note well the distant, brooding motive in the clarinets as this concerto opens, for the end of the last movement dissolves into a long
reflection on the same material, as though recasting its sinister qualities in an affirmative light. It is often held that the Cello Concerto
reflects its composer's longing for his homeland, and this may in part
explain the choice of keys, the melancholy, and tendency to return
again and again to his woods-and-groves idiom. But these are of course
constituents of Dvořák's high style, homesick or no: what is exceptional about the work is its symphonic scope and the substantial role
for the orchestra, an intimate, familial relationship between the soloist and his colleagues in the ensemble.

The clarinet melody introduces the principal material of a long,
rhapsodic orchestral exposition, expanding first into a *grandioso* statement for the full orchestra, then gradually turning to the warm and
memorable second theme in the solo French horn, carried on by the
solo clarinet. (This is one of the things I mean by "intimate relationship": the cellist will have the very same second theme, but Dvořák
is not afraid to have the solo winds share the limelight; it's a wonderful moment for both the wind soloists, with many more to come.) A
little polka serves to close the orchestra's half of the exposition. The
soloist, on entering, emphasizes from the first the triple stops, passagework, and leaps into extremes of register that show why the concerto is such a superb vehicle for the cellist—and how well the composer
had mastered his understanding of the instrument. The cellist has a
lively new transition of staccato sixteenths over bouncing bassoons,
and from here on things are exquisite indeed: the throbbing oboe and
bassoon at the next junction, the hushed second theme and passagework that follows it, the playful dialogue with the woodwinds, and
the headlong tumble into the orchestral tutti that concludes the exposition. But for one emotional swell, the development treats the quieter elements of the given material. The recapitulation occurs in reverse
order and in the major mode; in lieu of a cadenza comes a florid coda

for the cellist and victorious fanfares in the brass to conclude.

The second movement, in G major, begins as a simple song form, again for the clarinet. The cellist enters to reiterate the first phrase, then joins with the clarinets in a new phrase, soaring ardently into its highest reaches to peak and then retreat, panting, into a cadence; a reprise of the opening clarinet melody commences. The full orchestra with thundering trombone and tuba banish it with a grave gesture in the minor mode, but the soloist, unfazed, reenters with another delicate melody—this one based on a Dvořák song, much beloved by his sister-in-law, whom he knew to be terminally ill. Again, the thunder interrupts; again, the soloist carries on, and finally, French horns recapitulate the first half of the opening material. Now the cellist has the extended cadenza that was conspicuously lacking from the first movement, accompanied by all sorts of open-air warblings from the winds and distant thunder of timpani. Ever so quietly, the movement fades reluctantly away into this sylvan splendor.

The *Finale* opens with the approach of a sinister march, building into a great tutti with triangle. The cellist, never to be threatened, recasts the march into a resolute rondo theme. In fact there's little mystery, but a rather light-hearted romp, with a sweet contrasting section and a single strong return of the rondo at the center. At the end the rondo theme is expanded into a brass chorale. For a moment pointed references to the concerto's beginning are to be heard, but these are tamed and then swept away in the jubliant concluding bars.

Eight Slavonic Dances, OP. 46

1. *Presto* 2. *Allegretto scherzando* 3. *Poco Allegro* 4. *Tempo di Minuetto* 5. *Allegro vivace* 6. *Allegretto scherzando* 7. *Allegro assai* 8. *Presto*

Eight Slavonic Dances, OP. 72

1. *Molto vivace* 2. *Allegretto grazioso* 3. *Allegro* 4. *Allegretto grazioso* 5. *Poco adagio* 6. *Moderato, quasi Menuetto* 7. *Allegro vivace* 8. *Grazioso e lento, ma non troppo, quasi tempo di Valse*

For piccolo, flutes I-II, oboes I-II, clarinets I-II, bassoons I-II;
horns I-IV, trumpets I-II, trombones I-III; timpani, bass drum,
cymbals, triangle, glockenspiel; strings
Composed 1878 and 1886–87, first as piano duets; opus 46
orchestrated April–22 August 1878; opus 72 orchestrated
November 1886–5 January 1887
First performed (selections from op. 46) 16 May 1878, in Prague
at a concert sponsored by the Academy of Czech Journalists,
Adolf Čech conducting; selections from op. 72 first performed 6
January 1887 in Prague, Dvořák conducting
Published by N. Simrock (Berlin, 1878 and 1887). *Inexpensive
score* (of the opus 46 dances): Antonín Dvořák: *Slavonic Dances,
op. 46 in Full Score* (New York: Dover, 1987)
Duration: about 45 minutes for each opus

The opus 46 set of Slavonic Dances, played in England, France, and
Germany within a few months of their publication, established Dvořák's international popularity. They remain, along with the more refined
second set, opus 72, audience favorites and in their recorded form,
classical best-sellers; they are moreover among the most common cur-
tain-raisers, encores, and radio fillers in the classical repertoire. Clearly
Dvořák has captured in timeless fashion the essence of a folk tradition
that has universal allure.

For folk dancing lies at the very center of the Bohemian and Moravian cultures: circle dances, leaping dances, chases, galops, and
(increasingly, in the nineteenth century) polkas, typically accompanied by a tiny band of clarinet, violins, and bagpipe. They have names
like *furiant* (alternating $\frac{3}{4}$ and $\frac{2}{4}$, or $\frac{3}{4}$ with strong cross accents and
hemiolas), *dumka* (alternating slow and fast, melancholy and gay),
and such unpronounceables at *kvapík* (a galop: fast and in $\frac{2}{3}$) and *skočná*
(a hopping leap). It would be pointless to try to isolate them, in part
because Dvořák tends to mingle elements of several patterns in a single dance. Observe, instead, the strong prevalence of triple meter in
the dances, and how the polka-like movements in $\frac{2}{4}$ afford the necessary respite from all those threes. Note, too, another aspect of traditional Czech poetry and dance, the strongly accentuated downbeats of
phrases, whether the prevailing rhythms are short-long or long-short:
there's scarcely an upbeat to be found in music of this sort.

It's a music of contrasts: between major and minor, fast and slow, two groups of three beats and three groups of two. The forms, like the phrase groupings, are symmetrical (which heightens the effect of the metric ploys). Almost invariably there are two phrases of the main dance and a trio following. Dvořák is at his most unfettered here, and many of the tunes are among his best.

The most popular of the dances probably come from opus 46, particular the furious ones, nos. 1 and 8, the latter with its long subsiding coda and concluding presto. My own favorites are from opus 72: the tender *Allegretto grazioso,* no. 2, a slow waltz that begins with delicate violins over pizzicato rhythms and continues with a fluttery section for the woodwinds with violins, the whole in a particularly ravishing orchestration. This set ends unusually and well: the finale is actually the seventh dance, *Allegro vivace,* a brilliant polka with subplots and a stretto ending; the last dance, no. 8, is introspective and lingering, as though the composer is loathe to be done.

Edward Elgar

Born 2 June 1857 in Broadheath,
near Worcester
Died *23 February 1934 in Worcester*

The most important English composer between Purcell and Benjamin Britten, Elgar rose by virtue of his art to a prominence well above that of his inherited station in one of the most class conscious of modern societies. From humble beginnings in the provinces, he acceded to the ancient and honorable title Master of the King's Musick—first composer, that is, to the British Empire at the time of its maximum hegemony. His father, William Henry Elgar, was proprietor of the Worcester music shop Elgar Bros., later the organist of the Catholic church there. (He subsequently converted, and Edward Elgar was raised a Catholic.) Elgar had little formal education, but his practical experience as assistant organist to his father and pit musician elsewhere in the region taught him most of what he needed to know and gave him street wisdom as well. He sang in the local glee club and took violin lessons; from 1879 he was bandmaster for the insane asylum; from 1882, conductor of the Worcester Amateur Instrumental Society. In 1885 he succeeded his father as organist of St. George's Roman Catholic Church.

In 1889 he married a patrician, Caroline Alice Roberts. She encouraged him to undertake major compositions and maintained a quiet household where he could concentrate on composing music. Their period of residence in London was unsuccessful, for Elgar failed to attract either composition students or ongoing performances. In 1891 the Elgars returned to Worcestershire and took a house in the town of Malvern. Here his reputation began to grow, and his *Imperial March* for Queen Victoria's Diamond Jubilee in 1897 at last conquered London. In 1899 and 1900 he produced his two masterpieces, the "Enigma" Variations and *The Dream of Gerontius,* an oratorio to the poem of Cardinal Newman. The *Pomp and Circumstance* marches began to appear in 1901; in Elgar's *Coronation Ode* for Edward VII (1902) the stirring trio of the first march was given the text "Land of Hope and Glory," by Arthur C. Benson. The Elgars lived in Hereford and London from 1904 until his wife's death in 1920.

Elgar then retired to Worcester. Already decorated with the Order of Merit in 1911, he was knighted by George V in 1920 and made a baronet in 1931. He much enjoyed his dotage as a country gentleman, though he emerged from time to time to conduct and record his works. There is, for example, a fascinating 1932 recording of the Violin Concerto with Yehudi Menuhin, then 16 years of age, as soloist.

The major works for orchestra are the "Enigma" Variations; the five *Pomp and Circumstance* marches, op. 39 (1901–30); two symphonies (opp. 55, 1908; and 63, 1910), and concertos for violin and cello (opp. 61, 1910; and 85, 1919, respectively).

Variations on an Original Theme, OP. 36
("Enigma" Variations)

> *Enigma—C. A. E.—H. D. S.-P.—R. B. T.—*
> *W. M. B.—R. P. A.—Ysobel—Troyte—*
> *W. N.—Nimrod—Dorabella (Intermezzo)—G. R. S.—*
> *B. G. N.—* * *(Romanza)—E. D. U. (Finale)*
> [The movements are played without pause]

For piccolo, flutes I-II, oboes I-II, clarinets I-II, bassoons I-II, contrabassoon; horns I-IV, trumpets I-III; trombones I-III, tuba; timpani, snare drum, bass drum, cymbals, triangle; organ *ad libitum;* strings
Composed 1898–99 in Malvern; dedicated "to my friends pictured within"
First performed 19 June 1899 at one of Hans Richter's Orchestral Festival Concerts, St. James's Hall, London
Published by Novello & Co. (London, 1899)
Duration: about 30 minutes

The easy part is to identify the "friends pictured within." Elgar was, however, ambivalent about the work, grumpily arguing on the one hand that people should hear an abstract, pure theme and variations, while at the same time talking of "dark sayings" embraced therein and baiting us with all those initials and other mysterious allusions. Then he and his friends went on to identify themselves anyway. You might as well go ahead and read about them, memorialized as they were—like the otherwise ephemeral pictures at the exhibition—in a musical masterpiece. At length, however, you will probably be so taken with the fertility of invention unleashed in Elgar by the writing of variations that you may lose interest in which character is which.

Observe, at the start, the shape and structure of the theme, for these maintain a certain identity as the variations proceed. First there is a restless phrase built of three pairs of measures where the second bar rhythmically mirrors the undulations of the first; this begins in the minor mode and cadences in the major. The second phrase, of four bars, is built of a rather similar sequence that rises to a peak, then subsides into the third phrase, for all intents and purposes an embellished repeat of the first.

Variation I, C. A. E., has to do with Mrs. Elgar: Caroline Alice. Her music is richly scored, always passionate, perhaps somewhat nervous and reticent; and I hear many allusions to Brahms's *Haydn Variations* in the scoring at the start, and at the climax a clear reference to Wagner's *Liebestod.* H. D. S.-P. is H. D. Steuart-Powell, a pianist, whose finger exercises are reflected in a scherzo of the elfin manner. Richard Baxter Townshend (R. B. T.) was an amateur actor of buffoon roles: over a typically "clown of the orchestra" bassoon line, we hear the theme as a mazurka for oboe, then as a silly chromatic figure in the winds. William M. Baker (W. M. B.) was a temperamental country squire, and this movement was said by the composer to concern his scatterbrained summoning of carriages for his houseguests, slamming of the door, and subsequent tittering of the witnesses. Richard P. Arnold (R. P. A.), son of the poet Matthew Arnold, was a music lover given to melancholy conversation peppered with whimsical asides; this is one of the great variations in the set, particularly where, after the deep Brahmsian *largamente*s on the G-string of the violins, the whimsy breaks loose in the woodwinds and horns. Note particularly the charming passage for solo clarinet, with its tenuto at the beginning of each sextuplet. Elgar treats us to a reprise of this passage.

Ysobel is the violist Isabel Fitton, a pupil of the composer: thus a sensitive viola solo with a purposefully difficult string crossing at the beginning and, as Elgar put it, a touch of romance. (Tovey thought he detected here the "delicate aroma of a teacup.") Arthur Troyte Griffith was an architect and rather chaotic amateur pianist. Here, in a festive movement at dead center of the work, it is the timpani cross rhythms that most seize the ear. Such an expanse requires counterbalancing: Winifred Norbury (W. N.), secretary to the Worcester Philharmonic Society, was a sedate, tranquil lady yet fond of an occasional giggle. Nimrod, another of the priceless movements, recalls a summer evening walk with the critic August Jaeger. The opening is meant to suggest the beginning of the slow movement of Beethoven's *Pathétique* Sonata, the whole is of rich religious scoring, especially in the voicing of the French horns and bassoons at their entry. The title is a multicultural play on words: Jaeger is the German word for hunter, and Nimrod is a mighty hunter in the book of Genesis.

Dorabella was Miss Dora Penny, later the wife of the Steuart-Powell pictured above, nicknamed after the flighty heroine of Mozart's *Così fan tutte.* All the fluttering about between the violins and woodwinds is however the stuff of nineteenth-century ballet, offset to some degree by a contrastive center section and its reprise. (The charming Miss Penny / Mrs. Powell later wrote a monograph on the characters in the "Enigma" Variations.) G. R. S. was George Robertson Sinclair, organist of Hereford Cathedral. Actually the movement is said to describe Sinclair's dog Dan as he falls into the River Wye, paddles out, and barks with satisfaction at achieving dry land. The amateur cellist Basil G. Nevinson (B. G. N.) played in a trio with Elgar and is portrayed by a memorable cello variation with profound falls at the conclusion.

* * * was Lady Mary Lygon, who was at the time *en route* to Australia on a ship and thus could not be asked for permission to use her initials. We hear the clank of steam engines in the rattle of timpani hit with snaredrum sticks (or, as Elgar's timpanist preferred, big English pennies) and the piston-work in the viola section; the beginning of the clarinet melody, given in the score between quotation marks, is a citation from Mendelssohn's concert overture *Calm Sea and Prosperous Voyage.* The finale, E. D. U., is a self-portrait, the initials alluding to Lady Caroline's pet name for her husband, Edoo. It is a big, multifaceted movement citing passages from Lady Caroline's variation and from the great Nimrod movement. In proper English fashion, the pipe organ joins in the climax.

But Elgar would not explain the enigma. "Its dark saying must be left unguessed, and I warn you that the apparent connection between the variations and the theme is often of the slightest texture; further, through and over the whole set another and larger theme 'goes' but is not played."

Manuel de Falla

**Born 23 November 1876 in Cádiz
Died 14 November 1946 in Alta Gracia,
Argentina**

The most original and accomplished of the Spanish nationalist composers, Falla worked out the stylistic principles of his technique largely in the course of composing three works: the "symphonic impressions" called *Noches en los jardines de España* (Nights in the Gardens of Spain) and the two ballets, *El Amor brujo* (Love, the Magician, 1915) and *El Sombrero de tres picos* (The Three-Cornered Hat, 1919). That the Spanish elements are couched in a recognizably French idiom is one result of Falla's long residence in France (1907–14). There he made the acquaintance of Debussy and Ravel, composers who were themselves seduced by the irresistible lure of Spain. Another strong influence in those years was that of old Isaac Albéniz, resident in Paris since 1893. Like all ambitious nationalists, Falla was anxious that his art be a synthesis of native elements and international ones: viable, in short, universally.

He lived much of the rest of his life in Granada, surrounded by an intellectual circle that included the great Spanish poet Federico García Lorca, also an Andalusian. Andalusia was an area where west Asian, north African, and European cultures met and mingled. The musical manifestations of this crossing of cultures are found in its easily recognized dance rhythms, scale patterns, and instrumental practice. Andalusian music is that of the flamenco guitar and gypsy castanet; of the fandango, tarantella, sevillana; of florid vocalising about nighttime and magic.

These were the materials from which Falla's best art springs, though he was by no means ignorant of the rich heritage of classical music of the Spanish Middle Ages and Renaissance. His Concerto for Harpsichord with chamber ensemble (1923–26), written for Wanda Landowska, pays homage to these repertoires as well as to the music of Domenico Scarlatti, the pre-Classical keyboard composer who spent much of his career in Spain.

In 1939, weary of the Civil War and the certainty of pan-European conflict, Falla immigrated to Argentina, where he lived out his days in seclusion.

Noches en los jardines de España (Nights in the Gardens of Spain), Symphonic Impressions for Piano and Orchestra

En el Generalife (In the Generalife)
Danza lejana (Distant Dance)
En los jardines de la Sierra de Córdoba (In the Gardens of the Sierra de Córdoba)
[No pause between movements II and III]

For piano solo; piccolo, flutes I-II, oboes I-II, English horn, clarinets I-II, bassoons I-II; horns I-IV, trumpets I-II, trombones I-III, tuba; timpani, cymbals, triangle; celesta, harp; strings
Composed 1911–15, mostly in Paris; completed in Sitges, near Barcelona
First performed 9 April 1916, at the Teatro Real, Madrid, by the Arbós Orquesta Sinfónica, José Cubiles soloist; Enrique Fernández Arbós conducting
Published by Max Eschig (Paris, 1922)
Duration: about 25 minutes

The citadel called the Alhambra, perched on a plateau above Granada, is the palace from which the Moorish potentate governed. Here and in the environs are set Falla's three symphonic impressions. Among the outbuildings of the Alhambra is a villa called the Generalife, treasured by the Moorish princes for its water gardens, where one could gaze into a reflecting pool at the play of fountains and greenery, of light and shade.

Falla's first movement consists of a series of episodes that grow from (and return to) an undulating, typically Iberian figure heard at the very beginning in the viola and harp: now watery, now imbued with dance rhythms, now expansive, then introspective and improvisatory, and finally building into a pair of glistening, Debussy-like climaxes. In the second movement, the rhythmic and melodic motives of merrymaking heard in the distance are woven into a dialogue between the pianist and orchestra. It grows toward a feverish tempo, only to ebb away into reminiscences (in the celesta and high winds and strings) of what has gone before. Out of these grows a transition into the third movement, a savage dance with long glissandos in the twinkly instruments. The free passagework in the piano interludes is meant to suggest flamenco vocal improvisation. To conclude, a neo-Wagnerian "apotheosis" ending.

Noches en los jardines de España began as a series of solo piano nocturnes for Ricardo Viñes, the Spanish pianist then living in Paris, and is doubtless a homage to the balmy night-pieces of Debussy and Ravel. One of the composer's acquaintances said that the work sprang from a poem by Francis Jammes (1868–1938), poet of the French Pyrenees.

The work was later closely identified with the Polish pianist Arthur Rubinstein (1887–1982), who introduced it to the New World during an appearance in Buenos Aires. Do not expect a piano concerto: Falla's work is a suite of orchestral poems, where the piano has an important but not dominant role.

El Amor brujo (Love, the Magician), Andalusian Gypsy Scene in One Act

> *Introduction and Scene—Among the Gypsies (That Night)—Song of Heartsick Love—The Spectre—Dance of Terror—The Magic Circle (The Fisherman's Story)—Midnight (Sorceries)—Ritual*

Fire Dance (To Chase Away the Wicked Spirits)—Scene—Song of the Will-o'-the-Wisp—Pantomime—Dance of the Game of Love—Finale (The Morning Bells)

For voice (S.); piccolo, flutes I-II, oboe, clarinets I-II, bassoon; horns I-II, trumpets I-II, timpani, glockenspiel; piano; strings

Text and scenario by Gregorio Martínez Sierra (1881–1947), noted Spanish playwright and close associate of the composer

Composed 14 November 1914–15 April 1915 in Madrid. The original, one-woman version was revised in 1916 as a ballet with singing

First performed in its original version 2 April 1915 by Pastora Imperio at the Teatro Lara, Madrid, Moreno Ballesteros conducting; concert version first performed 28 March 1916 by the Orquesta Filharmónica of the Sociedad Nacional de Música, Bartolomé Pérez-Casas conducting

Published by J.& W. Chester, Ltd. (London, 1921)

Duration: about 25 minutes

It was natural for a Spanish composer to occupy himself with the ballet, for the Andalusian ethnic dance had long attracted the keen attention of classical dancers. During the nineteenth century the flamenco style and dances like the cachuca, jota, and fandango were cultivated for various sorts of theatricals, and dancers lacking a drop of Spanish blood were billed as the "the pearl of Seville" and "the star of Andalusia." Falla's particular concern here is with the *cante jondo* ("profound song," usually of anguish), the style of flamenco performance that embraces lavish wailing, exotic scales, guitar accompaniment, and much clapping of hands and stamping of feet.

The idea for the gypsy ballet was that of Pastora Imperio, a famous flamenco dancer and singer, who merely wanted what she called "a song and dance," a primitive *gitanería* ("gypsy piece"). Pastora's mother, Rosario la Mejorana, was also a noted flamenco artist, and Falla listened and took notes on their manner of performance as Martínez wrote down what he could of their inexhaustible lore of old gypsy tales.

This particular tale is of the gypsy Candélas, haunted by the thoughts of her dead, ne'er-do-well lover. Each time she embraces Carmélo, the new object of her affections, she sees the specter of her former mate. "Her memory of him," wrote Sierra, "is something like a hypnotic dream, a morbid, gruesome, maddening spell." It is arranged that another girl, Lucía, will woo the specter to divert his attention long enough for Candélas and Carmélo to exchange the kiss of perfect love. The spell is thus broken, dawn breaks, and the morning bells start to ring.

It is a tale of ancient ritual and black magic set in one of the gypsy caves of southernmost Spain. Candélas is found, at the beginning, reading her cards; she throws incense on the fire just before her ritual dance; a clock strikes twelve in the distance. The most famous passage, often excerpted, is the Ritual Fire Dance, of familiar melody and deftly understated crescendo. At the center is the Fisherman's Story, a "mystic circle" of calm, revolving harmonies that affords relief from the furies before and after. The poetic sentiments of Candélas's two songs are haunting indeed: in the first she sings of a dull flame in the soul which cannot be extinguished, in the second that "Love is a will-o'-the-wisp: you flee, and it pursues you." Falla never goes for long without his piano, which nearly always has the last word and often the critical role in the unusual and remarkably progressive harmonic twists with which the work abounds.

El Sombrero de tres picos (The Three-Cornered Hat)

Introduction
Part I: Afternoon—Dance of the Miller's Wife (Fandango)—The Grapes
Part II: The Neighbor's Dance (Seguidillas)—Dance of the Miller (Farruca)—The Corregidor's Dance—Final Dance (Jota)

For voice (Ms.); piccolos I-II, flutes I-II, oboes I-II, English horn, clarinets I-II, bassoons I-II; horns I-IV, trumpets I-III, trombones I-III, tuba; timpani, snare drum, bass drum, cymbals, triangle, castanets, tam-tam, xylophone; harp, celesta, piano; strings

Composed 1918–19 in Granada as the revision of a pantomime of 1917; scenario by Gregorio Martínez Sierra, after a novel by Pédro Alarcón (1833–91). The same novel served the librettist of Hugo Wolf's opéra, *Der Corregidor* (1895).

First performed 22 July 1919, at the Alhambra Theatre in London by Diaghilev's Ballets Russes with choreographer Léonide Massine as the miller and Tamara Karsavina as the miller's wife, Ernest Ansermet conducting; costumes and decor by Pablo Picasso

Published by J. & W. Chester, Ltd. (London, 1921); dedicated to Leopoldo Matos, Falla's lawyer, who negotiated the contract with Diaghilev. Two suites were drawn from the full ballet: these are the "Scenes and Dances from *El Sombrero de tres picos*" (Part I) and "Three Dances from *El Sombrero de tres picos*" (Part II).

Duration: about 35 minutes

Diaghilev's Ballets Russes took brief refuge from World War I in Granada and Seville, and there the Russian impresario's attention was drawn to Falla's work. He first hoped to fashion *Nights in the Gardens of Spain* as a ballet, but soon elected to adapt instead Falla's pantomime of 1917, *El Corregidor y la molinera* (The Magistrate and the Miller's Wife), for which he assembled a memorable team of collaborators. Falla, Diaghilev, the choreographer Léonide Massine, and the dance star Felix García toured Andalusia together to study the native musicians and dancers. None other than Picasso was engaged for the costumes and decor, which included a magnificent front-drop depicting a bullfight.

Shortly thereafter the ballet troupe found employment in London. By that time García had become too ill to dance, and his part was taken by Massine. On the afternoon of the first performance, Falla was summoned by telegram back to Madrid to his mother's deathbed. The Swiss conductor Ernest Ansermet stepped in to conduct. Falla's ballet was an overnight success.

The story takes place in the eighteenth century in a small Spanish village. The miller and his wife live in a mill-house by a bridge, their esplanade shaded by a vine from which hang enormous clusters of grapes. A naughty blackbird is caged there, and we see, too, a portion of the living quarters, dominated by an imposing conjugal bed. It is afternoon.

The homely miller and his beautiful wife flirt with the passersby. The corregidor enters, oblivious that the grotesque hat, symbol of his authority, is the object of collective derision. When the miller's wife returns a glove he has let fall, he is smitten. Later he returns to court the wife; she, pretending not to notice him, dances a purposefully erotic fandango. Then she tempts and teases him with a bunch of the grapes until he falls exhausted to the ground. The miller and his wife resume the fandango.

That evening is St. John's Night, a time of merrymaking. The neighbors come onstage and the miller dances a big solo piece (added for Massine). The corregidor's inquisitors arrive (to Beethoven's "fate knocking at the door" motive) and arrest the miller, as the guests flee. The miller's wife is left alone as a distant gypsy warns wives to bar their doors lest a devil come to call. Her song ends with the call of a cuckoo, followed by a cuckoo clock striking nine. The corregidor, having fallen in the water as he crossed the bridge, enters dripping wet, removes his clothes, and gets into the bed. Chaos ensues: the miller returns and infers the worst; the corregidor and the miller end up in each other's garments; the inquisitors pursue the wrong man; the merrymakers wrap the hated corregidor in a blanket and toss him around like a puppet.

Falla's music is gracious and restrained, based largely on traditional melodies, and with a host of technical clevernesses to reflect the action on stage. You can virtually see the ballet in your mind's eye, especially if you follow Falla's synopsis, where each new turn of events is cued to a number in the piano score. Indeed you must try, in a concert performance, to imagine the dancing, for otherwise the *jota* at the end, a castanet dance in triple meter, is the only really thrilling segment. The introduction, with its distant *olés* and clapping, was an addition demanded by Diaghilev to allow the audience to admire Picasso's front-drop when the curtains first parted.

Yet here as elsewhere in Falla, the orchestral brushwork is wonderfully delicate. Listen, for example, for the well music (complete with creaky winch) in the first tableau, accomplished with high piccolos and string harmonics. Strings are used in solos, pairs, or a half-section at a time, and though the work calls for a full brass section, the trombones and third and fourth horns enter for the first time in the concluding dance. The piano, as in *Nights in the Gardens of Spain,* provides the arabesques and arpeggiations demanded by the style. The guitar, whose textures and practices literally define the idiom, does not appear at all, and castanets are heard only at the beginning and end. Instead the whole orchestra conveys the spirit of a music dominated by one voice and guitar.

The first bassoon player, who portrays the wily corregidor instrumentally, should get a solo bow.

Gabriel Fauré

Born 12 May 1845 in
Pamiers, near Toulouse
Died 4 November 1924 in Paris

Grand maître of French music in the generation between Saint-Saëns and Ravel, Fauré quite dominated the traditional Paris venues, serving as organist to several of the major churches, director of the Conservatoire (though he had not been a student there), co-founder of an important new music association called the Société Nationale, composer of important works for the stage, and not a bad newspaper critic. He was (likewise in the French tradition) a fine teacher, among whose students were Ravel and Nadia Boulanger. But his seminal contribution was to sire a new generation of French song. He was, for example, the first to set the ravishing poetry of Paul Verlaine, and *La bonne chanson* (1894), his Verlaine song cycle for voice and piano, proves beyond a doubt his stature as a master of the *mélodie*.

Fauré was schooled in Paris for eleven years, primarily in church music, at the École Niedermeyer, and by the time he graduated at the age of 20 had garnered first prizes in virtually all the subjects they offered. After a brief period as organist in the provinces—he was dismissed from Rennes for playing a morning service still attired in his evening clothes—he returned to Paris to follow in the footsteps of Saint-Saëns, his most important teacher. Appointed substitute organist for Saint-Saëns at the Madeleine, he later acceeded first to the position of chorus master and then (1896) to that of first organist.

For a time Fauré was engaged to Marianne Viardot, daughter of the great singer Pauline Viardot; after she withdrew from the match, he married a straightlaced shrew, Marie Fremiet, from whom he often strayed. His adult life, however, is best characterized as a never-ending struggle with professional over-commitment.

Fauré, ever a great melodist, is equally adroit at crafting marvels of supporting texture. His experiments with modal scales and the subtlest forms of dissonance paved the way for some of the most imaginative strokes by Ravel and Debussy. Both Fauré works in the orchestral repertoire, the Requiem and the *Pelléas et Mélisande* suite, are relatively early ones. Additionally to be heard in the orchestra hall are the *Dolly* Suite, orchestrated in 1912 by Henri Rabaud (for use as a ballet) from a piano four-hand contribution to the nursery genre; and the suite *Masques et bergamasques,* op. 112, composed in 1920. My own favorite is the sultry *Pavane,* op. 50, of 1877.

Pelléas et Mélisande Suite, OP. 80

Prélude
Andantino quasi Allegretto [Fileuse (Spinning Song)]
Sicilienne (de Pelléas et Mélisande)
Molto Adagio [Mort de Mélisande]

For flutes I-II, oboes I-II, clarinets I-II, bassoons I-II; horns I-IV, trumpets I-II; timpani; harps; strings
Composed: 16 May–5 June 1898 at the invitation of Mrs. Patrick Campbell, the actress; first orchestration (unpublished) by Charles Koechlin; revised orchestration by the composer with Koechlin; dedicated to Princess Edmond de Polignac. The *Sicilienne,* op. 78 (1893) was added to the suite in 1909; it had originally been composed for the English cellist, W. H. Squire.
First performed with the play as incidental music, orchestrated by

Charles Koechlin, 21 June 1898 at the Prince of Wales Theatre,
London, Fauré conducting; the suite first performed in a
Concert Lamoureux, 3 February 1901, Camille Chevillard
conducting; the suite with the fourth movement first performed
1 December 1912 by the Société des Concerts du Conservatoire,
Paris, André Messager conducting
Published by J. Hamelle (Paris, 1901); *Sicilienne* incorporated
1909
Duration: about 20 minutes

It isn't especially surprising that Maeterlinck's surrealist play *Pelléas
et Mélisande* (1892–93) is remembered, at least by music lovers, mostly
in terms of Debussy's extraordinary opera: that is a historic meeting
of genius. Other composers, however, also tried their hands at *Pelléas
et Mélisande* music. Schoenberg wrote a symphonic poem after Maeterlinck's drama, and Sibelius and Fauré each wrote incidental music
for productions of the play. Fauré's *Pelléas et Mélisande* was the first of
them all.

Fauré composed his incidental music for the 1898 production in
London, where he often traveled to visit good friends. (Debussy had
declined the commission.) In the rush to be done on time, he enlisted
the help of his former student, Charles Koechlin (1867–1950), to
orchestrate the eight movements of his piano score for small theatre
orchestra. Later Fauré himself extracted three movements from the
incidental music to fashion a suite for full orchestra. As the *Pelléas et
Mélisande* suite achieved popularity in concert performances, he added
a fourth movement, his *Sicilienne* for cello and piano, opus 78, likewise orchestrated by Koechlin. The published editions of 1909 and
thereafter include that movement.

The *Pelléas et Mélisande* suite is an attractive example of Fauré's style
in that the miniatures are so similar to his vocal music—songs, that
is, without words. In the *Spinning Song,* for example, the oboe is the
(primary) singer, as is the flute in the *Sicilienne.* The melodies of both
clearly suggest utterances of the human voice.

The prelude music introduces the scene in which we find Mélisande
lost by a fountain in the forest, seized by yearning she cannot explain.
In the distance is heard the horn call of Golaud, who will discover
her there. The *Spinning Song* came before the famous love scene in the
third act where Mélisande at the window of her apartment and Pelléas

below first acknowledge their passion—to each other and to themselves. Listen for the rapid spinning figure in the upper strings, *pianissimo,* and for the conversational interplay of soprano and tenor melodies, particularly when the second theme wells up from solo clarinet and horn. The jealous Golaud kills his half-brother Pelléas and (it transpires) mortally wounds Mélisande at the end of act IV. Her dead march came as the last entr'acte and also during the scene at her bedside. The thematic contours are derived from the tenor melody of the *Spinning Song,* so closely associated with rapturous yet forbidden love.

Requiem (*Messe de Requiem*), OP. 48

Introït et Kyrie
Offertoire
Sanctus
Pie Jesu
Agnus Dei
Libera me
In Paradisum

For soloists (S., Bar.), chorus; flutes I-II, clarinets I-II, bassoons I-II; horns I-IV, trumpets I-II, trombones I-III, timpani; harps, organ; divided strings

Composed 1886–87 for strings with organ, harp, and timpani; unpublished; revised 1887–1900: enlarged for baritone and soprano with a *Libera me* of 1877, and reorchestrated with brass and woodwinds, 1900

First performed in the original version 16 January 1888 at the Madeleine; version II first performed 21 January 1893 at the Madeleine; version III first performed 12 July 1900 at the Trocadéro with Mlle Torrès, soprano, Jean Vallier, baritone, Eugène Gigout, organ, and the Lamoureux orchestra, Paul Taffanel conducting

Published by J. Hamelle (Paris, 1900–1)

Duration: about 40 minutes

Fauré's Requiem, a favorite of choruses everywhere, is unusual in that it omits the *Dies irae,* that terrifying centerpiece of the Requiem masses of Mozart, Berlioz, and Verdi. Rather the imagery is of untroubled slumber: that Fauré lingers again and again on the word "requiem,"

Latin for rest, is no coincidence, nor is the predominance of movements with serene texts (*Sanctus, Pie Jesu, Agnus Dei, In Paradisum*). About half the words come from less familiar passages in the Latin services for the dead, though in this and other respects Fauré's Requiem is squarely in line with the traditions of French funeral music. You should, indeed, endeavor to picture the Paris church of the Madeleine when you hear this work, for it was within that imposing though anachronistic edifice that Fauré spent much of his career, where the work was first performed, and where it served as the music for Fauré's own funeral.

The composer's view of death is conveyed in the prevailing homophonic textures and by the muted colors of the orchestration, which relies strongly on the sonorities of subdivided violas, cellos, bassoons, French horns, and the quieter ranks of the organ. The organ, supporting the structure, walks along in neo-Baroque fashion but for occasional eruptions of grander material. For the rest of the orchestra, it's largely a matter of counting rests. The two trumpets are used, sparingly, merely to enrich the French horn textures; flutes and clarinets appear only in the *Pie Jesu,* with trombones and timpani in the *Libera me* alone. Moreover, though harp-like arpeggios abound in the accompaniment figurations, the harps are to be heard only in the *Sanctus, Pie Jesu,* and *In Paradisum.* (The explanation for this lopsided orchestration lies partly in the long genesis of the work over three distinct versions, of which you need be concerned only with the third.)

Fauré's Requiem is, then, a soothing, almost passive composition. Note how often, for example, material is presented by the tenor section in unison of striking naiveté. The movements tend to be simple rounded structures. In the second, for instance, the solo baritone has, in the middle, a splendid *Hostias* intoned over pulsating strings, with on either side the imitative *Domine Jesus Christe.* The great movements are the *Libera me*—likewise for the baritone soloist, a stirring, noble march of reassurance in the face of reckoning—and just before it the *Agnus Dei,* a lullaby for tenors with a recollection of the opening *Requiem* toward the end.

The celestial movements (*Sanctus, Pie Jesu* with the single appearance of the soprano soloist, and *In Paradisum*) are a little syrupy, with the high violins, angelic sopranos, and harps all but inevitable in music of this sort. The French tend to think of paradise in pastel hues; there's always a harp and an organ to be heard, and women and children. Either you like this kind of thing or you don't; Fauré manages it about as well as any.

There's something private and quietly personal about Fauré's Requiem, perhaps the result of his having undertaken to compose it during the period when he lost both parents. Not all of us are heroes enough to merit the heroic Requiems of Berlioz or Verdi anyway: this tender work is a Requiem for everyman.

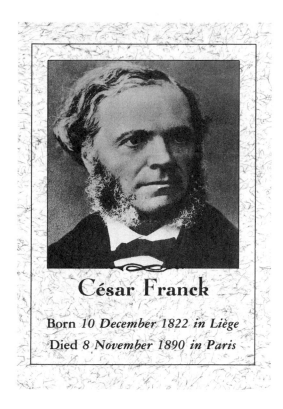

César Franck

Born *10 December 1822 in Liège*
Died *8 November 1890 in Paris*

Franck was by birth a Belgian, though most of his career was spent in and around Paris, and he became a naturalized citizen of France. His father urged music on the children rather zealously, and eventually had César enrolled in the Paris Conservatoire. But the father opposed his son's interest in composition, and partly for that reason Franck spent much of his life as a keyboard player and teacher, composing mostly between 5:30 and 7:30 A.M. and during summer recesses from his academic duties. His appointments as organist, culminating in 1858 with a prestigious post at the church of Ste.-Clotilde in Paris, were felicitous in that they brought him into daily contact with the distinguished organ builder Aristide Cavaillé-Coll, also a Belgian. At length, Franck was appointed professor of organ at the Conservatoire, from which post he led and molded the French organ school of the second half of the century. In terms of quantity, at least, his repertoire for organ significantly overshadows his symphonic composition.

Franck's orchestral style is thus for obvious reasons permeated with the dense chordal sonorities, rank-by-rank scorings, and parallelisms of motion familiar to him from the acoustical and mechanical properties of the pipe organ. The Symphonic Variations for Piano and Orchestra and the Symphony in D Minor have achieved enduring places in the orchestral repertoire; the symphonic poems *Le Chasseur maudit* (The Cursed Huntsman, 1882), *Les Djinns* (1884), and *Psyché* (1887–88) are worth hearing as well. Franck's other masterpieces include an oratorio called *Les Béatitudes* (1869–79), the Violin Sonata in A (1886), and the String Quartet in D (1889). All these works come from the last fifteen years of his life, the period of his greatest interest in composition.

Franck was not an especially practical man, oblivious to the politics of music-making in the most politically inclined of all musical capitals. He was uncomfortable to find himself at the center of artistic squabbles and being proclaimed prophet of the moderns. He preferred a quiet life with his students and his manuscript paper. His organ classes at the Conservatoire amounted to seminars in improvisatory composition instead of master classes on technique or repertoire. Though this did not please the technically minded, it had the effect that, one way or another, virtually the entire next generation of French composers benefitted from Franck's tutelage.

Symphony in D Minor

Lento; Allegro non troppo
Allegretto
Allegro non troppo

For flutes I-II, oboes I-II, English horn, clarinets I-II, bass clarinet, bassoons I-II; horns I-IV, trumpets I-II, cornets *à pistons* I-II, trombones I-III, tuba; timpani; harps; strings

Composed 1886–22 August 1888 in Paris; dedicated to Henri Duparc, the composer

First performed 17 February 1889 by the Société des Concerts du Conservatoire, Jules Garcin conducting

Published by J. Hamelle (Paris, 1896; posthumous). *Inexpensive*

score: César Franck: *Symphony in D Minor in Full Score* (New York: Dover, 1987)
Duration: about 45 minutes

It is difficult not to use the term Wagnerian to describe Franck's D-Minor Symphony, with its opening motto so like the Fate motive in the *Ring* and its subsequent obsession with rising four-note chromatics, so like *Tristan.* But in fact the *mélange* of references in this curious work from the very end of the composer's career includes hints of the Mendelssohnian scherzo, the improvisational practice of ninteenth-century organists, and a couple of direct references to late Beethoven as well. The thick textures, which can seem grossly overdoubled unless carefully handled by the performers, are in equal measure descended from mid-century grand opera styles and a function of the way organs work. The D-Minor Symphony is Franck's only effort in the genre.

What you remember, once you get beyond the titillation of its bigness, is Franck's wide-eyed frolic through the tonal system. The strong chromaticism of both the melodies and the chords that support them invites sudden blossom into some unthought-of but bright new tonal center, usually upward, and the violent wrenching of things back down into their proper key for a new theme group or for recapitulation. Franck speaks in long phrases that beg reiteration in varying guises.

The troubled three-note motto in the first bar, repeated in the second on a higher scale degree, is the germ from which Franck derives much of his subsequent melodic material. (Compare this motive to the very similar one at the beginning of Liszt's *Les Préludes;* see p. 321). The slow introduction, dominated by eerie instrumentation—low strings, horns, bassoons, and then tuba—portends the stormy eruption of an *Allegro,* which begins with the same motive. This is scarcely under way before you have a full repetition of all that has come so far, transposed up from D minor to F minor. When the sonata gets moving again—when you finally sense a structure in the making—it yields up a second theme in the strings, *cantabile,* and an unmistakably significant closing theme stated by the entire orchestra, now under full steam.

The recapitulation puts the motto opening in canon, with trumpets answering. Toward the end, Franck makes abundantly clear that the motto and the big closing theme are to be remembered, and the movement closes with that familiar Baroque inflection called a Picardy third—raising the minor mode into major.

This is cunning stuff, so far as it goes, but to my way of thinking rather prolix. The second movement, by contrast, seems a real conceptual triumph. Here Franck elides the two middle movements common to a symphony of the time—slow movement and scherzo—into one, such that in due course three "bars" of the scherzo equal one of the *Allegretto*. (This is accomplished by notating the scherzo figure in triplets in $\frac{3}{4}$.) It begins, in minor, as a slow march in triple meter over a repeating bass pattern, again neo-Baroque in manner. In the first of a series of variations over the bass, the English horn solo embraces suggestions of the motto from the first movement. (Here there are many parallels with passages from the *Variations symphoniques* for piano and orchestra, described below.) At the center of the movement appears the minor-mode scherzo with major-mode trio, from which grows a synthesis of all these elements and themes.

The third movement is one of those resolution-of-stress affairs, its melodies largely transformations of what has come before. The brass choir has a field day, especially in the tuba-dominated chorale which serves as the second subject. Reference to the main theme and scherzo of the second movement presage a series of triple-versus-duple ploys and the recollection of the other themes that you have probably been expecting to occur. The harp arpeggios at the end announce a last reminiscence of the various motives, now in their tamed state.

The premiere of Franck's D-Minor Symphony was for some weeks the talk of Paris. The Conservatory Orchestra disliked the work, and Vincent d'Indy reported the *bon mot* of one listener: "That was a symphony? Who ever heard of an English horn in a symphony?" Franck, for his part, said it sounded like he thought it would.

Variations symphoniques pour piano et orchestre

For piano solo; flutes I-II, oboes I-II, clarinets I-II, bassoons I-II; horns I-IV, trumpets I-II; timpani; strings
Composed 1885 in Azille
First performed   1 May 1886, by the Société Nationale, Paris, Louis Diémer, soloist, Jules Pasdeloup conducting

Published by Enoch frères & Costallat (Paris, 1893)
Duration: about 15 minutes.

Composers like Franck who are gifted improvisers take to variation practice like ducks to water. The Symphonic Variations constitute Franck's most convincing work for orchestra, their relatively limited structural demands perfect for his gifts. The tunes, harmonic colors, and textures are striking indeed. The form is less attention-getting than the easy synthesis of the themes, intertwined from the beginning, and the graceful, idiomatic work for the piano.

There are three big sections of approximately equal length: an introduction, variations on a theme, and a finale. In the first eight bars you hear the two most significant motives, a dotted figure for orchestra and its consequent, a simple, rather soulful four bars of drooping character stated by the piano.

Now the meter shifts into $\frac{3}{4}$, and what earlier seemed merely a transition now becomes a theme with six variations. Don't try to count them; enjoy, rather, the dialogue of orchestra and soloist, the gradual growth in intensity, the weaving in of the motives from the introduction, and the willowy scamper of the pianist over dense chord progressions in the strings.

The long trill in the piano and return of duple meter signal the beginning of the finale, a sonata-rondo of sorts, though again it does not pay to worry too much about this. A fine, pompous new version of the dotted figure makes its appearance in the piano, followed by a sextuple pulse in the piano along with a quadruple pulse in the orchestra. In the coda, orchestra and soloist chase each other to the final cadence.

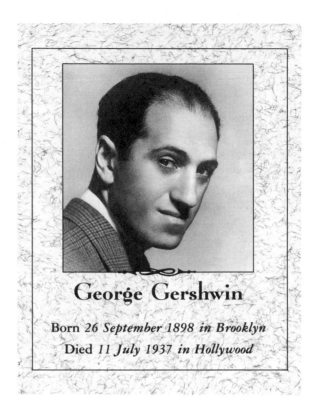

George Gershwin

Born *26 September 1898 in Brooklyn*
Died *11 July 1937 in Hollywood*

It's typical in essays like these to dwell on how poor and shrivelled were Gershwin's roots in Jewish Brooklyn, on the paucity of his formal study, and on his having had to plug songs in Tin Pan Alley. (Flog is more like it: Gershwin developed his improvisational fertility, it is said, to keep from going mad playing the same song over and over again on the sidewalk in front of Remick's publishing house.) The fact is that Gershwin's genius was clear by the time he was a teenager, and that in his twenties he was already enjoying the LA-New York-Paris life-style you know about from Scott and Zelda Fitzgerald and from *Citizen Kane. Swanee,* which he wrote when he was nineteen or twenty, sold over two million records—a hit single if ever there was one. His musicals *Lady Be Good* (1924), *Strike Up the Band* (1927), and *Of Thee I Sing* (1931; winner of a Pulitzer Prize)—to cite only three—earned big money and headlines in the newspapers. The movie *Shall We Dance?* (1937; Gershwin died before it was released) includes three good songs as well. In much of this he was inestimably assisted by his brother Ira (1896–1983), his principal lyricist.

Gershwin's masterpiece, *Porgy and Bess* (1935), is quite simply the most moving opera an American has yet produced. If you come from the South, as I do, you begin to weep uncontrollably at about *Summertime,* which is in the first scene. Bring plenty of Kleenex.

Gershwin spent much of his artistic maturity unnecessarily troubled by what he perceived as the weaknesses in his technical formation. Throughout his short career he was to be found trying to perfect his grasp of traditional principles with noted teachers, several of them serious about it, others bemused by his neurosis. ("Why do you want to be a Ravel," Ravel is said to have inquired, "when you are a perfectly fine Gershwin?") His great gift was that of melody: he could pull from his imagination tunes that exude the hopes and heritage of the nation: consider *Summertime* or the song of the Strawberry Woman in *Porgy and Bess,* the plantation-style English horn theme in the Piano Concerto, the "homesickness blues" in *An American in Paris.* He had the uncanny ability to fashion a kind of music that sits at the juncture of half a dozen styles and tastes, such that the net result seems distinctly all-American.

Gershwin's powers as an orchestrator were considerably greater than the gossip would have you believe. Ferde Grofé orchestrated the *Rhapsody in Blue,* it is true, and Gershwin had some help with other works, but that is part and parcel of the New York theater scene. His ability to notate legibly the complex material he improvised is just one proof of the magnitude of his technique. Gershwin's limitation was his discomfort with structures more complicated than the short song forms that came so naturally to him. Put another way, he had difficulty with the notion of development. And that patronizing Teutonic charge has been leveled for two centuries at gifted composers who were primarily melodists, including all Italians and most of the French. Gershwin is in good company.

The seriousness of his purpose, indeed, the intensity of his concerns, sets him a length ahead of Irving Berlin and Jerome Kern, the other fine songsmiths of his generation. It is one of the reasons he was so admired by the European establishment: Bartók, Ravel, Vaughan Williams, and even Berg and Schoenberg. (In Hollywood, Gershwin painted a picture of the latter as good as Schoenberg's own self-portraits.) Gershwin's tragedy is not, then, a matter of his humble beginnings or flaws of craft, but of his untimely death at the age of thirty-eight from brain cancer. He died during an operation to remove the tumor.

Beyond the Big Three orchestral compositions—*Rhapsody in Blue,* the Piano Concerto, and *An American in Paris*—there are an early Lullaby for String Quartet, a Second Rhapsody (the first being *Rhapsody in Blue*) for Orchestra and Piano (1931), a *Cuban Overture* (1932), and Variations for Piano and Orchestra on "I Got Rhythm" (1934). A suite from *Porgy and Bess* was left unpublished at his death; this was named *Catfish Row* by Ira Gershwin to distinguish it from the several orchestral syntheses of the opera then in vogue. The piano, at which Gershwin was at his best and most spontaneous, plays a major role in all of his music.

The Big Three, by the way, fit conveniently on a single disc and all too often make an obvious Gershwin Night at the symphony. My feeling about that is the same as for the *Brandenburgs:* these compositions are best savored one by one, and Gershwin Night should not be encouraged.

Rhapsody in Blue

> For flutes I-II, oboes I-II, English horn, clarinets I-II, bass clarinet, saxophones I-III, bassoons I-II; horns I-IV, trumpets I-III, trombones I-II, tuba; timpani, snare drum, bass drum, cymbals, bells; banjo; strings.
>
> Composed over three weeks in January–February 1924, New York, to a commission from Paul Whiteman for his big band; later revised and reorchestrated for symphony orchestra
>
> First performed in its original version 12 February 1924 by Paul Whiteman and his orchestra at the Aeolian Hall, New York; Gershwin, soloist
>
> Published by New World Music (New York, 1924)
>
> Duration: about 15 minutes

Gershwin was but one of many American artists given their big break by Paul Whiteman (1890–1967), the "King of Jazz." (Among the others were Benny Goodman and Bing Crosby.) Whiteman commissioned "something" from Gershwin for his 1924 Lincoln's Birthday concert of symphonic jazz in Aeolian Hall, New York—a historic event, this, with formidable ramifications for both popular and classical music in the United States. When the composer read in the New York *Herald-Tribune* that he was at work on a jazz concerto, he decided he had better get busy, and thereupon produced this famous blues for piano and instrumental accompaniment

Whiteman's orchestrator Ferde Grofé scored the work for jazz band, what we would today call a big band. He later redid the work in a couple of versions to enable performance by standard symphony orchestra. The famous clarinet glissando at the beginning was the contribution of one of Whiteman's reed players, Ross Gorman.

Three major themes are mingled in a free form related to the A-A-B structure of a conventional blues: the improvisational turn with which the work opens (clarinet), the shuffling blues melody you hear just afterward in the winds (clarinet, horn, tenor sax), and a strutting, marchlike business heard in the position of the second theme group over snapping pizzicati in the strings, banjo, and drum set with brushes. From this last grows, as a refrain some two-thirds of the way through, the soulful theme in strings and woodwinds with panting extensions in the horn—which you remember along with the clarinet gliss as the most impressive thing about *Rhapsody in Blue*. Little more need be said: in fact Gershwin seems almost impatient, thereafter, to bring the work to a prompt close.

Naturally there is a good deal of bluesy chromatic inflection of the melodies, and the soloist and orchestra generally alternate turns with the given material, as is customary in jazz practice. But what Gershwin is really about here is jazz rhythm: *Rhapsody in Blue* should be played with great freedom and swing, even by the stuffiest of philharmonic societies.

Gershwin was only twenty-five when *Rhapsody in Blue* became the rage of an era. From there, in the few years that were left to him, the central issue of his artistic life would be how best to fashion a mature style from this early victory. That is a nice kind of problem to have, but one that can be threatening as well.

Concerto in F for Piano and Orchestra

Allegro
Adagio; Andante con moto
Allegro agitato

For piano solo; piccolo, flutes I-II, oboes I-II, English horn, clari-
nets I-II, bass clarinet, bassoons I-II; horns I-IV, trumpets I-III,
trombones I-III, tuba; timpani, snare drum, bass drum, cym-
bals, slapstick, xylophone; strings
Composed 22 July–10 November 1925 in London and New York
First performed 3 December 1925 by the New York Symphony
Society, Gershwin, soloist, Walter Damrosch conducting.
Published by New World Music Co. (New York, 1927)
Duration: about 35 minutes

When Walter Damrosch, delighted by what he had heard in *Rhapsody in Blue,* commissioned a piano concerto from Gershwin, the composer had to confront the issue of building from his Broadway-tune and jazz-based improvisational style something that would pass muster in exalted circles. The New York Symphony was not, after all, Paul Whiteman's Orchestra: a certain traditional bent was to be expected of musicians and audiences alike. Many regard the Concerto in F— the old-fashioned title may contribute to this assessment—as Gershwin's highest achievement, though I find him more relaxed in the episodic structure of the rhapsody and the succession of separate numbers in *Porgy and Bess.* However that may be, his easy mingling here of Charleston, blues, barrelhouse, and now and then a hint of ragtime is carried off with such high spirit that you accept the idea without worrying too much about the sonata and rondo forms he thought he was using—which of course means that the piece works.

Brash percussion and winds in the first four bars announce an orchestral introduction of Charleston rhythms and a swinging theme that concludes with the opening percussion figure again. What appear at first to be languid, directionless musings by the piano soloist are soon perceived as outlining the principal theme. Agitated entries from the orchestra and then soloist swell to a full statement of this theme and a short cadenza: one thing you can always expect from Gershwin is that sooner or later in every movement, sometimes twice, he will let out all the stops in a full-blown statement of his best melody. The Charleston-and-swing from the start returns to commence the development; note particularly the episode that transforms this figure into something very close to the song "Fascinatin' Rhythm." This section settles into the wonderful *cantabile* passage stated by the English horn and strings, by turns indolent and gracious, an elegant transformation of the main theme. A bit of barrelhouse breaks out, accentuated with slapstick in the percussion, and works itself into a scherzando. After the general pause, at the grandiose recapitulation of the principal theme, you at last sense closure at hand. The pace quickens, with the various bits and pieces commingled in a brilliant finish.

The *Andante* is a blues, with sultry solo work by a trumpet player with felted mute. The main theme seems closely related to that of the first movement in the way it hovers around close intervals of a step or two; from one of the motives the trumpet player has essayed there emerges a faster blues for the piano. Here the strings strum a banjo-style accompaniment. A third theme, broad and tender, appears in the orchestra as though a refrain—all this is very similar in structure to the *Rhapsody in Blue*—before the movement subsides in the smoky atmosphere where it began, the solo work now taken by the flute.

Where the first two movements are driven by their strong melodic content, the third propels itself more by virtue of the hammering sixteenth-note rhythms it establishes in the first few bars. In form the movement is more or less a rondo. The xylophone statement toward the end introduces reminiscences of material from the first two movements, and the concerto concludes as it began, with the big timpani strokes.

Infusing old European forms with the zesty freedom of American jazz and theatre tunes was an obvious challenge to serious and imaginative composers, from Europeans like Stravinsky and Milhaud to the Americans Copland and Bernstein. Gershwin was as qualified as any to undertake the task. For all you will read of his struggles with the materials of high composition, his solution strikes me as representing something as typically American in attitude as Rachmaninov's concertos of roughly the same period are Russian or Bartók's Hungarian.

An American in Paris

For piccolo, flutes I-II, oboes I-II, English horn, clarinets I-II, bass clarinet, saxophones I-III, bassoons I-II; horns I-IV, trumpets I-II, trombones I-III, tuba; timpani, snare drum, bass drum, cymbals, triangle, taxi horns, xylophone; celesta; strings

Composed in early and middle 1928 in Paris and New York

First performed 13 December 1928 in Carnegie Hall by the New
York Philharmonic Symphony, Walter Damrosch conducting
Published by New World Music Co. (New York, 1929)
Duration: about 20 minutes

The idea for a "rhapsodic ballet" on an American tourist's impressions
of the French capital came to Gershwin during a visit to Paris in
1926. His American supporters, who wanted him to win over the
European musical circles, were delighted. Two years later he established himself with his sister and brother-in-law in the Hotel Majestic
to bask in the cosmopolitan artistic climate of Paris during those
day—in the company of Ravel, Stravinsky, Milhaud, Poulenc, Prokofiev, Walton, and Stokowski—and to compose *An American in Paris*.
This he managed to do, despite the inducements of Parisian society,
in a little over three months.

The compositional plan of *An American in Paris,* which he intended
to be "in the manner of Debussy and The Six," is not so different from
that of *Rhapsody in Blue:* it consists of a free stringing together of
episodes based on a handful of memorable tunes. In this case they are
the "walking theme" with which the work opens (you'll probably
think of Gene Kelly here) and its transformations, the famous "homesickness blues," and the bits of dance music one hears as the tourist
wanders from place to place. (Among these are quotations of the hot-
blooded song "La Sorella" in the trombones.) It's a work of atmosphere and panorama, with the street noise—note the four taxi horns
(pitched on A, B, C, and D), which I understand the composer to
have brought home with him—always prevailing.

Gershwin was happy for his listeners to read into the music whatever episodes they might care to imagine. The intricate program note
written by Deems Taylor for the first performance, quoted in the
score, goes on and on in its attempt to outline a diary of the American's activities, "swinging down the Champs-Élysées on a mild, sunny
morning in May or June," later (at the bridge passage) crossing the
Seine to the Left Bank, encountering a romantic interest, and so on.
Taylor writes, purply, of one section "so unmistakably, albeit pleasantly, slurred, as to suggest that the American is on the terrasse of a
café, exploring the mysteries of an Anise de Lozo." In an interview at
the time, however, Gershwin spoke more simply of the opening "gay
section," the "rich blues with a strong rhythmic undercurrent," and

the American's "spasm of homesickness" after having one too many in the café. This is followed by a coda where the "vivacity and bubbling exuberance" of Paris return as the tourist goes out into the open air and regains his equilibrium.

An American in Paris is wonderfully scored, by Gershwin himself, for mega-orchestra, complete with saxophones in three sizes, xylophone, celesta, the taxi horns, and a raft of extra woodwind. Surprisingly for a composer of Gershwin's leanings, there is no piano part.

Mikhail Glinka

Born *1 June 1804 in Novospasskoye,*
near Smolensk
Died *15 February 1857 in Berlin*

Glinka is called the Father of Russian Music in recognition of his diligent and greatly successful effort to establish the principles of a nationalistic style in a civilization theretofore dominated by foreign musicians. He was widely admired by his countrymen, upon whom he exerted a profound influence. The great writer Alexander Pushkin was Glinka's personal friend; of his foreign admirers, the most articulate was Berlioz, whose essays in the Paris press helped introduce him to the rest of the world.

Like most children of privilege in Russia of that era, Glinka studied piano, voice, and violin; he even had a few lessons with the noted Irish pianist, John Field (1782–1837). After earning his university degree Glinka travelled widely, again in the time-honored tradition of the well-bred. He sojourned in Italy and there made the acquaintance of Donizetti and Bellini and their operatic style.

On his return to Russia in 1834 he assiduously sought out subject matter appropriate for Russian opera. After a suggestion from the poet Vasily Zhukovsky he settled on a tale from the Time of Troubles, where the peasant Ivan Susanin saves the teenaged czar Michael Fyodorovich Romanov (reigned 1613–45) from Polish marauders. This was his first masterpiece, eventually called *A Life for the Tsar* (1836). His second was *Ruslan and Ludmila* (1842), to an exotic fairytale of Pushkin. After completing the two operas, Glinka traveled to Paris and Spain, returning home with two successful Spanish works in his portfolio of orchestral music, the *Capriccio brillante* on the *Jota aragonesa* (called Spanish Overture No. 1, 1845) and a Spanish Overture No. 2: *Summer Night in Madrid* (1848).

Overture to *Ruslan and Ludmila*

For flutes I-II, oboes I-II, clarinets I-II, bassoons I-II,
    contrabassoon; horns I-IV, trumpets I-II, trombones I-III;
    timpani; strings
Composed 1837–42 in St. Petersburg
First performed with the opera 9 December 1842 at St.
    Petersburg
Published by B. Schotts Söhne (Mainz, c. 1858)
Duration: about 15 minutes

In pagan Russia, the beautiful Ludmila is wooed by three admirers and eventually won, after a healthy dose of sorcery both good and evil, by the fair knight Ruslan. The first performances of the opera were poorly received, but it has since earned a place in the Russian repertoire and on the fringes of the international one.

The overture to *Ruslan and Ludmila* is a favorite curtain-raiser, the kind of *bonbon* that tends to begin seasons or serve as encore after a splendid evening. It opens with exclamatory chord progressions, *tutti*, interspersed with scrambling scales in the strings; from these grows the headlong charge into the first theme of the sonata, a rollicking, soaring affair and, above all, wickedly fast. The transitional passage hints (in the timpani solo and string pizzicatos) at how strongly the opening exclamations will go on to govern both the organization and the texture; it leads to the broad *cantabile* in lower strings and solo bassoon for a second theme, restated by the full orchestra. (The second theme is not in the usual dominant key, but in a soft, mediant one, F major; this lends the section some of its warmth. The same theme is in a similarly unexpected key when it recapitulates.)

The development deals mostly with the opening gambit, fragmenting it, juxtaposing a bit of the second theme in close imitation, and referring again and again to the rhythm of the first two bars. After the recapitulation, a fine coda confirms the ebullience of the principal theme, *più mosso*. All this portends a good love story with a happy ending.

Edvard Grieg

Born 15 *June 1843 in Bergen, Norway*
Died 4 *September 1907 in Bergen*

Grieg was the fourth of five children born to parents of comfortable circumstance. In 1858 the Norwegian violin virtuoso Ole Bull visited the Griegs, heard the young man play the piano, and encouraged the family to enroll him in the Leipzig Conservatory. There Grieg fell heir to the stylistic legacy of Mendelssohn and most especially Schumann, having been spellbound, for example, when he heard Clara Schumann play Robert's Piano Concerto. Despite the onset of the poor health that plagued him for the rest of his life, he mastered his instrument and began to compose promising works. He returned briefly to Norway in 1862 but almost immediately chose to establish himself instead in Copenhagen, the cultural capital of Scandinavia.

In that city, he moved in exalted intellectual circles, profiting from his association with the Danish composer Niels Gade and friendship with, among many others, Hans Christian Andersen. It was the young Norwegian composer Rikard Nordraak, however, who fired Grieg's nationalistic urges; together they formed a concert society to promote the Scandinavian repertoire. Shortly after Nordraak's sudden death in 1866 at the age of 23, Grieg—now disenchanted with Danish as well as German dominion over Scandinavian culture—returned to Norway to formulate a nationalistic style on his own. His enterprises, which enjoyed the strong spiritual support of both Ole Bull and the playwright Henrik Ibsen, were consistently successful; the Piano Concerto he composed on returning to Norway made him famous throughout the world. The Norwegian government in its gratitude provided him an annual stipend, leaving him ample time to compose.

For the remainder of his life, Grieg spent the spring and early summer composing at his home in Troldhaugen near Bergen, the late summer wandering in the mountains of Norway, and the fall and winter on international tours, during which he would appear as conductor, accompanist, or piano soloist for his own works. (He was in Bayreuth for the first performance of Wagner's *Ring,* of which he sent accounts back to the Bergen newspaper.) By disposition a miniaturist, Grieg left much of his best work in the form of songs and solo piano pieces (the latter organized in books of "Lyric Suites"). The important symphonic compositions include the Piano Concerto, op. 16 (1868), arrangements from his works for piano including the *Norwegian Dances,* op. 35 (1881), and the two *Peer Gynt* suites (opp. 46 and 55, 1876). These last enjoyed great popularity during Grieg's lifetime and continue to be favorites of the concert-going public.

Concerto for Piano and Orchestra in A Minor, OP. 16

Allegro molto moderato
Adagio
Allegro moderato molto e marcato
[No pause between movements II and III]

For piano solo; flutes I-II, oboes I-II, clarinets I-II, bassoons I-II; horns I-IV, trumpets I-II, trombones I-III; timpani; strings
Composed: 1868 in Sölleröd
First performed 3 April 1869 by the Copenhagen Court Orchestra, Edmund Neupert, piano, Holger Simon Paulli conducting

Published by E. W. Fritzsch (Leipzig, 1872)
Duration: about 30 minutes

The timpani roll in the first measure announces one of the most extraordinary solo entries in the literature: the three-octave tumble and rebound in A minor that nearly everyone associates with Grieg and by extension with Norway. In fact the opening of Grieg's concerto is in clear homage to the similar beginning of Schumann's Piano Concerto, a work likewise in A minor; any number of other specifics of the style seem descended from Schumann as well. The Norwegian folklike sensations result from rhythmic and metric devices which exert a strong influence on the thematic material, and of characteristic melodic shapes—though Grieg's melodies are newly fashioned, not borrowed from folk sources.

Though his biggest orchestral work, the concerto is both compact and traditional of form. The famous first theme yields to an animated transition and, for a second subject, a fervent statement from the cellos and brass choir. This passage, one of exceptional warmth, lends itself to embellishment and completion by the soloist. A turbulent development juxtaposes the material of the opening flourish and the first theme; after a fanfare from the trumpets, the piano enters to prepare the way for the recapitulation, the fanfares in the winds growing louder at first, then receding into a soft dynamic for the return. There is nothing especially striking about the formal procedure from here on, but it is worth noticing, at the recapitulation of the cello theme, how much less soulful it sounds only a few steps lower, but beneath the most brilliant range of the instrument. The cadenza embraces a recapitulation of the main theme, carried on by the orchestra when it sidles back in. Grieg continues trippingly to the end, *più allegro,* in a short coda. The piano returns to its opening cascades.

D♭ major, the key of the second movement, is about as far as you can go from A minor, the overall key of the work. This *Adagio* has the character of an intermezzo, the theme first stated by muted strings with punctuations from the horns and bassoons. The cadential close, reluctant to relinquish its grip, is surely meant to evoke herdsmen's horncalls and their echoes. The pianist has the improvisatory second subject; after a brief departure, the main theme returns in a much denser scoring, the melody in canon between the piano and the tenor instruments, and concludes in the same insistent cadence.

With a sudden fanfare, *pianissimo* but hair-raising in the way it affects the tonality, the clarinets and bassoons force the harmony back down into A minor and introduce the last movement. The main material is in the character of a waddling march based on a Norwegian dance (the *hulling*); the throbbing half-step suspensions in the piano part at first color the main pitches of the theme, then achieve identity as an important motive in their own right. After a little cadenza, there follows a Chopinesque interlude. More thrilling still is the moment when, after the full cadenza near the end, the duple march is thrust into a waltz-like *perpetuum mobile*. Grieg concludes, as is so common with nationalist composers, in a chorale of affirmation and triumph.

It was Liszt's not especially good idea to suggest some changes in the orchestration to Grieg during one of his visits to Italy. (A trumpet solo, for example, instead of cellos for the second theme of the first movement.) The first publication of the score incorporates these, but Grieg later thought the better of them and published a corrected version (1879) that returns to his original ideas.

Peer Gynt Suites, from incidental music to the drama by Henrik Ibsen

No. 1, OP. 46
Morning
Åse's Death
Anitra's Dance
In the Hall of the Mountain King

No. 2, OP. 55
Ingrid's Lament (or *The Bride's Plaint*)
Arabian Dance
Peer Gynt's Homecoming: Storm on the Coast
Solveig's Song

For piccolo, flutes I-II, oboes I-II, clarinets I-II, bassoons I-II; horns I-IV, trumpets I-II, trombones I-III, tuba; timpani, snare drum, bass drum, cymbals, triangle, tambourine; harp; strings

Composed 1874-75 in Fredensborg at the invitation of the playwright Henrik Ibsen (1828–1906), who had first suggested a tone poem. Eight of the twenty-three pieces of incidental music, op. 23, drawn into two suites, ops. 46 and 55

First performed with the play 24 February 1876 at the Christiana
Theatre, Oslo; suites first performed shortly afterward
Published by C. F. Peters (Leipzig, 1888; 1893)
Duration: about 20 minutes each

The peasant Peer Gynt, a figure from Norwegian history, is as luckless as Voltaire's Candide. Like many legendary rascals, he is a wom-
anizer, and sinister to boot. He abandons his wife Solveig to the
Norwegian forest, the better to seek out other pleasures, then returns
some four decades later to find redemption in her love. Withal, Solveig has remained faithful.

The excerpts are arranged in an attractive succession for concert
performance, not the order in which they occur in the play. Dawn
comes upon a desert in North Africa; the sun first peaks through the
clouds after the big climax, with the broad cello theme. Aside from
that, the movement, with its fine writing for solo winds, is built
entirely from repetition of the melody you hear in the first four bars.
The music for the death of Peer's mother Åse was heard both as an
entr'acte and during Peer's soliloquy at her deathbed. The movement
is for muted strings alone, rising heavenward, then falling dead away
in a sequence of chromatic motives. Anitra is an Arab girl whom Peer
encounters in the course of his African adventures. She dances a mazurka
and trio for his pleasure, accompanied by the muted strings of the
previous movement, now with divided violas and cellos and a single
triangle. The mountain king is ruler of the trolls, set to take vengeance on Peer for having seduced one of their maidens. There is a
big orchestral crescendo and climax on a single theme. At the end (in
the play, a chorus cries "kill him") blows fall, and you are meant to
imagine Peer writhing in agony.

The Second Suite is much the more complex and artful. Peer has
tired of Ingrid, a bride he seduced shortly after her wedding. Peer's
motive and a distant call of trumpet and four stopped horns frame her
melancholy song on the low strings, *cantabile.* The Arabians dance
with tambourine-dominated percussion and piccolos; the silky middle
section is a solo turn for Anitra. The wizened old Peer Gynt returns
to Norway on a boat. A storm blows up on the Norwegian coast, in
the middle of which you hear Peer's thoughts, quietly expressed in
the first violin and cello, of the sunny African dawn. Like all musical
storms, this one subsides, in this case into the last movement. It is

morning: the middle-aged Solveig spins cloth by her forest cottage, her pedaling reflected in the harp and low horns. Her song, now halting and wistful, now reveling in pleasant memories, affirms her confidence that her husband will someday return.

You may also hear the prelude to *Peer Gynt* as well as a "Dance of the Mountain King's Daughter" that was originally intended for the Second Suite. Grieg's traditional and tuneful idiom is in stark contrast to Ibsen's pessimistic modernism: it is testimony to the power of the composer's craft that Peer Gynt is now best remembered in terms of this delicious music of late Romanticism.

George Frideric Handel

**Born 23 *February 1685 in Halle, Saxony*
Died *14 April 1759 in London***

Handel, the son of a court employee in Halle, was eager to learn music and so was sent to study keyboard, oboe, and composition with the palace musicians. After a short time at the university of Halle, he joined the violin section in the opera orchestra of Hamburg. There he was able to absorb the popular Italian repertoire as well as the stage works of the resident conductor, Reinhard Keiser, and the music of Telemann. His own first two operas were produced in Hamburg in 1705; the following year he departed for Italy, where he spent half a decade perfecting his understanding of the Italian style, composing in it, and making the acquaintance of its master composers, notably Arcangelo Corelli. In 1710 he became Kapellmeister to the Elector of Hanover, but was absent from his job most of the time, beckoned by the cultural allures of London. While in England he curried favor

among the aristocracy; at home, he was on the verge of being repri-
manded when, in 1/14, the Elector of Hanover himself was invited
by the English Parliament to become King George I.

Handel spent the rest of his career in London, widely acknowledged to be the best composer since Purcell (d. 1695). He held a
royal annuity, served the Duke of Chandos (1717), and then became
director of the new Italian opera house called the Royal Academy of
Music (1720). For that house, and later for the King's Theatre in the
Haymarket, he composed and produced more than two dozen operas,
virtually the totality of his work in the 1720s and '30s. In 1739, as
the popularity of the Italian opera ebbed, he turned his attention from
opera to oratorio—large dramatic works for soloists, chorus, and
orchestra to biblical texts, but without scenery or costumes. This was
the period of *Saul, Israel in Egypt,* and *Messiah* (1742)—then, as now,
considered immortal works.

His eyesight failed in the early 1750s, though an assistant helped
him continue his work. Handel died shortly after conducting an Easter
performance of *Messiah* in 1759 and was buried with magnificent pomp
at Westminster Abbey.

Handel is very nearly the equal of Bach in his mastery of high
Baroque musical practice, yet Bach and Handel seemingly knew little
or nothing of the other's work. Handel's music is brighter and simpler than Bach's and therefore more direct and less demanding. He
had an innate feeling for vocal melody and a sense of pacing that
makes even the very lengthy oratorios seem much shorter than they
are. His major orchestral works include the *Water Music* (1717) and
Music for the Royal Fireworks (1749), *concerti grossi* for solo string and
wind instruments, and twelve organ concertos (1738 and 1740).

The Concerti Grossi

Six Concerti Grossi, OP. 3

No. 1 in B Major and G Minor
No. 2 in B Major
No. 3 in G Major
No. 4 in F Major
No. 5 in D Minor
No. 6 in D Major and Minor

For oboes I-II solo, violins I-II solo, flute and recorder solo (no.
3); strings, continuo with bassoons

Twelve Concerti Grossi, OP. 6

No. 1 in G Major	No. 7 in B Major
No. 2 in F Major	No. 8 in C Minor
No. 3 in E Minor	No. 9 in F Major
No. 4 in A Minor	No. 10 in D Minor
No. 5 in D Major	No. 11 in A Major
No. 6 in G Minor	No. 12 in B Minor

For strings and continuo

Assembled 1734 (in the case of opus 3) by the publisher from works extending back to, perhaps, 1710; opus 6 composed September–October 1739 (no. 1 dated 29 September; no. 11 dated 30 October), in London

First performances not documented

Published by John Walsh, Jr. (opus 3: London, 1734; opus 6: London, 1740). *Inexpensive scores:* George Frideric Handel: *Complete Concerti Grossi in Full Score* (New York: Dover, 1981)

Duration: between 10 and 15 minutes each

Comparatively little of Handel's instrumental music was published in any coherent fashion during his lifetime. How the dozens of movements of concerted orchestral music he left behind are supposed to fit together thus remains fairly baffling. In any case, two published sets of concerti grossi appeared during the 1730s. These show a composer at ease with the conventional Italian concerto as he had learned it from Corelli and others, yet keen to broaden its harmonic vocabulary and its formal possibilities. No composer was more skilled than Handel in manipulating the building blocks of ritornello practice, nor more inexhaustible of melodic invention.

The six Concerti Grossi, opus 3, have been known since Handel's time as "the oboe concertos." Such a subtitle is misleading, not only because there are true oboe concertos elsewhere in his oeuvre but because opus 3 calls for solo flute, recorder, and violin as well as the pair of oboes. The set was pieced together, from anthems and other works of 1710 and later, by Handel's publisher, a man of more commmercial sense than musical skill. Some of the resulting "concerti" are tonally dubious and it is not always clear which solo instruments are intended. Note the virtuoso passagework for two bassoons in the First Concerto. The Third Concerto works nicely for solo transverse flute and strings.

The opus 6 Concerti, by contrast, constitute a coherent series, composed at the peak of the composer's career, and published under the title *Twelve Grand Concertos in Seven Parts*. Bigger and more artful works than their predecessors, they are to be seen alongside the *Brandenburg Concertos* (see p. 65) as representing the best of the Baroque concerto style. The scoring is for strings and continuo alone, with a pair of violins as soloists. But if woodwind and brass color are sacrificed here, the nuances of texture become all the more vivid. Handel's formal designs are freely inventive: the concerti go from compact and traditional (no. 4, for example) to the leisurely, even sprawling works later in the opus. The most admired of the set is the Sixth Concerto, in G minor, with its long Musette. This is a movement that evokes the tiny bagpipe favored by aristocratic ladies fashionably playing shepherdess: a drone (or *bourdon*) supports a languid melody of limited range. Repeated statements of the musette theme alternate with contrastive passages, including one particularly fine display of rapid passagework in the violins.

In the Baroque repertoire, the scores are sometimes only outlines of the music that was meant to result. This is especially true of the slow movements here, where there should be extensive ornamentation and improvisation, rather than simple chord progressions. During the improvisations, in a good performance, the soloists will respond to each other's musical gambits as they go along, each trying in a friendly way to outdo the other.

Water Music

Suite 1 in F Major
1. *Ouverture* 2. *Adagio e staccato* 3. [*Allegro*] 4. *Andante* [*da capo* to 3] 5. [*Allegro*] 6. *Air* 7. *Minuet* 8. *Bourrée* 9. *Hornpipe* 10. [*Allegro*]

For oboes I-II solo, horns I-II solo, violins I-II solo; strings; continuo with bassoons

Suite 2 in D Major
11. [*Allegro*] 12. *Alla Hornpipe* 13. *Minuet* 14. *Lentement* 15. *Bourrée*

For oboes I-II, bassoon; horns I-II, trumpets I-II; strings; continuo

Suite 3 in G Major
16. [*Allegro*] 17. *Rigaudon* 18. *Trio* [*da capo* to 17] 19. *Minuet* 20. *Minuet II* 21. [*Allegro*] 22. [*Allegro*]

For piccolo recorder (20–21), flute, oboes I-II; strings; continuo
with bassoons
Composed 1715, 1717, and possibly 1736, in London
Apparently performed 22 August 1715 (First Suite); 17 July
1717 (Second Suite); 26 April 1736 (Third Suite), during royal
barge-trips, Handel conducting the court musicians of King
George I
Published by John Walsh, Jr. (London, c.1733) and in other
Walsh publications. *Inexpensive score:* George Frideric Handel:
Water Music and Music for the Royal Fireworks in Full Score (New
York: Dover, 1986)
Duration: entire work about 45 minutes

What, exactly "Handel's Celebrated Water Music" is, or was, is a
question to which there are no certain answers. Royal barge progresses—in which the King, usually surrounded by ladies of material
(and sometimes corporeal) substance, met the ships of visiting dignitaries, or travelled up- or down-river on holiday trips—were common
in England under George I, and he delighted in having his musicians
present to lend the necessary circumstance to such events.

The best documented of the water musics was heard on 17 July
1717, during a festivity described in the newspaper as follows:

On Wednesday Evening, at about 8, the King took Water at Whitehall
in an open Barge, wherein were also the Dutchess of Bolton, the Dutchess
of Newcastle, the Countess of Godolphin, Madam Kilmanseck, and the
Earl of Orkney. And went up the River towards Chelsea. Many other
Barges with Persons of Quality attended, and so great a Number of Boats,
that the whole River in a manner was cover'd; a City Company's Barge
was employ'd for the Musick, wherein were 50 Instruments of all sorts,
who play'd all the Way from Lambeth (while the Barges drove with the
Tide without Rowing, as far as Chelsea) the finest Symphonies, compos'd
express for this Occasion, by Mr. Hendel; which his Majesty liked so well,
that he caused it to be plaid over three times in going and returning. At
Eleven his Majesty went ashore at Chelsea, where a Supper was prepar'd,
and then there was another very fine Consort of Musick, which lasted till
2; after which, his Majesty came again into his Barge, and return'd the
same Way, the Musick continuing to play till he landed.

(The record does not show whether the doubtless exhausted players
got a good meal and a few days off after this night-long service on
behalf of the Royal Pleasure.)

Some years later the publisher John Walsh, anxious to make a quick guinea, began to sell suites of what he called *The Celebrated Water Musick,* and to include bits and pieces so designated in other collections. It appears, in short, that we are dealing here with three different suites organized by similarity of key and instrumental force; the three suites have been tentatively associated with river journeys of August 1715, the July 1717 evening, and April 1736, respectively. Even so, it is not always clear exactly how the movements are to be ordered. Thus the *Water Music* can be constructed in a variety of fashions, and the list of movements given above is but one of several possible solutions. A juicy and romantic version of the *Water Music* for full orchestra became popular some decades ago, and that most inauthentic of versions is still to be heard in the concert hall.

The First Suite begins with a brilliant French overture. Among the dances which follow are the famous *Allegro* with French horns in $\frac{3}{4}$ (mvt. 3), which because of the scoring and the echoes has an appropriately nautical lilt, and the lovely air with dotted rhythms (mvt. 6), now as traditional at weddings as the marches of Wagner and Mendelssohn. The Second Suite has trumpets as well as the horns and oboes, and contains (as did the First), a fine hornpipe—that somewhat rustic dance generally associated with sailors at play. The Third Suite is more tranquil, with solo work for transverse flute and piccolo recorder. Nearly all the dances in the Water Music are glad-hearted and majestic, as befits a kingly evening out.

Music for the Royal Fireworks

Ouverture: Adagio; Allegro
Bourrée
La Paix: Largo alla siciliana
La Réjouissance: Allegro
Menuetto I
Menuetto II

For a large force of performers, distributed, roughly, as follows: horns I-III, trumpets I-III; timpani I-III, [snare drums]; violins and oboes I, violins and oboes II, oboes III, violas, bassoons, cellos, and double basses I, bassoons and double basses II, and contrabassoon; continuo
Composed April 1749 in London
First performed 27 April 1749, in Green Park, London, to commemorate the Peace of Aix-la-Chapelle, concluded the previous October

Published by John Walsh, Jr. (London, 1749). *Inexpensive score:* George Frideric Handel: *Water Music and Music for the Royal Fireworks in Full Score* (New York: Dover, 1986)
Duration: about 20 minutes

Fireworks displays, like military parades, are the sort of free entertainment governments bestow on their citizenry from time to time in the hope of fostering patriotism and national contentment. The fireworks in this case had to do with a celebration in London of the Peace of Aix-la-Chapelle, concluded the previous October to end the War of Austrian Succession (1740–48). One of the treaty provisions guaranteed George I and his heirs right of succession in England and in their German territories; that alone was cause for jubilation.

Handel provided a French suite for the occasion: a substantial overture followed by the usual series of two-part dances. The Frenchness of the dance forms is most likely symbolic, and both titled movements—the siciliana called "Peace" and the gleeful movement before the concluding minuets, called "Rejoicing"—convey the spirit of the events and were probably coordinated with the fireworks display.

The instruments are of the loud, outdoor sort preferred by the king: oboes, trumpets, and horns in threes, bassoons and contrabassoons for the bass, and probably a great deal of improvised percussion. Strings must have doubled the wind parts, for the announced performing force consisted of nearly 100 musicians: 28 oboes, 12 bassoons, 9 horns, 9 trumpets, and over 40 strings. Improvisation in the French style is to be expected from a good performance.

The *Fireworks Music* was rehearsed before a huge crowd on 21 April 1749. It threatened rain on the 27th, but the music commenced at the proper time, only to be interrupted by a fire at one end of the scaffolding. By that time, though, Handel's music had already gained its following.

Messiah

Part I   [*Prophecy; Nativity*]
Part II   {*The Messiah as Redeemer*]
Part III   [*On Death and Resurrection*]

For soloists (SATB though some performances under Handel varied this scheme), chorus; oboes I-II, bassoon; trumpets I-II, timpani; strings; continuo

Text assembled from the Holy Bible by Charles Jennens (1700–73)

Composed 22 August–14 September 1741, in London; revised frequently thereafter

First performed 13 April 1742, in the New Music Hall, Dublin, Handel conducting; performed repeatedly thereafter under the composer's direction

Published by William Randall and John Abell, successors to John Walsh, Jr. (London, 1767). *Inexpensive score:* George Frideric Handel: *Messiah in Full Score,* edited by Alfred Mann (New York: Dover, 1989)

Duration: uncut, about two and a half hours, not counting intermissions

Messiah is probably the best, and certainly the most loved, of all oratorios; neither the Passions of Bach nor Haydn's *Creation* (see p. 285) have ever rivaled its popularity, though in the last century Mendelssohn's *Elijah* (see p. 362) was for a time considered its equal. What I find most intriguing about *Messiah* is the text of prophecy and revelation; despite the implication of the title, there is relatively little biographical accounting of the life of Christ. Handel seems especially taken with the redemptive meaning of the Messiah to the faithful: the promise of purification of the Sons of Levi, that the Lamb of God will deliver mankind from the sins of the world. The concept seems rather abstract for so popular a work, especially when we recall that *Messiah* (unlike the Bach Passions) was not intended as part of a devotional service, but rather as a middle-class entertainment, albeit a pious one, and but a short step removed from the stage of the Italian opera house.

Handel calls for an orchestra of strings, supplemented by oboes and bassoons and keyboard. This force is enhanced on two occasions by two trumpets and timpani ("Hallelujah" and the tremendous final choruses "Worthy Is the Lamb" and "Amen"), once by two trumpets alone ("Glory to God"), and once by solo trumpet ("The Trumpet Shall Sound"); the restraint of their deployment makes these passages majestic indeed. The *pifa,* or pastoral symphony (i.e., of the shepherds on Christmas Night), is a charming instance of orchestrational subtlety, evoking rustic instruments and melodies without recourse to the woodwinds. I think Handel is at his most profound, both musically and philosophically, in the beginning of part II, with "Behold the Lamb of God," the excruciating gravity of "He Was Despised," and the three successive choruses "Surely He Hath Born Our Griefs," "And With His Stripes," and "All We Like Sheep."

Audiences tend to lie in wait for the familiar choruses—"For Unto Us," "Hallelujah," and so on. But the triumph of *Messiah* is the uniformity of its greatness: do not miss the chromatic wanderings in "The People That Walked in Darkness," the busy accompanied recitative "And Suddenly There Was With the Angel," the grandeur of the French overture.

Handel conducted *Messiah* more than three dozen times and for each new performance would freshen things up, such that the number and disposition of soloists varied with the performance; so, too, did the musical texts, for from time to time he would insert new movements. Later on, *Messiah,* more than any other Baroque work, was submitted to merciless tampering: even Mozart put his hand to it, adding full woodwinds to the orchestra. Performances today range from historical reconstructions to festival offerings of the monster-choir-with-major-orchestra to the ubiquitous community singalong. It is a mark of the work's character that it survives all this attention with dignity and grace.

According to an altogether charming custom, we stand during the "Hallelujah Chorus" because (so the story goes) the king, and therefore the public, once rose to their feet at that point. Whether His Majesty was moved by a power greater than himself or was simply intending to go home at the end of part II has not been made clear.

Joseph Haydn

**Born *31 March 1732 in Robrau,*
*lower Austria***
Died *31 May 1809 in Vienna*

Haydn was one of twelve children born to musically inclined and religious artisans. (His brother Michael also became an excellent composer.) At the age of eight he went to Vienna to prepare for a career in music by becoming a choirboy at St. Stephen's Cathedral. In 1761 he entered the service of the wealthy princes Esterházy, who had a townhouse in Vienna, palaces in Eisenstadt and Forchtenstein, and, eventually, a lavish castle in the Hungarian swamps called Eszterháza. At the height of Prince Nikolaus Esterházy's patronage, Haydn prepared weekly operas and orchestra concerts for him as well as the daily ceremonial music. After Prince Nikolaus's death in 1790, Haydn settled in Vienna; immediately thereafter he accepted a tempting offer to come to London. He visited England in 1791–92 and 1794–95, writing there his best symphonies (the "London" or "Salomon" symphonies; Johann Peter Salomon was the impresario who had convinced him to make the trip). He was awarded a doctor's degree from Oxford University in 1791.

At the age of sixty-five, Haydn composed *Gott erhalte Franz den Kaiser* (God Save the Emperor Francis), which became the Austrian national hymn; the next year he wrote his masterpiece, *Die Schöpfung* (The Creation, 1798). This was followed by a second oratorio, *Die Jahreszeiten* (The Seasons, 1801). Haydn ended his days a venerated patriarch of music, having had promising pupils (including Beethoven), considerable wealth, and statues cast in his honor. He died just as Napoleon and the French were invading Vienna.

Much of what we consider the Viennese Classical Style originated from Haydn's pen. He was a consummate master of sonata form and orchestration. His work is characterized by unfailing inventiveness; by contrast with the music of Mozart (with whom he maintained a friendship), it has pronounced peasant-like elements and a fair share of bumptious good humor. Haydn wrote about 104 symphonies, the best-loved of which have distinguishing names attached to them. These are Symphonies 6, 7, and 8 (*Le Matin, Le Midi, Le Soir;* Morning, Noon, and Evening, 1761); Symphony No. 45 ("Farewell" Symphony, 1772); Symphonies Nos. 82, 83, and 85 (*L'Ours, La Poule, La Reine;* The Bear, The Hen, The Queen, three of the six Paris symphonies of 1785–86); Symphony No. 92 ("Oxford," perf. 1791); Symphony No. 94 ("Surprise," 1791); Symphony No. 100 ("Military," 1794); Symphony No. 101 ("Clock," 1794); and the last symphony, No. 104, called "London" (1795).

Haydn's finest works in other genres are his eighty-two string quartets, sixty piano sonatas, and the masses and oratorios described below.

Symphony No. 45 in F Minor ("Farewell")

Allegro assai
Adagio
Menuet: Allegretto
Finale: Presto Adagio

For oboes I-II, bassoon; horns I-II; strings
Composed late November 1772 in Eszterháza
First performed in late November 1772 at Eszterháza, Haydn
conducting the court orchestra

Published by J.-G. Sieber (Paris, 1784; parts only) and Forster
(London, 1786); score published by Le Duc (Paris, 1802)
Duration: about 25 minutes

The wives were left behind in Eisenstadt when Haydn and his band
of musicians—lusty and vigorous fellows in their prime—annually
went to summer from May through October at the Eszterháza estate.
Prince Nikolaus was right to take pleasure in his fabulous (and still
new) castle of 126 rooms, with adjoining opera house, outbuilding
for the musicians, an inn, a coffee house, and gardens with Chinese
pavilion. But when, at the beginning of November 1772, he announced
his intention to remain there for another two months, the musicians
made known to their Kapellmeister that further to delay their domestic pleasures was to risk a work stoppage. Haydn's solution ("I was
young and lusty in those days, too," he is said to have remarked) was
to compose this symphony-with-a-message: at the end, one by one,
the players blow out the candles on their music racks and leave the
room. The Prince took the hint: "If they all leave, we must leave
too," he said with typically aristocratic understatement, then went to
the antechamber to tell his musicians they could expect the necessary
carriages the next morning. Thus the appelation *Abschiedssymphonie,*
"Farewell" Symphony.

The work would be noteworthy even without the wittiness at the
end, for it is one of the spate of instrumental compositions from 1771–
72 that demonstrates the dawn of Haydn's mature style, perhaps best
summarized as an inexhaustible fertility and ongoing novelty of sonata
design in all its particulars. The choice of the key (F♯ minor) is unusual
(Haydn would not compose another symphony in the minor mode
until the Symphony in C minor, no. 78, a decade later) and the key
scheme of the movements correspondingly striking: F♯ minor, A major,
F♯ *major,* F♯ minor moving at the end to major.

The plunging minor triads that constitute the principal material of
the first movement and the almost angry syncopations that lie beneath
them are indicative of that affect called *Stürm und Drang* (storm and
stress). These qualities are, I think, made especially compelling by
the choice and relatively sparse deployment of wind instruments, which
seem to reinforce the urgency of the matter. The sonata form, too, is
uneasy: the arrival in the dominant, the customary position for a second theme, seems instead just another step in the working through

of the main theme; the true second theme appears in the development, and the recapitulation recasts altogether what had been in the exposition. The effect is something like a through-composed rumination on the first eight bars, governed by the spirit but not the specifics of the typical sonata.

The *Adagio* is a sonata of gracious sentiment and, likewise, some adventurous harmonic and formal twists. Muted violins state the theme: listen for the manner in which the grace notes are transformed into on-the-beat, short-long rhythms that come to figure prominently in both melody and accompaniment. In the minuet, where metric and dynamic contrast is at issue, the oboes and horns are given more than an articulative function: the horns state the theme of the trio, which I understand to be related to a Gregorian chant of which Haydn was fond. The finale, also a sonata, is in the hurried, almost skittish fashion common to the *Sturm und Drang*.

Suddenly, when the recapitulation has run its course, Haydn thrusts the well-established F♯ minor into F♯ major: a charming triple-meter and triplet-dominated *Adagio* ensues, like something from a chamber *divertissement* or *Nachtmusik*. Oboes and horns emerge with a prominent turn, then oboe I and horn II snuff their candles and go: "No more," says Haydn's manuscript. This leaves, of the winds, oboe II, horn I, and bassoon, the last of whom has for the first time (having theretofore doubled the cello part) his own line notated in the score. The basoonist exits after four bars; a few bars later the oboe II finishes and leaves; a bar after that the horn I is done. Now there are only the strings, and their departures commence after the double-bass player has his long and comic solo. The violists and assisting violinists soon are done as well, and the symphony would have ended with Haydn and his devoted concertmaster Luigi Tomasini playing the remainder, alone and very nearly in the dark.

Symphony No. 88 in G Major

Adagio; Allegro
Largo
Menuetto: Allegretto
Finale: Allegro con spirito

For flute, oboes I-II, bassoons I-II; horns I-II, trumpets I-II; timpani; strings

Composed 1787 in Ezsterháza, one of a pair (with Symphony No.
89 in F Major) for the violinist Johann Peter Tost to take to
Paris
First performed probably sometime in 1787, Ezsterháza, Haydn
conducting
Published by Artaria (Vienna, 1789; parts only) and others; score
first published around 1840 by Bock & Bock (Berlin). *Inexpensive
score:* Joseph Haydn: *Symphonies 88–92 in Full Score* (New York:
Dover, 1983)
Duration: about 25 minutes

The point of the slow introductions to Haydn's symphonies is that
the subsequent *Allegros* usually get underway in understated manner,
and the gravity at the start helps convey seriousness of purpose. Often,
too, there is some allusion to the thematic material that will follow,
thus further integrating the sections. That is the case with this G-
major Symphony, a very popular work in its own right, and a conspicuous forerunner of the great Symphony 104.

Here the strong sense of upbeat–downbeat in the *Adagio* prefigures
many of the thematic shapes we will encounter as the work unfolds.
The rusticity of the main theme in the *Allegro* is in equal measure a
function of the tune itself (a folk melody) and of its being always
stated in two voices: village bands dealt in this sort of thing, and we
are meant to make the association. To that end the French horns have
a strong presence, and drones of various sorts become conspicuous.
The arrival of the second group is made clear by the soft dynamic and
suddenly rather tame turn of events. Equally obvious of purpose is
the little closing melody in the oboe and bassoon. Decorating the
recapitulation is a new flute countermelody.

Variations on a theme constitute the second movement, a conceptual triumph that begins when Haydn selects solo cello and oboe,
separated by an octave, to govern the sonority. Each variation is a
more elaborate decoration of the theme; a contrastive section departs
from and then reconnects its statements. Haydn scores the second of
these as a tutti, where the trumpets and timpani are heard for the
first time in the symphony. These tuttis become turning points for
the remainder of the movement.

The spirited minuet, adored of Haydn's audiences, returns us to
rustic concerns. Here and elsewhere, when Haydn is composing in

this manner, the little tags at phrase endings are part of the cleverness; the trio has an evocative pipe melody over drones. The finale is
a sonata-rondo on a theme whose two eighth-note upbeats return that
same detail of the first movement to mind; note, in the long departure
that serves as a development, the episode where the theme is heard as
a canon between the lower instruments and violins

Haydn's previous six symphonies, nos. 82–87, had been ordered
for a Paris series called the Concert de la Loge Olympique. He composed the next two, nos. 88 and 89, with the Parisians very much in
mind, but the year was 1789 and Parisians were otherwise occupied.
Symphony No. 92, likewise in G major and likewise written for Paris
clientele, shares many other similarities with the 88th—though on
the whole it has a more colorful history. This later G-major Symphony is called the "Oxford" because it was the work Haydn conducted in the Sheldonian Theatre there after ceremonies of July 1791
to award him the degree of Doctor of Music, *honoris causa*.

Symphony No. 94 in G Major ("Surprise")

Adagio; Vivace assai
Andante
Menuet: Allegro molto
Finale: Allegro di molto

For flutes I-II, oboes I-II, bassoons I-II; horns I-II, trumpets I-II;
    timpani; strings
Composed 1791 in London
First performed 23 March 1792 at Salomon's Concerts in the
    Hanover Square Rooms, London, the composer conducting
Published by J. André (Offenbach, 1795; parts only); score
    published by Breitkopf & Härtel (Leipzig, 1808). *Inexpensive*
    score: Joseph Haydn: *Complete London Symphonies in Full Score*
    (Series I: Nos. 93–98), ed. Ernst Praetorius and H. C. Robbins
    Landon (New York: Dover, 1985)
Duration: about 25 minutes

Haydn's patron Prince Nikolaus Esterházy died in September 1790;
his less visionary successor, Prince Anton, dismissed most of the
orchestra. Haydn and his concertmaster Tomasini kept their positions, but having no responsibilities, returned to Vienna. Haydn's

retirement was of short duration: within weeks the London impresario Johann Peter Salomon, who was on the continent to search out talent for his concerts, came to "fetch" (he said) Haydn away to England. A lucrative remuneration was offered for Haydn's agreement to appear at the concerts and to compose for them six symphonies, a good deal of chamber music, and perhaps an opera while on British soil. Salomon and Haydn arrived in England at the beginning of 1791.

The concerts, on Friday evenings that spring, followed a formula where one or another of Haydn's new symphonies, billed as a "New Grand Overture," came just after the intermission, once the latecomers had arrived. (The problem of latecomers is as old as concert life itself.) Haydn profited well from his time in England, not just from his exposure to English society—and the crowds of refugees from the French Revolution—but also from hearing the excellent orchestras of London and, perhaps above all, discovering the music of Handel. Hearing *Messiah* and *Israel in Egypt* had formidable implications for the next chapter in his career. And his popularity with the English greatly enhanced his standing at home.

The surprise in the second movement of Symphony No. 94, a single *fortissimo* chord Haydn added to his manuscript to "make the women jump" (in one version of the story), is over and done in a trice. Yet people like to remember a composition with an anecdote attached—as in the case of the "Hallelujah Chorus"—and that is one reason the "Surprise" Symphony came to rival *The Creation* in popularity well into the next century. The work was a favorite of the Londoners even before the surprise existed at all, and it is thus perfectly acceptable, even sophisticated, to enjoy the remaining several hundred measures.

The symphony opens with the usual *Adagio*. This one, marked *cantabile,* imparts a particularly warm quality due to its wind-band scoring. The texture darkens the moment the strings respond; reference is made to one of these passages later in the exposition. The *Vivace,* in $\frac{6}{8}$, is spirited indeed, notably in the heavily syncopated second group and the sprightly closing material with oboe trill. In the development, most unusually, the timpani retunes one of its pitches in order to be able to articulate a *forte* climax, then tunes back to its original configuration.

The famous *Andante* is purposefully naive, a simple progress of increasingly ornamented variations of a tune quite like the ancestral *Twinkle, twinkle* (see p. 29), moving from C major to its *minore* and back again. Brass instruments with drums, of course, are at their most heroic in C major, and it is on those instruments that the movement relies for its majestic conculsion, the timpani maintaining its important role even as the music subsides. Like the first movement, the minuet is fast, with an extended B section that embodies a long departure, a return, and a short codetta; the trio features solo bassoon. Haydn chooses a rapid tempo for his finale as well; this is a sonata-rondo with its principal sections delineated by bars of rest.

Haydn withheld his G-major Symphony, even though it had been composed in 1791, until after his *Concertante* for oboe, bassoon, violin, and cello, usually called the *Sinfonia concertante* op. 84, could be performed (9 March 1792). The order of composition of the first six London symphonies was 96, 95, 93, 94, 98, [*Concertante*], 97.

Symphony No. 101 in D Major ("Clock")

Adagio; Presto
Andante
Menuet: Allegretto
Finale: Vivace

For flutes I-II, oboes I-II, clarinets I-II, bassoons I-II; horns I-II, trumpets I-II; timpani; strings
Composed early 1794 in London, the minuet in Vienna
First performed 3 March 1794 at Salomon's Concerts in the Hanover Square Rooms, London, the composer conducting
Published by J. André (Offenbach, 1799; parts only); score published by Breitkopf & Härtel (Leipzig, 1808). *Inexpensive score:* Joseph Haydn: *Complete London Symphonies in Full Score (Series II: Nos. 99–104)*, ed. Ernst Praetorius and H. C. Robbins Landon (New York: Dover, 1985)
Duration: about 30 minutes

Haydn had expected to return to England in 1793 but the necessary agreements were not reached until the fall of that year, so he did not arrive in London until February 1794. During his interlude in Vienna he began to compose the six new symphonies that would be needed abroad, and also during those months he and Beethoven had their brief and not especially successful experiment at being master and disciple. For the new season Salomon's concerts were moved to Monday evenings, February to May 1794, and during these, Symphonies No. 99, 100, and 101 were heard for the first time. Lacking suitable talent from the continent, he said, Salomon concluded his series at the end of the 1794 season. For the 1795 season, Haydn appeared in G. B. Viotti's Opera Concerts at the King's Theatre, which took the Monday evening slots vacated by Salomon. Here he presented his last three symphonies.

The history of music records few cases of composers who were as prolific in old age as Haydn. His powers continued to ripen; his energies were unflagging; his knack for tapping the enthusiasm of the public went unabated. The last six London symphonies operate on a more exalted intellectual plane still than the previous group and were yet even more popular. They are for a bigger orchestra, too, with pairs of flutes and clarinets and important work for the horns, trumpets, and timpani. (Until then, Haydn had not often used the clarinet.) And while he seems rather conscientiously to have brought his writing of symphonies to an end with this set, they are hardly his valedictory to composition: the two oratorios and six formidable masses were yet to come.

The Symphony No. 101 is, like the others in the set, formally inventive; something unusual happens in every movement. The nickname, which describes the ostinato accompaniment of the second movement, apparently comes from a 1798 Vienna transcription of the movement for piano, where it was called "Rondo: The Clock."

The slow introduction to the first movement begins in D minor; the rising scalar figure in the first two bars, metrically inconclusive for a time, soon finds itself transformed into the lilting figure with which the *Presto* begins. The $\frac{6}{8}$ meter here, which Haydn also uses for the first movement of the 103rd Symphony, is more commonly associated with rondo finales: its vivacity suggests a freedom from the customary first-movement gravities. Yet the *Presto* is very broad of scale, a third longer, indeed, than most of his other first movements. There is, for example, an exceptionally long transition between the first and second themes, though the second is more a matter of continuing elaboration of the given material than studied contrast. The imitative work in the development reappears in the recapitulation; note, too, how one purpose of the development is to reverse the upward-dashing eighth notes of the theme into downward scales.

The "clock" movement seems to conflate rondo and variation procedures: you listen with growing delight as the simple rounded phrase structure gives way to a loud, busy passage in the minor mode, then turns just as suddenly to one of the most elegantly wrought moments in all Haydn: a return of the main theme in the first violins, with the tick-tock accompaniment split between solo flute and bassoon some two octaves apart. For an instant after the empty bar, you think a second *minore* is taking wing, but instead there is a developmental statement in a most foreign key area before the movement concludes with a lavishly decorated restatement of the opening phrases.

The minuet, too, is a protracted affair—Haydn's longest. In the trio he offers a risible impression of the sleepy village band, with its hurdy-gurdy drones and piped solo. None of it quite works: the relentless drones from time to time imply the wrong harmony; the flute solo is altogether pointless; the violins go on too long; and the horns at the end of the trio hang on to their cadence point even when it manifestly clashes with the rest of the chord structure. On this sort of comedy Beethoven, too, was pleased to base the trio of the Sixth Symphony.

At first the strongly monothematic finale seems of ordinary sonata design, with the initial three notes achieving a strong motivic identity as it progresses. (The acute listener may note as early as the second phrase, however, some hints of contrapuntal delights to come.) An excited *minore,* reminiscent of harmonic turns in the first two movements, serves as a development; then, in lieu of an exact recapitulation Haydn constructs a passage in high counterpoint from the main subject. Not until after a tutti restatement and a second, quieter one does Haydn consent to let the movement end.

Symphony No. 103 in E♭ Major ("Drum Roll")

> *Adagio; Allegro con spirito*
> *Andante più tosto Allegretto*
> *Menuet*
> *Finale: Allegro con spirito*

> **For** flutes I-II, oboes I-II, clarinets I-II, bassoons I-II, horns I-II, trumpets I-II; timpani; strings
> **Composed** 1795 in London.
> **First performed** 2 March 1795 at G. B. Viotti's Opera Concerts in the King's Theatre

Published by J. André (Offenbach, 1799; parts only); score
published by Breitkopf & Härtel (Leipzig, 1806). *Inexpensive
scores:* Haydn: *Symphony No. 103 in E-flat Major ("Drum Roll"),*
ed. Karl Geiringer, A Norton Critical Score (New York:
Norton, 1974); Joseph Haydn: *Complete London Symphonies in
Full Score (Series II: Nos. 99–104),* ed. Ernst Praetorius and
H. C. Robbins Landon (New York: Dover, 1985)
Duration: about 30 minutes

The timpani roll in the first bar, and its treatment later on in the
work, is but the first of many imaginative features in this next-to-last
of Haydn's symphonies that remind us just how great his genius was:
after more than one hundred symphonies and in his sixty-third year,
his abilities seem anything but ravaged by time. The mysterious melody that follows, in the bassoon and low strings, is so set out that
you cannot quite fix the meter at first; moreover it hints at the famous
Dies irae tune, and this sinister suggestion is reinforced by the eerie
chromaticism which then ensues. In that context the spirited $\frac{6}{8}$ of the
sonata-allegro that follows, and its rather naive quality, come as
something of a surprise. Of similarly bright humor is the most prominent theme in the second group, a rustic melody stated by oboe and
violin over a waltz-like accompaniment. (The four bars that introduce
this come from the lugubrious introduction, and there is another reference to the slow introduction in the development after the first
fermata.) But a remarkable twist comes in the coda: here the drum
roll and the substance of the introduction are heard once more. The
merriment masks a good deal of serious thought about formal structure, and Beethovenian scope and process seem just around the corner.

One has the same response to the second movement, a theme and
variations that alternates between C minor and C major. (You will
usually read that this is a set of variations on two themes, the minor
one and the major one, but it all amounts to natural transformation
of the first theme.) Enjoy, especially, the low Cs in the bass line,
remembering that the double bass typically has E as its lowest note.
(The implication is that Haydn's bass players either had five-stringed
instruments or tuned their lowest string to a low C.) The fine violin
solo was for the great violinist Giovanni Battista Viotti, during whose
concert this symphony was first heard; after this comes the drums and

trumpets, held so far in reserve. The clarinets are not heard at all.

The minuet, too, is big, with a long development and recapitulation in its second strain. Note the tag on the first strain, which had by now become a Haydn trademark, the sort of thing I like to describe as a conspiratorial wink of composer to listener. The trio, built in roughly the same proportions as the minuet, has a music-box quality, the result of the interplay of the string voices doubled by solo woodwind.

What seems to be a simple horn call opens the finale, but we soon discover that its countersubject has become the theme of this highly imitative movement. The fugal treatment is sustained throughout, often with long-held notes above and below the figure in the winds. Here again, Beethoven's world seems not so distant: there is almost the sensation of Fate knocking at the door.

The "Drum Roll" Symphony has an alternative ending that has come down to us and which you may occasionally hear. More interesting is the question of the dynamic level of the first drum roll. The usual solution is to play it with a marked decrescendo, though there is some disagreement as whether eighteenth-century timpanists would have thought in such terms.

Symphony No. 104 in D Major ("London")

Adagio; Allegro
Andante
Menuetto: Allegro
Finale: Spirituoso

For flutes I-II, oboes I-II, clarinets I-II, bassoons I-II; horns I-II, trumpets I-II; timpani; strings

Composed: 1795 in London

First performed 13 April (probably) and 4 May 1795, London, at G. B. Viotti's Opera Concerts in the King's Theatre ("Dr. Haydn's Night")

Published by J. André (Offenbach, c. 1801; parts only); score published by Breitkopf & Härtel (Leipzig, 1807). *Inexpensive score:* Joseph Haydn: *Complete London Symphonies in Full Score (Series II: Nos. 99–104),* ed. Ernst Praetorius and H. C. Robbins Landon (New York: Dover, 1985)

Duration: about 30 minutes

Haydn either knew or suspected that his 104th symphony would be his last: the remark on the cover of his manuscript, "the 12th I have composed in England," has a ring of conclusiveness about it. There could not be a more fitting conclusion to his life's work as a symphonist, so cohesive are its elements, both within and among the four movements. We are comfortable, in short, in the knowledge that Haydn has had his ultimate say. But more is afoot here than mere valedictory: new aesthetic currents were in the air, and Haydn's sensitivity to the dawn of Romanticism is clear.

This is apparent in the glorious *Adagio,* with its minor mode and a seductive chromaticism that lingers on and on, and especially in the manner it accentuates the interval of a perfect fifth: the symphony returns to focus on this interval again and again. From the third and fourth bars of the gentle melody which constitutes the main theme of the *Allegro,* Haydn draws the motive which goes on to dominate the movement: four quarters and two half notes, moving up a step and returning. The main theme retains its control throughout, such that the second subject serves in effect merely to introduce closing material. The development is almost exclusively concerned with the quarter-and-half motive, exclusively in minor key areas; the recapitulation greatly varies the material from the exposition—note the statement for high winds insisting on the motto of quarters and halves. It is not a coincidence that the movement closes on the open fifths.

The *Andante* is in a rounded form (major–minor–major). The first section consists of two subsections, each repeated, during the course of which there is a clear return of the opening phrase. (This organizational premise is not so different from that which governs a minuet.) In the minor-mode section, interruptions of brass and timpani seem to refer to the slow introduction to the first movement. The charming fermata from the first section for bassoon and strings becomes in the restatement a tender reminiscence unwilling to relinquish its grip—and thus proto-Romantic of character.

The splendid minuet, in a peasant style of heavy footfall and miscellaneous jolts, is clearly a pleasantry: in the second part, after a long crescendo, the players begin to ruminate on the trills; suddenly the music stops in its tracks, and afterward the trill returns spread over two full bars. The trio sinks into a new major key, with pastoral figuration for the wind soloists and strings; at its conclusion there is a modulatory section to return to the original key (D major).

Much has been written of the tune-over-drones in the finale. Whether this had its origins in Croatian folksong (as seems likely, since Haydn had much to do with the Croatians in and around Eisenstadt) or is based on London street cries of "Hot Cross Buns" or "Live Cod" (as an English lady says in her not especially reliable memoirs) is irrelevant. Contrast to this merriness comes in the form of a broad phrase in half and whole notes, at the beginning of the second group. In the development the main theme is split in two, with its elements treated contrapuntally; this gives way after a bar of rest to the whole- and half-note theme, through which Haydn manages to ooze slowly through minor keys back into the recapitulation. He similarly broadens the recapitulation, intent to carry on as long as he can. The final statement comes over a long drone.

After which, in mid-August 1795, Haydn quietly returned to Austria.

Missa in tempore belli (Paukenmesse) in C Major (Mass in Time of War [Timpani-Mass])

> *Kyrie eleison*
> *Gloria*
> *Credo*
> *Sanctus*
> *Benedictus*
> *Agnus Dei*
>
> **For** soloists (SATB), chorus; flute, oboes I-II, clarinets I-II, bassoons I-II; horns I-II, trumpets I-II; timpani; strings with cello solo; continuo
> **Text** traditional Latin
> **Composed** Autumn 1796 in Eisenstadt and Vienna
> **First performed** 26 December 1796, at the Piarestenkirche, Vienna, in ceremonies celebrating the ordination of Johann von Hofmann, the composer conducting from the organ; repeated 29 September 1797 in Eisenstadt
> **Published by** Breitkopf & Härtel (Leipzig, 1802)
> **Duration:** about 55 minutes

Prince Anton Esterházy had died in 1794 after a very short time at the family helm. Haydn's new employer, the younger Prince Nikolaus, was anxious to reestablish the musical chapel. He asked of his celebrated Kapellmeister only an annual Mass for the nameday of his Princess Marie Hermenegild, *née* Lichtenstein. This was 8 September, a church celebration for the birthday of the Virgin Mary; Haydn's mass would typically be given the next Sunday. Between 1796 and 1802 Haydn composed for this contractual arrangement six marvelous masses, symphonic in scope, assured of technical command, and vividly heralding the new century. These were the St. Bernard Mass (1796), the Mass in Time of War (for 1797, though see below), the Lord Nelson Mass (1798), the St. Theresa Mass (1799), the "Creation" Mass (1801; so called because it quotes, at the *Miserere,* the music of "dew-dropping morn" from the oratorio); and the *Harmoniemesse* (1802, so called for its prominent use of wind band, or *Harmonie*). There is some uncertainty as to the order of composition and performance of the first two masses, since both were composed in 1796; now it seems probable that the "Mass in Time of War" was the one intended for performance on the princess's nameday in 1797. In fact, the Eisenstadt performance was delayed some three weeks in order to be presented during the visit to Eisenstadt of the Palatine Archduke Joseph, viceroy of Hungary.

In 1796 Austria remained at war with the French, and things were going poorly: by 1797 Napoleon had occupied Graz. What makes this a mass appropriate to a "time of war" are the persistent timpani strokes in the *Agnus Dei*—suggestions of distant strife, perhaps—and the particular urgency here of the plea for peace with which every mass concludes. The choice of key, C major, is optimistic, for C major is the key of victory.

The overall sound of the mass is colored by the bravura passagework for the soprano soloist. The orchestration, too, is striking, particularly that of the more lavish Vienna version, with its flute, clarinets (note the fine run at the beginning of the *Gloria*), and expanded horn parts. Haydn could customarily summon stronger forces in Vienna than in Eisenstadt; in the prince's band, for example, the horn players also played the trumpet parts, while in Vienna a pair of horns would double the trumpets.

After a sinister introduction, the *Kyrie* is set forth in what was for Haydn a rather typical monothematic sonata form. (The arrival of the second area occurs where the alto soloist is given the main theme.) The *Gloria* begins and ends in a fast $\frac{3}{4}$; these sections surround an arioso for the bass soloist, at "Qui tollis peccata mundi," with a lovely obligato for solo cello later joined by the flute. Here, as elsewhere in Haydn's masses, the words "miserere nobis" and "suscipe, deprecationem nostram" are declaimed homophonically, a texture that lends those sentiments great poignancy, as humankind begs collectively for mercy. The *Credo* is similar in structure to the *Gloria,* with big fugues at the beginning and end (at "Et vitam venturi saeculi"). In the middle are "Et incarnatus" for the solo quartet, led by the bass soloist, and the customarily exuberant "Et resurrexit," which returns to the initial major key and rapid triple meter.

The *Sanctus* begins slowly and with a Baroque-style walking bass, then turns abruptly to a vigorous "Pleni" with wind and brass, strongly tinted by the minor mode; its concision is meant as a foil to the great *Benedictus* which follows, a siciliana for the soloists. It is in the *Agnus Dei,* as I have noted, that our thoughts are drawn to troubled times. The big, affirmative Dona nobis dwells emphatically on the word "pacem"—an aspiration that must have been uppermost in the listeners' minds that year.

Missa in angustiis ("Lord Nelson Mass")

Kyrie eleison
Gloria
Credo
Sanctus
Benedictus
Agnus Dei

For soloists (SATB); chorus; flute, clarinets I-II, oboes I-II, bassoons I-II; trumpets I-III; timpani; organ; strings (the woodwind parts, added later, replace an obligato organ part)
Text traditional Latin
Composed 10 July 31–August 1798 in Eisenstadt
First performed 23 September 1798 in the Stadtpfarrkirche (town parish church), Eisenstadt
Published by Breitkopf & Härtel (Leipzig, 1803)
Duration: about 45 minutes

Haydn called the third of his six masses *in angustiis.* (*Angustiis* means "narrow"; "in times of difficulty" is the usual rendering, though *in angustiis* can have several meanings, perhaps including "composed in a short time.") The war with France continued. In early August 1798 the British admiral Lord Nelson, whose blockade of the French coast had failed long enough to allow Napoleon's huge expeditionary force into the Mediterranean, found the enemy fleet at anchor in Aboukir Bay at the mouth of the Nile. A pitched engagement of three days, 1–3 August 1798, ended in a great victory over the French. News probably reached the Esterházy court in Eisenstadt just before the first performance of Haydn's new mass; those who were there to hear it may well have made some obvious, though technically anachronistic, associations with the latest turn of military events. When the *Missa in angustiis* was played for Nelson during his visit to Eisenstadt in 1800, it became for all time the "Nelsonmesse" and is so identified in the inventory of Haydn's estate.

Where in the "Mass in Time of War" the military allusions were found in the timpani strokes of the *Agnus Dei,* here it is the trumpet fanfares and dark minor mode of the *Kyrie* and the particularly sinister low register of the trumpet that turn one's thoughts in that direction. Just as forceful is the end of the *Benedictus,* where the trumpets hammer away, interrupting the choral chant and then coloring, to chilling effect, the chorus's climax on a high B♭. The coloratura soprano line in the *Kyrie* is highly reminiscent of that for the "Mass in Time of War," though in this case we do not know the identity of the intended soloist.

The long movements, *Gloria* and *Credo,* are each subdivided into three parts. Both are as firmly in the major (D) as the *Kyrie* had been in minor: the effect is to introduce something of the festive Baroque, for this is the key of the great trumpet-and-drum choruses of Bach and Handel. The "Qui tollis" at the center of the *Gloria* is a solo aria for the bass, with gentle ornamentation in the accompaniment. The choral incantations here—"miserere nobis" and the urgent "suscipe, deprecationem nostram"—are as emphatic as they were in Haydn's previous mass. Around this section are matching ritornello sections on virtually the same material.

The *Credo* opens in the old-fashioned style, as eighteenth-century Credos often do, with a traditional church melody treated in canon. The "Et incarnatus" at the center is an aria for the soprano with obbligatos for cello and violin solo; at the words "crucifixus etiam pro nobis sub Pontio Pilato," there is a sharp turn to minor and reference to the opening of the *Kyrie.* This is followed by an excited "Et resurrexit," and there are melodic allusions to the previous movement. The soprano soloist begins to bring the movement to its close with her gleeful "et vitam venturi saeculi amen."

The slow *Sanctus,* with its unusual crescendo and diminuendo indications, introduces a faster "Pleni" and "Osanna"; the same "Osanna" returns after the *Benedictus.* But it is the *Benedictus* that dominates the second half of this mass with its formidable dimension and celebrated thunder of the trumpets and timpani. The soloists have the slow *Agnus* with a concluding fugal "Dona nobis pacem" for chorus.

Haydn's manuscript and his early performances included only the strings, brass, and timpani, with additional elaboration in the organ part, which Haydn himself would have played. This was because Prince Esterházy had dismissed all his wind players but for the fanfare band of three trumpets and drum. The published score of 1802 distributes the organ part to flute, oboes, bassoons, and horns. We can assume from a contemporary account that Haydn endorsed this arrangement, and it remains the version most often given in the concert hall.

The Creation (Die Schöpfung)

Part I   [*God Creates the Firmament and the Earth; Days 1–4*]
Part II   [*God Creates the Beasts of Sea and Land; Days 5–7*]
Part III   [*Adam and Eve in the Garden of Eden*]

For   three soloists (S. [the angel Gabriel, Eve], T. [the angel Uriel], B. [the angel Raphael, Adam), chorus; flutes I-III, oboes I-II, clarinets I-II, bassoons I-II, contrabassoon; horns I-II, trumpets I-II, trombones I-III; timpani; strings; continuo
Text   by an anonymous English poet and Baron Gottfried van Swieten, after the book of *Genesis* in the Old Testament and Milton's *Paradise Lost*
Composed   1795–98
First performed   29, 30 April 1798 at private concerts in the Schwarzenberg Palace in Vienna, Haydn conducting; first public performance 19 March 1799, in the Vienna Burgtheater
Published by   private subscription (Vienna, 1800) and by Breitkopf & Härtel (Leipzig, 1803). *Inexpensive score:* Joseph Haydn: *The Creation in Full Score* (New York: Dover, 1989)
Duration: about two hours

The work many consider Haydn's masterpiece is a direct descendent of Handelian oratorio. From his earliest days in England Haydn admired the great Handel oratorios; above all *Israel in Egypt,* with its frogs, flies, and hailstorms, influenced Haydn as he worked on *The Creation.* It had long been the impresario Salomon's plan to induce him to compose an oratorio for the English, and it was Salomon who brought him the libretto—one which had, in fact, originally been intended for Handel himself.

For each day of the week of creation, the English libretto suggested biblical recitative, commentary based on Milton, and a concluding chorus paraphrasing one of the psalms. Haydn carried the English text back to Austria, where he asked Baron Gottfried van Swieten to provide a German version. This was a good choice: Swieten, a former ambassador to Berlin and the keeper of the Imperial Library, was an enthusiastic promoter of Baroque music, and thus knew the territory well. He followed the English plan closely, and as he went along suggested to Haydn in the margin of his manuscript the sort of music he thought would be most appropriate. ("Because of the last three lines," he wrote of the aria, no. 16, "only the joyful twittering, not the long held tones, of the nightingale can be imitated here.") Swieten cut and altered his English source—though always leaving the King James biblical citations untouched—to fashion an English text that for the most part sits comfortably alongside his German. *Die Schöpfung / The Creation* is, then, for all intents and purposes bilingual. (This is trickier that it looks: if one is to write, as Haydn did, worm music, the English "worm" and German "Wurm" must fall in the same place, despite the grammatical differences between the two languages.) The English we use today was spruced up by Vincent Novello when the vocal score was published, but is still thick with Miltonian allusions.

Haydn excelled at word painting, such that the illustrative devices are apt to seize your attention early on. They begin, subtly, in the wondrous first bars of the overture, called by Haydn "Representation of Chaos," where life seems to stir for the first time with the bassoon arpeggio. At the word "light" of "And there was light" (no. 2), there blossoms an enormous C major from the full performing force. From there you will doubtless note, among others: the boisterous sea (no. 7); the "cheerful host of birds" and "th' immense Leviathan" (no. 19); and of course the tawny lion, flexible tiger, nimble stag, and noble steed of no. 22. Likewise, the choice of keys, instruments, and harmonic events is often dictated by particulars of the text.

For all its Baroquish picture-music, *The Creation* is emphatically a work of the nineteenth century. This, too, is announced in "The Representation of Chaos," Haydn's most erotic and extended slow introduction, of advanced harmonic idiom and forward-looking use of the orchestra. (Note, for example, the astonishing clarinet run and its consequent, some bars later, the descending chromatic scale in the flute.) "Chaos" is as successful an evocation of the mysterious void of the universe as you will find anywhere, comparable to the opening of Beethoven's Ninth and that of Stravinsky's *Rite of Spring.*

There is one further symbolism to be noted as well, and that is the tripartite nature of things: the three parts of the oratorio as opposed to the usual two, the use of three soloists (the angels Gabriel, Uriel, and Raphael) rather than the conventional four, and the recitative-aria-chorus structure that describes each of the days of creation. These reflect the deity in what is probably a nod toward Masonic ideals. The great trios and choruses with trio are indeed the focal points of the oratorio: "The Heavens are telling" (no. 14), "Most beautiful appear" and "The Lord is great" (nos. 19 and 20); and "Achieved is the glorious work" (no. 27).

The trouble with long pieces that begin so dramatically as *The Creation* is that the composer sometimes has difficulty sustaining the precedent. People often find part III, on Adam and Eve in the Garden of Eden, anticlimactic—even silly—by comparison with the celestial material that has come before. This view denies Haydn one of his fundamental premises: that Man is the most perfect creation of God. It is true that the love duet, "Graceful consort, at thy side" (no. 31), uses the rhetoric of the village band and pleasure garden. But the fall of Man only reconfirms the grandeur of God.

Creating a work of such dimensions drove Haydn, for once, to the limits of his legendary stamina. "I fell daily to my knees and asked God for strength to finish it," he said. He struggled through the first performance: "Sometimes my whole body was ice-cold, sometimes a burning heat overcame me, and more than once I was afraid that I would suddenly have a stroke." Yet the magnitude of the achievement was clear to everybody. "For the life of me," wrote one listener after the 1799 public premiere, "I wouldn't have believed that human lungs and sheep gut and calf's skin could create such miracles."

The Seasons (Die Jahreszeiten), Oratorio in Four Parts

Spring
Summer
Autumn
Winter

For three soloists (STB); chorus; piccolo, flutes I-II, oboes I-II,
    clarinets I-II, bassoons I-II, contrabassoon; horns I-IV, trumpets
    I-III, trombones I-III; timpani, snare drum, triangle; strings
Text by Baron Gottfried van Swieten after James Thomson's epic
    poem of the same name
Composed 1799–1800 in and around Vienna
First performed 24 April 1801 at a private performance in the
    Schwarzenberg Palace in Vienna, Haydn conducting; first public
    performance 29 May 1801, in the Vienna Redoutensaal
Published by Breitkopf & Härtel (Leipzig, 1802). *Inexpensive score:*
    Joseph Haydn: *The Seasons in Full Score* (New York: Dover,
    1986)
Duration: about two hours

It went almost without saying that a work as enormously popular as
The Creation of 1798 would foster a successor. *The Seasons,* too, has its
roots in England, for it is based on an epic poem of James Thomson
(1700–48)—a poem historians of English literature count among the
most interesting of the era. The German libretto was fashioned once
again by Baron van Swieten, who had the notion that the many
opportunities it offered for descriptive imitation (of animal sounds,
meteorological phenomena, and the like) would rouse the aging
Haydn to renewed compositional fervor.

In fact Haydn had had his fill of text painting and was annoyed by
the text of *The Seasons.* The country folk of the new work interested
him less than the archangels of *The Creation* had. When he got to the
lines "All hail, Industry, kind source of ev'ry gentle art," he complained that while he had been an industrious man his entire life long,
it had never occured to him that he would need to set industry to
music. In his declining years, Haydn would often remark that *The
Seasons* had overtaxed him and ruined his health.

However that may be, Haydn overcame, as composers must do,
the limitations of his libretto to create a coherent, often memorable,
work. Once you become accustomed to the fact that this oratorio will

seldom rival *The Creation,* you can begin to see its many strengths. For Haydn, in the wisdom of his years, confidently and compassionately portrays a convivial, simple humankind carrying out its daily tasks under God's benevolent gaze. Much of what made *The Creation* great is still there to be admired: the brilliant fugues, the trio textures, the advanced orchestration, and of course the symbolism at every compositional level. The rustic subject matter gives Haydn's sense of humor wider berth. This is apparent in Simon's aria, no. 4, where the farmer hastens forth in spring to plough his fields, whistling the famous melody from the "Surprise" Symphony; and, in the long *Autumn* portion, the drinking chorus where the fugue is carried on in the orchestra because the singers are too inebriated to make it on their own.

Each of the parts corresponds to one of the four seasons; each begins with an overture and recitative to suggest the season's attributes, with subsequent recitatives, arias, and choruses appropriate to the time of year. For a finale Haydn offers a unique double chorus with the three soloists. Listen especially for the great hunting chorus in *Autumn,* the many folk melodies, the merry rhythms which permeate the work, the slow and sultry tempos for *Summer.*

But what may well send a chill down your spine is the great aria at the end of *Winter,* where an old man looks back with nostalgia on his flowering spring, his summer's ardent strength, his sober autumn. Then he confidently turns forward, in the company of his virtue, to look on the promise of a second birth. The next glorious dawn, in the C-major chorus at the end, is that of Heaven. This is no less than Haydn's self-portrait, one of touching poignancy.

Paul Hindemith

Born *16 November 1895 in Hanau,*
near Frankfurt
Died *28 December 1963 in Frankfurt*

At the age of thirteen, Hindemith was admitted to the Conservatory in Frankfurt to study violin and composition. His gifts as a violinist and violist were prodigious, which was a good thing: after his father was killed in action in World War I, Hindemith supported himself and his family largely through his income as a performing musician. He went on to become one of the noted violists of his time.

Moreover, by the early 1920s Hindemith was widely recognized, especially through his appearances at the famous concerts of new music in Donaueschingen, as the best of the nation's young composers. In 1927, accordingly, he was appointed professor of composition at the Berlin Hochschule für Musik. This meteoric rise to celebrity as a performer-composer came to its climax in 1933–34 when, just as Hitler overtook Germany, Hindemith wrote his fine opera *Mathis der*

Maler. From 1934 on he was harassed by the Nazi regime, which branded his works as—among other things—Bolshevist. (In fact the central problems were that Hindemith's wife was Jewish, and that he continued to perform with Jewish players. It was also rumored that Hindemith had made his share of intemperate remarks about Hitler.) The Hindemiths left Germany for Switzerland in 1938.

In 1940 they emigrated to the United States, where Hindemith found a variety of good teaching posts, particularly at the Berkshire Music Center (Tanglewood) and Yale University. He was professor of music and director of the Collegium Musicum at Yale from 1940 to 1953, a particularly exciting era in that institution's long history of music making. The Hindemiths became American citizens in 1946. In 1950–51 he gave the prestigious Charles Eliot Norton Lectures at Harvard, subsequently published as *A Composer's World*. He divided his time, in his last years, between the United States and Switzerland.

Driven by a need for rigorous working out of his compositional principles (one of the things that made him a good teacher), Hindemith developed his philosophies of a modernistic style at a time when the very foundations of musical discourse were being rebuilt in other manners elsewhere. His idiom is resolutely tonal, with triads remaining the basic vertical sonorities, and with melodic and harmonic structures set forth according to hierarchies Hindemith thought were rooted in natural acoustics. The result is a music of complex themes pregnant with future promise, of high polyphony, well-balanced formal structures, and perhaps a certain paucity of rhythmic imagination. After *Mathis der Maler,* not a great deal changed in his basic premises, such that the majority of his familiar work embodies similarities of design that are easily recognized as the Hindemith sound.

A great believer in music of usefulness, Hindemith contributed significantly to the sonata and concerto repertoire for orchestral instruments, including notable additions to the literature for viola and cello. Additionally for orchestra there are the *Symphonic Dances* (1937), a Symphony in E♭, the *Symphonic Metamorphoses on Themes of Carl Maria von Weber* (1943), a symphony (and, later, opera) called *Die Harmonie der Welt* (1951), and the *Pittsburgh Symphony* (1959). There is also a wonderful Symphony in B♭ for Concert Band of 1951.

Symphony: *Mathis der Maler* (Matthias the Painter)

Engelkonzert (Angel Concert)
Grablegung (Entombment)
Versuchung des heiligen Antonius (Temptation of St. Anthony)

For piccolo, flutes I-II, oboes I-II, clarinets I-II, bassoons I-II; horns I-IV, trumpets I-II, trombones I-III, tuba; timpani, snare drum, bass drum, cymbals, small cymbals, triangle, glockenspiel; strings

Drawn from the opera *Mathis der Maler* in early 1934, before it was complete

First performed as a symphony 12 March 1934 by the Berlin Philharmonic, Wilhelm Furtwängler conducting; the complete opera first performed 28 May 1938 by the Zurich Stadttheater, Robert Denzler conducting

Published by B. Schott's Söhne (Mainz, 1934)

Duration: about 30 minutes

The painter Matthias Grünewald (d. 1528), master of the German Renaissance, was a near contemporary of Albrecht Dürer. Probably the best of his paintings is a multipaneled altarpiece done in the early sixteenth century for the monastery at Isenheim in Alsace, eastern France. The Annunciation and Nativity panels show a masterly, almost Flemish control of color and light; the Crucifixion, with its twisted, ravaged body of Christ, is of glacial stillness. In the hellish panels, by contrast, Grünewald creates a lurid turbulence of images. In sum, this powerful altarpiece, now displayed in Colmar, is well worth a visit.

Hindemith's opera on Grünewald's life and work was composed in a white heat, due in large measure to intimacies of intellectual stance shared between the Renaissance artist and twentieth-century composer. It is a tale, set during the Peasants' Revolt of 1524 and the dawn of Protestantism, wherein the artist discovers the futility of political and social engagement: the price of true art is the isolation of the artist. Hindemith drew his symphony from passages in the opera where Grünewald envisages the various panels of the altarpiece; it was finished and performed before the operatic *Mathis* was done.

To the left of the Virgin and Child in Grünewald's Nativity panel, angels in glorious raiment offer concerted music from their gilded pavilion. Hindemith's jubilant angel chorus, a sonata, begins with a slow introduction where the trombones state an old and apt tune, "Es sungen drei Engel" (There Sang Three Angels). The opening melody of the Allegro merits close attention, as it typifies Hindemith's imaginative intervallic structures, melodic open-endedness, and Baroque-style spinning out. The new theme you hear when the forward motion subsides and the texture broadens seems almost a mirror of the first. An innocent flute solo over light strings introduces the closing section of the exposition. In the development, where the two main themes are treated fugally as antecedent and consequent of each other, and in the recapitulatory synthesis as well, all these elements are woven together in a triumph of neo-Baroque imitative device. At length the slow-moving brass chorale returns, though now surrounded by the faster moving material from the other sections. Last reminiscences of the main thematic materials culminate in the breathtaking cadence for brass with triangle. The brilliance of the *Angel Concert* represents, to my mind, Hindemith at his very best.

The *Entombment* scene is obviously a meditation on death. One has the sense that the somber musings so well expressed in the first theme find a certain release in the tender dialogue of solo winds that follows. This sensation is reconfirmed by the adjustments to the passage at its recapitulation, where the violins soar gently from the bottom of their range heavenward.

The Temptation of St. Anthony, the most surreal of the Isenheim panels, has to do with the artist's temptations by the baser riches. (St. Anthony of Egypt was a hermit and prototypical monk, who endured unspeakable trials from all manner of devils.) A violent recitative introduces a long and complex movement imbued with sonata design, the exposition characterized above all by the near-continuous galloping rhythms in the accompaniment. At the center is a slow, intense episode for the strings, then a fast and crafty episode for brass, and various recapitulations, growingly harsh. The conclusion begins as a macabre dance in triple meter; out of this emerges, in the woodwind, the hymn *Lauda Sion Salvatorem* (Praise of Zion our Salvation). Temptation, in short, has been withstood: tribulation is banished with a glorious *Alleluia* from the brass.

Particularly interesting throughout *Mathis der Maler* is the deft deployment of the brass and percussion, and the thick, parallel voicing that often suggests the sound of a pipe organ. The contrapuntal practice is exceptionally fine, and Hindemith's strong sense of orchestral color makes the interplay of the voices, even in the densest passages, easy to perceive.

Symphonic Metamorphoses on Themes of Carl Maria von Weber

Allegro
Turandot: Scherzo (Moderato)
Andantino
Marsch

For piccolo, flutes I-II, oboes I-II, English horn, clarinets I-II,
   bass clarinet, bassoons I-II, contrabassoon; horns I-IV, trumpets
   I-II, trombones I-III, tuba; timpani, snare drum, bass drum,
   cymbals, small cymbals, triangle, tambourine, small gong,
   wood block, tom-tom, glockenspiel, chimes; strings
Composed: 1943 (score dated August 1943)
First performed 20 January 1944 by the New York
   Philharmonic, Artur Rodzinski conducting
Published by B. Schott's Söhne (Mainz, 1945)
Duration: about 20 minutes.

Like much of Hindemith's later music, the *Symphonic Metamorphoses* are meant to show off the post-Romantic orchestra—here with particular emphasis on the percussion. The themes for three of the movements come from piano duets by Carl Maria von Weber; the scherzo is based on the overture from Weber's instrumental music for a production of Schiller's *Turandot.* (This is a free translation of the same play Puccini used for his opera.) Weber found the Chinese tune he cites there in Rousseau's *Dictionnaire de musique* of 1768.

The Weber originals serve as mere starting points for Hindemith's invention. Both the first and the last movements are marches, by turns whimsical and rambunctuous; both begin simply with Weber's tunes and transform themselves—metamorphose—into intricate display as the role of Hindemith's countermelodies grows ever more significant. The lovely *Andantino,* based on a Weber siciliana, consists of increasingly ornamented treatments of the melody first begun in the clarinet; the restatement is dominanted by an obbligato for solo flute. The big movement, however, is the Chinese scherzo, where the simple tune works itself into a perpetual motion, ever grander in dimension. The wind and percussion work is for a time in the style of the Turkish band, with brash trills in the woodwind, snare drum, and triangle. When the percussion take over completely it is as though some huge musical clock has come unsprung, the last section discombobulating into irregular cycles of the constituent parts in multiple meters.

Gustav Holst

Born *21 September 1874 in Cheltenham*
Died *25 May 1934 in London*

An unassuming, almost reticent composer, embarrassed by the magnitude of his successes and never quite grasping the reasons for his failures, Holst was a teacher of merit, a central figure in English musical life, and a strong influence on the vivid English school of Britten and Tippett. Descended from a long line of European musicians, he was the son of a professional organist and pianist who pushed his son toward a career as piano soloist from all-too-early an age. He was happier when he became a village organist-choirmaster, a job that afforded him the opportunity to compose and conduct his own music. Holst studied composition with Sir Charles Villiers Stanford at the Royal College of Music, and owing to a neuritis of the right arm, abandoned the piano; instead he learned the trombone well enough to play professionally. Though he deemed his work as an instrumentalist "impersonal," it left him with an intimate knowledge of the orchestra and how it works. In 1905 he took a grueling job at the St. Paul's Girls' School in the London suburb of Hammersmith, a post he kept for the rest of his life. The income was steady, but so, too, was the struggle to find time to compose.

This was exacerbated by the unexpected triumph of *The Planets*, his first extended work to enjoy unequivocal praise. At midcareer—he was 45—he became a celebrity. After World War I, he returned from organizing concerts in the Middle East to unprecedented demand for works from his pen, recording contracts, and teaching assignments at august institutions of higher learning. Though he produced a host of important compositions thereafter, few of them were thought the equal of *The Planets*. His later music was held to be abstract and difficult.

For a weekend and summer composer, Holst was quite prolific, particularly in the vocal genres. His place in the instrumental repertoire is assured by *The Planets* and the First and Second Suites for Military Band (op. 28; 1909, 1911). (A popular prelude and scherzo for military band, *Hammersmith* [op. 52, 1930] has an orchestral transcription by the composer.) Less well known are four other works, *A Fugal Overture* and *A Fugal Concerto* (op. 40, nos. 1 and 2; 1922–23), *Egdon Heath,* a hommage to Thomas Hardy's *Return of the Native* (op. 47, 1927), and a Double Concerto for two violins and orchestra (op. 49, 1929). *Egdon Heath* takes wing from Hardy's description of "a place perfectly accordant with man's nature"; this Holst considered his best work.

Holst was a student and admirer of Hindu literature, having set his own translations from the *Rig Veda* (without knowing any authentic Indian music). Additionally he had a keen interest in English folklore, which he learned from its master, Cecil Sharp.

The Planets, OP. 32

> *Mars, the Bringer of War*
> *Venus, the Bringer of Peace*
> *Mercury, the Winged Messenger*
> *Jupiter, the Bringer of Jollity*
> *Saturn, the Bringer of Old Age*
> *Uranus, the Magician*
> *Neptune, the Mystic*

For female chorus (offstage); piccolos I-II, flutes I-IV, alto flute, oboes I-III, English horn, bass oboe, clarinets I-III, bass clarinet, bassoons I-III, contrabassoon; horns I-VI, trumpets I-IV, trombones I-III, tenor tuba, tuba; timpani, snare drum, bass drum, cymbals, triangle, tambourine, tam-tam, glockenspiel, chimes; xylophone, celesta; harps I-II, organ; strings

Composed 1914–16; arranged from a work for two pianos

First performed 29 September 1918 by the New Queen's Hall Orchestra in Queen's Hall, London, Adrian Boult conducting (this was a private performance given as a present by Balfour Gardiner, a patron of the composer); complete public performance 15 November 1920

Published by Goodwin & Tabb (London, 1921)

Duration: about 50 minutes

Holst's large-scale works before *The Planets* were not especially successful in their dealing with extended form and were, moreover, highly derivative—thick, one might say, with Wagnerian soup. ("He had a lot to unlearn," remarks his daughter Imogen.) It was his developing interest, from 1913, in astrology that appears to have opened new vistas: the contrasting characters of the planets suggested a lucidity of global structure that had so far eluded him. The seven-movement scale of the piece (Pluto was not discovered until 1930, and Earth is not included) is innovative indeed and has few predecessors, although Holst apparently knew Schoenberg's *Five Pieces for Orchestra*. The original manuscript, in fact, bears the title *Seven Pieces for Large Orchestra;* here the individual movements are headed not by the planet names but with what became the subtitles (*The Bringer of War,* etc.). "For instance, Jupiter brings jollity in the ordinary sense," he told the London press, "and also the more ceremonial type of rejoicing associated with religious or national festivities. Mercury is the symbol of mind."

In short, the subtitles, more than the planet names, are the key to the composer's descriptive intent. *Mars,* with its $\frac{5}{4}$ meter and incessant rhythmic motive, and *Saturn,* with its plodding accompaniment, are the dark movements. *Mars* is the more forceful, the rhythmic motto an underlying constant that sometimes clashes sharply with the ever-shifting tonality. (The violence of the movement, and the fact that *Mars* comes at the beginning of the work, was taken by wartime audiences to be commentary on the outbreak of World War

I; in fact, it had been sketched before the war began.) The motto never fully relents; even in the contrasting slow section toward the middle of the movement, the snare drum quietly plays a fragmented version of it. *Saturn* by contrast is static and cold. The melodic lines are compressed, and the harmony often approaches monotony as it oscillates between two chords. Slow, careful crescendos keep things from grinding to a halt, and a flirtation with a more animated tempo toward the end offers some respite from the chill.

Mercury, Jupiter, and *Uranus* are lighter in vein. *Mercury* is a nimble scherzo reminiscent of Mendelssohn and Berlioz. There is cleverness common to scherzos, including simultaneous subdivision of measures of fast $\frac{6}{8}$ into two groups of three and three groups of two; additionally Holst sometimes complicates the matter by superposing $\frac{2}{4}$, where four eighth notes take the space of six. In *Jupiter,* the flurry of strings at the opening goes on to accompany the strongly syncopated melody. This section is answered, after a pause, with a boisterous music-hall theme. The grand melody of the contrasting section is probably the most famous in the score (and, like the march *Pomp and Circumstance,* has had words added to it). *Uranus* is more impish. The four-note motive at the beginning introduces a dry, sardonic figure in the woodwind that goes on to control an exuberant play of the orchestral choirs.

Venus and *Neptune* are the tranquil movements. In *Venus,* Holst uses his two harps to great effect as they support a sensuous melodic undulation characterized for the most part by its minimalism. *Neptune* is the most abstract of Holst's conceptions, and appears to have made the greatest impression on his audience. The twinkle comes from the use of fast, quiet passagework in the strings and the harps, the arpeggios of the celesta, and the sustained percussion. Toward the end, a female chorus is heard offstage: they repeat the last measure of the work again and again as the stagedoor is slowly closed. "The sound," Holst instructs, "is lost in the distance."

The Planets is scored for monster orchestra, with women's chorus, organ, huge percussion battery, harps and celesta, and various unusual woodwinds including alto flute and heckelphone (a bass oboe). It is an impractical group to assemble, and thus a live performance of *The Planets* merits your excitement.

Charles Ives

Born *20 October 1874 in Danbury,*
Connecticut
Died *19 May 1954 in New York*

Ives was an authentic Yankee genius, eccentric and reclusive, who earned financial success in capitalistic enterprise and composed, during his spare time, a large body of radically progressive music. By choice he published very little and virtually never heard his works in live concert. He left behind confusing piles of manuscripts and contradictory instructions for dealing with them. Assessing the corpus of his work as a whole is a study still in its infancy.

The most important formative influence on Ives was his father George, a Connecticut music teacher who had been a bandmaster during the Civil War. From the family circle and his experience as church organist and bandsman, Ives absorbed the American military band repertoire, countless patriotic songs, Protestant hymnody, Negro spirituals, college songs, and the music of baseball and football. His father encouraged the children to experiment with strange musical effects—playing a simple song at the piano, for instance, with the left and right hands in different keys—and this sort of thing inspired Ives's lifelong interest in all kinds of clashing simultaneities. He was intrigued, for example, by the music of two bands intermingling and was delighted by the spatial effects of a passing parade.

Ives's higher education was at Yale University, where he showed himself a promising musician but otherwise poor student; he barely passed. After graduating he entered a New York insurance firm, eventually forming his own agency. For a time he played organ in a metropolitan Presbyterian church, then gave that up to devote more time to his composition. His health was fragile owing to a heart condition diagnosed in 1918, and this explains in part his somewhat curmudgeonly temperament and disinclination to go out. (Yet he lived for nearly 80 years, and at length succumbed not to his heart condition but to a stroke.) In 1919 he completed and published, at his own expense, the piano sonata called *Concord, Mass., 1840-60*, the four movements inspired by the great writers who lived there: Emerson, Hawthorne, the Alcotts, Thoreau. Within a few months he published a collection of *114 Songs* of 1888–1921. Both publications he gave away free to anyone who was interested. Regarding the *Concord Sonata* he soon published a companion volume of *Essays Before a Sonata* (New York, 1920), musings on poetry and patriotism. He retired from active composition in 1930, though he often returned to revise his works.

His music deals in an eclectic twentieth-century vocabulary: atonality, polytonality, some serialism, quarter-tones, free rhythms, chance elements, and the mutiplicity of textures that give nearly all his large music the sense of several things happening at once. He was obsessed by the "fate motive" in Beethoven's Fifth Symphony, by *Columbia the Gem of the Ocean* and *Nearer, My God, to Thee,* and he alluded incessantly to these and many other songs, sometimes so vaguely you cannot be certain what's on his mind. You have to learn to resist the "Name That Tune" syndrome with Ives: what is intriguing is his sense of music as an omnipresence of life, where tidbits of favorite melodies are apt to strike the ear without warning, then evaporate.

Ives composed four more-or-less complete symphonies (No. 1, 1896–98; No. 2, 1897–1902; No. 3, 1901–4 , winner of the Pulitzer Prize in 1947; No. 4, 1910–16), and an incomplete "Universe" Symphony. The "Holidays Symphony" is a "set of pieces for orchestra" composed from 1902 to 1912 and meant to stand alone as individual works if the occasion demands. *The Unanswered Question* and *Central Park in the Dark* likewise comprise an orchestral "set," as does *Three Places in New England*. The *Variations on "America,"* often played in William Schuman's arrangement for orchestra, were first composed for organ when Ives was 17. The rest of his music consists of songs (about 150), chamber music including some important violin sonatas, music for solo piano or organ, and works for church choir and glee club.

Three Places in New England

• *The "St. Gaudens" in Boston Common (Colonel Robert Gould Shaw and his Colored Regiment)*
Putnam's Camp, Redding, Connecticut
The Housatonic at Stockbridge

For piccolo, flutes I-II, oboes I-II, English horn, clarinets I-II, bassoons I-II, contrabassoon; horns I-IV, trumpets I-II, trombones I-III, tuba; timpani, bass drum, snare drum, cymbals, gong; piano, celesta, organ; harps I-II; strings

Composed c. 1908–14 in New York

First performed 10 January 1931 by the Chamber Orchestra of Boston in Town Hall, New York, Nicolas Slonimsky conducting (there had been a private reading, 16 February 1930, for the American Section of the International Society for Contemporary Music [ISCM]); reconstruction by James Sinclair for full orchestra first performed 9 February 1974 by the Yale Symphony Orchestra, John Mauceri conducting

Published by Mercury Music Corp., Inc. (Bryn Mawr, Pa., 1976); reduced orchestration published by Birchard (New York, 1935)

Duration: about 20 minutes

This orchestral triptych evokes patriots, settings, and events dear to the hearts of New Englanders. The first movement takes as its point of departure the monument erected by Augustus Saint-Gaudens in the Boston Common to honor Colonel Robert Gould Shaw (1837–63), commander of the fifty-fourth regiment of the Union Army, the first to consist of black soldiers. At the unveiling of the sculpture in

May 1897, William James spoke eloquently of Shaw's "lonely kind of courage, the kind of valor to which the monuments of nations should most of all be reared." Ives sets a prose-poem of his own at the head of the score ("Moving-Marching—Faces of Souls! / Marked with generations of pain," etc.). From the beginning we hear in the music the heavy footfall of soldiers, at one point slowing up, then regaining the original pace. ("Often," says Ives in the score, "when a mass of men march up hill, there is an unconscious slowing up. The drum seems to follow the feet, rather than the feet the drum.") The melodic allusions are to *Old Black Joe, Battle Cry of Freedom* ("Rally 'Round the Flag"), and *Marching Through Georgia.*

General Israel Putnam and his troops spent the winter of 1778–79 encamped outside Redding, Connecticut, where there is now a public park. We perceive the movement through the eyes of a child at a Fourth of July picnic there, sponsored by "the First Church and the Village Cornet Band." The child wanders away from the singing and the band, then falls asleep and dreams of the events long past: General Putnam himself comes over the hill. Here we have one of those sound collisions Ives so enjoys, with perhaps the best of his two-bands-at-once effects. The tunes are *The British Grenadiers* (the American version popularized, Ives tells us, by Putnam's soldiers), *Hail Columbia,* and *Semper Fidelis.* The craziness at the end is marked *con fuoco (as fast as playable).*

The Housatonic at Stockbridge takes its title from a poem by Robert Underwood Johnson, a portion of which is given in the score. ("Contented river! . . . / Thou hast grown human laboring with men / At wheel and spindle; sorrow thou dost ken.") The music commemorates a summer visit to Stockbridge, Connecticut, by Ives and his new wife, when they walked in the meadow and heard singing from the church across the river. "The mist had not entirely left the river bed, and the colors, the running water, the banks and trees were something that we would always remember." For the most part the movement is gently paced and delicate, with fragments of a hymn heard from both English and French horn, through a misty accompaniment; suddenly, there is a cataclysmic tutti chord and equally sudden fade.

Nicolas Slonimsky's first performances in New York and Paris used a small group of musicians from the Boston Symphony in a version reduced by Ives from the original full score. The 1935 publication is of this smaller version, in which a piano part covers for the excised orchestral lines. In the early 1970s James Sinclair readied a full score from the manuscripts at Yale; a number of recordings of this new version for full orchestra were subsequently issued.

Two Contemplations for Small Orchestra, generally called *The Unanswered Question* and *Central Park in the Dark*

I. *A Contemplation of a Serious Matter, or, the Unanswered Perennial Question*

For flutes I-II, flute III or oboe, flute IV or clarinet; trumpet or English horn or oboe or clarinet; solo strings
Composed 1906 in New York; revised in the 1930s
Published by Southern Music Publishing Co., Inc. (New York, 1953; rev. ed. 1986)
Duration: about 5 minutes

II. *A Contemplation of Nothing Serious, or, Central Park in the Dark in "The Good Old Summertime"*

For piccolo, flute, oboe, B♭/E♭ clarinet, bassoon; trumpet, trombone; snare drum, bass drum, cymbals; piano 1, piano 2 (two players); strings
Composed July–December 1906 in New York
First performed 11 May 1946 at the McMillin Academic Theater, Columbus University, with an orchestra of students from the Juilliard Graduate School, Edgar Schenkman conducting
Published by Bomart, Inc. (New York, 1949; rev. eds. Boelke-Bomart, Hillsdale, N.Y. 1973 and 1978)
Duration: about 8 minutes

Ives was always taken with the imponderables of life. The deceptively simple work he calls *The Unanswered Question* operates on three distinct plains: the tonal chord progression in the strings, the question as posed by the trumpet (the pitches are always the same but for the last note), and the responses of the woodwind quartet, usually but not mandatorily played on three flutes and a clarinet. It is the latter that draw our attention as they grow increasingly busy, opinionated, and stubborn. At the end, however, we are left with the stillness of the strings.

The woodwind ensemble travels at its own speed, without regard for the underpinning in the strings; it is as though the two groups are unaware of each other's existence. (For obvious reasons, two conductors are generally used.) Ives added a program to one of the versions of the score to the effect that the strings were to represent the Silence of Druids, knowing, seeing, and hearing nothing. The answers are those of human beings who, after contemplating the situation, mock the question.

In *Central Park in the Dark* the winds again move rapidly over sustained strings, but the effect is the opposite: here the background is atonal and the tunes tonal. The imagery is meant to suggest the sorts of things people might hear on a bench in Central Park some sultry summer evening "before" (Ives remarks) "the combustion engine and radio monopolized the earth and air." Over the nocturnal wending of the strings we hear sounds of a nightclub (a piano ragtime), passersby singing hit tunes, a band, and traffic: street cars, a fire engine, and so forth. A horse escapes from a cabman. Nighttime returns.

Both works have to do with Ives's courtship of Harmony Twitchell, the future Mrs. Ives (1876–1969). They were married in 1908.

Symphony No. 4

Prelude: Maestoso
Allegretto
Fugue: Andante moderato
Very Slowly: Largo maestoso

For chorus; piccolos I-II, flutes I-III, oboes I-II, clarinets I-III, optional saxophones (alto, tenor, baritone), bassoons I-III; horns I-IV, trumpets I-VI, cornets I-II, trombones I-III; timpani, snare drum, tenor drum, bass drum, cymbals, triangle, light gong, heavy gong, tom-tom, high and low bells; piano four-hands, celesta, organ, ether organ (theremin) *ad libitum;* strings with solo players

Composed 1910–16

First performance of movements I and II 29 January 1927 in New York by the Pro Musica Society (50 members of the New York Philharmonic), Eugene Goosens conducting; entire work performed 26 April 1965 in Carnegie Hall by the American

Symphony Orchestra, New York, Leopold Stokowski
conducting
Published by Associated Music Publishers, Inc. (New York,
1965); movement II published in Henry Cowell's *New Music*
Edition (San Francisco, 1929)
Duration: about 30 minutes

You're in for a shock if you've never heard Ives's Fourth, perhaps the
greatest and surely the most complicated manifestation of American
impressionism there is. Ives incorporated into it, during its long period
of genesis, many of his favorite principles, such that the Fourth Symphony offers a fine summary of his style. The four movements are
radically different in performing force (and thus wildy impractical to
rehearse), the first for chamber orchestra with chorus, the second for
the extended orchestra and assisting conductors, the third for a handful of winds, organ, and strings, and the fourth for the full orchestra
with chorus. Ives said that the work concerned the questions What?
and Why? posed in the first movement; the other three movements
supply different levels of response.

The Fourth Symphony is set in motion, after a cosmic orchestral
sigh, by violins and harp musing absently on the Lowell Mason hymn,
Bethany; this continues through the movement, and the tune goes on
to become a major component of the other movements. A solo cello
begins *In the Sweeet By and By.* A star is sighted, the symbol of both
Truth and Mystery: Ives began to think in these terms with the August
1910 appearance of Halley's Comet. The musical allusion is to the
Star of Bethlehem, for a chorus sings *Watchman Tell Us of the Night*—
of the "glory-beaming star." (Or does it? The score calls impishly for
"voices, preferably without voices"). "Watchman, tell us of the Night"
is, says Ives, an Eternal Question. Does this great celestial event bring
hope and joy or more problematic quantities? The possible answers
come in three movements: a comedy, a fugue of deep religious feeling, and a musical apotheosis.

The comedy, a scherzo, is another of Ives's Fourth of July movements, with quiet episodes built on Pilgrim hymns always swamped
by the brass and drums. The movement begins quietly with suggestions of dawn and, at the queasy string quarter-tones, yawns on awakening. The bustle begins: a screaming fanfare in the high winds
announces *Tramp, Tramp, Tramp* in the trombones. A ragtime march

breaks in, then a bit of *In the Sweet By and By*. All this culminates in an explosive statement of *Columbia, the Gem of the Ocean*. Now, to parody "polite salon music," there is cocktail piano with, as though from two different rooms, a solo violinist and violist plugging away in syncopation, still taken with the sweet by and by. The confusion grows complete: cornets launch into *Massa's in de Cold, Cold Ground*, the trombones into *Beulah Land*. After another explosion come echoes of the cocktail scene, as though a door has been closed and the street noises shut out; then a final orchestral potpourri of a half-dozen songs at once, including *Turkey in the Straw* and a bar of *Yankee Doodle*. Suddenly the bubble bursts, with the violas the last to dart away.

Ives notates the fugue in half notes, to give it an old formal look: one response to the questions of the prelude is religious ritual. The subjects are drawn from the hymns *From Greenland's Icy Mountains* and *All Hail the Power,* with solo horn or trombone as the celestial voice. When the movement begins to approach its climax the pipe organ enters, and with increasing dissonance the *Maestoso* is reached. At the end comes a quotation by the brass soloist of "And Heaven and Nature sing" from *Joy to the World*.

The last movement, an apotheosis of all that came before, begins with numerous references to the *Prelude:* the harps and violins form a distant choir, the double basses refer to the Mason hymn, and a "battery unit" of percussion players, oblivious to everything else, plays its tattoo. The momentum gradually builds, and at length the chorus reenters with a wordless rendering of *Bethany*. Nothing is left at the close but a glimpse of percussion and the distant violins.

Leoš Janáček

**Born *3 July 1854 in Hukvaldy, Moravia*
Died *12 August 1928 in Ostrava***

Janáček's youthful studies were in the Moravian capital of Brno, where he earned, as his father and grandfather had before him, credentials to become a school teacher. For much of the rest of his career he was a staff member at the Teacher's Institute of Brno and promoter of any number of enlightened musical enterprises in the city. During his early twenties, he travelled for further instruction to Prague, Leipzig, and Vienna, where he developed the beginnings of a solid compositional technique. Otherwise, owing to chronic monetary embarrassment, he did not profit much from the cultural offerings of the metropolitan capitals. An indefatigable activist from the beginning of his career, Janáček founded the Organ School in Brno and soon added to his duties a teaching position at the local Gymnasium.

His compositional life, as is so often the case with committed teachers, progressed in fits and starts. After many reverses, he began to discover the path to a viable style during the course of a field trip in 1888 to collect Moravian folk music. The opera *Jenůfa* is the result of long and systematic compositional rumination: elements of the folk repertoire flavor but do not overwhelm the work, and his theories of natural "speech-melody" for vocal lines—he took notes on the rhythms and intervals people used in ordinary speech—are channeled to great effect. *Jenůfa* was followed by other operas (on unusual, sometimes surreal subject matter) and a good deal of choral music. As he entered his seventh decade, Janáček was financially secure and well admired in Moravia. Elsewhere he was scarcely known.

That situation changed radically in May 1916, when a revised *Jenůfa* was staged in Prague to great public and critical acclaim. In its German translation and publication by a prestigious Viennese firm, the opera and its composer were soon known throughout the world. Janáček was 62. The rebirth of his compositional energies in those years is one of the most remarkable chapters in the history of Czech music. There were other reasons for the renaissance: for one thing he was buoyed by nationalistic pride, for Czechoslovakia was achieving its all too brief independence, and for another he had fallen in love—platonically, it seems—with Kamila Stösslová, a married woman half his age. Forthwith he completed three excellent operas, *Kát'a Kabanová* (1921), *The Cunning Little Vixen* (1924), and *The Makropulos Affair* (1926). There was another work in progress when he died. Of the many honors and recognitions that came his way he was proudest of his honorary doctorate from the university in Brno. He died unexpectedly of a pneumonia contracted during a holiday with Kamila and her son at his cottage in Hukvaldy.

Both works described below are products of these lusty years. Additionally in the concert hall you may hear *Taras Bulba* (1918), an orchestral rhapsody after Gogol on the story of the brave Cossack chieftain and his troublesome sons; *The Ballad of Blaník,* a symphonic poem (1920); and the Concertino for Piano and Chamber Orchestra (i.e., mixed sextet; 1925).

Sinfonietta

Allegretto
Andante
Moderato
Allegretto
Allegro

For piccolo, flutes I-IV, oboes I-II, English horn, E♭ clarinet, clarinets I-II, bass clarinet, bassoons I-II; horns I-IV, trumpets I-III, trombones I-IV, tuba; timpani, cymbals, glockenspiel; harp; strings; fanfare band in movements I and V: trumpets I-IX, tenor tubas I-II, bass trumpets I-II

Composed early 1926 in Brno; completed 1 April; dedicated at various stages to the Czech armed forces and to Rosa Newmarch, an English authority on Czech music.

First performed 26 June 1926 by the Czech Philharmonic Orchestra in Prague, Václav Talich conducting

Published by Universal Edition (Vienna, 1927)

Duration: about 25 minutes

The *Sinfonietta* opens with fanfares by a band of thirteen brass and timpani; these were composed for public exercises of a gymnastic society, similar to outdoor pageants Janáček had enjoyed as a child. So ruminating on his youth led him to compose, in short order, four other movements of a descriptive, cyclical work which became his most famous and, despite its relative brevity, longest orchestral composition.

According to its composer, the *Sinfonietta* describes "a man of today, free, fair, and joyful, with a strength and will to fight for his day"—whatever that may mean. (Nearly all Janáček's instrumental work has some degree of programmatic intent; the Concertino for Piano, for example, was said by the composer to make reference to hedgehogs, squirrels, and birds.) Here the vignettes are scenes of Brno past and present. The *Andantes* of the second movement, for example, suggest the majesty of a great castle. These alternate with faster band music of pointed rhythmic character, the dancing of children at play. The third movement remembers the Queen's Convent in old Brno, where Janáček had been a chorister. The lyric wind solos express "sacred peace . . . nocturnal shadows, the breath of the green hill." The trumpets reenter in movement IV, with a Bartók-like rhythm to describe the bustle of new Brno. This serves to introduce the last movement, an evocation of the town hall in Brno, symbol of centuries of enslavement yielded to government by the Slavonic people. The fanfares of the opening pages return, now under high trills elsewhere in the rest of the orchestra: the image is of the new nation's flags fluttering in the wind.

The *Sinfonietta* is an excellent place to begin one's consideration of the elements of Janáček's style: the pithy, repetitive motives that serve as the basic building blocks; their organization into sectional cells, often surrounded in the score with repeat marks; the oscillation of chord pairs (as at the beginning of the second movement or in the middle section of the third); the folk-imbued melodic configurations; the all-pervasive ostinato rhythms. The progress of keys is very free, with episodes of sudden and unexpected harmonic shift. (There are no key signatures.) Often you will become aware of mirrors in the underlying rhythmic patterns, where, for example, two eighths and a quarter in one bar will be answered by a quarter and two eighths in the next. The orchestration bears the unmistakable stamp of the village band; Janáček is given, too, to instrumental spacings that involve extremes of register, as in the high trills at the end of the work. New motives mutate from and interlock with what came just before, as cycle builds upon cycle. There is a primitive, almost minimalistic quality to such techniques, but in Janáček's case, the net effect always seems apposite to his compositional objectives.

Glagolitic Mass (M'ša Glagolskaja) (also called "Slavonic" and "Festival" Mass)

> *Introduction*
> *Gospodi pomiluj (Kyrie eleison)*
> *Slava (Gloria)*
> *Věruju (Credo)*
> *Svet (Sanctus)*
> *Agneče Božij (Agnus Dei)*
> *Organ Solo*
> *Intrada*

> **For** soloists (SATB); chorus; piccolos I-III, flutes I-IV, oboes I-II, English horn, clarinets I-III, bass clarinet, bassoons I-III, contrabassoon; horns I-IV, trumpets I-IV, trombones I-III, tuba; timpani, snare drum, cymbals, triangle, tam-tam, glockenspiel, bells; celesta, organ; harps I-II; strings
> **Text** in old church Slavonic
> **Composed** 5 August–15 October 1926 in Luhačovice and Brno, for the tenth anniversary of the Czechoslovak nation (1928) and the Exhibition of Contemporary Culture to celebrate it; this was also the millenium of St. Wenceslaus (d. 929)
> **First performed** 5 December 1927 in Brno; performed as well in

Geneva, 1928, for the first meeting of the International Music
Council
Published by Universal Edition (Vienna, 1928–29)
Duration: about 45 minutes

Janáček's nationalism was pan-Slavonic—he was, for example, an avid
student of Russian—and he saw in the use of old Slavonic, once the
common language of all his race, the means to suggest the strength
and dignity of his people. The Latin mass was translated into Slavonic
by venerable ninth-century churchmen using a new alphabet called
Glagolitic; the version used here was apparently pieced together by
Janáček and an associate. To celebrate the one-thousandth anniversary
of the life of Good King Wenceslaus, patron saint of Bohemia, Janáček wanted something more than a typical setting of the familiar
liturgical text: a festival excitement that included music for the arriv-
als and departures of the celebrants, the fancy organ improvisations
heard at the end of Mass, and above all a feeling of joyful brotherhood. (His imagined setting, he wrote colorfully, was of a cathedral
reaching to Heaven, star-topped fir trees its candles, its bells from a
herd of sheep, with thunder and lightning and music of nightingales,
thrushes, ducklings, and geese.) For all the jubilation, however, the
overall effect is one of simple piety, the handling of the chorus textures on the whole rather naive.

The festive introduction is constructed of interlocking cycles based
on the motive stated by the trumpets in the first two bars; winds and
percussion predominate. The theme of the *Kyrie,* first heard in the
cello in the opening measure, grows naturally from the introduction;
the chorus chants this figure again and again, interrupted by the
soprano's cry of "Christe eleison." (This is an excellent example of
Janáček's predilection for scoring by registral extreme; there are no
middle voices at the soprano's entry, only high treble and low bass.
Throughout the Mass, for that matter, the soprano and tenor have
the greater share of the solo work.) In the *Gloria,* or *Slava,* the angel
proclaims and reiterates over a twinkling accompaniment the message
brought to the shepherds in the fields: "Glory to God in the highest
and peace on earth to men of good will;" at length she is joined by
the chorus. After an orchestral interlude comes the remaining text,
shared between the soloists and chorus, with elated "amens" at the
close.

The "amens" carry into the *Credo* as well, and the motivic cycle that supports them is not so far removed from the bell-figures that have come before. Janáček dwells more dramatically, however, on the word *Věruju* (Credo, or "I believe") oscillating mystically beneath the tenor's declamations. Before the Crucifixus comes a vivid interlude for orchestra and organ on Christ's suffering; this is the occasion for the thunder and lightning. There is an exquisitely simple setting of the crucifixion text, with the resurrection passage assigned to women's voices. The *Věruju* returns, again with confirming "amens" from the chorus. This long movement summarizes, of course, the central tenets of Christian belief, and Janáček's apt setting is certain, strong, and wondrous.

A liquid *Sanctus* emphasizes a wide falling interval; the tempo accelerates and the peal of bells returns for the text "Heaven and earth are full of Thy glory." At length the alto soloist makes her first entry in the Benedictus, under the circumstances a stirring moment indeed. The *Agnus Dei,* too, begins with a ghostly orchestral figure (low instruments and high, again, with no middle). The chorus supplications, "Grant us Thy peace," are rendered in a homophonic *a cappella,* again of touching simplicity, the Slavonic people united in prayer. A flamboyant but very dark organ voluntary is succeeded by a brilliant recessional, with brass and timpani.

Zoltán Kodály

Born *16 December 1882 in Kecskemét,*
Hungary
Died *6 March 1967 in Budapest*

Kodály's accomplishments as composer, ethnologist pioneering in
the study of Hungarian folk music, and music educator are often
undervalued when he is compared with his countryman and collab-
orator, Béla Bartók. Bartók was the more interesting composer, but
Kodály, a natural academic, had such a long and productive life that
it is difficult to imagine any particular of Hungarian music left unaf-
fected by his influence. Aside from a half-year of study in Berlin and
Paris and concert and lecture tours abroad, Kodály spent most of his
life in Budapest. He was appointed to the faculty of the Academy of
Music there shortly after earning its Ph.D. degree, and from that base
he undertook the spectrum of activities that held his interest for six
decades. (During World War II the Kodálys harbored refugees, then
had to seek refuge themselves in a Budapest convent.) After the war

he enjoyed the life of an internationally distinguished musician and scholar, with attendant honorary degrees, decorations, and academy memberships. Moreover he lived to see many of his fondest dreams realized: the publication of a scholarly edition of Hungarian folk music, the adoption in the public schools of his principles of music education, and a thriving national choral movement.

Kodály gained recognition as a composer with his *Psalmus Hungaricus* (1923) for tenor, choruses, and orchestra, written for the 50th anniversary of the union of Buda and Pesth. His folk-opera (or Singspiel) *Háry János* of 1925–27 was similarly admired, the suite drawn from it soon played all over the world. The bulk of his orchestral music comes from the next decade: the *Dances of Marosszék* (1930); the very popular *Dances of Galánta* (1933), for the 80th anniversary of the Budapest Philharmonic Society; the *Variations on a Hungarian Folksong* (1938–39, popularly known as the "Peacock Variations" because the song is called "Fly, Peacock"), for the 50th anniversary of the Amsterdam Concertgebouw; and a Concerto for Orchestra for the 50th anniverary of the Chicago Symphony (1940). Kodály's last orchestral work is a Symphony of 1961. There is a large choral repertoire as well, for choral singing was at the heart of Kodály's notions of music education. His music is in a resolutely conservative idiom meant to accommodate the many Hungarian folk elements he wished to embrace; he is a master of rhythm and a fine orchestrator. Bartók minced no words about it, calling him "the most perfect embodiment of the Hungarian spirit."

The Kodály Method, a term too loosely bandied about by music teachers, denotes a system of music education that has as its overriding goal the achievement of universal musical literacy. Children are taught to read musical notation through the use of solfège syllables, and the repertoire is primarily folksong: cultures were defined, thought Kodály, by their folk music.

Suite from the opera *Háry János*, OP. 15

Prelude: The Fairytale Begins
Viennese Musical Clock
Song
The Battle and Defeat of Napoleon
Intermezzo
Entry of the Emperor and His Court

For piccolos I-III, flutes I-III, oboes I-II, E♭ clarinet, clarinets I-
  II, alto saxophone, bassoons I-II; horns I IV, trumpets I-III,
  cornets *à pistons* I-III, trombones I-III, tuba; timpani, snare
  drum, bass drum, cymbals, triangle, tambourine, tam-tam,
  glockenspiel, chimes, xylophone, celesta; piano, cimbalom;
  strings
Composed 1925–26 for a song play in five adventures by Béla
  Paulini and Zsolt Harsányi; the suite was extracted in 1927
First performed with the opera 16 October 1926 at the Royal
  Opera House, Budapest; the Suite first performed 15 December
  1927 in New York, Willem Mengelberg conducting
Published by Universal Edition (Vienna, 1927)
Duration: about 25 minutes

Háry János is a daydreaming veteran of the Napoleonic wars. The
composer writes:

> Day after day he sits in the tavern and recounts his incredible heroic feats.
> He is a true peasant, and his grotesque inventions are a touching mixture
> of realism and naiveté, of comedy and pathos. All the same, he is not just
> a Hungarian Baron Münchausen. On the surface he may appear to be no
> more than an armchair hero, but in essence he is a poet, carried away by
> his dreams and feelings. His tales are not true, but that is not the point.
> They are the fruits of his lively fantasy, which creates for himself and for
> others a beautiful world of dreams . . . We all dream of the great and
> impossible. Few of us master, like Háry, the courage to utter our dreams.

The orchestral sneeze at the beginning indicates, by Hungarian
tradition, that one is to take the ridiculous tale that follows with a
grain of salt. Napoleon's wife Marie-Louise has fallen in love with
Háry, and along with Háry's fiancée, Orsze, they go off in a carriage
to visit the court. At the Schönbrunn Palace, a musical clock strikes
the hour with a parade of lead soldiers. The *Song* is an authentic Hungarian melody, stated first by unaccompanied viola, then in further
strophes for solo woodwinds over improvisatory figurations: Háry and
Orsze are longing for their distant home. Napoleon has heard of his
wife's infidelity, and sets out with all his troops to avenge his honor.
Háry engages the French singlehandedly, and they are vanquished to
the last man—Napoleon himself. Háry agrees, this once, not to
decapitate the defeated leader: "Just sign a pledge that you'll never
annoy our emperor and terrorize our world again, so help you God."

The music is a comic quickstep for brass and percussion with violently shrill piccolos and a plaintive saxophone; after the very obvious moment of defeat comes a funeral march, where the quickstep melody turns into a dirge for saxophone.

The *Intermezzo* that reflects on Háry's military victory is, like the *Song,* strongly Hungarian in character. Both movements call for busy passagework from the cimbalom, a hammered zither of the sort you may well encounter in a Hungarian restaurant. Here there is also the influence of the *verbunkos,* a kind of ceremonial dance descended from soldier music the Austrians used to lure army recruits; the broad, heavy windup (*lassu*) inevitably springs out into faster, merrier material (*friss*). Now the Austrian emperor and court celebrate their triumph with a march. But Háry must renounce his pleasures: his new home awaits, and Orsze probably has dinner waiting.

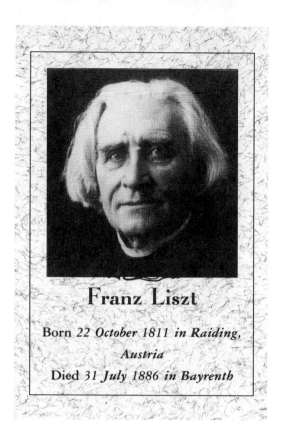

Franz Liszt

Born 22 October 1811 in Raiding, Austria
Died 31 July 1886 in Bayrenth

Patron of Berlioz, confidant of Wagner, father of Cosima Liszt von Bülow Wagner, essayist and correspondent, conductor, creator of the symphonic poem, and one of the founders of modern piano technique, the Hungarian virtuoso Liszt was numbered by his contemporaries as one of the three pillars (with Berlioz and Wagner) of "The Artwork of the Future."

His talents as a pianist were encouraged by his father (an employee of the Esterházy estate, where Haydn had worked), and he was sent to Vienna to study with Czerny and Salieri. He moved to Paris in 1827, where for eight years he consciously endeavored to be the Paganini of the piano. There he became lifelong friend to both Chopin and Berlioz, and there he met the first of his long-term companions, Marie, Countess d'Agoult. After a sojourn in Switzerland (where the Countess bore him three children, including the famous Cosima), he embarked on more than a decade of triumphant concert tours throughout Europe and to such exotic places as Ottoman Turkey. In 1848 he abandoned the life of the touring virtuoso to become court conductor to the grand duke of Saxe-Weimar. He soon took up residence with another aristocratic lady, Carolyne, Princess Sayn-Wittgenstein, who had left her husband and come to Weimar to form the liaison. In Weimar, Liszt supervised the first productions of Wagner's early operas as well as significant works by other composers. From 1861, his amorous attachment and the Weimar experience both having come to abrupt ends, he lived mostly in Rome, where by 1879 he had become deeply enough involved in the practice of Catholicism to take minor orders in the church. Thereafter he dressed in clerical garb and enjoyed being called the Abbé Liszt.

Though Liszt is arguably less important as a composer than as a proponent of modern art music, his oeuvre is considerable: there are significant choral works, songs, pieces for solo piano (many of them landmarks in the development of post-Romantic harmony), and, from early in his career, dozens of transcriptions for piano from the operatic and orchestral repertoires. His works for orchestra include the symphonic poems *Tasso* (1849, rev. 1854); *Les Préludes* (1848, rev. 1854), *Orpheus* (1853–54), *Prometheus* (1850, rev. 1855), *Mazeppa* (1851, rev. 1855), and eight others from the rich decade 1848–58; the *Faust-Symphonie* (1854–57) and Symphony on Dante's *Divine Comedy* (1855–56); and two piano concertos (1849, rev. 1856; 1839, rev. 1857) and a *Totentanz* for piano and orchestra (1849, rev. 1859).

Concerto No. 1 for Piano and Orchestra in E♭ Major

Allegro maestoso; Quasi Adagio; Allegretto vivace; Allegro marziale animato
[Played without pause]

For piano solo; piccolo, flutes I-II, oboes I-II, clarinets I-II, bassoons I-II; horns I-II, trumpets I-II, trombones I-III; timpani, cymbals, triangle; strings

Composed 1848–49; first orchestrated by Joachim Raff; revised 1853 and 1856; dedicated to Henry Litolff, peripatetic English composer-pianist and music publisher

First performed 17 February 1855 by the Weimar Court Orchestra, Liszt, piano, Berlioz, conducting

Published by Carl Haslinger quondam Tobias (Vienna, 1857).
Inexpensive score: Franz Liszt: *The Piano Concerti in Full Score* (New York: Dover, 1986)
Duration: about 20 minutes

Having settled himself in Weimar at the head of a small but accomplished ducal orchestra, Liszt summoned his legendary musical gifts in support of what was, given his record so far of display pieces and piano miniatures, an ambitious goal: to become a serious composer, in the extended orchestral forms of what we would now call the avant-garde. The body of orchestral works he composed or perfected in the decade from 1848 is formidable: twelve symphonic poems, the two concerti, and the great programmatic symphonies. At first it was slow going, for his experience with orchestras was on the whole quite limited; he received assistance in scoring from his disciples Joachim Raff and August Conradi. Soon enough he found his own way, and the final versions of all his major works are indeed his.

The First Piano Concerto, parts of which had been sketched in Paris in 1830, announces some of the principles of the new style, prevailingly monothematic and deliberately free from the traditional controls of sonata design. In a process called thematic transformation, the very limited thematic material is mutated and redeployed such that the works have both strong melodic unity and a dazzling melodic variety. Liszt's model here is Schubert's *Wandererfantasie,* in which a single composition, played without pause, is constructed from multiple submovements linked by thematic identities.

The *Allegro* begins with a dark, march-like motto in the minor mode which acts as a ritornello connecting solo cadenzas. From the beginning the cadenzas are colored by interjections from the orchestra; in the lyric middle section, there is a glorious exchange of the solo material by the clarinet, violin, and cello. The motto reasserts itself impetuously, first in the orchestra and then in hammering piano octaves, but this is subdued and in the end simply peters out. A new theme begins the slow movement, first heard in the strings, then taken over by the piano. The arioso is interrupted by another solo, after which we hear a third significant theme from the flute, over long trills in the piano.

The third movement is a march / scherzo with triangle. From here on out, you will recognize most of the thematic material: following the main statement there is a playful trio, a return to the impetuous hammerings of the first movement and the flute melody of the second. The fourth movement is a full-blooded march, with piccolos, cymbals, and full low brass, and conspicuous reference to the materials of the second movement.

It's enough to sense the general drift of the relationships without worrying too much about the particulars: your probable reaction will be to nod to yourself that this or that tune seems somehow familiar. With Liszt you must never forget to admire the technical virtuosity: let your imagination wander to the 1840s, when this Titan of the keyboard seduced an entire civilization with his dextral wizardry— or, better still, to that evening in February 1855 when Berlioz, the father of orchestral conducting, and Liszt, the century's musical godfather, first offered this concerto as a humble birthday present to a grand duchess.

Les Préludes, Symphonic Poem after Lamartine

For piccolo, flutes I-III, oboes I-II, clarinets I-II, bassoons I-II; horns I-IV, trumpets I-II, trombones I-III, tuba; timpani, snare drum, bass drum, cymbals; harp; strings

Composed 1848 in Weimar; revised in 1850 and 1854; dedicated to the Princess Carolyne Sayn-Wittgenstein, Liszt's mistress

First performed 23 February 1854 by the Weimar Court Orchestra, Liszt conducting

Published by Breitkopf & Härtel (Leipzig, 1856)

Duration: about 15 minutes

The title comes from one of the *Nouvelles Mélodies poétiques* (Paris, 1823) by the great Romantic poet Alphonse de Lamartine (1790–1869). His image is of a breeze that sets the lyre of song in motion, soothes the soul, and ultimately lifts our music, when our time is done, to celestial, Elysian heights. Lamartine called *Les Préludes* a "sonnet of poetry."

The rhetoric of spleen and isolation was much in the air during Liszt's time in Paris. When he began, in Weimar, to compose his series of symphonic poems on literary programs, it was to those heady days of French Romanticism that he turned for inspiration. The preface in the score, which was provided after the fact by Hans von Bülow and Carolyne Sayn-Wittgenstein, expresses a rather vague program where the trials of life are seen as preludes to the unknown hereafter: "What else is our life but a series of preliminaries to that unknown Hymn, the first and solemn note of which is intoned by Death?" It goes on to describe love as the dawn of being, the tribulations of our earthly existence, the serenity of the afterlife, and yet the necessity to answer the demands of life with our full consciousness.

Dull prose it is, in its struggle to summarize the amorous, pastoral, and military elements Liszt had already incorporated in *Les Préludes.* Actually the work has another program, having originally been composed as an overture to a series of four male choruses called *Les Quatre Eléments:* the North wind, the sea, the stars, and the earth.

You should file all this away in the recesses of your memory, turning your attention to the music alone, for *Les Préludes* requires none of it. It is, however, an excellent example of the way Lisztian thematic transformation works. Here, in a single, big sonata movement, the constituent sections form individual submovements. The slow introduction presents the principal theme, first as a lugubrious passage in the strings following just after the two pizzicatos that open the work; the rebound in the woodwinds makes a three-note motive from the theme. This material develops, at the entry of the harp, into a clearly directed transition. An Andante maestoso announces itself with clarion statements of the first thematic transformation and calls of trumpets and horns; at the shift to a compound triple meter, you hear the next transformation, a languid setting in the inner strings, soon joined by a dialogue of bassoon and French horn. There is a obvious change of key (C major to A major), then what is probably the most impressive setting of the material, a barcarole for horns and violas. A long and tempestuous development ensues, with emphasis on the clarion calls, then subsides into the gentleness of the woodwind choir. At the shift into $\frac{6}{8}$ a new submovement begins, marked by Liszt Allegretto pastorale but rather more like a scherzo than a true slow movement. The meter affords the opportunity to recapitulate the barcarole. The key returns to its original C major and the pace begins to quicken. Violin cascades and heroic statements in the brass announce the finale, which becomes a swashbuckling march with concluding Maestoso.

It's a fascinating design in its juxtaposition of heroism and agony, rooted as they are in common origins. There were more radical things going on in music composition during the years Liszt was at work on *Les Préludes,* but its fundamental notions lie at the core of nineteenth-century thought.

A *Faust Symphony* in Three Character-Pictures after Goethe, with Closing Chorus

Faust
Gretchen
Mephistopheles

For piccolo, flutes I-III, oboes I-II, clarinets I-II, bassoons I-II; horns I-IV, trumpets I-III, trombones I-III, tuba; timpani, cymbals, triangle; strings; the closing chorus calls additionally for tenor solo, male chorus, harp, and organ

Composed in its first version August–October 1854 for rather smaller orchestra; chorus added 1857, and a dozen measures were added to the slow movement in 1880; dedicated to Hans von Bülow

First performed 5 September 1857 in Weimar, Liszt conducting at a concert to celebrate the laying of the cornerstone for a monument to the Grand Duke of Saxe-Weimar, Karl August, patron of Goethe, and to the Weimar artists Goethe, Schiller, and Wieland

Published by J. Schuberth & Co. (Leipzig, 1861)

Duration: about 70 minutes

Berlioz had just published his *Huit Scènes de Faust* when Liszt, full of enthusiasm for the new *Symphonie fantastique* (December 1830), swept him off for dinner and conversation. They surely talked of *Faust* that night.

Liszt first began to sketch an orchestral *Faust* in 1840. In 1852 he suggested that Wagner expand his *Faust* overture, which Liszt had conducted, into a three-movement symphony. A few months later he had taken his own advice. (In turn, Wagner, then at work on the *Ring,* subsequently fashioned from Liszt's Faust theme his own Leit-motiv for Fate.)

Meanwhile Berlioz had expanded his Faust music into *La Damnation de Faust,* an evening-long symphonic legend, conducting portions of it in Weimar in November 1852. Eventually, Liszt and Berlioz exchanged dedictions of their *Fausts.*

The long, long *Faust-Symphonie* is without a doubt Liszt's best orchestral work. It is partly the psychology that attracts, for Liszt saw himself as Faust and Mephistopheles rolled into one: Mephistopheles as merely the negative side of Faust—or, as he put it, the spirit one denies in oneself.

Faust's movement begins, Lento assai, with two interlocking themes, the searching melody in the low strings and the motive of his love for Gretchen. (The cello theme embodies all twelve pitches of the chromatic scale and is thus looked on with great satisfaction by those who would search out the roots of the twentieth century.) The Allegro of the sonata, marked *impetuoso* in clear reference to Faust's character, opens with string theme and woodwind response related in both shape and affective quality to the themes of the slow introduction; there is confirming brass to conclude. The development is long and tortuous, as are Faust's ruminations in general, and the recapitulation embraces the implications of the opening Lento. It is symbolic that the Gretchen theme, though still uncertain, concludes the movement.

After that half-hour's worth of music, Gretchen's quiet movement is all the more welcome. After an uneasy introduction in the upper woodwind, the key settles and the solo oboe begins the aria accompanied by solo viola. The dialogue of woodwinds and strings, after the oboe cadenza, is said to reflect a scene in Goethe where Gretchen plays "he loves me, he loves me not" with a daisy. During an accelerando themes from the first movement are transformed into a character appropriate to Gretchen's. The aria recapitulates in a setting for four violins. One of Faust's motives is heard, softly, at the end, for he has found in Gretchen all he was longing for.

The scherzo for Mephistopheles is a mocking, malicious treatment of Faust's themes, grotesque laughter and all. Harsh pizzicatos (from a *Malédiction* Liszt had composed for piano and strings) introduce a rather cruel, fugal setting of the love theme. Gretchen's theme (in the woodwinds and horn) is swallowed up by the diabolic scherzo as it drives on and on. At the end, there is a last vision of Gretchen (cellos and horn) and a dead march in the brass; the male chorus comes onstage during the long timpani roll. The mystical chorus is in C major, with pipe organ, and we find in Heaven the contentment never enjoyed on earth. "What could not be achieved . . . is here accomplished," says the text. "Everlasting womanhood draws us on high." The tenor's tune is that of Gretchen's aria. And the text, hauntingly, was later used by Mahler at the end of his Eighth Symphony.

Gustav Mahler

Born 7 *July* 1860 *in* Kalischt (Kalište),
Bohemia
Died 18 *May* 1911 *in* Vienna

Distinguished during his lifetime primarily for his conducting, Mahler is now seen as the central figure in music between Brahms and Schoenberg and was, with Richard Strauss, among the last of the post-Wagnerian Romantics. After music studies at the Vienna Conservatory and courses in history and philosophy at the university, he held a series of increasingly prestigious conducting posts, at first assisting Anton Seidl and Arthur Nikisch, then as principal conductor in his own right. His tenure in Kassel (1883–85) was followed by posts in Prague (1885–86), Leipzig (1886–88), and the opera houses of Budapest (1888–91), Hamburg (1891–97; the symphony conductor there was Hans von Bülow), and finally Vienna (1897–1907). In collaboration with the noted set designer Alfred Roller, he led the Vienna Opera confidently into the twentieth century, not so much with new music as with gloriously modern productions of Wagner, Mozart, Beethoven, and Gluck. Mahler's tenure from 1898 as conductor of the Vienna Philharmonic concerts was controversial, for, despite his popularity with audiences, he was thought to be highhanded with the repertoire and his musicians alike. He resigned this post after only three seasons.

In 1907 Mahler came to the United States to be principal conductor of the Metropolitan Opera and later the New York Philharmonic (at a princely salary: $30,000 a year). His time in this country was not especially happy, either: his autocratic manner and free hand with limited funds caused bitter disputes with his boards of directors, and his health was in its ultimate decline. He conducted for the last time in New York on 21 February 1911, while suffering with a high fever. Eventually he was diagnosed as having a bacterial infection of the blood, incurable in those days. Thereupon he sailed for Europe and died in a Viennese sanitorium a few days after reaching home.

In part, he had simply burned himself out from the grueling demands of his two brilliant careers. Only during his summer retreats to the Austrian countryside could he find the periods of uninterrupted concentration necessary for his sort of composing; what little time was left to him during the season he spent orchestrating and correcting his music. He was, moreover, an obsessive perfectionist, given not merely to habitual retouching of details but to large-scale rewritings and reorchestrations even after his works had been performed and circulated. He composed exclusively in the genres of song and symphony, integrating the two so completely that it makes little sense to try to define the distinction. Mahler's tonal practice is, for its time and place, not very radical; his sonata forms, on the other hand, are matchless in originality. It is a music of contrasts and often violent interruptions, by turns traditional, naive, good humored, melancholy, positively depressing, and of course grandiose in the tradition of the loudest Wagner and Bruckner.

Mahler was a man of complex personality who worried excessively about love and death—and on one occasion spent the day in informal consultation with Freud. More pronounced than with Tchaikovsky is the sense that he is always edging toward the psychotic, but in the end his very conundrums give the music its exceptional power and depth. His large-scale work consists of ten symphonies, the last unfinished at his death, and *Das Lied von der Erde* (The Song of the Earth), a late symphonic work for soloists with orchestra. The Eighth Symphony in E♭ (1906–7; first performed in Munich, 1910) is commonly (but erroneously) called the "Symphony of a Thousand" in view of its large performing force of eight soloists, chorus, boy's chorus, organ, and monster orchestra with offstage bands. His Tenth Symphony was to have been in five movements; of these Mahler left an *Adagio* in reasonably good shape and another in a condition that approached being playable. Both movements were performed by the Vienna Philharmonic on 14 October 1924. Deryck Cooke later completed a performing version of the full work; this has been published (1976) and recorded; it may occasionally be heard in the concert hall. The orchestral songs are the *Lieder eines fahrenden Gesellen* (Songs of a Wayfarer), *Des Knaben Wunderhorn* (The Youth's Magic Horn), *Kindertotenlieder* (Songs on the Death of Children), and Five Songs to Texts of Friedrich Rückert (1901–2).

Mrs. Mahler, the former Alma Schindler, went on to become the mistress of the painter Oskar Kokoschka and subsequently married Walter Gropius the architect and Franz Werfel the writer.

Symphony No. 1 in D Major

Langsam, Schleppend
Kräftig bewegt
Feierlich und gemessen, ohne zu schleppen
Stürmisch bewegt
[No pause between movements III and IV]

For piccolos I-II, flutes I-IV, oboes I-IV, English horn, E♭ clarinet, clarinets I-III, bass clarinet, bassoons I-III, contrabassoon; horns I-VII, trumpets I-IV, trombones I-III, tuba; timpani (2 players), bass drum, cymbals, bass drum with cymbals mounted on top, triangle, tam-tam; harp; strings

Composed c. 1885–88 in Kassel and Leipzig; revised through 1906; originally there were five movements; the second, an Andante called *Blumine,* was removed c. 1896

First performed 20 November 1889 by the Budapest Philharmonic, Mahler conducting

Published by Josef Weinberger (Vienna, 1899). *Inexpensive score: Gustav Mahler: Symphonies Nos. 1 and 2 in Full Score* (New York: Dover, 1987)

Duration: about 50 minutes

The First Symphony and the *Lieder eines fahrenden Gesellen* (Songs of a Wayfarer; see p. 341) are works of simultaneous inception, stemming in part from an unhappy liaison between Mahler and the singer Johanna Richter during his brief tenure as music director in Kassel (1883–85). The songs were composed with piano accompaniments to be orchestrated later; in the delay the symphony emerged, borrowing—and orchestrating for the first time—some of the material from the songs.

Originally, the First was not called a symphony at all, but rather a Symphonic Poem in two parts and five movements. The first part, "From the Days of Youth," embraced three movements: "Spring without End," the Andante *Blumine* ("A Chapter of Flowers"), and "In Full Sail," the scherzo. In the second half, "The Human Comedy," were the funeral march, called "Aground" and the finale "Dall' Inferno al Paradiso." The published score of 1899 omits the program elements and the *Blumine* movement.

The first movement alludes strongly, in its long, slow introduction, to the opening of Beethoven's Ninth. But where Beethoven's initial passage turns out to harbor all the violence of Nature, Mahler flavors his open fifths with pastoral horns and a distant military fanfare. He then turns the falling interval into a cuckoo call. The high-pitched whine of the string harmonics, moreover, is decidedly post-Beethovenian. All the preparation is for an Allegro of meadows and fields, its principal material drawn from the second of the Wayfarer songs. In view of the length of the introduction, the exposition seems quite short and must be repeated for good balance. The development, which begins by returning to the slow motion and high whine of the opening, soon introduces important new material, a confident march heard in the quartet of French horns, *pianissimo*—not new, exactly, for there are antecedents in the ruminating horns of the introduction. For a Mahlerian development, what follows seems restrained and prevailingly carefree, even given the complexity of the motivic interaction. As the climax approaches, however, the trumpet calls are deflected into throbs and groans, emphasized in the bass, that begin the big crescendo to recapitulation. Rapturous flourishes of the trumpet calls from the introduction boil over into the French horn march, now quite martial. As is typical of Mahler's sonata forms, the materials from the exposition return in midstream, compacted, anxious to conclude. In this case the movement ends in an accelerando of the cuckoo figure and the rapid fire of general orchestral merriment.

The second movement is a plodding country dance, typically thought to be Breughelesque in connotation, with a genteel trio. In the first departure things take wing and end up riotously with uplifted bells in the winds, stopped horns, the kind of chaotic forward motion Mahler is given to marking "wild," and other tonalities clashing up against the interval so firmly established in the bass. The country dance can only return tentatively at first, then with growing confidence. The trio is suave, with erotic glissandos and rubatos in the interwoven melody lines and lovely work for solo cello. When the dance recurs for the last time, its vulgarities have been polished and civilized.

For his funeral march, Mahler had in mind a vaguely comic fairy-tale illustration, "The Hunter's Funeral Procession," in which a coffin—presumably that of the hunter—is borne forward by a parade of forest animals. The tune is the familiar round *Frère Jacques,* set in the minor mode over the continuous knell of a timpani ostinato. What comedy there is lies in the droll choice of soloists: double bass, bassoon, cello, tuba, and so on. A funereal tattoo is heard from the oboes, then the tolling of a tam-tam. The first of the trios begins as a lazy, possibly ethnic strain for oboes and trumpets, soon made mocking and lively (and Turkish) by the band and primitive bass drum and cymbals. A partial and very brief return to the round separates the two trios: the next turns to the major mode and cites the fourth of the Wayfarer songs, *Die zwei. blauen Augen,* likewise a cortege. Bits of the village-band episode have by now reasserted themselves and continue through the return of D minor and the procession recedes into the distance, with echoes in the timpani.

A terrifying orchestral thunderclap shatters the moment and sets the fourth movement into motion. The massive introduction carries on and on, as the triplet figures in the winds plunge ever deeper into the bass register. Finally, a savage march surges forth, eventually reaching a climax marked "with great ferocity." From its rubble emerges, as second subject, a songful passage for strings in a passive key. The long timpani roll and groaning cellos begin the development by reintroducing the atmosphere of the first movement. When it reaches the familiar fanfare, a firm D major with the tonic pitch sustained across the orchestra, and a happy peal of French horns, you sense a peroration in the making. Instead there is a dramatic return of first-movement motives and minor key, bird songs, and a lingering over the second subject before a proper recapitulation of the first. Once more the major-mode fanfares erupt over a sustained bass, this time culminating in a very long coda marked "triumphant." The way he goes on is probably excessive, but you can't deny the thrill when he gets to the end.

Symphony No. 4 in G Major

Bedächtig, nicht eilen
In gemächlicher Bewegung, ohne Hast
Ruhevoll
Sehr behaglich

For solo voice (soprano); piccolos I-II, flutes I-IV, oboes I-III, English horn, E♭ clarinet, clarinets I-III, bass clarinet, bassoons I-III, contrabassoon; horns I-IV, trumpets I-III, [no trombones or tuba]; timpani (2 players), bass drum, cymbals, triangle, glockenspiel, sleigh-bells, tam-tam; harp; strings
Text of movement IV from *Des Knaben Wunderhorn* (see p. 343)
Composed summers 1899–1900 in Maiernigg; the song used in the last movement was written in March 1892; revised 1906 for publication and, with the other symphonies, 1910
First performed 25 November 1901 by the Kaim Orchestra of Munich, Mahler conducting
Published by Ludwig Doblinger (Vienna, 1902); rev. ed. Universal Edition (Vienna, 1906). *Inexpensive score:* Gustav Mahler: *Symphonies Nos. 3 and 4 in Full Score* (New York: Dover, 1989)
Duration: about 55 minutes

The most intimate of Mahler's symphonies—the only one to lack trombones, for example—ends with a delicate song for soprano and orchestra, *Das himmlische Leben* (The Heavenly Life). So, too, do the other movements, each in its own way, seem innocent of the trials and tribulations before redemption so common with composers who view music as a journey. Yet the Fourth is a progressive work, too, especially in its melodic style of long-lined themes that pass from instrument to instrument as they unfold and then afterward live mostly in their constituent motives. Melodies often seem to be taken up in midstream, as though returning to thoughts too soon abandoned. The sonata forms are correspondingly flexible, softened always by Mahler's urge to transform and follow through as he goes along.

The symphony opens with sleighbells and circular woodwind figures, establishing for the movement its basic rhythmic pulse and good-natured orchestration. Segments of melody assemble into an expansive and gracious principal theme. A lurch forward in tempo and clarinets of shrill register effect the transition to the second subject, begun by cellos, *espressivo;* this is interrupted just short of closure by fragmentary digressions, then replaced—sleighbells and all—by an unusual return of the first theme. For a time it sounds as though the exposition is simply repeating, but little momentum is achieved and the music comes instead to a stop. Here, once more, the sleighbells: that this is the development becomes clear almost immediately, as hints of minor tonality and other unrests begin to be heard working themselves into ever more grotesque confrontations. Now, with ultimate assurance, the first violins settle gently into the recapitulation, not from the beginning of the main theme but from its third bar—an effect that delighted Mahler. Nor is the recapitulation ever quite note-for-note, but rather refashioned to sum up all that has come before, as the movement dances away with merry triangling.

Between the first and second movements the concertmaster switches to a violin tuned with its E string raised to F♯ to give it a tinny sound—"like a fiddle," the score says. In form the movement comes from the scherzo-and-trio family, with two trios. Additionally, the scherzo portions embrace a delicate middle section with shift to major mode and the sparkle of glockenspiel and harp. Mahler integrates the materials as he goes: the two quite different trios, for example, include a common clarinet theme. Note, at the end of the movement, the cello glissandos and, in the last bar, the sneer of high woodwinds.

The slow third movement is a "double" theme and variations, loosely after the *Adagio* of Beethoven's Ninth. From the warm initial phrase for low strings, marked "restful," grows a countermelody in second violins and then oboe; this goes on to a celestial close. Less settled is what follows, the second theme to be varied beginning quite slowly in the solo oboe over vestiges of the previous bass; the key has turned to the relative minor. Violins lead the melody to a Wagnerian high point, but both the statement and its reiteration end in bitter slides to hollow low notes at the orchestral floor. In the first pair of variations the major section becomes lighter and faster, the minor one still graver and more contemplative. The second pair becomes markedly faster all round, the first subject moving to a $\frac{3}{8}$ Allegretto, the second subject to a quite rapid $\frac{2}{4}$. Suddenly the French horns break the forward momentum, and the first theme is given a contemplative restatement. A flourish of French horns announces the theme of the last movement before reflections on the earlier melodies evaporate in a *pianissimo*.

Mahler's turn from this harp-and-string mist to the clarinet grazioso that introduces *Das himmlische Leben* is a captivating effect. The singer has four strophes, each concluding with a slow, wide-eyed, *sotto voce* cadence; separating these are recurrences of the sleighbells from the first movement. Rivulets of sixteenth notes decorate the orchestral textures from the beginning. Mahler demands, in writing, the conductor's utter discretion in accompanying the singer, who should in turn deliver her material with childlike and serene expression. Heaven, in fact, is lusty with dance and song, and St. Peter himself watches over the merriment. Good victuals are to be found there: in a delightfully confused symbolism wc find St. John releasing a "meek, innocent, patient, dear little lambkin" to be sacrificed for dinner, St. Luke slaughtering oxen, and St. Peter at the heavenly fishpond with his net and bait. The fruits and vegetables, we are assured, are of first quality; the wine is free. And no music can compare with the angel voices of St. Cecilia and her musicians.

Symphony No. 5 in C♯ Minor

PART I
1. *Trauermarsch: in gemessenem Schritt, Streng, Wie ein Kondukt*
2. *Stürmisch bewegt, mit grösster Vehemenz*

PART II
3. *Scherzo: Kräftig, nicht zu schnell*

PART III
4. *Adagietto: Sehr langsam*
5. *Rondo-Finale: Allegro*

For piccolos I-II, flutes I-IV, oboes I-III, clarinets I-III, bass clarinet, bassoons I-II, contrabassoon; horns I-VI, trumpets I-IV, trombones I-III, tuba; timpani, snare drum, bass drum, cymbals, triangle, tam-tam, glockenspiel; harp; strings

Composed summers of 1901 and 1902 in Maiernigg; revised
1904–10
First performed 18 October 1904 by the Gürzenich Orchestra of
Cologne, Mahler conducting
Published by C. F. Peters (Leipzig, 1905)
Duration: about 75 minutes

During the summers of 1901 and 1902, composing in a forest cottage
near his villa at Maiernigg, Mahler abandoned his infatuation with
the *Wunderhorn* songs (see p. 343)—and the singers he had required
for the Second, Third, and Fourth Symphonies—to write once more
for instrumentalists alone. Owing to its epic proportions, the symphony came to be known in some circles as the "Giant"—not to be
confused with "Titan," sobriquet for the First Symphony.

What may appear at first to be a perplexing table of contents—five
movements assembled under three Roman numerals—in fact describes
nicely the cool logic of the form, articulating its progress toward and
away from the pivotal scherzo. Part I consists of a funeral march and,
in the following movement, its working-out. Part II is the sprawling
scherzo. In part III, the famous *Adagietto* acts as a slow introduction
to the Rondo-Finale, and Mahler eventually interpolates its material
from the former into the latter. An overall tonal progress from C♯
minor to D major unifies the work: even if you do not sense the
particulars of this motion, you cannot be immune to the way the
profound resignation of the first movement lifts into the brilliant conclusion. In this respect the Fifth, though never overtly programmatic,
is clearly narrative (and probably autobiographical)—dwelling on the
familiar struggles, passions, and victory of the human experience.

The stern trumpet call that opens the first movement leads to the
percussive tattoo, for full orchestra, of a funeral dirge. (The moment
of brilliant major near the beginning is a chimera.) Two melancholy
themes in strings and woodwinds, closely related, form successive
strains of the slow march. Suddenly, after the distant trumpet, the
music lurches forward "as vehemently as possible." Though presented
as chaos unleashed, molten with harsh themes for the brass soloists
and woodwind choir (*Schalltrichter auf!*—with bells over stands), this
nevertheless amounts to something of a trio in typical march form.
The march recapitulates, truncated, varied, and redistributed in the
orchestra; the timpani solo introduces a second, truer, trio. A great

Wagnerian overflow and receding has the effect of subduing the trumpet. (Note, here, the *col legno* effect, where the strings are struck with the wood of the bow.) Its echoes are heard from a lone flute over the quiet rumble of bass drum. An abrasive C♯ in the lower strings summarily ends the movement.

Morbidity notwithstanding, what has come so far has been relatively simple of design and addressed the issue of development inconsequentially at best. The second movement allows the fury to take its full course. After the shrill, gutteral commotion at the beginning has spread through the orchestra it dissipates in a plummet of woodwind. A timpani roll returns us to the substance of the *Trauermarsch*, which manages to keep resurfacing in the developmental storm. During the recapitulation a new idea appears: a big brass chorale in D major that breaks forth from the raft of six horns and four trumpets with timpani and triangle, then pushes forward with mounting ecstasy to the spot Mahler marks "high point." But there it is simply left, and soon the sinister elements pass by once more in review. The overwhelming movement-pair dies out, *pianissimo,* in a sigh passed among the instruments and a little pizzicato cadence. A "long pause" follows, during which you are to ponder all you have heard.

In its metric character, the *Scherzo* with obbligato French horn suggests a Ländler, that Austro-Germanic folkdance, slower and more rustic than the waltz. The optimistic atmosphere, so different from part I, is best described in Mahler's words: "There is nothing romantic or mystical about it; it is simply the expression of incredible energy. It is the human being in the full light of day in the prime of his life." The melodies are bright, the counterpoint high; much is eventually made of the busy imitation for strings and clarinets that forms the departure from the main theme. The trio has the suave and slightly decadent character of the Viennese ballroom, as though the Ländler had been uprooted and acculturated. Afterwards, the good spirits of the Ländler begin to be deflected by the increasingly brooding quality of the horn solos. A long discourse ensues, including a waltz episode for pizzicato strings. A bass drum solo instigates the chase to the double bar.

Part III opens with the wonderful *Adagietto* for strings and harp. The melody bears strong resemblance to one of the Rückert-Lieder, *Ich bin der Welt abhanden gekommen.* A sudden *forte* and agitated turn of events indicate the beginning of the second section, during which the harp drops out (largely because of the frequent and violent shifts of key area, each of which would require resetting the pedals). When the harp returns, simultaneous with the major tonality, recapitulation has been reached.

Mahler writes *"attacca"* at the conclusion of the *Adagietto* and begins the *Rondo-Finale* in the French horn, on precisely the pitch where the violins had left off. The bassoon quotes *Lob des hohen Verstandes* (In Praise of Lofty Intelligence—the quarrel of a nightingale and a cuckoo), one of the *Wunderhorn* songs. Finally the horns commence the broad rondo theme, soon taken up by the rest of the orchestra. Toward the end the brass reassert the grand D-major chorale from the second movement. This time it triumphs, surrounded by cascades of the strings, and with that accomplished the music turns and flies away. You, in turn, having been captured by the many riches of this exceptional work, marvel that you have scarcely noticed the passage of a very long time.

Symphony No. 9 in D Major

Andante comodo
Im Tempo eines gemächlichen Ländlers, etwas täppisch und
*   sehr derb*
Rondo: Burleske (Allegro assai, sehr trotzig)
Adagio (Sehr langsam und noch zurückhaltend)

For piccolo, flutes I-IV, oboes I-IV, English horn, E♭ clarinet, clarinets I-III, bass clarinet, bassoons I-IV, contrabassoon; horns I-IV, trumpets I-III, trombones I-III, tuba; timpani (2 players), snare drum, bass drum, cymbals, triangle, tam-tam, glockenspiel, three low bells; harp; strings
Composed 1908–10, mostly in the summers of 1909 and 1910 in Toblach
First performed (posthumously) 26 June 1912 by the Vienna Philharmonic, Bruno Walter conducting
Published by Universal Edition (Vienna, 1912)
Duration: about 75 minutes

The compositional style of Mahler's last years—that of the Ninth, *Das Lied von der Erde,* and the unfinished Tenth—is, to my ear, less radical a turn from the midperiod than is usually held. Certainly they are all works about death: Mahler knew his heart condition to be life threatening, and he continued to grieve for the daughter he had lost in 1907. His fall from grace in Vienna, in part the work of anti-Semites, ended a great chapter of his life. But Mahler had after all been writing of life and death from the beginning, and I cannot help hearing the center movements of *Das Lied von der Erde* as very close kin of the *Wunderhorn* and Rückert Lieder.

What does change, demonstrably, is Mahler's psychology. "I see everything in a new light. I am completely agitated," he wrote, hearing on the one hand "concrete answers to all my questions" in the music around him, then feeling "that there are no more answers at all." One can hardly avoid reading aspects of farewell into the Ninth.

Another clearly audible feature is the assault of the Ninth on the boundaries of tonality and sonata practice: the harmonic phantasmagoria, with the themes less significant than motives they hold within, and counterpoint and orchestration taking precedence over particulars of form. The high twentieth century seems just around the corner, and Schoenberg was right to suggest that it was Mahler, and not he, who established the new direction.

There's a reasonably close parallel with Tchaikovsky's *Pathétique* (see p. 589): the huge, dark sonata at the beginning, the inner pairing of waltz and march, the third movement acting as finale and the fourth as tragic afterthought. The tonal progress is not of apotheosis, as in the Fifth, but of resignation. The *Rondo-Burleske* makes pointed allusion to two themes from Mahler's Fifth—those that open the second and third movements; there is probably, as well, a reference to a Strauss waltz. Surely the most moving citation occurs in the closing bars of the symphony, where Mahler quotes a melody from one of the *Kindertotenlieder*, a line associated with sunshine falling upon the heights where the absent children have gone to dwell.

That the Ninth is often a somber work is clear from the opening measures of the *Andante comodo*, a massive movement of a half-hour's duration. From the nervous bass notes of cello and horn grow first the semi-ostinato in the harp, then a horn call echoing with murmurs in the viola, and finally the main theme in the second violins. This, too, nods in resignation that colors—indeed, practically controls—so many of the elements to follow. In form the movement is a mix of sonata, rondo, and variation practices. A second theme emerges twice, tentatively with the shift of mode from major to minor near the beginning, then more properly and conclusively where the tempo accelerates. The development begins with the agitations from the first few bars of the movement, this time with muted trombones and tuba, and continues as the second theme—the more highly charged of the pair— tries to force its way to a resolution. A troubled climax is reached, and the whole process is repeated. This time the climax is bigger still—"highest power," says the score—then, "with maximum force," collapses. The music tumbles down into a recapitulatory dirge, subdued by dissonance.

Mahler's *Ländler* is a caricature "rather clumsy and quite coarse." At the *più mosso,* Tempo II, an impressionistic waltz asserts itself. Two closely related trios (Tempo III: "quite slow") are separated by a return of the waltz, all dominated by the same falling interval. The recapitulating follows its lengthy course, and the movement dissolves in bassoon percolations and, in the last bar, the odd sound of contrabassoon and piccolo, separated by five octaves.

The *Rondo-Burleske* is one of Mahler's greatest single movements, of often furious speed that demands great orchestral virtuosity. Mostly it is a grotesque fast march, with such intense counterpoint that each of the various thematic snippets seems inextricably interlocked with all the others. In the middle comes a passage of high string tremolandos and flutter-tongued flutes, with silvery rockets upward of violins and harp; the melody here reflects on the thematic contours of the entire work. The rondo intrudes ever more insistently on this quiet: percussion and bass voices begin to tick like a monstrous grandfather clock, and the tempo gains into a final Presto.

By the second phrase of the *Adagio,* the darkest register of bassoon and contrabassoon has begun to tint the ruminations of the string choir. All along in the Ninth we have sensed the urgency of melodic descent and the grip of Wagnerian ornament. What follows is an essay on these features. Your overriding sensation will of the extreme slow motion. When the strings are eventually joined by full brass and woodwinds, the mix becomes almost lurid: no orchestra but Mahler's ever sounds quite like this. After the central episode with English horn, there is a final climax with cymbal crash over which the violins linger ecstatically. Recapitulation begins *fortissimo,* then extends and subsides. The Ninth concludes with solo cello, the citation from *Kindertotenlieder,* and a dying away into a quintessential *pianissimo.* Even the creaking of the floor and the breathing of the players become part of the last stillness.

Das Lied von der Erde (The Song of the Earth)

Das Trinklied vom Jammer der Erde (The Drinking Song of
  Earthly Woe)
Der Einsame im Herbst (The Solitude of Autumn)
Von der Jugend (Of Youth)
Von der Schönheit (Of Beauty)
Der Trunkene im Frühling (The Drunkard in Spring)
Der Abschied (The Farewell)

For soloists (A, T); piccolo, flutes I-III, oboes I-III, English horn,
  E♭ clarinet, clarinets I-II, bass clarinet, bassoons I-III, contra-
  bassoon; horns I-IV, trumpets I-III, trombones I-III, tuba; tim-
  pani, bass drum, cymbals, triangle, tambourine, bells; harp,
  celesta, mandolin; strings
Text after Chinese poems of the eighth century, in the German of
  Hans Bethge: *Die chinesische Flöte* (The Chinese Flute), 1907
Composed in 1907–9, mostly summer 1908 in Toblach
First performed (posthumously) 20 November 1911 by the
  Munich Tonkünstler Orchestra, Bruno Walter conducting
Published by Universal Edition (Vienna, 1912; piano score in
  1911). *Inexpensive score:* Gustav Mahler: *Das Lied von der Erde in
  Full Score* (New York: Dover, 1988)
Duration: just over one hour

Mahler often described *Das Lied von der Erde* as a symphony or song-symphony, but purposefully avoided assigning it a number, so conscious was he of the cases of the three Viennese masters—Beethoven, Schubert, and Bruckner—whose ninth symphonies had been their last. Superstition apart, it made good sense to sidestep the issue of genre, for the usual terms do not suffice to describe this hybrid of song cycle and symphony. The irony is that Mahler's Ninth was indeed his last complete work; the tragedy, that he died before hearing either the Ninth or *Das Lied von der Erde* performed.

In the decline of his physical and emotional strength Mahler grew particularly receptive to the sentiments expressed in these verses from the ancient Chinese. The images are of earthly pleasures—youth, beauty, strong drink, friendship, sunshine, flowers, and breezes. Our opportunity to experience these delights is but fleeting, and at the end there is death. Yet in the certainty that the earth will blossom anew each spring, forever, there is to be found both a higher wisdom and a higher pleasure.

The Drinking Song of Earthly Woe is in three stanzas for tenor, each concluding with the refrain "Dunkel ist das Leben, ist der Tod" (Dark is life; dark is death), a little higher each time. The proposition is familiar: drink, sing, and make merry, for though the sky will always be blue and the spring is certain to blossom, we mortals have less than a hundred years to enjoy it. The orchestral introduction is emphatic and worldly and the overall scoring brilliant, emphasizing high registers in both the orchestral and vocal lines. Between the second and third stanzas comes an orchestral interlude of gripping symbolism— the blossoming continues without the singer. Over the course of the movement we encounter elements that characterize the work as a whole: freely varied strophes, mutation of tonality as the song progresses, and a prominent recurring melodic descent (a descending sixth).

While the tenor's three songs are lusty, those for the alto are wistful and pensive. In *The Solitude of Autumn* nature succumbs to its annual fading, to mists, frost, and icy wind, and the singer weeps in loneliness, seeking only rest and perhaps the sun to dry her tears. The scoring is bare: long, sad turns in the solo lines are set over almost continuously flowing eighth notes, and the solo part progresses in stepwise, rather resigned, quarter and half notes. At the invocation to the "sun of love" there is an outpouring from harp and winds; elsewhere all is cold.

Of Youth, for the tenor, is a true chinoiserie: at the end of a jade bridge to the island in a little pond stands a pavilion of green and white porcelain. Friends drink, chat, and write poetry in the gazebo, and all is mirrored on the pond's calm surface. The music has oriental melodic twists and an orchestration dominated by flutes and piccolos. You will inevitably compare the effect with that of the pagoda movement in Ravel's *Mother Goose Suite,* composed a few months later.

The most fetching attribute of youth is surely beauty. In the alto's second song, *Of Beauty,* maidens gather blossoms at the river bank and bask in golden sun. Young men pass by on horseback. One of the steeds shies and gallops, and the loveliest of the girls longs for its gallant rider. The music, still of oriental nuance, is playful, with the thunder of horse and rider one of the few big tuttis to be found in the center movements.

Intoxication is at issue in the tenor's last song, *The Drunkard in Spring.* The antidote to life's miseries, he argues, is strong drink and the drugged sleep that inevitably follows. A bird warbles of the springtime, but the singer would rather be drunk: "What has spring to do with me?"

Now comes *The Farewell,* a profound thirty-minute treatment of two related poems ("Waiting for a Friend" and "The Farewell of a Friend") that concludes *Das Lied von der Erde* by returning it to the cosmic gravities of the first movement. For altos this *tour de force* is the equal of Wagner's *Liebestod,* with which it has a good deal in common—poignant, bittersweet, brimming with the kind of nostalgia you also hear in Richard Strauss's *Four Last Songs* (see p. 564). From the first measures, where the oboe wends its plaint over the toll of tam-tam and low orchestral Cs (essentially the lowest sounds an orchestra can make), you know you are in for stark misery. These motives are soon joined by two others: falling chromatic sighs in pairs of winds and a faster, more curvacious chromatic descent by sixteenth notes. Tragedy is not so much at issue as resignation to fate: it is nightfall, the close of things; and as the world goes off to its well-earned slumber, the singer waits in utter darkness for the last meeting with a friend. The friend finally arrives and dismounts, and they share the draught of farewell. The friend sets forth toward the mountains, there to find peace for a lonely heart. All the cycle's subject matter— beauty, drink, youth—commingles, then concludes with the reminder that the earth will blossom again—forever . . . forever. . . .

Here lies Mahler's sustained and wrenching treatment of sentiments that lie deep in every listener's soul, especially during the orchestral episode that represents the long wait in the dark (after the line "O beauty! O, eternal love and life-drunk world!"). Note, too, the sonority of the mandolin ("I walk with my lute, hither and yon," says the text), which went on to become something of a vogue with the Viennese composers.

Lieder eines fahrenden Gesellen (Songs of a Wayfarer)

Wenn mein Schatz Hochzeit macht (On My Darling's Wedding Day)
Ging heut' Morgens über's Feld (This Morning I Went Through the Fields)
Ich hab' ein glühend Messer (I Feel a Burning Knife [in my Breast])
Die zwei blauen Augen ([My Darling's] Two Blue Eyes)

For solo voice (usually male); piccolo, flutes I-III, oboes I-II,
    English horn, clarinets I-III, bass clarinet, bassoons I-II; horns
    I-IV, trumpets I-II, trombones I-III; timpani, bass drum, cym-
    bals, triangle, glockenspiel; harp; strings
Texts by Mahler, though no. 1 seems to be based on a *Wunderhorn*
    poem
Composed December 1883–January 1885 in Kassel; orchestrated
    1891–95; revised c. 1892, 1896
First performed 16 March 1896 by the Berlin Philharmonic,
    Anton Sistermans, bass, Mahler conducting
Published by Josef Weinberger (Vienna, 1897) in vocal and
    orchestral scores. *Inexpensive score:* Gustav Mahler: *Songs of a
    Wayfarer and Kindertotenlieder in Full Score* (New York: Dover,
    1990)
Duration: about 15 minutes

The *Lieder eines fahrenden Gesellen* conclude Mahler's youth. Likewise,
if one isn't too picky about the chronology of their orchestration, they
can be heard as a sort of prelude to the nine symphonies. It is a cycle
of unrequited love, with autobiographical associations I treat briefly
in the section on the First Symphony (see p. 328). Aimless wandering
in such circumstances, where every new sensation draws the poet back
to his broken heart, has a long musical tradition with roots in Beethoven's *An die ferne Geliebte* (To the Distant Beloved) and more direct
lineage to song cycles by Schubert and Schumann as well. The way-
faring is not just physical and spiritual, but tonal as well, for each of
the songs ends in a different place from where it began. In the restraint
of the symphonic treatment, they foreshadow the intimate style of the
Wunderhorn and Rückert Lieder. Only at the end of the third song
("Woe, Woe: Would that I might lie in the dark grave") is there a
really big orchestral climax.

The woman for whom the Wayfarer yearns is marrying someone
else. He begs the flowers not to bloom on their wedding day, nor the
birds to sing; he will have no spring, but rather will grieve in his
room. The clarinet motive, in sixteenths, bespeaks the freshness of
spring, but the same melody in eighth notes becomes that of the
singer's petulant agony. He simply mocks the lilting $\frac{6}{8}$ at the center
of the song. Nature, at least, is happy in the second song, as finches
chatter and bluebells tinkle—music you may know from its use in
the first movement of the First Symphony. This rejuvenation, too, is
lost on the Wayfarer.

The song of the burning knife, cutting into the Wayfarer's breast, is a tempestuous $\frac{9}{8}$ for the full orchestra, with trumpets and trombones. Rather would he be lying in his grave, he says, and the music tumbles in that direction. The cycle concludes with one of Mahler's many cortege movements, again of material familiar from its reuse in the First Symphony. The Wayfarer, with thoughts of his darling's gaze uppermost in his mind, has set forth in pointless pursuit. Beneath a lime tree—the most Romantic of symbols—he takes his rest.

Songs from *Des Knaben Wunderhorn* (The Youth's Magic Horn)

1. *Der Schildwache Nachtlied* (The Sentinel's Night-Song)
2. *Verlor'ne Müh'* (Wasted Effort)
3. *Trost im Unglück* (Consolation in Sorrow)
4. *Wer hat dies Liedlein erdacht?* (Who Made Up This Little Song?)
5. *Das irdische Leben* (The Earthly Life)
6. *Des Antonius von Padua Fischpredigt* (St. Anthony of Padua's Sermon to the Fishes)
7. *Rheinlegendchen* (Little Rhine Legend)
8. *Lied des Verfolgten im Turm* (Song of the Prisoner in a Tower)
9. *Wo die schönen Trompeten blasen* (Where the Fair Trumpets Sound)
10. *Lob des hohen Verstandes* (In Praise of High Intellect)

   Das himmlische Leben (The Heavenly Life)
   Es sungen drei Engel (Three Angels Sang)
   Urlicht (Primeval Light)

   Revelge (Reveille)
   Der Tambourg'sell (The Drummer Boy)

For solo voice, piccolo, flutes I-II, oboes I-II, English horn, E♭ clarinet, clarinets I-II, bassoons I-III; horns I-IV, trumpets I-II, trombones I-III, tuba; timpani, snare drum, bass drum, cymbals, triangle; harp; strings

Texts collected by Clemens Brentano and Achim von Arnim (3 vols., 1805–8)

Composed 1892–99 as follows: nos. 1–4, January–26 April 1892 in Hamburg; nos. 5–7, summer–10 August 1893 in Steinbach; nos. 8–9, July 1898 in Vahrn–May 1899 in Vienna; no. 10, 12–19 June 1896 in Steinbach; *Das himmlische Leben, Urlicht,* and *Es sungen drei Engel* composed 1892, 1893, and 1895, respectively, and incorporated into the symphonies; *Revelge* composed July 1899 and *Der Tambourg'sell* composed August 1901 (these two later, longer songs postdate the first publication)

First performed as follows: nos. 1–2, Berlin, 1892; nos. 3, 4, 7, and *Das himmlische Leben,* 27 October 1893 in Hamburg; nos. 5 and 9, 14 January 1900 in Vienna; nos. 6 and 8 with *Revelge* and *Der Tambourg'sell,* 29 January 1905 in Vienna; no early performance traced for no. 10

Published by Universal Edition (Vienna, 1899; *Revelge* and *Der Tambourg'sell* added 1905)

Des Knaben Wunderhorn, a three-volume collection of traditional German song texts, was assembled in the first decade of the nineteenth century by the poet-folklorists Clemens Brentano and Achim von Arnim. By Mahler's day, the collection had already exerted strong influence on both literature (Heine, Eichendorff, the Grimm brothers) and music—especially through the intermediary of Heine's *Buch der Lieder,* from which came the texts of some of the best songs of the Romantic era. In fact, *Des Knaben Wunderhorn* was already somewhat passé, and it may well be that this enouraged the acutely personal and slightly abstract way he set his chosen texts.

Mahler's interest in the *Wunderhorn* poems originated during his years as a conductor at the Stadttheater in Leipzig, 1886–88. There Carl von Weber, grandson of Carl Maria, prevailed on him to complete the elder Weber's unfinished opera *Die drei Pintos.* Among the books in the Weber library Mahler found a copy of *Des Knaben Wunderhorn* that had belonged to the great composer.

Between 1887 and 1890 Mahler composed nine *Wunderhorn* songs for voice and piano. The ten (different) orchestral songs enumerated above were composed and performed in groups of two, three, and four between 1892 and 1898. Two further, and larger, settings come later: *Revelge* and *Der Tambourg'sell.* And three *Wunderhorn* songs were incorporated into the middle-period symphonies: *Urlicht* in the Second, which also has a scherzo based on the Fish Sermon; *Es sungen drei Engel* in the Third; and *Das himmlische Leben* in the Fourth.

There is, then, no fixed cycle called *Des Knaben Wunderhorn.* In the concert hall you will often hear a selection offered by two soloists, a male and a female, such that the several boy-girl songs can be sung in dialogue and the optional duet passages realized. These are piquant, sometimes tragic songs on subject matter ranging from fairytales to the more typical concerns of love and war. But the military songs are intimate and personal, the images not of bloodshed but of how battle affects individuals. And the lovers, usually adolescent, are inevitably unrequited. Most often, in fact, the lovers never meet, as in *Wasted Effort.* The forlorn young soldier of the *Sentinel's Night Song* cannot leave his post for the girl waiting in a rose garden. Other lovers meet at dawn in *Where the Trumpets Sound,* with the implication that despite their murmured assurances of a blissful life together, the young man will not survive the distant wars.

Among the most interesting of the narrative songs is *Das irdische Leben* (The Earthly Life), a song of hunger inevitably to be compared with *Das himmlische Leben,* the eating-and-revelry song at the close of the Fourth Symphony. Here, in a sort of rhetorical combination of "The Little Red Hen" and Schubert's *Erlkönig,* a hungry child cries for bread, to be put off day by day while the mother reaps and threshes and bakes the corn. By the time there is bread, the child has died. There is good humor, too: in *Lob des hohen Verstandes,* for example, a donkey tries to judge between the song of the nightingale and the cuckoo, with hee-haws in the clarinet. In another, St. Anthony addresses the fishes. Unlike his usual congregation, they come willingly to hear him preach; but once he is done the fish go back to their old ways— the pikes still steal, the crabs still crawl backward, the cod and carp still eat too much. But they liked the sermon.

It is the simplicity of the musical settings that so attracts, and the intimacy of the orchestration. Virtually all the orchestral instruments come sooner or later into play, but with restraint, their individual characters and profiles always paramount. The effect is as striking in its own way as a symphonic *fortissimo*: a single trumpet can evoke images of the battlefield, a triangle, the most indolent pleasures.

Kindertotenlieder (Songs on the Death of Children)

Nun will die Sonn' so hell aufgeh'n (Now shall the sun as brightly rise)

Nun seh' ich wohl, warum so dunkle Flammen (Now I see clearly, why such dark flames)

Wenn dein Mütterlein (When your dear mother [comes into my room])

Oft denk' ich, sie sind nur ausgegangen! (Oft do I think that they
   have just gone walking)
In diesem Wetter (In this foul weather)

For solo voice (usually Ms. or Bar.); piccolo, flutes I-II, oboes I-
   II, English horn, clarinets I-II, bass clarinet, bassoons I-II, con-
   trabasson; horns I-IV; timpani, tam-tam, glockenspiel; celesta,
   harp; strings
Texts by Friedrich Rückert (1788–1866)
Composed 1901 (nos. 1, 2, and 5) and summer 1904 (nos. 3 and
   4) in Maiernigg
First performed 29 January 1905 at a concert of the Vienna
   Union of Working Composers, with members of the Imperial
   Opera Orchestra and Friedrich Weidemann, baritone, Mahler
   conducting
Published by C. F. Kahnt (Leipzig, 1905); rev. ed. Universal
   Edition (Vienna, 1912). *Inexpensive score:* Gustav Mahler: *Songs of
   a Wayfarer and Kindertotenlieder in Full Score* (New York: Dover,
   1990)
Duration: about 25 minutes

I may use the word "haunting" too often in these pages, but if you
are not haunted for hours after hearing these inexpressibly tragic *Songs
on the Death of Children,* you could not have been listening closely.
(They should be programed at the end of a concert, or at least be
followed by an intermission.) Mahler has here set five of the nearly
500 poems written by Friedrich Rückert (1788–1866) in reflection
on the premature death of his two children. Mahler, too, knew where-
of he spoke, having lost several siblings to childhood disease. Further,
Mahler's beloved daughter Maria died suddenly in 1907, after the
composition and performance of the *Kindertotenlieder* but before their
publication. To posterity, at least, this tragedy gave the songs further
poignance.

As reflections of a bereaved father the songs are most appropriate
for the baritone voice; just as often, however, they are sung by a
mezzo-soprano and thereby gain the many additional associations particular to a mother's losss. As in the *Wunderhorn* songs, the scoring is
economical, the forms freely strophic, the tonal progress quite flexible. Phrases from the *Kindertotenlieder* find their way into Mahler's
later work, and in general sonority and dramatic purpose, the songs

are clear forerunners of similar work by Schoenberg, Berg, and Webern.

The saddest part of the death of a loved one is not so much the horror of the event itself as the frequency with which our thoughts subsequently turn to the life that has been lost, joining fond memories and open wounds. Rückert and Mahler both sensed this process implicitly. Events of daily existence—greeting the sun, foul weather, footsteps heard approaching a room—become, on reflection, images of the death, occasion for grief. In the first of the songs, for example, the brightness of the sunshine brings thoughts of light and life, extinguished. The four verse-pairs, rich with counterpoint of oboe and horn, are separated by double strokes of the glockenspiel—a knell that rings, too, in the left hand of the harp. After the words "ew'ge Licht versenken!" ([darkness] submerged in eternal light), there is brief orchestral brightness, but the singer can only greet it with agitation. Darkest of all is the low murmur of the clarinet.

In *Nun seh' ich wohl,* the parent sees in hindsight that the child's dark gaze hinted at the impending journey to distant realms; the eyes (*Augen,* an extremely expressive word in German) have become stars of night. The dominant sonority is that of the cello, the prevailing direction one of melodic ascent where virtually every phrase of the first song falls in lamentation; indeed the four-note rise that repeats itself again and again here is almost a Mahlerian hallmark. Just as idiomatic is the walking figure, in pizzicato cello and harp, that runs beneath *Wenn dein Mütterlein.* At the mother's approach the father finds himself turning to look at the spot where his daughter would have been. The major solo work is for English horn, the tessitura quite low and without violins. Here, just past the halfway point, you may well feel the cycle becoming almost unbearably intense.

We often delude ourselves that the unthinkable cannot have happened to missing children—that they have merely gone out to play and not yet come home. In fact, *Oft denk'ich* seeks to assure us that they have merely preceded us to a new home where parents and children will be united in sunshine. The music wanders, symbolically, in paired voices, and again there is the sound of the golden sun. Paradoxically the violent storm of *In diesem Wetter* results in similar assurance: in former times one would not have sent the children out in such weather, but now they are as safe as if they were at home. It begins as the only violent movement of the cycle. Mahler makes of the muted strings something sinister indeed, with divisi effects, pizzicatos, trills, tremolos, and harmonics. Each of the five strophes begins on the same low D with the same pelting rhythm for the words "In diesem Wetter"; yet the fifth stanza becomes a lullaby for children asleep as though in their mothers' arms. By now you are well aware that the poems have been arranged to conclude in a peaceful atmosphere, a process to which the celesta contributes markedly. Yet the recurrence of the glockenspiel figure from the first movement is chilling by implication, and the bass clarinet retains its ineffable pathos.

Felix Mendelssohn

Born 3 *February* 1809 *in Hamburg*
Died 4 *November* 1847 *in Leipzig*

The Bartholdy you sometime see attached to Mendelssohn's surname was added to the Jewish family name when Mendelssohn's father, a prominent Berlin banker, became a Lutheran. The composer's grandfather was the German philosopher Moses Mendelssohn.

Mendelssohn, one of the most fascinating characters of the early Romantic movement, was a man of refinement, intelligence, and great musical facility. He was well schooled in piano and violin, in foreign languages, and in art (his sketches are delightful). Moreover he was well travelled, having visited much of Europe before he was twenty. His most influential teacher at the famous Berlin Singakademie was Carl Friedrich Zelter, who introduced him to the music of Bach and took him to visit Goethe.

In March 1829 Mendelssohn conducted a performance of Bach's *St.*

Matthew Passion, an event that both established his reputation as a conductor and contributed to the general revival of interest in Bach. A few weeks later, he embarked on the first of his ten journies to England, where he appeared as conductor and piano soloist. His visit to Scotland that summer inspired the overture *Fingal's Cave* and, eventually, the "Scottish" Symphony. Mendelssohn was a favorite of the English in general and of Queen Victoria, to whom he gave piano lessons, in particular; it was the English, following the queen's precedent, who made his wedding march from the music for *A Midsummer Night's Dream* a standard recessional.

After two years of travel in continental Europe (1830–31), Mendelssohn, still only twenty-seven, accepted the post of conductor for the prestigious Leipzig Gewandhaus concerts; within a few years, he and his associates founded the Leipzig Conservatory as well. Yet for the rest of his career he remained an aristocratic vagabond, and a rather driven one at that, conducting and sojourning in Frankfurt, Berlin, London, and elsewhere. He was at the peak of his celebrity in 1846, when he conducted the first performances of his great oratorio *Elijah* in Birmingham: *Elijah* became one of the most popular works of the century. Yet the pressures of its composition, premiere, revisions, and subsequent performances in Germany and England had left him nervous and weak. In May 1847 he collapsed on learning of the death of his sister, Fanny Mendelssohn Hensel, also a composer. There followed what was apparently a series of strokes, to which Mendelssohn succumbed within the year. News of his untimely death shook the musical world, even as far away as the Americas.

Mendelssohn's compositions for orchestra include twelve early symphonies for strings and five mature symphonies, four excellent concert overtures including the great *Fingal's Cave* (1832), and the overture and incidental music for Shakespeare's *A Midsummer Night's Dream* (1826 and 1842). The numbering of the last three symphonies reverses the chronology of composition: the Third Symphony, "Scottish," was composed in 1842; the Fourth Symphony, "Italian," in 1833; and the Fifth Symphony, "Reformation," in 1832. This is the result of the "Scottish" and "Italian" symphonies having been published posthumously, with their order shifted in the process. Mendelssohn's two piano concertos (opp. 25 and 40, 1831 and 1837) remain popular, and the Violin Concerto (1844) is a pillar of the repertoire; *Elijah* has slipped a little, for reasons I discuss below. He also composed chamber music including a fine Octet, op. 20; works for solo piano; and organ and choral music.

Mendelssohn sometimes seems fettered by his strong senses of propriety and precedent, such that his music achieves the dramatic power of Berlioz or the emotional depth of Schumann less often than it might. But he is always rigorously capable and, when his inspiration runs free, can be thrilling indeed. In sonority and gesture, the opening bars of the *Midsummer Night's Dream* Overture quite epitomize the Romantic style; in form the Violin Concerto sets all sorts of precedents.

Symphony No. 3 in A Minor, OP. 56 ("Scottish")

Andante con moto; Allegro un poco agitato
Vivace non troppo
Adagio
Allegro vivacissimo; Allegro maestoso assai
[No pauses between movements]

For flutes I-II, oboes I-II, clarinets I-II, bassoons I-II; horns I-IV, trumpets I-II; timpani; strings

Begun July 1829 in Edinburgh, continued 1841–42, completed 20 January 1842 in Berlin; dedicated to Queen Victoria

First performed 3 March 1842 by the Leipzig Gewandhaus Orchestra, Mendelssohn conducting

Published by Breitkopf & Härtel (Leipzig, 1843). *Inexpensive score:* Felix Mendelssohn: *Major Orchestral Works* (New York: Dover, 1975)

Duration: about 40 minutes

As was the custom for scions of well-bred families of the nineteenth century, Mendelssohn completed his artistic formation with a grand tour of Europe and Great Britain. Travel is always a superb finishing school, and Mendelssohn's came at a time when musical language across the continent was mutating by leaps and bounds. His letters home are filled with observations on the artists he encountered, the music he heard, and the various landscapes, colors, and folk practices that drew his attention along the way. It was a time of one inspiration after another, and later he often returned to the sketches he had made *en route* for the substance of a major composition.

In 1829, during his first trip to Great Britain, Mendelssohn traveled to Scotland, then as now a strangely timeless land bursting with the kinds of imagery that seduced those of Romantic inclination. There he met Sir Walter Scott, already venerated as a father of Romanticism; at Holyrood Castle in Edinburgh, overgrown palace of Mary, Queen of Scots, he first conceived the material for the Andante that begins the "Scottish" Symphony—a passage redolent with the pensiveness and wonder of our promenades in history's abandoned corridors. From this germinal phrase grows a good deal of the material to follow.

But it was to be many years before the symphony was completed and performed. The "Scottish" Symphony in fact represents Mendelssohn's valedictory in the genre. It is also his symphonic masterpiece—novel yet convincing of formal organization (the movements, for example, played without interruption), vivid of orchestration and melody. Yet for all the exoticism of locale, it isn't worthwhile to search for a particular story: what you are probably meant to envisage is a collage of images of Scotland past and present—suggestions of its tempestuous political history, its folk idioms, and (not least) its ever-changing weather.

While there are some obvious bows to Classical practice in the fifty-odd-bar *Andante,* the prevailing sensation is of being suspended over evolutions of the languid opening material. The sonata proper begins with the new tempo and meter, an *Allegro un poco agitato* in $\frac{6}{8}$ with first theme elaborating the melody of the *Andante.* A leisurely transition begins with the trumpeting tutti and continues in a near-fugal texture; the closing theme, squarely in E minor (not the C major you might expect), hints at a barcarole rhythm. From the motivic counterpoint and fragmentation in the development emerges a broad countermelody in the cellos, over which, eventually, the recapitulation commences. During the coda there is an obvious storm at sea, with timpani thunder; surges and ebbs from the violins overlap those in the low strings. There is a brief reprise of the opening Andante and a pizzicato close.

The second movement is equally imaginative in form—part scherzo, part highland fling, with motion by relentless sixteenth notes. It's a frantic, almost fiendish showpiece, slipping from time to time (especially at the second theme) into the string *pianissimo* staccato at which Mendelssohn always excels. Note that the main theme is based on that of the first-movement *Andante;* once again there is a pizzicato conclusion. Now the pizzicatos become a guitar-like accompaniment to the main theme, for violins, of the third movement. Not only the funereal character of the second episode but also the swells and sighs of the violin line give the movement its strong introspective cast.

The final movement, once marked "warlike," seems to evoke some undertaking of battle or brigandry—a typically post-Beethovenian struggle and working out. The second theme, heard in the woodwinds over continuous triplets in violins or violas, is a version of the now familiar motto opening; at the close of the movement this is heard again in the solo clarinet over drones in the strings, much subdued. Then the $\frac{6}{8}$ returns in major mode, and the motive which has so long dominated the work achieves its resolution. Mendelssohn meant this passage to sound like a male chorus of thanksgiving, the precedent clearly that of Beethoven's "Pastoral" Symphony. The effect is, in my view, anticlimactic and a little trivial; but that is a minor flaw in what is otherwise a symphony of exceptional imagination and craft.

Symphony No. 4 in A Major, OP. 90 ("Italian")

Allegro vivace
Andante con moto
Con moto moderato
Saltarello: Presto

For flutes I-II, oboes I-II, clarinets I-II, bassoons I-II; horns I-II, trumpets I-II; timpani; strings
Composed winter 1830–31 in Italy; completed in Berlin, winter 1832–March 1833; revised from time to time thereafter until the composer's death.
First performed 13 May 1833 by the Royal Philharmonic Society, London, Mendelssohn conducting; revised version first performed 1 November 1849, posthumously, by the Leipzig Gewandhaus Orchestra
Published by Breitkopf & Härtel (Leipzig, 1851; posthumous). *Inexpensive score:* Felix Mendelssohn: *Major Orchestral Works* (New York: Dover, 1975)
Duration: about 30 minutes

Despite its great popular success Mendelssohn himself had mixed opinions of his "Italian" Symphony. Troubled by what he saw as flaws in its design—now in the center movements, now in the first and last—he withheld it from publication and, moreover, never conducted it in Germany. Given his fastidiousness and general conservatism, Mendelssohn's dilemmas in one sense argue the work's principal strength, for it is in the very spontaneity of organization that the Italian Symphony distinguishes itself.

The brilliant, expansive, and quite famous melody which succeeds the initial thump of strings is brightly colored by the relentless eighthnotes of the winds. As early as the section that connects the two statements of this main theme, you sense the beginnings of a Haydnesque, anything-goes sonata form. Similar digressions complicate the bridge passage, and then the cool, rather understated second theme is soon set upon and overtaken by the first again (though in the appropriate key). At the very beginning of the development comes a new subject in the minor mode; the counterpoint that follows turns into a kind of fugue-scherzo, with interjections of a motive summarizing the principal theme. A more sinister tutti on the same material subsides to allow for the crescendo to recapitulation, such that a triumph over adversity seems to have taken place. (This structure foreshadows some of the tactics of the last movement.) All three themes recur in the recapitulation, in the order they were first encountered. Because of the unusual turn of events in the development, it's important to have taken the repeat of the exposition; moreover, there is some interesting material in the first ending that you would not otherwise hear.

The second movement, in D minor, is meant to suggest a procession of monks chanting their litanies—a scene common to the Italian countryside. Mendelssohn's opening unison, heard again at the reprises and coda, is typical of chant intonations, and the tune set over the "walking" bass is said to be a Czech hymn. The scoring is of great delicacy, with the principal melody stated in octaves of viola, clarinet, and bassoon, and at the turn to the second theme and major mode a ravishing close harmony of the two clarinets over French horns. The subtlety of dynamic nuance, with accents, swells, and certain falls away, is equally striking. Evolving as they go, the two subjects alternate without much by the way of note-for-note recapitulating. There are structural freedoms, too, in the minuet and trio, where the second strains of both halves work themselves through without strict repeats; otherwise the underlying form is scrupulously traditional. In the trio the almost Bohemian fanfares for horns and bassoons become by the second strain quite martial figures with trumpets and timpani. These are recollected, *piano* and *pianissimo,* in the final bars of the movement.

You may well have expected that the third movement would have been a scherzo—Mendelssohn was, after all, a master of that idiom—and been correspondingly surprised to find a minuet. Now you will understand the reason, for the finale is a super-scherzo, a wild saltarello of the sort that in the nineteenth century swirled round public piazzas on feast days. That it is presented in the minor mode gives the movement a certain countrification, as does the piping of winds in parallel thirds. Meanwhile the strings tend to lurch out of the prevailing triplet figure into falling eighths, and calls of brass and woodwind offer another contrasting idea. In lieu of true development and recapitulation comes a long, carefully paced crescendo to peroration, from *pianissimo* to *fortissimo;* the triplets become legato and continuous, in tarantella fashion. After the long pedal point in the bass instruments, the original saltarello reestablishes itself, and as the work winds down we hear very obvious references in the woodwinds to the first movement's theme, swept into the fray just as the dance begins to exhaust itself. But brigandly movements seldom just fade away, and suddenly there is a sharp crescendo and strong finish.

Symphony No. 5 in D Minor, OP. 107 ("Reformation")

Andante; Allegro con fuoco
Allegro vivace
Andante
Choral (Ein feste Burg ist unser Gott); Allegro vivace; Allegro
   maestoso
[No pauses between movements III and IV]

For flutes I-II, oboes I-II, clarinets I-II, bassoons I-II, contrabassoon and serpent; horns I-II, trumpets I-II, trombones I-III; timpani; strings

Composed for the most part in 1830; the symphony was begun in 1824 in England and completed in April 1832 in Berlin

First performed 15 November 1832 by the Berlin Singakademie Orchestra, Mendelssohn conducting

Published by N. Simrock (Bonn, 1868; posthumous)

Duration: about 30 minutes

Mendelssohn intended this symphony, at once academic and pro-grammatic, to commemorate the tricentenary of the Augsburg Confession by which the Protestant faith had been defined in 1530 and the Lutheran Church officially established. But he found little enthusiasm for this notion in Berlin, where the celebration was to take place, and the repertoire eventually chosen included nothing by Mendelssohn. Dissatisfied with certain elements of the work, he laid it aside after the first performance and never returned to it. (The first publication was more than two decades after his death.) In Paris, too, there was discontent: the Société des Concerts du Conservatoire dropped the symphony from an announced program after one rehearsal, explaining that it was too studied, too formal, and lacking in melody.

However that may be, the "Reformation" Symphony affords an instructive look at Mendelssohn's compositional priorities during a time when he was under the spell of Lutheran church music. His performance of the *St. Matthew Passion,* on 11 March 1829, had for example led him to a systematic analysis of Bach's styles and proce-dures. The obvious genuflections are in the use of Martin Luther's chorale *Ein feste Burg ist unser Gott* (A Mighty Fortress is Our God) in the finale and the various occurrences of the "Dresden" Amen. But there are other allusions to past practice as well: the slow movement strongly suggests a Baroque arioso, and there is something of the chorale prelude in the finale. Likewise the harmonic relationships are grand and churchly, as when the last movement opens in G and con-tinues in D in the fashion of a sweeping Amen.

The work opens quietly as a brooding melodic motive begins in the lower strings and spreads in layers through the orchestra. The motive changes shape in the woodwinds to become a kind of fanfare, answered by the Dresden Amen in the strings. With the sudden shift into minor, rapid duple meter, and a theme born of the fanfares, a sonata-allegro structure has begun. It is a long, tempestuous move-ment, possibly meant to suggest thoughts of the Protestant wars. First group, bridge, and second group join seamlessly and with little or no repose; the restless development, concerning itself almost exclu-sively with the first theme, builds to a great climax with trumpets and drums and a downward lunge of strings. At this juncture the Dresden Amen settles over and quiets the fury. The recapitulation, as though humbled by this piety, begins softly, unlike the exposition, and is quite brief.

A light minuet (or scherzo) and trio follows here, rather than in the customary third-movement position, as though to offset the rigors of the long movement just concluded. As in the "Italian" Symphony, Mendelssohn is given to digression, such that the second phrases of both minuet and trio leave more the impression of following one's nose than close adherence to a given form. The brevity of the third movement, a simple rounded aria form for first violins and rudimentary accompaniment in the supporting strings, suggests such Baroque antecedents as the slow movements of the Bach orchestral suites. When, in the final bars, a melody from the first movement is quoted, we can see in retrospect how the rhythmic and melodic character. has been derived from material that has come before.

This proceeds without pause to the chorale *Ein feste Burg* as slow introduction to the last movement. The first four notes of the chorale should bring to mind the fanfares of the opening movement, for the two figures are inversions of each other. A $\frac{6}{8}$ Vivace on phrases from the chorale effects the transition into the *Allegro maestoso,* clearly meant to be in the tradition of the heroic finale to Beethoven's Fifth. We are never far from the chorale, which is treated contrapuntally in the development section and then in purest homophony for the statement that brings the symphony to its majestic end.

Concerto for Violin and Orchestra in E Minor, OP. 64

Allegro molto appassionato
Andante
Allegro molto vivace
[No pause between the movements]

For violin solo; flutes I-II, oboes I-II, clarinets I-II, bassoons I-II; horns I-II, trumpets I-II; timpani; strings
Composed 1838–16 September 1844 in Berlin and Leipzig for Ferdinand David, Mendelssohn's concertmaster, to whom the work is dedicated
First performed 13 March 1845 by the Leipzig Gewandhaus Orchestra; Ferdinand David, violin; Niels Gade conducting
Published by Breitkopf & Härtel (Leipzig, 1845). *Inexpensive score: Great Romantic Violin Concertos in Full Score* (New York: Dover, 1985)
Duration: about 25 minutes

"I want to do you a violin concerto," Mendelssohn wrote to his distinguished concertmaster Ferdinand David in 1838: "I have one in E minor in my head, and the opening won't leave me in peace." That was six years before the work was achieved; in the interim David supported the enterprise with his enthusiasm and technical advice. The Violin Concerto proved to be Mendelssohn's last orchestral work and probably his most influential. For it is a noble creation at a time when the concerto was more often a vehicle for dazzling but routine displays of technical prowess, and its assessment of the principles of the genre is both fresh and engaging. The solo part is, to be sure, for a virtuoso, but its technical challenges draw less attention than the overall strength and solidity of Mendelssohn's compositional craft.

This much is clear from the opening measures. After a bar and a half of restless accompanimental figuration (much in the mold of Mozart's G-Minor Symphony, see p. 382), the solo violin enters with a long, soaring melody in the upper register—and, moreover, pointedly lacking in pyrotechnics. There has been no orchestral ritornello. You are lured to think that the next section, the wandering figure in quarter notes first stated by oboe and violins, is the second group, but this is in fact a transition: the shifting harmony—the wandering, indeed—indicates that the true second subject has not yet been reached. It is the slow fall of the solo violin across three octaves to its low G that introduces the new theme, in the woodwinds, *pianissimo* and *tranquillo*. By the end of the exposition the main theme has returned, to be confirmed in the new, major key. The development juxtaposes motives from this principal melody and the bridge, a process carrying on typically enough when, in a novel twist, the (fully notated) solo cadenza begins. Nor does the cadenza end conventionally; instead the orchestra creeps in with the recapitulation beneath the soloist's arpeggiated passagework. Roles have thus been reversed: the theme is now in the orchestral violins as the soloist provides the accompaniment. The main subjects are restated without elaboration—another Mendelssohn hallmark, this, as though he is impatient with the notion of recapitulating at all—in order to make room for the concluding accelerando and presto, presaged by loud trills of the woodwinds and violins.

The *Andante* continues without interruption, a solo bassoon having held the transitional pitch from the first movement's final chord into the progression that introduces the next. This is a rounded aria form with an extended, developmental center section that traverses moments of sadness and agitation. At its conclusion, the soloist and orchestra muse quietly on the theme of the first movement until fanfares announce the *Allegro molto vivace* in E major. Even for a finale, Mendelssohn is prepared to rely on his scampering idiom, and insists throughout on the dancing first theme, which quite overshadows the little march figure that passes for a second subject. In the development the soloist presents what seems to be new material, but this is heard to be a countermelody of the first theme when the two are presented simultaneously. Once again the recapitulation is short and to the point, thus making way for the soloist's fancy coda and stratospheric high E—three octaves and then some above middle C—just at the end.

Die Hebriden (The Hebrides) or *Fingalshöle* (Fingal's Cave), OP. 26, Concert Overture

For flutes I-II, oboes I-II, clarinets I-II, bassoons I-II; horns I-II, trumpets I-II; timpani; strings

Composed 1829–32 in various places in Europe including Scotland; first version dated 16 December 1830, revision dated 20 June 1832; dedicated to the Crown Prince of Prussia, later King Friedrich Wilhelm IV

First performed 14 May 1832 by the London Philharmonic Society, Thomas Atwood conducting

Published by Breitkopf & Härtel (Leipzig, 1835). *Inexpensive score:* Felix Mendelssohn: *Major Orchestral Works* (New York: Dover, 1975)

Duration: about 10 minutes

The Hebrides, Outer and Inner, are islands of enchanting name and appearance off the western coast of mainland Scotland. Just off Iona (where Macbeth, according to legend, is buried) lies the tiny island of Staffa. Here in a huge basalt cave the third-century hero Fingal, legendary defender of Ireland from the invading Danes, had his lair. (The Gaelic bard Ossian, celebrated of the Romantics, was Fingal's son. But there's more myth than fact here, and the Ossianic lore of the 1760s was actually the work of the Scottish poet James Macpherson.) You reach Fingal's Cave in a tiny boat, and the seascape is often overhung with threatening clouds.

Mendelssohn visited Fingal's Cave in August 1829, painted some watercolors there, and sketched in a letter to his family the rolling-sea motive that became the cornerstone of the concert overture. *Die Hebriden* doubtless influenced Wagner in *Der fliegende Höllander* (The Flying Dutchman), an opera of the sea, and in some respects it is the godfather of all the other sea pieces treated in this book. What is most interesting about this motive is how it serves for both accompanimental and melodic figuration.

Like Mendelssohn's other programmatic works, the overture suggests incident less than atmosphere. Using the relatively circumscribed orchestra of the late eighteenth century (two horns, two trumpets, no trombones) and a generally straight sonata form, Mendelssohn nevertheless manages to create strongly Romantic effects: the ebbs and flows, the glistening *pianissimo*s in the treble instruments, and most of all the warmth of the tenor voices. A slower, rather melancholy figure in woodwinds effects transition to the wonderful second theme, a *cantabile* that blossoms up from the cellos and bassoons into the range of the clarinet. The exposition ends on a heroic note, with brass and timpani and surges of the lower strings; in the development there emerges a little scherzando on the main theme, *pianissimo* and staccato, bouncing from strings to wind band and back. After a stormy climax the recapitulation begins beneath glistening oscillations of the treble instruments. It's a stunning conclusion, less a return to what has gone before than the end of an adventure. The second theme now becomes a recollection of the clarinets, softly and as though from a distance. There is an animated coda and quick dissolve to the pizzicato cadence.

All this—the seascape, the play of light and shadow, the narrative use of orchestration, the reminiscing—is about as fundamentally Romantic as music comes. Too often we think of Mendelssohn as reserved, brainy, perhaps somewhat foppish. He himself fretted that his overture was too much about counterpoint and too little about seaspray: that is why he rewrote it on two occasions, leaving behind multiple versions. It is true that both the makeup of the orchestra and the formal design are a little polite. To my mind this cachet of respectability in fact adds an intriguing dimension to what is already dashing by any measure. In that regard Mendelssohn is a nineteenth-century Haydn: beneath all that propriety lurks a complex psychology you want to know better.

Music for Shakespeare's *A Midsummer Night's Dream*,
OPP. 21 (1826) and 61 (1842)

Ouverture: Allegro di molto
Scherzo: Allegro vivace
[*Notturno.*] *Con moto tranquillo*
Hochzeitmarsch (Wedding March): *Allegro vivace*

For flutes I-II, oboes I-II, clarinets I-II, bassoons I-II; horns I-II,
  trumpets I-III, trombones I-III, ophicléide; timpani, cymbals,
  triangle; strings
Composed (the overture) 1826, dedicated to the Crown Prince of
  Prussia; (incidental music) 1842, published excerpts dedicated
  to the composer's friend Heinrich Conrad Schleinitz, board
  member of the Gewandhaus orchestra
First performed (the overture) 20 February 1827 by the Stettin
  court orchestra, Karl Löwe conducting; first performed as
  incidental music with the Shakespeare play 14 October 1843 at
  the New Palace, Potsdam, Mendelssohn conducting
Published by Breitkopf & Härtel (Leipzig, 1830 [overture], 1842
  [excerpts]). *Inexpensive score:* Felix Mendelssohn: *Major Orchestral
  Works* (New York: Dover, 1975)
Duration: about 35 minutes

In the days before recorded sound, live orchestras were a part of all
good theater companies, and a pit was to be found in every house. It
was not uncommon to invite noted composers to provide music for
important productions: Beethoven did it for Goethe's *Egmont,* Berlioz
for *Hamlet,* Grieg for Ibsen's *Peer Gynt,* and so on. Later Prokofiev
pioneered in composing a similar kind of music for the movies. The
incidental music for a play usually consists of an overture, music for
scene changes and entr'actes, music for any stage pantomimes, and
settings of any songs sung by the characters.

Mendelssohn had devoured Shakespeare, in both English and German, long before he was asked to compose incidental music for *A
Midsummer Night's Dream.* In fact he was only 17 when, in an inspired
response to his adolescent Shakespearean fervor, he wrote the *Midsummer Night's Dream* Overture.

All the magic of Oberon and Titania's fairy world is summarized
in the four quiet chords of the winds, harmonized and voiced in a
manner for which there is virtually no precedent. It's a "once upon a

time" beginning, drawing the listener with a few deft strokes into the dreamlike, fantastic atmosphere of the play. In similar manner the first theme, in its airy darting about of violins, conjures images of the enchanted wood outside Athens. The allusions go on: suggestions of *Figaro*-like wedding music, the galloping of Theseus's hunt, a great snore of the ophicléide (nowadays played on a tuba), love music for the second theme. Nor can you fail to note the hee-haw, in the rustic closing theme, of Bottom transformed into an ass. The development drifts gently off to sleep, thence into a reprise of the opening chords. After what sounds like the final cadence of the recapitulation comes another brilliant stroke: the fairy music begins again, the music drifts off once more, and we return at the end to the magic chords from which dreams begin.

Seventeen years after composing the *Midsummer Night's Dream* Overture, Mendelssohn was invited by the Prussian Royal Theater to compose incidental music for a new production of Shakespeare's play. He provided more than a dozen bits and pieces, including three substantial entr'actes: the *Scherzo* (to introduce the second act, the first of the fairy scenes), *Nocturne* (for the close of the third act, where the lovers drift into their drugged sleep), and *Wedding March* (before act V, which begins with a processional). These are often drawn together with the overture into a kind of concert suite.

The *Scherzo,* in a loose sonata form, has much the same impishness as the overture, but here the woodwinds are the instigators, with the strings stating much of the second-group material. French hornists everywhere treasure the *Nocturne,* with its memorable solo work enriched by the sonority of bassoons and clarinets. Upper strings do not enter until the rather restless departure section, after which the return of the French horn reconciles the contrasts, with a soothing, silvery close for flutes and high violins. The *Wedding March* you can whistle, of course, but the length of the interludes and trios generally omitted by church organists may come as a suprise.

Elijah, OP. 70, oratorio after the words of the Old Testament

PART I
[*Elijah Predicts Drought—Elijah Raises the Widow's Son—The Contest on Mount Carmel—Elijah Brings Rain*]

PART II
[*Jezebel Orders Elijah's Death—Elijah Flees to Mount Horeb—Elijah Is Swept by a Whirlwind into Heaven*]

For soloists (B [Elijah], T [Obadiah, Ahab], S I [the widow, an angel), S II, A [an angel, Jezebel], boy soprano); chorus (SATB, with some divided choruses, an angel trio, and a double quartet); flutes I-II, oboes I-II, clarinets I-II, bassoons I-II; horns I-IV, trumpets I-II, trombones I-III, ophicléide; timpani; organ; strings

German text prepared by Pastor Schubring, after passages from the Old Testament of the Lutheran Bible; the skillful English translation was by William Bartholomew, following the King James Version

Composed spring–summer 1846 at the invitation of the Birmingham Music Festival

First performed 26 August 1846 at the Birmingham Town Hall, Mendelssohn conducting

Published by N. Simrock (Bonn, 1847)

Duration: about three and a quarter hours

Elijah, Mendelssohn's last major work, is to my way of thinking his best. Complete performances are, unhappily, nowhere near so common in this century as in the last, a function in part of the modern impatience with concerts that go on past 11 P.M. But good orchestras will program *Elijah* occasionally, and a number of the movements are mainstays of the church repertoire: the quartet "Cast thy burden upon the Lord," the *a cappella* trio "Lift thine eyes," the arias "If with all your hearts" and "O rest in the Lord."

Elijah, the Hebrew prophet of King Ahab's reign, sought to turn the Children of Israel away from the idolatrous worship of foreign gods. Of Elijah's complex tale, the central episode is the contest on Mt. Carmel with the prophets of Baal: the Lord alone is able to send fire from heaven, and the Israelites are thus persuaded to have no other gods before the Lord. To this and the other incidents in the story of Elijah Schubring added texts from elsewhere in the Old Testament (and, in one case, the gospel of St. Matthew) to construct a libretto at once narrative and contemplative. The subject matter, having significance for Christians and Jews alike, was ideal for a composer of Mendelssohn's cultural persuasions; the genre allowed him to revel in his affinities for both Bach and his predecessor in the English affection, Handel.

The precedents intermingle. *Elijah* is Handelian in the way its text is assembled from the Bible alone, without added poetry. The chorus often works quite like the crowd choruses in the Bach passions, and, as in the passions and the Haydn oratorios, the soloists take character parts. There is, however, no narrator in the manner of Bach's evangelists.

Part I begins with drought and ends with a rainstorm. Before the overture begins, Elijah delivers the curse of drought, to be lifted when the people return to the Lord, God of Israel. The stern wind chords at the beginning suggest a prophecy not to be ignored, and the intervallic sequence immediately following becomes the motive of Elijah's curse. (This recurs in the chorus "Yet doth the Lord," no. 5, at the words "His curse has fallen down upon us," and again in the recitative at the beginning of the contest scene.) Not just the surprise opening, but the horror of what follows—a turbulent fugal overture with thundrous descent of trombones to the low A pedal; then the mighty chorus of woe, "Help, Lord!"; the wailing recitative "The deep affords no water;" the women's lament "Zion spreadeth her hands for aid"— give the start of *Elijah* a dramatic effect that should leave you trembling.

Obadiah, in the famous recitative "Ye people, rend your hearts" and aria "If with all your hearts," urges the Israelites to return to God; Elijah is called from the wilderness. Only in the scene between Elijah and the widow is there the opportunity for true duo writing, and the shift of means is rendered all the more striking by Mendelssohn's beginning the movement in confrontation ("What have I to do with thee, O man of God?") and concluding it in rapturous close harmony. Elijah then challenges the priests of Baal, determined to mock their impotence. ("Call him louder!" he teases, wondering if perhaps Baal "is in a journey; or, peradventure, he sleepeth.") His aria reflecting on the triumph, "Is not His word like a fire?" is obviously modeled on "For He is like a refiner's fire" in *Messiah*. The people having been won over, Elijah then prays for rain, the clouds finally gather, and the people offer their monumental chorus "Thanks be to God: He laveth the thirsty land." (I once conducted a memorable performance of *Elijah:* lightning and thunder began outside the hall, and a driving rain commenced as if on cue. The effect was sensational.)

Part II, gentler and more serene than the first, treats Elijah's flight from the wrath of Jezebel, his sojourn in the wilderness, and—for Mendelssohn the climax of the story—the "still, small voice" of the Lord on Mount Horeb. At the conclusion Elijah, in a fiery chariot, is swept to Heaven by a whirlwind. The soprano aria which opens the second part ("Hear ye, Israel!") was written for Jenny Lind and centers on the high F Mendelssohn admired in her voice. But she did not, in fact, sing the role until after Mendelssohn's death, and Madame Caradori-Allan, who did sing it, found it "unladylike."

Elijah has its occasional flaws of dramatic continuity, to be explained in part by the confusion in which the last portion of the libretto arrived and was set. Yet as he composed it, Mendelssohn—who had always been a great melodist—was in particularly fine control of harmonic vocabulary, counterpoint, and deployment of the large performing force. The palette of vocal sonorities is most imaginative, both in the changing character of the full choruses and in the chamber groupings—trio, quartet, double quartet; and the women's duet with chorus ("Zion spreadeth her hands" / "Lord, bow Thine ear") is a triumph of tone color. For its part, the orchestra offers on the one hand tender, comforting arabesque accompaniments of such choruses as "Blessed are the men who fear Him" and "He, watching over Israel," and on the other, unforgettable music of fire, flood, and whirlwind.

Darius Milhaud

Born *4 September 1892* in *Aix-en-Provence*
Died *22 June 1974* in *Geneva*

At the Paris Conservatoire, Milhaud became a disciple of modernism even while studying the *fin-de-siècle* style of his teachers, Vincent d'Indy, Charles Widor, and Paul Dukas. Simultaneously he moved in a circle of intellectual aristocrats dominated by the Catholic poet Paul Claudel; this led to his appointment in early 1916 as attaché to Claudel, new head of the French legation in Brazil. In the following months, Milhaud added South American rhythms and textures to a vocabulary already rich with provençal idioms, and the adventure instilled in him his lifelong passion for travel and the exotic. On his return to Paris he fell into the retinue of Erik Satie and Jean Cocteau and through them was linked with the affinity group that came to be called *Les Six*. (The other five were Georges Auric, Arthur Honegger, Francis Poulenc, Germaine Tailleferre, and the now-forgotten Louis

Durey.) Les Six was more a journalistic convenience than anything of philosophical substance; in fact, its members shared few stylistic traits. But they did enjoy each other's company, and the group photographs succeeded in suggesting to the world the existence of a new French school.

In 1922 Milhaud visited the United States to give concerts and lectures, absorbing as he went not just the American academic culture but the popular and ethnic as well. The French liked to think that they had found in Milhaud a successor to Ravel and found it symbolic that Milhaud delivered an oration at Ravel's burial. But Milhaud thought his purported mentor's work unbearably precious—"music in a corset," he said—and cultivated not that sort of elegance but vibrant modernism, albeit in the disciplined fashion of composers born and bred at the Conservatoire. He was militantly anti-Wagnerian, anti-Romantic. The extent of Milhaud's stature is still argued, but he was incontestably the dominant French composer of his era, which I would define as lasting well into the 1950s.

When the war broke out, the Milhauds came to live in the United States. From 1940 he taught at Mills College in Oakland; after 1947 he divided his time between Paris, where he was professor of composition at the Conservatoire, and northern California. He was a demanding but popular teacher of many Americans who went on to achieve distinction in the field, creating around himself and Mills, moreover, an exciting atmosphere which is still remembered with deep affection. Eventually, he retired to Paris and Geneva.

His style is influenced, first of all, by Provence: "For Milhaud," writes his biographer in *The New Grove*, "all roads lead back to Aix." His Jewish ancestry fostered a sympathy for disenfranchised peoples that explains in some measure his predilection for black Americans and their music. But mostly it is his worldliness, his disinclination to dismiss anybody's music as unworthy of attention, that gives Milhaud's work its character; and his ear for the music embodied in the sounds around him was acute. It was for this reason that he took such pleasure in his Paris flat in the boulevard de Clichy overlooking the Place Pigalle—a locus raffish with the noises of crowds, street carnivals, and hustlers.

His opus numbers exceed 440. He enjoyed experimenting with stage forms, film, and even tape; he welcomed and advanced polytonal practices; he was a splendid melodist, quick to pen a good refrain, agile in arranging and rearranging his works for various combinations.

Too little of his music remains in the orchestral repertoire. In addition to his three dozen operas and ballets, he wrote twelve symphonies (1940–62), many concertos, and, from his early years, six chamber symphonies. Aside from the two ballet scores discussed below, his most popular works are the *Saudades do Brazil* of 1920–21 (originally for piano), a *Suite provençale* of 1936, and a *Suite française* of 1944–45 (originally for band). His autobiography is entitled *Notes Without Music* (1949). Milhaud was a man of arresting appearance. Confined to a wheelchair by arthritis, he is typically pictured seated—a position from which he conducted. His girth was commensurate with his immobility, but these he carried with dignity and a zest for life that everybody found contagious.

Le Bœuf sur le toit (The Ox on the Roof), OP. 58

For piccolo, flutes I-II, oboe, clarinets I-II, bassoon; horns I-II, trumpets I-II, trombone; tenor drum (i.e. *tamburin,* a Provençal drum), bass drum, cymbals, tambourine, güiro [see below]; strings

Composed 1919 in Paris and Aix-en-Provence; dedicated to Jean Cocteau

Ballet first performed 21 February 1920 in Paris by the Ballets of the Théâtre des Champs-Elysées, Vladimir Golschmann conducting; scenario by Jean Cocteau, who directed; scenery by Raoul Dufy

Published by Max Eschig (Paris, 1950)

Duration: about 20 minutes

It was Mardi Gras season in Rio de Janeiro when Milhaud arrived for his Brazilian sojourn. Already a devotee of popular and ethnic styles, he was precisely the sort of person apt to be infected by the epidemic good humor of the carnival music in the streets. The title of *Le Bœuf sur le toit* apparently comes from the folklore of Brazil, and the music is an assemblage of more-or-less authentic dance tunes—sambas, tangos, and maxixes—for an ensemble that looks like a proper chamber orchestra but sounds like a Latin American street band.

Milhaud originally intended his music as a *cinéma-symphonie,* a sort of all-purpose background music for a silent film—perhaps something by Charlie Chaplin. The literary adventurer Jean Cocteau disapproved of that idea and instead suggested a surrealistic pantomime of clowns and acrobats who move in a slow motion that deliberately contradicts the musical rowdiness of the score. The Shah of Persia funded the production.

The setting is the Do-Nothing Bar, an American establishment of the Prohibition years. Demimonde characters make their entrances: a boxer, a black midget, a fashionable lady, a redheaded woman in a man's suit, a bookie, a gentleman, and of course, the bartender. When a policeman enters, the room is suddenly transformed into a milk bar. But the policeman's suspicion is nevertheless aroused, so the bartender turns on an overhead fan and decapitates him. The mannish woman dances with the head, Salome-style. The customers exit. The bartender reassembles the policeman and gives him the bill.

None of which has anything whatever to do with oxen on roofs, tangos, or Charlie Chaplin.

Milhaud, quite typically, organizes his rudimentary dance tunes into a rigorous if giddy formal structure governed by some dozen recurrences of the opening theme and its merry rasping percussion. (The score calls for a "guitebaro," which Milhaud identifies as a Puerto Rican instrument; the güiro, a ridged gourd scraped with a stick, is the usual approximation, but a cheese grater does just as well.) What results is something of a rondo, with returns of the samba theme separated by various slower episodes, most of then tango-ish. Meanwhile the tonality progresses through all twelve major keys. Just as the work threatens to disintegrate into endless cycles the tempo quickens for the coda. There is a single change of meter, for the little waltz that occurs at the half-way point.

From a mechanical point of view this kind of procedure is elegant, even dainty. Nor can the vivacity of the dance patterns fully account for the sense of barely contained chaos. This is, I think a function of the polytonality: mad (and quite routine) superpositions in some of the voices of material in the "wrong" key—as in the woodwind tag to each refrain, or the chromatic material that snakes up from the clarinet and flute in the first departure section. The ear keeps trying to correct for what is in fact a nonproblem, the effect not so much outrageous as droll.

In fact, the surrealism of title, score, and scenario managed to provoke a typically Parisian *scandale.* Dufy's backdrop, with the ox peering from the roof into the bar, his tail coiled round the chimney, lingered in the mind's eye. Soon enough there was a cabaret in Paris called Le Bœuf sur le Toit (which still thrives) and similar *boîtes* elsewhere in the world. Milhaud found himself cast as the *enfant terrible* of new music.

Shortly after the premiere Milhaud arranged the score as a *"cinéma-fantaisie"* for violin and orchestra, dedicated to and first performed by the violinist René Benedetti. This version, in its 1962 revision, is occasionally heard as well.

La Création du monde (The Creation of the World), OP. 81

Modéré   ♩ = 54
I.   ♩ = 62
II.   ♩ = 54
III. *Vif* ♩ = 104
IV.   ♩ = 108
[No pause beween the movements]

For piccolo, flutes I-II, oboe, clarinets I-II, saxophone, bassoon; horn, trumpet I-II, trombone; timpani, battery including small, high drums, small snare drum, snare drum, tabor, bass drum with pedal symbal, cymbals, tambourine, metal block, wood block; piano; strings soli without viola; often played with augmented strings
Composed 1923 in Paris; dedicated to Paul Collaer and Roger Desormière, Belgian promoter of new music and French conductor, respectively
First performed with the ballet 25 October 1923 in Paris by the Swedish Ballet, Vladimir Golschmann conducting; scenario by Blaise Cendrars, settings and costumes by Fernand Léger
Published by Max Eschig (Paris, 1929)
Duration: about 20 minutes

American jazz became a European vogue in the wake of World War I, and it is from this period that ragtime and blues begin to turn up in the music of Stravinsky and the Parisians. The authentic commodity remained in short supply, its essence culled from visiting Americans, phonograph records, and a London club or two. Milhaud, always an intrepid tourist, had first discovered jazz in London in 1920. Two years later in New York, he reveled in American popular music, ranging from that of Paul Whiteman and his orchestra to what he heard in Harlem clubs. His wide-eyed company for one foray into Harlem included the Italian composer Alfredo Casella and the Dutch conductor Willem Mengelberg. "We were the only white folk there," he noted with pleasure.

When the vagabond writer Blaise Cendrars suggested that he compose the score for a ballet on African myth, Milhaud responded with the altogether inspired notion that the music should sound like New York-style jazz. *La Création du monde,* then, is a sort of African *Rite of Spring,* throbbing not with primeval jungle rhythms, but with the accultured, prevailingly cool sounds of the Harlem nightclub. It is among the earliest and certainly the most interesting of the European jazz compositions; *La Création du monde,* moreover, predates *Rhapsody in Blue* by about a year. Milhaud wrote copiously and well for another half century, but he never surpassed the brilliant imagination of *La Création.*

The band has a Dixieland makeup with prominent solos for alto saxophone and characteristic work for trumpet, clarinet, tailgate trombone, bass, and a splendid battery of percussion. The twisting motives and languid saxophone in the introduction are meant to suggest the primordial soup, out of which a trombone glissando thrusts from time to time: here and elsewhere comparisons with Stravinsky come to mind. Probably the cleverest of the movements is the lively one that follows, a good conservatory fugue based on the lick in the double-bass, answered in turn by trombone, saxophone, and clarinet. The next movement returns to the undulations of the opening, the saxophone melody now taken by the flute, with a reminiscence of the fugue subject in the cello and, everywhere, tongue-in-cheek allusions to the bluesy codetta "Good evening, friends." Of particular interest are the flutter-tongued figures just at the end.

The miniature march—or shuffle—which follows seems to pay hommage to the style of Stravinsky's *L'Histoire du soldat* (The Soldier's Tale). A slower interlude leads to the Dixieland finale, where for the first time the music seems to work itself free of French discipline and understatement and gather into something really wild. At the end (sometimes identified as a fifth movement) the undulations, reminiscences, and twinklings resume and fragment away, concluding with the flutter-tongues and the plaintive saxophone.

Onstage the scene is dominated by giant, primitive figures of the African deities Mzamé, Mebère, and Nkwa. A mass of blackness in the center of the stage begins to boil and heave. A leg, then a torso emerge from the seething heap; scenic abstractions of trees and beasts shoot up from the ground. Finally, a man and a woman materialize and dance to the ritual music of creation. Together they greet, in the quiet music of the conclusion, the dawn of the first spring.

La Création du monde also exists as a suite for piano and string quartet, opus 81b, fashioned by Milhaud in 1926 and performed in Baden-Baden the following year by the Kolisch quartet.

Wolfgang Amadeus Mozart

Born 27 *January 1756 in Salzburg*
Died 5 *December 1791 in Vienna*

Nicolas Slonimsky, the limpid lexicographer, summarizes Mozart as "supreme genius of music whose works in every genre are unsurpassed in lyric beauty, rhythmic gaiety and effortless melodic invention"; the music historian Joseph Kerman numbers him "with Bach and Beethoven . . . the greatest of Western composers." Mozart seems to have been endowed with genuine musical genius, possibly the most prodigious in the history of music; his technical capabilities were immense, his imagination all but limitless—though he worked much harder at composition than legend would have you believe. He died before he was thirty-six, yet his collected works take the same shelf space as Bach's and Haydn's.

His father Leopold Mozart was a gifted musician in his own right and was able to recognize and nourish the exceptional talents of both

Mozart and the older sister they fondly called Nannerl. Mozart made his first concert tour at the age of six; within a few years he could boast of having played before most of the monarchs of Europe. Maria Theresa herself gave him welcome to the imperial court in Vienna, where it was assumed by the Mozarts and royalty alike that he would one day enjoy a handsome appointment. When he was fourteen, Mozart visited Italy, assimilating like composers before and after him the Italian operatic repertoire, orchestral practice, and churchly counterpoint. In Rome, for example, he heard and notated from memory the "secret" and famous *Miserere* sung only at the papal chapel. By now he had begun to compose excellent stage pieces. The death of his patron, the archbishop of Salzburg, led to intolerable conditions there, and he left on another journey, this time through Munich to Paris, hoping to find a suitable and permanent position. Instead there were reverses: his mother died in Paris, and the rupture with Salzburg became definitive. Mozart thereupon settled in Vienna to practice his trade and, ever hopeful of imperial generosity, refused grander offers for employment elsewhere. He married Constanze Weber in 1782.

He had less than a decade to live, but the few years from 1782 to 1791 were a time of astonishing accomplishment, embracing the bulk of his best composition alongside literally hundreds of public appearances. We generally measure his career by the steady progress of his operas, some successful, all distinguished. These include *Die Entführung aus dem Serail* (The Abduction from the Seraglio [Harem], 1782), *Le Nozze di Figaro* (The Marriage of Figaro, 1786), *Don Giovanni* (1787), *Così fan tutte* (roughly, Women Are Like That, 1790), and *Die Zauberflöte* (The Magic Flute, 1791). In 1790 Mozart bid a last farewell, as it turned out, to his friend Haydn when the patriarch embarked for London. Mozart then went to Prague for the coronation of the new Emperor Leopold II as King of Bohemia. He returned to Vienna, fatigued and already overworked, to face the composition and production of *Zauberflöte*. Meanwhile he had been tendered a mysterious commission for a Requiem Mass; he collapsed while composing it and died before it was done.

Mozart works through the possibilities of sonata form, as it was understood in Viennese circles, as preemptively as Bach had done with canon and fugue a few decades before. His understanding of how drama can be fashioned from the play of tonality within relatively limiting conventions of form and rhythm makes the whole notion of instrumental music seem anything but abstract. Mozart himself never seems close to exhausting the idiom, yet except for Haydn's works virtually everything else composed at the same time along similar lines seems trivial by comparision. Along with his operas the most influential of Mozart's compositions are probably the twenty-eight (or so) concertos for piano, symbol of the triumph of Viennese Classicism and the death of the Baroque. Others hold the symphonies (forty numbered ones, and perhaps a half dozen others) to be preeminent; some favor the string quartets and quintets. I wouldn't waste my time arguing those sorts of supremacies.

Mozart's formidable output was systematically catalogued by Ludwig von Köchel in 1862, from whence come the K. numbers, roughly chronological and extending through K. 626. These are invaluable in distinguishing Mozart's works from each other and in suggesting their order. The catalogue has been revised on several occasions to reflect advances in our understanding of the chronology and authenticity of the corpus. Many K. numbers changed accordingly; mostly, however, we go on using the original numbers that musicians have relied on for well over a century.

Symphony No. 29 in A Major, K. 201 (186a)

Allegro moderato
Andante
Menuetto
Allegro con spirito

For oboes I-II; horns I-II; strings
Composed score dated 6 April 1774 in Salzburg
First performed probably in Salzburg in the spring of 1774
Published by A. Kühnel (Leipzig, 1811)
Duration: about 15 minutes

The A-Major Symphony is one of the best of the Salzburg works and, with the Bassoon Concerto, K. 191, among the earliest Mozart in the repertoire. It is a small work in both duration and performing force, the paired oboes and horns characteristic of Mozart's intimate orchestrations; and the chamber-like use of the strings serves to remind us that the boundaries between symphony and quartet remained indistinct. The overall atmosphere is that of what we call the *style galant:*

gracious, elegant, and compact, but with a certain earnestness as well.

Octave leaps downward and caressing rebounds, strung together in rising sequence, constitute the main theme of the first movement. The basic motive lends itself to imitation at the half bar, such that the figure begun in the violins is soon mirrored in the violas and cellos with concomitant thickening of the texture. An equally mundane subject, likewise for violins, of five repeated pitches and an arpeggiated triad introduces the second group; a third theme begins the process of closing the exposition and enriching it with fuller tutti work. The development occupies itself with reversing directions of the given materials; recapitulation is carefully prepared, but in the event seems a rather effacing retreat into the amiability of the first theme. (Mozart puts repeat signs around the development and recapitulation: these should be observed more often than they are.) In the coda, the imitating of the main theme comes to the fore—violins shadowed by cellos, then violas—and begins to cycle.

Violins are muted in the *Andante*, a movement of refined double-dotted melody and walking bass, not dissimilar to the clock movement in Haydn's No. 101 (see p. 275). In the second half of the opening phrase, the second violins take the melody while the firsts carry on in a striking obbligato that achieves thematic prominence as the movement continues to unfold. Where in the first movement the oboes and horns merely supplied the whole-note thickening, here they confirm the end of each new statement, as though given the power to assent to the progress of things. The string players remove their mutes for the last four bars, a *forte* on the main thematic materials.

Dotted rhythms, too, strongly inflect the minuet, in which the logical end of each strain is extended by exclamatory punctuation from oboes and horns. The first violins put a similar kind of tag on the trio, but the effect is a good deal less assertive. The finale is a hunt rondo in $\frac{6}{8}$, with commensurate French horn work. Here, too, there are spirited tags at the end of each section, where the motivic downward-plunging scales reverse, after empty downbeats, into upward rockets.

Symphony No. 36 in C Major ("Linz"), K. 425

Adagio; Allegro spiritoso
Poco Adagio
Menuetto
Presto

For oboes I-II, bassoons I-II; horns I-II, trumpets I-II; timpani; strings

Composed score dated 3 November 1783 in Linz

First performed 4 November 1783 in the municipal ballroom of Linz, Mozart conducting; the orchestra may have been that of Count Johann Thun

Published by J. André (Offenbach, 1793; parts only). *Inexpensive score:* Wolfgang Amadeus Mozart: *Later Symphonies: Full Orchestral Score of Symphonies 35–41* (New York: Dover, 1974)

Duration: about 25 minutes

It is said that the "Linz" symphony was written in a day or so, as Mozart had arrived for his concert in that pastoral Austrian town with nothing new to offer. I find the "Linz" the most charming of the later symphonies—though others are, to be sure, more "important"—both for the brightness of its keys and the gallantry of its melodies. On the whole it seems to confirm the notion that Mozart thought the symphony a happy genre, perhaps a shade less serious than the keyboard concerto. Symphonies of this period are appropriately played by an orchestra of about six violins I, six violins II, three or four violas, three or four cellos, three double basses, and whatever winds are called for in the score. Mozart doubtless conducted from the piano keyboard—there were always piano concertos on his programs—and probably played along, continuo fashion, from time to time.

Mozart's introductory Adagios are usually there to lend gravity to movements that go on to become airy and bright. Here the chromatic inflections add a hint of mystery, but this is dispelled altogether by the breezy *Allegro*. The first group of the sonata contrasts the gracious phrases for strings with the martial winds and timpani. Immediately on arriving at the second group, Mozart deflects the tonality into the minor mode, then returns to the proper area through a seizing whiff of C major in woodwind and brass. As a result of this kind of digression, the closing materials in both exposition and recapitulation are drawn out with splendid tutti hammerings and trills and a conclusiveness you cannot miss.

One should register, if possible, the lovely rise of key from the first movement to the second (C to F), so striking that I would not allow latecomers to be seated here but would carry straight on. This is a $\frac{6}{8}$ *Adagio* rich with allusions to its Baroque ancestors, triplet decorations all around, and in both groups prominent articulation from wind and brass in octaves. ("Group" is an appropriate word to use for this kind of sonata, for there are many themes and motives.)

A minuet of strong, perhaps halting, upbeat returns the key to C major, the dotted figures of the phrase endings reminding us of similar effects in the first movement. The trio features solo oboe, then oboe with bassoon, all doubled by first violins. A *Presto* in duple meter concludes the symphony, incorporating the devices favored by the virtuoso orchestra of Mannheim: crescendos, "rockets" (see p. 393), nervousness in the inner strings. Enjoy in particular the very last bars, where the violins dive to their low G, then rebound in triple stops.

Symphony No. 38 in D Major ("Prague"), K. 504

Adagio; Allegro
Andante
Finale: Presto

For flutes I-II, oboes I-II, bassoons I-II; horns I-II, trumpets I-II; timpani; strings
Composed dated 6 December 1786, Vienna, in Mozart's manuscript catalogue of his works
First performed 19 January 1787 in Prague
Published by Cianchettini & Sperati (London, c. 1800) and J. André (Offenbach, 1800; parts only). *Inexpensive score:* Wolfgang Amadeus Mozart: *Later Symphonies: Full Orchestral Score of Symphonies 35–41* (New York: Dover, 1974)
Duration: about 25 minutes

We know little enough of the circumstances surrounding Mozart's composition of a symphony for the city of Prague. Apparently he finished the work in Vienna in early December 1786, and we know him to have arrived in Prague at the beginning of January. The thing that may be Praguish about the symphony is its lack of minuet, possibly having to do with municipal prejudices against dancing, but more likely because the three-movement symphony was customary there. It lacks clarinets, too, but the wind writing is memorable nevertheless, and the work for the two bassoons is some of the suavest to be found anywhere.

The *Adagio* reiterates the tonic pitch, D, as insistently as will the *Allegro* to come. So, too, are the falling chromatics in the violins to be recalled later on. The horn call with timpani evolves into a drum-roll that prepares the elision of the slow introduction and the sonata allegro. The *Allegro* opens by ambling forward with syncopated Ds in the violins that gather momentum into a true melodic cell, evoking a military response in the winds and brass, leading finally to a spirited tutti with sixteenth-note flourishes. The idiom is quite like that of the overture to *The Marriage of Figaro*—which had been a great success in Prague (Mozart had found the populace talking about "nothing, nothing but *Figaro!*"); the prevailing melodic motive, on the other hand, is suggestive of *The Magic Flute* overture. What may sound like a restatement of the initial ambling and first theme is in fact at a higher pitch level and begins the bridge; the second group commences with the new, liquid melody in the first violins and is immediately nudged into the minor mode for a few measures by the bassoons. The flourishes that close the exposition are the same as those that ended the first theme. The development begins an exchange of descending scalar motives which the themes then join and dominate, the various subjects merging into and out of each other with nonchalance and consistently imaginative linkage.

In the *Andante* the chromaticism we had glimpsed in the slow introduction of the first movment is much intensified. Both halves of the first phrase, for example, end in rising chromatic scales. The movement is an unhurried sonata, pausing to muse over this and that soft-spoken point, elegantly ornamented, with a richness of sonority that noticeably deepens the impact of the symphony we are coming to know. Trumpets and timpani are useless here.

In the first four bars of the *Presto,* Mozart articulates the principal issues of the movement: the triadic motive in the violins, begun off the beat and mimicked at once in the voices below; the syncopated falls; the hammered resolutions. The wide intervals open the symphony up and blow away the stepwiseness of the preceding movements. Winds, as they have done elsewhere, continue to veer into the minor mode. Stepwise motion appears momentarily with the second theme, but the principal motive returns almost immediately. Gruff tutti remarks volley with the triadic motive in the development, and there is enough emphasis on this matter for the recapitulation to commence with the second theme. Despite such freedoms throughout the "Prague," it is a work of pleasing symmetry, with such close connections from movement to movement that we are always able to keep the totality in mind as the constituent parts unfold.

Symphony No. 39 in E♭ Major, K. 543

Adagio; Allegro
Andante con moto
Menuetto: Allegro
Finale: Allegro

For flute, clarinets I-II, bassoons I-II; horns I-II, trumpets I-II;
timpani; strings
Composed dated 26 June 1788, Vienna, in Mozart's manuscript
catalogue of his works
First performed possibly in Dresden and / or Leipzig in the spring
of 1789, Mozart conducting
Published by Cianchettini & Sperati (London, 1807) and J. André
(Offenbach, 1797; parts only). *Inexpensive score:* Wolfgang
Amadeus Mozart: *Later Symphonies: Full Orchestral Score of
Symphonies 35–41* (New York: Dover, 1974)
Duration: about 30 minutes

Mozart had not composed new symphonies to be performed in Vienna
since moving there in 1781, preferring instead to quench the public
thirst for his piano concertos. (The "Haffner" Symphony, K. 385 of
1782, was originally part of a serenade; the "Linz" and "Prague" Symphonies were composed for out-of-town.) Why he should suddenly
have produced, in the summer of 1788, the three stunning symphonies that conclude his work in the genre is not certain. Possibly he
intended the pair in flat keys, the E♭ Major and G Minor, for concerts
that summer or the following season and (as can happen when composers work themselves into white heat) just kept going. Perhaps a
published opus was being born. But a summer concert in 1788 failed
for lack of subscribers, and the Lenten concerts of 1789 do not appear
to have included new symphonies. Talk of a London season, of the
sort Haydn was soon to have, came to naught.

Mozart's concert programs in Germany in 1789 and 1790 may have
included all three works, though the vexing habit of citing merely "a
new symphony of Herr Mozart" in handbills and the press and of
Mozart himself referring to new works without identification reduces
us to mere speculation. There is evidence in the manuscript score for
one or more performances of the G-Minor Symphony, probably in
Dresden on 14 April 1789 and perhaps at the Leipzig Gewandhaus
on 12 May, where at least one and possibly two of the others were

offered. In Frankfurt on 15 October 1790, in conjunction with the coronation of the Austrian emperor, one of the new symphonies was heard on the same program with the "Coronation" Concerto, K. 537 (see p. 390).

All three symphonies are complex of design, more severe than the "Prague," and on the whole more progressive. Relationships between movements are stronger; the finales acquire new weight and gravity. There results a new sense of symphonic process, where cumulative musical issues gather toward resolution at the end. Beethoven was quick to discern and exploit this new direction in compositional thought.

Mozart's choice of key and orchestral force for this symphony tells us what he is up to. E♭ major is a key of outward high spirits but of warmth and subtlety as well. The single flute is there to be given solos; the absence of oboes precludes the old, if reliable, effects for oboe and horn; the striking work for paired clarinets shows his growing fascination with that instrument. (The great Clarinet Quintet, K. 581, follows a few months later.)

The *Adagio* opening is quite royal, with falling scalar figures in the violins that foreshadow later developments. With the timpani roll, the transition has already begun; chromatic twists darken the passage as it wends toward resolution, settling gently into the *Allegro*. This is a sonata movement of generally slow harmonic motion and a certain degree of understatement. The $\frac{3}{4}$ meter is as unusual for a Mozart first movement as the general motion by quarter-note rhythms. Striking, too, is the number of different melodic gambits. The second group, which begins over horns and double-basses, seems insecure, a feeling reinforced when the very figure that clinches the new key—the baubling eighths and sixteenths at the end of the exposition—deflects into the development and begins to migrate all over the place. This excursion is brief; suddenly there is an empty bar, then a splendid chord progression of woodwinds into the recapitulation.

It is, however, with the *Andante con moto* that the E♭ Symphony begins to soar, achieving in its great length a sustained elegance and clarity of design that pretty well epitomize the dynamic of Viennese Classicism. The white-wigged beginning, for example, is a perfect example of the antecedent-consequent eight-bar phrase, each new turn balancing every other. The entire statement, like the next, is repeated. The second section, more than twice as long, carries the same material away from its stability into suggestions of tonal unrest, then settles back into a reprise of the opening material. The movement is long, on account of the slow tempo and the dual repeats; now there is a developmental excursion to a new key and second theme. As in the first movement, and with similar effect, the second subject plays out over sustained horns and basses. Once this pedal breaks, the movement turns directly to a recapitulation copiously ornamented by the winds.

The minuet is of the rollicking sort, violins charging up and down the staff, with a famous trio melody for the two clarinets and flute. The finale—though marked *Allegro,* it comes off more like a *Presto*—is monothematic, the second theme being a refashioning of the first. Things become by turns syncopated, lopsided, donkeyish, with the development ending in an empty measure. And the last few measures are so abrupt as to leave you with a toe or more in the air.

Symphony No. 40 in G Minor, K. 550

Molto Allegro
Andante
Menuetto: Allegretto
Allegro assai

For flute, oboes I-II, clarinets I-II, bassoons I-II; horns I-II;
   strings; the clarinets were added later, presumably in 1791,
   when the flute and oboe parts were slightly rewritten
Composed score dated 25 July 1788 in Vienna; the autograph was
   later owned by Brahms
First performed probably 14 April 1789 in Dresden (see
   Symphony No. 39, above). The version with clarinets
   performed 16 and 17 April 1791 at a benefit concert of the
   Vienna Society of Musicians (with nearly 200 players), Antonio
   Salieri conducting, but the score shows evidence of an earlier
   performance with clarinets.
Published by Cianchettini & Sperati (London, c. 1810) and J.
   André (Offenbach, 1794; parts only). *Inexpensive scores:*
   Wolfgang Amadeus Mozart: *Later Symphonies: Full Orchestral
   Score of Symphonies 35–41* (New York: Dover, 1974); Mozart:
   Symphony in G Minor, K. 550, ed. Nathan Broder, A Norton
   Critical Score (New York: Norton, 1967)
Duration: about 35 minutes

You remember the opening of the G-Minor Symphony as vividly as the first sentence of *Jane Eyre* or *Gone With the Wind.* The restless agitato of the first two bars and the theme that follows, at once sinister and graceful, have a way of lingering in the mind as a universal truth. The entry of wind instruments as the statement culminates—nowadays we almost always use the clarinets—is equally dramatic. The restatement is cut short by an energetic bridge; the empty measure announces the second theme, shared by the winds and strings. One of Mozart's stormiest developments stresses the first theme, fragmenting it into a troubled palpitation. The moment of recapitulation is not a moment at all, but rather a drawn-out event, for the theme begins over the point of maximum harmonic unrest; not until the second full bar does the harmony settle back into G minor. (Szell's recording with the Cleveland Orchestra is of strong impact here: almost imperceptibly he stretches this delicious moment out, then breathes deeply.) But Mozart is not through with his surprises: when the second theme is done recapitulating it does not cadence but surges into an eight-bar chromatic ascent, such that the movement seems to lift itself into its closing materials.

The *Andante* is a sonata movement in $\frac{6}{8}$ that rises out of the repeated eighth-notes in the violas, imitated by the second, then the first violins. Built into both themes are chromatic and rhythmic sighs, and the strong grip of pairs of thirty-second notes, often in falling cascades. These give the movement its filigree.

Minuets usually are stately or rustic retreats from the graver concerns of the other movements, but here the metric tension (called *hemiola*) and minor key have grave effect as well. The major-mode trio offsets this somewhat, and the arched phrases have a tranquilizing effect; yet at the *da capo,* of course, the G minor reasserts its grip. Nor is there release to be found in the finale. In fact there is a close affinity between the triadic theme and that of the minuet (and, for that matter, movement III of Beethoven's Fifth Symphony). The rush of eighth notes begins to take control during the transition; the second theme asserts some brightness, but the agitations return and gain precedence. The development is correspondingly intense and almost as formidable a display of counterpoint as in the more celebrated finale of the "Jupiter" Symphony; the empty measure separates development and recapitulation.

The G-Minor Symphony has intrigued countless essayists with its pent-up melancholy, its storm and stress. In that respect, it is a vital precursor of Romanticism: Wagner, for example, thought it pivotal.

Symphony No. 41 in C Major ("Jupiter"), K. 551

Allegro vivace
Andante cantabile
Menuetto: Allegretto
Molto Allegro

For flute, oboes I-II, bassoons I-II; horns I-II, trumpets I-II; timpani; strings
Composed score dated 10 August 1788 in Vienna
First performed probably spring 1789 (see Symphony No. 39, p. 380)
Published by Cianchettini & Sperati (London, c. 1810) and J. André (Offenbach, 1793; parts only). *Inexpensive score:* Wolfgang Amadeus Mozart: *Later Symphonies: Full Orchestral Score of Symphonies 35–41* (New York: Dover, 1974)
Duration: about 30 minutes

It was the impresario Salomon—Haydn's Salomon—who described Mozart's last symphony as the "Jupiter," or so it seems from an 1829 entry in the diary of the English publisher Novello. He and his wife made a pilgrimage to visit Mozart's widow in Salzburg where, he wrote:

> Mozart's son said he considered the Finale to his father's Sinfonia in C— which Salomon described as the Jupiter—to be the highest triumph of instrumental Composition, and I agree with him.

"Jupiter," in any event, serves nicely for a C-major symphony of epic proportion.

The fierce opening gambit, three forceful tonic Cs with ornamenting upbeats, is immediately diffused by the gentle violin counterfoil, tried again on G, then swept into an aristocratic tutti with the ornaments in the opposite direction. The restatement is *piano,* with a new countermelody in flute and oboe. The carefully prepared second group affords the first sustained lyricism; suddenly, after an empty measure of the sort we expect to portend remarkable turns, there is a C-minor triad surging into a strong cadence and a soaring close—or so it seems.

In fact this abruptly changes direction and peters out, to be succeeded by a courtly, square closing passage. We hear more of this very passage at once, after the woodwinds have begun the development by sallying into a distant key. The recombining of melodies and related imitative ploys in the development foretell important things.

The *Andante cantabile,* in F major, is cast in the sonata form with short development common to Classical slow movements: But the primary interest here lies in the arioso style of melody, which twists and turns in graceful, ever more complex arabesques. The minuet centers on a descending figure of chromatic nuance; the trio is quirky of phrase and enigmatic of conclusion.

In the celebrated finale Mozart unleashes the full measure of both his fancy and his technique. It opens with a naive melody on the first four notes of the major scale. At once the sonata becomes permeated by high counterpoint. Each new motive is swept into the contrapuntal web and revealed to have all sorts of crafty connections to everything else. The second group, for example, reduces by half the opening notes values and is an inversion of the first theme's shape. Already the motives suggest fugal design. So far, however, Mozart has reveled in a kind of fugue-imbued symphonic writing for which there is a certain degree of precedent in the Viennese literature. But at the coda, the five main ideas are gathered into a true fugue—a genuinely extraordinary display of the most learned counterpoint. The display is short-lived, but the result is grand. The glories of *Zauberflöte* and the Requiem were yet to come, but Mozart achieves with the "Jupiter" Symphony one of his surest triumphs.

Concerto for Piano and Orchestra No. 23 in A Major, K. 488

Allegro
Adagio
Allegro assai

For piano solo; flute, clarinets I-II, bassoons I-II; horns I-II; strings

Composed score dated 2 March 1786 in Vienna; there is a cadenza for the first movement by Mozart

First performed at one of the Lenten concerts of 1786, Mozart playing the solo part and conducting from the keyboard

Published by J. André (Offenbach, 1800; parts only). *Inexpensive*

score: Wolfgang Amadeus Mozart: *Piano Concertos Nos. 23–27 in Full Score* (New York: Dover, 1978)
Duration: about 25 minutes

During the high season in Vienna, which began in Advent and carried on through Lent, the nobles who gathered there from all over central and eastern Europe would vie to present memorable concerts. Mozart's participation as pianist or conductor was highly prized, and between these and his own Lenten subscription concerts he would appear dozens of times each year. Such intense booking demanded an ongoing supply of new piano concertos from his pen. In late autumn, accordingly, he would begin to think about the following Lent and typically would have his last concerto for the season ready a day or so before its premiere.

In fact of the twenty-seven numbered piano concertos in Mozart's oeuvre, well over a dozen appear to have been written for the Lenten seasons from 1782 to 1786. After the concerto for Advent 1786 (K. 503 in C; see p. 389) the demand seems to have dropped off, and Mozart returned to the genre only twice more, for K. 537 in D and K. 595 in B♭ (see pp. 390 and 391). I pass over the D-minor Concerto, K. 466, with regret. The nineteenth century favored this one over all the others, and Beethoven used it as a model for his Third Concerto.

It is a formidable repertoire in which the composer tends to be at his most individual. Nowhere, certainly, was he more at ease than seated at the piano before an orchestra he would proceed to conduct and then join as soloist. A Mozart concerto is not on the whole ostentatious, the solos often consisting of material no more elaborate than passagework or melody in the right hand and simple accompaniment in the left. Mozart played along during the opening orchestral ritornellos, and would also have provided a good deal of ornamentation for which there is no indication in the score. The cadenzas he would usually improvise on the spot, perhaps having sketched out some preliminary ideas in advance, and afterward would play along with the orchestra to the end. A good performance of a Mozart concerto, then, will imitate these practices, though it makes good sense to use a Mozart cadenza if one exists.

K. 488 is the most personable of the trilogy of 1785–86. The themes are charming, the writing for winds (in an orchestra lacking oboes, trumpets, and timpani) glamorous in the five-part ensembles and in the trio work (flute, first clarinet, and first bassoon) as well. A half-dozen different melodies are to be heard in the orchestral ritornello and are taken up in turn by the soloist. After a beat of silence in the solo exposition the second theme finally emerges softly in the strings. The development is brief, led by the wind choir in alternation with the soloist and strings; the solo gleefully and with mounting excitement advances on the recapitulation. Following the restatement of the second theme there is a lovely extension for the clarinets and bassoons.

The *Andante* is pensive and reticent, in F♯ minor and $\frac{6}{8}$, and is begun by the soloist. Ignoring the metric character established by the piano in the first dozen bars, the orchestral response rises in an emotional sequence of overlapping laments. Flute and first clarinet begin the second theme over triplets—another new feature—from the second clarinet. The winding down of an already memorable movement is of gripping effect: the left hand of the piano alternating with the bassoons, diaphonous cadences with string pizzicatos, and a last lingering over the lament. A hunt rondo would be inappropriate; instead there is a duple-meter *Presto,* begun and altogether dominated by the piano. The strings, in fact, have very little to do, for one after another the merry themes are proposed by the pianist and the winds, with the obviously confident solo part at length coming up with the idea that brings things to closure. But if you are a principal wind player there's nothing better than K. 488 and its companion, K. 491, discussed below.

Concerto for Piano and Orchestra No. 24 in C Minor, K. 491

Allegro
Larghetto
[*Allegretto*]

For piano solo; flute, oboes I-II, clarinets I-II, bassoons I-II; horns I-II, trumpets I-II; timpani; strings

Composed dated 24 March 1786, Vienna, in Mozart's manuscript catalogue of his works

First performed 3 April 1786 in a subscription concert, Mozart

soloist and conducting from the keyboard; repeated April 7 in
an academy concert at the Burgtheater, Mozart soloist and
conducting

Published by J. André (Offenbach, 1800; parts only). *Inexpensive
score:* Wolfgang Amadeus Mozart: *Piano Concertos Nos. 23–27 in
Full Score* (New York: Dover, 1978)

Duration: about 30 minutes

Mozart is at his most profound in the key of C minor. In K. 491 we
hear him confront, as if under cover of darkness, universals of the
innermost spirit, and after hearing it, find ourselves obsessed with its
subjects and arguments for many hours. Certainly the orchestral ritornello of the first movement is one of the more engrossing in the concerto repertoire. The mystery of the twelve-bar theme lies in its overall
quietude, low register, unison presentation in strings and bassoon,
and disjunctures of shape that emphasize the darkest intervals embedded in the minor key; also there is a lugubrious use of rhythmic values
in $\frac{3}{4}$ time, the long notes at the start yielding to lurches, empty space,
and filler. The restatement is a violent tutti. Now the wind players
undertake the first of their many episodes—do not fail to note the
presence of trumpets and timpani—first considering the given subject, then introducing a languid new phrase in dialogue of flute and
bassoon. A rather similar dialogue of strings and woodwinds begins
closure, and a stern dotted-rhythm tutti achieves it. The piano does
not dispute but rather enriches these musings. When the solo part
reaches the second group, in E♭ major, one's first impression is of a
stock eight-bar choral progression, mirrored in the woodwinds. But
this broadens into a huge digression, with new themes, an eyebrow-
raising return of the main theme in E♭ *minor,* and for that reason,
extended closing materials to reconfirm the major mode. The development then proceeds to puzzle through false recapitulatory gestures
and a cycle of purplish tutti surges and solo responses. After the
recapitulation and cadenza—often the one by Johann Nepomuk
Hummel—comes a fragile *pianissimo* close.

The *Larghetto* commences in the piano with rather squarely wrought
phrases suggestive of the theme of a theme and variations: four bars
of solo repeated in the wind, a short departure, and a return of the
four-bar subject. But then comes a sublime episode for the woodwinds, doubling and then quadrupling the original note values. Returns

of the main theme continue to alternate with bewitching departures in the winds; the closing theme is of inestimable grace, as the solo bassoon offers the arpeggiated ("Alberti") bass figures usually associated with the left hand on the piano.

The oriental flavor of the third movement comes from its suggestions of a Turkish march, with emphasis on hollow trumpets and timpani. The march tune is varied in successive statements, reaching at its peak a pompous *forte* for all concerned, and the subsidary sections have the corresponding feel of march trios. The second of these veers off into an episode featuring, one last time, the solo winds. Yet another novelty is in store, for the cadenza ends with the soloist shifting into $\frac{6}{8}$ for a last variation of the theme and an extended coda.

Concerto for Piano and Orchestra No. 25 in C Major, K. 503

Allegro maestoso
Andante
[*Allegretto*]

For piano solo; flute, oboes I-II, bassoons I-II; horns I-II, trumpets I-II; timpani; strings
Composed 1786, dated 4 December 1786, Vienna, in Mozart's manuscript catalogue of his works
First performed probably 5 December 1786 at an academy concert in the Casino, a hall in Vienna
Published by Constanze Mozart (Vienna, 1797; parts only). *Inexpensive scores:* Wolfgang Amadeus Mozart: *Piano Concertos Nos. 23–27 in Full Score* (New York: Dover, 1978); Mozart: *Piano Concerto in C Major, K. 503,* ed. Joseph Kerman, A Norton Critical Score (New York: Norton, 1970)
Duration: about 35 minutes

This is the last of the twelve great piano concertos of the mid-1780s (K. 449 to K. 503) and was completed just two days before the "Prague" Symphony, with which it shares certain principles of proportion. (For example, both have unusually long first movements.) The choice of C major leads, in turn, to the bold proportions of the work, and both features make it fitting for what effectively marked the end of an epoch. Afterward, there appears to have been a slacking of interest in the genre on the part of both Mozart and his public, and both remaining concertos are less exalted of purpose.

That it is meant as a noble concerto is clear from the fanfare opening; its inner mystery is suggested by the inflections of minor early on and, a little later, the minor-mode march that constitutes the second theme of the orchestral introduction. While the solo exposition does not particularly avoid chromatic alterations, the second subject, in oboes and bassoons, is a simple thing; return to the march is witheld for the development. By the conclusion of the exposition, however, the solo part has gathered into brilliant two-handed passagework. On the whole the melodic style features short motives—the three repeated notes, for example—over extended treatment of the themes.

The *Andante,* in the tradition of the romanza, juxtaposes the extreme simplicity of the opening triadic gesture with a developing complexity of ornamentation, first in the flute solo and second violin accompaniment, then in the piano. The theme of the rondo is drawn from the gavotte in the ballet music for the opera *Idomeneo.*

Concerto for Piano and Orchestra No. 26 in D Major ("Coronation"), K. 537

Allegro
Larghetto
Allegretto

For piano solo; flute, oboes I-II, bassoons I-II; horns I-II, trumpets I-II; timpani; strings

Composed dated 24 February 1788, Vienna, in Mozart's manuscript catalogue of his works

First performed probably 14 April 1789 in Dresden; performed 15 October 1790 at Frankfurt to celebrate the coronation of Leopold II as emperor

Published by J. André (Offenbach, 1794). *Inexpensive score:* Wolfgang Amadeus Mozart: *Piano Concertos Nos. 23–27 in Full Score* (New York: Dover, 1978)

Duration: about 35 minutes

K. 537 became the "Coronation" Concerto after its Frankfurt performance in conjunction with the coronation of the Austrian emperor Leopold II, brother of the unfortunate Marie Antoinette. In fact, the work had been intended for the 1788 Lenten concerts in Vienna, but apparently was not played.

With this work, Mozart returns to a more formulaic concerto structure. The progress of themes is anything but taut, the wind players given little to do, as if, some suggest, Mozart were wary of instrumentalists he might encounter on the road. There is, nevertheless, a certain brilliance to the D-major key. What results is an airy first movement, competent if typical in its solo passagework, and unassuming of orchestral accompaniment.

The *Larghetto* is a simple rounded movement with long stretches of unaccompanied piano solo; the digressive middle section, by contrast, carries on over continuous eighth-note accompaniment in the strings. The long rondo, with gavottish upbeats like K. 503, undergoes serious challenges from minor key areas. But your attention is most drawn by the virtuosity of the long thirty-second-note figurations for the soloist.

Mozart did not circulate this concerto (or K. 503) in manuscript; as a result the right hand part is often skeletal and requires fleshing out. Long stretches of the left hand, moreover, are left entirely blank in the autograph. These were filled in by the publisher André, whose text became the customary reading.

Concerto for Piano and Orchestra No. 27 in B♭ Major, K. 595

Allegro
Larghetto
Allegro

For piano solo; flute, oboes I-II, bassoons I-II; horns I-II; strings
Composed dated 5 January 1791, Vienna, in Mozart's manuscript catalogue of his works; cadenza to movements I and cadenzas in movement III (two, one after each fermata) by Mozart
First performed 4 March 1791, at a concert of the clarinetist Joseph Bähr at Jahn's Hall in the Himmelpfortgasse, Vienna
Published by Artaria & Co. as op. 17 (Vienna, 1791). *Inexpensive score:* Wolfgang Amadeus Mozart: *Piano Concertos Nos. 23–27 in Full Score* (New York: Dover, 1978)
Duration: about 35 minutes

Mozart's last two instrumental works were concertos, this one a shade anticlimactic, the Clarinet Concerto K. 622 invigorated with discovery at every turn. To be noted in the piano concerto are the guileless, mostly untroubled idiom to which he had returned with K. 537 and the continued absence of clarinets. The wind writing is, however, a little more significant, and there are some imaginative touches in the tutti work. The introductory first bar, for example, like that of the G-Minor Symphony, is highly unusual, and tonal excursions in and around the soloist's episode in (B♮) minor are hair-raising indeed.

In the *Larghetto,* another ternary romanza, the piano part is the quintessence of simplicity, the orchestra providing the richnesses of texture: the sustained wind lines in the center section, for example, particularly as it passes through the glamorous key of G♭ major. The rondo is dominated by a single carefree tune of arpeggiated triads, quite similar to spring songs Mozart composed a few days later. There are some jolting modulatory passages, but again the ear is most taken by the virtuosity of the solo passagework.

The Concertos for Winds

Concerto for Bassoon and Orchestra in B♭ Major, K. 191 (186e; 1774)

Concerto No. 1 for Flute and Orchestra in G Major, K. 313 (285c; 1778)

Concerto No. 2 for Flute (or Oboe) and Orchestra in D Major, K. 314 (285d; 1778)

Concerto No. 2 for French Horn and Orchestra in E♭ Major, K. 417 (1783)

Concerto No. 3 for French Horn and Orchestra in E♭ Major, K.447 (1783–86)

Concerto No. 4 for French Horn and Orchestra in E♭ Major, K. 495 (1786)

Concerto for Clarinet and Orchestra in A Major, K. 622 (1791)

Inexpensive scores: Wolfgang Amadeus Mozart: *Concerti for Wind Instruments in Full Score* (New York: Dover, 1986)

The passage of two centuries has found little to challenge the supremacy of Mozart's concertos in the repertoire for solo wind instruments: flute, oboe, clarinet, bassoon, and horn. He wrote them, mostly, to amuse the soloists—noble dilettantes on the one hand and his instrumentalist friends on the other—and their invited guests. As a result their outlook is typically unperturbed, their scale smallish. The sequence of movements is conventional: a concerto-sonata first movement with orchestral ritornello, an Andante, and a rondo. The usual orchestration is for strings with pairs of oboes and horns, but without clarinets, trumpets, and timpani—the "light" orchestra of the time. All are in major keys.

Mozart composed his Bassoon Concerto in June 1774, when he was 18, possibly at the request of the aristocratic amateur Baron von Dürnitz. The solo part percolates, in the first movement, through an expansive main theme and a second subject of typical bassoon passagework that takes care to descend now and then to the instrument's lowest notes. (Despite its ungainly appearance and unholy association with irritable grandfathers, the bassoon is a remarkably agile instrument.) The *Andante* may well remind you of "Porgi amor," the Countess's aria at the beginning of act II of *The Marriage of Figaro,* which it precedes by many years; the third movement is a rondo in the minuet style, with the solo part beginning in courtly triplet arpeggiations and then becoming markedly faster and more intricate. Throughout Mozart revels in the bassoon's ability to bounce with ease over intervals wider than an octave.

Mozart composed the two flute concertos to a commission from a Dutchman named De Jean, an amateur who wanted "three short, simple concerti" and some flute quartets. They met in November 1777 in Mannheim, a court city celebrated for the accomplishments of its orchestra, and both concertos embrace such elements of the Mannheim style as fast, upward-bursting scales in the violins (the "Mannheim rocket") and what was for the time the unusually dramatic device of crescendo. Mozart, who was not fond of the flute to begin with, complained bitterly of having "to write for an instrument I cannot bear." At length he finished two of the required concertos (by dint of refurbishing, for the second, an earlier concerto for oboe) and at least two of the quartets. De Jean received the hand-me-down with displeasure and found the second movement of the first concerto too difficult, so paid only half the promised sum. By the time the matter was considered closed by both parties, two years later, Mozart had composed a substitute second movement, the Andante K. 315 (285e), and may have begun the third concerto.

The First Concerto is the more rigorous; it has a big first movement textured with rapid orchestral passagework, particularly in the second violins. All of the significant motives are stated in the orchestra ritornello: the opening flourish, the transitional chains of interlocking major thirds, the cocky little rise of dotted eighths and sixteenths for the second subject. A pair of flutes replaces the oboes for the *Adagio non troppo,* with muted upper strings and a good deal of pizzicato in the bass; the soloist's aria is richly ornamented, and again there is important passagework for second violins. The rondo is in the minuet style, much like the third movement of the Bassoon Concerto. Here rocket figures in the violins are taken up by the soloist, who also alludes to the interlocking-third motive in the first movement.

The Second Flute Concerto is presumably the same as the lost Oboe Concerto in C, composed the previous year for the oboist Giuseppe Ferlendis. The solo flute's first entry is quite dramatic, pausing for four bars of high D while the strings carry on beneath. The tune of the last movement is equally familiar as Blonde's aria "Welche Wonne, welche Lust" from act II of *Die Entführung aus dem Serail* (1782).

A French hornist's solo repertoire consists largely of two concertos by Richard Strauss and three Mozart concertos and the horn quintet. Mozart may have composed as many as seven horn concertos, of which three are preserved complete and a fourth (the First Concerto) pieced together. These works were composed for a colorful character named Joseph Leutgeb (c. 1745–1811), horn player from Salzburg who, after some quite successful solo appearances in Paris, moved to Vienna to become a cheese merchant. (In this enterprise he had the financial backing of none other than Leopold Mozart—whose son Wolfgang, in turn, looked to Leutgeb for loans.) Mozart poked unmerciful fun at his friend: the manuscript of K. 417 is headed "W. A. Mozart took pity on an ass, ox, and fool"; the rondo to K. 386b concludes in catty Italian "Finished! Thank God! Enough! Enough!" and with an unflattering portrait; the autograph of K. 495 is written in four different colors of ink, as though one were insufficient to a person of limited mental powers.

The concertos are for valveless horn, on which chromatic alterations to the tonic scale had to be produced by stopping the air column with the hand in the bell. All make considerable use of signals of posthorn and hunting horn, especially in the rondos. The best of them is usually held to be the Third Concerto, K. 447, with its lovely Romanza in the rich and unusual key of A♭ and with clarinets and bassoons instead of oboes and horns. My own favorite movement is the rondo of the Second Concerto, which dwells on woodsy fanfares and trills and graces, and near the end introduces one of Mozart's most ardent closing themes.

(Concerning Leutgeb's cheese shop it is worth noting that Mozart's multitalented librettist Lorenzo Da Ponte was also, for a short time, a purveyor of comestibles. After coming to New York in 1807, he became a grocer, but short on acumen for that trade took the safer course of teaching Italian at what is now Columbia University. He died in 1838, at the age of ninety, after writing some fine memoirs; in his old age he saw the first New York production of *Don Giovanni*.)

Mozart wrote the Clarinet Concerto for Anton Stadler (1753–1812), one of the two brothers whose mastery of the clarinet and basset horn—and whose Masonic activity—had drawn them into the composer's innermost circle. Stadler accompanied Mozart to Prague in September 1791 to play the clarinet solos written for him in *La Clemenza di Tito;* the Clarinet Concerto was done in October, just a few weeks before Mozart's death. Essentially it his last complete work.

His experience with the clarinet family, scarcely older than Mozart himself, was already long and happy. For the concerto he chose a placid manner, restrained themes, and an orchestra with flutes instead of oboes. The soloist plays almost continuously, with no breaks at all in the second movement. Naturally enough the emphases are on the clarinet's intricate tone color and its agility in moving from one extreme of register to another. Passagework tends to cover two octaves, sometimes two and a half, at a stretch. The second and third movements demonstrate the dualism of character Mozart saw in the clarinet, the *Adagio* serene and deep, the rondo growing almost comic as the clarinet edges ever closer to the limits of the range, leaps across the staff, plummets happily into its basement.

Sinfonia Concertante for Violin, Viola, and Orchestra in E♭ Major, K. 364 (320d)

Allegro maestoso
Andante
Presto

For violin and viola solo; oboes I-II, horns I-II; strings with violas
    I-II.
Composed summer 1779 in Salzburg; cadenzas in movements I
    and II written out by Mozart
First performed probably in Salzburg in the fall of 1779,
    probably with the concert-master Antonio Brunetti, violin, and
    Mozart, viola
Published by J. André (Offenbach, 1802; parts only). *Inexpensive
    score:* Wolfgang Amadeus Mozart: The Violin Concerti and the
    Sinfonia Concertante, K. 364, in Full Score (New York: Dover,
    1986)
Duration: about 30 minutes

The *symphonie concertante,* a concerto-like composition for multiple
soloists and orchestra, is represented in the standard repertoire only
by Mozart's for violin and viola. The *concertante* is a step-child of the
concerto grosso of fifty years previous, and enjoyed great vogue in the
1770s in Paris and Mannheim—cities Mozart visited during his travels of 1777–78. He liked the idea of virtuosi in a joint display of
their accomplishments and accordingly produced in the following
months a spate of works in the *concertante* style, among them this
Sinfonia Concertante and its companion, the Concerto for Two Pianos
(K. 365 [316a], also in E♭). Not dissimilar in scope is the Concerto
for Flute and Harp (K. 299 [297], 1778) composed for the Parisian
Duc de Guines and his daughter. (A concerto for a gentleman dilet-
tante of the flute and a properly bred young woman at the drawing
room harp has much to say of the society of the time.) But neither of
the double concertos is actually called *concertante,* and of the five works
Mozart may have begun with that title, only this one is preserved
complete. Its descendants are such works as the Beethoven Triple
Concerto and the Brahms Double.

Mozart himself was to play the viola part. To put the soloists on
an equal footing—so the conventional explanation goes—he calls for
the violist to tune all four strings up a half-step. The idea was to
provide the solo part an extra measure of brilliance, that it not be
engulfed by the two separate viola lines in the orchestra. (Considerations of this sort are less urgent now than in the days of small violas
and old-fashioned bows and strings.) In any case the combination of
the princely violin with its more reticent sibling, along with the five-
part string textures in the orchestra, results in an engaging and altogether unique tone color.

Formally, the Sinfonia Concertante is free-wheeling. The ritornello of the first movement, for example, begins in the stasis of long note values and slow harmonic progress and takes a long time to unfold. Mozart thought the key of E♭ major quite serious and demanding great subtlety of treatment, an idea we begin to grasp when the soloists gently emerge from the trilled thrusts of cellos and violas. The movement progresses in sections articulated by pauses and decorated turns, always governed by principles of the good sonata. The cadenza is by Mozart, as is the one in the second movement.

The *Andante* is a serene essay in C minor, mostly for the soloists and articulating interjections from the pair of oboes; it is without a development. In the rondo the orchestra is given square-cornered march figures, material rendered insignificant by the snappier figures in the solo parts. Here the soloists alternate rather than join, trading suggestions and riposts over buzzing accompaniments. In one sense the skirmish was won before it began, for we would not dare to imagine, as it was too often thought in those days, that the viola is an instrument best given to violinists past their prime.

Eine kleine Nachtmusik (A Little Night Music) in G Major, K. 525, Serenade

Allegro
Romanze
Menuetto: Allegretto
Rondo: Allegro

For solo violins I-II, viola, cello, and double-bass; often played by string sections of symphony orchestras
Composed dated 10 August 1787, Vienna, in Mozart's manuscript catalogue of his works
First performed presumably in Vienna, 1787
Published by J. André (Offenbach, c. 1827; parts only). *Inexpensive score:* Wolfgang Amadeus Mozart: *Complete Serenades in Full Score,* Vol. II (New York: Dover, 1990)
Duration: about 15 minutes

The closing decades of the eighteenth century sired countless descendants of the Baroque dance suite, called by such titles as serenade and divertimento. Shallower in purpose than the symphony or concerto, they are correspondingly freer in design and with as many movements as might be deemed necessary to fill the time allotted for music from the terrace, gallery, or behind the potted plants. Too often they are routine and formulaic. It is a mark of Mozart's genius that whatever their social prestige—and these were works of slight public measure—his efforts in the genre invariably bear the stamp of high art.

We do not know the occasion for which this work, from the nocturnal branch of the serenade family, was composed. Certainly there is little to connect it with the formidable serenades for wind band (K. 375 and 388 [384a] of 1781–82). Yet its perfections, on a much smaller scale, cannot be ignored.

The *Allegro* is a sonata of triadic call to attention and gallant themes, with the merest 20 bars of not very developmental development. A minuet, now lost, came in the second position. The *Romanze* in the center is a good example of the kind of aria-style movement so beautifully represented in the French horn concertos as well. The trio of the minuet grows out of the eighth-note melody in its second strain. A cheery *Rondo* on a preexisting Viennese tune convokes the idiom that in a few year's time would be forever associated with the brainless but lovable bird-man Papageno in *The Magic Flute*.

The Opera Overtures

Overture to *The Marriage of Figaro*, K. 492 (1786)
Overture to *Don Giovanni*, K. 527 (1787)
Overture to *The Magic Flute*, K. 620 (1791)

It is surely with his operas that Mozart's achievement becomes Olympian. His contribution to the lyric stage is of inestimable sublimity. From a precedent repertoire positively hidebound with tradition—stand-there-and-sing affairs of static plots and an endless succession of *da capo* arias, where it didn't much matter if your attention flagged for ten or fifteen minutes—he crafted an altogether visionary music theatre. Characters grow and the action progresses during almost every phrase. Stock recitative-aria pairs are less and less inevitable, and soporific stasis is no longer to be tolerated. (I'll admit a number of exceptions to these hackle-raising characterizations of what is called opera seria but stand firmly by my conviction that much of that repertoire is best left to decompose.) Some of the most memorable characters in all music drama—the eunuch Osmin in *The Abduction from the Seraglio;* virtually the whole cast of *Don Giovanni,* with its wicked but charming Don, his luckless servant Leporello, the wronged noblewoman Donna Anna, the clammy-handed statue; the stoical countess in *The Marriage of Figaro;* Papageno and Monostatos and Sarastro in *The Magic Flute*—are creations by Mozart and his gifted librettists. The ensemble finales are particularly fine.

In view of Mozart's uniform mastery of every operatic detail, it isn't especially surprising that the opera overtures are unsurpassed. What is, I think, coincidental to his goal is how well these adapt themselves to concert performance. For they are not the sort of overtures, like those of *Die Meistersinger* or *The Mikado,* that proffer a potpourri of familiar melodies from the opera, nor do they summarize in microcosm the progress of a story, as Beethoven does in *Egmont* and *Leonore No. 3.* We are attracted, for one thing, to sonata style at its tightest, and to being reminded of the general atmosphere of the great tales that would follow in the opera house. And of course they are great curtain raisers, always first on a concert program, breathless in their anticipation of what is to follow. All three are excited works, with rapid Allegros of virtually continuous eighth notes. Two, *Don Giovanni* and *The Magic Flute,* have slow introductions reminiscent of their not-so-distant precursor, the French overture.

At issue in *The Marriage of Figaro* is Count Almaviva's intent to exercise the wedding-night *droit du seigneur.* (The story is really about the rapprochement of count and countess, with a tidy dose of French republicanism tossed in for the edification of the Viennese aristocracy.) The overture bustles in preparation for the wedding: its busy opening—played ever faster, these days, by ever more accomplished orchestras, but tough for the bassoon players nonetheless—broadens into allusions to the peal of wedding bells. Such elaboration as there is comes in the extension of the second theme, followed by a closing theme again of nuptial tint. The recapitulation follows straight away, without true development. Note the coda's torrent of descending scales, and pause to consider how (or whether) the wind players manage to tongue that rapidly. For the opera, the overture merges, "attacca subito," into a scene where Figaro, with his yardstick, tries to find a place in his tiny chamber for the marital bed.

Sinister chords at the start of the *Don Giovanni* overture foreshadow the Don's well-deserved but nasty end. Within the severe chord progressions that follow we hear restless passagework surge and ebb in the second violins. (This Andante returns, reinforced by the lugubrious tones of the three trombones, midway into the second-act finale, when the Stone Guest does in fact answer Giovanni's cavalier invitation to dinner.) The Allegro shifts abruptly into a quick major-mode sonata with, in the development, a false—that is, wrong-keyed—reprise. The original version of the overture leads directly into the first number, where we find poor Leporello bewailing an employment that consists mostly in standing guard. (Beethoven based one of his Diabelli Variations on this aria, "Notte e giorno faticar.") The concert ending to the overture consists of a dozen bars to finish in the correct key; you may from time to time hear longer endings fashioned by others, including one by Mozart's publisher J. André.

The Magic Flute, on the one hand a fantasy of magic creatures and enchanted musical instruments, is on the other a serious tale of discovering Enlightenment virtues: honesty, fidelity, and dignity. From its opening bars the opera also alludes strongly to Freemasonry. Here three mystic chords foreshadow the many triangles to come (three ladies, three boys, three priests; "be steadfast, patient, and silent," the boys tell Tamino). This *Dreimalige Akkord*—"three-fold chord"—is also heard at the beginning of act II, after a lugubrious procession with basset horns and trombones and before Sarastro's grave invocation to Isis and Osiris. The Allegro is presented in the manner of a fugue exposition. And the fugue "subject" is the only true theme; the second group consists of the same melody answered by a new resolution in the flute. In the center comes the *Dreimalige Akkord* again, followed by brief return of the opening materials. The crescendo at the end is reminiscent of the orchestral style Mozart had discovered in Mannheim, with a brilliant final cadence based on the main theme. He first conducted *The Magic Flute* on 30 September 1791, just nine weeks before his death.

Requiem, K. 626

> *Introit: Requiem*
> *Kyrie*
> *Dies irae; Tuba mirum; Rex tremendae; Recordare; Confutatis;*
>   *Lacrimosa; Domine Jesus; Hostias*
> *Sanctus*
> *Benedictus*

Agnus Dei
Communion

For soloists (SATB), chorus; basset horns I-II, bassoons I-II; trumpets I-II, trombones I-III; timpani; strings; continuo (organ)
Composed late 1791 in Vienna; completed by Joseph Eybler and F. X. Süssmayr
First performed 14 December 1793 in the Vienna Neustadt as the work of Count Walsegg-Stuppach, Walsegg conducting;. shortly afterward given by Constanze Mozart as her husband's work
Published by Breitkopf & Härtel (Leipzig, 1800). *Inexpensive score:* Wolfgang Amadeus Mozart: *Requiem in Full Score* (New York: Dover, 1987)
Duration: about one hour

As everybody who has seen *Amadeus* knows, a stranger in black came to see Mozart during the summer of 1791 to commission a Requiem Mass on condition that the composer keep his identity secret. Mozart, working feverishly—so the story goes—to finish two operas for the fall (*Die Zauberflöte* and *La Clemenza di Tito*), was certain that the messenger of Death had come to call. The Requiem was to be his own.

According to Mozart's letter describing the events, the stranger was clothed in grey. But that letter is a forgery, and in any case there exists a perfectly ordinary contract drawn between the composer and the perpetrator of the ruse, one Count Walsegg-Stuppach. Walsegg's purpose was to present the new Requiem, in memory of his late wife, as his own composition—or, possibly, as a guessing game for his house musicians. This he eventually did, some two years after Mozart's death.

Nor is there much indication that Mozart's last months were quite as miserable as legend would have you believe. His letters to Constanze, who early that summer was in the spa-town of Baden approaching her next confinement, are on the whole optimistic and mirthful. In late August they went together to Prague for performances of *Don Giovanni* and the premiere on 6 September of *La Clemenza di Tito*. In Vienna on 30 September *Die Zauberflöte* had its first performance; just afterward Mozart composed the great Clarinet Concerto, K. 622, for Anton Stadler. The Requiem Mass was merely the next work in this burst of masterpieces—a burst you can carry back as far into the 1780s as you like.

Mozart had been ill in Prague, and as the autumn progressed his condition worsened; in mid-November he took to his bed with a high fever. Feeling somewhat improved on the evening of 4 December 1791, he gathered three friends to his bedside to sing through parts of the Requiem with him. Later that night, however, he took a violent turn and succumbed shortly after midnight, apparently to complications of rheumatic fever. The notion that Mozart was poisoned is a romantic fabrication; the tradition that Salieri was the culprit is the dubious legacy of Rimsky-Korsakov's opera *Mozart and Salieri* (1898), after a poem of Pushkin. And while we are on this subject the truth about Salieri is that he was an exceptionally significant and not especially villainous character in music history: court conductor in Vienna for nearly three decades, teacher of Beethoven, Schubert, and Liszt, and founder of any number of the institutions of Viennese musical life. And he cheered heartily at the first performance of *Die Zauberflöte*.

What is rather difficult to explain is why the widow Mozart did what she did with her husband's incomplete score. Not that the decision to have another hand complete it is surprising: she had been left virtually destitute, and Walsegg's fee was still to be earned. But the obvious candidate for the task was F. X. Süssmayr, who had been Mozart's amanuensis in preparing the performance material for *Die Zauberflöte* and who may have written the recitatives for *La Clemenza di Tito*. Perhaps an affair of the heart was at issue, for he had accompanied Constanze to Baden; she later explained simply that she had been angry with him and could not remember why. So she took Mozart's manuscript to a less advanced pupil, Joseph Eybler.

Mozart had finished the first movement altogether (with some of the mechanical fillings in done by his apprentices); the chorus parts and figured bass were drafted through the *Hostias,* along with a little of the orchestration—the violin part in the *Dies irae* and *Rex tremendae,* for example, and indications for the trombone solo in the *Tuba mirum.* The overall continuity was relatively well established through the breathtaking rise to climax at bar 8 of the *Lacrimosa,* where Mozart's draft breaks off. The *Sanctus, Benedictus, Agnus Dei,* and *Communion* (Lux aeterna / Cum sanctis tuis) would need to be written from scratch.

Eybler completed the orchestration through the first phrase of the *Lacrimosa,* after which true composition was required. That he would not or could not do, so he returned the manuscript to Constanze. Mozart's colleague Maximilian Stadler (a composer, not one of the clarinet- and basset horn-playing Stadlers) had meanwhile orchestrated the *Domine* and *Hostias* following a copy of the score he had made for safekeeping.

It was at this juncture that Süssmayr was at last entrusted with Mozart's Requiem. The manuscript evidence shows that he adapted the existing orchestrations, composed the missing movements, and reset for the Communion the music Mozart had composed for the *Introit* and *Kyrie*. There is precedent in Mozart and elsewhere in the Classical period for such reuse; later, with both Berlioz and Verdi for example, it became almost traditional. Süssmayr held that he and Mozart had "often discussed" how the Requiem might be completed in the event of the master's death, though maintained that the repetition was his own idea. (Constanze said that it was Mozart's.)

Thus has Süssmayr's altogether serviceable but occasionally stodgy completion of the Requiem become its traditional text. Touching up his work has been standard practice, however, for nearly two centuries. Among recent endeavors are a deft and pleasing retreatment by the Munich scholar Franz Beyer, whose rounding off of the otherwise abrupt Osannas seems worth adopting.

It's a pretty sensational twist of history when the last, unfinished work of a master composer is a Requiem mass, and for that reason alone all the above needs saying, especially in view of *Amadeus* and its not altogether unwelcome intrusion into the popular culture. But the Requiem is to be savored on its own terms, and you may need to remind yourself to let all the historical speculation recede to the background. Attend, instead, to the remarkable reconciliation of Baroque styles with high Classicism: the old-fashioned counterpoint of the *Introit* and *Kyrie,* for example, couched in the incomparably Viennese tones of the quartet of basset horns and bassoons and the trombone trio. (The basset horn, a sort of alto clarinet, had made the scene in the 1770s; Mozart was fond of the instrument because of its connection with Free Masonry, which he practiced.) The fugue subject of the *Kyrie,* so like "And With His Stripes" from *Messiah,* seems to have been drawn directly from another Handel oratorio.

Mozart's great sensitivity to the text is clear both from its organization into movements and from the more localized text-paintings. The terrors of "Confutatis maledictis" are immediately offset by the plaintive "Voca me"; the fugue at "Quam olim Abrahae promisisti" is appropriately confident, even rollicking. But far the most poetic bars have no text at all: the mystic dialogue of winds at the start, perfect for a Requiem and unique to the literature.

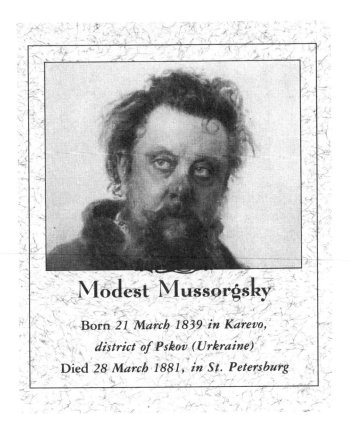

Modest Mussorgsky

Born *21 March 1839 in Karevo,*
district of Pskov (Urkraine)
Died *28 March 1881, in St. Petersburg*

Though Rimsky-Korsakov was certainly the most productive and probably the most glamorous of the Russian nationalist composers, Mussorgsky was the one with the best raw instinct for capturing in musical terms the soul of Russia. As a child he had piano lessons from his mother; his higher education was at a military academy. During his active duty in the army he met and was strongly influenced by the excellent composer Alexander Dargomyzhsky (1813–69) and through him extended his circle of acquaintances to include César Cui (1835–1918), Mily Balakirev (1837–1910), and the chief polemicist of the nationalist movement, Vladimir Stasov. While occupying various bureaucratic posts in the government—with the Ministry of Communication from 1863, the Forestry Department from 1868—Mussorgsky acquired the skills of composition in fits and starts: some lessons from Balakirev, an avid study of Beethoven and Schumann, advice from Rimsky-Korsakov and Stasov. He took seriously his having been named by Stasov as one of the "mighty handful" and as a result pondered deeply and well on how he might best sustain the movement. Like Gershwin, Mussorgsky thought himself faulty of technique. Actually he was an authentic primitive, whose unpolished imagination is the very foundation of his genius. That genius was compromised by the alcoholism that confused his last years, and in a powerful portrait by Ilya Repin made toward the end he appears half-crazed, ravaged—even bewitched. He died a week after his forty-second birthday, leaving a great deal of work unfinished.

His masterpiece is *Boris Godunov* (1874), the story of a czar's guilt at having achieved his throne by murder. It is a moving treatment, as well, of the social upheavals in Russia at the start of the seventeenth century, the onset of the Time of Troubles. This was an era Mussorgsky rightly saw as having parallels with his own. *Boris* is particularly significant for the way it incorporates the musical qualities of Russian speech, and Mussorgsky's innate sense of the psychology of guilt and power makes for a powerful drama indeed. His two subsequent operas were unfinished: *Khovanshchina*, completed and orchestrated by Rimsky-Korsakov (1886), and *The Fair at Sorochinsk*, completed by Cui (1917). Mussorgsky's two works in the central orchestral repertoire are *A Night on Bald Mountain* (1860–66, reorchestrated by Rimsky-Korsakov and first performed posthumously), and *Pictures at an Exhibition* as orchestrated by Ravel.

Mussorgsky's greatness was thus made known to the world by others: even *Boris Godunov* achieved its international following in the form revised and reorchestrated after Mussorgsky's death by Rimsky-Korsakov. Nowadays the preference is growing for Mussorgsky's music in its original state (where that can be reconstructed), for the later refinements inevitably mask the great resonance of his own voice.

Pictures at an Exhibition, orchestrated by Maurice Ravel.

Promenade—Gnomus (Gnome)—*Promenade—Il vecchio castello* (The Old Castle)—*Promenade—Tuileries—Bydlo* (Polish Ox-Cart)—*Promenade—Ballet des Poussins dans leurs coques* (Ballet of Unhatched Chicks)—*Samuel Goldenberg und Schmuyle—Limoges: Le Marché* (Marketplace at Limoges)—*Catacombae: Sepulcrum Romanum* (Catacombs: Roman Burial Place)—*Con*

mortuis in lingua mortua (With the Dead in a Dead Language)—
La Cabane sur des pattes de poule (Baba-Yaga) (The Hut on
Chicken Feet: Baba-Yaga)—*La Grande Porte de Kiev* (The Great
Gate at Kiev)

For piccolo, flutes I-II, oboes I-III, English horn, clarinets I-II,
    bass clarinet, alto saxophone, bassoons I-II, contrabassoon;
    horns I-IV, trumpets I- III, trombones I-III, tuba; timpani,
    snare drum, bass drum, cymbals, triangle, tam-tam, rattle,
    whip, bells, glockenspiel, xylophone, chime; harps I-II, celesta;
    strings
Composed 1874 for piano after the death on 23 July 1873 of the
    painter and architect Victor Hartmann, artist of the pictures;
    orchestrated by Ravel in 1922
First performed 19 October 1922 in a Koussevitzky concert at the
    Paris Opéra, Serge Koussevitzky conducting
Published by Editions Russes de Musique (Paris, 1929), later
    Boosey and Hawkes (London and New York, 1942)
Duration: about 30 minutes

Mussorgsky composed this series of descriptive miniatures after an
exhibition commemorating the life and work of the artist Victor
Hartmann (1834–73). Originally it was for piano, much in the vein
of Schumann's *Carnaval;* Ravel's superb orchestration of 1922 is the
most successful of a half-dozen such efforts.

Linking the musical evocations of the ten pictures is a passage called
Promenade "in the Russian fashion," suggestive of the thoughtful wandering of the viewer from image to image. Consequently, the simple
quarter- and eighth-note rhythms fall into unusual and varying phrase
lengths, and the meter tends to change from bar to bar. Later statements of the promenade are transformed to suit the surroundings.

The scowling gnome in the first picture is actually a nutcracker.
Frenetic scurrying erupts from the low strings, then a twinkle of falling chord-pairs over string glissandos of the supernatural sort and a
ponderous theme of wide interval and thick scoring. Already Ravel's
deft orchestration, here with rattle, whip, xylophone, celesta, and
harmonics in harp and strings, is integral to the effect. *Il vecchio castello,* with its solo alto saxophone, is the mournful song of a troubador
by the walls of a ruined medieval castle. *Tuileries* describes the squab-
bling of boys, then girlish twitter, in the historic old gardens that

open forth from the Louvre. In *Bydlo,* a magnificent solo for baritone tuba over a heavy hooves-and-wheels ostinato in the bass suggests the lumbering approach and passing by of the Polish oxcart.

The *Ballet of Unhatched Chicks,* a scherzo and trio, is Mussorgsky's reflection on Hartmann's design for an Easter-egg ballet, an etude on the delicate sonorities, with flutter-tonguing in the flute. Two Polish Jews argue on a street corner in the ghetto: Goldenberg is wealthy and pompous, the beggar Schmuyle aptly described by the nattering trumpet. The flurry of French horns turns our attention to the bustle of the marketplace in Limoges, prosperous city of south central France.

Now we turn to the rendering of the Roman catacombs beneath Paris, the music a slow, sinister progression of chords for the winds and double basses, hinting a melody only at the climax. The mysterious version of the promenade tune, here titled "with the dead in a dead language," suggests a turning away to meditate on death in general and, presumably, that of Hartmann in particular. The last two vignettes are the most extended: angry music for the witch Baba-Yaga at her hut, grinding bones to feed her captives; and the *Great Gate of Kiev*—an architectural design for a structure to honor Czar Alexander II, never built—the music a great hymn, interspersed with suggestions of Russian chant and heavy on the bell effects.

A Night on Bald Mountain, Concert Fantasy

> **For** piccolo, flutes I-II, oboes I-II, clarinets I-II, bassoons I-II; horns I-IV, trumpets I-II, trombones I-III, tuba; timpani, bass drum, cymbals, tam-tam, bell; harp; strings
>
> **Composed** 1867 in St. Petersburg and dated 23 June 1867, the eve of St. John's Night; revised by the composer and, in 1880, by Rimsky-Korsakov
>
> **First performed** 27 October 1886 by the Russian Symphony Society, St. Petersburg, Rimsky-Korsakov conducting
>
> **Published by** W. Bessel et Cie. (St. Petersburg and Moscow, c. 1912)
>
> **Duration:** about 10 minutes

However much you may wish to associate the *Night on Bald Mountain* with Halloween, these satanic revels actually take place on St. John's Night, which is on June 24 in high summer. (Falla's *The Three-Cor-*

nered Hat takes place on the same night; see p. 228.) The composer's program summarizes the merry-making as follows:

> Subterranean sounds of supernatural voices.—Appearance of the spirits of darkness, followed by that of Satan himself.—Glorification of Satan and celebration of the Black Mass.—The Sabbath revels.—At the height of the orgies the bell of the village church, sounding in the distance, disperses the spirits of darkness.—Daybreak.

The music is less a response to that scenario than an orgy of devilishness in something approaching typical sonata form, with a big recapitulation and a coda for the churchbell and break of day. The melodic material is limited to the loud, black declamation that comes in the low brass early on and the spirited bacchanale introduced later in the woodwinds and French horns. Virtually all the rest is atmosphere of one sort or another. Any first-year theory student can come up with such notions, yet the *Night on Bald Mountain* is a compelling study of texture and voice: the whirlwind of violins at the beginning, the high woodwinds with piccolo so reminiscent of other diabolicism in nineteenth-century music, and the incessant scamper of eighth notes, all of it sagging under the weight of dense, dense doublings. Not much happens, all told, and I could be convinced that it is a trivial piece, Walt Disney notwithstanding. But everybody likes a good ghost story, and by the end you have been swept into the, so to speak, holiday spirit.

Niccolò Paganini

Born 27 October 1782 in Genoa
Died 27 May 1840 in Nice

Paganini's legendary technical capabilities on the violin, meteoric progress through the capitals of western Europe, and precipitous decline in both health and reputation summarize the heroic aspect of Romanticism. His personal appearance summarized the satanic: ravaged by disease, cadaverous of facial feature, his skeletal, long-limbed frame clothed in ill-fitting black, he seemed an ambassador of the underworld—Mephistopheles incarnate. It was an impression he encouraged.

His parents, poor but industrious and music-loving, withheld supper until their children had finished a grueling practice each day. His advanced studies were with the leading virtuosos of Genoa and Parma, and by the age of twelve Paganini was demonstrating his prodigious abilities to the public and had already begun to compose. In 1801 he moved with his brother to Lucca, where they found orchestral positions, and there Paganini occupied himself for the better part of a decade with a relatively quiet routine of playing, teaching, and composing. In the last week of 1809, after having exhausted the possibilities of Lucca, he took to the road as a wandering virtuoso—a harsh career of difficult living conditions, exorbitant physical demands, and frequent "duels" when other virtuosos were encountered *en route*. In 1813 he took Milan by storm, then continued his peregrinations through Italy for another fifteen years. His beloved son, Achille, was born in 1825 of a liaison with the soprano Antonia Bianchi.

In 1828, confident of his prowess, Paganini invaded foreign soil: Vienna, then Prague, Warsaw, and much of Germany, where with few exceptions he triumphed blindingly. He reached Paris and London, with the cholera epidemic, in 1831. The concurrence of these developments did not go unnoted: the advance of each was reported with military precision, and anticipation of the one matched the dread of the other. Paganini's decline began in 1834, when for legitimate reasons—among them a cancer of the throat that first left him unable to speak and ultimately killed him—he refused to appear in some benefit concerts. Such gestures from an artist reputed to be among the wealthiest in the profession inflamed the already volatile press; by the time he returned to Paris in 1837, his reputation as skinflint and monetary adventurer was pretty well universal. In 1834, he had commissioned a viola concerto from Berlioz, a work that became *Harold en Italie;* on hearing it for the first time in 1838, he was overcome with emotion and next day sent Berlioz the gift of 20,000 francs that enabled him to compose *Roméo et Juliette.* So much for greediness. A few weeks later Paganini fled, pursued by the police, to sort out his financial and legal affairs in Nice. He died there shortly afterward. In his estate were instruments of Amati, Guarneri—his favorite violin was a Guarneri del Gesù of 1742—and eleven by Stradavarius.

Paganini's innovations of technique, regarded during his time as simple wizardry, amount to a rewriting of the instrument's vocabulary. The most recognizable of these are the left-hand pizzicato, the ricochet (in which the bow is bounced during the stroke, producing rapid staccato pitches), and double-stop harmonics. (Double stop means, of course, playing pitches on two strings at once; a harmonic is the very high pitch that results from forcing the string, by a light touch at the proper spot, to vibrate in fractions of its overall length).

He was fond of the deep sounds of the G-string, the lowest of the violin's four, and given to breaking the other three to show how he could finish a work on one alone.

He was among the few who grasped, early on, the depth of Berlioz's genius; Liszt learned from Paganini the very priniciples of Romantic virtuosity. Both Chopin and Schumann were captivated by the idea of Paganini, and both paid him homage in their own compositions. He guarded the secrets of his trade jealously, refusing to allow his works to be published, distributing the manuscript parts at the last possible moment, and playing only fragments of his own part during the rehearsals. The virtuosos who heard him play rapidly assimilated his technique in their search to broaden the horizons of the instrument, but not until a selection of his works was published in full score in 1851 were violinists able to analyze how the legend had been achieved.

Paganini appears to have composed at least a half-dozen concertos for violin and orchestra, of which the first two, in D major and E minor, have been celebrated and in print since the nineteenth century. The second movement of the E-minor concerto, called *La Campanella* or *La Clochette* (The Little Bell), is equally well known in its bravura piano transcription by Liszt. Of the remainder of his works, most are variations on music by other composers; certainly the most significant is the collection of 24 Caprices for solo violin, published by Ricordi in 1820 as Paganini's opus 1.

Concerto No. 1 for Violin and Orchestra in D Major, OP. 6

Allegro maestoso
Adagio espressivo
Rondo: Allegro spiritoso

For   violin solo; flutes I-II, oboes I-II, clarinets I-II, bassoons I-II; horns I-II, trumpets I-II, trombones I-II; timpani, bass drum, cymbals; strings

Composed   c. 1817–18 in Italy; the original orchestral parts are in E♭ major, because Paganini tuned his violin up a half-step for added brilliance

First performed   29 March 1819 in Naples, Paganini conducting and playing the solo part

Published by B. Schott's Söhne (Mainz, 1851) and Schonenberger
(Paris, 1851)
Duration: about 35 minutes

The important thing about a Paganini concerto, obviously, is the solo
part—nice Italian melodies and serious pyrotechnics, supported but
never challenged by the orchestra. Lovers of the Italian opera will find
the idiom altogether familiar, a sort of *bel canto* for violin, extravagant
and often ardent of display in the solo line yet otherwise innocent of
complexity. Here the orchestra begins with a solid ritornello of Ros-
sinian verve and theatricality—and with cymbals. (The ritornello is,
however, often cut by more than half.) The solo exposition begins *con
forza,* the wide intervals of the first eight bars defining from the outset
the extremes of range that will be on display. But it is the tail of the
tune that wags the rest, a sunny Mediterranean romp for the violin in
double-stops of parallel thirds. The same effect follows the second
theme and is of course recapitulated later on. The development finds
the orchestra rather mechanically circling through various harmonic
areas, then settles into a *maggiore* (in this case, B major) over guitar-
like pizzicatos in the strings, a gloss on the second theme. A tarantella soon emerges, with prominent violin double-stops and ricochet
falls, its two episodes separated by a solo version of the *maggiore.* Only
the second theme recapitulates, following which come the cadenza and a brief orchestral coda. (The cadenza is apt to be by one of
the twentieth-century virtuosi, Paganini having left none written down.)
Stay alert, during the trills that conclude the exposition and then the
recapitulation, for the pair of left-hand pizzicatos just at the cadence.

Paganini's next movement, *Adagio espressivo,* is in fact greatly like
an operatic *scena* of the time, the sort of thing where a character wanders onstage during the orchestral introduction, then ruminates on a
thought, ornamenting it with ever greater novelty and determination
as the work progresses. That's precisely what happens here, *con espres-
sione* and at one point even *con passione,* with some very nice turns of
phrase on the G-string. The last movement, in duple meter, is a
march-rondo, as was the fashion of the time for display pieces. The
thirty-second-note upbeats in the theme are played with ricochets of
the bow; elsewhere the emphasis is on the very high register, with
long stretches in harmonics and an episode in double harmonics. (Those

driven to distraction by so-called ultrasonic devices—burglar alarms and stoplight trippers, for example—had best not listen to this movement with headphones.)

In violin concertos by really distinguished composer—think of Beethoven, Mendelssohn, Brahms, and Tchaikovsky—you are seized as much (or more) by the architecture of the work as by the soloist's abilities. In a Paganini concerto, you tend to forget the composition in your amazement at all the things a violin can do. Pianists have eighty-eight keys under their ten fingers; violinists, four fingers on four strings of what is, after all, one of the smaller instruments. (For that matter, if you stop to think about it, drawing horsehair over catgut is a pretty primitive and somewhat risible way of making a sound to begin with.) Here we have a working range of four octaves, a fine palette of registral effects, chords of two, three, and four notes, and all the rest. That one so often rediscovers the violin on hearing a Paganini concerto shows that at least some of the Paganini mystique lingers on.

Krzysztof Penderecki

Born *23 November 1933 in Debica, Poland*

Penderecki (pronounced "-etsky") had excellent training in music at the High School (i.e., Conservatory) for Music in Kraków, then studied at the university there. In 1959 he made a clean sweep of the Polish Composers Union competition, winning in all three prize categories, and was catapulted to a certain international celebrity. (Of the central European nations, Poland has always been the most sympathetic to agressively modern music; developments there are disseminated rapidly through the Warsaw Festival of Contemporary Music, one of the most important of its kind.) He was named to the faculty of the music school, then taught for a time at the Hochschule für Musik in Essen, West Germany, and in the 1970s at Yale and in Aspen. For three decades, Penderecki has been one of the significant

European composers, his work measured alongside that of Stockhausen, Xenakis, Messaien, and Boulez.

Penderecki has eschewed serialism and other strict "systems" in favor of a style that welcomes the musical possibilities of almost any sort of sonority: clusters of sounds, all manner of dissonance, events governed not so much by the composer's notation as by the spirit of the moment, shouting and moaning, and so forth. He composes music on global, sometimes mythic subject matter which he expresses not so much in terms of theme and harmony as in a wash of sonic effects. He is particularly inventive in his writing for strings and for voices in chorus. In addition to a great deal of music for relatively traditional groups of live musicians, he has composed with tape and synthesized sound.

His works for instrumental ensemble include the *Emanations* for two string orchestras (1958), *Anaklasis* for 42 strings and percussion (1960), the fine *Polymorphia* for 48 strings (1961), a Canon for 52 string instruments and tape (1962), and what is perhaps his masterpiece to date, a *St. Luke Passion* (1963–65) for large choral forces and orchestra, written for the Münster Cathedral. This last is but one of numerous sacred works on metaliturgical themes for singers, chorus, and orchestra. His Pittsburgh Overture was composed for the American Wind Symphony (of Pittsburgh) in 1967; a second symphony, called *Christmas Symphony,* was premiered by the New York Philharmonic in 1980.

Threnody for the Victims of Hiroshima

> For 52 strings: 24 violins, 10 violas, 10 cellos, and 8 double basses, each enumerated and distributed variously as the work progresses
> **Composed** 1959–61 in Warsaw, the majority in 1960
> **First performed** 31 May 1961 by the Warsaw Radio Orchestra
> **Published by** Polskie Wydawnictwo Muzyczne (i.e., Polish Music Publishing House; Kraków, 1963)
> **Duration:** about 10 minutes

The *Threnody* (i.e., dirge) is a study of the sonoric possibilities of the string choir. Here Penderecki investigates nuances of timbre, methods of attack and decay, quarter-tone divisions of the whole step, and the highest pitches—harmonics—the strings can obtain. The syntax is that of motivic cells and clots of sound that rise and fall, grow wider and narrower, break into rhythms and then return to an amorphousness quite similar to white noise. The 52 players are organized into changing subchoirs according to the structure of the cells; at the end they cover the 52 quarter-tone pitches between the C an octave below middle C and C♯ an octave above (with 24 quarter-tones to the octave.) Enough of this was revolutionary, more than a quarter of a century ago, to have earned the work a wide following and frequent performance. It was recognized with a citation from UNESCO in 1961.

It's a pity that the score, a wonder to behold, is not often seen by the listener, for (like all scores) it shows the very logical structure of musical events that on a single hearing or two may seem inexplicable. The convention of the score as time line is retained, with a staff of one or more lines for each instrument group and some imaginative graphic representations of the ultramodern sounds. A thick black line, for example, shows the width of the cluster; as it narrows to a point, the cluster converges on a single pitch, and to show a rising glissando, the black line juts upward. The passage of events is specified in real time, not beats of measure, each event lasting a certain number of seconds. The width and length of vibrato is indicated by the amplitude of wavy lines. And so forth.

Generally speaking the work progresses from the nonspecific whines at the beginning to the horrifying chord at the end in a series of blobs and splashes that rise to a climax during the section before the final chord. At roughly the five-minute mark it becomes very specific with regard to pitch and rhythmic attack, and correspondingly percussive. Gradually, from there, the blanket of tone clusters settles over again.

The *Threnody* is supposed to be harsh, presumably apocalyptic, in view of its memorial function, and you are not likely to miss the implications of the many siren-like effects. Sounds like these take some getting used to, for such a work investigates the interstices between music and noise. It's neither disorganized nor unmusical, however, and in the end it all makes good sense. Indeed it is a work of terrifying impact.

The dawn of synthesized music and computer-controled variables has made such efforts as these seem, with the passage of time, somewhat old-fashioned. Nowadays you hear more intricacy in movie soundtracks and television commercials. But as music for live performers goes it remains quite novel, and is worth some attentive and scrupulous listening.

Walter Piston

Born *20 January 1894 in Rockland, Maine*
Died *12 November 1976 in Belmont,*
Massachusetts

Piston attended the Mechanic Arts High School in Boston and the Massachusetts Normal School of Art, from which he graduated in 1916 with a degree in architectural drawing, and for a short time was a draftsman with the Boston elevated railway. Along the way he taught himself violin and piano and earned a living playing these (and later, saxophone) in theatre pits and dance bands. This unconventional start to a decidedly cerebral career in classical music served him well, leaving him with an innate affection for ensemble performance—and with calligraphic skills, as shown by his scores, worth venerating. Moreover he met the future Mrs. Piston, née Kathryn Nason, at art school.

The remainder of World War I he spent in the Navy. Following the Armistice and some months of freelance playing, he enrolled at

Harvard to complete his technical formation in music under the tutelage of the noted Archibald T. Davison, graduating *summa cum laude*
in 1924. He thereupon used a John Knowles Paine Travelling Fellow-
ship for two years of study in Paris with Nadia Boulanger and Paul
Dukas. On his return to the United States, Harvard, astutely, appointed
him to its faculty, of which he remained a member for the rest of his
life.

The Boston / Harvard milieu was ideal for Piston, his association
with the Boston Symphony Orchestra in the Koussevitzky years intimate and rewarding. Commissions of orchestral music from the
Koussevitzky Music Foundation and of chamber music from the Elizabeth Sprague Coolidge Foundation assured an uninterrupted and
enviable productivity. Academically inclined by nature, he was both
a stimulating teacher and a gifted author of didactic texts. Among
his students were Leonard Bernstein and Elliott Carter; among his
books, treatises on analysis, harmony, and counterpoint that are still
in use.

Piston's music is prevailingly tonal and highly contrapuntal,
embracing an encyclopedic and meticulous understanding of orchestral device, at least as it was understood in academic circles of his
time. He avoided the Americanisms that give Copland and, say,
Gershwin, their immediacy, such that his symphonic work is purer,
perhaps more austere. At the same time he was an eclectic: there are
undeniably American elements, for example, in the writing for wind
band and in the strong syncopations that now and then interrupt his
generally regular rhythmic flow. You hear hints of Stravinsky, Bartók, and Prokofiev (all of whom were likewise cultivated by Koussevitzky), and of the French style both past and contemporaneous. He
experimented, too, with twelve-tone techniques, though seldom
composed extended structures in that idiom. He is at his best, I think,
in his very fast movements, where he shows particularly imaginative
control of motion, texture, and rhetoric.

Piston wrote eight symphonies, the third and seventh of which
won Pulitzer Prizes (1948, 1961). Much of the rest of his work is in
the form of concert pieces and multimovement concertos for solo
instruments; he wrote almost nothing for the voice. In both amount
and breadth of accomplishments, Piston's was an impressive career,
recognized by his election to the national academies and copious hon-
orifics of other sorts—about as many as an American composer can

get. Of his clutch of honorary degrees he was probably most pleased with that of Doctor of Music, *honoris causa,* from Harvard herself.

Suite from the ballet *The Incredible Flutist*

> *Introduction: Siesta in the Market Place—Entrance of the Vendors—Entrance of the Customers—Tango of the Merchant's Daughters—Arrival of the Circus—Circus March—The Flutist—Minuet—Spanish Waltz—Siciliana—Polka Finale*

For piccolo, flutes I-II, oboes I-II, English horn, clarinets I-II, bass clarinet, bassoons I-II, contrabassoon; horns I-IV, trumpets I-III, trombones I-III, tuba; timpani, snare drum, bass drum, cymbals, triangle, tambourine, glockenspiel; piano; strings

Composed 1938 for a ballet by Jan Veen [Hans Wiener]

First performed with the ballet 30 May 1938, by the Jan Veen Dancers and the Boston Pops Orchestra, Arthur Fielder conducting; the suite first performed 22 November 1940 by the Pittsburgh Symphony Orchestra, Fritz Reiner conducting

Published by Associated Music Publishers, Inc. (New York, 1938)

Duration: about 20 minutes

When a circus comes to town, the trials and tribulations of daily life are suspended. Good humor settles in, as if by magic. Romance blossoms. Anyway, that is the premise of *The Incredible Flutist,* one of Piston's very few ventures into the world of music that tells a story. The ballet is merry and unfailingly clever, hummable, a sequence of crowd scenes and familiar sorts of dances. The suite consists of about half the music of the full ballet; both are fast-moving and action packed.

The setting is an anonymous but presumably Iberian village as siesta time draws to its close. Things begin to come to life, in the introduction, with a sleepy oboe solo. A fluttery march for woodwinds and percussive vamp announces the arrival of the street merchants, and this extends into a scene of three brief but bustling episodes. Quiet returns for a moment with a tiny cadenza for flute and reprise of the oboe solo, then the customers descend on the market place to a barrage of French horns, trumpet, and winds, with a ponderous countermelody in tuba and low strings. All this flies by, yielding in short order to the seductive tango of the merchant's daughters—a terrific number, this, with a little bolero at the center and very suave scoring. You can see where the young Bernstein learned some of his trade.

Now, at the halfway point, the circus arrives. (The transition is virtually identical to the one that preceded the tango.) The scoring of the circus march is for brass band with clarinets and piccolo, but, Ives-fashion, you are likely to hear only snatches of the tune through the din. This particular racket comes from all the other members of the orchestra, who are instructed to cheer wildly and, one of them, to bark like a dog at the end. A typical cast of characters has arrived onstage: the ringmaster, jugglers, a monkey trainer and monkeys— and an incredible flutist. During the curvaceous solo, minuet, piano cadenza, and the big Spanish waltz that concludes the middle section, he charms in succession (I gather) the snake dancer, the snake, and one of the merchant's daughters. An assignation is arranged for eight that night.

A clock strikes eight in violas, piano, and horns, the atmosphere redolent with couples in love. Incredible flutist and merchant's daughter dance to the siciliana of solo woodwind, piano, and strings. (In a subplot of the full ballet, a widow and the merchant exchange a kiss that's been in the making for years; the widow faints; the flute playing revives her.) A polka strikes up in the band. The circus departs, leaving behind it pleasant recollections for all and, for a few of them, some rather more erotic memories.

Francis Poulenc

Born 7 *January 1899 in Paris*
Died 30 *January 1963 in Paris*

The milieu of Poulenc's youth was that of Debussy, Ravel, and the Stravinsky ballets; his texts, the poems of the Symbolists and later Apollinaire and Éluard. He profited from his comfortable circumstance and family connections to study piano with Ricardo Viñes, the era's leading interpreter of new music. But it was the eccentric Erik Satie who captured his fancy and to whom he dedicated his first published work, the *Rapsodie nègre* for baritone voice and chamber ensemble of 1917. This earned him notoriety and a spot among the progressives promoted by Cocteau and Satie as *Les Nouveaux Jeunes* and then as *Les Six* (enumerated on p. 366). After military service in World War I, Poulenc had his only formal instruction in composition, three years of harmony lessons from Charles Koechlin—the same Koechlin who had served as Fauré's orchestrator. The rest of his style he assimilated from the aesthetic climate of Paris at one of its intellectual plateaus—impressionism, symbolism, eccentricity—and from visits, during his formative years, with Schoenberg in Vienna and Casella in Rome.

Poulenc became famous with *Les Biches,* a nonsense ballet in the Cocteau-Satie vein, where young girls dally about a couch and are visited by men in bathing suits. Yet for all the wit and urbanity to be found there, Poulenc was at heart an elegant composer in the lineage of Fauré. Song came to dominate his world when, in 1935, he began to accompany the French tenor Pierre Bernac, composing many new works for him over the course of time. After World War II they concertized throughout Europe and in several visits to the United States. Otherwise Poulenc led a quiet, solitary bachelor's life divided between his apartment overlooking the Luxembourg Gardens on the Left Bank and a country house in the Touraine.

His work is assured, suave, melodically inventive, and often of glossy buoyance, with hints of Bizet and of Milhaud's provençale manner. Two of Poulenc's operas have established themselves in the repertoire: *Les Mamelles de Tirésias* (1947) and *Les Dialogues des Carmélites* (1957). For orchestra there are the Concerto for Harpsichord and Chamber Orchestra (1929), Concerto for Two Pianos and Orchestra (1932), Concerto for Organ, Strings, and Timpani (1941), and Piano Concerto (1950). A fine *Stabat mater* for soprano, chorus, and orchestra (1950) predates the famous *Gloria* of 1959; between them came the *Dialogues des Carmélites,* which concerns the fate of a group of nuns during the French Revolution. This rather dramatic turn to religious subject matter results in part from the death of a friend in the late 1930s.

Suite from the ballet *Les Biches*

Rondeau
Adagietto
Rag-Mazurka
Andantino
Finale

For piccolo, flutes I-II, oboes I-II, English horn, clarinets I-II, bass clarinet, bassoons I-II, contrabassoon; horns I-IV, trumpets I-III, trombones I-III, tuba; timpani, small snare drum, snare drum, bass drum, cymbals, triangle, tambourine, glockenspiel, celesta; harp; strings

Composed 1923 in Paris; reorchestrated May 1939–January 1940; dedicated to Misia Sert (see p. 455)

First performed with the ballet 6 January 1924 in Monte Carlo at the Théâtre de Monte-Carlo, Édouard Flament conducting, and 26 May 1924 at the Théâtre des Champs-Élysées, Paris, André Messager conducting; decor and costumes by Marie Laurencin; choreography by Bronislava Nijinska

Published by Heugel & Cie. (Paris, 1940; piano-vocal score of complete ballet, Paris, 1924)

Duration: about 20 minutes

It was Stravinsky who first brought Poulenc to the attention of Diaghilev. *Les Biches,* composed for the Monte Carlo period of the Ballets Russes, was to be a décor ballet after the designs of Marie Laurencin (1885–1956), friend of Apollinaire and idol of the cubists. The setting is a drawing room in white with a baby blue sofa; it is afternoon on a hot summer day. Three sporting youths proceed to enjoy the company of a dozen or so elegant women. It is a study in coquettishness—*biche* means doe—and of a kind of flirtation innocent "in appearance only." You are encouraged either to think nothing of it or to think the worst, and it is worth remembering in the latter regard that Louis XIV took his various pleasures in his *parc aux biches.*

Poulenc retouched the score, which had been his first orchestral composition, in 1940, and at that time fashioned a suite from the full ballet by omitting the overture and three choral songs. The idiom is meant to be neo-Baroque. Yet in the opening rondeau for the entry of the girls, the trumpet theme is a good deal more provençal than Baroque, the lurching fourth-beat spondees far too lively for white wigs. At the center comes a stylish interlude for the tenor instruments, shifting from $\frac{4}{4}$ into $\frac{2}{4}$ and slowing finally into a calmer episode in $\frac{3}{4}$. The rondo theme returns and rattles on until cut short by a wisp of strings and upper woodwinds. Easily the most attractive movement of *Les Biches* is the *Adagietto,* where the rocking of octaves at the beginning of the oboe solo and the reiterations of pitch at the end of it have the effect of cycling a rudimentary eight-bar phrase into perpetual motion. Subsequent excursions lead the tonality far afield and back again. Between the movements comes a little gloss on the woodwind figure that opened the suite, a sort of afternoon wake-up call.

The *Rag-Mazurka,* so far as I can make out, has characteristics of neither ragtime nor mazurka, sounding rather more like a gigue. At the English horn subject, Poulenc has confused raffishness for raggishness. Another woodwind gloss separates this movement and the *Andantino,* where there actually is a strong syncopated component. The effect is quite like that of the opening rondeau, but with falling motives replacing the trumpet's upward sixteenths. The finale is a Presto gigue, opposing motion by triplets with passages in continuous eighths.

Gloria

> *Gloria*
> *Laudamus te*
> *Domine Deus*
> *Domine Fili unigenite*
> *Domine Deus, Agnus Dei*
> *Qui sedes ad dexteram Patris*
>
> For soprano solo; chorus; piccolos I-II, flutes I-II, oboes I-II, English horn, clarinets I-II, bass clarinet, bassoons I-II, contrabassoon; horns I-IV, trumpets I-III, trombones I-III, tuba; timpani; harp; strings
> Text from the traditional Latin liturgy
> Composed December 1959 in Paris to a commission of the Koussevitzky Music Foundation; dedicated to the memory of Serge and Natalie Kousssevitzky
> First performed 20 January 1961 by the Boston Symphony Orchestra and the Pro Musica Chorus, Charles Munch conducting
> Published by Editions Salabert (Paris, 1960)
> Duration: about 30 minutes

A *Gloria* should be brilliant, brassy, and exuberant. Poulenc's, which comes from the end of his career, mingles these qualities with interludes of breathtaking quiet and tenderness. There are some obvious parallels with Vivaldi's famous *Gloria,* and the excitement at the beginning has the strong flavor of Janáček. Where it comes to the declamation of the text, atmosphere counts for more than technical precision. The Latin prosody is in fact so consistently out of kilter that in a curious way these antique sentences have been given a new life, as though the singers, breathless with enthusiasm, were encountering them for the first time. A sure hand is at work here, with little winks and nods and intimacies shared with his listeners as the confident old fellow trots out the technique acquired over a lifetime.

The idiom is neo-Classical and tonal, yet moves zestfully into and out of far distant keys. Poulenc's building blocks are succint motivic cells, typically two-bar phrases, that through repetition and combination with other such cells build themselves into his structural arches. The meters change freely. In the first movement, for example, groups of four sixteenths, now and then doubled into bubbles of eight thirty-seconds, underpin nearly every bar. Note, too, the sparkle of the two piccolos. The final mark of punctuation, based on the initial fanfares, is borrowed from Stravinsky.

In the first bar of the *Laudamus te* the interlocking pitches of the two trombone parts, one on the beat, one off, describe a figuration that carries jauntily on beneath the choral litany. At the center, after a long fermata, comes a moment of repose with the "Gratias agimus tibi" for sopranos alone and a *pianissimo* reponse in the strings; the initial gambit returns to gain volume and enthusiasm. Poulenc took his share of criticism for this sort of indelicacy, and responded by reminding his detractors of what worldly pleasures Renaissance society found in churchly things. Offsetting the rambunctiousness is the *Domine Deus,* introduced by a quiet octet of winds. The soprano soloist enters *pianissimo,* the "Domine" high and sweet and the "Deus" low and caressive; and the maternal refrain *Pater omnipotens,* backed by an echo of loving woodwind solos, is exquisite in its grace.

Domine Fili unigenite is another essay in Poulenc's jolly, sauntering mode, as though little had changed since the days of *Les Biches*: chorus parts seem merely set down over a pre-existing ballet movement. (Here, in the score, a subtle notation for the singers: every "Jesu Christe" is followed by an exclamation point.) In the fifth movement, after a long and elegant orchestral prelude, the soprano reenters with a text parallel to that of the third—"Domine Deus, Agnus Dei," like the earlier "Domine Deus, Rex coelestis." The *pianissimo* entry is the same as before, as is the wide range covered, but here the solo rises in direction to end on high As. The solo motives cycle on and on, but the placid choral responses are just as significant and offer, moreover, all the cadence points. The finale begins with the *a cappella* choral sentence "Qui sedes ad dexteram Patris, miserere nobis," at which point comes a reminiscence of the opening pages of the work. A long and animated Allegretto ensues. After a sustained fermata the soloist enters with the Amen, outlining and filling in, once more, the interval of an octave and answered by a choral Amen. Now the forward motion is suspended in a world of Debussian pointillism, marked "extraordinarily calm" and "sweetly murmured." The fanfares return for the last Amens.

None of this should have been written in 1959. Poulenc's *Gloria* would be more appropriate from a historical point of view had it been composed in 1913. But that will not matter in a hundred years' time, any more than it matters today that the B-Minor Mass was hopelessly anachronistic in 1750.

Sergei Prokofiev

Born *27 April 1891* **in** *Sontsovka, Ukraine*
Died *5 March 1953* **in** *Moscow*

Prokofiev studied composition in Moscow with Reinhold Glière (of *Red Poppy* fame) and in St. Petersburg with Rimsky-Korsakov and others; at the St. Petersburg Conservatory from 1904 he also studied piano and conducting. Completing his compositional studies in 1909, he went on to win the Rubinstein Prize in 1914 with his First Piano Concerto and then to earn a degree in conducting. After the Revolution of 1917 he traveled widely as a concert pianist, appearing in Japan, the United States, and Paris. In 1921 he came back to this country for the first performance of *The Love for Three Oranges* by the Chicago Opera Company, which was a failure with the American critics. After living in Paris for nearly ten years, he returned to Russia in 1932, taking only short concert tours abroad for the rest of his life. Prokofiev's last American visit was in 1938, during the course of which he studied cinema techniques in Hollywood.

His works, though sometimes experimental, are tonal and otherwise conservative of manner. It is a style of diverse character traits—good humored, political, witty, given to burlesque, and imbued with the heritage of the classical ballet—asserting themselves in easy coexistence and short succession. By the same token Prokofiev is a composer of contrasts, the jocular suddenly turning tragic, the rigorous evaporating into naiveté.

His career is usually divided according to his places of residence: the early period in Russia, to 1918; the fifteen years abroad, era of the second through the fourth symphonies and of the fourth and fifth concertos; and the return to Russia in 1932, with *Romeo and Juliet,* the operas, *Peter and the Wolf,* and the symphonies after the Fifth. Prokofiev was industrious and accordingly prolific, leaving few genres untouched. His most popular works are the third of his five concertos for piano (1921), the *Classical Symphony* (1916) and Fifth Symphony (1944), *Peter and the Wolf* (1936), ballet music for *Romeo and Juliet* (1936) and the suite from an unfinished film called *Lieutenant Kije* (1934)—all described below. Additionally there are two important Violin Concertos (D major, 1917; G minor, 1935).

Prokofiev died on the same day, practically at the same moment, as Stalin.

Symphony No. 1 in D Major, OP. 25 ("Classical")

Allegro
Larghetto
Gavotte: Non troppo Allegro
Finale: Molto vivace

For flutes I-II, oboes I-II, clarinets I-II, bassoons I-II; horns I-II, trumpets I-II; timpani; strings

Composed 1916–17; completed 10 September 1917; dedicated to Boris Asafiev (1884–1949), distinguished historian and music critic, composer, and friend of the composer

First performed 21 April 1918 by the Court Orchestra of Petrograd (St. Petersburg), Prokofiev conducting

Published in the west by Boosey and Hawkes (London and New York, 1926). *Inexpensive score:* Sergei Prokofiev: *Four Orchestral Works* (New York: Dover, 1974)

Duration: about 15 minutes

Prokofiev's classicism is more a matter of rhetorical clarity than slav-ish imitation of Viennese practice: where, after all, is there a gavotte in the Viennese symphony? The instrumentation is that of Haydn's London symphonies, to be sure, and Prokofiev's avowed intent was "to write a symphony as Mozart or Haydn might have written it." But then he went on ". . . had either one of them been a contempo-rary": neoclassicism was, after all, in the air, and in that sphere the new twists are what validate the old forms.

The *Classical Symphony,* from Prokofiev's twenty-fifth year, is by no means his first orchestral work. Before it had come two unpublished symphonies (the second rewritten as the Fourth Piano Sonata), the first two piano concerti (opp. 10 and 16 of 1911–12 and 1912–13), and the First Violin Concerto, op. 19 (1916–17).

Tradition, I suppose, takes the mirthful *Allegro* almost exactly twice as fast as the composer's metronome mark. It's a scales-and-triads kind of piece, fashioned, that is to say, from the primary elements of the tonal vocabulary and in the simplest sonata form. The opening gesture, for example, consists of arpeggiations of the D-major tonic triad followed by what amounts to a descending D-major scale. At the second statement, just afterward, you can sense that you are in a corner of the twentieth century, for the phrase has slid down a step into C. And there are extra beats, beginning with the transitional material in flute, to be felt here and there. The second theme is in the proper dominant key (A major) and consists of slight and elegant material for the first violins over staccato bassoon, the constituent pitches separated horizontally by rests and vertically by two-octave disjunctures. Following an affirmative and rather Mozartian closing passage, an empty bar separates exposition from development. The moment of melodic recapitulation is likewise clear, but here there is a characteristically laconic detail, for it starts in C and only lifts into D with the flute solo.

The *Larghetto* has the character of a Haydn Andante in rhythm and texture, with deliberate introductory bars and then a gently descend-ing scalar melody in the first violin, restated by flute. The secondary material is in continuous sixteenths, first with bassoon, then involv-ing all the woodwinds and finally—as Haydn would often do—the brass and timpani. Prokofiev redecorates this material as he recapitu-lates it, then restates the short introductory passage as a coda.

The ponderous initial footfalls of the *Gavotte* portend nothing grave, and despite all the downward plunges the melody is actually rising toward its cadence. The drone trio incorporates an obviously ethnic melody; the gavotte returns, this time quietly and in the woodwinds. Prokofiev expanded the movement for his *Romeo and Juliet* ballet by adding a second trio, and you will sometimes hear the later version at this point. The *Finale,* a mad scramble of a sonata, treats three main elements: the opening dash of the violins, the hammering crescendo in the woodwinds, and the little second theme in the flute solo—all of which go by so fast that you may not even notice the dividing lines. Nor are you likely to have given a moment's thought to the epochal events of 1917, though the *Classical Symphony* was composed, poetically speaking, within earshot of the Revolution.

Symphony No. 5 in B♭ Major, OP. 100

Andante
Allegro marcato
Adagio
Allegro giocoso

For piccolo, flutes I-II, oboes I-II, English Horn, E♭ clarinet, clarinets I-II, bass clarinet, bassoons I-II, contrabassoon; horns I-IV, trumpets I-III, trombones I-III, tuba; timpani, snare drum, tenor drum, bass drum, cymbals, triangle, wood block, tam-tam; harp, piano; strings

Composed summer 1944 at Ivanovo, a country house and estate west of Moscow operated as an artists' colony by the Composers Union

First performed 13 January 1945 by the Moscow State Symphony Orchestra, Prokofiev conducting; American premiere 9 November 1945 by the Boston Symphony Orchestra, Serge Koussevitzky conducting

Published in the west by Edwin F. Kalmus (New York, 1946), in Russia by the State Music Publishers (Moscow, 1946)

Duration: about 40 minutes

Prokofiev's decision to return to the Soviet Union, taken sometime in the early 1930s, was motivated not so much by ideology—though he thought he could live with Soviet policies, and managed pretty well—

but by the altogether understandable desire to go home. Sojourns in the USSR from December 1932 led finally to his resettling permanently with his wife and family in Moscow in 1936. For a time Prokofiev maintained his international mobility, despite the Soviet's cultural isolation in those years. But his 1938 tour of Europe, England, and the United States was his last. Thereafter his circumstances changed radically, due partly to the evacuation of artists from Moscow at the beginning of the war, partly to the decline of his health after a series of heart attacks, and partly to a liaison with the young woman, Mira Mendelson, who became his companion for the rest of his life. Prokofiev's wife, a Spanish soprano who called herself Lina Llubera, was eventually sent to a concentration camp and later, in 1976, allowed to immigrate to the United States.

Much had changed in the fifteen years since Prokofiev had composed the Fourth Symphony. The Fifth he called a work "about the spirit of man," to celebrate freedom, happiness, and strength. How much such assertions were those of political necessity, I cannot say. Certainly there is a measure of narrative in its expanse and its various humors, but the real pleasures of the work are those of symphonic composition in the abstract: the admirable melodies, fresh orchestral sonorities, and strong formal tactics.

The first movement, an *Andante* of well-delineated sonata design, opens with a broad, wide-intervaled melody in the flute and bassoon that expands with the growing participation of the low brass into a landscape of great majesty. At the *più mosso,* with a shift from triple into duple meter, a new group of materials begins to be unveiled, first a transitional phrase for flute and oboe, then a climax with brass and piano, and finally a closing animato that introduces fast note values separated by thumps of low wind. The intermingling of these ideas in the development helps realize the potential pent up in what is, after all, an enormous orchestral force. The arrival at recapitulation is a forceful tutti closing in, from top down and bottom up, on the main theme—this time *fortissimo* in the brass choir with a roll of cymbals. The majesty continues to mount in a Gershwin-like exaltation of the second theme and thundrous closing chords with full percussion.

In the center movements, Prokofiev's winsome humor comes to the fore. The second, *Allegro moderato,* offsets the sprawl of the first movement in lively, perhaps equestrian rhythmic manner and a clever, comic tune first heard in the clarinet. (It's the sly chromaticism and bouncing close that make it funny.) Novel instrumental effects fly by: the patter of snare drum and woodblock, a flashy rip that passes from first clarinet to second and back, buffoonery in the low brass. The tune eventually doubles into longer note values in bassoons, then dissolves; between two slower statements for woodwind and horns comes a trio in triple meter, spacious and low of melody, again begun by clarinet and gathering toward an industrial statement for full orchestra with piano, harp, and percussion. A rather more complex version of the opening material serves for recapitulation and a finely paced crescendo of the full forces.

In the *Adagio,* Prokofiev is concerned with cycling figures in various species of triple meter, where a sort of carousel waltz keeps trying to open out. It's a long movement with fine tuttis, prominent percussion and low brass and, at one point, the same sort of rapid plummets downward and rebounds up that had informed parts of the second movement. The fading out at the end recalls the opening, the final cadence a magical progression of four simple triads sinking in the strings while arpeggiating upward in the clarinets.

Despite the indication *Allegro giocoso* for the last movement, the long note values in effect yield a slow introduction, and the cello section, divided into four parts and moving still more slowly, muses on the melody that began the symphony. A burlesque *giocoso* kicks in with a flightly clarinet melody accompanied by the horn quartet. The sonata structure is similar to that of the first movement, with a prominent transitional theme of new rhythmic character (begun by the oboes) and a strong arrival of the secondary key area (solo flute). The development begins at the sudden return to the slow note values and low textures of the introduction and memories of the first and third movements, then goes on to set up the recapitulation and boisterous finale close.

The Moscow premiere was unforgettable: victory over the Nazis was at hand, and Prokofiev had to wait a moment for the sound of distant artillery to subside. The Boston premiere, on 9 November 1945, was likewise historic: a rapprochement between Prokofiev and the orchestra after the cool reception it had accorded the Fourth Symphony, and, as the war was just over, a victory celebration.

Concerto No. 3 for Piano and Orchestra in C Major, OP. 26

Andante; Allegro
Andantino
Allegro ma non troppo

For piano solo; piccolo, flutes I-II, oboes I-II, clarinets I-II, bassoons I-II; horns I-IV, trumpets I-II, trombones I-III; timpani, bass drum, cymbals, tambourine, castanets; strings
Composed 1917–21, mostly 1921 in Etretât, on the Brittany coast; several of the themes come from works composed in pre-Revolutionary Russia
First performed 16 December 1921 by the Chicago Symphony, Prokofiev, soloist; Frederick Stock conducting. It was, however, a Paris performance in 1922, with Serge Koussevitzky conducting and Prokofiev as soloist, that launched the international popularity of the work.
Published by A. Gutheil (Moscow, 1923)
Duration: about 30 minutes

Prokofiev's Third Concerto, which precedes the Ravel concertos by about a decade, remains one of the most popular of the twentieth century. Like most piano concertos, it was written at least in part to demonstrate the composer's own prowess as soloist, and from the beginning, he meant it to be a big work dominated by the solo part. Its genesis is a long story, with sketches going back well before the First World War and the *Classical Symphony* together with an obvious attempt to reconcile Parisian modernism and Soviet populism. It is his only concerto in the standard three-movement design.

The high, searching theme of the *Andante,* for clarinet and then violins and flute, becomes a principal element of the first movement as a whole. The soloist enters in the *Allegro* with such ebullience that you may fail to note the simplicity of its two-line construction. The foil to that proposition comes soon enough, first with the *fortissimo* chords and bouncings-back exchanged between the soloist and strings, then at the visually impressive spot where the pianist pounds out a passage of thick chords spread over the whole range of the instrument. This has been a transition to the second group, where the woodwinds, with castanets and string pizzicatos, state a waddling march. The rest of the movement is similarly clear of design: a bright scherzando, a delectation on the opening *Andante,* a sudden turn to the faster tempo and quick passagework that clearly anticipates climactic recapitulation. In fact development and recapitulation are, as is often the case in Prokofiev, simultaneous operations. Once the recapitulating has been accomplished there's a dramatic glissando and fall in the piano and a moment where the forward motion relents; the dashing scalar charge from the end of the development leads this time to the final cadence.

The waddling that had characterized the second theme in the first movement is likewise a feature of the *Andantino,* here rendered ever so slightly grotesque by the octave-falling grace notes. Five variations follow: the first, mostly for piano, with the theme at the end, then a tempestuous variation with piano and brass. The center variation involves rhapsodic triplet figures in the solo part and, in the winds, a treatment that transforms the theme by inverting its direction—a process that continues in the contemplative fourth variation and the almost violent Russianness of the fifth. For a coda Prokofiev restates the theme, still in the woodwind, but this time quietly and twice as slow.

The contours of the bass ritornello that opens the last movement evoke the clarinet theme from the beginning of the first movement. Its wide intervals and seesawings back and forth seem to describe a circularity of overall motion; the second thematic motive, introduced in piano and first violins, is at last angular in its sharp initial turn and rocket fall. Hammering reiterations of the accompanying chords begin to be felt by the end of the exposition. The elements develop as they go, with the slower passages in the middle confirming their close relationship with passages in the first and third movements. Overall the form is rondo-like, with each return of the main theme longer than before. Recapitulating takes the form of more and more conspicuous revolutions of the initial theme, with the pounding ostinato coming to the fore at the end.

Peter and the Wolf, OP. 67, Symphonic Tale for Children

> For narrator; flute, oboe, clarinet, bassoon; horns I-III, trumpet, trombone; timpani, snare drum, bass drum, cymbals, triangle, tambourine, castanets; strings

Text by Prokofiev
Composed April 1936 in Moscow; completed 24 April
First performed 2 May 1936 at the Moscow Children's Theater,
    Prokofiev conducting, Mme. Bobovra (a last-minute substitute
    for Natalia Satz, the theater director) narrating
Published in the west by Boosey & Hawkes (London and New
    York, 1942). *Inexpensive score:* Sergei Prokofiev: *Four Orchestral
    Works* (New York: Dover, 1974)
Duration: about 30 minutes

Disobeying one's grandfather is always a bad idea, but in this case
only the duck loses. Prokofiev's association of the characters with solo
instruments works so well that a sizeable percentage of the concert-
going public imagines the clarinet to be cat-like and the bassoon
crotchety. *Peter and the Wolf* is a marvelous score. Do not become so
engrossed in the story that you neglect to notice the technical cleverness of the music: the clash of the motives, for example, in the quarrel
between the duck and the bird, or the lowering of the lasso, where
the little chromatic figure begun in muted violins settles down into
the cellos and basses. Once the rope is tightly fastened around the
wolf's tail, the story needs only its finale, in this case a plump Russian
march for the hunters, transformed, after Peter's little waltz of satisfaction at already having caught the wolf, into a triumphant procession. Peter's theme is now to be heard in the formerly wolfish horns
as each of the characters passes by for our review—though in the case
of the duck, of course, we must listen *very* closely.

There are doubtless some moral and perhaps even political overtones in such lines as "Boys like Peter are not afraid of wolves." Yet
"what was important to me," the composer writes, "was not to tell a
story, but to have the children listen to the music. The story was
merely a pretext." The narrative is usually preceded by a short demonstration of which instruments plays what character. Trendy narrators—politicians and their spouses, especially—detract from the proper
effect; the best have been the great character actors, like Basil Rath-
bone and Cyril Ritchard. The Walt Disney version, by the way, gets
things all wrong and moreover reorders and cuts the music.

Ballet Suites from *Romeo and Juliet*

> Suite No. 1, OP. 64BIS
> *Folkdance: Allegro giocoso*
> *Scene: Allegretto*
> *Madrigal: Andante tenero; Andante assai*
> *Minuet: Assai moderato*
> *Masquers: Andante martiale*
> *Romeo and Juliet: Larghetto; Andante*
> *Tybalt's Death: Precipitato; Presto; Adagio drammatico*
>
> Suite No. 2, OP. 64TER
> *Montagues and Capulets: Andante; Allegro pesante; Moderato*
>   *tranquillo; Allegro pesante*
> *The Child Juliet: Vivace; Più tranquillo (quasi andantino); Più*
>   *animato; Più animato (Vivace I)*
> *Friar Laurence: Andante espressivo*
> *Dance: Vivo*
> *Romeo and Juliet Before Parting: Lento; Andante; Adagio; Poco*
>   *più animato; Adagio; Andante*
> *Dance of the Girls From Antilles: Andante con eleganza*
> *Romeo at Juliet's Grave: Adagio funebre; Adagio*
>
> For piccolo, flutes I-II, oboes I-II, English horn, clarinets I-II,
>   bass clarinet, tenor saxophone, bassoons I-II, contrabassoon;
>   horns I-IV, trumpets I-II, cornet *à pistons,* trombones I-III,
>   tuba; timpani, snare drum, bass drum, cymbals, triangle,
>   tambourine, maracas, bells, xylophone; harp, piano; strings; in
>   the Second Suite there are parts for celesta and a viola d'amore
>   *ad libitum.*
> Composed early 1935 to a commission from the Kirov Theater of
>   Leningrad; completed 8 September; revised through 1936
> First performed the First Suite, 24 November 1936 by the
>   Moscow Philharmonic, Prokofiev conducting; the Second Suite
>   first performed 15 April 1937 in Leningrad, Prokofiev
>   conducting; the complete ballet first performed 30 December
>   1938 at the municipal theatre of Brno, Czechoslovakia; a Kirov
>   production followed on 11 January 1940
> Published by State Music Publishers (Moscow, 1938); a third
>   suite was assembled in 1946 as opus 101
> Duration: about 30 minutes each

Prokofiev's works for the stage and screen number in the dozens and
include the operas, incidental music for plays of Pushkin and Shake-

speare, music for films of Sergei Eisenstein (*Alexander Nevsky* and *Ivan the Terrible*), and ballets for Paris, Berlin, and Moscow. Of the nine ballets the most ambitious were the seventh and eighth: *Romeo and Juliet* in four acts (later three), and its successor *Cinderella,* opus 87 of 1945. From both Prokofiev drew orchestra suites and piano pieces.

His initial response to the Kirov commission was to wonder how a *Romeo and Juliet* ballet might end. ("The dying cannot dance," he mused.) His solution, to which the stage director had agreed, was to compose a happy ending, but this did not find favor with the producers in Leningrad; in Moscow the Bolshoi thought the music—more than two decades after *The Rite of Spring*—undanceable.

Gleaning what he could from the failure Prokofiev drew two suites of seven excerpts each, opus 64, and a series of 10 pieces for piano, opus 75. Thus the world became familiar with the *Romeo and Juliet* music long before the ballet was staged. After a second attempt to arrange a Leningrad production failed in 1937, the premiere was given to the theatre in Brno, Czechoslovakia.

The two famous suites are assembled from here and there in the complete ballet, dwelling on the festival scenes, love music, and death scenes. Moreover, the suites are typically regarded as pick-and-choose turf for the conductor, so that it is possible to hear a suite assembled uniquely for a particular concert offering. More's the pity, for the development of the musical motives, as Juliet discovers her passion and Romeo his ardor, is lost in the shuffle.

The movement titles are pretty well self-explanatory. The *Folk Dance,* which begins act II, suggests a Mediterranean tarantella. *The Death of Tybalt,* with its violent harmonies and demise in a progress of fifteen deadly chords, is particularly famous. So, too, is the ball scene at the Capulet house, here called *Montagues and Capulets.* Generally speaking the first suite is the lighter of the two, consisting mostly of intermezzo dances from the earlier acts arranged in no particular order. The second comes more or less in order of the action and embodies some serious treatment of the motives associated with the title characters—the maturing of Juliet's theme, for example. But I find the lovers' inability to part not so much serene as tedious.

You may be surprised, having grown accustomed to thinking of Prokofiev as a Soviet composer, at the Frenchness of *Romeo and Juliet*— the parallels of sonority and structure with, say, the practice of Poulenc and Milhaud. Partly this is a matter of Prokofiev's own associations with Paris during his period as an emigré; partly, though, it's that the epigrammatic character dance for subsets of the troupe is demanded by the genre itself, which was by that time a thorough fusion of Russian and French heritage anyway. As for the Bolshoi's reservations, suffice it to say that Prokofiev's *Romeo and Juliet* has become a pillar of classical ballet, routinely inviting the attention of the world's best choreographers.

Suite from the music for the film *Lieutenant Kije*, OP. 60

Kije's Birth: Andante assai
Song: Andante
Kije's Wedding: Allegro fastoso
Troika Song: Moderato
Kije's Burial: Andante assai

For baritone, *ad lib.;* piccolo, flutes I-II, oboes I-II, clarinets I-II, tenor saxophone (in absence of a singer), bassoons I-II; horns I-IV, trumpets I-II, cornet *à pistons,* trombones I-III, tuba; timpani, snare drum, bass drum, cymbals, triangle, tambourine, sleighbells, celesta; harp, piano; strings

Composed summer 1933, mostly in Paris, for a film by the Leningrad director Alexander Feinzimmer; suite extracted 1934, dated 8 July

First performed 21 December 1934 in Moscow, Prokofiev conducting

Published by A. Gutheil (Moscow, 1935); published in the west by Boosey and Hawkes (London and New York, 1947). *Inexpensive score:* Sergei Prokofiev: *Four Orchestral Works* (New York: Dover, 1974)

Duration: about 20 minutes

Feinzimmer's film was never finished, so Prokofiev published the symphonic suite as his opus 60 and the two songs with piano accompaniment as opus 60bis.

The story dates from the early nineteenth century and stems from the misunderstanding of a verbal report given the czar by his military advisors. The monarch misunderstands the words "Poruchiki zhe" (the lieutenant, however. . .) as "Poruchik Kizhe"—Lieutenant Kije. It is easier to invent a life and career of a non-existent army officer than to inform the autocrat of all the Russias that he has erred. A farce is born and our hero killed off as quickly as possible; the music is correspond-ingly good humored and boisterous, the military allusions under-stated in keeping with the fictitious nature of things.

Kije's "birth" is imagined in terms of a distant bugle call (offstage cornet) and the music of fife and drum. The oboe melody in the sec-ond strain of the march is Kije's motive, to be heard several more times in the movements to follow. Battle music breaks out, with much trumpeting and some cannon fire, followed by the return of Kije's theme, the fife-and-drum march, and the bugle call. The Song comes in versions with and without baritone solo; the text is of a gray dove pining for his absent mate. In the all-instrumental version, the baritone solo part is taken over by the unusual and altogether success-ful pairing of double bass and tenor saxophone. Each successive strain of the Slavic lament is subtly different of orchestration, texture, and key. For instance the very first doubling of the melody, by a solo violist, gently ornaments as it goes, in an age-old improvisatory prac-tice called heterophony; for the last statement there is fluttering dec-oration by the flute.

Kije's wedding music is framed—beginning, middle, and end—by a proper nuptial salute in the winds and percussion and a quickstep for cornet solo. The tuba and horn accompaniment is a cliché; more interesting are the countermelodies in the winds, the weaving in of Kije's theme in the saxophone, and, at that point, the military figures in the strings. The *Troika Song* begins with its climax, followed by the jingle of a three-horse sleigh. Kije's theme is almost immediately combined with a Russian drinking song (a rather piggish text about a woman's capacity to engage the attention of multiple partners). In the funeral dirge are to be heard, not surprisingly, the distant bugle call, a slow march on Kije's theme, and recollections of the romance and wedding march.

The *Kije* music, in sum, is trivial. But it's the very nature of a farce, and part of the fun, to be simple minded.

Sergei Rachmaninov

Born _1 April 1873, Semyonovo,_
near Novgorod
Died _28 March 1943, Beverly Hills,_
California

Rachmaninov received his general education and preliminary training in music at the St. Petersburg Conservatory. His advanced work was at the Moscow Conservatory, where he studied piano with Alexander Siloti and composition with Anton Arensky; there, too, he met Tchaikovsky, whose most direct spiritual descendent Rachmaninov proved to be. His early reputation as both piano virtuoso and composer was built largely on the C♯-Minor Prelude from the opus 3 _Morceaux de fantaisie,_ written when he was nineteen. Otherwise it was a slow beginning, marred by failures of his early efforts, including a bitter reverse with the First Symphony. ("The Seven Plagues of Egypt," César Cui had called it, and in his despair, Rachmaninov was driven to consult a psychopathologist. It was later said that the conductor of the performance, the otherwise distinguished musician Alexander Glazunov, had been drunk at the time.) In 1906, fearing the political climate at home, Rachmaninov resettled in Dresden, undertaking from there a series of hugely successful concert tours. He made his American debut at Smith College in 1909 and during that season gave the first performance of his Third Piano Concerto in New York. In subsequent years he was twice offered and twice declined the post of conductor of the Boston Symphony Orchestra.

Rachmaninov had returned to Russia in 1909 to conduct at the Bolshoi Theatre, but after the 1917 Revolution he and his wife immigrated to Switzerland. In 1935 they moved to New York and from there to Los Angeles.

His performances have been well preserved in recordings that show the Lisztian fire of his piano technique and both the passion and precision of his conducting. The demands of his career as a performer correspondingly limited the number of his compositions: he is one of those composers who earned an estimable stature on the strength of a half-dozen popular works. He wrote three symphonies (in D minor, opus 13, 1895; E minor, opus 27, 1906–07; and A minor, opus 44, 1935), four piano concertos (in F♯ minor, opus 1, 1891, later revised; C minor, opus 18, 1900–1; D minor, opus 30, 1909; and G minor, opus 40, 1914–26, revised 1941), and the Rhapsody on a Theme of Paganini, opus 43 (1934). Additionally, there are three operas, wonderful songs, a set of Symphonic Dances, opus 45 (1940), and a choral symphony, opus 35 (1913), called *The Bells,* after the poem of Edgar Allan Poe.

Concerto for Piano and Orchestra No. 2 in C Minor, OP. 18

Moderato
Adagio sostenuto
Allegro scherzando

For piano solo; flutes I-II, oboes I-II, clarinets I-II, bassoons I-II; horns I-IV, trumpets I-II, trombones I-III, tuba; timpani, bass drum, cymbals; strings

Composed summer 1900 in Italy (movements II and III); movement I added, 1901, in Moscow; dated 21 April 1901; dedicated to "Monsieur N[ikolai] Dahl," Rachmaninov's physician

First performed 27 October 1901 by the Moscow Philharmonic, with the composer as soloist, Alexander Siloti conducting

Published by Alexander Gutheil (Moscow, 1901). *Inexpensive score:*
Serge Rachmaninoff: *Piano Concertos Nos. 1, 2, and 3 in Full
Score* (New York: Dover, 1990)
Duration: about 35 minutes

The Second Piano Concerto marks Rachmaninov's return to productive composition and mental stability after three years of depression
brought on by the failure of his First Symphony at its premiere in
March 1897. In the summer of 1900 Rachmaninov vacationed in
Italy with the great bass Chaliapin and there composed the second
and third movements of the concerto; a successful reading in December induced him to go on to compose the first movement. Rachmaninov's first orchestral masterpiece comes just eight years after the
Pathétique, Tchaikovsky's last.

Each movement of the Second Concerto is in a sonata-based form,
the structural turning points amply highlighted. The soloist begins
alone: a lugubrious progression of eight thick chords—the low notes
approach the bottom of the keyboard—serves as a prelude to the surging cortege that constitutes the first theme. This becomes more eloquent still, as Rachmaninov's themes are inclined to do, when the
cellos and then violins begin to extend the tune in wave after wave
and peak upon peak and enough hairpin crescendos and decrescendos
to keep a half-dozen music typographers busy for a week. An accelerando, climax, and moment of rubato in the violas indicate the arrival
of the second theme, in E♭ major: another of Rachmaninov's splendid
melodies, and Lisztian in its presentation over wide arpeggios in the
left hand. The development is animated, bringing faster tempi and
note values to prominence and building to a climax just before the
recapitulation. Now the cortege is given a Cossack setting. The second theme recurs in the solo French horn; the diaphonous coda strongly
foreshadows one of the Paganini Variations.

The *Adagio sostenuto* commences in the minor key with which the
first movement closed, then over the four bars of orchestral introduction slides into E major. This is essentially a single-themed movement based on the material heard in the solo flute and clarinet over
the undulating, metrically ambiguous accompaniment in the piano.
When the secondary key area is at last reached (by the first violin
choir over the piano, fading away to *niente* after each surge), the soloist
embarks on an enraptured soliloquy which ultimately merges into

developmental material. The entry of the trombone and tuba marks the start of a long accompanied cadenza. Note, after the short recapitulation, the building blocks of the wonderful coda: the fervor of the piano, the filigree in flutes and clarinets, the sighs of the violins.

The first subject of the *Allegro scherzando* comes after three dozen bars or so of introduction and a cadenza in the piano. The famous second theme, first heard in oboe and viola, became a popular song of the big band era. (What makes this work so memorable is the composer's uncanny ability to string together one melody after another. These are inevitably simple of rhythmic design and square of phrase, but just as inevitably they go on to pant and throb, often in the soulful tenor register of cello and solo wind. Rachmaninov had a particular feel for how this can be accomplished in the context of a concerto for piano.) There's a long working-out, with the scherzando elements breaking in repeatedly, in one case fugually. The work culminates, very like Gershwin and almost as if by foregone conclusion, with a majestic statement of the second theme.

Rhapsody on a Theme of Paganini for Piano and Orchestra, OP. 43

> For piano solo; piccolo, flutes I-II, oboes I-II, English horn, clarinets I-II, bassoons I-II; horns I-IV, trumpets I-II, trombones I-III, tuba; timpani, snare drum, bass drum, cymbals, triangle, glockenspiel; harps; strings
> **Composed** 3 July–18 August 1934, at Senar (from the initials of Rachmaninov and his wife), his villa near Lucerne, Switzerland
> **First performed** 7 November 1934 in Baltimore by the Philadelphia Orchestra, Rachmaninov soloist, Leopold Stokowski conducting
> **Published by** Edition TAIR (New York, 1934)
> **Duration:** about 25 minutes

Rachmaninov's Rhapsody, his last work for piano and orchestra, consists of 24 variations on a theme found in the last of Paganini's Solo Caprices, opus 1. (Liszt, Schumann, and Brahms wrote variations on the same theme.) It begins, however, not with the Paganini tune but with an allusion to the finale of Beethoven's "Eroica" Symphony: after an eight-bar introduction, you hear the first variation (marked "Preceding"), a skeletal outline of the theme. Both the ploy and its deft orchestration with harp, glockenspiel, and expanded percussion suggest the composer's considerable maturation since the Second Concerto. Paganini's theme is stated, appropriately, by the violins, the piano carrying on in the manner of the preceding variation. The sprightly character of the melody and the holes it contains are ideal for a scherzando treatment of motives, darting about and peeking through, and this is precisely what occurs in the next four variations (II–V).

In the next group (variations VI–X) Rachmaninov becomes as Mephistophelian as Paganini himself, introducing the Gregorian *Dies irae* and progressively more violent considerations of it. And a piano rhapsody of these implications must surely pay homage to Liszt: variation XI–XV accomplish this, first with Lisztian improvisation all over the keyboard, then with an obviously Hungarian "minuet," a military variation with prominent trumpet, and a fleeting scherzando for the soloist alone. The tonality thickens noticeably with the addition of four new flats (B♭ minor / D♭ major, variations XVI–XVII), the setting for the famous variation you've been waiting for. This serves the conventional function of a *maggiore,* indicating that the process is nearing its end. The original speed and key return for the last group (variations XIX–XXIV), with a short cadenza before variation XXIII and a huge statement of the *Dies irae* at the close. Note, in the last two bars, the piano's wink of farewell.

Maurice Ravel

Born 7 March 1875 in Ciboure, Pyrenees
Died 28 December 1937 in Paris

Ravel's family moved to Paris from the Basque region when he was a child; at the age of fourteen he entered the Paris Conservatory, where he studied piano with Charles de Bériot (dedicatee of the *Rapsodie espagnole,* Ravel's first orchestral masterpiece) and composition with Gabriel Fauré. Within two years he had won a first prize in piano, but what was deemed a brazen and offensive grammar (which is to say, progressive musical vocabulary) kept him from winning the *prix de Rome* in composition, though he sat for it four times. The resulting scandal—his excellence as a composer had already been established through such works as the *Pavane pour une infante défunte* of 1899 and the orchestral song cycle *Shéhérazade* of 1903—led ultimately to the resignation of Conservatoire's director, Théodore Dubois, and a rethinking of institutional priorities there. Diaghilev's commission of *Daphnis and Chloé* in 1909, however, properly recognized Ravel's stature as a composer of note. The modernism of his harmonic language and delicacy of his orchestration led him to be thought a disciple of Debussy, and indeed they shared a certain outlook on the musical issues of the day and above all a lucidity of thinking. But Ravel insisted that his technical principles were conceived and matured independently, and was right to observe that the foundation of his style had been achieved before Debussy composed his most interesting work.

Though frail of constitution and hermetic of disposition, Ravel volunteered for service during World War I and was allowed to work in the ambulance corps. Nor could he ignore the demands of celebrity, which led him to undertake concert tours of western Europe, England (where, in 1928, he was given an honorary degree by Oxford University), Scotland, and North America. In 1932 he was involved in a taxi wreck which appears to have aggravated a brain disorder from which he may already have been suffering for many years. An operation was attempted in 1937 at a Parisian clinic, but Ravel never recovered consciousness.

Most of his orchestral works began as compositions for piano. (And he left two-piano arrangements of *La Valse* and the *Boléro*, originally for orchestra.) It is a mark of his greatness that virtually all of them have achieved a permanent place in the repertoire. These are the *Rapsodie espagnole* (1907–8), *Pavane pour une infante défunte* (1910), *Ma Mère l'oye* (Mother Goose, 1911), *Daphnis et Chloé* (1909–12), the *Valses nobles et sentimentales* (1912), *Alborada del gracioso* (1918), *Le Tombeau de Couperin* (1919), *La Valse* (1919–20), *Tzigane* (a rhapsody for violin and orchestra, 1924), *Boléro* (1928), and the two piano concertos (1929–31). The celebrated orchestration of Mussorgsky's *Pictures at an Exhibition* (see p. 406) dates from 1920.

Rapsodie espagnole

Prélude à la nuit (Prelude to Night)
Malagueña
Habanera
Feria (Celebration)
[No pause between movements I and II]

For piccolos I-II, flutes I-II, oboes I-II, English horn, clarinets I-
II, bass clarinet, bassoons I-III, sarrusophone; horns I-IV, trumpets I-III, trombones I- III, tuba; timpani, snare drum, bass
drum, cymbals, triangle, tambourine, castanets, tam-tam, xylo-
phone, celesta; harps I-II; strings
Composed 1907; orchestrated 1907–1 February 1908; dedicated
to the composer's teacher, Charles de Bériot
First performed 15 March 1908 in a concert of the Colonne
orchestra at the Théâtre du Chatelet, Édouard Colonne
conducting
Published by A. Durand & fils (Paris, 1908). *Inexpensive score:*
Maurice Ravel: *Four Orchestral Works in Full Score* (New York:
Dover, 1989)
Duration: about 20 minutes

Like the other Spanish pieces treated in this volume, Rimsky-Korsakov's *Capriccio espagnol,* the Falla works, and Chabrier's *España,* the
Rapsodie espagnole seeks to capture Iberian motion and color in musical
terms. (Like Bizet, Ravel had not visited Spain.) But though he makes
certain references to both Rimsky-Korsakov and Chabrier, the character of the *Rapsodie espagnole* is radically different, evoking through
hints and fragments what comparable works state flat out. We tend
to be leery of the term Impressionism to describe French music of the
early twentieth century, but here it is apt: the bright yet curiously
distant rhetoric has a number of obvious parallels with poetry and
painting of the time.

The *Prelude to Night* opens in a surrealistic haze with a four-note
descent in the strings; the motive, which cycles through the entire
movement, will be heard in the *Malagueña* and *Feria* as well. From
this nocturnal mist emerge other suggestions: mysterious pairs of chords,
shimmering melodic turns of Spanish flavor, and marvelous improvisations for a pair of clarinets and then a pair of bassoons, suggestive
of the Andalusian gypsy idiom and evoking similar effects in Rimsky-
Korsakov's *Capriccio espagnol.* The clarinet melody that blossoms from
the chord pairs will reappear prominently at the center of last movement. The detail of sonority is ravishing: note, for example, how the
harp and violin glisten beneath the bassoon improvisation, and how
toward the end of the cadenzas the two clarinets and two bassoons
slip just out of kilter.

The *Malagueña* likewise begins distantly, as the guitar-based dance pattern establishes itself in the low instruments. (The bass clarinet is not unusual in orchestras of this time; less common is the sarrusophone, heard a little further along in the movement. The authentic instrument, named after its inventor M. Sarrus, is a sort of double-reed saxophone, but the part is more often played on the contrabassoon.) The decorative figurations grow more complex throughout the orchestra until finally the trumpet, doubled rhythmically by tambourine, states a true tune. This is then developed into an animated tutti, the first we have heard so far, and with seven percussionists, no less. But the forward momentum ceases, an English horn solo is heard, the cycling of the first movement reappears, and the *Malagueña* concludes as quietly as it began.

You will recognize the dance pattern of the *Habanera* at once from its ancestor in *Carmen,* and despite the lethargic tempo, the effect is similarly provocative. The dance is reticent at first, building toward something bigger, then dissolving through an ostinato on the five-note rhythm of the principal melody.

Feria, the longest of the movements, develops into the bold ethnicity we have been expecting all along from a Spanish rhapsody. The main sections are built from three ideas: the repetitive flute figure near the beginning, the castanet-like turn for the three trumpets a few pages later, and the headlong perpetual motion in the winds as the momentum gathers. In the center, the English horn has an interlude similar to the one it had had in the *Malagueña.* However, it's the wild glissandos and arabesque work that seize your attention: at the end, the multi-octave surge and fall, and final exclamation point should lift you from your seat.

Audience reaction to the first performance of the *Rapsodie espagnol* was divided between the music lovers in the cheap balcony seats, who demanded an encore, and the socialites in the chic seats, who did not. A cry was heard from the balcony: "Tell them that it's Wagner and they will find it very good."

Ma Mère l'oye (Mother Goose)

Pavane de la Belle au bois dormant (Sleeping Beauty Pavane)
Petit Poucet (Tom Thumb)
Laideronnette, Impératrice des Pagodes (Laideronnette, Empress of Pagodas)

Les Entretiens de la Belle et de la Bête (Conversations of Beauty
and the Beast)
Le Jardin féerique (The Enchanted Garden)

For piccolo, flutes I-II, oboes I-II, English horn, clarinets I-II,
bassoons I-II, contrabassoon; horns I-II; timpani, bass drum,
cymbals, triangle, tam-tam, xylophone, keyboard glockenspiel,
celesta; harp; strings
Composed originally for piano, four-hands, 1908–10;
orchestrated, 1910; enlarged into a continous ballet, 1911;
dedicated to Mimie and Jean Godebski, children of his friend
Cyprien Godebski, for whom the piano version had been
written; the ballet dedicated to Jacques Rouché, director of the
Théâtre des Arts, "en amicale reconnaissance."
First performed as a ballet 28 January 1912 at the Théâtre des
Arts, Paris, Gabriel Grovlez, conducting; scenario by Ravel;
choreography by Jeanne Hugard
Published by Durand et Cie. (Paris, 1912). *Inexpensive score* (suite):
Maurice Ravel: *Four Orchestral Works in Full Score* (New York:
Dover, 1989)
Duration: suite, about 15 minutes

You will usually hear Ravel's *Mother Goose* as an orchestral suite that
closely follows the original work for piano, four-hands. For the ballet
Ravel added to the five original movements a prelude and spinning-
wheel dance at the beginning, reordered the five original movements,
and connected them with new transitional interludes. The full ballet
score is certainly worth hearing for the prelude alone, which amalga-
mates the themes of the various episodes, and for its sudden turn in
one of the interludes to the shimmering world of an oriental empress
and her subjects, the Pagodas.

The original Mother Goose tales (1697) were by Charles Perrault,
who had told "The Sleeping Beauty," "Little Red Riding Hood,"
"Puss in Boots," and the others to his children. (The English Mother
Goose and her very fine gander were developed after Perrault's title,
a half century later, by the publishers of the nursery rhymes.) Ravel's
title and first two movements come from Perrault. The pagoda movement is based on a tale by Perrault's contemporary the Countess
d'Aulnoy, while "Beauty and the Beast" is by a moralist of the next
generation named Marie Leprince de Beaumont. Excerpts from their
stories appear in the score.

Sleeping Beauty's pavane lasts only twenty bars, a rounded form (as are all five movements) of open-ended solo melodic turns over a walking bass with string pizzicatos—she is, of course, sleepwalking. Like Hansel and Gretel, *Tom Thumb* scattered bread crumbs in the forest to mark his return path, only to discover that the birds had eaten them. Wandering phrases in parallel thirds support the melody begun in the solo oboe, the meter vacillating between $\frac{2}{4}$ and $\frac{3}{4}$; this reaches a gentle peak about a third of the way in. The bird calls of the second section are offered by the concertmaster, playing glissandos in harmonics, and by the piccolo and flute.

Laideronnette is an oriental empress, serenaded at her bath by her subjects, little creatures playing on theorbos and viols made of nutshells. A five-pitch, or pentatonic, scale lends the melody its oriental flavor; in this case, it is the scale of the black notes on the piano, a point made clear at the two big climaxes with xylophone, where Ravel alludes to the ditties children work out on the black keys. ("Peter, Peter Pumpkin Eater" it was, when I was a kid.) The writing for percussion and harp, like some red-lacquered clock gone amok in its chiming, is unexcelled.

The *Conversation of Beauty and the Beast* is self-explanatory: Beauty has the naive little waltz, a reference to Satie's *Gymnopédies* (see p. 483), while Beast is the growling of the contrabassoon. At the return of the waltz, the two themes join, a device that occurred in the reprise of the pagoda movement as well—indicating in this case that Beauty has accepted the Beast's proposal of marriage. With the long harp glissando, triangle stroke, and Beast theme transformed into harmonics for the solo violin, we may be reasonably certain that the Beast has been transformed into a Handsome Prince. In *The Enchanted Garden,* Prince and Princess Charming (the former Beast and [Sleeping] Beauty) are sent to live happily ever after by the Good Fairy. The apotheosis ending, again with percussion and harp, may as well be heard as the peal of wedding bells.

Daphnis et Chloé, Suites No. 1 and 2 ("Symphonic Fragments") from the ballet

Suite No. 1
Nocturne—Interlude—Danse guerrière (Warrior's Dance)

Suite No. 2
Lever du jour (Dawn)—*Pantomime*—*Danse générale*
[No pause between the movements]

For wordless chorus; piccolo, flutes I-II, alto flute, oboes I-II,
English horn, E♭ clarinet, clarinets I-II, bass clarinet, bassoons
I-III, contrabassoon; horns I-IV, trumpets I-IV, trombones I-
III, tuba; timpani, small snare drum, snare drum, bass drum,
cymbals, triangle, tambourine, castanets, tam-tam, wind
machine, glockenspiel, celesta; harps I-II; strings with violin
solo
Composed 1909–12 to a commission from Diaghilev
First performed (Suite No. 1) 2 April 1911 at a concert of the
Colonne Orchestra, Paris, Gabriel Pierné conducting; the ballet
first performed 8 June 1912 by the Ballets Russes at the Théâtre
du Chatelet, Pierre Monteux conducting; scenario and
choreography by Michel Fokine; décors and costumes by Léon
Bakst
Published by Durand & Cie. (Paris, 1911, 1913). *Inexpensive
edition* of the full ballet score: Maurice Ravel: *Daphnis and Chloe
in Full Score* (New York: Dover, 1989)
Duration: Suite 1, about 15 minutes; Suite 2, about 20 minutes

Daphnis and Chloé, one of Ravel's most extended compositions and
almost surely his best, pictures what the composer called the "Greece
of my dreams." The last word in that formulation is as important as
the first: Ravel's conception is now distant and serene, now voluptu-
ous, tinted always by the play of color and light. Though written as
a ballet score, it is anything but a collage of set pieces: a composer's
symphonic *tour de force,* rather, virtually certain to overshadow the
staging and décor.

Daphnis and Chloé was one of the many scores commissioned by
Sergei Diaghilev, whose Ballets Russes had thundered into Paris in
1907; by the 1909 season he had managed, in a strategy both artistically meritorious and politically shrewd, to commission musical scores
from most of the interesting composers working there. The choreography was to be by Michel Fokine, Diaghilev's ballet master during
this period, whose great accomplishments were the *Polovtsian Dances,
Les Sylphides, Scheherazade, The Firebird, Petrushka,* and *The Dying Swan.*
It was however a painful collaboration, with disagreements between
Fokine and the rather meddlesome Ravel over the scenario and cho-

reography, and with the dancers complaining (as they must have done for much of the work written for them) of the difficulty of counting the beats. (Ravel suggested, for the long bacchanale in $\frac{5}{4}$, that they simply chant the syllables Ser-gei-Dia-ghi-lev; this was an absurd idea, as you will discover if you try it for yourself.) *Daphnis and Chloé* had but two performances that season, largely because the public was more interested in paying to see Nijinsky's scandalous behavior in *Afternoon of a Faun,* which had just opened.

The story, adapted from an early Greek tale, had enjoyed a certain vogue in France under Louis XIV. Daphnis and Chloé, abandoned as children on the island of Lesbos, have been raised by shepherds. Daphnis has fashioned pan-pipes to play for Chloé, who found his music irresistably seductive; they have fallen in love. In the first of the ballet's three scenes Daphnis outdances his rival Dorcon to earn Chloé's kiss, then retains his virtue despite the erotic advances of Lyceion. Chloé is meanwhile captured by pirates; Daphnis, in vain pursuit, swoons before the grotto of the nymphs. In scene 2, set in the pirates' camp, Pan and his warriors rescue Chloé. In scene 3, at dawn, Daphnis wakes and mourns for the lost Chloé; shepherds enter with the rescued damsel; Daphnis and Chloé pantomime the tale of Pan and Syrinx; there is a grand bacchanale.

The two suites are simply long, uninterrupted extracts from the ballet score, comprising the end of the first scene and first half of the second for Suite No. 1 and the whole of the third scene for Suite No. 2. (For those who have the full score cited above: the first suite commences at rehearsal figure 70 and continues to the double bar just before 131; the second suite begins at rehearsal 155 and goes to the end.)

Suite No. 1. Daphnis lies prostrate at the grotto, into the surrounding rock of which have been sculpted statues of three nymphs. Another rock vaguely resembles the god Pan. At each of the three cadenzas (flute, horn, clarinet) one of the statues comes to life; they consult with each other (wind machine and string glissandi) and begin their slow, mysterious dance. Both prominent musical ideas, the palpitating chords in the flute choir and the subsequent figure for oboe and clarinets, have had strong identity since the beginning of the ballet. The nymphs invoke Pan, whose presence is celebrated by the wordless chorus, offstage. The distant horn and trumpet calls begin the transition to the scene in the pirates' lair. The coarse and violent warrior's dance begins with the thumping eighth-note figure, continues in a faster section with rapid passagework melody in woodwinds, then combines the two ideas. Pandemonium reigns as the men of the offstage chorus begin to howl: the effect reminiscent, to my ear, of the bacchanale from *Samson and Delilah*.

Suite No. 2. Of all the exceptional music composed for the Ballets Russes, the daybreak sequence, Ravel's greatest triumph, surely contends with *Afternoon of a Faun* and portions of *The Rite of Spring* for first place. Daphnis is still prostrate at the grotto; the murmur of rivulets falling from the rocks (woodwinds, harps) is the only sound to be heard. Dawn comes up (low strings) and the birds begin to sing (three solo violins, piccolo). The florid piccolo solo indicates a shepherd passing by with his flock; another shepherd passes at the solo for E♭ clarinet. Chloé appears, escorted by shepherdesses, and, at the big climax, they fall into each other's arms at last. During the oboe interlude a wise shepherd explains that Pan has rescued Chloé in memory of his own quite similar love for the nymph Syrinx. Daphnis and Chloé begin their mime of the story of Pan and Syrinx. She darts into the reeds; he fashions pan-pipes, and with the virtuoso flute solo their big dance begins. Chloé at length dances herself into the arms of Daphnis, and in the languid interlude they pledge their undying love. Bacchantes with tambourines enter. Joyous tumult, in $\frac{5}{4}$.

La Valse

.

> For piccolo, flutes I-II, oboes I-II, English horn, E♭ clarinet, clarinets I-II, bass clarinet, bassoons I-II, contrabassoon; horns I-IV, trumpets I-III, trombones I-III, tuba; timpani, bass drum, cymbals, triangle, tambourine, castanets, tam-tam, bells; harp; strings
> **Composed** December 1919–March 1920; dedicated to Misia Sert, née Godebska, literary socialite; Ravel numbered Misia, her three husbands, and her brother Cipa among his intimates
> **First performed** 12 December 1920 by the Lamoureux Orchestra of Paris, Camille Chevillard conducting; Ravel and Alfredo

Casella gave the first performance of the version for two pianos
in Vienna, 23 October 1920
Published by Durand (Paris, 1921)
Duration: about 15 minutes

Ravel convalesced slowly from dysentery contracted during the war,
a period of illness doubtless complicated by his incipient neurological
disorder. His first work after *Le Tombeau de Couperin* of 1914–17 was
the "choreographic poem" *La Valse,* completed in 1920. The idea of
a work in homage to Johann Strauss goes back many years; by 1914
there was a title, *Wien* (Vienna), and the notion of an "apotheosis of
the Viennese waltz, . . . a fantastic and fatal kind of Dervish's dance."
By 1920, the score was called simply *La Valse,* the former title having
been deemed inappropriate after the war. The preface reads:

> Through whirling clouds can be glimpsed now and again waltzing cou-
> ples. The mist gradually disperses, and at letter A [in the score] a huge
> ballroom filled with a great crowd of whirling dancers is revealed. The
> stage grows gradually lighter. At the *fortissimo* at letter B the lights in the
> chandeliers burst forth. The scene is an imperial palace about 1855.

There is something of the macabre in Ravel's fantastic vision of the
waltz, the dalliance of an irrelevant civilization soon to vanish. The
main material is developed from a motive first stated by bassoons
amid confused rumblings in lower strings. This gradually transforms
itself into a full orchestral statement. From here on the *tutti* sections
alternate with restrained, trio-like material punctuated at times by
brass, in a Straussian series of waltz episodes. Everything from the
midpoint is a restatement and transformation of the waltzes into a
kind of delirious motion—the "fatal whirling" that culminates in the
chromatic and metrically shocking final cadence. As usual, the
orchestration is a garden of delights, for example the multitude of
effects given the harps and the many imitations of the harp elsewhere
in the orchestra.

Diaghilev intended for a time to produce *La Valse* with Stravinsky's
Pulcinella, but it was not danced as a ballet until 1926, when it was
produced by the Royal Flemish Ballet in Antwerp, Belgium. Ida
Rubinstein's company danced the work to a scenario by Ravel and
choreography by Bronislava Nijinska; this was first performed 23 May

1929 at the Paris Opéra. Subsequently George Balanchine choreographed a shining version for the New York City Ballet.

Boléro

> For piccolo, flutes I-II, oboes I-II, oboe d'amore, English horn, E♭ clarinet, clarinets I-II, bass clarinet, saxophones (sopranino, soprano, tenor), bassoons I-II, contrabassoon; horns I-IV, D trumpet, trumpets I-III, trombones I-III, tuba; timpani, 2 snare drums, cymbals, tam-tam; harp, celesta; strings
> **Composed** July 6–October 1928; dedicated to Ida Rubinstein
> **First performed** 22 November 1928, by the orchestra of the Paris Opéra at a dance recital of Ida Rubinstein, Walther Straram conducting; choreography by Bronislava Nijinska; first concert performance in Paris 11 January 1930, the composer conducting the Lamoureux Orchestra
> **Published by** Durand (Paris, 1929)
> **Duration:** about 15 minutes

This erotic showpiece for mega-orchestra, dubious sire of minimalism, was written to commission from the dancer / choreographer Ida Rubinstein. Ravel composed it during the seaside holiday he took following his grueling North American tour of 1928. The idea was to try to find as many ways of expressing what he called a "particularly insistent" melody without recourse to any development—one long and gradual crescendo. Six large cycles of the two-part tune progress from a sultry statement by flute solo over the incessant bolero figure in the drum to the immense final episode, which requires thirty-six lines of score. The bolero rhythm is highly stylized, several stages removed from the real thing. Among the exceptional settings of the tune are those for high bassoon and tenor saxophone solos, the statements coupled in parallel fifths in the manner of a pipe organ, and in one case a three-way coupling (C major in celesta and horn, E major in piccolo I, and G major in piccolo II). Equally impressive are the dozens of ways guitar strumming is suggested, as for example the quadruple-stopped pizzicati of the inner strings at the very end. The hair-raising rise of tonality near the end, after all the "automatic elements" that have come before, seems orgiastic.

Ravel, for his part, was rueful over the unparalleled public enthusiasm for *Boléro,* which he feared would be reckoned his only masterpiece. "Alas," said he, "it contains no music."

The Piano Concertos

Concerto for the Left Hand (in D Major) for Piano and Orchestra

Lento—Più lento—Allegro

For piano solo; piccolo, flutes I-III, oboes I-II, English horn, E♭ clarinet, clarinets I-II, bass clarinet, bassoons I-II, contrabassoon; horns I-IV; trumpets I-III, trombones I-III, tuba; timpani, snare drum, bass drum, cymbals, triangle, wood-block, tam-tam; harps; strings

Composed 1929–30 in Paris; dedicated to Paul Wittgenstein
First performed 5 January 1932 by the Vienna Symphony Orchestra, Paul Wittgenstein, piano, Robert Heger conducting
Published by Durand & Cie. (Paris, 1931)
Duration: about 18 minutes

Concerto for Piano and Orchestra in G Major

Allegramente
Adagio assai
Presto

For piano solo; piccolo, flute, oboe, English horn, E♭ clarinet, clarinet, bassoons I-II; horns I-II, trumpet, trombone; timpani, snare drum, bass drum, cymbals, triangle, woodblock, whip, tam-tam; harp; strings

Composed 1929–31 in Paris; dedicated to Marguerite Long
First performed 14 January 1932 by the Lamoureux Orchestra in the Salle Pleyel, Marguerite Long, piano, Ravel conducting
Published by Durand & Cie. (Paris, 1932)
Duration: about 23 minutes

Ravel's two piano concertos, for all intents and purposes his last major compositions, were conceived and written simultaneously. They come two decades after the ballet that made him famous, a decade after *La*

Valse, and more than two years after the *Boléro.* The composer's 1927–28 concert tour of North America—a "crazy" trip, in his words, with enthusiastic audiences, breathtaking scenery, and horrid food—had been so successful that there was talk of a second, during which the Boston Symphony Orchestra might premiere a piano concerto with the composer as soloist. For some time he had been pondering a concerto for the French pianist Marguerite Long (1874–1966, pupil of both Ravel and Debussy and professor at the Conservatoire from 1920), who had played the first performance of *Le Tombeau de Couperin* in 1919.

Meanwhile the Austrian pianist Paul Wittgenstein (1887–1961; brother of the philosopher) approached Ravel for a different sort of concerto: one for the left hand alone. Wittgenstein's right arm had been amputated following a wound sustained during the opening weeks of the war. Undaunted, he went on to have an important career playing works that had been adapted or written especially for him, including Ravel's concerto, two works by Richard Strauss, Prokofiev's Fourth Piano Concerto, and Britten's Diversions on a Theme, opus 21.

Ravel had meant to play the first performance of the G-Major Concerto himself, but saw that he lacked the stamina after his grueling labors on the pair of concertos. Thus Marguerite Long gave the first performance, conquering audience and critics alike in "the finest artistic manifestation of the season." (The critic Emile Vuillermoz complained that Ravel's conducting was "badly timed" and "lacked clarity and elasticity," but he had nothing but praise for the man as composer.) Disobeying his doctor's order of complete rest, Ravel then embarked on a four-month European tour to conduct the new concerto with Long as soloist.

The Concerto for the Left Hand is scored for the larger of the two orchestras. An introduction presents a lugubrious dotted theme in the contrabassoon, joined by a blues-like melody in horns. Gradually it becomes clear that the introduction is built over an unchanging sustained note, E, in the bass instruments. The form is traditional, of Schumannesque themes alternating with a toy march in $\frac{6}{8}$ meter that eventually transforms itself into a scherzo. Reprises of the march and scherzo, along with some restatement of the opening material, lead into the difficult and magnificent cadenza. (In the passage halfway into the cadenza, one hand plays three voices: melody lines on top and bottom, with accompaniment in the middle. Here and throughout the concerto, the pedal-work—an obvious area for exploration in a one-handed piece—is particularly detailed.) The opening blues theme provides the material for the conclusion.

The G-Major Concerto is a rather smaller work, though Ravel thought it "a concerto in the truest sense of the word: I mean that it is written very much in the same spirit as those of Mozart and Saint-Saëns." There are also jazzy rhythms, chords, and blue-notes, and hints of Gershwin and possibly Stravinsky along with the usual Spanish and Basque elements that permeate Ravel's mature style. Cadenzas for harp and woodwind precede the solo cadenza in the first movement. The second movement closely resembles that of a Mozart concerto—though Ravel told Mme Long that it had been written "two measures at a time, with frequent reference to Mozart's Clarinet Quintet." The third movement is witty and fast, with three short, nimble themes: the shrill flute whistle, a syncopated triadic dance begun by the piano in the bass clef, and a march in $\frac{6}{8}$.

Ottorino Respighi

Born *9 July 1879* in Bologna
Died *18 April 1936* in Rome

From his violin masters in Bologna, Luigi Torchi and Giuseppe Martucci, Respighi absorbed that city's musical heritage, as old as the violin itself. In the first years of the new century he visited St. Petersburg, where he played viola in the opera orchestra, and met Rimsky-Korsakov, with whom he studied composition. After further and rather pointless studies with Max Bruch in Berlin, he moved in 1913 to Rome, where he taught and composed for the rest of his life. For a time he was a professor and then director of the Conservatorio di Santa Cecilia, but resigned in 1925–26 to devote his career to composition and conducting. During that season and again in 1932 he made concert tours of the United States.

Respighi's work is that of an adroit crafstman, pleasant, un-threatening, successful—but without the psychological complexity that usually attends artistic greatness. His genius is his sense of typically Italian melodic beauty, which he expresses with an orchestrational vigor similar to that Rimsky-Korsakov and Richard Strauss.

His compositions includes the four-part symphonic poem *Le fontane di Roma* (The Fountains of Rome, 1916), *I pini di Roma* (The Pines of Rome, 1924), *Feste romane* (Roman Festivals, 1928), and orchestrations of works by older composers: *Gli ucelli* (The Birds, 1927) and three sets of "Ancient Airs and Dances for Lute" (1917, 1923, 1931). A portion of his international prominence was earned for him by Toscanini, who championed his works.

I pini di Roma (The Pines of Rome), Symphonic Poem

I pini di Villa Borghese (The Pines of the Villa Borghese)
Pini presso una catacomba (Pines Near a Catacomb)
I pini del Gianicolo (The Pines of the Janiculum)
I pini della via Appia (The Pines of the Appian Way)
[No pauses between movements]

For piccolo, flutes I-III, oboes I-II, English horn, clarinets I-II, bass clarinet, bassoons I-II, contrabassoon; horns I-IV, trumpets I-III, trombones I-IV; timpani, 2 snare drums, bass drum, cymbals, small cymbals, triangle, tambourine, rattle, tam-tam, glockenspiel, celesta; harp, piano, organ; strings; the song of the nightingale in the third movement was originally provided on a disc ("gramophone-nightingale"); the last movement calls for straight trumpets or bugles (pairs of *"buccine, flicorni"*: soprano, tenor and bass)
Composed 1923–24 in Rome
First performed 14 December 1924 by the Augusteo Orchestra, Rome, Bernardino Molinari conducting
Published by G. Ricordi & Co. (Milan, 1925)
Duration: about 20 minutes

The *belvedere* near the Villa Borghese, atop the Spanish steps, commands a breathtaking vista of the Eternal City; Respighi suggests as well (according to notes supplied by his librettist, Claudio Guastalla) rowdy boys playing soldier. The pines near a catacomb are redolent with memories of the Christians who assembled there to pray in secret and who lie buried in the vaults beneath. A funeral dirge in the wind choirs alludes to their chanted prayers. The Janiculum is one of the seven hills of Rome, where you may wander through ageless gardens and past magnificent palaces: the movement evokes such a midnight promenade, the warm night air filled with the song of a distant nightingale. The fourth scene treats the approach, down the ancient Appian Way, of Roman legions. Fierce rhythmic ostinatos and insistent brass and percussion define the unseen army; with a great crescendo, the procession comes into view.

Respighi and his large orchestra revel in this panoply of sonic and visual images, with opulent orchestration, good tunes, and a strong sense of the composer's almost childlike glee as he turns the pages of his picture book. It was above all the permanence of the pines that attracted Respighi: the fact that they had presided over these comings and goings for centuries. He called his country villa The Pines.

Nicolai Rimsky-Korsakov

Born *18 March 1844 in Tikhovin,*
near Novgorod
Died *21 June 1908 in St. Petersburg*

Rimsky-Korsakov was born to aristocratic parents and led a privileged childhood that included lessons with the local music masters. At the age of twelve he was sent to the Naval Academy in St. Petersburg, where during the course of his studies he first became acquainted with Balakirev, Borodin, and Cui (see p. 131). After graduating in 1862 he went to sea on active duty, though he did some composing as well. In 1865 he settled in St. Petersburg, serving simultaneously in the Navy and as a teacher of composition at the St. Petersburg Conservatory; he retired from the Navy in 1873 to become government inspector of military bands. As a teacher he was exceptionally gifted and could number among his pupils nearly the whole of the next generation of Russian composers, including Stravinsky. He was rather less successful at conducting but did a lot of it, anyway. Two of his more significant appearances were in Paris, for the 1889 Universal Exhibition (of Eiffel Tower fame) and, thirteen months before his death, for Diaghilev's first Paris season. Also in 1889 he was swept by a St. Petersburg production into the world of Wagner's *Ring;* thereafter he devoted his composition almost exclusively to opera.

Rimsky-Korsakov's work descends directly from Glinka's, and he wrote proudly (if a little inaccurately) of having achieved his brilliant effects without extending the Glinka performing force. His virtuoso orchestration is the hallmark of his style—that, and his fascination with Russian folksong and orientalia. Of his operas the orchestral repertoire retains "musical pictures" and suites: *Sadko* (1867, rev. 1869, 1892), *Tale of Tsar Sultan* (1903), *Mlada,* with its great Cortege of the Nobles (1903), and *Le Coq d'or* (or *The Golden Cockerel,* 1907). Rimsky-Korsakov also composed three symphonies (No. 1 in E♭ Minor, 1861–65, rev. and transposed to E minor, 1884; No. 2, "Antar," 1868, rev. 1875, 1897; No. 3 in C Major, 1866–73, rev. 1886), the three popular orchestral works treated below (*Capriccio espagnol, Scheherazade,* and the *Russian Easter Overture*), and choral music and songs. His selfless efforts to preserve the work of his late colleagues—he completed, orchestrated, or revised for performance Borodin's *Prince Igor,* Mussorgsky's *Boris Godunov, Kovanshchina,* and *Night on Bald Mountain,* and Dargomyzhsky's *The Stone Guest*—constitute, in and of themselves, a repertoire of note.

Capriccio espagnol, OP. 34

Alborada (Song of Dawn): *Vivo e strepitoso*
Variazioni: Andante con moto
Alborada: Vivo et strepitoso
Scene e canto gitano (Scene and Gypsy Song): *Allegretto*
Fandango asturiano
[Played without interruption]

For piccolo, flutes I-II, oboes I-II, English horn, clarinets I-II, bassoons I-II; horns I-IV, trumpets I-II, trombones I-III, tuba; timpani, snare drum, bass drum, cymbals, triangle, tambourine, castanets; harp; strings with violin solo

Composed summer 1887 in Nikol'skoye, a summer residence; completed 4 August 1887

First performed 12 November 1887 at a Russian Public Symphony concert, St. Petersburg, Rimsky-Korsakov conducting

Published by M. P. Belaieff (Leipzig, 1888)
Duration: about 15 minutes

The vogue for Spanish music started among the Russians with Glin-
ka's *Jota aragonesa* and *Night in Madrid,* products of his two years in
Spain, 1845–47. Rimsky's caprice was begun as a sequel to his own
Fantasy on Russian Themes for violin and orchestra of 1886.

Alborada is the Spanish aubade, the morning song typically offered
with pipe and tabor beneath a fair maiden's window. This particular
morning's song would wake the dead with its riotous enthusiasm and
sheer numbers—a full orchestra with five percussionists in lieu of pipe
and tabor. The clarinet has the solo piping over excellent pizzicato
work, and a splashy solo turn by the concertmaster draws this first
appearance of the *Alborada* to an end. The *Variations* are on the lovely
Andalusian theme given by the four horns: an improvisatory dialogue
of the English and French horns (the French horn echoes in stopped
notes, a technique achieved by blocking the air column with the right
hand), soulful variations by the string and woodwind choirs, and a
lingering close beneath willowy chromatics in the solo flute.

The *Alborada* returns, this time with trumpet flourishes and harp.
Now Rimsky considerably extends the violin and clarinet solos, with
a fountain of clarinet arpeggios at the end. The strumming and vocalising common to the start of gypsy scenes is here suggested by the
brass over a snare drum roll. The violin soloist's cadenza improvises
on the same material, from which is born a brief but animated dance
figure in flute and clarinet. But this is no sooner stated than it digresses
into three more cadenzas, for flute, clarinet, and harp. At last the
long-pent-up dance is fully unleashed, gathering force as it goes, then
merging into a fandango with castanets. A second reprise of the *Alborada* serves as the coda, the tempo now faster than ever.

The title, incidentally, is a bizarre translation into both Italian and
French of the Russian for "Caprice on Spanish Themes."

Scheherazade, OP. 35, Symphonic Suite from *A Thousand and One Nights*

Largo maestoso (The Sea and Sinbad's Ship)
Lento (The Story of the Kalendar Prince)
Andantino quasi Allegretto (The Young Prince and the Princess)

Allegro molto (Festival at Baghdad; The Sea; The Ship Goes to Pieces on a Rock Surmounted by a Bronze Warrior; Conclusion)

For piccolo, flutes I-II, oboes I-II, clarinets I-II, bassoons I-II; horns I-IV, trumpets I-II, trombones I-III, tuba; timpani, snare drum, bass drum, cymbals, triangle, tambourine, tam-tam; harp; strings

Composed July 1888 in Nyezhgovitsy, a summer residence; dedicated to Vladimir Stasov

First performed 9 November 1888 at a Russian Public Symphony concert, St. Petersburg, Rimsky-Korsakov conducting

Published by M. P. Belaieff (Leipzig, 1889). *Inexpensive score:* Nikolay Rimsky-Korsakov: *Scheherazade in Full Score* (New York: Dover, 1984)

Duration: about 40 minutes

Scheherazade is of course Rimsky-Korsakov's delectation on the *Arabian Nights*. The Sultan Schahriar, persuaded of the faithlessness of women, has vowed to execute each of his wives after the first night. (So goes the argument at the head of the score.) For 1001 nights, however, the Sultana Scheherazade delays her fate by weaving tales of many marvels—of Sinbad and Ali Baba and Aladdin and the rest, of handsome princes and lithe princesses—and at length her husband forgets his bloody plan. Rimsky later withdrew the movement titles, arguing that they had been merely "guideposts" to attract the listener's fancy. Nineteenth-century composers often pulled this stunt, but once established such stories are hard to erase from the collective memory.

In this case, the composer had good reason on his side, for *Scheherazade* is better heard as four interlinked segments of the same tone poem than as four separate stories. Two motives recur through the work, the sultan's blustery tenor-and-bass theme of the first six bars, and the violin solo that so clearly represents the sultana's voice as she unravels a new tale to distract him from his stated purpose. Between them comes a once-upon-a-time progression in the woodwinds certainly to be associated with the very similar curtain-raising effect in Mendelssohn's *Midsummer Night's Dream* music. The first movement develops into a fantasia on the two themes. A new pair of ideas is introduced at the *tranquillo:* the deliberate quarter-note figure in clarinets and bassoon and its riposte in the solo flute. The nautical effects are very tame, based on a rolling $\frac{6}{4}$ meter. The second movement is a showpiece for the solo woodwinds, who state the capricious theme in brisk triple meter and minor key, once the sultana's cadenza is done. A stern pronouncement from the trombones is briefly developed, but this is deflected into a clarinet cadenza of three successive sections. Confusion breaks out in the skittish Vivace, and the trombone theme undergoes a long treatment. The three-part cadenza is heard again from the bassoon, then once more (and most interestingly) in the string sections; these improvisations separate episodes in a progressive interweaving of the thematic elements. By the third movement, which turns to the major mode with a winsome theme in $\frac{6}{8}$, we begin to understand that the new melodies are transformations of what has come before: they have a familiar ring despite their new surroundings. The dandy effect here is the series of steeply-arched arabesques for the solo woodwinds and their rather more assertive counterpart in the violins. An animated dance setting with full percussion springs loose, interrupted after a time by Scheherazade's cadenza and a particularly stunning version of the arabesques, where the flute and clarinet travel in octaves over harp glissandos. A return of the Sultan's motive introduces the furious Baghdad scene, a collage of the themes and effects that have occupied our attention in the preceding movements. Scheherazade's cadenza is heard one last time at the close, as is the Mendelssohnian chord progression for the high woodwinds.

Rimsky's Arabian nights are long, too long, and by the end you may be tempted to scream if you hear the solo violin begin to spin tales again, however marvelous. The tunes are nice, but there aren't many of them. You get seduced anyway: Rimsky's skill at orchestration is legendary for good reason, and no one is better at evoking the romance of Araby. You must object if the violin cadenzas, flawless though they may be, are loud and vulgar with vibrato, as is too often the case: the lady telling the story was buxom, enticing, and seductive.

Russian Easter Overture, OP. 36

> For piccolo, flutes I-III, oboes I-II, clarinets I-II, bassoons I-II; horns I-IV, trumpets I-II, trombones I-III, tuba; timpani, bass drum, cymbals, triangle, tam-tam, glockenspiel; harp; strings

Composed 6 August 1887–20 March 1888 in St. Petersburg;
dedicated to the memory of Mussorgsky and Borodin
First performed 15 December 1888 at a Russian Public
Symphony concert, St. Petersburg, Rimsky-Korsakov
conducting
Published by M. P. Belaieff (Leipzig, 1890)
Duration: about 15 minutes

Rimsky-Korsakov's three big orchestral works, of which this is the
last, were composed during the same two-year period, 1887–88. It
was a time of rebound from a hiatus caused in part by his activities of
behalf of the publishing firm of M. P. Belaieff and in part by the
work he had undertaken as musical executor for his late friends Mussorgsky and Borodin. Once the series was done a prolonged period of
neurasthenia set in, doubtless prompted by illness in the family and
the subsequent loss of his mother and two of his children. But Tchaikovsky's death in 1893 left Rimsky-Korsakov in a position of unchal-
lenged seniority among Russian composers, and his sense of obligation
to the cause of nationalism renewed his energy. Thereupon he went
on to write the outstanding series of operas that constitutes his last
period, and where his most mature work is to be found.

A proper translation of the title and subtitle of Rimsky's opus 36
is "Russian Easter Festival, overture on liturgical themes." The themes
he had found in an eighteenth-century collection of canticles for the
Russian Orthodox liturgy; the sonorities he knew from the monastery
at Tikhvin, his birthplace. At the head of the score is a "program"
consisting of the first two verses of Psalm 68 ("Let God arise, let his
enemies be scattered"), the passage from the gospel of St. Mark where
Mary Magdalene and her companions discover the white-robed angel
in Christ's tomb, and the composer's own vivid images of Easter jubilation: a heavenly "Resurrexit" sung by angels and trumpeted by archangels to the flutter of seraphim wings, an earthly "Resurrexit" chanted
by priests in temples to clouds of incense, the light of numberless
candles, and the chiming of triumphant bells.

That about says it all. The introductory section, through the clarinet arpeggio and slow glissando of the harp, is meant to evoke the
mystery of the empty tomb. After the initial statement by the woodwinds, much of the chanting is given to the trombones, though near
the beginning there are statements by the unusual grouping of two

bassoons with tuba. A lively sonata structure follows, among the themes of which is one that doubtless alludes to Glinka's *Ruslan and Ludmila* overture and another very like the Kremlin bells in *Boris Godunov*. The harp, glockenspiel, tam-tam, and other percussion come to the fore as the bells become more and more jubilant, and at the end the tonality veers into an ecstatic D major.

Gioacchino Rossini

Born *29 February 1792 in Pesaro*
Died *13 November 1868 in Paris*

Urbane traveling superstar, Rossini forged the tenets of the sensationally popular *bel canto* opera of the nineteenth century. The son of provincial north Italian musicians, he sang and played well enough by the age of ten to supplement the family's pitiful income. He took composition lessons and established his credentials in Bologna; in 1810—still only eighteen—he received his first commission, an opera for the Teatro San Moisè in Venice. For the next twelve years he composed three or four operas annually, for Venice, Milan, Rome, and Naples—some three dozen in all. In 1822 he married his *prima donna* Isabella Colbran, formerly the mistress of the impresario to whom he was under contract. It was a poor match: they separated in 1837, and Rossini remarried shortly after her death in 1845. He met Beethoven during a successful season in Vienna, 1822–23, saw to the production in Venice of his last opera for Italy, *Semiramide* (1823), then left for what turned out to be a highly profitable engagement in London.

On their way to England, the Rossinis passed through Paris, where he was offered a 40,000-franc salary as director of the Italian opera company. Subsequently, he held various sinecures from the French government, and for the coronation of Charles X in 1825 he composed *Il viaggio a Reims.* The 1829 production at the Opéra of his greatest work, *Guillaume Tell,* was the triumph of the decade—at which juncture, having proved his point and earned his fortune, he simply retired. He lived in Italy for nearly two more decades, then in 1855 returned to Paris to spend the rest of his life in the luxury of his villa in the posh suburb of Passy.

Rossini loved the company of his admirers and the trappings of his wealth. His sense of humor was boundless, his *bons mots* the talk of Paris. During the last years he held the most exclusive *soirées* in town, becoming, as one writer has put it, his own apotheosis.

Apart from a lovely *Stabat mater* (orchestrated version 1841–42), Rossini is best remembered in the concert hall for the overtures from his operas, a half dozen of which have become staples of the repertoire.

The Opera Overtures

La Scala di Seta (The Silken Ladder)
First performed 9 May 1812, Teatro San Moisè, Venice

L'Italiana in Algeri (The Italian Girl in Algiers)
First performed 22 May 1813, Teatro San Bendetto, Venice

Il Barbiere di Siviglia (The Barber of Seville)
First performed (as *Almaviva*) 20 February 1816, Teatro
Argentina, Rome

La Cenerentola (Cinderella)
First performed 25 January 1817, Teatro Valle, Rome

La Gazza Ladra (The Thieving Magpie)
First performed 31 May 1817, La Scala, Milan

Guillaume Tell (William Tell)
First performed 3 August 1829, Paris Opéra

For theatre orchestras of varying size, generally piccolo, flutes I-
II, oboes I-II, clarinets I-II, bassoons I-II; horns I-IV, trumpets
I-II, trombones I-III; timpani, snare drum, bass drum,
cymbals, triangle; strings; *La gazza ladra* uses a second snare
drum, often offstage; *Guillaume Tell* has an English horn part
Duration: about 10 minutes each

Rossini composed his operas like lightning: it is said that he would
rather write a new page than get out of bed to pick up a leaf that had
fallen to the floor. The overtures came last of all, usually during the
rush before opening night. Thus, while not exactly written by formula, they are often built of tried-and-true organizational principles.
Typically they begin with a maestoso or slow introduction and continue, briskly, in sonata fashion: first and second themes, a prominent
closing theme, brief modulatory transition, recapulation, and a coda
più mosso. The closing themes, both in the exposition and recapitulation, are the occasion for the celebrated Rossini crescendo, in which
successive repetitions of four- or eight-bar phrase groupings grow from
piano to a climactic *forte,* thickening dramatically in texture and
orchestration as they go.

Il barbiere di Siviglia is Rossini's comic masterpiece, the one with
Figaro's famous aria "Largo al factotum" and Rosina's "Una voce poco
fa." Its overture measures up to the accomplishment in every respect,
with witty themes and memorable writing for the solo woodwind and
French horn. The four-note repetitions in the theme of the Maestoso
recur in the crescendo to excellent effect. Equally fine is the overture
to *La gazza ladra,* which opens with drum rolls and a march where
the phrases keep spinning off into little triplet cadences for the wind
players. The first theme of the Allegro, though notated in $\frac{3}{4}$, comes
off with all the triplets as if in a fast $\frac{9}{8}$ that presumably suggests the
magpie's teasing. (The plot revolves around a lost necklace, which in
fact has not been stolen by the maid but by the bird, who hid it in a
tree.) Trombone players are understandably fond of the climaxes here.

William Tell, unlike the Italian comedies, is an opera in French
derived from an important work of literature, Friedrich Schiller's play
of the same name. The settings are the Alps and shore of Lake Lucerne
during the Austrian oppression; the complex story concerns Arnold's
love for Mathilde, daughter of the Austrian governor Gessler, the
Swiss uprising against the oppressors, and of course the heroism of

Tell with his bow and arrow. At the end, revolution in full swing, Gessler's boat is caught in a storm on the lake; he manages to reach safety, only to be killed by one of Tell's arrows. Rossini's overture, a triumph in orchestration and clarity of expression, begins with a glorious evocation of the Swiss landscape. A cello quintet describes the sunrise, a storm blows up, tranquility returns with the pastoral of English horn and flute. The galloping Allegro begins.

Camille Saint-Saëns

Born *9 October 1835 in Paris*
Died *16 December 1921 in Algiers*

Saint-Saëns was a child prodigy whose gifts are invariably compared with Mozart's. He had perfect pitch, played the piano and composed for it from the age of three, performed Mozart and Beethoven concertos at ten, enrolled in the Paris Conservatory at twelve, and won the first prize in organ three years later. Though a student of Fromental Halévy (composer of the fine opera *La Juive*) and protégé of Berlioz from his teens, Saint-Saëns was most profoundly influenced by Liszt, whose friend and strong proponent he became. He served nearly two decades as organist at the Madeleine and taught for five years at the École Niedermeyer, where his pupils included André Messager, later an influential conductor, and the young Gabriel Fauré. With the latter he became intimate, nurturing Fauré's career and in due time becoming a family favorite. Saint-Saëns's career as recitalist, conductor, and orchestral composer was virtually without failures. It lasted, morever, for three quarters of a century: ponder, for a moment, the notion of a man who knew Berlioz and Liszt in their prime having survived Debussy, *Le Sacre du printemps,* World War I, and the dawn of the movies. When Saint-Saëns died Aaron Copland was twenty-one.

His wide-ranging interests led him down every conceivable avenue of musical life. He was a capable music critic, editor of the works of Baroque master Jean-Philippe Rameau, sometime poet and playwright, and in his prime the preeminent French composer. He was a tireless advocate of serious instrumental music in a culture dominated by music for the stage. Perhaps his most significant contribution to the future of his art was the organization in 1871 of the Société Nationale de Musique, a new music society that over the years gave first performances of works by every significant French composer from Franck to Ravel. He was, perhaps understandably, a curmudgeon where it came to the modernisms of Debussy and his successors; nevertheless the grand old Saint-Saëns was venerated by musicians the world over, for he symbolized a bygone age. And you have to admire anybody who, in his eighties, would voluntarily steam away from Europe to give his first concert tour of South America.

Saint-Saëns's major works for orchestra include three symphonies (op. 2, 1855; op. 55, 1878; and op. 78, with pipe organ, 1886), several symphonic poems of which the most popular is the *Danse macabre* (op. 40, 1874), and an armload of concertos: five for piano, three for violin, and two for cello. Of these the best entrenched in the repertoire are the Second and Fourth Piano Concertos, opp. 22 (1868) and 44 (1875), and the First Cello Concerto, op. 33 (1872); additionally, there is a very popular Introduction and Rondo Capricioso for violin and orchestra, op. 28 (1863). Of the unusual circumstances surrounding *The Carnival of the Animals* you will read below. The theatre works of Saint-Saëns were rather less successful, but *Samson et Dalila,* op. 47 (1877) is a masterpiece.

Symphony No. 3 in C Minor, OP. 78 ("Organ Symphony")

I. *Adagio; Allegro moderato; Poco adagio*
II. *Allegro moderato; Presto; Maestoso; Allegro*
[No pause between the two movements in each section]

For piccolo, flutes I-III, oboes I-II, English horn, clarinets I-II,
bass clarinet, bassoons I-II, contrabassoon; horns I-IV; trumpets
I-III; trombones I-III, tuba; timpani, bass drum, cymbals, triangle; organ, piano (four-hands in one passage); strings

Composed early 1886 in Paris; dedicated to the memory of Liszt,
who died on 31 July 1886, between the first performance and
the publication

First performed 19 May 1886 by the London Philharmonic
Society, Saint-Saëns conducting (the rest of the program,
including Beethoven's Fifth Piano Concerto with Saint-Saëns as
soloist, was conducted by Sir Arthur Sullivan)

Published by Durand Schoenewerk & Cie. (Paris, 1886)

Duration: about 50 minutes

It was altogether natural for Saint-Saëns to incorporate the piano and
the pipe organ into his orchestra, for he was a virtuoso performer on
both. It was just as appropriate for him to dedicate the work to Liszt,
who had admired the score during his last visit to Paris. Nor, finally,
is it suprising to discover a composer of Saint-Saëns's predilections
grappling here with the confrontation of symphony and tone poem.
Of the curious organization, four movements in two, he writes:

This symphony is divided into two parts. Nevertheless it embraces in
principle the four traditional movements, but the first is altered in its
development to serve as the introduction to the Adagio, and the scherzo
is connected by the same process to the finale. The composer has sought
to avoid to some extent the interminable reprises and repetitions which
are leading to the disappearance of instrumental music.

The Organ Symphony exemplifies Saint-Saëns's shrewd control of
instrumental color and atmosphere—serene at times, as in the second
movement where the organ first enters, then sweeping and majestic
when the brass and organ are allowed their full volume. Elsewhere it
can be driving, sometimes violent, as the in first *Allegro* and the scherzo.
Metric ambiguities, particularly in the scherzo, perplex the listener
as to the location of the downbeat—effects made more striking by the
way a pipe organ articulates every beat with uniform strength.

The motive that begins the first *Allegro* (after the brief introduction, *Adagio*) goes on to dominate the work as a sort of *idée fixe* that
reappears in every movement; the first four notes are equivalent to
those of the *Dies irae* chant. Much of the material seems purposely

derivative: the introduction is Wagnerian in tonal idiom, while the *Allegro* has some obvious parallels with the opening of Schubert's *Unfinished*. The scherzo, built from a transformation of the principal motive, is reminiscent of Mendelssohn's practice, and the metric ruses, like the passage in simultaneous $\frac{6}{8}$ and $\frac{2}{4}$, seem derived from Berlioz. A proper product of the Conservatoire, Saint-Saëns writes learned fugues of great craft: the one in the finale, for example, includes a phrase that was foreshadowed at the end of the scherzo. Few ventures in orchestration are as original as the grand introduction to the last movement—where the piano, four-hands, erupts in a *presto*. The symphony goes on to conclude in an orgy of C major.

In some respects, though, it is the second movement that most intrigues, a passive theme and variations over chords in the organ. The pizzicato in the low strings restates the motive from the first movement, and its prominent half step receives an extended treatment.

Danse macabre, OP. 40

> For solo violin; piccolo, flutes I-II, oboes I-II, clarinets I-II,
>   bassoons I-II; horns I-IV; trumpets I-II; trombones I-III, tuba;
>   timpani, bass drum, cymbals, xylophone, triangle; harp; strings
> Composed early 1874 in Paris; finished October; dedicated to
>   Mme Caroline Montigny-Remaury (1843–1913), virtuoso
>   pianist and often the composer's partner for four-hand
>   performances
> First performed 24 January 1875 at the Théâtre du Chatelet in
>   Paris, Édouard Colonne conducting
> Published by Durand Schoenewerk & Cie. (Paris, 1875)
> Duration: about 10 minutes

This *Dance of Death* follows from a tradition held in great esteem by nineteenth-century composers, and the sequence of events is much the same as in Mussorgsky's *Night on Bald Mountain* and the last movement of Berlioz's *Fantastique* (see pp. 408 and 113, respectively). The clock (a harp, or bell, or tam-tam) strikes midnight; Death tunes his violin—with the E-string lowered to E♭, more for symbolic than musical reasons, I think. The skeletal revelry has two themes: the bone-rattling xylophone tune and the lugubrious waltz for the strings in their tenor register. The xylophone was so new, incidentally, that the composer describes it in the score and tells where one may be obtained.

Preceding the music in the published score is a trivial poem by one Henri Cazalis: "Zig, Zig, Zag," it goes, "Death plays a dancing tune on his violin." Winter wind howls, the night is dark, the trees shudder; skeletons darts through the shadows; the bones of the dancers clack. Suddenly the dance stops and everyone flees, for the cock has crowed.

Le Carnaval des animaux (The Carnival of the Animals), Grande Fantaisie zoologique

Introduction et Marche royale du lion—*Poules et coqs* (Hens and Roosters)—*Hémiones (Animaux véloces)* (Tibetan Mules: Fast Beasts)—*Tortues* (Tortoises)—*L'Éléphant*—*Kangourous*—*Aquarium*—*Personnages à longues oreilles* (Persons With Long Ears)—*Le Coucou au fond des bois* (The Cuckoo From the Depths of the Wood)—*Volière* (Aviary)—*Pianistes*—*Fossiles*—*Le Cygne* (The Swan)—*Final*

For pianos I-II; flute, clarinet; harmonica (played on celesta), xylophone; strings

Composed February 1886 in Paris

First performed at a private *soirée* of Mardi Gras 1886 given by the cellist Charles Lebouc; the instrumentalists, one on a part, included the flutist Paul Taffanel and Saint-Saëns at the piano; given again several days later by the Society "La Trompette" at the publishing house of A.-P. Lemoine and on 2 April at a *soirée* to honor Liszt; first public performance 26 February 1922, the first Mardi Gras after the composer's death, Gabriel Pierné conducting the Orchestre Colonne

Published by Durand & Cie. (Paris, 1922; posthumous)

Duration: about 25 minutes

Saint-Saëns dashed off his most popular work, his "grand zoologic fantasy," for a few friends to play at a Mardi Gras party, never intending it to be more than a jolly *bonbon*. Though *The Carnival of the Animals* continued to circulate privately, Saint-Saëns, anxious lest it damage his standing, forbade its publication, and an opus number was never assigned. A specific provision in his will removed the interdiction, and his publishers put the score on sale just after his death. It lent itself to performance by small orchestra and soon became a favorite of audiences everywhere.

As a matter of fact *The Carnival of the Animals* should interest adults more than the children for whom it is usually programmed, since some aspects of the imagery are relatively sophisticated. Anybody can write elephant and kangaroo music, I suppose, but the acquarium and aviary movements, and of course the justly celebrated music for the swan, are memorable achievements indeed. (This last served for the famous solo ballet, *The Dying Swan*, choreographed by Michel Fokine for Anna Pavlova in 1907.) For all the foolishness there's real personality to be found among these animals—even a certain nobility.

A brief introduction and fanfare leads us to the lion cage, where we hear great chromatic roars in pianos and lower strings. Hens argue and a cock crows; Tibetan mules—the two pianos, racing—are those restless ones that gallop in circles around their enclosure. Ancient tortoises are given the "can-can" and another short passage from Offenbach's *Orpheus in the Underworld*, played ever so slowly in the low strings. Such silliness continues in the waltz for the elephants, where the references are to the *Ballet des sylphes* from Berlioz's *La Damnation de Faust* and the scherzo from Mendelssohn's *Midsummer Night's Dream*. The kangaroo music, like that of the mules, is for pianos alone.

To my ear, the wonderful aquarium setting is about as liquid as music gets, a striking combination of piano arpeggios, glissandos in the celesta, and muted strings, with sparkles in the flute and clarinet. The donkey's bray is self explanatory, interrupting this series of delicate vignettes with a moment of vulgar comedy. The clarinettist goes offstage for the cuckoo calls, as the two pianos offer forest music; this merges into the fluttery bird music with florid solo work for the flute— another incontestible triumph of scoring.

The strong implication of the movement where the pianists practice their scales is of course that they, too, belong behind bars. Now comes the series of three well-paced movements that draws the work to its end. The fossil display is an assemblage of familiar, and by inference prehistoric, tunes: the *Danse macabre* xylophone solo, *J'ai du bon tabac* (a French folktune beloved of bored pit musicians, who would play it as a mark of disapproval during third-rate operas), *Ah vous dirai-je maman* ("Twinkle, Twinkle"; see p. 29), *Au clair de la lune;*

and one of Rosina's arias from the *The Barber of Seville* (the clarinet solo). Even Saint-Saëns recognized the merit of the swan music, for cello and the two pianos: it is the one excerpt he did allow to be published. Our visit to the zoo reaches its end in a *furiant* that recollects the previous themes. The donkeys have the last whinny.

Erik Satie
Born *17 May 1866 in Honfleur*
Died *1 July 1925 in Paris*

Where eccentricity is concerned, Satie was the genuine article, yet few could question—then or now—that behind his antic exhibitionism lay real genius and formidable implications for art music. He was a dilatory student at the Paris Conservatory and ultimately a dropout. He pursued an interest in gothic religion even as he was being seduced by the avant-garde at the café Chat Noir in Montmartre. He developed from 1890 an intimate and psychologically complex friendship with Debussy that lasted for two decades. In 1898 he moved to a new outpost of bohemianism, the suburb of Arcueil, trudging each day from there to Montmartre to play cabaret piano. His early composition was limited for the most part to café tunes, a cabaret style distilled in the seven movements of *Trois Morceaux en forme de poire* (Three Pieces in the Shape of a Pear, 1903), for piano duet.

Between 1905 and 1908, with unaccustomed seriousness of purpose, he studied with Vincent d'Indy and Albert Roussel at the Schola Cantorum. His reputation began to soar in 1911 with successful performances by Ravel of his piano Sarabandes (1887) and by Debussy of the orchestrated *Gymnopédies*. Shortly afterward the famous pianist Ricardo Viñes began to play his works and, from 1915, Jean Cocteau to promote his career. Satie reacted to the attention with a barrage of piano pieces of zany title and content—*Embryons desséchés* (Dried Embryos, 1913), for example—and with the ballet *Parade,* wherein he was the junior partner in a galactic collaboration with Cocteau, Sergei Diaghilev, Leonid Massine, and Picasso. By then no one could ignore his ideas: the epigrammatic rhetoric, the purity of means, and his advanced sense of the absurd.

It was in fact around Satie and Cocteau and the scandalous exchange of slanders that followed the typewriter and pistol shots in *Parade* that the younger generation of composers gathered; eventually these were called (by Henri Collet, a critic) *Les Six*—Milhaud, Poulenc, and the others (see p. 366). Later Satie and Milhaud formed a School of Arcueil that included the composer Henri Sauget and conductor Henri Desormière. In the interim he completed what is usually said to be his masterpiece, the cantata *Socrate* for four sopranos and chamber orchestra (1919), and ended his career with two more controversial ballets, *Mercure* and *Relâche* (both 1924, the latter including a surrealistic film). When he died, of alcoholism, Milhaud and some friends went to his lodgings to find in his single room only a few pieces of furniture, a rickety piano, his dozen matched gray velvet suits, and his papers. It was through Milhaud's intervention that Satie's musical manuscripts were saved.

As Stravinsky put it: "He was certainly the oddest person I have ever known, but the most rare and consistently witty person, too. . . . With his pince-nez, umbrella, and galoshes he looked a perfect schoolmaster, but he looked just as much like one without these accoutrements."

Gymnopédies, orchestrated by Claude Debussy

> *Lent et grave*
> *Lent et douloureux*
>
> For flutes I-II, oboe; horns I-IV; cymbals; harps I-II; strings with solo violin

Composed for piano, February–2 April 1888; nos. 1 and 3 orchestrated by Debussy in late 1896
First performed 20 February 1897 by the Société Nationale, Gustave Doret conducting
Published by Rouart, Lerolle, & Cie. (Paris, 1919)
Duration: about 3 minutes each

Satie composed his three *Gymnopédies* for piano in 1888. One day in 1896 Satie and Debussy were guests at the home of the conductor Gustave Doret. When Satie bungled his attempt to play the *Gymnopédies* Debussy, coming to the rescue, was won over by them; Doret, in turn, conceived the notion of having them orchestrated. Debussy accordingly scored the third and the first, reversing their original order, for the concert of February 1897; the second was later orchestrated by Roland-Manuel, among others. But it is the two Debussy settings that have earned a following in the concert hall. Satie himself had sketched a few bars of an orchestration with pizzicato strings and harps, and empty staff lines that show he meant to go on with oboe, clarinets, and voices; this probably dates from the early 1890s, before he and Debussy had met.

The *Gymnopédies* are meant to evoke ritual dances by naked Spartan youths in honor of Apollo. Both are quiet and slow, in a languid triple meter that possibly alludes to the sarabande dance pattern. The melodies are of statuesque curves arranged in irregular phrase lengths, weaving through the flute, oboe, and first violins; the rest of the orchestra provides a docile accompaniment. Debussy's accomplishment in the second of the dances, where to Satie's original he adds the harp arpeggios and light strokes of a drumstick on a cymbal, is particularly alluring.

It was almost inevitable that Debussy would be rebuked for omitting one of Satie's triptych and altering the character of the other two, but such objections are ultimately beside the point. And in the diaphonous languor of their orchestral dress they afford an arresting example of musical slow motion.

Arnold Schoenberg

Born *13 September 1874 in Vienna*
Died *13 July 1951 in Los Angeles*

Schoenberg began his musical career as a violinist; the principles of good composition he absorbed while playing chamber music and from a few lessons with the composer Alexander von Zemlinsky, whose sister Mathilde he married in 1901. By the beginning of the twentieth century, Schoenberg had written a number of successful works and on their merit had established himself as a teacher of composition. The most notable of his pupils were Alban Berg and Anton Webern; the confluence of these three masters came to be known, in retrospect, as the Second Viennese School—the homage, of course, being to the galactic trio of old Vienna, Haydn, Mozart, and Beethoven. In 1912 Schoenberg completed *Pierrot lunaire,* three sets of seven poems set for five instrumentalists and a speaker, who declaims her text in *Sprechstimme* (notated musical contours without specific pitches).

In 1923 he began to compose in a system he called at first "music of twelve tones," in which he wrote for most of the rest of his life. (This system of serial music is summarized in Chapter 4.) After the death of his wife Mathilde in October 1923, he married Gertrud Kolisch, sister of the illustrious violinist and chamber musician, Rudolf Kolisch, who was at the time his pupil. Their daughter Nuria married the Italian composer Luigi Nono, also a serialist.

Fleeing from the Nazis in 1933, Schoenberg came to the United States and eventually settled in Los Angeles. He taught at both UCLA and the University of Southern California, thus profoundly influencing a new generation of American composers. Schoenberg wrote important theoretical and pedagogic texts, including *Style and Idea* (1950). He was also an accomplished painter, so much so that the best likenesses of him are his own self-portraits.

His works for orchestra include *Verklärte Nacht,* originally a string sextet; the symphonic poem *Pelléas et Mélisande,* written without knowledge of Debussy's opera; two chamber symphonies (opp. 9B and 38), concertos for violin and for piano, and the Variations for Orchestra, op. 31. Equally important are his orchestral songs; his *Gurrelieder* for soloists, chorus, and orchestra; *A Survivor From Warsaw,* for speaker, men's chorus, and orchestra; *Pierrot lunaire;* and four operas.

Verklärte Nacht (Transfigured Night), OP. 4

For string orchestra

After a poem of the same title by Richard Dehmel (1863–1920)

Composed September 1899 as a string sextet (violins I-II, violas I-II, cellos I-II); arranged 1917 for string orchestra; revised 1943

First performed the chamber version 18 March 1902 by the Rosé Quartet and members of the court orchestra, Vienna; the orchestral version first performed in March 1918 by the Leipzig Gewandhaus Orchestra, Arthur Nikisch conducting

Published by Universal Edition (Vienna, 1917)

Duration: about 25 minutes

Formulations that begin, "If only Schoenberg had kept writing in the style of *Verklärte Nacht* . . ."—or, in the case of Stravinsky, *The Fire-*

bird—are still common. Yet both were, after all, early works, and good composers always mature. Indeed, the twenty-five-year-old Schoenberg here demonstrates such consummate understanding of the artistic principles he inherited from Wagner, Brahms, and Richard Strauss that it would have been astonishing had he *not* gone on to propose changes in the very foundations of musical style. That is what the most serious composition is all about. Besides, both Schoenberg and Stravinsky remind us again and again that a composer's only choice is to compose in the one "style" he knows—his own personal assessment of the issues at hand.

Schoenberg and Richard Dehmel, a writer of sensual, impressionistic, and socially meaningful verse, maintained a friendship and a correspondence. It was natural enough that Schoenberg should undertake to set his poems: three of the Four Songs, opus 2, likewise of autumn 1899, are to Dehmel texts. What was daring was to compose an untexted poetic reflection for string sextet, since with few exceptions chamber music is given to the most abstract modes of musical expression. Schoenberg wanted the work to have integrity of both dimensions, descriptive and absolute; the proof of his success is that on hearing a live performance Dehmel himself forgot to follow the lines, so absorbed was he in Schoenberg's luxuriant musical poetry.

A couple walks through the bare, cold forest, bathed in moonlight. The woman speaks: she, having longed for the fulfillment of motherhood, is carrying another man's child. Now she is ashamed, and life's revenge is that she has met her present companion. They walk on. The man speaks: the moonlight is the splendor of the universe, the cold dispelled by the warmth they share. And that warmth will transfigure the child into their own creation. They embrace and go on walking, now in the vast brilliance of night.

Schoenberg's setting consists of two sonatas connected by a transitional interlude, suggesting in turn the five units of dramatic action: the woman's confession and the man's response separated, introduced, and concluded by promenade passages. The obvious ritard shortly into the score indicates the end of the introduction, wherein the various atmospheres have been established. With the viola solo the exposition of the woman's stanza begins, and you should not underestimate the expanse of the first half as it progresses through its transitions, subsidiary themes, development and recapitulation. The center has been reached when the texture greatly thins and the note values broaden into quarters and halves; after a few bars comes the clear allusion to the opening promenade music, followed by a short but prominent cadenza in the first violin and two equally portentous empty bars. With the compassionate cello solo, the man's rather shorter stanza begins and the second sonata starts unfolding. The magnificent lunar nightscape at the end is of incomparable delicacy. But it's easy enough to imagine how a composer of Schoenberg's genius might conclude afterward that the old Wagner-Strauss transfiguration close had reached the end of its useful life.

Verklärte Nacht was deemed too audacious for the Vienna Composer's Guild (*Tonkünstlerverein*) concerts, where it might ordinarily have been played. But the sublimities of technique and organization and instrumental control could not long be denied—nor the power of the poetic interplay of cold and warm, dark and light, femininity and masculinity. The orchestral version of *Verklärte Nacht* makes these relationships, in my view, clearer still. The music has another life as the score of Anthony Tudor's ballet *Pillar of Fire*, where the story is somewhat different but the mood very much the same.

Five Orchestra Pieces, OP. 16

Vorgefühle (Premonitions): *Molto Allegro*
Vergangenes (Yesteryears): *Andante*
Sommermorgen an einem See (Farben) (Summer Morning by a Lake [Colors]): *Moderato*
Peripetie: Molto Allegro
Das obligate Rezitativ (The Obligatory Recitative): *Allegretto*

For (revised version) piccolos I-II, flutes I-III, oboes I-II, English horn, E♭ clarinet, clarinets I-II, bass clarinet, bassoons I-II, contrabassoon; horns I-IV, trumpets I-III, trombones I-III, tuba; timpani, bass drum, cymbals, triangle, gong, xylophone, celesta; harp; strings; first version for a still larger force of quadrupled winds with contrabass clarinet and a large brass section with 6 horns and 4 trombones

Composed 23 May–August 1909 in Vienna; revised by the composer for conventional orchestra in December 1949; revised edition dedicated "to the memory of Henri Hinrichsen, a music publisher who was a grand seigneur"

First performed 3 September 1912 at a London Promenade Concert, Henry Wood conducting

Published by C. F. Peters (Leipzig, 1912); revised edition
published by C. F. Peters Corp. (New York, 1952)
Duration: about 20 minutes

The original orchestration requires an expanded instrumental force,
including woodwinds in fours, six horns, and four trombones. Today
you will almost certainly hear Schoenberg's revision of 1949 for an
orchestra of conventional size. Schoenberg supplied the movement
titles to please his publisher, purposefully keeping them "very technical or very obscure." These he regarded as a necessity of publication
and not, he says, "to provide poetic atmosphere."

The Five Pieces come between Schoenberg's abandonment of tonality and his formulation of the principles of composing in twelve tones.
The music that results here, put simply, consists of ongoing mutation
of the motives stated early in each movement. One result is that the
music seems to simmer in a state of constant metamorphosis. In *Premonitions,* for example, you hear most of the operative material in the
first three bars: the theme in the cello, the delicate passagework, and
the hollow open fifth in the clarinets. After the ritard the ostinato
bass, organized in groups of three eighth notes, and the low chord in
bassoons and bass clarinet carry on through most of the rest of the
movement. The absence of tonality, that is, has been met with increased
detail and significance of other materials of composition, notably
rhythm, instrumental color, and, in this case, rapidly shifting dynamic
levels. *Yesteryears* presents a single melody over dissonant chordal harmony, the counterpoint increasing in complexity as the movement
develops.

Colors is perhaps the most unusual of the studies, where chords
change their color by subtle manipulation of the orchestration. The
rate of pitch change builds, the colors thus twinkling more, until
they become an impressionistic swirl. "The changes of chord," writes
Schoenberg, "have to be done with the greatest subtlety, avoiding
any accentuation by the instruments entering, such that only the change
of color is perceived." No theme or melody is attempted, though the
chord changes end up having a motivic effect. In the 1949 version
the movement is subtitled *Summer Morning by a Lake,* and, elsewhere,
Schoenberg called it *The Changing Chord.*

Peripetia is, in Greek literature, a sudden reversal of circumstance.
The movement is brief and violent, in effect canceling out the tran-

quility of *Colors*. Keep your eyes on the percussion section at the end: the percussionist is instructed to produce a "tremolo with cello bow on the edge of a cymbal." The Finale is *The Obligatory* (or perhaps "fully-developed" or "endless") *Recitative,* returning to the melodic style of the second movement, and with suggestions of the dance.

Variations for Orchestra, OP. 31

Introduktion: Mäßig, ruhig
I.   *Moderato*
II.   *Langsam*
III.   *Mäßig*
IV.   *Walzertempo*
V.   *Beschwingt*
VI.   *Andante*
VII.   *Langsam*
VIII.   *Sehr rasch*
IX.   *L'istesso tempo, aber etwas langsamer*
Finale: Mäßig schnell

For piccolos I-II, flutes I-IV, oboes I-IV, English horn, E♭ clarinet, clarinets I-IV, bass clarinet, bassoons I-IV, contrabassoon; horns I-IV, trumpets I-III, trombones I-IV, tuba; timpani, snare drum, bass drum, cymbals, triangle, tamtam, tambourine, bells, xylophone, flexatone, harp, celesta, mandolin; strings

Composed May 1926–20 September 1928; sketched in Berlin, completed at Roquebrune, French Riviera

First performed 2 December 1928 by the Berlin Philharmonic Orchestra, Wilhelm Furtwängler conducting

Published by Universal Edition (Vienna, 1929)

Duration: about 20 minutes

Both artistic heritage and the "laws" Schoenberg had developed drew him to variation procedures. His Viennese predecessor Brahms had been a master of variation technique, and one of the implications of his own theorizing was that it could effectively replace the tonally-driven sonata structure. Here, in his first twelve-tone work for orchestra, Schoenberg practices what he calls developing variation, where the character of each new variation is born of all that has come before, growing generally in speed and size toward a massive finale. (It's not that revolutionary an idea, with precedents, for example, in Beethoven, Brahms, and Elgar.) The interesting twist is Schoenberg's use of the hallowed B–A–C–H motive (that is, B♭–A–C–B♮), heard prominently in the solo trombone toward the end of the introduction and grandly in the finale. This represents, I think, a simple salute to the Leipzig master, not confession of a secret model. Composers love to build this sort of reference into their music; hiding the *Tristan* chord (see p. 631) in love scenes is equally common.

After a slow, prevailingly delicate introduction, the cello section states the theme over restful chords elsewhere. The nine variations that follow are easy to distinguish from one another on the basis of marked changes of texture, tempo, and orchestration. The second variation, for example, is for the principal players, where the first had been for full orchestra. (This alternation of chamber and full ensembles goes on.) The third introduces a brittle ostinato in sixteenths and prominent percussion—notably the flexatone, a souped-up musical saw; the fourth is a merry waltz, with the four sixteenths from the previous movement serving as a kind of bolero accompaniment in harp, celesta, and mandolin.

Variation V is the big central movement, of slow motion and broad theme in the violins, dwelling on the interval of the half step; VI is a short Andante. Variation VII is a contemplation of orchestral transparency, the solo line in the bassoon and the filigree reflecting textures we have heard in the introduction. A rude variation follows, with canonic devices in the winds, and these canons continue, subdued, in the ninth variation.

Now the finale, with the B–A–C–H motive sounding first in the tremolo of violins and, shortly afterward, with greater insistence in the cello and double-bass; a scherzando ensues, then, as the work begins to draw to a close, a Presto with increased emphasis on the original motive. The finale, which is as long as the sum of all the variations, is the ultimate development, where according to the composer the "images move toward each other, link up to form a circle, and in anticipation of the conclusion enforce the adoption of a new form."

The long gestation of the Variations, Schoenberg tells us, has to do with his having lost his train of thought in 1926; two years later he stumbled on an old sketch that reestablished his direction. This is the fate of builders, he says: "to have a plan of construction, to lose it and, what is worse, to find it again."

A Survivor from Warsaw, OP. 46

> For narrator; unison male chorus; piccolos I-II, flutes I-II, oboes I-II, clarinets I-II, bassoons I-II; horns I-IV, trumpets I-III, trombones I-III, tuba; timpani, military drum, bass drum, cymbals, triangle, tambourine, tam-tam, castanets, bells, chimes, xylophone; harp; strings
>
> Text by the composer
>
> Composed 1946–23 August 1947 in Los Angeles to a commission from the Koussevitzky Music Foundation; dedicated to the memory of Natalie Koussevitzky.
>
> First performed 4 November 1948 by the Albuquerque Civic Symphony, Kurt Frederick conducting
>
> Published by Bomart Music Publications (New York, 1949)
>
> Duration: about 10 minutes

Perhaps the blackest atrocity of Nazism was the leveling of the Warsaw ghetto in February 1943. The numbers are appalling: of the half-million Jews originally walled up in the space of a few city blocks, most by then had starved or been sent to the camps. The insurrection that February was fought largely in the sewers and tunnels under the streets. Every Jew, eventually, was killed or herded away.

Schoenberg's cry of outrage may surprise you in its economy, for there's nothing so immediately frightful as, say, the screaming in Penderecki's *Threnody for the Victims of Hiroshima* (see p. 416). Yet *A Survivor From Warsaw* is a work of equal terror. Harsh trumpet calls and obsessive drumming—both in the percussion and in the percussive effects spread throughout the orchestra—define the bloody surrounding. The narrator, in *Sprechstimme,* begins his account as though in a daze, unable to recall how he survived the sewers. Reveille sounds; the Jews, exhausted, old, and ill, try to evacuate. But it is too late. The soldiers, barking their orders in German, beat everyone and leave the fallen to die. The rest are lined up and sent away—faster and faster, like a stampede of wild horses—to the gas chambers. Suddenly, in the midst of the chaos, the Jews begin to sing the ancient

Hebrew creed: *Shema Yisroel* ("Hear, o Israel: the Lord thy God is one god," etc.).

If you believe that serial music is powerless to express such profundities, take a close listen here. Virtually every nuance of the text is illustrated in the surrounding music. The stampede of wild horses, for example, in confused triplet rhythms; the commotion of the fleeing Jews and arrival of the soldiers as described in a long and, for Schoenberg, uncommon episode for percussion; the dignity of the choral *Shema* rising through the collapse as the Jews go to their certain death. Everywhere there is violence: unusual trills and flutter tongues in the winds, biting *col legno* (with the wood of the bow) and *sul ponticello* (at the bridge) in the strings. And, always, the drumming rhythms.

Franz Schubert

Born 31 *January 1797 in Vienna*
Died 19 *November 1828 in Vienna*

Son of a Viennese schoolmaster, Schubert learned the violin, singing, and piano from members of the family and was destined for a
career in elementary school teaching. He entered the Imperial Semi-
nary as a choirboy in 1808, at the age of 11, and duly impressed his
colleagues and teachers with his musical aptitude and skill on the
violin. (The rather forbidding formal name of this institution, the
k. k. Stadtkonvikt, doesn't mean what you might think.) The school
orchestra met every night after dinner, and in the course of their
rehearsing covered the major repertoire of Haydn, Mozart, and Beethoven. These *soirées orchestrales,* so to speak, were a major formative
influence; another began when Schubert was taken on as a pupil by
Antonio Salieri, mentor of Beethoven and Liszt. By 1814 he was
teaching in his father's school and well embarked on his musical career;

that year, indeed, he composed one of his best songs, *Gretchen am Spinnrade* (Gretchen at the Spinning Wheel, to a text from Goethe's *Faust*).

Little by little Schubert gave up school teaching in favor of serious composition, making Vienna his permanent home after 1818. A coterie of admiring friends encouraged and helped support him; his reputation grew steadily. The success of the Schubertiads, evenings of his solo song and chamber pieces played before a drawing room filled with friends, was legendary. Schubert and Beethoven, incidentally, only met once toward the end of their careers, though Beethoven spoke highly of Schubert's songs. Toward the end of his life, Schubert enjoyed a degree of financial and artistic success mostly attributable to his lieder. His great works in other genres, however, were almost totally ignored. Not until the last months of his life was there a concert of his orchestral music.

In 1827 Schubert began to decline from an unspecified brain disorder, perhaps syphillitic in origin; in November 1828 he contracted typhoid and died, at the age of thirty-one. At his own request he was buried a few yards from Beethoven. (Now, in a different cemetery, the graves of Beethoven, Schubert, and Brahms are proximate to each other.) He had composed music for less than two decades.

The only native Viennese of the Viennese composers, Schubert was also the least formally schooled in composition. But his industry and imagination, his unsurpassed gift of melody, and his radical ideas on harmonic structure were intellectual challenges all but the equal of Beethoven's. His working habit was to sketch out quantities of ideas, then return to them later for fleshing out and completion. When he died in mid-career, dozens of pieces were left unfinished. Since his major instrumental works had not so far been performed, there was considerable confusion (which has lasted well into the present century) about exactly what he had composed. The "Great" C-Major Symphony was not performed until 1839; the two movements of the "Unfinished" were not heard in public until 1865. This situation accounts in part for the bizarre numeration of the Schubert symphonies. The scholar Otto Eric Deutsch has dealt with the many mysteries of Schubert chronology by creating a catalog in which each work is given a D. number.

Schubert wrote seven complete symphonies and fragments of six others, six fine masses for chorus and orchestra, the incidental music to a play called *Rosamunde,* and a number of operas (all of them post-humously produced, and in which are found some of Schubert's most interesting ideas). Deustch, *The New Grove Dictionary,* and informed program annotators have adopted the following numeration of the symphonies: Symphony No. 5 in B♭ Major (D. 485), Symphony No. 6 in C ("Little C-Major," D. 589), Symphony No. 7 in E Minor (D. 729: unfinished, but not *the* Unfinished), Symphony No. 8 in B Minor ("Unfinished," D. 759), and the Symphony No. 9 in C ("Great C-Major," D. 944). Also, of course, there are the 600 songs, solo piano music, and exquisite string trios, quartets, and quintets.

Symphony No. 4 in C Minor ("Tragic"), D. 417

Adagio molto; Allegro vivace
Andante
Menuetto: Allegro vivace
Allegro

For flutes I-II, oboes I-II, clarinets I-II, bassoons I-II; horns I-IV, trumpets I-II; timpani; strings
Composed spring 1816 in Vienna; completed 27 April 1816
First performed (posthumously) 19 November 1849 at the Leipzig Book Exchange, A. F. Riccius conducting (no known performances during the composer's lifetime)
Published by Breitkopf & Härtel (Leipzig, 1884). *Inexpensive score:* Franz Schubert: *Four Symphonies in Full Score* (New York: Dover, 1978)
Duration: about 30 minutes

It isn't really tragic, though Schubert himself decribed the Fourth Symphony that way. Restless and unsettled are, rather, the terms that come to mind. Though by no means slight, it has neither the scale nor the depth of sentiment and subsequent release or transfiguration required for true tragedy.

The first movement seems almost operatic. The slow chromatic introduction with long, ominous chords at the beginning and in the middle and little triplet falls from the high wind, suggests influences from the stage and oratorio of the preceding generation. The *Allegro vivace* is nearly monothematic in its singular emphasis on the dashing initial subject: every new idea seems to telescope out from it, and things are going by so fast that you may not even notice the new key and putatively contrastive theme; the repeat of the exposition thus comes as a surprise. Where the development begins, with the loud unison sequence based on the main theme, is clear enough; but then comes a statement that sounds suspiciously like recapitulation, and isn't—for the working out continues. *Then* comes something that sounds note-for-note recapitulatory, all right, but in a different register than before: lower, a shade tamer. In fact, in a standard Schubert ploy, the recapitulating begins in the "wrong" key. This allows the harmonic relationships of the exposition to continue to flourish at the end, there to set up the big C-major conclusion that had been approached but then deflected in the exposition.

In the *Andante,* Schubert contrasts the intimate and reassuring material stated by the string choir in the first section with the urgent upward thrusts and sixteenth-note accompanying textures at the sharp turn to the minor mode. The principal material retains its basic identity for each of its three episodes—beginning, middle, and end— while the recapitulation of the second section involves both an adjustment of key and horizontal extension. But it is not so much the ordering of the segments that carries the movement as all the lingerings, mostly in the woodwinds, once the statements have been got out of the way: the woodwind dialogues, the seams at the junctures, the poetic turns of the harmony, and the way the continuous sixteenths carry into the last statement of the main theme, then at the end slow into triplets.

All the two-by-two accents and unusual chromatic shifts in the minuet (or is it more like a Beethoven scherzo?) may keep you from hearing the $\frac{3}{4}$ and the true phrase shapes until the much clearer downbeats of the second strain. The trio begins in square fashion with rural scoring and instrumentation but goes on with striking tonal digressions and Romantic surges of the upbeat figure. One's bearings become well enough established that the *da capo* has an unusually revelatory character. A good performance will push right ahead, allowing the stormy finale to well up from the cellos and bassoons. Here the primary sensation is once more of restlessness, as the driving eighth notes of the accompaniment never really stop. This becomes extravagant—and delightful—beneath the sighs of the intermediate theme and positively swashbuckling as it reaches victory at the second group. The harmonic ingenuity that has characerized the whole symphony continues unabated, such that when the final C major is achieved, you cannot help thinking of Beethoven.

Symphony No. 5 in B♭ Major, D. 485

Allegro
Andante con moto
Menuetto: Allegro molto
Allegro vivace

For flute, oboes I-II, bassoons I-II; horns I-II; strings
Composed September–3 October 1816 in Vienna
First performed in the spring of 1816 in a salon concert at the home of Otto Hatwig, Vienna—as was the Sixth ("Little" C-Major) Symphony; Schubert played viola; first performed before the public 17 October 1841 in the Theater in der Josefstadt, Vienna, Michael Leitermayer conducting
Published by Breitkopf & Härtel (Leipzig, 1885). *Inexpensive score:* Franz Schubert: *Four Symphonies in Full Score* (New York: Dover, 1978)
Duration: about 30 minutes

Schubert's Fifth, a jewel of rare clarity, is very nearly the last "little" symphony of the great age of Viennese Classicism. Just how delicate it is can be demonstrated by comparing it with Beethoven's Eighth, also considered a smallish work and its near contemporary. In this case the scale is matched by a corresponding restraint of the orchestral force, which lacks clarinets, trumpets, and timpani and boasts only a single flute. Schubert's middle symphonies, the Third through the Sixth, were probably written for the orchestra of two dozen or so that had grown from the Schubert family string quartet. When they outgrew Schubert's dwellings they eventually moved to the drawing room of the violinist Otto Hatwig. There the Fifth Symphony was first performed.

Concision, properly handled, can result in rare power of expression. That much is clear from the four opening bars, where the plainest of chord progressions in the winds and the scamper of violins beneath unveil a dainty first theme in the fashion of the old *style galant,* echoed in the bass instruments; the winds enter again at the end of the phrase. Not that what follows is remotely fragile. Early on the melody is colored by chromatic alteration, and in the restatement the flute suggests a new countermelody; in the tutti bridge echoes between the outer voices are quite forceful. The position of the second theme is made clear by the half bar of rest that precedes it. As before, strings begin and are joined by winds, and now the intensifying chromaticism is stronger still, prominently affecting the unusual decrescendo cadence. So it is not surprising when the distant tonality (D♭ major) that has been so frequently suggested comes to the fore at the beginning of the development. This sort of thing is not old fashioned at all, but decidedly Romantic.

Similar harmonic vocabulary, indeed, is to be heard in the *Andante con moto,* where the wistful thematic material, sighing with thirty-second-note falls and turns, is tinted with chromatic nuance of accompaniment in nearly every bar. The harmonic shift for the second big section is something sensational. After an excursion of great tonal fluidity the main theme returns unadorned and then richly ornamented. Both the excursion and the theme recapitulate.

The minuet should remind you of the third movements of Mozart's G-Minor and of Beethoven's Fifth. Every particular that lends the minuet its stern weight is deflected in the trio—major of mode and not minor, arpeggiating down where the minuet had risen, and legato rather than marcato. Note, as well, the long and developmental extension of the minuet's second phrase.

The *Allegro vivace* is a bright, many-themed sonata with internal repeats that give it some rondo-like characteristics. Just after the theme is stated, for example, there is a leisurely departure and return enclosed in repeat brackets. The purple patch is the transition. After the fermata comes the true second theme and a merry closing passage in triplets, with a repeat back to the purple patch. Once all that is achieved, the process of developing and recapitulating carries on in the traditional manner.

Symphony No. 8 in B Minor ("Unfinished"), D. 759

Allegro moderato
Andante con moto
[*Allegro:* unfinished]

For flutes I-II, oboes I-II, clarinets I-II, bassoons I-II; horns I-II, trumpets I-II, trombones I-III; timpani; strings

Begun 30 October 1822; abandoned toward the end of the year; promised when half complete to the Styrian Music Society of Graz in gratitude for an honorary membership, April 1823

First performed (posthumously) 17 December 1865 by the Vienna Gesellschaft der Musikfreunde, Johann Herbeck conducting

Published by C. A. Spina (Vienna, 1867). *Inexpensive scores:* Franz Schubert: *Four Symphonies in Full Score* (New York: Dover, 1978); Schubert: *Symphony in B Minor ("Unfinished")*, ed. Martin Chusid, A Norton Critical Score (New York: Norton, 1971)

Duration: about 30 minutes

After the Sixth Symphony, a smallish work, Schubert felt obliged to demonstrate his seriousness of purpose by way of a *große Symphonie*. The "Unfinished" was the fourth of five attempts: the others include two abandoned efforts in D major, a Seventh Symphony for large orchestra in four movements some three-quarters complete, and the "Great C-Major" Symphony. (Reconstructive operations have been performed by Brian Newbould on all the manuscript sources that lend themselves to fleshing out, and recorded by Neville Marriner and the Academy of St. Martin in the Fields.)

Schubert set aside the work on his B-Minor Symphony at the end of 1822, more than five years before he died. He had completed and scored the first two movements and sketched a good deal of the scherzo, with the melody line complete through the first half of the trio. The first twenty bars of the scherzo, about two pages' worth, had been fully scored. The closing months of 1822 also marked the onset of Schubert's ill health. His failure to finish the work may thus have something to do with its negative associations.

The autograph manuscript passsed from the composer to his friends Josef and Anselm Hüttenbrenner, possibly in payment of a debt. Unaccountably, the work was kept from the public for more than forty years, though progressively more specific allusions to it appear in the press beginning in the 1850s. The first performance in Vienna in 1865 was followed by offerings in Leipzig, London, and Graz, and a score and parts were soon published.

And so it was that after Schubert's death there were rumors of another symphony, on a par with the "Great C-Major." The romance of the tale is not the least of the factors which led to the immense popularity of the "Unfinished" in the late ninteenth century. Yet its reputation—legend or no—is justly earned, for the B-Minor Symphony is by any measure one of Schubert's masterworks.

Most listeners know of the "Unfinished" by the great cello theme in the first movement, an inspired melody by a composer revered as a writer of song. The first movement's structure, though, is worthy of rather more detailed attention, most of all for its contrasts of texture and its outbursts of pathos—the passages seen by one writer as eruptions of a volcanic temperament lurking just beneath a usually tranquil demeanor. In this movement, Schubert is on the whole less concerned with balance and symmetry than he is with harmonic adventure and novel thematic juxtaposition.

The movement opens with an eight-bar phrase, part introduction and part main theme, in the cellos and basses; this dual role will have greater meaning later in the movement. The next thematic idea, set over the pulsating strings, is the melancholy tune in oboe and clarinet. With an abrupt cadence in B minor, horns and bassoons modulate during the space of three chords to the discernably passive key of G major. Now occurs the famous theme, interrupted by a bar's pause and an explosion of harmonic color—a purple patch. The next section, developmental in character, yields to a codetta, but rather than a formal closing figure in the style of Haydn and Mozart, Schubert refashions and concludes the interrupted second theme.

The development dwells on the musical material of the opening eight bars, treating it with ever increasing harmonic and textural urgency and introducing an insistently percussive dotted figure. All at once the tempestuousness subsides into recapitulation. But it is not the very beginning of the exposition that we hear, but rather the oboe-and-clarinet theme. Those first eight bars, so formidably treated in the development, are saved for the coda. The effect is to leave the placid second theme surrounded by mystery.

In the second movement, *Andante con moto,* the constituent themes develop as they go. As before, the tonality is adventurous. Particularly intriguing, for a movement in E Major, is the appearance in the coda of a taste of A♭ major—light years away from Classical norms, and a good reminder of the way Schubert draws the curtain on Viennese Classicism by planting one foot, at least, firmly in the future.

Symphony No. 9 in C Major ("Great C-Major"), D. 944

Andante; Allegro ma non troppo
Andante con moto
Scherzo: Allegro vivace
Allegro vivace

For flutes I-II, oboes I-II, clarinets I-II, bassoons I-II; horns I-II,
trumpets I-II, trombones I-III; timpani; strings

Composed in all probability, during the composer's summer
holiday in Gmunden and Gastein in 1825; the autograph score
bears the date March 1828

First performed (posthumously) 21 March 1839 by the Leipzig
Gewandhaus Orchestra, Mendelssohn conducting

Published by Breitkopf & Härtel (Leipzig, 1840). *Inexpensive score:*
Franz Schubert: *Four Symphonies in Full Score* (New York: Dover,
1978)

Duration: about 45 minutes

With the "Great C-Major," Schubert finally finished the *große Symphonie* he had essayed so often in the 1820s without success. Never before had he written on such a scale, or controlled so deftly materials such as these. In it he shows a consummate understanding of the principles of space, rhythmic vitality, and forward propulsion. Schumann, with his customary insight, wrote of the first performance in 1839: "I say quite frankly that he who is not acquainted with this symphony knows but little of Schubert." It was worthy, he thought, to be compared to the greatest in Beethoven.

You get a sense of the proportions involved when the introductory *Andante* seems so disinclined to hurry anywhere. Unison horns state the principal theme quietly and unaccompanied, and for that matter there seems little imperative in the elementary rhythms and contours it describes. The last two measures, echoing the one just before, are positively unnerving in their stasis. The woodwinds extend the idea and then fade away. Only then does there come a *fortissimo*, a gesture that allows the more typical function of slow introductions—getting to the *Allegro*—to begin. During the soft woodwind restatement two further elements are introduced in the accompaniment, the triplets in the violins and dotted rhythms in the bass.

In fact, these become the controling motives of the *Allegro*, built of the pounding unisons in the strings answered by a crescendo of triplets—harmonized, but not especially melodic—in the winds. In due course a new subject is heard from the band, the vaguely Hungarian figure begun by the pairs of clarinets and bassoons in parallel intervals, and under the circumstances the shift into motion by quarter notes is radical. The development brings together the three motives of course, but what is gripping is the fall away in volume and then the great crescendo to recapitulation. Schubert extends an already expansive movement still further with a long coda, *più mosso,* that returns to the initial horn theme.

These elemental rhythms continue their hold. In the *Andante* it is a matter of continuous eighths, contrasted with the pert turns and ornaments of the oboe theme. Again the atmosphere is vaguely exotic, the suggestion of the long swell and fade perhaps that of some passing procession.

The *Scherzo* is about four times bigger than the typical Viennese third movement, each of its sections carrying on for pages. What extends the length is all the trading around of material; the first section takes plenty of time getting to the new key and introduces a new theme along the way; the second works the main theme into all sorts of guises, including a striking series of gambols down through the orchestral voices. The eight-bar introduction to the trio is nothing more than a crescendo of reiterated pitches, setting the stage for the many repetitions to follow and announcing the prominence of the wind.

You know by now you are in for a giant finale. It is a massive sonata with all the suggestions of victory that can be unleashed. There are many allusions to the other movements: the colloquy of triplets and dotted figures, the winds in parallel thirds, the repeated notes that introduce and characterize the second theme. And, of course, all the interest in visiting Romantic key areas.

Schubert never heard a complete performance: the C-Major Symphony was abandoned by the ordinarily courageous Gesellschaft der Musikfreunde as too difficult. The manuscript passed to Schubert's brother Ferdinand, who made its existence known to Schumann. He, in turn, brought it to Mendelssohn's attention, and this led to the first performance by the eminent Gewandhaus Orchestra of Leipzig though, it is said, severely cut.

Overture and Incidental Music from *Rosamunde,* OP. 26
(D. 797)

Overture: Andante; Allegro vivace
Entr'acte Music I: Allegro molto moderato
Entr'acte Music II: Andantino
Ballet Music I: Allegro moderato; Andante un poco assai
Ballet Music II: Andantino

For flutes I-II, oboes I-II, clarinets I-II, bassoons I-II; horns I-II,
    trumpets I-II, trombones I-III; timpani; strings; the overture
    has four horns
Composed winter 1823 in Vienna
First performed 20 December 1823 with the play *Rosamunde* at
    the Theater an der Wien; the overture is that of *Die Zauberharfe*
    (The Magic Harp, D. 644), first performed 19 August 1820
    (see below)
Published by C. A. Spina (Vienna, 1866–67)
Duration: overture, about 10 minutes; incidental music, about 15
    minutes

Rosamunde, Princess of Cypress, a four-act play by Helmina von Chézy,
opened in December 1823 and closed two nights later. Though the
text has been lost, newspapers of the time give all-too-accurate accounts
of the plot. The Princess Rosamunde, raised secretly as a shepherdess,
has been denied her rightful throne. The handsome prince Alfonso
survives a shipwreck and pirates, and succeeds in redirecting a letter
written in poison ink from its intended victim, Rosamunde, back to
the villain. Rosamunde and Alfonso are wed and accede jointly to the
throne of Cyprus.

    Schubert's incidental music includes the overture and three entr'actes,
ballet music, a romanze, and choruses of ghosts, shepherds, and hunters. The romanze and subsequently the choruses were offered for sale
in the 1820s with a four-hand arrangement of the overture to *Die
Zauberharfe,* D. 644. But it was not until 1867, when uncovering
Schubert sources was at the height of its vogue, that two noted English
tourists in Vienna—Arthur Sullivan, the composer, and George Grove,
the lexicographer—drew attention to the original performance material. The complete incidental music was revived at a concert of the
Gesellschaft der Musikfreunde that December.

    The traditional orchestral suite is comprised of the overture, the famous *Andantino* entr'acte, and the concluding ballet music II, to which either of the other two movements may be added. The overture, which is in C major, begins with a slow introduction typical of theatre pieces of the time—minor mode, a sinister chord progression, a pastoral theme that develops into a transition—and continues as a brisk sonata. Its particular interest lies in how close Schubert gets to the Rossini style on the one hand (the ostinato of cellos beneath the lyric theme for clarinet and bassoon becomes a galloping crescendo), and to the rhythmic and harmonic world of the *Midsummer Night's Dream* on the other. The coda shifts into a fast $\frac{6}{8}$.

The famous lullaby melody of entr'acte II was a favorite of Schubert himself: it appears, too, in the second movement of the A-Minor String Quartet, D. 804 (1824) and in the third of the Four Impromptus for piano, D. 935 (1827). In structure the entr'acte resembles a symphonic third movement with two *minore* trios. The second of these is drawn from the song *Der Leidende*, D. 432 (1816). Ballet music II is the last-act *divertissement*, a contradance of Hungarian sentiment. The first section moves into the minor mode and out again to a drone episode for clarinet and flute before its tutti close; the band trios turn to $\frac{6}{8}$, then effect a retransition to $\frac{2}{4}$ for the *da capo*.

Entr'acte music I is an overture-length sonata, commencing with triplet upbeats and a unison advance on the dominant key and a fermata. Ballet music I begins with the identical passage, then goes on with a half-dozen sections for dancing based on the motives from the entr'acte. The concluding *Andante un poco assai* is actually a separate movement, much in the style of entr'acte II and highly appropriate for drawing into the concert suite.

Mass No. 6 in E♭ Major, D. 950

> *Kyrie: Andante con moto, quasi Allegretto*
> *Gloria: Allegro moderato e maestoso*
> *Credo: Moderato*
> *Sanctus: Adagio*
> *Benedictus: Andante*
> *Agnus Dei: Andante con moto*

> **For** soloists (SATTB); chorus; oboes I-II, clarinets I-II, bassoons I-II; horns I-II, trumpets I-II, trombones I-III; timpani; strings
> **Composed** June–September 1828 in Vienna

First performed 4 October 1829 in the Dreifaltigkeits-Kirche of
Alser, Vienna, Ferdinand Schubert conducting
Published by J. Rieter-Biedermann (Leipzig and Winterthur,
1865)
Duration: about 65 minutes

The works of Schubert's last weeks were the *Schwanengesang,* the great
C-Minor String Quintet, three piano sonatas, and the Mass in E♭.
The mass was completed, probably, by the beginning of October. On
4 November he had his first and only lesson in counterpoint with
Simon Sechter, the foremost master of theory in Vienna; in just over
two weeks, he was dead.

The previous June he had begun work on a sixth mass for presentation by a new Society for the Performance of Church Music, founded
that October. Instead it was given posthumously, on the society's first
anniversary, 4 October 1829, in the parish church of Alser, a Viennese suburb. Schubert's brother Ferdinand conducted.

Schubert was right to consider the mass one of the best examples
of his striving "for the highest in art," and to think it on a par with
his three operas and the great C-Major Symphony. Few choral works
of the period show such sustained and exquisite lyricism, or such an
active role for the orchestra. The sonority of the two clarinets and
three trombones, associated both with Freemasonry in Vienna and
with music at the graveside, is utterly breathtaking. Most memorable, to my ear, are the quiet passages: the *Kyrie,* the "Gratias agimus
tibi" in the *Gloria,* the loving *Benedictus,* and the wonderful closing
Dona nobis pacem. At the very center of the work, in the *Credo,* is an
exquisite barcarole for soprano and two tenors ("Et incarnatus est"),
with sinister choral reponses of the Crucifixus text. Though put off
until the *Benedictus* and *Dona nobis pacem* at the end, the work for solo
quartet is equally lovely.

Contrasted with these riches are the savage, perhaps morbid thrusts
of the G-minor "Domine deus" in the *Gloria* and the closely related
C-minor *Agnus Dei.* A third structural element is the fugue for chorus
doubled by the instrumental force. Both the "Cum Sancto Spirito" in
the *Gloria* and the "Et vitam venturi saeculi, amen" are long, full-
blown displays of the most rigorous device and craft. Schubert's contrapuntal dexterity makes you wonder why he thought he needed
lessons.

We too seldom find the Viennese masses—those of Mozart, Haydn, Schubert, and Beethoven—programed by our symphony orchestras. That situation is particularly disappointing in the case of Schubert's E♭ Mass, which concludes and in a way summarizes his work.

Robert Schumann

Born 8 June 1810 in Zwickau
Died 29 July 1856 in Endenich, near Bonn

Schumann was, with Berlioz, Mendelssohn, and Liszt, a founder of Romanticism in music; like them he possessed a keen intelligence, excellent education, literary accomplishment, and expertise as a performer. He was the fifth child born to well-bred parents who owned a publishing house and lending library. By the time he left Zwickau to matriculate in law at the University of Leipzig, Schumann had shown gifts in both music and creative writing; even in his teens he was passionately fond of Schubert's music and the eccentric prose of Jean Paul (i.e., Jean Paul Richter).

It is said that at the university Schumann failed to attend a single lecture in law. During a year of study at the University of Heidelberg, he made the acquaintance of a circle of music lovers and learned a great deal of repertoire during soirées of chamber music. Upon returning to Leipzig, he took lodging with the eminent piano teacher, Friedrich Wieck. His life was growing progressively unhappy: Wieck was more interested in the professional promise of his daughter Clara, and Schumann was meanwhile developing addictions to drink and tobacco, uncertain about sex, and increasingly certain that he suffered from the mental disease that ran in his family. Nevertheless, he had begun to produce fine compositions confirming his wide acquaintance with recent trends in musical style, notably those set by Paganini (whom he had heard) and Chopin. In 1832, after of an injury to his right hand, he had to abandon whatever hopes he had ever entertained for a career as virtuoso pianist.

A flirtation and short engagement in 1834 to a young woman named Ernestine is immortalized in one of Schumann's greatest compositions for solo piano, *Carnaval,* in which she and her hometown figure among the musical portraits and epigrams. This was also the year he founded the *Neue Leipziger Zeitschrift für Musik* (New Leipzig Newspaper for Music), signing his editorial columns either Florestan, Eusebius, or Master Raro, testimony to the wide range of his critical attitudes and a hint of his schizophrenia. His true love was Clara Wieck; after several years of passionate correspondence, courtship, and legal wrangling with Clara's father, the two were married in 1840. Their happiness was expressed in Schumann's "year of song" (during which he wrote song cycles to poems of Heine and Eichendorff, *Frauenliebe und -leben,* and *Dichterliebe*) and, shortly thereafter, the completion of his First Symphony.

For six years (1844–50) the Schumanns lived in Dresden, where Robert taught piano students privately and composed assiduously. Schumann then succeeded Ferdinand Hiller as director of musical activities in Düsseldorf. It cannot be said that he was a success as conductor, and his increasingly psychotic episodes—involving cosmic noise and the cries of angels and devils—hindered his professional standing. In desperation he threw himself into the Rhine; rescued by fishermen, he was sent to a nearby asylum, where two years later he died. Brahms, who had met the Schumanns in 1854, attended Clara and her family during this tragic period; their attachment may have been romantic, but it was so tactful that we can discern only its traces. They separated gracefully, and Clara devoted the rest of her days to assuring performance and publication of her husband's works. A great piano virtuoso and gifted composer, Clara is, withal, one of the noblest figures in the history of music.

Schumann composed four symphonies: B♭ major, op. 38 (1841), C major, op. 61 (1846), E♭ major, op. 97 (1850), and D minor, op. 120 (1851). The Piano Concerto in A Minor, op. 54 (1845), is one of the most popular of the nineteenth century; additionally, Schumann composed a successful Concert Piece for Four Horns, op. 86 (1849), and a Cello Concerto, op. 129 (1850).

Symphony No. 1 in B♭ Major, OP. 38 ("Spring")

Andante un poco maestoso; Allegro molto vivace
Larghetto
Scherzo: Molto vivace
Allegro animato e grazioso
[No pause between movements II and III]

For flutes I-II, oboes I-II, clarinets I-II, bassoons I-II; horns I-IV, trumpets I-II, trombones I-III; timpani, triangle; strings
Composed 23 January–20 February 1841 in Leipzig; dedicated to Friedrich August, King of Saxony
First performed 31 March 1841 by the Leipzig Gewandhaus Orchestra, Mendelssohn conducting
Published by Breitkopf & Härtel (Leipzig, 1853). *Inexpensive score:* Robert Schumann: *Complete Symphonies in Full Score* (New York: Dover, 1980
Duration: about 35 minutes.

Schumann composed this work, sketched in four days, under the influence of a springtime poem by Adolf Böttger (1815–70). The movements originally had titles ("Spring's Awakening, Evening, Merry Playmates, Spring's Farewell"), but as composers often do, Schumann had second thoughts about the program and withdrew it. By that time, however, he had written to several friends of the spring theme. Once before he had begun a symphony, only to abandon it; now, in his first year of marriage, Clara was urging him to undertake symphonic work again. "It isn't my turn to keep the diary this week," she wrote in mid-January 1841, "but when your husband is writing a symphony he must be excused from other things."

On the first pass it's not clear whether the horn and trumpet fanfare, stark and in unison, bodes good or evil. When in the third bar the rest of the orchestra dives in with the great waves that come next, the association with positive elemental forces establishes itself well. The introduction works through various atmospheric allusions, including a prominent chromatic fall in the flute and oboe, and then gurgles, presumably avian, in the flute and clarinet. A tumbling crescendo in the horns effects the elision to the *Allegro*, thus releasing the pent-up excitement implied by both the program and the fanfares. In my view this is one of Schumann's best movements, the dancing merriment enhanced by all the scampering in the first group, the wiggle in the violas underneath the second theme, and, as the momentum builds to cadence, a breathtaking sally away from the promised goal. There's serious working out of challenges in the development—note the entry of the triangle—that culminates in the opening fanfare, now even more vigorous than before. Here Schumann embarks on a flight of fancy: the first theme doesn't really recapitulate so much as carry on developmentally. The second theme goes by in more or less traditional fashion; then, at the acceleration, there begins what sounds for a while like true finality in the home key and a proper last dealing with the theme. But things get digressive again and veer off into a luscious Romantic outpouring for which there has been no precedent established. Eventually the fanfare pushes through to allow for an intrepid close.

The *Larghetto* is a series of reflections on the long theme stated by the first violins, less symmetrical than fluid of turn, and with ornaments of consummate delicacy. Stanzas for cello and woodwinds are linked by freer modulatory passages; the textures are progressively opulent. The solemn progression in the three trombones at the very end starts as though intending to confirm a *religioso* cadence, but in fact is a premonition of the *Scherzo*. In the *Scherzo*, too, Schumann makes of a traditional form something of great novelty. The chromaticism and metric tensions are common enough, but it's unusual to have a true second theme in the *Scherzo* and pretty much unprecedented to have two different trios. The first of these, in duple meter, has the same rhythmic impetus that powered the first movement; the second introduces material that sounds as though it should have come in the *Scherzo* proper, with little if any trio character. Another suprise: after the first strain of the *Scherzo* returns, there begins a coda based on the second strain but lifted into the major mode, followed and concluded by memories of the first trio.

The bold introductory gesture of the last movement becomes thematic in due course, though the principal material is, for the most part, in the character of a cordial polonaise. The elfin turn in the minor mode serves in part to reintroduce the opening figure on its way to becoming the closing theme. The development becomes stormy, with trombones, almost at once; this clears with the distant horn calls and flute cadenza. After a straightforward recapitulation, the storminess returns for a moment, but only to set up a closing resolution of stress.

Symphony No. 3 in E♭ Major, OP. 97 ("Rhenish")

Lebhaft
Scherzo: Sehr mäßig
Nicht schnell
Feierlich (Solemn)
Lebhaft

For flutes I-II, oboes I-II, clarinets I-II, bassoons I-II; horns I-IV, trumpets I-II, trombones I-III; timpani; strings

Begun 2 November 1850 in Düsseldorf; completed in five weeks, by early December

First performed 6 February 1851 by the Düsseldorf Orchestra, Schumann conducting; performed later in the month in Cologne and again in Düsseldorf in early March

Published by N. Simrock (Bonn, 1851). *Inexpensive score:* Robert Schumann: *Complete Symphonies in Full Score* (New York: Dover, 1980)

Duration: about 35 minutes

In September 1850 the Schumanns moved to the Rhineland, where Robert was to become music director of the Düsseldorf orchestra. It was a radical change in their lives. Late in September they visited the ancient and honorable city of Cologne, overwhelmed by their first sight of the august cathedral there, bathed in sunlight. Anxious to make a good first impression on the proud folk of the Rhineland, Schumann began a symphony "of the Rhine": the "Rhenish."

Schumann dwells on the majesty of his chosen key and the imposing character of French horns, trumpets, and timpani. The first movement is a large sonata with no repeat and a prominent but quite false recapitulation before the real thing. The second movement, marked *Scherzo,* is in fact a Ländler, a bucolic folk-waltz, which Schumann meant to suggest morning on the Rhine. The third is a sonata-imbued intermezzo of three themes. The fourth, an "extra" movement, which serves to anticipate the finale, has to do with the Cologne Cathedral itself; the Schumanns had seen it in readiness to elevate the local archbishop to the rank of cardinal, and Robert subsequently headed his manuscript "like the musical accompaniment for a solemn ceremony." Trombones enter here for the first time. Their chorale broadens into a fugal development in triple time, then a magnificent, slower recapitulation. The last movement is one of provincial mirth; at the end, in the French horns, there is a brief reference to the very first theme of the symphony.

Note, too, the movement titles in German, for the first time in Schumann's symphonic work.

The orchestration of the Schumann symphonies has traditionally been considered problematic of balance and figuration. Themes, for example, are often scored in octaves the way the thumb and little finger might legitimately emphasize them on the piano, but a pale effect when distributed to violin and cello. Schumann sometimes loses track of his brass registers, with resulting shrillness or heaviness. But I think some of our dissatisfaction has to do with the common knowledge that Schumann went mad, an extension of the kind of thinking that says because Beethoven was deaf, he couldn't have meant this or that. The conductor's careful attention to the issues of balance will usually offset the problems, and it is no longer acceptable to perform Schumann's works as rescored by others.

Concerto for Piano and Orchestra in A Minor, OP. 54

Allegro affettuoso
Intermezzo: Andantino grazioso
Allegro vivace
[No pause between movements II and III]

For piano solo; flutes I-II, oboes I-II, clarinets I-II, bassoons I-II;
    horns I-II, trumpets I-II; timpani; strings
Composed May 1841 and June–July 1845 in Leipzig and
    Dresden; dedicated to Ferdinand Hiller

First performed 4 December 1845 by the Dresden Orchestra,
 Clara Schumann soloist, Ferdinand Hiller conducting
Published by Breitkopf & Härtel (Leipzig, 1862). *Inexpensive score:*
 Robert Schumann: *Great Works for Piano*
 and Orchestra in Full Score (New York: Dover, 1982)
Duration: about 30 minutes

Schumann composed the first movement of his celebrated Piano Concerto in just over a week in May 1841, calling it Fantasia in A Minor
for piano and orchestra. The genesis of the concerto, therefore, is part
and parcel of that especially fertile period in Schumann's life which
began with his marriage to Clara and the so-called "year of song" and
perhaps reached its peak that January with the "Spring" Symphony.
Clara, more than eight months' pregnant with their first child, gave
the premiere of the Fantasia at a concert of the Leipzig Gewandhaus
Orchestra that August.

After the move to Dresden in late 1844 and a subsequent period of
disorientation and despair, Schumann was drawn again to the piano;
in June and July of 1845 the concluding rondo and finally an intermezzo were composed. Clara played the first performance of the complete concerto on 4 December 1845 and again for a Gewandhaus concert
of New Year's Day 1846. It went on to become the centerpiece of her
repertoire, played in all the musical capitals of Europe. Any number
of the next generation's masters counted hearing her play the Schumann Concerto as critical to their artistic formation.

At first, the solo part threatens to overwhelm the work, when
attention is immediately drawn away from the orchestra's single chord
to the flourish for the piano. Conventions of the concerto form then
go on to be abandoned left and right. Schumann struggled with this
issue, to the extent that despite several attempts he never completed
another keyboard concerto. In his other works for piano and orchestra,
the orchestra's role is, in fact, secondary. But here the solution is
effective, and competition is not the issue, cyclisicm is: the first four
notes of the main theme—its motivic germ—recur, transformed and
mutated, at critical junctures in all three movements.

This is first stated by the winds. The soloist takes the restatement,
then goes on to development of the theme. A transitional passage
begins to gather momentum, but the new key area is marked not by
contrastive melodic material but rather references to the main theme

in a wonderful series of clarinet solos, the exposition concluding in a triumph based on material we have heard before. The development continues in this vein, with insistent references to what has now become a melody of obsessive character; so, too, does the recapitulation, which is very nearly an exact replication of what came before. The cadenza, after its initial display, settles on a cadential trill almost at once, but this proves to be only the halfway point: there is to be considerably more examination of the materials at hand. What follows as orchestral coda—the piano, for once, accompanies—is a minor-mode march on the four-note germ.

The *Intermezzo* seems cast in the mold of the second movement of Beethoven's Fourth Concerto, a conversation between soloist and orchestra. Here the statements of the piano are coquettish and feminine, counterbalanced by the broad, masculine phrases first introduced by the strings. References, both major and minor, to the motto introduce the third movement. This is a one-to-a-bar rondo, where the first theme begins with a transformation of the unifying melody. But what particularly delights is the contrastive material, a little march in duple meter uncomfortably superposed over the prevailing triple. From there the movement evolves into a *perpetuum mobile* as the pianist, not to be dissuaded, fends off each attempt at closure. Even within fifty bars of the end, the piano seems to insist that such a fine adventure must not, just yet, come to an end.

Concerto for Cello and Orchestra in A Minor, OP. 129

Nicht zu schnell
Langsam
Sehr lebhaft
[No pause between the movements]

For cello solo; flutes I-II, oboes I-II, clarinets I-II, bassoons I-II; horns I-II, trumpets I-II; timpani; strings
Composed October 1850 in Düsseldorf
First performed 9 June 1860 by the Leipzig Conservatory Orchestra, Ludwig Egbert soloist, Alfred Wieman conducting a concert to mark the fiftieth anniversary of the composer's birth
Published by Breitkopf & Härtel (Leipzig, 1854). *Inexpensive score: Great Romantic Cello Concertos in Full Score* (New York: Dover, 1983)
Duration: about 25 minutes

Schumann's Cello Concerto is not one of your thunder-and-lightning showpieces but rather a tame sort of reverie, as though improvised by the soloist and a few friends in some mid-century drawing room. Like all fine concertos, however, it is particularly apt for the solo instrument, investigating by turns the cello's capacity for lyric tenor melody on the one hand and its refined sort of wit on the other. The movements are played without pause, thereby suggesting various analogies with the one-movement keyboard fantasy of the era.

The woodwind chords take the place of an orchestral introduction, by this time a well-tested opening strategy. This understatement draws us straight into the solo exposition, a spilling out of melody across some two dozen bars and all the various registers of the cello. Scales eventually rocket upward to complete the segment, an idea incorporated into the orchestral tutti that follows. Here for the first time, the tempo marking "not too fast" having indicated another understatement, some forward momentum begins to build. But this is no more a music about tuttis than about virtuoso indulgence, and the new theme simply resumes the process the orchestra had interrupted. The cellist's turn to triplets evokes a similar response from the orchestra. About the only formal event that elicits a jolt comes as the strongly felt buildup to the main internal cadence is deflected, just at its point of arrival, into the development. Both the merge into recapitulation and the restating of the second theme in the major mode are accomplished with consummate subtlety.

The return of the woodwind chords begins an interlude that effects the modulation to the second movement, *Langsam* (slow) and in F major. Pizzicato accompanying figures and the ongoing breadth of melody in the solo part suggest a sort of serenade. The magic effect here is the way you begin to sense the emergence of a second solo line, that of the principal orchestral cellist. Ultimately the soloist begins to play double stops and the orchestral cello fills in the middle. So much for Schumann's limits as an orchestrator.

Again, at the crucial juncture, come the woodwind chords, this time going on, as does the soloist, to reflect on the theme of the first movement. A brief written-out cadenza leads into the last movement—lively, strong-rhythmed, folkish of scoring and meter. The prevailing idea is of filling in the space between the groups of three orchestral strokes, the cello springing up through quick arpeggiations. The resulting dialogue affords the cellist some quite satisfactory display work, especially toward the cadence points. What does happen is not a full-fledged cadenza but a rather modest elaboration of the cadence point before the quick coda with triplets. Too often a soloist will wedge some five-minute digression into one of the interstices.

Roger Sessions

Born *28 December 1896 in Brooklyn*
Died *16 March 1985 in Princeton,*
New Jersey

Sessions studied piano with his mother, a usual enough way to begin. But by the age of thirteen he had written his first opera *Lancelot and Elaine;* the following year he enrolled at Harvard, there to master his counterpoint under Archibald T. Davison. As was the custom for young American composers of his obvious promise, Sessions had intended to further his studies abroad, in this case with Ravel. The war in Europe, however, caused him instead to go to Yale, where in 1917 he earned a second bachelor's degree with Ives's mentor Horatio Parker. His artistic formation was completed with Ernest Bloch, from whom he studied privately in New York. Sessions began his teaching career at Smith College (1917–21), then became Bloch's assistant and later successor at the Cleveland Institute of Music (1921–25). (The substantial influence of Bloch is to be heard in Sessions's dense textures and melodic expanse.) But from the beginning Sessions had little difficulty establishing a personal idiom: he was able, for example, to absorb the advances of Stravinsky and Schoenberg as they happened without compromising his own principles—above all his often-described search for "the long line."

The success of Sessions's incidental music for a play called *The Black Maskers* (1923; orchestral suite, 1928) led to a string of fellowships that supported his long, and long-delayed, sojourn in Europe: from 1925 to 1933 he lived and worked in Florence, Rome, Paris, and Berlin. During periodic return visits to New York he coproduced the influential Copland-Sessions Concerts of new music (1928–31). His First Symphony was successfully launched by Koussevitzky and the Boston Symphony Orchestra in 1927. From 1933 Sessions taught at prestigious American institutions of higher learning—Boston University, Princeton, the Berkeley campus of the University of California, Harvard, and Juilliard—and had become by mid-century probably the most influential composition teacher in the nation. Among his pupils were Milton Babbitt, Leon Kirchner, Andrew Imbrie, and David Diamond.

Sessions's orchestral compositions include nine symphonies (the first, 1927; the last, 1978) of which the Third (1957) is particularly fine; a Concerto for Violin (1935), interesting in that the orchestra lacks violins altogether; a Piano Concerto (1956); a Double Concerto for violin, cello, and orchestra (1971); and the Concerto for Orchestra treated below. The opera *Montezuma* (1941–63) represents both the culmination of his middle period and the dawn of his vigorous last years, from which era the cantata *When Lilacs Last in the Dooryard Bloom'd* (1970) is but one of the masterpieces. Everybody who has thought seriously about American art music realizes that Sessions's work is (as Copland put it) one of its cornerstones. His orchestra pieces are of legendary difficulty, but the modern virtuoso orchestra is a dauntless assemblage, and these days you can hear your Sessions live.

When Lilacs Last in the Dooryard Bloom'd

Part I   *Introduction: Poco Adagio* [*The Lilacs, the Star, the Thrush*]

Part II   *Andante e pesante* {*The Funeral Train*}

Part III   *Poco Adagio* [*"Come, lovely and soothing Death"*]

For soloists (S., Contr., Bar.), chorus; piccolo, flutes I-II, alto
flute, oboes I-II, English horn, E♭ clarinet, clarinets I-II, bass
clarinet, bassoons I-II, contrabasoon; horns I-IV, trumpets I-II,
trombones I-III, tuba; timpani, military drum (muffled),
Chinese drum, tambourin provençal, tenor drum, bass drum,
suspended cymbal, tambourine, wood block, maracas, whip,
glockenspiel, tubular bells, xylophone, marimba, vibraphone,
celesta, harp, piano; strings

Text by Walt Whitman, a poem added to later editions of *Leaves
of Grass*

Composed 1967–2 January 1970, mostly in Princeton; the idea
and some of the sketches go back to the 1920s; commissioned
by the University of California, Berkeley, for the centenary
commemoration of its founding; dedicated to the memory of
Martin Luther King, Jr., and Robert F. Kennedy

First performed 23 May 1971, in Berkeley, California, by the
Symphony Orchestra and Chorus of the University of California,
Berkeley, Helene Joseph, soprano, Stephanie Friedman,
contralto, Allen Shearer, baritone, James Cunningham
conducting

Published by Merion Music, Inc. (Bryn Mawr, Pa., 1974)

Duration: about 40 minutes

The lilacs were in bloom on the day of Lincoln's death, 15 April
1865, a memory of the fallen hero that pervades this most aromatic
of works. The sounds in Whitman's great poem are the lament of a
lone thrush in the distant swamp, the clatter of the funeral train as it
wends its way through the American heartland from Washington to
Springfield, and the deafening silence of the throngs of citizens that
lined the route to pay their last respects to Lincoln, the "great star
disappear'd." Every American knows this scene, which is as firmly
rooted in our collective identity as the slow progress of the funeral
caisson that bore John Kennedy's coffin to the Capitol. (Hindemith's
setting of the same text was written in memory of Franklin Delano
Roosevelt and performed in 1946.)

Whitman's majestic poetry runs the curious risk of being too musical to function successfully as a cantata text. His rhythms and phrase
structures, recurring motives, and climactic peaks seem to demand
response from the composer at every turn; the images (here "the cold,
transparent night," "sea-winds, blown from east and west," "the gor-

geous, indolent, sinking sun") are so amenable to picture music as to threaten a composition's collapsing under their weight. (Whitman himself thought his style operatic.) Sessions's success is a function of his selectivity: the text painting is there in abundance enough to sustain and enhance the poetry—the "tolling bells' perpetual clang," for example, or the "carol floating with joy"—but elsewhere long stretches are set as relatively unencumbered declamation by the soloist or chorus.

The cantata is in three parts, a short introduction and two longer movements, one on the funeral train and one of reflection on the meaning of death. It is spellbinding from the first measure, where flute and clarinet state the motive associated with the lilacs in specific and with April and springtide in general. Another prominent motive is the song of the thrush, "a shy and hidden bird, solitary," first heard in the flute, piccolo, and glockenspiel at the entry of the soprano.

The second movement is bold and huge, national in scope, as the funeral train passes "the show of the States themselves, . . . With processions long and winding, and the flambeaus of the night, With the silent sea of faces." It begins with as industrial a locomotive music as was ever composed, then goes on to reflect Whitman's ecstasy at the expanse of the American nation. The chorus acts as the bereaved citizenry, yet the central moment (for baritone solo) is the poet's, as he lays his sprig of lilac on the coffin. Note, too, the sublime quiet of "sea winds, blown from east and west" and the explosion of "mighty Manhattan." At the end the lilac, with mastering odor, hovers over the emptiness.

The third movement centers around the quatrain that begins "Come, lovely and soothing Death," a line music lovers are likely to associate with the Lutheran chorale *Komm' süsser Tod.* The setting constitutes the first extended passage for the contralto soloist, on the whole a tranquil and "glad serenade." But this yields to the terrible vision of the slain, and the throbbing choral refrain of the word "suffered" will haunt you long after the work is done. The cantata comes to rest with "Lilac and star and bird, twined with the chant of my soul. There in the fragrant pines, and the cedars dusk and dim," lingering in the low winds.

Sessions had bought a copy of Whitman's *Leaves of Grass,* he says, on arriving at Harvard in 1911; the sketches for a "Lilacs" cantata date from the 1920s. But these were set aside until the blossom of Sessions's seventh decade. What results from this encounter of nineteenth- and twentieth-century singers of songs *par excellence* is a masterpiece for all time.

Concerto for Orchestra

Allegro—Largo—Allegro maestoso

For piccolo, flutes I-II, oboes I-II, English horn, E♭ clarinet, clarinets I-II, bass clarinet, bassoons I-II, contrabassoon; horns I-IV, trumpets I-III, trombones I-III, tuba; timpani, side drum, military drum, tenor drum, Chinese drum, cymbals, triangle, tambourine, tam-tam, whip, woodblock, bells, xylophone, vibraphone; harp; strings

Composed 1979–16 August 1981 to a commission by the Boston Symphony Orchestra for its centennial; dedicated "to Seiji Ozawa, also in memory of all of his illustrious predecessors who built and maintained the Boston Symphony Orchestra"

First performed 23 October 1981 by the Boston Symphony Orchestra, Seiji Ozawa conducting

Published by Merion Music, Inc. (Bryn Mawr, Pa., 1983)

Duration: about 15 minutes

For its fiftieth anniversary in 1931, the Boston Symphony Orchestra under Koussevitzky placed a series of commissions with eminent composers, a project that yielded such excellent works as Stravinsky's *Symphony of Psalms*. For the centennial celebration of 1981, a similar series was commissioned from a dozen successful orchestral composers (Leonard Bernstein, Donald Martino, Leon Kirchner, Peter Maxwell Davies, and Michael Tippett, among others). Sessions, by then eighty-five, obliged with the Concerto for Orchestra, writing in the program note of his gratitude for all that the BSO had meant to him for seventy years. He was a subscriber at fourteen, and the BSO had gone on to offer first performances of his First and Third Symphonies—the latter in fact composed for the orchestra's seventy-fifth anniversary. The Concerto for Orchestra won Sessions his first, and in the opinion of many, sadly overdue Pulitzer Prize.

That Sessions chose to write a concerto for orchestra for this anniversary occasion was doubtless a nod toward Bartók's famous concerto, likewise composed for the BSO (see p. 654). Here, however, work for the choirs of woodwinds, brass, and strings takes precedence over vignettes highlighting individual sections of the orchestra (in the manner of Bartók, or Britten in *The Young Person's Guide*); the net effect is to observe that the full orchestra is a good deal more than the sum of its parts. The predominant role of the strings is, interestingly, to mold together and unify the material in the winds and percussion; they have very little solo work of their own.

The Concerto defines its wide-intervalled melodic contours and festive spirit in its first bars, with Americanisms of rhythm that all but suggest a Copland-style hoedown. In the *Allegro,* described by the composer as alternately playful and lyrical, the woodwinds have the major role, though the xylophone is significant in articulating the structural divisions. The lyrical sections include lovely solo work for the oboe; the last of these, begun by solo horn and clarinet, gathers into an allargando, the first climax, and the biggest statement of the fast material. As this subsides xylophone and piccolo begin the transition to the *Largo,* succeeded by a trumpet solo in a long rise from just below middle C over nearly two octaves.

The slow movement then features the brass: the first trombone begins a theme broadened and answered succesively by horns, tuba, and trumpets. Episodes of rapid woodwind work separate statements of the more leisurely material, which eventually grows to the biggest climax in the concerto. The *Allegro maestoso* begins with another prominent trumpet figure and the return of the xylophone. This last movement is one of great spirit, the dominating motive built from four repeated sixteenths. Just at the end is a great slowing of tempo and thickening of texture, a coda that peaks at a tutti *fortissimo* and then slips away until nothing is left but the triad of clarinet and two horns.

Dmitri Shostakovich

Bŏrn *25 September 1906 in St. Petersburg*
Died *9 August 1975 in Moscow*

The first—and best—Russian composer whose work falls entirely under the Soviet regime, Shostakovich left a spectacular body of instrumental music: progressive, original, highly personal work that managed, one way of another, to survive a repressive and sometimes capricious government censorship. Like all the best Soviet artists, Shostakovich too often found his work in political disfavor, despite his own innate sympathy for the theory of socialism: in 1936 his opera *Lady Macbeth of Mtsensk* was attacked by *Pravda* for its "bedlam of noise," "leftist distortions," "sensationalism" and all the rest in an inflammatory article called "Muddle Instead of Music." Rehabilitated after the Fifth Symphony he then became a target of the 1948 nationwide movement to relieve art of its "formalist perversions." (Yet in the meantime he had won the Stalin Prize for his Piano Quintet of

1940.) Things improved somewhat after the death of Stalin, though Khrushchev launched an attack on the Thirteenth Symphony (1962, text by Yevtushenko) for its suggestion of continued anti-Semitism in Russia, and for neglecting to mention the other victims of Nazi atrocity, Ukrainians in particular. But politics seldom succeeds in controling art, and Shostakovich never ceased to search for viable paths for his compositional thought. His is quite simply one of the major voices of twentieth-century music.

After piano lessons from his mother, a professional pianist, Shostakovich enrolled at age thirteen at the State Conservatory in Petrograd. Though he came from a family of status, he had barely survived the Revolution and its associated hunger and pestilence and spent the remainder of his life in more or less fragile health. After his father's death he supported the family as a movie-house pianist, while earning degrees in composition in 1923 and piano in 1925. (The First Symphony, his graduation thesis, was performed with great success in 1926 in both Moscow and Leningrad; in the West one of its major promoters was Tuscanini.) In 1927 Shostakovich won the International Chopin Competition in piano; by 1930 he had completed his graduate studies.

His middle period embraces the war years and those of political disfavor, where, after the Fifth Symphony, his music consists mostly of patriotic works and film music. The Tenth Symphony of 1953 inaugurates his remarkable late period, two decades in which masterpiece followed upon masterpiece—six symphonies, three concertos, ten string quartets, and so forth.

Even in the late works, his language is mostly tonal and metric, but the intricate rhythm, free dissonance, and dense counterpoint lend the music a markedly contemporary sound. Of his fifteen symphonies, the most frequently programmed is the Fifth (1937), with its powerful finale; the Seventh Symphony ("Leningrad," 1941) is a grand and symbolic work, composed while that city was under siege by the Germans during World War II. Shostakovich also composed concertos (for violin, piano, and cello), operas (*The Nose,* 1930; and *Lady Macbeth*), and film scores.

He was dour of appearance and understandably reluctant to acknowledge his artistic likes and dislikes in public. Never did he consider himself anything other than an obedient servant of a political philosophy he supported, though beginning in the 1960s, his work suggests strong disillusion with the Soviet system. His son Maxim Shostakovich (b. 1938), a pianist and conductor, has become an important exponent of his father's work.

Symphony No. 5 in D Minor, OP. 47

Moderato
Allegretto
Largo
Allegro non troppo

For piccolo, flutes I-II, oboes I-II, E♭ clarinet, clarinets I-II, bassoons I-II, contrabassoon; horns I-IV, trumpets I-III, trombones I-III, tuba; timpani, snare drum, bass drum, cymbals, triangle, tam-tam, bells, xylophone, celesta, harps I-II, piano; strings

Composed 18 April–20 July 1937 in Leningrad
First performed 21 November 1937 by the Leningrad Philharmonic, Yevgeni Mravinsky conducting
Published by Muzgiz (Moscow, 1939)
Duration: about 45 minutes

The Fifth Symphony is subtitled "a Soviet artist's practical creative reply to justified criticism"—the composer's attempt, that is, to rehabilitate himself after *Lady Macbeth* by forging a music of "socialist realism." It was conceived, he said, "lyrically from beginning to end," to suggest the stabilizing progress of a life's journey from tragedy at the beginning through resolution in a climactic finale of optimism and joy. (In the Soviet Union, the Fifth has been called the "Hamlet" Symphony.) With it commenced Shostakovich's middle period. He was in his early thirties.

There was not much new, in the 1930s, about a life-cycle symphony with its memories of childhood, "ironic smile over the irrevocable past" (in the case of the second movement), suffering, and resolution. Richard Strauss had mined that vein pretty thoroughly; Mahler's psychological orientation is similar, and the music is better. But it's precisely the lucidity and optimism of the Fifth that has earned it an unshakable place in the symphonic repertoire. Under the circumstances it makes more sense to admire how Shostakovich, who was nothing if not loyal to tenets of the Party, came up with such a workable solution to his dilemmas.

The first movement is a sonata of several very strong thematic elements: the opening motive, in the introductory bars, of wide intervals and prominent dotted rhythms, the chains here and elsewhere of the three-note motive that grows from it, and the true theme—the long melody in the first violins after the movement opens. There is, too, an important thumping eighth-note figure in the first violins; these reiterated eighths go on to accompany the second group, which begins in the strings (at the entry of the harp) in a melody of wide intervals and very long note values.

What transpires in the exposition can be deemed either leisurely or lethargic, depending on your degree of charity. Forward motion begins to gather, though almost imperceptibly at first, with the development: the French horns have a version of the first theme in their lowest register and *forte,* as though keen to force their way out; the piano is added. The tempo quickens, as do the prevailing rhythmic values, and the tame little quarter-eighth-eighth accompaniment figure works itself into a fiery tatoo in the brass. At the climax the main theme is heard as a fat Russian march, developing in volume and orchestral breadth into a bold recapitulation of material that had at first been stated quietly indeed. The second theme recapitulates as a dialogue for flute and horn solo, and this becomes the vehicle by which the movement at last reaches closure, with rising chromatics in the celesta.

The scherzo is neoclassic in the Prokofiev manner, but more rotund, with bouncing, vulgar rusticity, dozens of extra beats, and heavy on the band instruments. Its formal arrangement is free enough that you needn't try to follow the traditional scheme.

Shostakovich is said to have written the *Largo* in a three-day paroxysm. It's typical to associate the string sonority—violins in three sections, violas and cellos in two—with Mahler, but where it concerns the melody and counterpoint a better comparison, I think, is with Samuel Barber. The interlude episodes are dialogues for duo or solo winds. There's a big climax on the principal theme, and a slow fade at the end, with harp and celesta.

The last movement is one of the celebrated finales in the literature: a pulsating rumble of timpani underscores the initial theme, which goes on to dominate the movement. Things build to a huge tutti where the xylophone enters, then begin to decelerate and ultimately to dissolve, in something like a mirror image of the first movement.

Ultimately, however, the eighth-note pulses hold sway. There's a thunderous arrival in the major mode to close, with heroic brass and a sweep that will remind you of Sibelius and Tchaikovsky. It can be argued, I suppose, that all this pounding takes the place of inspired formal control that by the end the movement has simply fallen apart. But there's no denying its impact.

Symphony No. 10 in E Minor, OP. 93

Moderato
Allegro
Allegretto
Andante

For piccolo, flutes I-II, oboes I-III, English horn, E♭ clarinet, clarinets I-II, bassoons I-II, contrabassoon; horns I-IV, trumpets I-III, trombones I-III, tuba; timpani, snare drum, bass drum, cymbals, triangle, tambourine, tam-tam, xylophone; strings
Composed summer–25 October 1953 in Komarovo village, gulf of Finland
First performed 17 December 1953 by the Leningrad Philharmonic, Yevgeni Mravinsky conducting
Published by State Music Publishers (Moscow, 1960)
Duration: about 50 minutes

There's a mystique, of course, about tenth symphonies: by Shostakovich's era the number of composers who never got that far included not just Beethoven and Schubert but Bruckner and Mahler as well. Yet the time was ripe, in 1953, for Shostakovich to undertake a new symphonic work. The worst memories of the war had begun to fade, and with them some of the passions associated with the great Seventh Symphony of 1941. The Eighth Symphony was a decade old and the Ninth approaching that mark, and neither had been greatly popular.

The new symphony was to be a music of peace and resistance to war; of the dawn of a better world. Some of this amounted to politics as usual: the Tenth was yet another gesture of "rehabilitation"—and a successful one, for Shostakovich went on to be recognized as a "People's Artist" of the Soviet Union. Yet what resulted is a mature masterpiece, with the sort of universality senior symphonists can so often muster. It contains some of his best music.

The first movement is vast, some twenty-five minutes in length. But it is likewise simple. Sonata form, which Shostakovich had set out to use, at length escaped him: instead he found himself obsessed by the gruff first theme, in the low strings. This builds, extends, and transforms itself, reaches its immense climax with squealing winds (here, as throughout the movement, in a remarkable exercise of orchestral timbre), then merely reverses itself and dies. By contrast with the sprawling *Moderato,* the scherzo is short, frantic, and very obviously interrupted before completing any repetitions.

The phrases of the folklike *Allegretto* are passed from instrument to instrument, notably the wind soloists, now tranquil, now mysterious in texture. The horn solo and its echo introduce a brief, developmental Largo, after which the tempo rebuilds into recapitulatory gesture, a climax, and a dissolve.

The finale begins with an introductory *Andante,* again for wind soloists, and continues with an energetic Allegro. At the center, in trumpet and trombone, there is a strong statement of Shostakovich's monogram DSCH (D–E♭–C–B), and this goes on to be woven into the fabric as a focal point of the vigorous conclusion.

Symphony No. 13, OP. 113

.

I   *Babi Yar: Adagio*
II   *Humor: (Scherzo) Allegretto*
III   *At the Store: Adagio*
IV   *Fears: Largo*
V   *A Career: Allegretto*
[Movements III-V played without pause]

For bass solo, chorus of basses (unison); piccolo, flutes I-II, oboes
     I-III, English horn, E♭ clarinet, clarinets I-III, bass clarinet,
     bassoons I-III, contrabassoon; horns I-IV, trumpets I-III,
     trombones I-III, tuba; timpani, snare drum, bass drum,
     cymbals, triangle, castanets, tambourine, woodblock, whip,
     tam-tam, glockenspiel, bells; xylophone, celesta, harps I-II,
     piano; strings
Text by Yevgeny Yevtushenko (b. 1933)
Composed March–April (mvt. I) and July 1962 in Moscow;
     completed 20 July 1962
First performed 18 December 1962 by the Moscow Philharmonic

Orchestra and men of the Russian A Cappella Choir and Gnesin
Musical-Pedagogic Institute at the Large Hall of the Moscow
Conservatory, Vitaly Gromadski, bass; Kyril Kondrashin
conducting
Published in *Soviet Composer* (Moscow, 1971)
Duration: about one hour

Shostakovich's Eleventh and Twelfth Symphonies (called, respectively, "The Year 1905" [referring to an early, failed revolutionary
movement] and "The Year 1917") show the composer obediently toeing
the realist line. Their compositional style is older and easier than that
of the Tenth; both were welcomed in Russia and greeted with disap-
pointment in the West. The Thirteenth Symphony, by contrast, was
novel of concept and inflammatory—not least, for its implied strong
criticism of the Soviet way of life. The pairing of Shostakovich and
dissident poet Yevgeny Yevtushenko was in itself electrifying. And
it was an exciting time for Russian art in general: Solzhenitsyn's *One
Day in the Life of Ivan Denisovich* (1962), for example, is contemporaneous.

Babi Yar laments the Jews massacred during the Nazi occupation
of Kiev in 1945. Shostakovich read Yevtushenko's *Babi Yar* in a Russian literary magazine in September 1961. The idea of a texted symphony on the subject of civic morality grew therefrom, with the
additional texts taken from Yevtushenko's *A Wave of the Hand.* It was,
under the circumstances, a courageous essay, virtually inviting political response. The texts were not distributed at the first performance,
nor were reviews permitted, and permission to publish the work was
withheld. (It was seven years before the performance material was
allowed to circulate in the West.)

As a generic mingling of cantata and symphony, the Thirteenth
was, wrote the composer "in many respects new to me as far as form
goes"—though both the Second and Third Symphonies require a chorus.
The progress of the movements is formally pleasing, with the rigorous
first movement offset by a scherzo, two slow movements, and a finale.
And the treatment of the voices is imaginative as well, with the chorus
always in unison recitations and the solo part tending toward speech
rhythms and contours.

It is, however, the tolling of the bell that strikes the sharpest note
of agony, and in turn of protest. Not until that is done does the

chorus enter with its condemnation of Russian anti-Semitism, a vile thing, says the poet, in a good land. (Yevtushenko was forced to substitute a more politically acceptable text before a second performance was allowed on 10 February 1963, but the music was unchanged.) "There is no memorial at Babi Yar," it begins. "The sheer cliffs stand as the gravestone. It makes me afraid." In the music you hear reflections of the text: the sounds of spring, a kiss as the ice breaks, the wind whistling through the wild grass at Babi Yar.

Humor, the second movement, attacks hypocrisy in the ruling class—a stratum of society that has managed to survive the overthrow of czars and kings. Humor cannot be bought, the text argues, and even when condemned to death returns merrily to dance. The E♭ clarinet and solo violin are the prominent soloists in this scherzo. *At the Store* concerns the deprivation of Russian women struggling to feed their families. The slow theme in the low strings, then violas, represents the trudge of feet as freezing shoppers mill about in long lines, their hard-earned money crumpled in their hands. They have endured too much, and it is shameful to cheat them at the scales. The woodblock, presumably, suggests the injustice.

In the second of the slow movements, the solo tuba introduces a choral incantation on secret fears, and the things that one does not dare write down. The bells toll again. And the finale is a biting look at the folly of a genius (like Galileo) in the modern society. "He who is unwise is more wise," insist the singers, to pizzicato strings, and the soloist concludes in pride at making his career without having to work at it.

Symphony No. 14, OP. 135

De profundis: Adagio
Malagueña: Allegretto
Die Lorelei: Allegro molto
The Suicide: Adagio
On the Watch: Allegro
Madame, Look!: Adagio
At the Santé Jail: Adagio
Zaporozhye Cossacks' Reply to the Sultan of Constantinople: Allegro
O Delvig, Delvig!: Andante
The Poet's Death: Largo
Conclusion: Moderato

For soloists (SB); tom-toms I-III, castanets, woodblock, whip,
glockenspiel, xylophone, chimes, vibraphone; celesta; 10 violins, 4 violas, 3 cellos, 2 double basses

Texts by Federico García Lorca (I, II), Guillaume Apollinaire (III-
VIII), Wilhelm Küchelbecker (IX), and Rainer Maria Rilke (X,
XI); various translators into Russian

Composed spring 1969 in Moscow; dedicated to "dear Benjamin
Britten as a token of profound respect from a cordially devoted
D. Shostakovich, 1 December 1969, Moscow"

First performed 29 September 1969 by the Moscow Chamber
Orchestra in Leningrad, with Galina Vishnevskaya, soprano,
and Yevgeny Vladimirov, bass, Rudolf Barshai conducting

Published by State Music Publishers (Moscow, 1971) and Edwin
F. Kalmus (New York, 1969)

Duration: about 50 minutes

The Fourteenth Symphony is, like Mahler's *Das Lied von der Erde,* a
meditation on death, an orchestral song cycle about as tragic as they
come. Limiting the performing force to two soloists, nineteen strings,
and percussion is one of those master strokes that instead of constrict-
ing possibilities opens up a world of unexpected sonority. Shostakovich's novel subdivisions of the string choir, the cold rattle of the
woodblock and the insistent tolling of bells—all these go to underscore the truths of death with powerful acuity. And these and other
identities, notably the recurring allusions to the opening melodic figure, make the designation "symphony" apt.

Above all, the Fourteenth is an adventure in poetry. (A composer's
knack for choosing texts is one sure measure of his art.) Here the
choice of three modern, West European poets and a nineteenth-
century Russian is ingenious: García Lorca (1898–1936), arrested and
shot by Franco's troops only a few weeks after confidently declining
refuge in New York ("Nobody kills poets," he had said); Apollinaire
(1880–1918), the French literary cubist, who knew of prison first-
hand; the great German lyric poet Rainer Maria Rilke (1875–1926),
a tragic figure who died from blood poisoning after pricking his finger
on a rose bush. The most poignant poem is the one in Russian, addressed
from prison by one Küchelbecker to a fellow poet, Delvig. "What
comfort is there," he asks, "for talent among villains and fools?"

You think, for a while, that the composer's role in all this is clin-
ical and distant; only gradually do you understand his genius at allow-

ing the poetry to speak, underlining in music only its most poignant turns. The García Lorca pair progresses from the somnolent *De profundis* of "a hundred fervent lovers" in eternal sleep beneath the red-sanded roads of Andalusia to the violence of Death stalking in and out of a tavern in a macabre malagueña. Six settings of Apollinaire follow. In the first, the Lorelei of Rhenish myth is banished to a convent by the bishop in a conversation underscored by brusque cellos and xylophone, following which we hear in the music the horseback journey to the convent, the Lorelei paused at her rock, the death knell before she leaps to her death, and her funeral song. In *The Suicide,* the soprano and cello weave a hypnotic, miserable evocation of three lilies on her unmarked grave, their beauty, like hers, accursed. *On the Watch* is a percussive dirge, as the soprano foresees the certainty of her lover's death in battle. *Madame, Look!* observes the bass: "you have lost something." But it is only her heart, and she laughs mockingly at a love cut short by death.

Now the texts become bleaker still: the distress of the isolated prisoner, with only his mind for company; the Cossacks' violent response to the Sultan of Constantinople—a rotten cancer, mocks the bass, born in filth, and covered with scabs; and the great outburst "O Delvig, Delvig!" of resonant and melancholy string sonority. The work ends, still dwelling on the austerity of the strings, with Rilke's *The Poet's Death* and *Conclusion.* A skeleton rattles before the release in death and chilling last silence.

It is a work of bitterness and pessimism, carrying forward the disenchantment so obvious in the Thirteenth Symphony. And yet it is a monument to the composer's great friendship, in his last years, with Benjamin Britten, to whom the work is dedicated. Shostakovich's last symphony, the Fifteenth, followed in 1971.

Jean Sibelius

Born *8 December 1965 in*
Hämeenlinna (Tavastebus), Finland
Died *20 September 1957 in Järvenpää*

Sibelius is the very symbol of his nation—a distant land of sad history, noble myth, and bitter cold; his heroic stature was not compromised when at length the mainstream of composition passed him by, but was instead confirmed for all time. Indeed the passage of a half century has seen his symphonic work adopted, the world over, into the core repertoire.

He studied music with the local bandmaster, though by the time he did, he had already begun to compose on his own. He was sent to the University of Helsinki to study law, abandoning that for studies in composition with Martin Wegelius at the Helsinki Conservatory (now the Sibelius Academy), and then with Busoni in Berlin and Goldmark in Vienna. Although the Sibelius family spoke Swedish and his studies were mostly in German, Sibelius was by birth and persuasion a son of Finland. Possibly because he never studied with a teacher of assertive personality, he was able to write in a personal, and therefore national, style from the start. By 1892, when he returned to Finland and began to teach at the Helsingfors Conservatory, his music was already dominated by the subject matter of Finnish legend. His symphonic poem *Finlandia* (1900) became so identified with the independence movement that the Russian government eventually forbade its performance at politically sensitive events.

Supported by an annual stipend from the government, Sibelius settled in 1904 at a country house in Järvenpää just north of Helsinki, where with few interruptions he lived and worked for the rest of his career. From time to time he would go abroad to conduct his works, but in general the Sibelius repertoire was made known to the world through performances by the Helsinki Philharmonic Orchestra under its founder, Robert Kajanus. It was Kajanus who first took the repertoire to western Europe and, eventually, the United States. In 1914 Sibelius himself ventured to America to offer his work at the Norfolk Music Festival and to receive an honorary doctorate from Yale University.

Like Brahms, he came late to composing symphonies. Like Bach, his compositional interests were out of fashion by the time he reached middle age. He had a remarkable ability to rethink the principles of symphonic composition, however, such that the overall progress of his work, from the tone poems and First Symphony through the flood of activity in 1926—the Sixth and Seventh Symphonies and *Tapiola*—is extraordinary indeed.

In the late 1930s, Sibelius ceased to compose and lost whatever interest he ever had in contemporary musical developments (though he continued to follow the work of Prokofiev and Shostakovich). He promised an Eighth Symphony to Koussevitzky for a Boston Symphony Sibelius cycle, then for a project to record his complete symphonic work, and finally to Thomas Beecham. Whatever he had finished was apparently destroyed according to his wishes at his death, just before his 92nd birthday.

There is nothing shameful, of course, with puttering in one's garden. Sibelius had long been in poor health, and his later life was complicated by alcoholism. He was kindred of spirit with Brahms, Tchaikovsky, and Dvořák, and they had been gone for half a century. And a chronological anachronism is of less concern with every decade that passes.

Of the seven symphonies, the Second (in D major, op. 43, 1901) and the Fifth (in E♭ major, op. 82, 1915) are the most frequently performed. Equally popular with audiences are the *Karelia* overture and suites (opp. 10 and 11, 1893), which describe the cheery populace of a southeastern province of Finland, and some dozen symphonic poems, among them the ones treated below. The Violin Concerto, op. 47 (1903, rev. 1905) is well ensconced in the literature. His incidental music includes suites for *Pelléas and Mélisande, Twelfth Night,* and *The Tempest.*

Symphony No. 2 in D Major, OP. 43

Allegretto
Tempo Andante, ma rubato
Vivacissimo
Finale: Allegro moderato

For flutes I-II, oboes I-II, clarinets I-II, bassoons I-II; horns I-IV,
    trumpets I-III, trombones I-III, tuba; timpani; strings
Composed 1901–2, mostly in Rapallo, Italy
First performed 8 March 1902 by the Helsinki Philharmonic
    Orchestra in Helsingfors, Sibelius conducting
Published by Breitkopf und Härtel (Leipzig, 1903)
Duration: about 40 minutes

The Second Symphony owes its great popularity to attractive themes and rich hues, set forth in a formal scheme of almost ponderous grandeur—the whole an essay that deals simultaneously in pastorality and patriotism. Every gay melody or serene reflection is offset by some surge of trouble or melancholy of the sort we naturally associate with a populace threatened by enslavement. The scoring is heavy-handed (and sometimes problematic), the decoration copious; in the last movement the relentless scales that lap around the melody eventually engulf it. The brass choir surges forth again and again, now with chorales, now with heraldry, but until the very end these always recede again into mystery, chill, or darkness.

Note well the repeated-note pulsations of the first passage, for they return in other guises later on. These introduce a sprightly dance of the woodwinds, echoed by horns. From this gentility blossoms a fanfare in bassoons, a dark recitative in violins, and the accelerating pizzicati that introduce the second group. The second theme is more urgent, with prolonged high note and throbbing fall and punctuated by stabs of the first woodwind theme. Development of these materials takes the form of a long crescendo into the majestic brass chorale at the center of the movement. The pastoral character returns in an abbreviated recapitulation.

The low pizzicato figures at the beginning of the *Andante* carry on beneath the lugubrious melody of bassoons and the roll of timpani. Just as the oboe and clarinet suggest an extension of the theme, the texture and speed intensify into an argument of fragmentary motives. The brass lash out, then fade away, and the harmony lifts dramatically upward into an affirmative new statement. This ends in the unrest of violins, without resolving. A considerably varied recapitulation begins by assigning the bassoon theme to low trumpet and flute; this time the brass chorale is bigger still, broadening into a lofty cadence, still in the minor mode.

The third movement is a nocturnal scherzo, decidedly sinister. The main counterpoint is a quadruple figure thrust atop the prevailing sextuple motion. A yearning trio for solo oboe grows, at the entry of the trombones, into the richest brass work so far. Sibelius slightly alters the repeat of the scherzo, such that the phrase structure is more puzzling still. At the spot where before a trio had so gorgeously flowered, the movement shifts direction into a thrilling transition to the finale, and arrives there not just without pause but in magnificent release.

The ensuing hymn is interrupted by victory calls in the trumpet; the phrase extends itself into an arioso of tenor-register strings. A menacing second group merely sets up the long drive over relentless minor scales to another statement of the hymn. Afterward the orchestra retreats to regather its forces—again with the minor scales for the glorious, soaring close.

Symphony No. 5 in E♭ Major, OP. 82

Tempo molto moderato; Allegro moderato
Allegro moderato quasi allegretto
Allegro molto
[Little if any pause between the movements]

For flutes I-II, oboes I-II, clarinets I-II, bassoons I-II; horns I-IV, trumpets I-III, trombones I-III; timpani; strings

Composed 1914–15 in Järvenpää; revised 1916 and 1919
First performed 8 December 1915 by the Helsinki Philharmonic
    Orchestra, Robert Kajanus conducting at a gala concert to
    honor the composer on his fiftieth birthday
Published by Wilhelm Hansen (Copenhagen, 1921)
Duration: about 35 minutes

The central novelty of the Fifth Symphony is its combining of the initial two movements into one: at about the halfway point the $\frac{3}{8}$ broadens into a Largamente, the high woodwinds introduce a livelier notion in parallel thirds, and after this altogether imperceptible seam a scherzo takes wing. Originally these had indeed been two separate movements, but in retrospect Sibelius could see that the symphony had grown into an essay on how diverse material can be generated from the same basic cells; after the first performance, he joined the two movements, then in 1919 refined things into the version we know today and conducted its first performance that November. The effortless flow that results belies the great effort that went into it.

The second movement is a set of variations on the theme stated by the winds, though the seamlessness may make it difficult for you to distinguish the turning points. There is a restful quietude to the movement, a certain humility, dominated as it is by the benevolent theme. By contrast, the finale is energetic, brilliant, and intense. Short motives work themeselves into themes, then disappear into the accompaniment as new episodes telescope forward. The frantic pace never relents. Beware of the ending, a climactic chord followed by a series of sharp thrusts with long spaces between. Count six of them before applauding.

Sibelius's fiftieth birthday was for all intents and purposes a national holiday, crowned by the premiere of the Fifth. It was meant as a celebration of life, jubilant and optimistic. The despair of the Fourth Symphony had no place. Now he was writing of "this life that I love so infinitely, a feeling that must stamp everything I compose."

The Swan of Tuonela, OP. 22, no. 2

For English horn solo; oboe, bass clarinet, bassoons I-II; horns I-
    IV, trombones I-III; timpani, bass drum; harp; strings
Composed summer 1893 in Kuopio

First performed 13 April 1896 by the Helsingfors Philharmonic
Orchestra, Sibelius conducting
Published by Breitkopf & Härtel (Leipzig, 1901)
Duration: about 10 minutes

The *Kalevela* is the Finnish national epic, its many legends and thousands of verses transmitted orally through the centuries by the peoples of Finland, Lapland, and north Russia. It was assembled into a written narrative and published in the mid-nineteenth century by the philologist Elias Lönnrot (1802–84). In the mythical land of Kaleva, the hero Lemminkäinen and his two brothers, earthly representatives of the gods, seek their fortunes.

Sibelius had first intended to compose a full opera, *The Building of the Boat,* on the Lemminkäinen legends. This project he abandoned in favor of a group of symphonic poems, the Four Legends from the *Kalevela,* op. 22: *Lemminkäinen and the Maidens of Saari, The Swan of Tuonela, Lemminkäinen in Tuonela,* and *Lemminkäinen's Return.* It's a tale of heroic deeds, sorcery, and—always—bitter cold. And many bizarre incidents: in the third of the legends, for example, Lemminkäinen has been murdered and hacked to pieces, and his mother travels to the underworld with a magic rake to put him back together.

This underworld is Tuonela, surrounded by a black river. Upon the rapid currents of these waters of death a swan glides majestically. Lemminkäinen's task is to kill the swan with a single arrow in order to win the hand of the Daugher of the North; but there is no archery here, and the rest is the subject matter of *Pohjola's Daughter,* op. 49.

The swan's song is a soliloquy for the ever plaintive English horn and orchestra—not a narrative at all, but rather a tableau. The division of the strings into thirteen parts (violins I and II into four each, the violas and cellos in two, and double-basses) and the metamorphoses of register, harmony, and tune have much to say of the river's depth and constant, quiet motion. Even as the English horn phrases broaden, the curves of contour and the triplet motives retain their identity. There's ample time for this image to settle in. At the climax the English horn is doubled by the oboe. Just afterward the other woodwinds enter for the first time; impetus gathers with the pizzicatos in the first violins toward the passage where a distant horn call and its echoes are heard over harp arpeggios and the roll of drums. A death knell begins in low brass and percussion, and there is a great *cantabile* of unison strings. But this is more a vision of things to come than the death of the swan: the English horn solo returns, and the movement concludes in the icy, sombre majesty with which it began.

Finlandia, OP. 26

For flutes I-II, oboes I-II, clarinets I-II, bassoons I-II; horns I-IV, trumpets I-III, trombones I-III; timpani, bass drum, cymbals, triangle; strings

Composed 1899 in Helsinki for a series of tableaux celebrating Finland's history

First performed 14 December 1899 for a gala of the Press Pension Fund at the Swedish Theatre in Helsinki, Sibelius conducting

Published by Breitkopf & Härtel (Leipzig, 1905)

Duration: about 10 minutes

Composing patriotic music to stir the hearts of one's countrymen is a noble endeavor. Haydn did it, and so did Tchaikovsky, Elgar, and Sousa, to name those who come first to mind. Composers can also fan the flames of nationalism among oppressed peoples (Chopin with the Poles, for instance, and Berlioz and Liszt with the Hungarians). Sometimes the effect is inadvertent: to have composed in *Finlandia* an overtly inflammatory work seems to have taken Sibelius by surprise. But he had the courage of his convictions and thus both the man and the composition became a kind of rallying point for a political idea whose time had come.

The Finns were nomadic hunters and fishers who settled in the area during the first century A.D., forcing the resident Lapps northward. Finland had operated since the twelfth century under a policy of benign neglect from Sweden; from the early nineteenth century, after the Napoleonic wars, it had carried on in like manner as a relatively autonomous grand duchy of the Russian empire. That changed with the accession in 1894 of the new Russian czar, Nicholas II. In the February Manifesto of 1899 Russia curtailed the civil rights of the Finns. In Helsinki that year the press organized a political demonstration veiled as a pageant of dramatic tableaux on Finnish history, for which Sibelius was asked to compose incidental music. The music for the fourth tableau, "Finland Awakes," became *Finlandia* when published the following year. Three of the others are published as *Scènes historiques* I, opus 25.

Finlandia, very like the most famous of Elgar's *Pomp and Circumstance* marches, always surprises audiences because the familiar tune comes so late in the piece. The violent chords at the beginning are typically heard as howls of aggression; these are met with hymnlike strains in the winds and strings. Threatening brass and percussion come with the increase of tempo, and a strife develops. A march of growing assurance swells up and is repeated. Now, at last, the famous anthem, as though a trio, in noble dignity and reverence. A quick reprise of the march concludes in an apotheosis cadence with a phrase of the anthem, augmented in value, in the brass choir.

Finland declared its independence from Russia a couple of weeks after the Russian Revolution. Its autonomy was recognized by the Soviet Union in October 1920.

Bedřich Smetana

Born *2 March 1824 in Litomyšl*
Died *12 May 1884 in Prague*

Smetana came from that sort of prosperous provincial family—his father was a brewer—in which it's not necessarily a good thing to want to be a musician. His father discouraged Smetana's plans accordingly, though the lad had been playing in string quartets by the age of five and composing for them shortly after. At the age of eighteen, he moved to Prague to study piano and theory, supporting himself as music teacher to an aristocratic household. He began to be noted as a pianist, especially for his interpretations of the Chopin repertoire, but his compositions were received indifferently. In Prague, too, he first heard Liszt play, and the two became close friends. Liszt helped him set up a music school in 1848, a year of pan-European revolution that found Smetana at the barricades. In 1856 he was appointed conductor of the Göteborg Philharmonic Society in Sweden, a position he was anxious to accept in view of the stasis of his career at home. On one of his journeys back to Prague, he visited Liszt in Weimar and heard the first performance of the *Faust* Symphony. Like so many other composers of mid-century, Smetana found in Weimar both intellectual stimulus and a direction for the future.

In 1860 Bohemia achieved a degree of political independence from Austria; Smetana was invited to return to Prague to help establish a national theatre and opera company. *The Brandenburgers in Bohemia* (1862–63) was his first major contribution to the nationalist movement. On the heels of its production in January 1866 came his masterpiece, *The Bartered Bride*, premiered on 30 May 1866. In the years that followed Smetana continued his assiduous composition of nationalist opera, worked on his Czech, and oversaw the transformation of the Provisional Theatre into a permanent National Theatre with its own house. He was dismissed in 1872 because of a dispute over repertoire, and thereupon turned his attention to an epic symphonic work on national themes. This became *Má vlast* (My Fatherland, 1872–79), a cycle of six tone poems.

His personal life had never been especially happy. Three of his children and his first wife died in the 1850s; his second marriage was a failure. By the mid-1870s his deafness, caused by advancing syphilis, began to affect his career; the finale of his string quartet "From My Life" refers to the high-pitched whine that had begun to dominate his hearing. He retained his faculties long enough to attend the first performance of his opera *Libuše* on 11 June 1881, though having grown reclusive and eccentric, he was not offered a free ticket. In late April 1884, after several episodes of violent behavior, he had to be confined at the Prague insane asylum, where he died three weeks later. His funeral, however, was an event of appropriately national significance.

The Moldau (Vltava), from My Fatherland (Má vlast)

The Two Sources of the Moldau—Forest Hunt—Peasant Wedding—Moonlight: Nymphs' Dance—St. John's Rapids—The Moldau in its Greatest Breadth—Vyšehrad

For piccolo, flutes I–II, oboes I–II, clarinets I–II, bassoons I–II; horns I–IV, trumpets I–II, trombones I–III, tuba; timpani, bass drum, cymbals, triangle; harp; strings

Composed late November–8 December 1874 in Prague; the cycle
was dedicated to the city of Prague
First performed 4 April 1875, by the orchestra of the Prague
Provisional Theatre, Adolf Čech conducting; the entire cycle
first performed 5 November 1882 in Prague, Čech conducting
Published by Fr. A. Urbánek (Prague, 1880)
Duration: about 15 minutes

My Fatherland, or *My Country,* is Smetana's cycle of six symphonic
poems on subject matter dear to the Czechs: Vyšehrad, the great castle of Bohemian kings—a place, said Smetana, of glory, tournaments,
battles, and finally ruin; the great river Moldau, which flows through
Prague; the Hussite wars of the fifteenth century; the Bohemian woods
and meadows. Smetana composed the cycle in order, with *Vyšehrad*
conceived gradually between 1872 and 1874, the three succeeding
poems done in white heat over the next few months, and the pair of
Hussite movements completed in 1878–79, after his abilities has
slowed.

The Moldau was not the most popular of the cycle to the Czechs
themselves, but since has captivated listeners everywhere with its
innocent but stirring imagery. The river has two sources, suggested
by intertwining flutes at the beginning. Clarinets and eventually strings
gather into the flow, and the regal theme is presented by the violins.
In successive episodes that crescendo and subside again the river passes
a hunt and a peasant wedding—neither of these especially original,
but charming nonetheless. My favorite is the glistening moonlight
scene where the river seems to lose its impetus as nymphs languor-
ously bathe. The full brass enter majestically yet *sempre pp.* (You seldom hear this much brass play this softly, and a good conductor can
stretch this passage out to bewitching end.) After a restatement the
river billows with great tonal and textural unrest through the rapids
and on to Prague. The mode shifts to major as the Moldau reaches its
greatest breadth, and where the imposing Vyšehrad castle looms, the
motive that unifies the cycle is stated with heroic pride. Then the
river flows out of sight into the Elbe.

Má vlast is now traditionally played each year in Prague on 12 May,
the anniversary of Smetana's death, to open the annual spring music
festival.

Overture and Dances from *The Bartered Bride*

For piccolo, flutes I-II, oboes I-II, clarinets I-II, bassoons I-II; horns I-IV, trumpets I-II, trombones I-III; timpani, snare drum, bass drum, cymbals, triangle; strings
Composed (the opera) July 1863—15 March 1866 in Prague; revised January 1869–September 1870
First performed with the opera 30 May 1866 by the Prague Provisional Theatre, Smetana conducting
Published by Umelěcké Beseda (Prague, 1872); overture published by Ed. Bote and G. Bock (Berlin, 1887)
Duration: about 20 minutes

Smetana composed eight operas altogether, of which *The Bartered Bride* is the second and far the most famous. It gained its reputation in Bohemia as he put it through numerous revisions, and enjoyed more than a hundred performance during his lifetime.

The young lovers are Jeník and Mařenka, their future blackened when the marriage broker arranges a match between Mařenka and the village idiot Vasek, younger son of the wealthy landowner Tobias Mícha. Jeník barters away his interest in Mařenka for 700 florins, on the condition that the groom must be Tobias Mícha's son. In so doing he wins the bride—and the money—for himself, for he is none other than the landowner's long-lost elder son.

Smetana was so excited by the idea that he wrote the overture before seeing the complete libretto. It proceeds Vivacissimo from the first to last, much in the spirit of the overture to Glinka's *Ruslan and Ludmila* (see p. 251). The merry unison thrust at the beginning settles back after a few bars, fragmenting into lesser pokings out of the strings in low register. From this the second violins flee in a scatter of continuous eighth notes. As though in pursuit, each of the other voices enters imitatively, and the resulting crescendo builds into a climax at the second thematic element, a figure of strong syncopation suggestive of the dance. The dance imagery continues in the gleeful closing theme that makes a metric joke of pairs of quarter notes. That's all, really: the hint of a lyric countermelody dissipates, and scamper, imitation, and climax are what matters.

The polka comes at the end of act I, where the young people dance on the green. After a start-and-stop introduction the amiable little dance begins its course, staccato over a pizzicato accompaniment, with grace notes at every turn. The trio introduces the undulation of a wide legato interval in the strings which the woodwinds then summarize in their broader melody. Note the dainty work for triangle and cymbals.

The furiant, which takes place in the local tavern, is based on one of those three-against-two figures of which Dvořák is so fond; in the middle of the movement the tension eases into rather straighter waltz music. In the last scene of *The Bartered Bride* itinerant circus performers give a preview of their work on the town green. The "Dance of the Comedians" is a *perpetuum mobile* in the general manner of the overture: the rapid scamper, the tutti climax, and in this case, trio sections of high syncopation.

Johann Strauss, Jr.

Born *25 October 1825 in Vienna*
Died *3 June 1899 in Vienna*

He was the eldest son of the first Johann Strauss (1804–49), who was himself a prince of waltzes, founder of the family's dynasty of dance orchestras, and author of the famous *Radetzky March*. The second son, Josef Strauss (1827–70) was also a good composer. The brothers were close, Josef later serving as Johann's second in command. The third brother was Eduard Strauss (1835–1916), who had his own orchestra and succeeded Johann as conductor of the court balls.

But it was Johann Strauss, Jr., who became known the world over as the waltz king. Their father had expected all three sons to enter business, and the younger Johann was thus forced to learn violin and composition on the sly—aided and abetted by his mother—while he worked in a bank. By 1844, at the age of nineteen, he had his own orchestra at a café-casino in the suburbs and there began to essay waltzes of his own composition. They were, from the first, wildly popular with the Viennese public.

Five years later, at his father's death, their two orchestras were amalgamated. His newly enlarged band toured Austria, Germany, and Poland, and had a highly profitable engagement at the public park in St. Petersburg—profitable both monetarily and in terms of significant works composed for these occasions. From 1863 Strauss was imperial director of the court balls, which culminated each spring with the most fashionable of them all, Fasching (Mardi Gras); by his mid-forties he could consider himself an international celebrity. He appeared in Paris for the Exhibition of 1867 and later that season in London, then in 1872 visited the United States to conduct huge festival concerts in New York and Boston. The Boston event, on 4 July 1872, was part of Patrick S. Gilmore's Peace Jubilee celebrating the end of the Franco-Prussian war. Among the twenty-two thousand (!) performers at the biggest of the concerts were dozens of assisting conductors, organ, canon, and at the anvils in the Anvil Chorus, a hundred representatives of the Boston fire department. Strauss later wrote the *Centennial Waltzes* for the hundredth anniversary of the Declaration of Independence.

From 1871 Strauss composed operetta as well. *Die Fledermaus* (The Bat, 1874) and *Der Zigeunerbaron* (The Gypsy Baron, 1885) found success, but otherwise, his long list of dramatic works is forgotten, his knack for setting text having been limited. His music for the pleasure garden and ballroom, however, was universally acknowledged to be without peer: the four hundred or so waltzes as well as marches, polkas, quadrilles, and a very popular *Perpetuum mobile,* op. 257. Of the polkas—French polkas, fast polkas, and polka-mazurkas—we recall *Pizzicato-Polka,* composed with his brother Josef; *Tritsch, Tratsch,* op. 214; and *Unter Donner und Blitz* (Thunder and Lightning), op. 324. The titles alone tell you much about of the idiom and the era: *Paroxysms, Extravagances, Accelerations,* even an *Electro-magnetic Polka.* There were quadrilles on everything from folksongs to motives from French grand opera and Verdi. (A quadrille, as the name suggests, was a type of square dance.)

Among Strauss's friends and admirers were both Brahms ("You must go to the Volksgarten . . . He's a master!") and Wagner. Schoenberg, Berg, and Webern on one occasion rescored a series of his waltzes. He is, in short, part and parcel of the very meaning of Vienna, and at his death not an eyebrow was lifted when he was buried alongside Brahms and Schubert.

Waltzes

An der Schönen, Blauen Donau (On the Beautiful Blue Danube), OP. 314
Composed 1867 in Vienna
First performed 10 March 1867 by the Strauss-Kapelle at a
    benefit concert in the Volksgarten, Vienna, for Josef and Eduard
    Strauss, Johann Strauss conducting
Published by C. A. Spina (Vienna, 1867)
Duration: about 10 minutes

Geschichten aus dem Wienerwald (Tales from the Vienna Woods), OP. 325
Composed 1868 in Vienna
First performed 18 June 1868 by the Strauss-Kapelle at a benefit
    concert, with fireworks, in the Volksgarten for Josef and Eduard
    Strauss, Johann Strauss conducting
Published by C. A. Spina (Vienna, 1869)
Duration: about 12 minutes

Wein, Weib, Gesang (Wine, Women, and Song) OP. 333
Composed 1869 in Vienna; Dedicated to Johann Herbeck,
    conductor at the imperial court
First performed 2 February 1989 by the Strauss-Kapelle and
    Vienna Men's Choral Society at a costume ball
Published by C. A. Spina (Vienna, 1869)
Duration: about 6 minutes

Emperor Waltzes, OP. 437
Composed 1888 in Vienna on the occasion of the fortieth
    anniversary of the reign of Emperor Franz Joseph
First performed 19 October 1889 to inaugurate a new hall in
    Berlin
Published by N. Simrock (Berlin, 1889)
Duration: about 12 minutes

For piccolo, flutes I-II, oboes I-II, clarinets I-II, bassoons I-II;
    horns I-IV, trumpets I-II, trombones I-III, tuba; timpani, snare

drum, bass drum, cymbals, triangle; harp; strings; *Tales from the Vienna Woods* has a solo zither part as well; both *The Blue Danube* and *Wine, Women, and Song* have *ad libitum* chorus parts.
Inexpensive edition: Johann Strauss, Jr.: *The Great Waltzes in Full Score* (New York: Dover, 1989)

Each of the titles—*Tales from the Vienna Woods, On the Beautiful Blue Danube,* and so on—actually embraces a group of five or six waltzes. An introduction foreshadowing the main themes is followed by a big crescendo to the first waltz. Each of the waltzes is in two strains, usually with a *da capo;* the series is connected with appropriate introductions and transitions and follows a scheme of closely related keys. Strauss's particular contribution to the form was to introduce such symphonic elements as thematic cross-referencing and development. In the coda, for example, the main themes are recalled as the waltz wind down, though there is always a brilliant close. The whole process takes something on the order of ten or fifteen minutes, such that two waltzes and a polka constitute an hour's worth of dancing. Strauss offered many an interlude and earned a good deal of money playing just such sets.

Too long for encores, too inconsequential for most concerts, the Strauss waltzes work best in exactly the venues for which they were intended: the fancy-dress ball and the dance pavilion. The performance practice is actually quite intricate, with anticipation of the second beats in the inner parts, lifts with delayed downbeats, and great ritards and springings free. The waltzes should gain in momentum and glamour as they progress—there is usually a last whirl with snare drum and cymbals—and then subside in the memories of spent passion. The style has a good deal to do with Viennese parlance. An acquaintance of mine says that if you want to know how to play a certain figure you must pronounce the word *Zwirnknäulerl* (a ball of string). And so, she says, "It needs a born Viennese to conduct these waltzes and polkas, and the players had better be native."

Nothing else changes, not the basic orchestration, nor the formal organization, nor least of all, the meter. Each of the waltzes, however, has a tale to tell: the surging *Emperor Waltzes* in joint hommage to the Prussian and Austrian monarchs, the *Blue Danube* as the sensation of the 1867 Paris Exhibition, *Wine, Women, and Song* in Boston— both these last, incidentally, with *ad libitum* chorus parts. The best,

I think, is *Tales from the Vienna Woods,* with its long, pastoral introduction, flute cadenza, zither solo, and timeless tunes.

You must pity the double bass and trombone players, who have
the boom, and the violas, second violinists, and French horns, who
have the chick-chick—for pages on end. But the latter of these play,
arguably, the central part: for it is they who delay all the second beats
the fraction of an instant that adds the froth.

Richard Strauss

Born *11 June 1864 in Munich*
Died *8 September 1949 in*
Garmisch-Partenkirchen

Son of the principal horn player in the Munich court orchestra, Richard Strauss had the opportunity to study music at court, where he became a facile pianist and promising young conductor. Moreover he was already composing significant music in his teens: this included some of his most popular songs, the Violin Concerto in D minor, opus 8 (1880–82), and the first of his two horn concertos in E♭ (1882–83). During a visit to Berlin in 1883 he met the great conductor Hans von Bülow and soon became his assistant. Strauss's conducting career gained serious momentum when he succeeded von Bülow in Meiningen; thereafter he had important posts in Munich, Weimar, Berlin, and Vienna, and eventually appeared as guest conductor (usually of his own works) with all the major European orchestras. He visited the United States twice: in 1904, when he conducted at Carnegie Hall and in Chicago with his wife, Pauline, as soprano soloist;

and again in 1921. On the podium he was an autocrat, but his technical wizardry and the depth of his expressivity earned him universal admiration of musicians and public alike.

Once he had left Munich, his compositions began to reflect the stylistic influences of Berlioz, Liszt, and Wagner. It is no accident that the orchestral pieces which followed took Liszt's descriptive tone poems as a model. Thereafter nearly all of Strauss's music has a story-line or text. His impressive series of symphonic poems extends from the late 1880s to the end of the century: *Macbeth* (1887); *Don Juan* (1889), his first great success, written when he was twenty-five; *Tod und Verklärung* (Death and Transfiguration, 1890); *Till Eulenspiegels lustige Streiche* (Till Eulenspiegel's Merry Pranks, 1894–95); *Also sprach Zarathustra* (Thus Spake Zarathustra, 1896); *Don Quixote* (variations for cello, viola, and orchestra, 1898), and the autobiographical *Ein Heldenleben* (A Hero's Life, 1899). The subsequent orchestral works, a *Domestic Symphony* (1904) and an *Alpine Symphony* (1915), have a lesser place in the repertoire by reason of their too-literal text painting and their demand for alphorns, wind machines, cowbells, and the like. The Second Horn Concerto comes from near the end of Strauss's career, in 1942, as does the haunting *Metamorphosen* for 23 strings, 1945.

With the turn of the century, Strauss concentrated on opera: *Salome* (based on Oscar Wilde's play, 1905), *Elektra* (1909), his masterpiece *Der Rosenkavalier* (The Knight of the Rose, 1911), *Ariadne auf Naxos* (1912), and *Die Frau ohne Schatten* (The Woman Without a Shadow, 1919). For *Elektra, Rosenkavelier,* and *Die Frau ohne Schatten* his librettist was Hugo von Hofmannsthal, with whom he developed one of the most successful collaborations in the annals of opera. The waltz suites from *Der Rosenkavalier* and the Dance of the Seven Veils from *Salome,* op. 54 (1905) are popular extracts from this repertoire. Additionally, there is an orchestral suite drawn from Strauss's incidental music for a production in German of Molière's *Le Bourgeois Gentilhomme* (op. 60, 1918).

Strauss loved writing music and was exceptionally facile at it. The mind boggles to consider the amount of ink consumed in the mere notation of these long, dense, and difficult scores. You must not let Strauss's occasional bouts of self-indulgence and climactic overkill get on your nerves: his descriptive effects, and the orchestral writing that goes with them, are always clever and very often inspired, and no one, not even Mahler, understood so well the principles of Wagnerian counterpoint. You must take him for what he offers, remembering always that Strauss was presiding over the sunset of a golden age.

Strauss briefly held an appointment—apparently without his consent—with the Nazi government. Actually he spent most of the war at his villa in Garmisch, and in 1948 he was officially exonerated of collaborating with the National Socialists.

Don Juan, OP. 20, tone poem after Nikolaus Lenau

> For piccolo, flutes I-IV, oboes I-II, English horn, clarinets I-II, bassoons I-II, contrabassoon; horns I-IV, trumpets I-III, trombones I-III, tuba; timpani, cymbals, triangle, bells; harp; strings
>
> Composed   May–30 September 1888; dedicated to Ludwig Thuille (1861–1907), boyhood friend of Strauss, later a distinguished composer
>
> First performed   11 November 1889 by the Weimar Court Orchestra, Strauss conducting
>
> Published by   Jos. Aibl Verlag (Munich, 1890). *Inexpensive score: Richard Strauss: Tone Poems: Series I* (New York: Dover, 1979)
>
> Duration: about 20 minutes

Strauss earned his first true celebrity with three tone poems he composed in his early twenties: *Macbeth, Don Juan,* and *Death and Transfiguration.* They introduced, it was clear, a composer of great promise and invention, as gifted in melodic and contrapuntal dexterity as he was in brilliance of orchestration. The public found certain elements of *Don Juan'*s subject matter shocking, it is true, but there could be no denying the arrival on the scene of a new virtuoso composer.

The scenario is by Nikolaus Lenau, wherein the Don is not so much a cad, in the fashion of Mozart's Don Giovanni, as an idealist smitten by "the endless charms of beautiful women." Nor is the text a narrative story, but rather a poem on the mysteries of love. The music treats the passions of the heart: longing, quest, the thunderbolt of discovery, fulfillment, and ultimately death.

Don Juan's character is suggested by two themes, that of the solo violin at the beginning, invoking loneliness and unsettled desire, then the big horn theme of pursuit. The woodwind episodes are meant as vignettes of the women in the Don's life. There is a troubled, confrontational development, then the love music for solo oboe—a third theme—with cellos and violas, and its culmination in a new, fourth theme for horns, later enriched with trombones. In the recapitulation the horn theme is heard at a higher scale degree, and thus more assured, and this spirit of confirmation is emphasized by the glissando figure in the harps. At the end, death comes in stern chromatics and tempestuous, minor-mode tremolo. Finally, to quote Lenau, "only silence remains."

Tod und Verlkärung (Death and Transfiguration), OP. 24

For flutes I-III, oboes I-II, English horn, clarinets I-II, bass clarinet, bassoons I-II, contrabassoon; horns I-IV, trumpets I-III, trombones I-III, tuba; timpani, tam-tam; harps I-II; strings

Composed 1888–18 November 1889 in Munich; dedicated to the composer's "dear friend Friedrich Rösch," author of the program of *Ein Heldenleben*

First performed 21 June 1890 at the Music Festival of the Allgemeiner Deutscher Musik-Verein in Eisenach (Bach's birthplace), Strauss conducting

Published by Jos. Aibl Verlag (Munich, 1890). *Inexpensive score:* Richard Strauss: *Tone Poems: Series I* (New York: Dover, 1979)

Duration: about 25 minutes

Close on the heels of *Don Juan* came *Death and Transfiguration,* to the composer's own scenario. The saccharine poem at the head of the score is the work of Strauss's friend Alexander Ritter, and did not inspire the composition but rather was provided later. In a letter of 1894, Strauss wrote:

It occured to me to present in the form of a tone poem the dying hours of a man who had striven toward the highest idealistic aims, maybe indeed those of an artist. The sick man lies in bed, asleep, with heavy irregular breathing; friendly dreams conjure a smile on the features of the deeply suffering man; he wakes up; he is once more racked with horrible agonies; his limbs shake with fever; as the attack passes and the pains leave off, his thoughts wander through his past life; his childhood passes before him, the time of his youth with its strivings and passions and then, as the pains begin to return, there appear to him the fruit of his life's path, the conception, the ideal which he has sought to realize, to present artistically, but which he has not been able to complete, since it is not for man to be able to accomplish such things. The hour of death approaches, the soul leaves the body in order to find gloriously achieved in everlasting space those things which could not be fulfilled here below.

The narrative meaning of the succession of episodes is obvious enough: at the beginning we envisage the artist on his sickbed, of labored pulse and breath, struggling, sometimes violently, with the inevitable. Memories of his life pass by in review: his innocent childhood (the oboe and harp), the enthusiasm of his youth, the awakening of his passion. But the affliction renews its assault, defied by the first theme of the artist and his art. Death triumphs at the strike of the tam-tam, but from the emptiness rises the transfiguration, a soaring hymn mingled at times with reminiscences of childlike purity. Strauss argues for faith in an afterlife of victory and in the permanence of the art we leave behind.

Till Eulenspiegels lustige Streiche (Till Eulenspiegel's Merry Pranks), OP. 28, after the Old Roguish Manner, in Rondo Form

For piccolo, flutes I-III, oboes I-III, English horn, D clarinet, clarinets I-II, bass clarinet, bassoons I-III, contrabassoon; horns I-IV, horns I-IV in D *ad libitum;* trumpets I-III, trumpet in D *ad libitum,* trombones I-III, tuba; timpani, snare drum, bass drum, cymbals, triangle, large rattle; strings

Composed   1894–95 in Munich; manuscript dated 6 May 1895; dedicated to the composer's "dear friend Dr. Arthur Seidl," the conductor

First performed   5 November 1895 by the Gürzenich Orchestra of Cologne, Franz Wüllner conducting

Published by   Jos. Aibl Verlag (Munich, 1895). *Inexpensive score: Richard Strauss: Tone Poems: Series II* (New York: Dover, 1979)

Duration: about 20 minutes

Till Eulenspiegel was a rogue in medieval North German legend, to whose exploits Strauss was originally attracted as possible subject matter for an opera.

The tone poem begins with the musical equivalent of the age-old formula "Once upon a time, long ago, and far away." Till's first theme is the famous French horn solo, an insouciant romp through the instrument's several registers, technically difficult and of much greater metric complexity than you may be aware without looking at the music. Till's second motive, a thumb-nosed sneer in the clarinet, sets his adventures in motion. What follows is more or less a rondo structure, with returns of the solo motives separating the episodes of the story.

The first adventure begins with Till on horseback, galloping through the countryside. He rides into a crowded and noisy village marketplace, cracking his whip and upsetting goods and stalls. The townspeople scurry off in all directions, and Till rides away.

Next, he disguises himself as a priest and begins to preach the merits of the sober life, but his sassy motive in the clarinet indicates a rather different and more characteristic frame of mind. At the violin glissando he throws off his clerical robes to declare his interest in a young woman among his listeners, but she rejects his advances. Doctors and professors arrive, to a halting march with academic canons, to dispute with Till, but these he mocks as well.

Till is a jokester in a land of respectability, and his irreverence will not do. The drum rolls signal his being brought to trial on trumped-up charges. Till pleads his innocence three times, but he is found guilty by the judge and hanged forthwith. We hear the life leaving our hero as the clarinet squeals and the orchestra applauds. But then there is a little reprise of the French horn theme: Till's lusty spirit lives on in all of us.

Also sprach Zarathustra (Thus Spake Zarathustra), OP. 30, tone poem freely after Friedrich Nietzsche

[Preamble]—Of Those of the Unseen World—Of the Great Longing—Of Joys and Passions—The Dirge—Of Science—The Convalescent —The Dance Song—The Song of Those Who Come Later

For piccolos I-II, flutes I-III, oboes I-III, English horn, E♭ clarinet, clarinets I-II, bass clarinet, bassoons I-III, contrabassoon; horns I-VI, trumpets I-IV, trombones I-III, tubas I-II; timpani, bass drum, cymbals, triangle, glockenspiel, bell in low E; harps I-II, organ; strings

Composed 4 February–24 August 1896 in Munich

First performed   27 November 1896 at a concert of the Frankfurt
Museum Orchestra, Strauss conducting
Published by   Jos. Aibl Verlag (Munich, 1896). *Inexpensive score:*
Richard Strauss: *Tone Poems: Series II* (New York: Dover, 1979)
Duration: about 35 minutes

The philosophy of Friedrich Nietzsche (1844–1900)—ideas about the
eclipse of tragedy by rationalism, the meeting of Apollonian and
Dionysian modes of thought, the merits of intellectualism shaped by
passionate love of art—permeates modern thought in many ways. His
volume *Also sprach Zarathustra* (subtitled "A Book for All or None")
was written 1883–84, as he despaired of finding a suitable mate, and
published in 1892. In this rhapsody on the mysteries of life, he pro-
motes the idea of a Superman who would come to lead mankind from
a world of suffering into a utopian society of elevated pursuits.
Nietzsche's book was thus only a few years old when Strauss first
discovered it.

The composer is quick to note that the symphonic poem merely
takes its point of departure from Nietzsche, intending to suggest the
progress of mankind from its origin through its religious and then
scientific phases to a more exalted plane of existence. Nevertheless an
excerpt from Nietzsche's text appears at the head of the score to indicate, at least, the programmatic meaning of the opening and last
pages. Zarathustra (that is, Zoroaster, the prophet of Persian myth),
weary of his wisdom, elects to return to dwell with mankind and, by
inference, to lead it forward. At the end of the work Zarathustra's
descent is abundantly, perhaps egregiously, obvious; so, too, is the
apotheosis which follows.

The work emerges from the famous trumpet call into a galactic
climax, familiar to you from the movie *2001: A Space Odyssey,* for
which it served as soundtrack along with György Ligeti's *Lux Aeterna.*
The first big section suggests religious mysteries, first in the hollow
transition of the bass instruments, then in an ecstatic episode for strings
and organ. Just before this, the French horn figure is marked "Credo
in unum deum"; just afterward the organ has a short figure marked
"Magnificat."

The *Great Longing* begins in the string choir and goes forward with
the triplet-dominated figure that bubbles up from the cello and bassoons and surges upward through the orchestra with ever increasing

chromaticism and intensity. The music works itself into the major key and becomes flirtatious in the passage on joys and passions: innocent pleasures, these, in which a fundamental truth is to be found. The grave song, or *Dirge,* returns to the minor mode and is given to the oboe solo.

Of Science is, appropriately, an academic fugue, followed by the necessary period of convalescence. The episode for flutes and trilled clarinets represents Zarathustra's vision of a dance of Cupid and the wood nymphs. As the bell tolls midnight, the wandering into the future begins. There is the magnificent descent of Zarathustra, with wild plunge of trumpets, and the work concludes in a tonal mixture as the harmony cadences in B major while the basses maintain their low C. Of these sorts of mysteries is born new truth.

Strauss's aural imagination never ceases to amaze you, as he wanders from his pseudosacred mode through heroism, waltzing, and general impishness—not to mention fuguishness. But it can well be argued that this sequence of what are essentially mood musics is grossly overdone, and it certainly goes on a long time. There are plenty of people in the world who can't stomach it. I tend to muse on where it all came from and where it was going. Not much further, is the answer, though occasionally there is a premonition or two of Bartók.

Don Quixote, OP. 35, Fantastic Variations on a Theme of Knightly Character

Introduzione, Tema con Variazioni, Finale

For viola and cello solos; piccolo, flutes I-II, oboes I-II, English horn, E♭ clarinet, clarinets I-II, bass clarinet, bassoons I-III, contrabassoon; horns I-VI, trumpets I-III, trombones I-III, tenor tuba, tubas I-II; side drum, bass drum, cymbals, triangle, tambourine, bells, wind machine; harp; strings

Composed October 1896–29 December 1897 in Munich; dedicated to the composer's friend Joseph Dupont

First performed 8 March 1898 by the Gürzenich Orchestra of Cologne, Friedrich Grützmacher, solo cello; Franz Wüllner conducting

Published by Jos. Aibl Verlag (Munich, 1898). *Inexpensive score:* Richard Strauss: *Tone Poems: Series I* (New York: Dover, 1979)

Duration: about 35 minutes

The idea here is that Don Quixote, the doddering adventurer, is portrayed by the cello soloist and his rather more practical sidekick Sancho Panza by the viola. The incidents come from the great novel of Cervantes (1547–1616), source of aphorisms, *bons mots,* and wry observations of all sorts. Strauss's music is of correspondingly good humor.

The work takes the form of ten variations on the theme, an effective solution to the problem of setting a series of episodes that always involves the same two characters. From the opening bars, the knightly allusions and melodic eccentricity suggest the pleasantly disordered character of our hero, never completely crazed, but never quite stable, either. The string motives gather confidently together at first, then back down again in a cozy eighths-and-sixteenths figure in close harmony, as the long introduction becomes increasingly fanciful. The formal introduction of characters comes after the first big climax: the Don's material, already familiar to us, in the solo cello (carried on by solo violin) in D minor; Sancho Panza has a silly tune in F major for the bass clarinet and tuba, soon joined by the viola soloist.

In the first variation, the motives intertwine as the Don and Sancho Panza set out on their adventure tilting at windmills. The Don encounters the army of the Emperor Ali-fanfaron: a bold advance in the strings and woodwinds denotes the beginning of variation II; the hushed tremolandos in the violas and bleating in the brass and woodwinds—one of Strauss's more comical effects—indicate that the "army" is merely a flock of sheep. A shepherds' call is heard in the woodwinds, and our heroes are pelted with stones.

In the long third variation Sancho urges the Don to come to his senses: a big viola solo is followed by a passionate development. The D-minor tonality returns with the fanfares and a long-held D in the bass instruments at the beginning of variation IV. Here brass and bassoons suggest the chanting of the band of monks the Don believes are abducting a likeness of the Madonna; there is a skirmish, and another defeat. The Don slips from consciousness at the end of variation IV (the long, low glissando in tuba and then contrabassoon), then dreams of the beautiful Dulcinea in the course of a lovely orchestral cadenza (tremolandos in the winds, long chords in the low brass, cello solo, and timpani; then a magic glissando in the harps and burst of violins). The true Dulcinea, who enters on a donkey with variation VI, is an ugly creature, though the Don imagines she is merely under some spell. Variation VII is a brilliant orchestral evocation of a windstorm, complete with a wild ride of the blindfolded lovers on a magic horse. But the wind is merely a blacksmith's bellows, and we know from the continuous low D in the double-basses that the wooden horse has never moved. The next misadventure, variation VIII, takes place in a rowboat and finds them getting soaked in a thunderstorm; in the ninth, the Don disputes esoterically with two wizards—actually monks—in a mawkish dialogue of the two bassoons. Variation X deals with the Don's last defeat, where a friend induces him to give up knight-errantry and enter his retirement. He dies, at the little obbligato figure for clarinet and the slow glissando in the last bar of the cello part, with at least a little wisdown, and the final cadence is a fond one. "For if he like a madman lived," writes Cervantes, "At least he like a wise one died."

Ein Heldenleben (A Hero's Life), OP. 40

The Hero—The Hero's Adversaries—The Hero's Companion—The Hero's Deeds of War—The Hero's Works of Peace—The Hero's Retirement

For piccolo, flutes I-III, oboes I-IV, English horn, E♭ clarinet, clarinets I-II, bass clarinet, bassoons I-III, contrabassoon; horns I-VIII, trumpets I-V, trombones I-III, tenor tuba, tuba; timpani, small snare drum, large tenor drum, bass drum, cymbals; harps I-II; strings with solo violin

Composed 2 August 1898 in Munich–27 December 1898 in Berlin; dedicated to Willem Mengelberg and the Concertgebouw Orchestra of Amsterdam

First performed 3 March 1899 at a concert of the Frankfurt Museum Orchestra, Strauss conducting

Published by F. E. C. Leuckart (Leipzig, 1899). *Inexpensive score: Richard Strauss: Tone Poems: Series II* (New York: Dover, 1979)

Duration: about 45 minutes

Don't be in a hurry when you approach this last of the Strauss tone poems, which goes on as long as a Brahms symphony but with a good deal less breathing space. The composer's idea was that, Beethoven's "Eroica" Symphony having faded from the repertoire, it would be good to do a new piece in the same key (E♭) and along the same

lines—"with lots of horns" but without the funeral march. For subject matter he chose no less a hero than himself, with the puckish
remark that he found his own life as interesting as that of Napoleon,
or Alexander the Great. Such a notion would be offputting were it
not that Strauss is exceptionally good at it. The impression you come
away with, rather, is that the composer's self-esteem was reasonably
healthy: after all, most people are most passionate about themselves,
and those who bother to analyze themselves in heroic terms are probably worth paying some attention to.

Strauss began *Ein Heldenleben* just after finishing *Don Quixote,* the
sketches show, and finished it on the eve of his move to become director of the Berlin Philharmonic. You can sense him at a stylistic turning point, with the size of the orchestra, which is among the largest
in the repertoire, stretched almost beyond practicality.

The composition has four big subdivisions, with linking transitions and digressions, that amount to movements on the four central
issues of the program: the hero, the wife, war, peace. At the same
time an overarching sonata form is at work: the hero motive as first
theme, that of the adversaries as transition, of the wife as second
theme, of war as development, and the works of peace as recapitulation. The coda represents retirement and fullfillment. Strauss did not
include the subheadings in the published editions of the score, but
spoke of them often enough to his friends and biographers that he
might as well have.

The hero's theme is a dashing soar upward through the string sections, from cellos to first violins, merging seamlessly as they go. From
this extravagant theme are drawn any number of motives that return
to the fore later in the work. The wide gaps of silence, at about the
five-minute mark, and the ensuing thrombosis articulate the end of
the first section. The flurry of woodwinds and the hollow parallel
intervals in the tenor and bass tuba are the "very sharp and pointed,
snarling" motives of the adversaries; the hero's theme is deflected into
the minor mode.

The violin solo begins the portrait of the hero's companion. This
is none other than the composer's wife, Pauline: complex, delicate,
coquettish, yet at times perverse—to use the composer's language—
"at every moment different from how she had been just before." One
is scarcely concerned with the less flattering implications, so imagi-

native is the work for solo violin and so perplexing its thematic and tonal implications. And the ardent night scene which follows is to be savored above everything else in the work. Time virtually stands still as this triumph of eroticism, with stunning downward glissandos in harps and portamentos in the winds, plays itself out.

Just after the motive of the adversaires insinuates itself, offstage trumpets issue a call to battle. The confrontation takes place over a powerful rattling tatoo in the percussion and a near-Ivesian clash of tonalities; one of the themes here is from *Don Juan*. Things become cacophonous on every plane, including metrically. You can't miss the chromatic tumble of the adversaries defeated, nor the powerful return of the E♭ tonality and the recapitulation of the hero's theme.

There follows, to begin the process of drawing things to a close, the remarkable section devoted to the hero's works of peace, an amalgam of some three dozen wisps and snippets from Strauss's previous work. The citations will seem familiar even if you cannot quite place them all; the most recognizable are those from *Till Eulenspiegel* and *Death and Transfiguration*. A last rattle from the adversaries—and a quick pommeling—is followed by the coda of resignation and fulfillment. At the end the solo violin sails up to its highest E♭; in the final bars, the French horns have the same pitch four octaves below, and there's a *Zarathustra*-like close for brass and rolls of percussion.

First Sequence of Waltzes from *Der Rosenkavalier*

For flutes I-III, oboes I-III, clarinet in D / E♭, clarinets I-II, basset horn, bassoons I-III; horns I-IV, trumpets I-III, trombones I-III, tuba; timpani, snare drum, bass drum, cymbals, triangle, glockenspiel; harps I-II; rings

Composed for the opera in 1909–10; waltz sequence I, with new concert ending, arranged 1944; scored dated 26 October 1944 in Garmisch-Partenkirchen and dedicated to Dr. Ernest Roth (also the dedicatee of *Im Abendrot;* see below); waltz sequence II, from act III, extracted 1934; additionally, there is a *Rosenkavalier* Suite (published 1945) and music for a 1925 film on the opera

First performed 4 August 1946 by the Philharmonia Orchestra of London, Erich Leinsdorf conducting; the opera had first been

performed 26 January 1911 at the Royal Opera, Dresden, Ernst
von Schuch, conducting
Published by Boosey & Hawkes (London, 1947)
Duration: about 12 minutes

Strauss's *Der Rosenkavalier* is a bittersweet story of an aging noblewoman (the Feldmarschallin) who loses her young lover (Octavian) to
a girl his own age (Sophie). (All three characters are sopranos, such
that the prevailing tone quality in the opera is unlike any other, and
their trio at the end is one of the loveliest passages in all music.)

Der Rosenkavalier contains some of Strauss's most gorgeous music.
The central incident, from which the opera draws its name, occurs
when a silver rose is sent by the bumbling Baron Ochs to the young
Sophie Faninal in token of their engagement. One did not present the
rose oneself, according to Viennese tradition, but rather sent a lieutenant. Ochs chooses Octavian, but when the handsome lad and the
beautiful girl set eyes on one another, all previous understandings
become null and void.

Waltz music permeates every scene of *Der Rosenkavalier,* which in
several respects seeks to evoke the essence of old Vienna. The waltzes
come and go, seldom quite complete, and in the suites are woven
together with such freedom that little is exactly like the operatic original. The horn call and response at the beginning of the first waltz
sequence is that of the sunrise and lazy dalliance of Octavian and the
Marschallin at the beginning of act I; the delicate, highly chromati-
cized figure for flutes and glockenspiel that of the silver rose. A half-
dozen waltzes are presented in the course of the suites with, in the
first, a polka associated with Baron Ochs. Both are fancy works for
mega-orchestra with hair-raising harmonic twists and a sort of *fin-de-
siècle* abandon you may well associate with Ravel. Strauss is older and
wiser here than in the tone poems: every moment is to be savored,
and (unlike the tone poems) the waltzes are over too soon.

Four Last Songs

Frühling (Spring)
For flutes I-II, oboes I-II, English horn, clarinets I-II, bass
clarinet, bassoons I-III; horns I-IV; harp; strings
Text by Hermann Hesse

Completed June 18–July 1948 in Pontresina, Italy; dedicated to
Dr. Willi Schuh and his wife

September
For flutes I-III, oboes I-II, English horn, clarinets I-II, bass
clarinet, bassoons I-II; horns I-IV, trumpets I-II; harp; strings
Text by Hermann Hesse
Completed 20 September 1948 in Montreux, Switzerland;
dedicated to Maria Jeritza Seery and her husband

Beim Schlafengehen (Time for Sleep)
For piccolos I-II, flutes I-II, oboes I-II, English horn, clarinets I-
II, bass clarinet, bassoons I-II; horns I-IV, trumpets I-II,
trombones I-III, tuba; celesta; strings
Text by Hermann Hesse
Completed 4 August 1948 in Pontresina; dedicated to Dr. and
Mrs. Adolf Jöhr

Im Abendrot (At Dusk)
For piccolos I-II, flutes I-II, oboes I-II, English horn, clarinets I-
II, bass clarinet, bassoons I-II, contrabassoon; horns I-IV,
trumpets I-III, trombones I-III, tuba; timpani; strings
Text by Joseph von Eichendorff
Completed April 6 May 1948 in Montreux; dedicated to Dr.
Ernest Roth

First performed 22 May 1950, posthumously, by the
Philharmonia Orchestra in the Royal Albert Hall, London,
Kirsten Flagstad, soprano; Wilhelm Furtwängler conducting
Published by Boosey and Co., Ltd. (London, 1950)
Duration: about 25 minutes

These were, as the title suggests, old Dr. Strauss's last compositions.
The Eichendorff text was the first to be set, in May 1948, with the
three Hesse songs composed over the course of the following summer,
concluding with *September*. Strauss assembled and retouched the set
between April and September 1949, again in Montreux and Pontresina; the order in which they were left was, however: *Im Abendrot,
Frühling, Beim Schlafengehen,* and *September*. A fifth song, incomplete,
was found among his papers at the time of his death, on 8 September
1949.

They are poignant songs of love, nature, and death, intimately associated with the composer's wife, Pauline, a professional soprano who had often sung her husband's lieder. The texts are progressive: in his more than two hundred songs Strauss had never before set either Hesse or Eichendorff. And the musical treatment is, for a patriarch, adventurous as well, with the soprano line inextricably fused with the orchestral voices, now interwoven in rich counterpoint, now floating above the sea of instrumental sonority, now swept away in it. Collectively the set describes a journey through the seasons and into the autumn of life and toward its peaceful conclusion. Sentiments such as these can too easily become saccharine and indulgent, but instead Strauss discovers a serene rhetoric that is at the same time intensely ardent.

Frühling is a triumph of text painting: the substance of virtually every phrase, at times every word, is reflected in the music. It blossoms from the half-light in which the poet has waited for spring, then lifts to the soprano's top register for the word *Lüften* (breezes) and floats and warbles there at the word *Vogelgesang* (birdsong). The orchestra bathes the scene in the sunlight mentioned in the text, and the soprano reaches her highest pitch on the word *Wunder*. Poem and music quiver in the marvelous presence of spring, and there is a sustained orchestral close.

September carries with it a tinge of melancholy, as summer longs for repose. You hear the golden leaves fluttering down from the acacia tree and feel not just the general downward fall, but the marked slowing of the rhythmic values at the end, the dramatic low-pitched setting of the word *Ruh* (repose), and the solemn closing of summer's eyelids.

So far the songs have dealt primarily with nature's life cycle: the birth of spring, the falling asleep of September. These are given a human connection with *Beim Schlafengehen,* where death is seen as the ultimate repose from life's weary journey. The opening is low and somber, with the soloist entering in midphrase. Between the second strophe and the last comes an orchestral interlude with solo violin, presumably symbolic of the soul ascending. The soprano returns as before, in mid-phrase; the text of the soul winging toward the magic realm of night prompts an ethereal vocal line that settles to its low point at the word *tief* (deep), then floats to a high B♭ at on the line "deep and ever to dwell." Poet and composer look forward with dignity to the final rest.

Im Abendrot begins in the brilliant and erotic hues of the setting sun; companions of a lifetime wander hand in hand toward the setting sun. At every new phrase you hear the words in the music: the pause beside the silent landscape, the song of the two skylarks, the weariness of the journey. And finally, at the tempo indication *immer langsamer* (ever slower), the climactic line *ist dies etwa der Tod?* (is this, perhaps, death?). The French horn at the end cites a motive from *Tod und Verklärung,* and the two larks sing once again.

Igor Stravinsky

**Born 17 June 1882 in Oranienbaum,
near St. Petersburg
Died 6 April 1971 in New York**

Stravinsky, majestic voice of the new century, was probably among the dozen most influential composers in the history of music. The son of a leading bass with the Imperial Opera, he grew up in a cultivated intellectual and artistic milieu. He went to the university to study law, but turned his attention to music composition when he became a student of Rimsky-Korsakov. Two of his early works for orchestra, *Feu d'artifice* (Fireworks, written for the wedding of Rimsky's daughter, 1908) and a *Scherzo fantastique* (1909), so impressed the impresario Sergei Diaghilev that he commissioned Stravinsky to write a ballet score on Russian subject matter for the forthcoming Paris season of the Ballets Russes. The result was the first of three ballets for the company that catapulted Stravinsky into the first rank of international celebrity: *The Firebird* (1910), soon followed by *Petrushka* (1911) and

Le Sacre du printemps (The Rite of Spring, 1913). The subject matter of *Le Sacre,* its barbaric rhythms, and harmonic modernisms so shocked the Parisian public that a riot ensued at the first performance.

Stravinsky spent the years of World War I in Switzerland, where he gradually developed what has come to be known as his neoclassic style. The most famous of the works from this period are the musical play *L'Histoire du soldat* (The Soldier's Tale, 1918) and the ballet *Pulcinella* (1920), the latter based on themes Stravinsky believed to be by Giovanni Battista Pergolesi. He returned to Paris, which he regarded as the font of all modernism, frequently in the 1920s and in 1934 became a French citizen.

But in those days, no one of his leanings could long deny the lure of the United States (monetary, of course, but cultural and social as well). He had already begun to compose for American audiences with the classical ballet *Apollon Musagète* (1928, commissioned by the Elizabeth Sprague Coolidge Foundation and first performed at the Library of Congress) and the *Symphony of Psalms* (1930, for the fiftieth anniversary of the Boston Symphony). In late 1934 he visited Massachusetts to deliver, in French, the Charles Eliot Norton lectures at Harvard (*Poetics of Music,* 1948); in 1939 Stravinsky immigrated to the United States and settled in Hollywood. In the years that followed, he revised and republished his most important Europeans works in order to give them an American copyright and corresponding income.

Among the dozens of provocative works he composed in this country is a more-or-less traditional opera, *The Rake's Progress* (1951, to a libretto by W. H. Auden and Chester Kallman, based on a series of engravings by Hogarth). He returned to Russia for a visit in 1962 and received a hero's welcome there, despite the fact that his music had been all but ignored in his native land. The Stravinskys moved to New York shortly before the master's death in 1971; his remains were flown to Venice, site of the premiere of *The Rake's Progress,* and buried alongside Diaghilev's in the Russian portion of the cemetery on the island of San Michele.

Few composers have maintained such continued dominion over musical composition throughout their lives, or been so willing to investigate fresh stylistic issues with each new undertaking. (Monteverdi is perhaps the best comparison.) Among Stravinsky's works for large instrumental ensemble are the *Symphonies of Wind Instruments,* in memory of Debussy (1920), the two Suites for Orchestra (1917–25,

1921), the Concerto for Piano and Winds (1924), the *Dumbarton Oaks Concerto* (1938), the Symphony in C (1940), the *Ebony Concerto* (1945, a clarinet concerto for Woody Herman), and the *Variations: Aldous Huxley in Memoriam* (1965). The great works for orchestra and chorus include the cantata *Les Noces* (The Wedding, 1923), *Canticum sacrum* (1956) and the *Requiem Canticles* (1966; performed in 1971 at the composer's grave).

My favorite Stravinsky story concerns the *Circus Polka* Stravinsky composed in 1942 for the Ringling Brothers and Barnum and Bailey Circus. It was billed as a "Ballet of the Elephants: Fifty Elephants and Fifty Beautiful Girls in an Original Choreographic Tour de Force featuring Modoc, première ballerina, the Corps de Ballet and Corps des Eléphants." Balanchine, the choreographer, telephoned Stravinsky to ask for a polka. "Elephants," he said. "How old?" inquired Stravinsky. "Young." "If they're very young," replied Stravinsky in a flash, "I'll do it."

L'Oiseau de feu (The Firebird), symphonic suite from the ballet

1919 Version
Introduction—The Firebird and Its Dance—Variations (of the Firebird)—Rondo of the Princesses (Khorovde)—Infernal Dance of the Subjects of King Kastchei—Lullaby (Berceuse)—Finale

1945 Version (with material added at the beginning)
Introduction—Prelude and Dance of the Firebird—Variations (The Firebird)—Pantomime I—Pas de deux (Firebird and Ivan Tsarevitsch)—Pantomime II—Scherzo (Dance of the Princesses)—Pantomime III—Rondo (Chorovod)—Infernal Dance—Lullaby (Firebird)—Final Hymn

For flutes I-II, oboes I-II, clarinets I-II, bassoons I-II; horns I-IV, trumpets I-II, trombones I-III, tuba; timpani, bass drum, cymbals, triangle, xylophone; piano, harp, strings; the 1945 version adds snare drum to the original orchestration

Composed November 1909–18 May 1910 in St. Petersburg to a commission from Diaghilev; a suite drawn from it in 1910, without the lullaby and finale, then in 1919 reorchestrated for small orchestra with those two movements added; complete ballet revised for large orchestra 1945; dedicated "to my dear friend," i.e., Andrei Rimsky-Korsakov

First performed with the ballet 25 June 1910 in Paris, Gabriel
  Pierné conducting; scenario and choreography by Michel Fokine
Published by Éditions Russes de Musique (Berlin, 1912); the
  1945 version published by Schott (Leeds & New York, 1946) as
  a suite. *Inexpensive score:* Igor Stravinsky: *The Firebird in Full Score
  (Original 1910 Version)* (New York: Dover, 1987)
Duration: about 30 minutes

Stravinsky had not yet turned twenty-seven when, in February 1909,
Serge Diaghilev heard *Fireworks,* his wedding offering to Rimsky-
Korsakov's daughter and Maximilian Steinberg. Diaghilev was quick
to involve Stravinsky in the affairs of his company, first by inviting
him to score a portion of the new Chopin ballet *Les Sylphides* and to
come to Paris for its performance. Subsequently, after both Glazunov
and Tcherepnin had declined similar offers, Stravinsky was given the
commission for a new ballet to be premiered during the 1910 Paris
season of what was by then being called the Ballets Russes.

In *The Firebird,* the evil King Kaschei retains his spell over his
subjects through the power of a magic egg preserved in an ornate
casket. Coming one night upon Kaschei's garden, the handsome prince
Ivan Tsarevitch captures a firebird, and in exchange for its life the
bird leaves him a magic tailfeather. He then stumbles upon thirteen
enchanted princesses; hoping to attain the most beautiful of them, he
allows himself to be lured to the palace and surrounded by Kaschei's
infernal subjects. The next morning he is to be placed under the
wicked spell. With the magic tailfeather Ivan summons the firebird
and learnes from it the secret of the egg. Ivan opens the box and
smashes the egg; the ogre dies. All the spells are broken, and Ivan
and the beautiful princess will marry and rule the kingdom.

This is, of course, exotic and colorful subject matter and is matched
with a musical score of commensurate brilliance, wherein it's easy to
hear the mantle of the glittering Rimsky-Korsakov being passed on
to Stravinsky. The ballet suite begins by evoking Kaschei's magic
garden by night with glissandos of strings over the fingerboard, an
effect of which Stravinsky was especially proud. In the dance of the
firebird there is a set of variations on a characteristic Russian song
with ornate decoration in the winds. The round dance of the princesses, or Khorovde, juxtaposes two folk songs; its orderly conclusion
is shattered by the beginning of the Infernal Dance, in which the

visceral rhythmic character of *The Rite of Spring* is strongly foreshadowed. The angry episode and its reprise surround a quieter central passage, then a return. The famous *berceuse,* or lullaby follows, for solo violin and tender orchestra accompaniment. Tremolos effect the transition into the finale, a glamorous wedding processional affirming the rich future of the prince and princess.

Petrushka, Burlesque in Four Tableaux

First Tableau: The Shrovetide Fair
    The Magic Trick—Russian Dance
Second Tableau: Petrushka's Room
Third Tableau: The Moor's Room
    Dance of the Ballerina—Waltz
Fourth Tableau: The Shrovetide Fair That Evening
    Dance of the Nursemaids—Dance of the Coachmen and Stable
    Boys—The Mummers

For piccolos I-II, flutes I-II, oboes I-III, English horn, clarinets I-III, bass clarinet, bassoons I-III, contrabassoon; horns I-IV, cornets I-II, trumpets I-II, trombones I-III, tuba; timpani, snare drum, bass drum, cymbals, triangle, tambourine, tam-tam, xylophone, glockenspiel; harps I-II, piano, celesta; strings

Composed winter 1910 in Beaulieu-sur-mer—26 May 1911 in Rome; dedicated to Alexandre Benois; rewritten 1947 to secure the copyright and to adapt the ballet for smaller orchestra (in this version the piano has a greater role)

First performed 13 June 1911, by the Ballets Russes at the Théâtre du Châtelet, Paris, Pierre Monteux conducting

Published by Éditions Russes de Musique [Boosey and Hawkes, Inc. in the west]; revised edition published by Boosey and Hawkes, Inc. (London, 1947). *Inexpensive scores:* Stravinsky: *Petrushka,* ed. Charles Hamm, A Norton Critical Score (New York: Norton, 1967); Igor Stravinsky: *Petrushka in Full Score, Original Version* (New York: Dover, 1988)

Duration: about 35 minutes

Stravinsky's second ballet for Diaghilev took shape in the composer's imagination when, as he was composing an unrelated work, the image of an exasperating puppet kept coming to mind. It was clear that *The*

Rite of Spring would not be ready for the 1911 season, so Stravinsky suggested the puppet story to Diaghilev, who had a scenario prepared and engaged Michel Fokine for the choreography and Vaclav Nijinsky for the title role. Petrushka of the Mardi-Gras fair is common to many folk traditions, not so different from Punch of Punch and Judy shows or Pulcinella of the Italian *commedia dell'arte*—"the immortal and unhappy hero," Stravinsky called him, "of every fair."

The score is a masterpiece, overflowing with memorable descriptive vignettes; a fresh harmonic idiom that yields, in the scene in Petrushka's room a wonderful bitonal sonority (simultaneous chords of C and F♯ major) generally called "the Petrushka chord"; and fine rhythmic and metric effects, particularly in the unmitigated confusion of crowd scenes. In its entirety the enormous orchestra exudes the effervescence of the Shrovetide Fair; in smaller groupings—drone and winds for the barrel organ, glockenspiel for the music box, the pair of clarinets for Petrushka's curse—the orchestration can be more vivid still. A good deal of the melodic material comes from Russian folksong, popular French melody (in the second of the organ tunes, for example), and, for the waltz, the music of the Viennese composer Joseph Lanner (1801–43).

The ballet score is very effective as a concert piece, but it is important to imagine the story as it goes by:

Tableau I. The curtain rises on a fairground, to one side of which is a little puppet theater of the sort often found in European parks and gardens. It is Mardi Gras (Shrovetide); the weather is still cold. Tipsy merrymakers lurch by. A magician-puppeteer enters and beckons the crowd toward the theater. An organ grinder and dancer appear; she dances to the hurdy-gurdy, beating time on her triangle, as though a doll herself. The puppeteer again tries to attract the crowd; the revelers return.

Drummers announce the beginning of the puppet show. With a flick of his wrist (*The Magic Trick*), the old puppeteer raises the curtain. Three puppets lie on stage: Petrushka, the Moor, and the Ballerina. The puppeteer plays his flute to bring the dolls to life. The puppets dance a Russian Dance (*trépak*) together.

Tableau II. *Petrushka's Room.* A door opens and Petrushka is kicked into the room, falling in a heap on the floor. He comes to life and curses his fate. The Ballerina enters and for a moment they dance together. Then she abandons Petrushka to his miserable loneliness.

Tableau III. *The Moor's Room.* The Moor, a comic villain, dances a characteristic solo. The Ballerina enters to dance and play a cornet; she waltzes with the Moor. The jealous Petrushka quarrels with the Moor, and the Ballerina faints. The Moor, much the stronger of the two, shoves Petrushka from the room. Darkness falls.

Tableau IV. *The Fair That Evening.* A group of nursemaids dances, then an animal trainer with his bear. A rich merchant, with gypsy girls on either arm, jovially tosses money to the merrymakers; stable boys and coachmen enter to dance with the nursemaids. Carnival-maskers approach, with mummers costumed as pigs and goats. Confusion erupts in the puppet theater: Petrushka rushes out, chased by the Moor, with the frightened Ballerina unable to separate them. The Moor strikes Petrushka with a Turkish sabre and he falls to the ground, his skull broken. Police fetch the puppeteer, who shakes the lifeless doll and, remorseless, shrugs. The crowd drifts away.

The old magician stands there alone and begins to drag the limp puppet toward the theater. But Petrushka's ghost, standing on the roof of the theater, sneers at him and thumbs his nose. The terrified puppeteer drops the doll and flees. Snow begins to fall.

Le Sacre du printemps (The Rite of Spring)

I. The Adoration of the Earth
Introduction—Augurs of Spring (Dance of the Young Girls)—
Ritual of Abduction—Spring Rounds—Ritual Games of the Two
Rival Cities—The Procession of the Oldest and Wisest Ones—The
Kiss of the Earth (The Wise Man)—The Dancing Out of the
Earth

II. The Sacrifice
Introduction—Mystical Circles of the Young Girls—The Naming
and Honoring of the Chosen One—Evocation of the Ancestors—
Ritual of the Ancestors—Sacrificial Dance (the Chosen One)

For piccolos I-II, flutes I-III, alto flute, oboes I-IV, English horn,
    E♭ clarinet, clarinets I-III, bass clarinets I-II, bassoons I-IV,
    contrabassoons I-II; horns I-VIII; piccolo trumpet, trumpets I-

IV, bass trumpet in E♭, trombones I-III, tubas I-II (tenor and
bass); timpani, bass drum, cymbals, triangle, tambourine,
tamtam, güiro, antique cymbals in A♭ and B♭; strings; extra
tuba parts played by horn players

Composed 1911–8 March 1913 in Ustilug (Russia) and Clarens
(Switzerland); dedicated to Nicolas Roerich, the painter

First performed 29 May 1913 by Diaghilev's Ballets Russes at the
Théâtre des Champs-Élysées, Paris, Pierre Monteux conducting;
choreography by Nijinsky

Published by (1921 version) Éditions Russes de Musique
[assigned to Bookey and Hawkes, Inc. in the West]; revised
edition published by Boosey and Hawkes, Inc. (London, 1947).
Inexpensive score: Igor Stravinsky: *The Rite of Spring in Full Score*
(New York: Dover, 1989), a reprint of the State Music
Publishing House edition (Moscow, 1965)

Duration: about 40 minutes

One of the things Stravinsky loved most about Russia, he wrote, was
"the violent Russian spring that seemed to begin in an hour and was
like the whole earth cracking," and it was with this altogether audible
image of vernal rebirth in mind that he began to consider a new
ballet. The rudiments of *The Rite of Spring* had come together just
after *The Firebird,* but at the same time Stravinsky's compositional
technique was undergoing significant stylistic changes: the music was
to be different, even formidable, and took its own time coming.

There is little to the plot of *Le Sacre du printemps.* Spring begins to
blossom, and with it emerge the denizens of an Asian plane. There
are ritual dances and tribal games, the arrival of the venerated elders,
and the choosing and sacrifice, by dancing herself to death, of a young
maiden—this last the only solo number in the ballet. All of it takes
place in an atmosphere of high mysticism and ceremony. *Le Sacre du
printemps,* lasting just over half an hour, goes by very quickly indeed.

The music of each section is built of short melodic motives, all of
them quite tonal, joined together horizontally and vertically in a
kaleidoscope of sonic events: you have the strong sense of the ritual
circles throughout the work. The rhythmic language is astonishingly
fecund: nothing, perhaps, in the history of rhythm so well defines its
era as the randomly placed accents in the *Augurs of Spring* near the
beginning, and nothing so astounds the amateur scorereader as the

changing meters, in virtually every bar, of the sacrificial dance at the end. Stravinsky's handling of orchestral timbre is no less absorbing: the primeval textures at the start, the heavy plod of the cortege of elders, the occult shapes of all sorts in the second half. What harshness there is, and what may seem at first an impenetrable modernism, is accomplished mostly through piling together contrasting keys (in the ritual games of the rival cities, for example, the superposition of two different musics), melodies, and meters. It doesn't take too many hearings for all that to become clear, nor for some of the most significant principles of the music of this century to take root in your understanding.

The scandal that surrounded the first performance—where Nijinsky, choreographing a major and very difficult work for the first time, lost his *sang-froid,* and the altogether uncomprehending public stampeded into the streets—lends a certain excitement to the story of *Le Sacre du printemps.* How remarkable it is, nevertheless, that a work that once seemed the pinnacle of orchestral virtuosity (beginning with that high bassoon melody, which commences on the C above middle C), is now in the repertoire of every orchestra, greeted by musicians as just another day's work.

A magnificent reconstruction of the original sets, costumes, and choreography was undertaken by the Joffrey Ballet and premiered in 1987. It is worth hooking up your VCR well in advance for the televised performance. And the version for two pianos, which served for the rehearsals, is now available in several excellent recordings.

Symphony in C

Moderato alla breve
Larghetto concertante
Allegretto
Largo; Tempo giusto, alla breve
[No pause between movements II and III]

For piccolo, flutes I-II, oboes I-II, clarinets I-II, bassoons I-II; horns I-IV, trumpets I-II, trombones I-III, tuba; timpani; strings

Composed autumn 1938–summer 1940 in Europe and the United States; score—"Composed to the Glory of God [and] dedicated to the Chicago Symphony Orchestra on the occasion of the

Fiftieth Anniversary of its existence"—dated 19 August 1940;
commissioned by Mrs. Robert Woods Bliss

First performed 7 November 1940, by the Chicago Symphony
Orchestra, Stravinsky conducting

Published by Schott and Co., Ltd. (London, 1948)

Duration: about 30 minutes

It took Stravinsky a long time to write the Symphony in C—and a
longer time still, if you discount a youthful Symphony in E♭, to get
around to writing a symphony at all. The genre was out of vogue, for
one thing; for another, the stakes are always high when a composer
known mostly for stage works turns away from scenarios and texts to
write in purely abstract terms. The long approach to the Symphony
in C began in 1920 with the *Symphonies of Wind Instruments,* dedicated
to the memory of Debussy (for Debussy's great work for two pianos,
En Blanc et noir, had carried a dedication to Stravinsky); and continued
with several concertos, the most important of which is the "Dumbarton Oaks" Concerto for chamber orchestra (named after the venue of
the first performance, the country estate near Washington, D.C., of
the patrons, Mr. and Mrs. Bliss).

Once commissioned, the Symphony in C was four very bleak years
in the writing. The Second World War was imminent; tuberculosis,
still in those days a dread disease, had struck Stravinsky and his family. At first he ignored the physicians' advice to join his wife and
daughters at the sanatorium in Sancellmoz, Switzerland, and thus it
was in Paris, in the fall of 1938, that the first movement was composed. Shortly afterward his wife Catherine, his elder daughter Ludmila, and his mother all died of the disease; finally Stravinsky was
induced to join his younger daughter Milena at Sancellmoz. There
the second movement was composed.

Once the war had broken out, Stravinsky accepted Harvard's call
to deliver the Charles Eliot Norton lectures, and thus the third movement was composed in Massachusetts. As it turned out, he was in the
United States to stay. In early 1940 his former mistress Vera de Bos-
set arrived in this country and they were married. A few months later
they settled in Holywood, where the last movement of the Symphony
in C was completed. Stravinsky, in one of his many pronouncements
on his life and work, suggests that the symphony has, as a result, a
European half and an American half, but this supposed geographical

distribution need not be taken particularly seriously.

A motto, characterized by the rise of a half-step or step and the fall of a fourth is central to the structure of this spare but by no means short work. You hear it prominently and repeatedly in the oboe melody near the beginning; it is also present in the opening sally of the first two bars and, more slowly, in the riposte just following. A sonata is underway, a structure of apparently old-fashioned form, strong tonality, and almost juvenile simplicity of rhythms—mostly eighth notes. The orchestra, moreover, is Beethoven-sized, not the awesome ensemble of the ballets. Yet these primitivisms are mere the scaffolding: the music involves itself with routine challenges of your expectations by displacing expected events, adroit reweaving of the cells and strands in the manner of the ballets, and advanced harmonic complexes—as, for example, the dozen huge cadential chords at the end of the movement.

The *Larghetto* suggests, in its florid ornamentation and generally Italianate conventions, the inner movement of a Baroque concerto. Again the motto has an important structural role. An interjection for three violas, *dolce cantabile,* shortly precedes the second section, nervous in both melody and accompaniment, and twice as fast; in the reprise, the *dolce cantabile* is for cello trio, and the movement concludes with highly Baroque turn for oboe and bassoon. The cadential figure is adopted, without pause, by the low strings to begin the scherzo, a chain of episodes in the fashion of a ballet intermezzo but with decidedly one-legged metric irregularities. Pounding string chords and a *Petrushka*-like oscillation of the winds separate the episodes, and the movement concludes with high counterpoint in the brass.

The *Finale* begins with a lugubrious dialogue of the two bassoons over horn and trombone. After a few bars the *Tempo giusto* sets in with a fast scalar theme short on downbeats but full of promise for eventual contrapuntal treatment; this culminates in a loud statement of the theme from the first movement. Faster note values break through over the pedal point in the bass, leading to a second theme in the oboe and a *fortissimo* statement of the main theme in the bass instruments. The bassoons and horns from the beginning reassert themselves to begin the promised fugal treatment, which Stravinsky says he dropped "like a very hot potato." The big climax in C major—the only full-scale tutti in the work—leads to the coda, a long decrescendo with circles of the motto chords in wind.

Symphony of Psalms

Exaudi orationem meam
Expectans, expectavi Dominum
Laudate Dominum
[Played without pause]

For chorus (preferably including children); piccolo, flutes I-V, oboes I-IV, English horn, bassoons I-III, contrabassoon; horns I-IV, trumpets I-V, trombones I-III, tuba; timpani, bass drum; pianos I-II; cellos, double basses

Text chosen by Stravinsky from the Vulgate (i.e., Latin Bible): verses 13-14 of Psalm 38, 2-4 of Psalm 39, and Psalm 150 in its entirety; these are equivalent to King James Psalms 39:12-13, 40:1-3, and 150

Composed January–15 August 1930 in Nice and Charavines—"Composed to the glory of God and dedicated to the Boston Symphony Orchestra on the occasion of the fiftieth anniversary of its existence"; the commission had come from Serge Koussevitzky

First performed 13 December 1930 by the Brussels Philharmonic Society, Ernest Ansermet conducting; and 29 December 1930 by the Boston Symphony Orchestra, Koussevitzky conducting

Published by Éditions Russes de Musique (Paris and Berlin, 1931); then Boosey & Hawkes, Inc. (London and New York; rev. 1948, mostly technical corrections and a tempo change or two)

Duration: about 25 minutes

In 1926 Stravinsky had taken the requisite instruction and become a communicant of the Russian Orthodox Church. This sudden turn toward cult in a man of decidedly secular tastes is a good indication of the many complexities of his character. "One hopes to worship God with a little art if one has any," he wrote, and went on to inscribe the words "Composed to the glory of God" at the head of several scores of the period. It was thus that he ignored the advice of his colleagues to compose for the Boston Symphony Orchestra "something popular," and instead chose to set texts from Psalms for chorus and an instrumental ensemble of winds and low strings, without violins and violas.

He began with the fast parts of the third movement, his view of Elijah's chariot being swept to heaven in a ball of fire. ("Never before had I written anything quite so literal as the triplets for horns and piano to suggest the horses and chariot.")

In the first movement nearly every detail is colored by the interval of the third (E–G, for example): it is of these that the opening wiggles in the woodwinds are built. The speed of this figure halves (into eighths and sixteenths) to accompany the chanted *Exaudi,* mostly on the pitches E and F, as it unfolds with relentless confidence. This confrontation of excitement with calm yields an atmosphere of burning intensity, appropriate to a text of exaltation. This is Stravinsky's magic at its best, the kind that sends a shiver up the spine.

The second movement is a celebrated double fugue in four sections, beginning with a long exposition the composer later (and wrongly) came to think "too obvious, too regular, and too long." The choral fugue is tighter; then the orchestra returns in a faster statement, leading to a grand pause and forceful restatement. There is a ravishing soft close, with the chorus in unison as the fugue continues at one speed in the high trumpet and twice as fast in the cello and bass.

Cycles continue to operate in the last movement, with warm cadences in C major. A reverent Alleluia serves to introduce the spellbinding oscillations of the Laudate. Suddenly there is the violent charge of the chariot music, and the introduction of cymbals and tuba. At the center the hushed Alleuia returns and then a developed recapitulation. The last Laudate is a triumph of construction, with a canon in the voices that covers a cycle of six bars and beneath it an ostinato bass that revolves in groups of four bars.

Requiem Canticles

Prelude
Exaudi
Dies irae
Tuba mirum
Interlude
Rex tremendae
Lacrimosa
Libera me
Postlude

For contralto and bass solo, chorus; piccolo, flutes I-III, alto flute, bassoons I-II; horns I-IV, trumpets I-II, trombones I-III; timpani (two players), xylophone, vibraphone, bells; celesta, harp, piano; strings

Composed 1965–13 August 1966, mostly in Hollywood; dedicated to the memory of Helen Buchanan Seeger

First performed 8 October 1966 at Princeton University by the New York Concert Symphony Orchestra and the Ithaca College Choir, Elaine Bonazzi, contralto, Donald Gramm, bass, Robert Craft conducting

Published by Boosey & Hawkes (London, 1967)

Duration: about 15 minutes

Stravinsky considered the *Requiem Canticles* music of his "last, or last-ditch," period, and imagined he was safe in thinking it "the first mini- or pocket-Requiem." His original title was to have been *Sinfonia da Requiem,* but this he abandoned in view of the fact that "I seem to have shared too many titles and subjects with Mr. Britten already."

Stravinsky's sketchbook of the period is full of obituaries for his acquaintances, and this work, like several that preceded it, was memorial in its implications. He surely sensed the imminence of his own death. It seems possible, moreover, that each movement constitutes a musical farewell to a different friend. In 1968 Stravinsky gave Balanchine permission to use the score for a ballet in memory of Martin Luther King but he was unable to complete the new movement he had envisaged; in 1972 Jerome Robbins choreographed another ballet to the *Requiem Canticles* for the great commemorative Stravinsky Festival of the New York City Ballet.

The *Requiem Canticles* is a symmetrical arrangement of two groups of three movements with prelude for strings, interlude for winds, and postlude for percussion. (The permutation of instrumental colors is much like that in the *Variations: Aldous Huxley in memoriam* of 1964.) The structural intervals are drawn from two twelve-tone series. It is a concise, epigrammatic work, with the text presented for the most part as vocal parlando or chanted incantation. The *Exaudi,* for example, consists of the single word, with the melody in the harp; the *Dies irae,* merely of shouts and their echoes with a *fortissimo* run in the orchestra. As in almost every setting of the Requiem text, the Tuba mirum is for trumpets, here over a simple bass. The most sustained sung melody is that of the contralto's *Lacrimosa,* long and tragic, low of pitch, set against the contrasting register of a quartet of flutes. In the macabre postlude, flutes and horn intone cycles of a funereal chord progression over the dark percussive tattoo.

Piotr Tchaikovsky

Born 7 *May 1840 in Votkinsk*
Died 6 *November 1893 in St. Petersburg*

Votkinsk, where Tchaikovsky's father was an inspector of mines, lies hundreds of miles northeast of Moscow as the Urals begin to lift—a place of severe yet boundless majesty. The family moved to St. Petersberg when Piotr was eight. On graduating at age nineteen from the prestigious School of Jurisprudence he, like his father, entered government service. Two years later, however, he became a student at the new St. Petersburg Conservatory, and though he had started late was composing significant music by his thirtieth birthday. (The first version of the fantasy-overture *Romeo and Juliet,* for example, is from 1869.) In 1866 he moved to Moscow to teach harmony at what was soon to become the Moscow Conservatory; there he was influenced by Mily Balakirev and Nicolai Rubinstein, though his Western "classicism" was incompatible with the nationalism then in fashion.

The rest of his life he spent composing, teaching, and writing newspaper criticism.

He was a quiet man, preferring his hermitage at Klin and the very small circle of his intimates—his brothers, the Rubinsteins, his publisher P. I. Jurgenson—to the attentions of the aristocracy and public. Of his infatuation with the singer Désirée Artôt (1867) and his brief and unconsummated marriage to Antonina Milyukova (1877) you will read below. His extraordinary relationship with his patroness, Nadezhda von Meck, was conducted for fourteen years (1876–90) entirely by correspondence; it was mutually agreed that they would never meet face-to-face. He was widely traveled and correspondingly well met—and cosmopolitan by heritage, having been born to a mother of French extraction. He knew the *Ring* and *Carmen* from live performances and numbered Brahms, Saint-Saëns, Grieg, and Mahler among his friends.

In 1888 he was granted a lifetime pension from the czar, in recognition of his many contributions to the stage and concert hall. Tchaikovsky visited the United States in 1891 to conduct concerts in New York (including one for the inauguration of Carnegie Hall), Philadelphia, and Baltimore; in 1893 he was given an honorary degree from Cambridge. His morbid temperament, especially in his last years, was caused partly by the difficulties of coping with his homosexuality. On at least one occasion he attempted suicide, and his death from cholera was the result of his drinking contaminated water during an epidemic, possibly on purpose. The authorities are still arguing about the details of Tchaikovsky's demise, however, and the account that appears in *The New Grove* is not necessarily the last word.

His accomplishment is equally impressive in all four of the extended forms in which he composed: opera, ballet, symphony, and concerto. In the symphonies Tchaikovsky favors many-themed, rather Brahmsian sonata forms that allow his orchestrational gifts and swings of mood full play. The sentiments that lie at the core of these works are not so much nationalistic as global: those of fate, struggle, death. Yet he is not averse to adopting ethnic tunes and inflections; stylistically he is thus at once a son of Russia and the most international of the Russians—before or since.

His greatest works are the Fourth, Fifth, and Sixth ("Pathétique") Symphonies, the opera *Eugene Onegin* (1879), the ballets *Swan Lake* (1877), *Sleeping Beauty* (1890), and *The Nutcracker* (1892), and the concertos for piano (1875, 1882) and violin (1881). The one-movement works are rather less substantial, though several remain popular favorites in the orchestral repertoire.

Tchaikovsky was not a happy man, yet his bursts of genius are as apt to be warm-hearted as despairing: the Fifth Symphony and *Sleeping Beauty* are contemporaneous, as are the "Pathétique" and *Nutcracker*. And he remained active and prolific to the end. It does not matter that the Russian nationalists counted him out, for however pathfinding it may have been, their music was in essence based on little more than exotic subject matter and glamorous orchestration: Tchaikovsky, by contrast, occupied himself with the universals.

Symphony No. 4 in F Minor, OP. 36

Andante sostenuto; Moderato con anima (in movimento di Valse)
Andantino in modo di canzona
Scherzo, Pizzicato ostinato: Allegro
Finale: Allegro con fuoco

For piccolo, flutes I-II, oboes I-II, clarinets I-II, bassoons I-II; horns I-IV, trumpets I-II, trombones I-III, tuba; timpani, bass drum, cymbals, triangle; strings

Composed May 1877–7 January 1878 in Klin and San Remo, Italy; dedicated to "my best friend" (i.e., Mme von Meck)

First performed 22 February 1878 in Moscow by the Imperial Russian Musical Society, Nicolai Rubinstein conducting

Published by P. I. Jurgenson (Moscow, 1877) and D. Rahter (Hamburg and Leipzig, 1880). *Inexpensive score:* Peter Ilyitch Tchaikovsky: *Fourth, Fifth and Sixth Symphonies in Full Score* (New York: Dover, 1979)

Duration: about 45 minutes

It would be best if you were to hear the Fourth Symphony as a grip-of-destiny piece in the lineage of Beethoven's Fifth and disregard as much as possible of the story telling that goes with it. Yet some of that is inevitable, since the Fourth represents for Tchaikovsky a turning point both musical and psychological. The important thing is not to lose track of the magnitude of the achievement in purely symphonic terms: after all, countless works of art—most of them, possibly—are to one degree or another autobiographical. Associating the

Fourth with the doleful turn of events in the composer's life during its genesis can enrich our understanding of the music but must not comprise our only approach to it.

In September 1876 Tchaikovsky, feeling that his social condition demanded it, reached the decision to marry at the first reasonable opportunity. His intimate correspondence with Mme von Meck, documenting this and many other concerns of heart and mind, began in December. Sometime that winter he undertook his fourth symphony—"our symphony," he told her in a program and dedication they would not make public. It would confess the thousand shifting movements of his soul, he wrote, unburdening it through music. By March he had begun serious drafting, and the first movement was finished in June.

The previous May a student at the Conservatory, Antonina Milyukova, had written to proclaim her admiration for Tchaikovsky; in July they were married. This domestic arrangement, we know with the certainty of hindsight, was doomed from the beginning. Tchaikovsky and his wife had separated within three months, and in October he made a half-hearted attempt at suicide by wading into the frigid Moscow River up to his waist, waiting to catch his death of cold. Having survived the crisis, and supported by a new stipend from Mme von Meck, he retreated south to recover in the Swiss Alps. There he completed the second, third, and fourth movements of the Fourth and dated the score in San Remo on 7 January 1878. In Milan the next day, he bought a metronome to use for setting the tempo indications. Tchaikovsky was not present for the first performance a few weeks later in St. Petersburg, but was resting in his Florence hotel after a long day at the Ufizzi galleries.

The trumpets and horns in the opening measures present the Fate motive, here envisaged as the force which prevents us from attaining happiness. Its primary musical role, indeed, is to interrupt conventional sonata procedures with its stern reminders. In maintaining its identity from movement to movement—this is Tchaikovsky's first effort at cyclic composition along such lines—the Fate motive acts as a kind of germ of everything to follow. The point of the first movement is to suggest life as a balance between severity and fleeting happiness. The principal theme is a turbulent waltz, interrupted by the Fate theme at the end of the exposition, in the development, and at the climax toward the end. Our fleeting dreams are suggested by the second theme, begun by clarinet and extended in the strings. In the coda a chorale tries to reconcile the conflicting materials.

The second movement deals with suffering, solitude, and memories: "sad and somehow sweet to sink into the past," a study of melancholy in dark minor mode, with a middle section in major; the indication is *in modo di canzona*. In the third the imagination is to draw free pictures ("after we have drunk wine," the program suggests). This is a wonderful scherzo with themes arranged by families: the string pizzicatos, the woodwind countermelodies, and the military figures for brass. The woodwind theme in the trio is meant as the street song of a drunken peasant. All these pass by and are gone, superpositioned once at the end, but with the military suggestions there kept at a distance.

The last movement is a velocitous finale for virtuoso orchestra, though still hinting at the sinister elements that have been close by since the beginning. "If you truly find no joy within yourself, look for it in others," reads the program, which goes on to describe the merrymaking of a peasant festival. The Russian folksong which constitutes the second theme is authentic. Just before the coda, the Fate motive is heard one last time followed by a finish in reckless abandon.

Symphony No. 5 in E Minor, OP. 64

Andante; Allegro con anima
Andante cantabile, con alcuna licenza
Valse: Allegro moderato
Finale: Andante maestoso; Allegro vivace

For piccolo, flutes I-III, oboes I-II, clarinets I-II, bassoons I-II; horns I-IV, trumpets I-II, trombones I-III, tuba; timpani; strings

Composed late May–26 August 1888 in Klin; dedicated to Theodor Ave-Lallement, a board member of the Hamburg Philharmonic Society

First performed 17 November 1888 by the St. Petersburg Philharmonic Society, the composer conducting

Published by P. I. Jurgenson (Moscow, 1888) and D. Rahter (Hamburg, 1889). *Inexpensive score:* Peter Ilyitch Tchaikovsky: *Fourth, Fifth and Sixth Symphonies in Full Score* (New York: Dover, 1979)

Duration: about 50 minutes

Tchaikovsky undertook a Fifth Symphony in the spring of 1888, following a long concert tour; it comes a full eleven years after the Fourth. Like that work it was to be a symphony of Fate, but in the Fifth there is not so much disputation as what the composer termed "complete resignation before . . . the inscrutable predestination of Providence." He complained to Mme von Meck, of working "without ideas, without inspiration," and fretful of the reverses a performance might bring. Perhaps, he feared, his muse was exhausted. But the long days of work at the summer house in Klin, sketching in the morning, seeking inspiration as he walked in the woods, and concluding his day's work by teatime, were fruitful, and the symphony was done by the end of the summer. It was successfully performed in St. Petersburg late that autumn and repeated with equal success shortly afterward in Prague.

The throaty clarinet theme at the beginning is a motto motive that over the course of the symphony progresses from the plaintive cast it has here toward true jubilance at the end. The *Allegro* begins as a lugubrious barcarolle of bassoon and clarinet, pointedly syncopated. Strings arrest the forward motion in a passage of brooding temperament; a merry bubbling of winds, said to suggest a hurdy-gurdy figure, completes the transition to the second group. This is an elegant waltz in the best Tchaikovsky fashion, carrying itself away to an eloquent climax, as good as anything in *Sleeping Beauty* or *Nutcracker*. The horns, returning to the hurdy-gurdy motive, lead into a lusty development, and again to recapitulation. There seems at first a greater urgency in the recapitulation, but gradually the movement merely dissipates into the lowest orchestral register.

"Shall I embrace Faith?" Tchaikovsky had written in his sketches for the second movement, and the famous French horn solo at the beginning has a correspondingly religious and consoling quality about it. The chord progression that introduces the movement grows naturally from the void of the first; the solo strophe is built of long and elegant phrases, carefully balanced, with the interstices filled in from time to time by the clarinet. The oboe offers the first riposte, its suggestions mirrored by the horn, and eventually there blooms a lavish restatement of the celebrated theme in the richest register of the cellos, now with copious woodwind elaboration. After a tutti and the thunder of timpani, the movement turns to consider subsidiary material, alternated among the orchestral sections. The ominous motto is heard from the trumpets. Strings return to the main theme with heightened filigree from winds; this time the big climax with timpani is more ecstatic still, and the motto explodes once more before retreat into the lowest orchestral register.

The third movement is a waltz of winsome melody. The bassoon, in its high register, carries it afield; from this episode a trio of much faster note values dashes away. The restatement mingles the waltz and scherzo themes for a moment, and toward the end the motto returns, solemn but comfortable in the clarinet and bassoon.

The finale, too, begins with the motto motive, growing in successive repetitions—for there is not enough of it to constitute a real theme—into a majestic climax. The main theme proper is a strident plunking of quarter notes, prevailingly a descending minor scale. The march qualities are emphasized by the second subject for the band instruments, and at the center comes another trumpeted statement of the motto, now copiously decorated. What follows is not so much development as building toward peroration: where the tempo lurches forward, the motto takes over all but completely, and the end is reached in a setting of progressive ebullience.

Tchaikovsky was dissatisfied with the Fifth Symphony, finding its effects exaggerated and its many thematic repetitions superfluous. Ultimately he left conducting it to others. But his objection, if valid at all, can only apply to the somewhat formulaic exuberance of the finale. Elsewhere the melodic fertility and inspired use of the orchestral instruments assure the Fifth a certain place among his masterworks.

Symphony No. 6 in B Minor ("Pathétique"), OP. 74

Adagio; Allegro non troppo
Allegro con grazia
Allegro molto vivace
Finale: Adagio lamentoso

For piccolo, flutes I-III, oboes I-II, clarinets I-II, bassoons I-II; horns I-IV, trumpets I-II, trombones I-III, tuba; timpani, bass drum, cymbals, tam-tam; strings

Composed 16 February 1893–31 August 1893 in Klin; dedicated to Vladimir Lvovich Davidov, the composer's nephew

First performed 28 October 1893, by the Imperial Russian
Musical Society of St. Petersburg, Tchaikovsky conducting
Published by P. I. Jurgenson (Moscow, 1894). *Inexpensive score:*
Peter Ilyitch Tchaikovsky: *Fourth, Fifth and Sixth Symphonies in
Full Score* (New York: Dover, 1979)
Duration: about 50 minutes

For what was to be his last symphony, Tchaikovsky intended to write
a "symphony with a program—but a program that will remain an
enigma to all. Let them guess for themselves." His original idea had
been to call the work merely "A Program Symphony," but the day
after the first performance—possibly because the premiere had left
the public puzzled and unconvinced—he asked his brother Modest to
provide a descriptive subtitle. The initial suggestion, "Tragic," became
"Pathetic" more or less as an afterthought—and the composer's final
instruction, indeed, was that the symphony should merely carry its
dedication to Davidov, with no subtitle at all. We know little else
about the enigmatic program, but one can hardly escape the conclusion that the near complete despair of parts of the "Pathétique," and
its lighter moments as well, are essentially autobiographical.

The Sixth Symphony came quickly to Tchaikovsky, with the first
movement sketched in only four days. He was buoyed by the certainty
that he had arrived at a new level of quality in his composition, and
for a time the issues of his personal life were forgotten in the euphoria.
The finished symphony he termed "the best of all my works to date.
. . . I love it as I have never loved any of my musical offspring."

What is remarkable about the "Pathétique," in view of Tchaikov-
ky's generally conservative stance regarding orchestral argument, is
its novelty of form. From the earliest stages of composition, he had
intended to conclude the work with a sorrowful Adagio of great expanse,
and what emerged was, in fact, a successful solution to the age-old
problem of how to end a work of this size. That decision once reached,
other intriguing solutions fell naturally into place. The dance movement, a waltz in $\frac{5}{4}$, was appropriate to the second position. And thus
it became the role of the third movement to accomplish at least some
of the functions of the symphonic finale: it begins as a scherzo, becomes
a march, and ends in conclusive triumph.

But it is the memorable theme in the first movement that comes
to mind when most people hear the word "Pathétique"—not in fact

the principal theme, but the second. What you hear in the bassoon of the opening bars is a low, slow version of the first theme. The *Allegro* takes wing from there, haltingly at first and given to darting away. Suggestions of the famous theme are heard early in the transition, then swept along into the furious climax. Just afterward the famous melody simply settles over the moment, and after all the scrambling that has come before, its solidity and assurance are welcome characteristics indeed. The quiet excursion of the woodwind solos and fervent restatement of the theme are shattered by the sharp thrusts that begin the development. This works itself into such confrontation—the trombone intonations, incidentally, cite a Russian chant for the dead—that you will probably take the beginning of the recapitulation for the climax of the development. Then comes the fullest and most glamorous setting of the second theme, followed by a compassionate coda for brass over string pizzicato, rich with longing and pathos.

It is appropriate to hear the "Pathétique" as plumbing the depths of human existence, though you should remember that *The Nutcracker* is contemporaneous with the first sketches for the symphony. What cannot be forgotten, by way of biographical cachet, is that the first performance was a failure, and that ten days later, just before a triumphant second performance, Tchaikovsky was dead.

There's an interesting footnote to the story of the "Pathétique." In May 1893, when he went to England to be awarded (along with Saint-Saëns) an honorary degree from Cambridge, Tchaikovsky found himself seated at table next to the young American conductor Walter Damrosch. By the end of the meal, it was agreed that Damrosch would conduct the first American performance of the symphony on which Tchaikovsky was then at work. To everyone's surprise a package containing the score and parts arrived in New York just after the news of Tchaikovsky's death, and Damrosch was thus able to lead the New York Symphony Society in a dramatic American premiere, 16 March 1894.

Concerto No. 1 for Piano and Orchestra in B♭ Minor, OP. 23

Allegro non troppo e molto maestoso; Allegro con spirito
Andantino simplice
Allegro con fuoco

For   piano solo; flutes I-II, oboes I-II, clarinets I-II, bassoons I-II;
    horns I-IV, trumpets I-II, trombones I-III; timpani; strings
Composed   November 1874 in a month; scored dated 21 February
    1875; substantially revised 1889; dedicated (after Nicolai
    Rubinstein, the intended dedicatee, had declared the work
    unplayable) to Hans von Bülow, who gave the premiere
First performed   25 October 1875, by the Boston Symphony
    Orchestra, Hans von Bülow, piano, Benjamin Johnson Lang
    conducting
Published by   P. I. Jurgenson (Moscow, 3rd revised edition, 1879)
Duration: about 40 minutes

Tchaikovsky has a way of going about things that to an unusually
broad spectrum of listeners seems immediate, appealing, unforgettable: he is, in a word, popular, and nowhere any more so than in what
we tend to think of as *the* Tchaikovsky Concerto. (In fact there are
two other true concertos and a number of concerto-like compositions
for soloist and orchestra.) Its impact has much to do with expanse and
nobility, especially of the solo part. What you remember most, after
the echo has faded, is the radiant opening melody, sung forth by the
strings, exultantly doubled (and later redoubled), floating over the
choir of winds, and surrounded by the thundering chords of the piano.
The pianist then, in an ornamented version of this famous melody,
veers off into a brief cadenza; a still more majestic setting of the main
theme follows, so set out that once heard it can never be quite forgotten. Now spent, the introduction falls away into the *Allegro:* we have
passed through a triumphal arch to arrive at less settling material,
and in the minor key.

We never hear from these first affirmations again, but a similarly
majestic section at the very end of the concerto, likewise in major,
provides a strong sense of balance at the end of the work.

The *Allegro con spirito* begins as a nervous affair with its theme
stated, at first, in hiccups. The pianist's passagework, as this idea
develops, is interrupted by snippets in the winds that foreshadow a
second theme; the tempo relents, and the full subsidiary episode occurs,
first stated by the clarinet. (Tchaikovsky said that he heard an itinerant musician play this melody at a fair.) Out of this episode grows a
new melody in the strings, fragments of which provide most of the

transitional passages for the rest of the movement; woodwind and timpani herald yet another cadenza-like digression by the piano and subsequent closure of the exposition on a delicate *pianissimo.*

The development occupies itself with juxtaposing fragments of the three main themes, arriving at a peak in fireworks and cascades: a thunderclap in the timpani begins the taut crescendo to the altogether brusque recapitulation, which Tchaikovsky treats as though meeting an unwanted obligation. By this time it is clear that the movement is progressing inexorably toward a big cadenza. Furious quadruple-octave-work in the piano brings the movement to its close.

To offset such intensity, Tchaikovsky offers in the second movement a diaphonous melody in flute over pizzicato strings, lingering memories of a waltz. Note, just after the piano's first statement, the little metric ploy of falling wedges that seem for a moment to thrust the beat out of kilter: a little later these work themselves into a ruthless scherzo, *prestissimo,* though this frightening turn of events serves merely to set up a charming merry-go-round waltz in the new fast tempo. The little chanson we hear, *Il faut s'amuser et rire* (Laugh and enjoy yourself) is associated with the singer Désirée Artôt, to whom Tchaikovsky had once proposed marriage; it also has close affinities with the flute theme from the beginning. A return of the scherzo material dissolves into the cadenza; the first large section returns, gloriously closed by the oboe.

The lively Russian dance that follows is derived from a Ukranian melody ("Come, come, Ivanka"); a variant of this tune, stated *furioso* and *forte* by the full orchestra, rounds off each main section. The second theme seems, at the outset, somewhat routine; more interesting is the subsequent broad dotted figure (an idea we hear again in the Fourth Symphony). The movement soon develops an unmistakable momentum: timpani, celli, and double basses alight on a long-held pitch over which fragments of the main theme, and then another quadruple-octave affair in the piano, zero in on the second subject— the one that had at first seemed so routine. Now, spread across the orchestra and piano, it returns us to the majesty of the concerto's beginning, though Tchaikovsky does not deny himself the luxury of a charge to the last double-bar.

When the composer showed his work to its intended soloist, Nicolai Rubinstein, the great Russian pianist found it worthless, vulgar, and unplayable. (Vulgar is the only charge that might hold up; I suppose it could be argued that Tchaikovsky's fondness for thunder and lightning leads him at times into questionable territory.) "I replied," wrote Tchaikovsky, "that I would not alter a single note, and that I would have the concerto pubished as it then stood." Subsequent events made liars of them both: von Bülow's great success in Boston showed that the concerto could indeed be played, yet Tchaikovsky later revised the score extensively. As for Rubinstein, he freely admitted the error of his first perceptions and became an ardent champion of the concerto.

Concerto for Violin and Orchestra in D Major, OP. 35

Allegro moderato
Canzonetta: Andante
Finale: Allegro vivacissimo
[No pause between movements II and III]

For violin solo; flutes I-II, oboes I-II, clarinets I-II, bassoons I-II; horns I-IV, trumpets in D I-II; timpani; strings
Composed 17 March–11 April 1878 in Clarens, Switzerland; dedicated to Leopold Auer, then Adolf Brodsky, both violin virtuosi
First performed 4 December 1881 by the Vienna Philharmonic Orchestra, Adolf Brodsky, violin, Hans Richter conducting
Published by P. I. Jurgenson (Moscow, 1879). *Inexpensive score: Great Romantic Violin Concertos in Full Score* (New York: Dover, 1985)
Duration: about 35 minutes

Tchaikovsky's great Violin Concerto is a work of rebound from his ill-advised marriage, and his ensuing psychological collapse. Its genesis was nourished by the arrival in Switzerland of the young violinist Joseph Kotek, Tchaikovsky's go-between in his relationship with Mme von Meck. Together they had played Édouard Lalo's *Symphonie espagnole* for violin and orchestra, and in the first days of April 1878 they began to work through the drafts of the concerto. Thereafter the saga is quite like that of the Piano Concerto: declared unplayable by one who should have known better, first performed outside Russia, and adopted forthwith as a pillar of the repertoire. In this case the villain was the original dedicatee, Leopold Auer, who taught at the St. Petersburg Conservatory. Auer assured Tchaikovsky that the solo part was "awkward, unpleasant, and impracticable," and refused to play the work. Thus it was that the first performance fell to Adolf Brodsky.

In a repertoire already brimming with difficult solo parts, the Tchaikovsky concerto manages to propose a new level of pyrotechnic display: in the great rapidity of the passagework, the extremes of register, the multiple stops, the ceaseless trills and motion by chromatics. This is especially true in the immense first movement, which overwhelms the rest of the work. A story-teller's beginning in the orchestra serves mostly to get things underway; within a few bars the timpani roll makes it clear that the soloist's entry is at hand, first in a short recitative, then with the magnificent theme proper. Longing, tender, wide of phrase, and given to darting away in improvisatory drifts, this principal theme is one of Tchaikovsky's great achievements. It goes on through extended episodes before reaching the second subject, still in the solo violin. When the orchestral tutti is finally reached, it merely suggests strains of a march, then turns at once toward the development. The very similar tutti that comes next sets the stage for the big cadenza, followed by a recapitulation that begins quietly in the flute and gathers energy toward the close. It is not what one would call an intimate marriage of soloist and orchestra: the solo part ends up dominating every section.

Tchaikovsky had some difficulties with the second movement, discarding a *Méditation* eventually published as a solo movement for violin and orchestra, opus 43, no. 1. The canzonetta that replaced it is in a simple aria form that investigates the lower register of the violin. A sonata-rondo concludes the work, by returning to the animated concerns of the first movement. Here it seems certain that Tchaikovsky was following the general structure of the Mendelssohn Violin Concerto.

I said above that the Violin Concerto achieved a quick place in the repertoire. That is true, but not until after the Viennese critic Eduard Hanslick, violently assailed the work as a "rare mixture of originality and crudity, of inspiration and wretched refinement," with the violin "beaten black and blue" and with an "audible, odorously Russian, stench." So much for the critics.

Suite, opus 71a, from the ballet *The Nutcracker*, OP. 71

Miniature Overture
Characteristic Dances
  March—Dance of the Sugar-Plum Fairy—Trépak (Russian
  Dance)—Arabian Dance—Chinese Dance—Dance of the Reed
  Flutes—Waltz of the Flowers

For piccolo, flutes I-III, oboes I-II, English horn, clarinets I-II,
  bass clarinet, bassoons I-II; horns I-IV, trumpets I-II, trom-
  bones I-III, tuba; timpani, cymbals, triangle, tambourine,
  glockenspiel, celesta; harp; strings
Composed February 1891–4 April 1892; suite developed
  January–21 February 1892
First performed as a suite 19 March 1892 at a concert of the
  Imperial Russian Musical Society, St. Petersburg, Tchaikovsky
  conducting; the "fairy ballet in two acts" first performed 18
  December 1892 at the Imperial Theatre, St. Petersburg;
  scenario by Marius Petipa after Dumas *père* and E. T. A.
  Hoffmann
Published by P. I. Jurgenson (Moscow, 1892) and D. Rahter
  (Hamburg, 1892); characteristic dances published by P. I.
  Jurgenson (Moscow, 1896). *Inexpensive score:* Peter Ilyitch
  Tchaikovsky: *Nutcracker Suite in Full Score* (New York: Dover,
  1987)
Duration: about 20 minutes.

The story is a perennial holiday favorite: Uncle Drosselmeyer, alder-
man and amateur toy maker of sinister appearance, fashions a nutcracker in the likeness of a soldier as a Christmas gift for his niece and
nephew. After a merry open house and the unwrapping of gifts, the
niece, Clara, falls asleep and dreams that the Christmas toys have
come to life. (In the ensuing tableau, the giant Christmas tree and
fireplace dwarf the dancers to create the illusion of the toy ballet.)
The nutcracker, now a handsome prince, defends Clara against the
mice and their king. Clara becomes his princess, and in the enchanted
palace of the Kingdom of Sweets, they watch the sequence of character dances that conclude with the *Waltz of the Flowers.*

Only in the case of *The Nutcracker* could Tchaikovsky be induced
to extract an orchestral suite from his ballet music. For it he chose
the *Miniature Overture* (so-called because it lacks a development), the

children's march from act I, and the evocative dances from act II. (The *Arabian Dance* is subtitled *Coffee;* the *Chinese Dance, Tea.*) It is not merely that the each excerpt is memorable of melody and appropriate to the magic of the Christmas season: Tchaikovsky also shows, throughout, his keen mastery of orchestration. This is most noticeable, perhaps, in the *Dance of the Sugar-Plum Fairy,* with its celesta and bass clarinet. Elsewhere note the suave low reeds and tambourine over the drone bass in the *Arabian Dance,* the flute work in the *Dance of the Reed Flutes,* and the atmospheric use of the full orchestra: in the delirium of the Russian *Trépak* (the famous Cossack squat-kick dance), for example, and in the joyous abandon of the waltz.

"Sugar-Plum Fairy," incidentally, is a charming mistranslation. A *dragée* is not a gum-drop at all, but rather that sort of pastel-colored, sugar-coated almond that the French present to each other on festive occasions. "Reed Flutes" doesn't tell the whole story, either, for a *mirliton,* or kazoo, is also a cream-puff pastry.

1812: Ouverture solennelle, OP. 49, Festival-Overture

> For piccolo, flutes I-II, oboes I-II, English horn, clarinets I-II, bassoons I-II; horns I-IV, trumpets I-II, cornets *à pistons* I-II, trombones I-III, tuba; timpani, snare drum, bass drum, cymbals, triangle, tambourine, glockenspiel; strings; military band *ad libitum;* cannon fire and church bells
>
> **Composed** 12 October–19 November 1880 in Kamenka, to a commission from Nicolai Rubinstein for a Festival Overture to open an Exhibition of Arts and Crafts
>
> **First performed** 20 August 1882 in the new Moscow Cathedral for its consecration, Ippolit Karlovich Altani conducting
>
> **Published by** P. I. Jurgenson (Moscow, 1882)
>
> **Duration:** about 15 minutes

On 7 September 1812 the Grand Army of Napoleon met General Kutuszov and his Russian forces at the Battle of Borodino, a little south of Moscow. When the dead could be counted, their number came to more than eighty thousand, with both armies crippled. The Russians, in a brilliant strategy, withdrew behind Moscow, and Napoleon arrived to find the city on fire. There was nothing in Moscow to sustain his legions or to warrant his occupation, and the historic and terrible French retreat into the bitter winter began on October 19. With that the Napoleonic empire had begun to collapse.

It was Nicolai Rubinstein who suggested that Tchaikovsky compose a commemorative patriotic work to be performed in the open air, and the notion of using cannon fire and the Kremlin bells grew naturally out of the proposition. In fact, the first performance took place just short of the seventieth anniversary of the retreat from Moscow, in conjunction with the consecration of the new Moscow Cathedral, which had been commissioned in 1812.

The musical allusions are obvious enough: to the *Marseillaise* and Russian Hymn ("God Preserve the Czar"), of course, and to the bugling and drum tattoos of the Russian army, the military strife, and the elation of victory. Most of the rest of the thematic material is nationalistic, as well, including the Russian chant used for the opening Largo, suggestions of several folksongs, and, for the lyrical second subject of the sonata, a citation from one of Tchaikovsky's operas (*The Voyevoda*, 1869). It's a composition of greater craft than artistry, and Tchaikovsky himself doubted its artistic merit. But the reason he gave was curious in the extreme: he found it, he said, "without much warmth of enthusiasm."

Romeo and Juliet, Overture-Fantasy after Shakespeare

For piccolo, flutes I-II, clarinets I-II, English horn, bassoons I-II; horns I-IV, trumpets I-II, trombones I-III, tuba; timpani, bass drum, cymbals; harp; strings

Composed 7 October–27 November 1869; revised summer 1870 and in the early 1880s; dedicated to Mily Balakirev, who had suggested the idea.

First performed (in its successive versions) 16 March 1870 at a concert of the Imperial Russian Musical Society in Moscow, Nicolai Rubinstein conducting; 17 February 1872 in St. Petersburg, Eduard Nápravník conducting; 1 May 1886 in Tbilisi, Mikhail Ippolitov-Ivanov conducting

Published by Ed. Bote and G. Bock (Berlin, 1871; rev. ed. 1881). *Inexpensive score:* Peter Ilyitch Tchaikovsky: *Romeo and Juliet Overture and Capriccio Italien in Full Score* (New York: Dover, 1986)

Duration: about 20 minutes

A cold chorale in clarinets and bassoons, meant to suggest Friar Lawrence in his cell, opens this majestic tone poem. It continues to unfold, with harp arpeggios, rather in the manner of Rimsky's *Sheherazade,* as though a narrator were telling a story. The introduction closes with a musical question mark, and a violent first group breaks out—the dueling of the rival families in the streets of Verona. But the brawling is overtaken and shamed by the great English horn and viola theme (known to one generation of Americans as "Our Love"). The passage broadens over throbbing horn, and the orchestration thickens. Then, in the developmental passage, the fury breaks out again. Again the love theme displaces it, now in a grand statement with the orchestra fully unleashed. In the coda a funeral knell is followed by an apotheosis ending of the lovers united in death.

Romeo and Juliet always seems to invoke fervent response from composers who turn to it, and Tchaikovsky's Overture-Fantasy is probably his first masterpiece. Many music lovers consider it to contain, quite simply, the best love music there is.

Serenade for Strings in C Major, OP. 48

Pezzo in forma di Sonatina: Andante non troppo; Allegro moderato
Valse: Moderato, Tempo di valse
Élégie: Larghetto elegiaco
Finale (Tema Russo): Andante; Allegro con spirito

For string orchestra
Composed 21 September–4 November 1880 in Kamenka; dedicated to Konstantin Karl Albrecht, a friend of long standing and Tchaikovsky's landlord
First performed 30 October 1881 in St. Petersburg, Eduard Nápravník conducting
Published by P. I. Jurgenson (Moscow, 1881)
Duration: about 30 minutes

Tchaikovsky's usual domain was that of the grander forms: concerto, symphony, opera, ballet. The rhetoric he found most personal was an epic Romanticism of power, turmoil, the welling up of tragedy and Fate. But there was a gentler side to him as well, one that urged simplicity of concept and obedience to the classical norms. This other world is represented by the String Serenade and the four suites for orchestra, all of which come between the Fourth Symphony of 1877–78 and the Fifth of 1888.

The String Serenade, which pleased Tchaikovsky, was composed simultaneously with *1812,* which did not. (It was also played during the same Moscow Exhibition for which *1812* had been written.) Here the composer was amused by the prospect of investigating the ground that lies between the string quartet and symphony. The result is a bright work, firmly in the major mode, with an eighteenth-century flavor that mingles Baroque details with suggestions of the style of Mozart and Haydn. At the center is the most admired of the movements, a thoroughly Romantic waltz not so different from those in *The Nutcracker* and *Sleeping Beauty.*

The thematic content of the *Andante non troppo* with which the sonatina begins and ends has less to do with the first movement than the last, where it recurs to lend a certain cyclicism to the overall structure. Architectually speaking the sonatina is true to form in lacking a development section: the second subject, a sort of perpetual-motion figure in sixteenths, is succeeded forthwith by a note-for-note reprise of the richer, slower first theme. But there's a fair share of internal development along the way, notably in the long transition between the first and second themes.

Tchaikovsky takes particular care with the seams between the movements. The ascending scalar theme of the elegy, for example, makes strong allusion to that of the preceding waltz, and the high *pianissimo* with which the movement concludes becomes the point of departure for the finale. "Elegy" in this case has less to do with lamentation than with nostalgia. The pensiveness is to be found in the first theme; the *cantabile* second theme, in the viola and cello register, is untroubled altogether, and there is an elegant long close over a low pedal point.

The finale begins with a slow introduction based on a traditional Volga hauling song, the end of which, in another clever seam, is turned into the theme of the *Allegro.* What follows has all the lilt of a Haydn symphony. The cello theme seems at first to afford the kind of contrast second groups should, but as it turns out the two subjects are constructed such that they can combine with each other in counterpoint, both in the development and recapitulation. Fugatos break out, with pedal points and allusions in modern terms to the old-fashioned harmonic progress by circle of fifths. The opening of the first movement returns.

Tchaikovsky's work serves as the score for George Balanchine's famous white ballet of 1935, *Serenade.*

Capriccio italien, OP. 45

For piccolo, flutes I-III, oboes I-II, English horn, clarinets I-II, bassoons I-II; horns I-IV, trumpets I-II, cornets *à pistons* I-II, trombones I-III, tuba; timpani, bass drum, cymbals, triangle, tambourine, glockenspiel; harp; strings

Composed 16 January–27 May 1880 in Rome; dedicated to Carl Davidov, famous Russian cellist

First performed 18 December 1880 by the Imperial Russian Musical Society, Moscow, Nicolai Rubinstein conducting

Published by P. I. Jurgenson (Moscow, 1880) and D. Rahter (Hamburg and Leipzig, 1881). *Inexpensive score:* Peter Ilyitch Tchaikovsky: *Romeo and Juliet Overture and Capriccio Italien in Full Score* (New York: Dover, 1986)

Duration: about 15 minutes

Tchaikovsky was pleased with the themes of the *Capriccio italien,* some of which he found in a published collection and others among the street songs he overheard during his Roman holiday in the winter of 1880. The opening for solo trumpet imitates the bugle call Tchaikovsky heard from his hotel every sunset. This and the dark Mediterranean melody that carries on in the vocal register of the strings go to make up a long preamble. Tempo and texture shift, from vague suggestions of guitar and castanet into lazy, meridional motion for the famous melody in the two oboes, then the cornets—what is waggishly called the "spaghetti" theme. The orchestration grows lush, especially at the brilliant rising scales in the strings.

A shift into duple meter and fast tempo, with galloping accompaniment, announces an episode of chase figures. From this emerges the more important melody in the strings, over gracious figuration in the winds brass, percussion, and harp. There is a return to the preamble, then a fast tarantella with reprises of the other themes. The speed continues to gather until the metric collapse.

One would not speak here of sophistication of form, but rather of ingenuity in stringing together of a medley of borrowed tunes. But Tchaikovsky is able to move so freely from one to the next, and so sunnily, that you do not stop to ponder the graver issues.

Michael Tippett

Born 2 *January* 1905 *in London*

Sir Michael Tippett's fine music figures less prominently in the rough-and-tumble of American concert life than it should; in England, as critics used to say, his name is on every lip.

His father having retired from successful business ventures, the family led a peripatetic life that took them from Suffolk to France to Italy. After early studies with his mother (who had been a Suffragette) and the governess, Tippett returned to Edinburgh and Lincolnshire for schooling. In 1923 he found his way to the Royal College of Music—neither he nor the family knew quite how to go about becoming a composer—where he studied composition and conducting, the latter with Adrian Boult and Malcolm Sargent. Through his conducting he learned the English stage repertoire and the mechanics of performance; his experience as music director for a work-camp of the unemployed reinforced his leftist politics and pacifist instincts. In 1932 he began his long affiliation with Morley College, an institution strongly committed to the London underprivileged, where he led what became the South London Orchestra. The College was nearly destroyed in the October 1940 bombings; shortly afterward Tippett registered as a conscientious objector. Refusing his wartime assignment, he was sentenced in 1943 to three months in the prison at Wormwood Scrubbs.

Under his guidance the concerts of old and new music sponsored by Morley College had become a feature of London cultural life. Anxious for more time to compose, Tippett resigned from Morley in 1951 to accept a less demanding post as a commentator for the BBC.

The first of his compositions usually counted as masterpieces are the Concerto for Double String Orchestra (1938–39) and the oratorio that immediately succeeded it, *A Child of Our Time* (1938–41). These were followed by an opera that established his prominence as a composer for the stage, *The Midsummer Marriage* (1946–52, first performed 1955). For orchestra his work includes four symphonies (First Symphony, 1944–45; Second, 1956–57; Third, with soprano soloist, 1970–72; Fourth 1976–77); the great success of the Third Symphony in Boston, New York, and Chicago under the composer's baton in 1974 led to the commission of the Fourth by the Chicago Symphony, who gave its premiere in 1977. Additionally, there are a *Fantasia on a Theme of Handel* for piano and orchestra (1939–41), a Piano Concerto (1953–55), a *Fantasia Concertante on a Theme of Corelli* for string orchestra (1953), a Concerto for Orchestra (1962–63), and a Triple Concerto for string trio and orchestra (1978–79). The suite of Ritual Dances from *The Midsummer Marriage* (1953) has also earned a place in the repertoire. Tippett's later operas are *King Priam* (1962), *The Knot Garden* (1970), *The Ice Break* (1977), and *New Year* (1989, premiered by the Houston Opera). The librettos for all these works are his own.

By the late 1950s it was clear that Tippett was one of the major symphonic and operatic composers of our time, and the appropriate honors were not long in coming: appointment as Commander of the Order of the British Empire (C.B.E.) in 1959, a knighthood from Queen Elizabeth in 1966, and honorary membership in the American Academy of Arts and Letters in 1973. From 1969 until 1974 he led and revitalized the prestigious Bath Festival. He entitled his volume of reminiscences *Moving into Aquarius* (2nd ed. 1974).

Of the three style periods into which Tippett's works are typically organized, the first is conservative, tuneful, and in some respects neo-classicist; the second harsher and more intense; and the third eclectic, expansive, and technically assured. Blue notes and jazz rhythms are to be found throughout his music, alongside sonata forms and liberal suggestions of the heritage of Monteverdi, Corelli, and Handel. Mostly, however, you are attracted by Tippett's eloquent post-Romanticism and his sweeping mastery of the symphonic idioms. You invariably sense youself in the presence of a highly cultivated and articulate artist.

A Child of Our Time, Oratorio

Part I   [*The Climate of Oppression*]
Part II   [*The Story*]
Part III   [*Reflections on the Story; the Healing*]

For soloists (SATB); chorus; flutes I-II, oboes I-II, English horn, clarinets I-II, bassoons I-II, contrabassoon; horns I-IV, trumpets I-III, trombones I-III; timpani, cymbals; strings
Text by the composer
Composed 1939–41 in London
First performed 19 March 1944 by the London Philharmonic Orchestra, Morley College Choir and London Region Civil Defence Choir, and soloists at the Adelphi Theatre, London, Walter Goehr conducting
Published by Schott & Co., Ltd. (London, 1944)
Duration: about one hour and a quarter

Since the end of World War I, Tippett, a man of pacifism and compassion, had meant to compose a dramatic work that would in some way condemn the political expediencies that make scapegoats of innocent and oppressed peoples. By the mid-1930s, as Hitler was reaching the height of his power, he had settled on the idea of a work in the manner of a Bach passion, where reflection on the meaning of the story would be as important as the narrative itself. Tippett found his subject matter some months later in an apocalyptic episode that seemed to summarize his blackest thoughts and, in turn, helped him formulate the thrust of what became one of his deepest and most profound works.

In late October 1938, Poland, unable to meet the Nazi demand to repatriate all Polish Jews then resident in Germany or Austria, announced the requirement of a special visa for admission into the country. The German government thereupon arrested thousands of Jews and abandoned them at the Polish border, where they soon began to succumb to hunger and disease. In Paris, a seventeen-year old boy named Herschel Grynspan, himself facing deportation, learned that his family were among those at the Polish frontier. On November 7 he went to the German embassy in Paris, gained access to an undersecretary named Ernst vom Rath, and shot him. The German reprisal, which began on the night of November 9, close on vom Rath's death, was one of the most vicious pogroms of the Nazi regime. To Tippett, Grynspan was the symbolic Child of our Time.

Of none of this is there specific mention in Tippett's oratorio: "I knew from the first," he writes, "that the work itself had to be anonymous and general, in order to reach down to the deeper levels of our common humanity." At this juncture Tippett sent a detailed scenario to T. S. Eliot, asking him to fashion the libretto. That Eliot refused the task was probably a good thing, in view of what Tippett went on to accomplish, here and elsewhere, as his own librettist. In fact the subtitle of A Child for Our Time—"the darkness declares the glory of light"—is borrowed from Eliot, and further on there are lines from Wilfred Owen (the young World War I poet whose poems Britten used for the War Requiem), Yeats, and the Bible.

The musical fabric makes other sorts of allusions. The three-part structure is modeled on that of Handel's Messiah, though in some respects the better parallel is with Israel in Egypt, which likewise opens with a bitter chorus of oppression. Tippett imitates Bach's use of church chorales in the passions, by setting Negro spirituals at similar junctures. This is a poignant stroke, indeed, and the rudimentary, almost primitive treatment of the borrowed material adds immeasurably to the effect. The spirituals are Steal Away; Nobody Knows the Trouble I See; Go Down, Moses; I'm Gonna Lay Down My Heavy Load; and, at the end, Deep River—songs of the enslaved, to be sure, but likewise of salvation in adversity.

Part I is a scena for alto and chorus, narration, and a chorus of the oppressed, with anguished laments of the tenor and soprano soloist. We find the world in winter, turning on its dark side, with an iciness relieved only by the warmth of *Steal Away*. In Part II, "a star rises in mid-winter;" the scapegoat, the child of our time. The boy's relatives cry toward him, and in desperate response he shoots the official. The terrible taking of vengeance follows. In Part III, the cold has deepened; the child, too, has been cast off. But where in the first part humanity had been lost "as seed before the wind, . . . carried to a great slaughter," here winter is seen as "the secret nursery of the seed."

At least, writes the composer, we are seed. "And if we are carried to a great slaughter, this may be a true collective sacrifice from which a new attitude and reconciliation may spring."

Symphony No. 4

> For piccolos I-II, flutes I-II, oboes I-II, English horn, clarinets I-II, bass clarinet, bassoons I-II, contrabassoon; horns I-VI, trumpets I-III, trombones I-III, tubas I-II; timpani, snare drum, tenor drum, bass drum, cymbals, suspended cymbal, triangle, tom-tom, wood block, maracas, claves, wind machine, glockenspiel, xylophone, marimba, vibraphone; harp, piano; strings
> **Composed** 1976–18 April 1977, to a commission from the Chicago Symphony Orchestra; dedicated to Ian Kemp, a noted British musicologist and Tippett's biographer
> **First performed** 6 October 1977 by the Chicago Symphony Orchestra, Georg Solti conducting
> **Published by** Schott & Co., Ltd. (London, 1977)
> **Duration:** about 30 minutes

The composer calls this a "birth to death" symphony, thereby suggesting the kind of symphonic discourse—statement, growth, and wane—we associate with Mahler, Richard Strauss, and Tchaikovsky. There is another stimulus as well, one that must be unique in all the literature: for a half-century earlier at an anthropology museum Tippett had seen a time-lapse film of a living rabbit embryo. The plasmic quiver and subsequent cell division came again to mind as he composed the opening passage of the Fourth, where the wind machine suggests a sort of cosmic panting.

For the most part it's a lively, eager work. The extreme velocity of several of the most significant passages, combined with the overall fast pacing of the episodes, make it all seem to hurry past, and the moments of repose are few and far between. The orchestral sonority is bold, owing in part to the strong presence and penetrating character of the pitched percussion—the marimba, xylophone, and glockenspiel—and in part to the prominent brass, notably the six horns and two tubas. Indeed the recurring and quite recognizable horn episode, sounding at first much like the opening of Richard Strauss's *Also sprach Zarathustra* (see p. 557), articulates several of the most significant turning points. Three quite perceptible principal metric identities (called by the composer Tempo 1, Tempo 2, and Tempo 3) identify the subdivisions of the symphony; these are connected by developmental passages and conclude in a summarizing finale that draws the various elements together at the end.

After the mysterious, visceral opening with humanoid sighs of the wind machine comes the exposition of rapid material, first for brass and then for strings with interjecting plunks of the piano; ultimately the violins and violas divide into eight parts, Sibelius fashion, then restate the material that began the section. Following the presentation of the important French horn themes, the music becomes quieter and more thinly scored, with harp and piano arabesques, excellent woodwind passagework, and solo viola, cello, and oboe. The new marcato section, Tempo 2, begins in low strings and timpani: "tough, strict," the score demands. There is a homophonic tutti with brass and a big climax with snare drum.

At Tempo 3, the bassoon and clarinet set forward in a scherzo. (Here the composer has written "light! flying!" in the score.) Triplet figurations in the woodwinds and percussion grow more and more confused, the trumpets punctuating the discourse. After the string choir returns there are twinkling cadenzas with oboe and viola solos. The wind machine and brass begin the transition to the finale. There's a significant crescendo into an episode for percussion and strings, with sharp brass chords as the final synthesis of materials begins. The winding down is quite dramatic, concluding with a last exhale of the wind machine.

Tippett has written a difficult score, particularly with regard to its speed, and you can tell he had orchestras like the Chicago in mind to play it. But there can be little question as to what he wants: score and parts are filled with directions—"power," "vigour," "with lyric grace," "radiance," and so forth. One finds oneself paying considerably more attention to these nuances and to the elements of the orchestral conversation than to the purported treatment of life and death.

Edgard Varèse

Born 22 December 1883 in Paris
Died 6 November 1965 in New York

High prophet of the Electronic Age, Varèse dreamed with uncanny accuracy of civilizations dominated by technology, of a time when the many avenues of music making would be electrified. No thinker was more influential than he in establishing the framework for those very developments.

His parents expected he would become an engineer. After math and science studies in Turin, where the family had gone to live, Varèse enrolled at the Schola Cantorum of Paris in 1904 to study composition with Vincent d'Indy and theory with Albert Roussel; later there were lessons with Charles-Marie Widor at the Conservatoire and advice from Debussy. From 1908 he lived in Berlin, at that time a locus of progressive musical thought due in large measure to the work of the iconoclast Ferrucio Busoni. There Varèse wrote a series of big Romantic works, all of which were apparently either destroyed by the composer himself or lost in a fire. He served briefly in the French army during World War I but was discharged in 1915 for medical reasons; thereupon he settled permanently in the United States, finding there a rapidity of pace and an excitement in matters scientific and technological that suited his thoroughly modern temperament. After failing as a conductor, and chronically short of cash, he devoted his energies to promoting performances of new music. The most notable of his ventures was the International Composers' Guild (from 1921) and its successor the Pan American Association of Composers, which he organized with Charles Ives, Henry Cowell, Carlos Chávez and Nicolas Slonimsky—an American "mighty handful" if ever there was one. In 1925 he bought the house on Sullivan Street in New York where he lived until his death; in 1926 he became an American citizen.

Though he thought of his lineage as one extending back to music of great antiquity, Varèse virtually personifies the term avant-garde. He was a tireless experimenter who enjoyed collaborating with acousticians and engineers (the inventor Léon Theremin, for instance), to discover new sonic possibilities. His innovations in manipulating blocks of sonority, or sound masses, of characteristic rhythms, volumes, and registers are thought by many to be as significant to the progress of compositional thought as the advances of Stravinsky and Schoenberg.

Varèse wrote primarily for instrumental ensemble, though he was prone to avoid the string sections, finding them "too expressive." Among his works are *Amériques* (1918, the first piece he composed in this country; the title, he said, was meant to be "symbolic of discoveries"); *Offrandes* for soprano and orchestra (1921); *Hyperprism* for small orchestra and percussion (1923; the concept is of a prism projected to the fourth dimension); *Octandre* for eight players (1923); *Intégrales* for woodwind, brass, and percussion (1925); *Arcana* for large orchestra (1925–27); *Ionisation* for percussion ensemble (1931); and *Ecuatorial* (1934) for bass voice, winds, percussion, and two ondes Martenot, to a sacred Mayan text. There followed a hiatus and rebirth in the new field we now call electronic music—what he called "organized sound." *Déserts* (1954) is for winds, percussion, and stereophonic tape. His swan song was a *Poème électronique* for the Philips Pavilion at the Brussels World's Fair (1958): the architect Le Corbusier's three-peaked structure was meant to suggest a circus tent outside and a cow's stomach within, and Varèse's three channels of sound were played over 400 speakers as visual images were projected onto the walls.

Arcana

For piccolos I-III, flutes I-II, oboes I-III, English horn, heckelphone, E♭ clarinets I-II, clarinets I-II, contrabass clarinet, bassoons I-III, contrabassoons I-II, horns I-VIII, trumpets I-V, trombones I-IV, tuba, contrabass tuba; timpani, 6 percussionists (drums, cymbals, gongs, woodblocks, coconut shells, rattle, xylophone, glockenspiel—some 39 instruments, all told); strings

Composed 1925–February 1927 in New York; the ending was revised in 1960

First performed 8 April 1927 by the Philadelphia Orchestra, Leopold Stowkowski conducting

Published by Max Eschig (Paris, 1931); revised edition published by Franco Colombo, Inc. (New York, 1964)

Duration: about 20 minutes

The title means "secrets" or "mysteries": alchemy, for example, was an arcane branch of knowledge. The score is preceded by a citation from the *Hermetic Astronomy* of Paracelsus, a sixteenth-century Swiss physician and alchemist. It describes the cosmos as arranged under an apocalyptic star beneath which are the ascendant star, the four elements, and imagination; the last of these begets a new star and a new cosmos. Varèse intended thus to pay tribute to science and the advancement of knowledge, but took care to observe that the music was not to be heard as commentary.

The thudding motive in the first two-bars, so reminiscent of the Infernal Dance in Stravinsky's *Firebird,* constitutes what Varèse called an eleven-note *idée fixe.* Because of its many recurrences and its position in the bass of the ensemble, commentators (following the first program note) tend to describe the work as a passacaglia-like structure. But this is not really apposite, for the *idée fixe* exerts almost nothing of a passacaglia's control. In view of the fluid combinations of rhythmic and melodic cells the better parallel is with Stravinsky's Paris ballets, to which, I think, *Arcana* makes frequent allusion. Varèse also quotes a motive from his own *Intégrales* (the French horn figure after the first fermata) and includes, about a third of the way in, an episode for percussion that foreshadows the sound of *Ionisation*.

Few works are as violent or, for that matter, as loud. The orchestra numbers in excess of 120, with great extension in the wind and percussion of a sort that outdoes even Stravinsky. There's particular heaviness in the lowest register—contrabass clarinet, two contrabassoons, bass and contrabass trombone and tuba, and the field of double-basses— and an opposing shrillness from the three piccolos and two E♭ clarinets at the top. All this led critics and audiences to complain of cacophonous tumult, unendurable screaming, and merciless disharmony. *Arcana* is, without question, explosive.

But the compositional procedure at work is straightforward enough, and, on the whole, easy to discern. The sound masses are built of discrete cells that rearrange themselves, assimilate, and synthesize as they go. The dozen or so sections are clearly delineated by abrupt changes of texture, fermatas, or empty bars. There's enough recurrence of previous material to lend a good sense of overall coherence. And the degree of rhythmic and orchestrational invention to be found in the hundreds of constituent cells is, in a word, deafening.

Ionisation

For 13 percussionists (see below), with celesta and piano
Composed 1931, dated Paris 13 November 1931
First performed 6 March 1933 at the third Pan American Concert in Carnegie Hall, New York, Nicolas Slonimsky conducting
Published by the New Music Orchestra Series (San Francisco, 1934)
Duration: about 6 minutes

I count more than three dozen instruments in the battery for this famous and in some respects epochal composition, which after more than a half century remains the best thing in the repertoire for percussion. The most striking are the high and low siren (the score gives a manufacturer and part number) and the string drum, or lion's roar, where the sound comes from the friction of a string drawn through the drumhead. Additionally there are conventional drums, cymbals, gongs, tambourine, triangle, slapstick, güiro, woodblocks, claves, maracas, bongos, cowbells, sleighbells, chimes, and anvils—often in pairs, high and low or shallow and deep.

As anyone who has heard an African or Polynesian drum band knows, an orchestra of percussion can create convincing and extraordinarily complex musical structures from the counterpoint of rhythms, volumes, and tone colors available to it. You can, that is, have motives and formal sections and the like without specifically pitched melody. In fact *Ionisation* has some very interesting pitch components: the rise and fall of the sirens in particular, but also the play of high and low voices. And the dramatic introduction, near the end, of the instruments of true pitch (the chimes, celesta, and piano) is a central formal event. Even here, however, texture is of greater concern than melody: the pitches of the thick chords run together as they continue to vibrate, and the pianist's forearms keep pounding out clusters in the bass. It's a very Ivesian sound.

The form is of clearly articulated sections—percussion instruments are nothing if not articulate—that grow in volume and complexity as the work progresses. The first *fortissimo,* for example, is reached near the midpoint, during which quintuplet rhythms are prominently introduced. Intensity slackens a little with the reappearance of the sirens; after the metallic fermata comes a penultimate section with slapstick and the conclusion with piano and bells.

The adulation with which *Ionisation* was received in certain New York circles was the first wave of what has become something of a Varèse cult. "Every age has its characteristic sound," he held, and what might be called the metropolitan heat of *Ionisation* may well be the characteristic sound of his own. That seems a more sensible assessment of things than to look for some cosmic interpretation of the title.

Ralph Vaughan Williams

Born 12 October 1872 in Down Ampney,
Gloucestershire
Died 26 August 1958 in London

Though Vaughan Williams was the son of a clergyman of relatively modest circumstance, his lineage was substantial: there was a dynasty of jurists on his father's side and, on his mother's, the Wedgwoods (of china fame) and Charles Darwin. An aunt gave him early instruction in piano and the rudiments of composition; at boarding school he studied the violin, viola, and piano. His advanced training took place at both the Royal College of Music and Cambridge, where he studied composition with Hubert Parry, Charles Villiers Stanford, and Charles Wood, the nation's most accomplished teachers at the time. In 1897 he had lessons with Max Bruch in Berlin, then returned to Cambridge to take the Doctor of Music degree.

All of which left him, he thought, with amateurish technique and without a clear sense of compositional direction. He found his inspiration, as his friend Holst did at about the same time, in the music of Elgar and in collecting English folksong.

In 1908, reasonably well established and approaching middle age, he studied for three months with Ravel in Paris. That experience gave rise to a series of works of new vision and craft: the song cycle *On Wenlock Edge* (1909) to poems from A. E. Housman's *A Shropshire Lad,* the Fantasia on a Theme by Thomas Tallis (1910), and what he called his *London Symphony* (No. 2, 1914), an impressionistic and descriptive treatment of metropolitan sounds that incorporates songs of the music hall and the Westminster Chimes.

After the First World War, during which he served as an artillery officer, he became a ubiquitous presence on the English musical scene, equally at ease at the podium, in the classroom, before the microphones of the BBC, composing for films. From 1905 he was conductor of the Leith Hill Festival in the London suburb of Dorking, a position he retained for most of his career. At the height of his career he also led the London Bach Choir (1920–28) and taught composition at the Royal Conservatory of Music (1919–39). He visited the United States on three occasions: once in 1922 to conduct his Fourth Symphony at the Norfolk Festival in Connecticut (Sibelius had come there in 1914), in 1932 to teach at Bryn Mawr, and finally in 1954 on a lecture tour of American universities. On this last occasion he was accompanied by the second Mrs. Vaughan Williams, *née* Ursula Wood, his secretary and later his biographer; they had been married in 1953, when the composer was eighty-two. His vitality was indeed spectacular: the Eighth and Ninth Symphonies come from the same period.

Vaughan Williams was a populist (and, despite his parentage, an atheist), given to a relatively conservative style that is inevitably to be compared with that of Sibelius, whom he much admired. It embraces hints of French impressionism but more significantly employs a melodic and harmonic idiom that devolves naturally from his interest in folk music. Within these boundaries he moves with great freedom and ingenuity. His command of modal counterpoint, for example, serves the style admirably.

He composed nine symphonies; some of them bear titles: the *Sea Symphony* for chorus and orchestra to a text of Walt Whitman (his first, 1903–09); the *Pastoral Symphony* (No. 3, 1922); and the *Sinfonia Antarctica* (No. 7, 1949–52), which grew from the film score for *Scott of the Antarctic* (1948). Of all of them the Fourth, in F minor (1935), is often considered his best; his most popular work for chorus, however, is the Christmas cantata *Hodie*, for soloists, chorus, and orchestra (1953–54).

Fantasia on a Theme by Thomas Tallis

> For two string orchestras: the second orchestra consists of nine players (double string quartet and bass), placed at a distance from the first; the solo quartet parts are played by the principals
> **Composed** June 1910 for the Gloucester Festival that year; revised 1913 and 1919
> **First performed** 6 September 1910 at the Gloucester Festival, the composer conducting
> **Published by** Goodwin & Tabb (London, 1921); later Boosey & Hawkes
> **Duration:** about 15 minutes

Tallis's theme, "Why fum'th in fight?", is the third of nine hymn tunes he composed for Archbishop Matthew Parker's *The Whole Psalter translated into English Metre* (London, 1567). Thomas Tallis (c. 1505–85) was an organist and composer at the Dover Priory, in London, and at Waltham Abbey, later a Gentleman of the Chapel Royal under Henry VIII, Mary, and Elizabeth I. Vaughan Williams was attracted to the tune while working as editor on *The English Hymnal,* where it serves for hymn 92, "When rising from the bed of death."

The melody is interesting: modal, metrically complex, elegantly shaped, perhaps a little stern. Vaughan Williams achieves marvelous registral and textural effects in treating it, and the subtle antiphony often leaves you wondering where a particular echo came from. The very idea of the work, thoroughly of its time and place yet dwelling in a golden age four centuries earlier, is imaginative in the extreme. Other composers—Respighi and Rimsky come to mind—had tried rather similar effects, but none with such sophisticated result.

After the two-bar chordal introduction, *molto sostenuto,* the theme emerges from the low strings beneath the static high note in the violins. The many repeated pitches, suggestive of chant, impart the ecclesiastical quality. The restatement is prevailingly homophonic, tinted with the tremolandos in the uppermost voices, though toward the end the second violins begin a very gentle ornamentation in rippling sixteenths. Echoes begin to cycle between the orchestras.

The episode for viola and violin solo presents the second phrase of Tallis's theme, with responses from the orchestras. A short polyphonic digression is undertaken by the solo quartet, and the antiphonal forces proceed to develop this material and lead it into an expansive homophonic climax. In the third section, the violin and viola solos continue, this time not in alternation but contrapuntally. The coda recollects an earlier closure, then cadences beneath the arpeggiated ascent of the solo violin.

Fantasia on *Greensleeves*

For flutes I-II; harp; strings
Arranged 1934 by Ralph Greaves from an interlude in the opera
    Sir John in Love, 1924–28
First performed 27 September 1934 at a Vaughan Williams
    Promenade Concert in Queen's Hall, London, the composer
    conducting (the opera was first performed 21 March 1929)
Published by Oxford University Press (London, 1934)
Duration: about 5 minutes

The ever-popular song *Greensleeves* came to prominence in the late sixteenth century and was cited by Shakespeare in *The Merry Wives of Windsor.* The text had first appeared in a famous anthology called *A Handefull of Pleasant Delites* (1584).

As music director for 1913 productions at Stratford-upon-Avon, Vaughan Williams used the song in both *Richard III* and *The Merry Wives of Windsor.* In act III of his opera *Sir John in Love,* based on *The Merry Wives,* he gives the tune to Mistress Ford. Ten years later this setting was excerpted and refashioned for a Prom concert, one of those music-for-everybody fests that traditionally launch the London season.

This version of *Greensleeves* has become more or less the industry standard by virtue of being just sweet enough to evoke thoughts of rosy medievaldom without quite sliding into sentimentality. The patina of antiquity results from placing the tune in the middle of the musical fabric for the most part, with discants above and plucking strings below. The harp and flute solo are employed for angelic effect at the beginning and again toward the end; elsewhere the harp participates in the plucked effects. For the first verse the song is in the second violins and violas, and in the even warmer pairing of violas and cellos for the verse at the end; both verses have the concluding refrain in the violins. At the center, there is a folk tune of rather similar contour, *Lovely Joan*.

Giuseppe Verdi

Born *10 October 1813 in*
Le Roncole, near Parma
Died *27 January 1901 in Milan*

From the most modest beginnings as a village shopkeeper's son, and by dint of slavish labor and shrewd business acumen, Verdi rose to the summit of nineteenth-century opera. A century later the corpus of his work still dominates the lyric stage, and nowadays we are inclined to regard his gifts as a musical dramatist on a par with Wagner's.

His promise attracted the patronage of Antonio Barezzi, merchant of nearby Busseto. Barezzi supported Verdi's early studies in Milan, artistic capital of Italy and home of the great opera house, La Scala. After two unhappy years in Milan, Verdi returned to become organist in Busseto and marry Barezzi's daughter Margherita. Their daughter Virginia died in infancy, and in 1840, while Verdi was trying once more to conquer Milan with a comic opera, his wife and son succumbed to a fever.

Despairing of his future, Verdi resolved to abandon composition. Then, according to his own account, his eye fell on the line "Va pensiero sul'ali dorate"—Go, my thought, on wings of gold—from a manuscript libretto on his desk. The resulting opera, *Nabucco* (1842), was his return to life and his first major success at La Scala; it was followed by *Ernani* (1844) and *Macbeth* (1847), both based on librettos by Francesco Maria Piave, with whom Verdi collaborated for nearly 20 years. He reached a quite profitable arrangement with the publisher Giulio Ricordi, and during the decade he called his galley years saw his work produced all over Italy and in London and Paris as well. His companion since *Nabucco* had been the soprano Giuseppina Strepponi; they were married in 1859.

With *Rigoletto* (1851) he became the reigning monarch of the stage. There followed two equally impressive accomplishments, *La traviata* and *Il trovatore* (both 1853). His choice of an opera concerning the assassination of Gustav III, king of Sweden, was thought to condone attempts on the life of Italy's foreign monarch, Napoleon III. He was thus forced by the censors to change the setting of *Un ballo in maschera* (A Masked Ball, 1859) to Boston! The result was that, with *Un ballo,* Verdi became something of a hero in the growing movement for a unified, independent Italy. His name became an acronym for a nationalist slogan: Vittorio Emmanuale, Re D'Italia (Victor Emmanuel, King of Italy).

Meanwhile there had been productions in Paris of *Les vêpres siciliennes* (The Sicilian Vespers, 1855), in Venice of *Simon Boccanegra* (1857), in St. Petersburg of *La forza del destino* (The Force of Destiny, 1862), and in Paris again of *Don Carlos* (1867). *Aïda* was produced in Cairo on Christmas Eve, 1871, in conjunction with the opening of the Suez Canal.

After a hiatus of fifteen years, Verdi, then 73 years of age, composed his masterpiece, *Otello* (1887), to Arrigo Boito's adaptation of the Shakespeare play. This was followed by an equally exceptional work, the comedy *Falstaff* (1893), again to a text of Boito based on Shakespeare's *Merry Wives of Windsor.* Verdi died quietly of old age; two years earlier he had established a retirement home for musicians in Milan, to be supported after his death by the income from his estate.

Verdi's Requiem Mass for the writer Alessandro Manzoni is frequently programed by symphony orchestras and their choruses. (Toscanini gave a particularly stunning performance of the work in New York on the fiftieth anniversary of Verdi's death in 1951.) His String Quartet (1873) is often played as a concert piece, as is the rousing overture to *La forza del destino*.

Messa da Requiem

Requiem
Dies irae (9 sections)
Offertorio
Sanctus
Agnus Dei
Lux aeterna
Libera me

For soloists (SMsTB); chorus; piccolo, flutes I-II, oboes I-II, clarinets I-II, bassoons I-IV; horns I-IV, trumpets I-IV, offstage trumpets I-IV, trombones I-III, tuba; timpani, bass drum; strings
Composed 1874 in Sant'Agata, in memory of Alessandro Manzoni
First performed 22 May 1874 at the Church of San Marco, Milan, Verdi conducting
Published by Ricordi (Milan, vocal score 1874, rev. 1875; full score 1913). *Inexpensive score:* Giuseppe Verdi: *Requiem in Full Score* (New York: Dover, 1978)
Duration: a little over an hour and a half

Shortly after Rossini died in 1868, Verdi proposed that a Requiem Mass be prepared collaboratively by the best Italian composers and performed on the first anniversary of his death, the traditional occasion in Europe for unveiling monuments and literary tributes. The score was completed in due course but never performed. Verdi's contribution had been the *Libera me*.

This movement and the thoughts that had yielded it were eventually gathered into Verdi's Requiem Mass of 1873–74, a memorial to the great nationalist poet Alessandro Manzoni, a man whom the composer revered. Verdi had expected *Aïda* of 1870–71 to be his farewell to composition, but a few weeks after Manzoni's death on 22 May 1873, at the graveside, he resolved to return to work. "It is a heartfelt impulse, or rather a necessity," he wrote, "to do all in my power to

honor this great spirit whom I valued so highly as a writer and venerated as a man." But the memory of Rossini, too, is very much at
issue here, and there is from time to time motivic homage to Rossini's
Stabat mater.

The centerpiece of Verdi's conception of the Requiem text is the
massive second movement, which constitutes nearly half the work.
This is a setting of the medieval sequence, or prosa, *Dies irae, dies
illa,* a poem of seventeen rhymed three-line strophes, a concluding
quatrain (*Lacrymosa*), and a last unrhymed liturgical formula (*Pie Jesu,
Domine*). Verdi envisages a frightening apocalypse, indeed, insisting
on the *Dies irae* section three times here and once again at the close of
the composition. With its bass-drum explosions and rapid passagework fleeing in all directions, the section should terrify you with its
graphic suggestion of the "Devil chasing you to Hell" (as the critic
David Cairns put it). Nor are Gabriel's trumpets in the *Tuba mirum*
especially comforting. But Verdi offsets the horror with passages of
tenderness and an occasional glimmer of optimism—as with the *Offertorium,* which begins as a consoling barcarole.

Each of the soloists makes a noble entry in the *Kyrie eleison,* after
which they are parsed out, in all their permutations, with such seeming inevitability that you scarcely notice the great care the composer
has taken to assure each an equal share of the action. (Opera composers are quite skilled at this sort of thing.) The bass, like an angel of
death, has the first solo of the *Dies irae,* albeit a brief one, at the
words "Mors stupebit." Then comes the mezzo's stern aria on the
proffering of the Book of the Dead (*Liber scriptus*), in which all things
are written, nothing hidden. At the center of the movement, the
soprano joins the mezzo-soprano for the *Recordare,* with its striking
cello-dominated climax; there follow the big solos for tenor (*Ingemisco,*
a plea to be numbered not with the goats but among the lambs), and
bass (*Confutatis maledictis,* begging to be spared from the acrid flame
of Judgment Day). Meanwhile there are fine trio and quartet passages,
and, in the profound *tuttis* of the *Salve me* and *Lacrymosa,* a scoring
that allows the soprano's several high B♭s and Cs to float over the
mass of performers with crystalline clarity.

Offertorium (no. 4) and *Lux aeterna* (no. 6) are for soloists and orchestra without chorus. The soprano does not sing in the *Lux* because the
solo work in the last movement (*Libera me, no. 7*) is given to her
alone. There she represents harried humankind, troubled by hellish

presentiments and seeking, tentatively at first, then with growing assurance, her place among the saved.

Note the many cross-references in both the musical and the liturgical texts. The verse structure of the *Agnus Dei,* for example, suggests to Verdi three delicately varied strophes of his simple refrain; in the *Offertorium,* the recall of the line "Quam olim Abrahae promisisti" affords him a full-scale recapitulation of his menacing dead march. In the *Libera me* there is both a recapitulation of the bass-drum scattering from the second movement and an *a cappella* setting with the soprano solo of the opening Introit text.

The Requiem properly bows to ecclesiastical tradition: chanted declamation pervades the somber sections, and there are two full-blown fugues, in the *Sanctus* and the concluding *Libera me.* Yet essentially it is operatic, of course, the ancient and honorable liturgy serving as a profound libretto. This makes it a fine concert vehicle for the superstars of the opera, such as Jessye Norman and Luciano Pavarotti and their peers.

Verdi's Requiem is, in short, a masterpiece of the genre, a work of "universal catastrophe, destruction, terror, and despair," writes *New Yorker* critic and Verdian, Andrew Porter, "then hope at its most urgent and poignant."

Antonio Vivaldi

**Born 4 March 1678 in Venice
Died c. 25 July 1741 in Vienna**

Vivaldi studied violin and composition with his father, and as a young man entered the priesthood. (He was called "the red priest," after the color of his hair.) From 1703 to 1718 his principal appointment was as *maestro di violino* at a Venetian orphanage for girls called the Ospedale della Pietà, and he retained some form of association with the school for the rest of his life. Much of his solo and ensemble music was composed for the concerts at the Pietà. He owed his celebrity outside Italy to Estienne Roger, music publisher of Amsterdam, whose edition of Vivaldi's twelve concertos for violins called *L'estro armonico* (op. 3, 1711) was the best-selling music title of the early eighteenth century. Roger and his successors went on to publish ten of Vivaldi's twelve opuses; *La cetra,* two books of concertos dedicated to the Emperor Charles VI, led to Vivaldi's affiliation from 1728 with the imperial court in Vienna. In the second half of his career he worked in Mantua and Rome as well as Venice, and in the course of premiering his operas traveled throughout northern Italy and as far as Prague and Dresden. In 1740 he left Venice on a journey of uncertain purpose that took him by late June 1741 to Vienna. There he died a month later and, having exhausted his considerable fortune, was buried in a pauper's grave.

His reputation was that of a man driven more by money than morality, a paragon of vanity, unpleasant to be around and dishonest to boot.

Vivaldi wrote more than seven hundred instrumental works, composing them faster, he boasted, than they could be copied. Some five hundred or so are concertos, about half for violin solo; Vivaldi is thus a critical figure in the history of the Baroque concerto. (Bach, for example, sometimes copied out Vivaldi scores. You often hear his transcription for organ of the popular A-Minor Concerto for two violins and orchestra.) The most frequently performed of Vivaldi's work remains the cycle depicting the seasons of the year, *Le Quattro Stagioni*. Additionally, he composed dozens of operas, cantatas and the like, chamber music, and a very popular *Gloria* for soloists, chorus, and orchestra. A complete (and very confusing) edition of his instrumental works has been published by Ricordi, edited by the Italian scholar Gian Francesco Malipiero. Because of the complexity of the sources and the many self-borrowings in Vivaldi's work, arranging it in any useful order has been a daunting task.

Le Quattro Stagioni (The Four Seasons), OP. 8, Nos. 1–4

La primavera (Spring)
L'estate (Summer)
L'autunno (Autumn)
L'inverno (Winter)

For violin solo, strings, and continuo
Composed in the early 1720s; dedicated to Count Venceslao (i.e., Wenceslaus) von Marzin (or Morzin) of Bohemia
First performed according to the published dedication by Morzin's orchestra c. 1725
Published by Le Cène (Amsterdam, 1725)
Duration of the set: about 40 minutes

Vivaldi's opus 8, which appeared in 1725 or thereabout, is a two-volume collection of twelve concerti grossi titled *Il cimento dell'armonia e dell'inventione* (The Ordeal Between Harmony and Invention). The first four of them are *The Four Seasons*.

Preceding each concerto is a "demonstrative sonnet," possibly by Vivaldi himself, that describes the musical images to follow. (These poems and their translation should appear in your concert program.) Letters placed in the margin by the poems correspond to similar letters above the systems of score, making the intended imagery of specific musical passages clear; moreover lines of text in both the full score and the published parts reiterate the references. The truth is that this music can seem a little silly if you fail to imagine the scenes the composer had in mind.

Vivaldi's tactic is to suggest the general character of each season in the opening ritornello, then attend to the specific imagery in the episodes for the solo players, relying heavily, as this kind of description always does, on weather music and animal sounds. Each concerto is in the typical succession of three movements, fast-slow-fast. What is unusual is the freedom of interplay between the orchestral ensemble and the soloists in place of strict alternation, and the significant solo work for the cello and harpsichord. Both features are the natural result of music that follows a programmtic text.

Spring. I: The arrival of spring, bird songs, the play of fountains, the murmur of sweet breezes, lightning and thunder of a spring rainstorm, the storm subsiding, bird songs again. II: A goatherd sleeps, foliage rustles, the faithful dog (viola) barks. III: Pastoral dance with pipes and drones as nymphs and shepherds frolic in a meadow.

Summer. I: Scorching sun, the burning torpor making flora, fauna, and human beings droop; cuckoo, turtledove and finch; sweet zephyrs, impetuous winds; a shepherd frets over the forthcoming tempest. II: The weary shepherd knows no rest; lightning and thunder; a swarm of flies. III: A summer hailstorm crushes the crops.

Autumn. I. The song and dance of peasants delighted with the harvest; they drink heartily of Bacchus's cup, then fall asleep. II: One by one, they cease their sport and sleep. III: A hunt; entry of the hunter at dawn, with horn and hounds; the bewildered beast tires, is set upon by the dogs, and shot; the beast falls and dies.

Winter. I: Shivering, in mounds of snow; cruel winds; we stamp our feet, teeth chattering. II: Contented days by the fireside, while outside there is driving rain. III: Walking on ice; bravely we step out, taking care not to fall, then fall anyway; we get up and run again; breaking ice; wind howling through the bolted door; the war of winds.

This is a big dose of musical picture-making to face all at once, and in any event twelve ritornello movements at a sitting can test your patience. (For that matter, I dislike hearing the *Brandenburg Concertos* played altogether.) But in this case there is very little choice but to hear Vivaldi out, and you can take the time to muse on how much easier this sort of thing could be managed in later eras, when there were more graphic resources available to an orchestral composer. Besides, the sleeping goatherd and his faithful dog is an inspired bit of part-writing.

Richard Wagner

Born 22 May 1813 in Leipzig
Died 13 February 1883 in Venice

Creator of the so-called "music drama," Wagner composed opera almost exclusively, most of it based on dark, mythical subject matter. Seldom has there been so egocentric a composer: unlike most of the composers treated here, Wagner as a person was both disagreeable and often duplicitous. (Vivaldi is, I suppose, his closest rival on this score.) Yet his effect on the composition of music was as great as Beethoven's had been. Not until Stravinsky would there be another composer of such revolutionary impact.

He showed pronounced interest in literature and opera from an early age and was educated at good schools in Dresden and Leipzig. His time at the University of Leipzig was inconsequential, his formal training in composition modest; the remainder of his life he spent, as he had spent his youth, in and around the theatre. At the beginning of his career he worked for opera houses in Magdeburg, Königsberg (where he married an actress, Minna Planer), and Riga; then lived unhappily as a bohemian in Paris (1839–42), sending reports of musical life back to the Dresden newspaper and doing odd jobs for music publishers at low compensation. His operas *Rienzi* (1842) and *Der fliegende Holländer* (The Flying Dutchman, 1843) were produced in Dresden to enough enthusiasm to warrant his appointment as Kapellmeister to the Saxon court. There he produced *Tannhäuser* (1845), completed *Lohengrin* (1848), and began the libretto, "Siegfried's Death," that evolved into the tetralogy *Der Ring des Nibelungen.*

Wagner imprudently became involved in the Dresden revolt of 1848–49 and was forced to flee to Switzerland. The next decade saw a spectacular development in his dramatic theory and compositional practice: manifestos on "Art and Revolution" (1849) and "The Artwork of the Future" (1849; also "Opera and Drama," 1856), *Das Rheingold,* and *Die Walküre.* In the mid-1850s, Wagner fell in love with Matthilde Wesendonck, the wife of a friend; they took up residence together, and he completed three more compositions under her spell: *Siegfried* (the third opera in the *Ring*), *Tristan und Isolde* (1859), and five settings of Matthilde's poems.

From 1859 to 1862 he lived in Paris, still the center of the operatic universe, during which time a production of *Tannhäuser* with added ballet music was an abysmal failure. Eventually Wagner was granted amnesty to return to Germany and in 1864 established residence in Munich under the patronage of the "mad" Ludwig II of Bavaria. There he began a liaison with Liszt's daughter, Cosima, wife of the conductor Hans von Bülow. (Bülow conducted the first performances of *Tristan* just two months after his wife had given birth to Wagner's child.) In 1865 Wagner and Cosima settled in a lovely villa on Lake Lucerne in Switzerland, where he completed *Die Meistersinger* (1868) and the last of the *Ring* operas, *Götterdämmerung.* They were married on 25 August 1870, following Minna's death and Cosima's divorce from von Bülow.

In 1872 the town of Bayreuth, north of Munich, offered Wagner land on which to build the festival theatre of his dreams. By 1876 his theatre, the Festspielhaus, and his home, Wahnfried, were finished. The completed *Ring des Nibelungen* was offered in August of that year. He finished his last opera, *Parsifal,* in 1882. Seeking a cure for his ill health he went to Venice for the winter, but died there of a heart attack in February.

Wagner wrote volumes and volumes of prose and poetry, including a tedious autobiography and a somewhat more important treatise on conducting. For orchestra there are overtures and marches, all but the wind *Trauermusik* for Weber pretty well forgotten, and the charming *Siegfried-Iydll* treated below. (His *American Centennial March* was premiered in Philadelphia in 1876.) The excerpts from his operas most commonly heard in the concert hall are the *Rienzi* Overture, the overture and Venusberg Music from *Tannhäuser* (written to give the Paris Opéra production its mandatory ballet), the preludes to act I and III of *Lohengrin,* the "Ride of the Valkyries," from *Die Walküre,* "Siegfried's Rhine Journey" from *Siegfried,* the prelude and "Liebestod" from Tristan und Isolde, and the prelude to *Die Meistersinger.*

Prelude and "Liebestod," from *Tristan und Isolde*

For piccolo, flutes I-III, oboes I-II, English horn, clarinets I-II, bass clarinet, bassoons I-IV; horns I-IV, trumpets I-III, trombones I-III, tuba; timpani; harp; strings

Composed 1857 in Zurich

First performed (the prelude only) 12 March 1859 in Prague, with an ending by Hans von Bülow, who conducted; with the Wagner ending, 25 January 1860 at the Théâtre-Italien, Paris, Wagner conducting; with prelude followed by transfiguration 10 March 1863 in St. Petersburg, Wagner conducting

Published by Breitkopf & Härtel (Leipzig, 1860; the two excerpts joined, 1882). *Inexpensive score:* Wagner: *Prelude and Transfiguration from Tristan and Isolde,* ed. Robert Bailey, A Norton Critical Score (New York: Norton, 1985)

Duration: about 15 minutes

So enigmatic is the first chord of the *Tristan* prelude, so suggestive of love potions and unfulfilled longing and eroticism, so succint a statement of everything the opera is about, that the sonority has ever since been called the "Tristan chord." It slides upward and pushes down simultaneously, moves but does not—for the moment—resolve, and in the opera you go on to hear it stab through the dense textures at virtually every significant turn of events.

Moreover the whole opening gambit—blossom and wither of cello, Tristan chord in the winds and its slackening—is repeated three times at successively higher pitch levels. The fragmentation ends in repetitions of a quizzical two-note cell, then seems on the verge of exploding into a cadence. But this is diverted into the long, despondent cello phrase. Not until the very close of the opera (to give away the secret at once) will the Tristan chord find true resolution. There it is not diverted into melancholy but transfigured into bliss, soaring past the minor key it has always implied into celestial major.

All this has to do, of course, with the uncontrolled passion Tristan and Isolde have conceived for one another. (This is the magic work of a philtre, the sort of excuse for unseemly conduct medieval legend seems to require; the story, I've always thought, is a good deal more powerful if you just ignore it.) It is a deadly passion, too, for Isolde is the bride of King Mark of Cornwall, Tristan's employer. Virtually all of act II of *Tristan und Isolde* is devoted to their illicit rendezvous by night, where they begin to understand that only in the endless night of death can their love be fully consummated. At dawn their love making is indeed interrupted by the arrival of King Mark and his retinue, and Tristan is dealt a fatal wound.

Which brings us to Isolde's "Liebestod" at the end of act III. Tristan manages to survive just long enough to witness Isolde's return, then expires in ecstasy. Isolde cradles his head and begins her own transfiguration, the music drawn from the act II love duet: "How softly and gently he smiles. . . . Do you not see, friends, how he shines? . . . Do I alone hear this melody rising up? Should I thus plunge into the ocean of sound, the all-encompassing world of the earth spirit, drown, sink unconscious?—highest lust." She collapses over his body as the curtain falls.

It is, of course, a music of barely concealed sexuality. Wagner is nowhere better than here in the prelude as he uses musical syntax to describe universal imponderables, or in the "Liebestod" as the music lifts in its every parameter—orchestrationally, harmonically, melodically, and poetically—to a new plane. The idea of coupling the two excerpts was Wagner's own, a possibility that first occurred to him in October 1862 in the wake of several performances of the prelude alone. You miss, of course, the four hours in the middle, some of the most glorious music ever written.

Prelude to Act III of *Lohengrin*

For flutes I-III, oboes I-III, clarinets I-III, bassoons I-III; horns I-
IV, trumpets I-III, trombones I-III, tuba; timpani, triangle,
cymbals, tambourine; strings
Composed (the opera) early 1846–April 1848, mostly in Dresden
First performed with the opera 28 August 1850 in the Grand-
Ducal Theater of Weimar, Liszt conducting (because Wagner
was in exile, wanted by the law)
Published by Breitkopf & Härtel in lithographed facsimile of a
copyist's manuscript score (Leipzig, 1852); the dedication of
this edition is to Liszt, who had given the first performance;
prelude engraved by Breitkopf & Härtel (Leipzig, 1872–73)
Duration: about 3 minutes

Lohengrin is an opera that, broadly speaking, treats the triumph of
Christianity over paganism and celebrates the merits of steadfast love.
The setting is Antwerp, of the Belgian duchy of Brabant, in the tenth
century. The intricate story, a conflation of two different legends,
centers around the false assertion that Elsa of Brabant has murdered
her brother, heir to the dukedom. A knight arrives in a swan-drawn
boat to defend Elsa's honor in trial by combat. She agrees to marry
him if he is victorious, and he elicits from her the vow that she will
never ask his name. Ortrud, Elsa's wicked stepmother, arouses her
suspicions by denouncing her champion as a magician. Following their
wedding in the Antwerp cathedral, she asks her husband the forbidden question; he reveals that he is Lohengrin, second son of Parsifal,
the knight of the Holy Grail. Having answered, he must go away.
The swan reappears and is transformed into Elsa's missing brother,
the rightful heir. She swoons into his arms as she watches her husband
disappear down the river, his boat now drawn by the dove of the Holy
Grail.

The prelude to act III is meant to evoke the exhilaration of the
wedding ceremony and feast. (The finale of act II that just precedes it
is Elsa's wonderful procession to the cathedral, with its antiphonal
trumpet flourishes at the end; the first scene of act III begins with the
famous wedding march that leads Elsa away from the festivity to her
bridal chamber.) The opening triplets charge across the orchestra into

a euphoria of high strings and winds. Cellos, bassoons, and French horns present the familiar, swashbuckling theme, joined in the repeat by trombones and at the climax by triangle and tambourine. A trio-like center section suggests processional music, with an expansive countermelody in the cellos and then a prominent figure for solo clarinet. The abbreviated recapitulation focuses, *tutta forza,* on the tenor theme, bringing the trombones and tuba to the fore.

Siegfried-Idyll

For flute, oboe, clarinets I-II, bassoon; horns I-II, trumpet; strings (one on a part, or small ensemble; first performed one on a part)

Composed late November–December 1870 at Tribschen, Wagner's villa near Lucerne; dedicated to Cosima Wagner, the composer's wife

First performed 25 December 1870 by thirteen musicians at Triebschen, Wagner conducting

Published by B. Schotts Söhne (Mainz, 1878)

Duration: about 20 minutes

On 6 June 1869 Cosima Liszt von Bülow gave birth to a Wagner's son, Siegfried. She was thirty-one years old; Wagner was fifty-six. For Christmas Day, 1870, Cosima's birthday, her doting husband composed his *Siegfried-Idyll*—the reference being to their son, not the operatic hero. Early that morning thirteen musicians, who had been surreptitiously rehearsed in Zurich and at their villa Tribschen in Lucerne by Hans Richter, crept up the stairs of the villa and woke Cosima and the baby with their gentle offering. Wagner conducted; their guest Friedrich Nietzsche was present as well. Later in the day the *Siegfried-Idyll* was played twice more, along with a Beethoven sextet and the Wedding March from *Lohengrin.*

The little fantasy draws on tunes from Wagner's opera, *Siegfried,* with which Cosima was by then conversant, as well as on a familiar lullaby. It is symbolic in other ways, as well: the manuscript is titled "Tribschen-Idyll, with Fidi's Bird-song and an Orange Sunrise, presented as a Symphonic Birthday Greeting to his Cosima by her Richard, 1870." Fidi was Siegfried's nickname, and the orange sunrise refers to the play of sunlight on the orange wallpaper in the nursery on the morning of Siegfried's birth—thus the birds and the sunrise music in an intermezzo of rather typically Wagnerian counterpoint and melody. Wagner, given to more epic passions, was not usually this sentimental, but on the whole it becomes him.

Prelude to *Die Meistersinger von Nürnberg*

For piccolo, flutes I-II, oboes I-II, clarinets I-II, bassoons I-II; horns I-IV, trumpets I-III, trombones I-III, tuba; timpani, cymbals, triangle; harp; strings

Composed (the opera) autumn 1861–62 in Vienna, Biebrich, and Lucerne; the sketches go back to 1845 in Marienbad

First performed (the prelude) 1 November 1862 by the Leipzig Gewandhaus Orchestra, Wagner conducting; the opera first performed 21 June 1868 at the Royal Opera House, Munich, Hans von Bülow conducting

Published by B. Schotts Söhne (Mainz, 1866)

Duration: about 10 minutes

Die Meistersinger was first envisaged by Wagner as a worldly companion to the more mythical *Tannhäuser,* both of which involve gaining the hand of a loved one by the singing of a song. The setting is Nuremberg in the middle of the sixteenth century. A guild of mastersingers—a baker, goldsmith, cobbler, grocer, and the like—annually awards a prize to the song that best accords with their rules of good poetry and composition. Hans Sachs tutors the young Walther von Stolzing in the rudiments of song. (Both Sachs and Walther were drawn from history.) The villain is the town clerk, Beckmesser, who acquires Walther's poem in a ruse. All three of them admire the lovely Eva, promised by her father to the winner of the morrow's contest. (In one memorable scene Sachs, the cobbler, marks the errors in Beckmesser's song by hammering on a pair of shoes. The shoes are finished well before Beckmesser is done singing.) At the end, of course, Walther's song wins the prize, as Hans Sachs, the wizened master, looks on benevolently. *Die Meistersinger* is Wagner's sunniest work, with dance music, traditional aria forms, and many choruses and chorales.

The leading motives are comparatively few. Of these the most significant and first to be conceived—originally for the last act of *Tristan,* where Isolde's ship is finally sighted—was the seven-note chain of descending fourths that forms the basis of Walther's prize song. Then there are the fanfare motives for the guild and its banners, love themes, and various suggestions of medieval Germany in springtide.

Much of this the prelude suggests in microcosm. The key, C major, and the martial quadruple meter are trappings of nobility and the opening that of the procession of the guildsmen, massive in homophony and radiant brass. Suggestions of Walther's prize song are heard in the flute and clarinet, followed by cascades of violins that lead to the fanfares associated with the guild's banner. There follows further rumination on the prize song, a warm and lofty theme in violins and winds embracing the prominent chain of falling intervals. An intricate development follows, with sudden shifts of harmony and a playful dialogue on the opening processional stated in much faster note values. In the big drive to recapitulation the fanfare theme (in woodwinds and inner strings), the processional (in bassoon, tuba, and double-basses) and the prize song (in clarinet, violin, and cello) are joined in an elaborate web. This culminates in the exaltation of the brass and strings, another affirmation of the prize song, and the grand close with triangle.

Carl Maria von Weber

Born 18 November 1786 in Eutin,
near Lübeck

Died 5 June 1826 in London

Weber is generally held to be the pathfinder of German Romanticism in music and was easily the most important precursor of Wagner. It's worth noting how his advances parallel and in some cases extend beyond those of Beethoven, who both preceded and survived him. He was a first cousin by marriage of Constanze Weber, Mozart's wife, and the family encouraged him to follow in Mozart's footsteps. For a time he played in his father's theatre productions, then took lessons in composition from Michael Haydn. An early opera was produced when he was fourteen; thereafter he led an itinerant life of conducting appointments in Breslau, Karlsruhe, Stuttgart, Mannheim, and Darmstadt. He toured extensively as a piano virtuoso, held a brief but important appointment in Prague, and finally was named by the King of Saxony as musical director of the opera in

Dresden—a job later held by both Liszt and Wagner.

His greatest and most influential work was the opera *Der Freischütz* (The Free Shot—a story about a hunter who makes a pact with the "black huntsman," 1821). It was followed by *Euryanthe* (1823) and *Oberon* (1826). Though seriously ill with tuberculosis, Weber went to London to conduct the first performances of *Oberon;* after a dozen performances he had to give up, and died a week later. His remains were moved from London to Dresden in 1844, on the occasion of which Wagner wrote a splendid funeral march for winds on themes from *Euryanthe.*

Weber was a piano virtuoso, a good critic, and a prescient conductor. His importance to Romanticism, particularly in the theatre, comes from his having successfully challenged the prevailing trends of Italian and French opera; in his use of medieval Germanic subject matter and folkish-sounding song, his brilliant orchestrational colors, and experimentation with leading motives, he opened up new avenues of operatic composition.

For orchestra his great successes were in the concerto form and its offshoots: the works treated below, as well as movements for orchestra with clarinet, bassoon, horn, flute, and cello solo. The overtures to *Freischütz* and *Euryanthe* are popular concert pieces as well, but *Freischütz,* especially, loses a good deal if you don't know the story that goes with it—that the brooding, plunkish theme, for example, is that of the black huntsman, Samiel. These overtures are available in an inexpensive score: Carl Maria von Weber: *Great Overtures in Full Score* (New York: Dover, 1986).

Concerto No. 1 for Clarinet and Orchestra in F Minor, OP. 73

> *Allegro moderato*
> *Adagio ma non troppo*
> *Rondo: Allegretto*
>
> For clarinet solo; flutes I-II, oboes I-II, bassoons I-II; horns I-III, trumpets I-II; timpani; strings
> Composed April–17 May 1811 in Munich, to a commission for a pair of concertos by King Maximilian of Bavaria; dedicated to Heinrich Bärmann, the clarinetist
> First performed 13 June 1811 by the Munich Court Orchestra,

Heinrich Bärmann, clarinet, Friedrich Kaufmann conducting
Published A. M. Schlesinger (Berlin, 1822)
Duration: about 20 minutes

The connections between Mozart's career and Weber's extend well beyond their indirect family relationship. Both spent their impressionable years in vagabondage, demonstrated their maturity with operatic masterpieces, and died too young. And each made significant contributions to the repertoire for clarinet, in those days a newcomer to the orchestra, by virtue of personal friendship with a gifted player.

The concerto opens, as does Mozart's C-Minor Piano Concerto, K. 491, with the dark contours of the minor tonality arpeggiated out in the cello and basses. This sort of opening demands a tutti *fortissimo* and gets it at the fermata; the full orchestral statement follows and extends itself, as far as the cadence in strings. The entry of clarinet is marked *con duolo*—with sadness. With the high tessitura of the opening, the rapid turn to the throaty register at the triplets, and finally the relentless plunge toward the bottom of the clarinet's range, Weber shows his understanding and sympathy for the personality of the solo instrument. A roll in the timpani alone and an empty bar allow for the rather abrupt arrival of the second theme group. This proves unstable, such that what sounds likes the closing section of the exposition, intrepid and dotted, actually slides into uncharted territory and ends up in the development. When the clarinet enters softly on its lowest pitch, the development is clearly underway. Unconventional, too, is the process of recapitulation: as the clarinet gathers full steam, it becomes clear that the development is over, an impression confirmed by the call of French horns. What follows is, however, a reminiscence of the second theme. Most of the clarinet's melodic recapitulation, in fact, takes place over the sustained tension of the low pedal, and full release is not achievewd until the closing orchestral tutti. The clarinet exits flamboyantly, starting near the bottom of the range and charging relentlessly to the top. As the movement fades into a *pianissimo,* the soloist returns to muse on one of the motives, now in its lowest register.

Weber is consistently bothered by the constraints of first-movement forms, much preferring the freedom slow movements can afford and the unfettered merriment of finales. Here the *Adagio* begins as a typical aria for the soloist over restrained orchestral accompaniment.

A dialogue in the minor mode begins in the woodwinds and strings, with passagework in the solo part; this is followed by a spellbinding episode in E♭ for the clarinet and three horns, a brief recapitulation, and closure with the horns. Weber is like that: always reveling in orchestral sonority, voice by voice, timbre by timbre.

He is at his best, I think, in his rondos, spirited little affairs with the outdoorsy north-German quality that served him so well in *Freischütz*. Here the clarinet sallies forth with a gleeful, showy tune characterized by the octave leaps and returns. The long developmental episode in the middle turns to minor, then, just as it appears to be settling back, slides recklessly into an orchestral trumpeting in a different key. This proves to have been a diversion on the way to recapitulating: the soloist begins the last statement of the rondo and the big tutti confirms arrival. The clarinet concludes in a relentless rise from its lowest F to its highest, three octaves away.

Konzertstück for Piano and Orchestra in F Minor, OP. 79

Larghetto ma non troppo—Allegro passionato—Tempo di Marcia—Presto giojoso

For piano solo; flutes I-II, oboes I-II, clarinets I-II, bassoons I-II; horns I-II, trumpets I-II, trombone; timpani; strings

Composed February 1818–June 1821 (the day *Der Freischütz* opened) in Dresden and Berlin; dedicated "to Her Royal Highness, the Princess Marie Augusta of Saxony, with deepest respect"

First performed 25 June 1821 at the Royal Theater in Berlin, Weber conducting

Published by the Bureau de Musique [Peters] (Leipzig, 1823)

Duration: about 20 minutes

Konzertstück means simply "concert piece," with the implication "in one movement." Weber's short but influential opus 79 amounts to a piano concerto, in this case a progress in four submovements from a searching start through the bravura at the end. There is, moreover, a story attached—but a rather trivial one. I reveal it here with some reluctance, for it comes down to us through an account by Weber's pupil Julius Benedict, and the composer left no indication of it in the published score. But the story was well known to Weber's followers and was soon imitated by others.

The lady of the manor dreams idly of her long-absent husband, away on a crusade. She has a vision of his lying wounded on the field of battle (*Allegro passionato*), then (presumably at the plunges that end the movement) swoons away in a dead faint. A military march is heard in the distance; she recognizes her husband, alive and well, as the soldiers with their crosses and banners come into view. She sinks into his arms (interlude after the march). Victory; endless bliss (*Presto giojoso*).

We know, too, that Weber had planned his *Konzertstück* as a progress of passions: Separation—Lament—Suffering—Reunion—Consolation—Triumph.

Pairs of flutes, clarinets, and bassoons open the work in dreamy melancholy and prominently accented dissonance. The pianist enters with the same material, marked *con duolo*. From here the movement is primarily the soloist's, with allusion to the harp-like quality of revery and an arresting variety of figurative device. The countermelody in the flute and clarinet, as the passage draws to an end, foreshadows material in the next section. The closing chord in the piano is reiterated by the woodwinds to open the *Allegro passionato,* into which the soloist charges with great violence and with what is, to my ear at least, a prominent allusion to Beethoven's Piano Sonata in D minor, opus 31, no. 2—likewise a turbulent affair. A sonata structure ensues, with chromatic fireworks at the end.

The transition to the march takes place during a simple five-bar Adagio for bassoon solo and strings. The march begins naively for horns and clarinets; strings join the restatement. A glissando of some three-and-a-half octaves erupts from the piano: the moment, of course, where the lady recognizes her husband in the returning force. The march, accordingly, becomes *fortissimo*. With "great agitation" the piano responds, and this constitutes the transition to the last movement. Here the main theme is fashioned of octaves in the right hand over chords in the left; for the rest it's mostly a matter of velocity. Just before the recapitulation there is an orchestral tutti of disruptive key and, to conclude, chromatics that should remind you of the similar display in the first movement.

Invitation à la valse, orchestrated by Berlioz

For piccolo, flute, oboes I-II, clarinets I-II, bassoons I-IV; horns
  I-V, trumpets I-II, cornets *à pistons* I-II, trombones I-III;
  timpani; harps I-II; strings
Composed by Weber as *Aufforderung zum Tanze: Rondo brillant,*
  summer 1819 in Dresden; arranged by Berlioz in 1841
First performed 7 June 1841 by the Paris Opéra orchestra,
  Pantaléon Battu conducting
Published by A. M. Schlesinger (Berlin, 1842), who had
  published the piano version in 1821
Duration: about 10 minutes

Weber told his wife the simple story when he played her his "rondo
brillant" for piano: the dancers approach each other with bows and
curtsies, waltz, and take their leave. However ingenuous you may
find the idea, be aware of how significant it was to the nineteenth
century, not so much for the story but because it marks the arrival of
the waltz in the repertoire of the concert hall. There can be no dance
form more symbolic of Romanticism than the waltz: close dancing
and passionate, sometimes giddy, and the linked bodies inevitably
separating in reluctant farewell. That about summarizes things.

Berlioz scored the *Invitation à la valse* for full orchestra to serve as
ballet music for the Paris Opéra's production of *Der Freischütz.* He
was at the peak of his own orchestral élan and had been smitten with
Weber since his youth. The arrangement was one of Berlioz's most
popular concert offerings—and the confluence of composers is as
charming as that of Mussorgsky and Ravel.

Anton Webern

Born 3 December 1883 in Vienna
Died 15 September 1945 in Mitttersill,
near Salzburg

Webern, who reveled all his life in the mountainous Austrian out-of-doors, composed his first works during the pleasant summers of his teens, spent at the family's country house in the Carinthian Alps. On finishing Gymnasium—his graduation present was a trip to hear Wagner opera in Bayreuth—he undertook advanced work under the musicologist Guido Adler at the University of Vienna. There he earned a Ph.D. in 1906 for his dissertation on the Renaissance master Heinrich Isaac—an immersion in the principles of counterpoint, notably canon, that strongly influenced his emerging compositional style. Between 1904 and 1908 he studied with Schoenberg, composing his rather Brahmsian Passacaglia for Orchestra, opus 1, as a sort of graduation exercise. He went on to become, with Alban Berg, an intimate member of Schoenberg's intellectual family. What is remarkable, however, is the degree of interdependence among this triumvirate of the so-called Second Viennese School, for each confidently went his own way in turbulent times—both artistically and politically—and their collective repertoire is as noteworthy for its differences as for its similarities.

Webern supported himself as a conductor, first of the spa orchestra at Bad Ischl, then in Teplitz, Danzig, Stettin, and Prague. In 1918 he resettled in Vienna (in the suburb of Mödling) and became a central figure in organizing and conducting the Society for Private Musical Performance, Schoenberg's series of new music concerts to which critics were not invited. His social philosophies attracted him, as well, to organize a Viennese workers' orchestra and chorus. Webern's eminence in the field of new music was recognized by his appointment in 1927 to an advisory and conducting post with the Austrian Radio; additionally, he was featured on BBC broadcasts from 1929.

All told, Webern's complete oeuvre lasts about three hours, the product of a consuming quest for brevity and concision. Generally it can be seen as representing a progress from post-Romanticism through free atonality to serial composition in twelve tones following Schoenberg's principle. His particular contributions were in promoting symmetrical forms and divisions of the twelve-tone row and in approaching serial organization of the musical parameters beyond pitch: notably rhythm, dynamics, and mode of attack. Of his thirty-one published opuses, those for orchestra include the Passacaglia, opus 1 (1908); the Six Pieces, opus 6 (1909); the Five Pieces, opus 10 (1911–13); the influential Symphony, opus 21 (1928); and the Orchestral Variations, opus 30 (1940). Additionally, he composed a Concerto for nine instruments, opus 24 (1931–34); exceptional works for solo voice with instrumentalists; and three cantatas (opp. 29, 31, and post.) for soloists, chorus, and orchestra to texts of Hildegard Jone.

Webern's workers' organizations were dissolved by the Nazis in 1934, and in 1938 he lost his job with the radio. He lived through the war years in seclusion in Mödling, devoting himself mostly to his gardening. After their son was killed in an air raid, the Weberns fled from Vienna to their daughter's house near Salzburg. Apparently misunderstanding the terms of the postwar curfew, Webern stepped out of the house to smoke one evening and was shot to death by an American military policeman.

His work was created quietly and deliberately, the response of a rigorous thinker to what he saw as the artistic necessities of the era; it was performed for the most part in obscurity, and received by the public with indifference. After the war, however, the implications of his achievement dawned, as though overnight, on serious composers the world over—not so much the brevity of the style as the wondrous openness of its textures, the understanding of how dramatic a silence can be, the power of disjunctions of register, the interplay of an orchestral dialogue established pitch by pitch: in short, the seemingly total control of the details of composition. His music in all its complexity seems a natural response to the rules formulated to control it, strikingly in parallel with much more recent notions about how intelligent systems work. That so prophetic an orientation came from a man whose sensibilities lay so obviously in the tradition of Schubert and Brahms and Wagner and Mahler, one whose intellect swam in a sea of old-fashioned canons and passacaglias, and whose heart was spontaneously drawn to texts of strong Romantic character—all this says a great deal indeed about how artistic creativity wends its inexorable way into the future.

Five Pieces for Orchestra, OP. 10

Sehr ruhig und zart
Lebhaft und zart bewegt
Sehr langsam und äusserst ruhig
Fliessend, äusserst zart
Sehr fliessend

For piccolo, flute, oboe, E♭ clarinet, clarinet, bass clarinet; horn, trumpet, trombone; snare drum, bass, drum, cymbals, triangle, cowbells, low bells, glockenspiel, xylophone, celesta, harmonium; mandolin, guitar, harp; violin solo, viola solo, cello solo, double bass solo

Composed 28 June 1911–6 October 1913 in Vienna

First performed 22 June 1926 at the Zurich Festival sponsored by the International Society for Contemporary Music (ISCM), the Tonhalle Orchestra, Webern conducting

Published by Universal Edition (Vienna, 1923)

Duration: about 6 minutes

Impatience is not quite the right word to describe Webern's attitude toward such ordinary compositional procedures as development and growth: rank hostility is more like it. He was so disinclined to dabble with the further implications of a well-made structure that he came to believe that a theme, once properly stated, had little further purpose—or, more sweepingly (and in a slightly different context), that "once the twelve notes had run out, the piece was over."

Webern's Five Pieces, opus 10, exemplify his passion for the ultimate delicacy of nuance—the perfect *pianissimo,* you might say—and for absolute concision. (It will take you longer to read these remarks than to listen to the whole work.) They represent, too, a step in his progress toward serialism: his inclination to twelve-tonishness is clear, but the specifics of technique have yet to emerge. Here his melodic practice emphasizes the interval of the half-step, usually displaced by just over or just under an octave. The "orchestra," too, is compact, with a single player per part even in the strings; you will probably note the absence of much activity in the bass register, and that the brass are always muted.

The work affords a good opportunity for studying Webern's almost bewildering subtlety of orchestration. The first gesture of the first piece, for example, consists of six pitches: a B for harp and muted trumpet; a C for celesta, harp harmonic, and viola harmonic; a B♭ for harp and flutter-tongue flute; and three notes in the glockenspiel. The mandolin, for which Mahler and Schoenberg showed affection as well, has a prominent role. One of the most enchanting sounds, indeed, is the twinkling accompanimental texture in the third movement, for mandolin and guitar tremolandos, harp and celesta ostinato, and the roll, "scarcely audible" (then "dying away") of cowbells, low bells, and bass drum.

The fourth piece is a singularly striking case of Webernian principles at work: it lasts for only six bars, about a quarter of a minute. Yet its wispiness does not suggest lack of substance: the three clear melodic phrases (mandolin, trumpet / trombone, violin) form a coherent and satisfying statement, and by the end you have grasped that the accompanimental figure is one of various patterns of repeated pitches. The term epigrammatic applies.

Both of the rapid movements, nos. 2 and 5, actually reach a *fortissimo,* though in neither case can Webern quite bring himself to write a true *tutti.*

Symphony, OP. 21

Ruhig schreitend
Variationen (Theme and 7 Variations)

For clarinet, bass clarinet; horns I-II; harp; strings
Composed November 1927–August 1928; dedicated to the
composer's daughter, Christine; used to fulfil a commission
from the American League of Composers, June 1929
First performed 18 December 1929 by the Philadelphia
Orchestra, Alexander Smallens conducting
Published by Universal Edition (Vienna, 1929)
Duration: about 10 minutes

The many intricate relationships afoot in this short work, Webern's
first serial essay for orchestra, result from his overriding concern with
symmetry. Symmetries exist on horizontal and vertical planes, orchestrationally, and so forth—so many of them, in fact, that you may
return to the work again and again before you begin to understand all
that's going on.

One of the ultimate symmetries of structure is the palindrome,
where at its midpoint a statement turns back and mirrors itself horizontally. Both movements of the Symphony involve formal palin-
dromes, and the twelve-tone row Webern uses is itself palindromic
for the interval pattern of the second six notes is an exact mirror of
the first six. (These become audible, to the willing ear, as a sort of
melodic motive.) Another kind of symmetry, at work in the first
movement, is that of canonic practice, where the leading voice dictates exactly what the follower must do. The scoring, for four winds
and the four string sections, with a harp in between, suggests a sort
of double quartetness of still another kind of bilateral design.

But for all these devices what will probably seem most novel on a
first hearing is the overall linear organization of the symphony, where
the melodic progress is fashioned of individual pitches linked across
wide vertical intervals and over horizontal expanses peppered with
rests. Webern's treatment of musical space, in short, is radical indeed,
and it requires that you suspend your typical mode of equating line
with a particular segment of the performing force. The polyphonic
interplay is perceived in the mix of registers, timbres, and dynamics

that defines this unique kind of sonority. As an impressionistic tactic, it quite outdoes the French.

The first movement embraces a kind of sonata form, but this is less clear to the ear than the canons operating in the winds and strings: the viola, for example, answers the cello note-for-note, but by contrary motion. A similar relationship exists between the second and first horn and then the clarinet and bass clarinet. In the second half there occurs a prominent palindrome: the cello leaps up nearly an octave, the harp in the low bass turns around on itself, and the cello goes back where it came from, all this enlosed with fermatas. Once that has happened, everything else turns back, note for note, and what had come before, comes again. ("My end is my beginning," as Guillaume de Machaut put it in a similar composition centuries before.) The final section begins where the string soloists remove their mutes.

The second movement consists of a theme based on a mutation of the original row and seven variations of the usual sort: by tempo, scoring, and texture. In the eleven-bar theme, you may sense the mirror at work when the four eighth notes in the middle return immediately to the dialogue of quarters. By the time one has heard the tiny fourth variation, which pivots between the fermatas, it may have become clear that each of the variations is a palindrome as well. And what follows the midpoint clearly mirrors and balances the first half.

A third movement was projected for the Symphony, but Webern abandoned work on it in August 1928.

PART THREE

Some Great Orchestras and Their Conductors

Some

Great

Orchestras

The orchestras described below were selected by quantitative measures: age, historical significance of recordings, and size of annual budget. On that last score it must be said that too many of today's music organizations seem destined to function under never-breaking clouds of financial uncertainty. But function they do, and thrive in their artistry, such that even were I to include entries of a few paragraphs on every active professional orchestra in the United States alone, it would fill a book.

Many of the conductors names you will encounter below appear again and again as they circulate from one great orchestra to the next. Conductors were peripatetic long before the jet-setters took over: consider the careers of Antal Doráti (Dallas, Minneapolis, Stockholm, the BBC in London, the National in Washington, D.C., and Detroit),

Seiji Ozawa (Chicago, Toronto, San Francisco, and Boston), or, for that matter, Mahler. This is not always a question of ladder climbing or even *Wanderlust;* eventually, a fine conductor will usually succumb to the temptation of molding yet another ensemble in his or (too infrequently) her image. By mid-century the joint phenomena of relatively short directorial tenures and frequent visiting sojourns for conductors—"principal guest conductor" becomes a common title, and even the French began to use the term *le guest-conductor*—meant that committed concertgoers, especially in metropolitan areas, could count on experiencing a broad segment of the world's best conducting in a relatively short span of time. Whether or not the modern concept of jet-setting is a good thing is certainly open to dispute: the recent work of Charles Dutoit in Montreal and Simon Rattle in Birmingham argues persuasively for staying put, as did the long tenures of Eugene Ormandy in Philadelphia and Maurice Abravanel in Utah. But both audiences and orchestras enjoy reveling in the discovery of a new *maestro.*

Academy of St. Martin-in-the-Fields. Established in 1958 by Neville Marriner, the orchestra takes its name from the London church on Trafalgar Square where it first gave concerts. The core group, devoted primarily to the eighteenth-century repertoire, consists of about a dozen strings players and a harpsichordist; the full orchestra numbers between three and four dozen. From 1975, in view of his engagements elsewhere, Marriner passed most of the conducting duties to Iona Brown, who held the title concertmaster-director from 1974, leading performances from her seat at the head of the violin section. Kenneth Stillito succeeded to that position in 1980. The Academy of St. Martin-in-the-Fields can claim a part in the modern-day popularity of the Haydn and Mozart repertoire; any number of their recordings (on the Philips label) have been best-sellers.

Amsterdam Concertgebouw Orchestra. The Concertgebouw Orchestra first offered concerts in its famous hall in 1888, a few years after the establishment of a Concertgebouw Gezelschap (that is, Concert-Building Society). Orchestra and hall were synonymous until after World War II, when they became separate enterprises; and where at first the society was supported entirely by private subscriptions and gifts, now the orchestra enjoys governmental subvention. Willem Mengelberg took the podium in 1895 and led the orchestra until 1945. His electrifying performances of Beethoven and devoted championing of Mahler, Strauss, and Debussy brought the orchestra the prominent stature it continues to hold. Mengelberg's successors were Eduard van Beinum (1945–59) and Bernard Haitink (1961–88; jointly with Eugen Jochum, 1961–64, and Kiril Kondrashin, 1979–81). When Haitink left to become musical director of the Royal Opera House at Covent Garden, Riccardo Chailly was named chief conductor.

The Concertgebouw has recorded extensively for Philips on discs noted for both artistic merit and technical quality.

Atlanta Symphony Orchestra. Under the patronage of the venerable Atlanta Music Club (founded 1915), the present group emerged in 1947 from a successful Atlanta Youth Orchestra conducted by Henry Sopkin. On Sopkin's retirement in 1966, the Symphony became fully professional, attracting Robert Shaw as music director (1967–88); his successor since 1989 is Yoel Levi. The orchestra plays in Symphony Hall, part of a Memorial Arts Center established to honor the memory of some hundred Atlanta art patrons who died in a 1962 plane crash during a chartered tour.

Baltimore Symphony Orchestra. Established in 1914 as an enterprise of the city of Baltimore, and apparently the first American orchestra to be subsidized by local government, it gave its inaugural concert on 11 February 1916. Gustave Strube, who was a faculty member of the Peabody Conservatory in Baltimore, conducted the orchestra until 1930; among his successors was Howard Barlow (1939–42), known to radio listeners as conductor of the CBS Symphony Orchestra (1927–43) and to early television audiences from the "Voice of Firestone" series. An even closer association with the Peabody Conservatory (where many of the players are faculty members) was formed by Reginald Stewart, simultaneously director of the Conservatory and conductor of the Orchestra (1942–53). Stewart's sucessors were Massimo Freccia (1952–59), Peter Herman Adler (1959–68), and Brian Priestman (resident conductor, 1968–69). Under the Romanian conductor Sergiu Commissiona (1970–84), the Baltimore Symphony came to national prominence for its performances of new music. Since 1985, David Zinman has continued and broadened that commitment to strong programming; in 1987 he led the ensemble on a very successful tour of the Soviet Union.

Berlin Philharmonic Orchestra. The Berliner Philharmonisches Orchester was founded in 1882, though since the eighteenth century there had been a thriving court orchestra in Berlin, along with many amateur societies. (A 1939 census counted 81 orchestras in that city.) At the time of its centenary in 1982, the orchestra had had only four long-term conductors: Hans von Bülow (1887–94), Arthur Nikisch (1895–1922), Wilhelm Furtwängler (1922–45, 1952–54), and Herbert von Karajan (1955–89). The founding conductor was Franz Wüllner (1882–85), and Joseph Joachim and Karl Klindworth shared the podium afterward (1884–86). Claudio Abbado succeeded Karajan in 1990.

The orchestra's original hall, called the Philharmonie, was destroyed in 1944 during World War II; after seasons in several different halls, among them the converted movie theatre Titaniapalast, the orchestra moved in 1963 into its present home, the new Philharmonie by the Tiergarten. Under Karajan the Berlin Philharmonic was noted for its impetuous performance style, notably with the Beethoven symphonies. These and dozens of other significant recordings are issued by DGG, the Deutsche Grammophon Gesellschaft.

Boston Symphony Orchestra. Boston enjoyed a thriving musical culture throughout the nineteenth century, one that relied heavily on German repertoire and German musicians. Such organizations as the Handel and Haydn Society, Germania Orchestra, and the Mendelssohn Quintette Club brought many of the great pieces in the repertoire to the attention of prosperous Bostonians not so long after their first performances in Europe. The Boston Symphony was founded in 1881 by Henry Lee Higginson, who wished to establish a resident orchestra committed to the best repertoire and to ticket prices modest enough that they would attract a large public. The concerts were to be on Saturday evenings, with Friday afternoon rehearsals open to the public. (The series of open rehearsals has since become the Friday Afternoon Concerts.) Symphony Hall, considered to have the most perfect acoustics in the United States, was opened in September 1900.

Among the prominent conductors of the Boston Symphony have been Arthur Nikisch (1889–93), Pierre Monteux (1919–24), Serge Koussevitzky (1924–49), Charles Münch (1949–62), Erich Leinsdorf (1962–69), William Steinberg (1969–72), and, since 1973, Seiji Ozawa. The Boston Symphony commissioned many of the century's significant orchestral compositions, including Stravinsky's *Symphony of Psalms* and a number of other works composed for the fiftieth anniversary celebrations in 1930; for the centenary in 1980, another dozen major commissions were made.

Summer concerts by members of the BSO have taken place since the earliest years of the society; these became the Boston Pops concerts of May and June, lively events with champagne *à table* and general merriment all around. Later in the summer the BSO's famous rural revelry takes place, the Berkshire Music Festival in Tanglewood, as important in pedagogy as performance, and a closely watched springboard for young conductors and soloists.

Chicago Symphony Orchestra. Only a few years younger than the New York Philharmonic and Boston Symphony, the Chicago Symphony has perhaps the most American roots of any of the so-called Big Five. It was founded in 1891 as the Chicago Orchestra by the American conductor Theodore Thomas, who had given concerts in Chicago as early as 1869. After Thomas's death (1905) the ensemble was called the Theodore Thomas Orchestra, taking its present title in 1912.

The Chicago Symphony occupies the elegant Orchestra Hall near the shore of Lake Michigan, opened in 1904 and built by subscriptions from the public; that the Chicago Symphony occupies its own hall rent-free, unlike the majority of American orchestras, has been a major factor in its positive fiscal standing over the years.

Conductors of the Chicago Symphony this century have been Frederick Stock (1905–42), Artur Rodzinski (1947–48), Rafael Kubelík (1950–53), Fritz Reiner (1953–63), Jean Martinon (1963–68), and Georg Solti (1969–90). Solti's tenure was particularly brilliant, with repertoire, recordings, and numerous tours that positioned the Chicago Symphony firmly at the center of American musical life. Daniel Barenboim became music director in 1991.

The Chicago Symphony has been active in a wide variety of educational enterprises since its inception. Chief among these are the Civic Orchestra, a young people's orchestra from which many members go on to become professional players, and the series of radio and now televised broadcasts in existence since the first days of broadcasting. A summer series, the Ravinia Festival, has been offered in Ravinia Park north of Chicago since 1936.

Cincinnati Symphony Orchestra. The roots of the Cincinnati Symphony extend back to the organization of the Cincinnati May Festivals in 1873 and the construction of Music Hall in 1878 (remodeled 1971). The orchestra was constituted in 1895 for a concert series under Frank van der Stucken, Anton Seidl, and Henry Schradieck. Van der Stucken continued as conductor until 1907, when a labor dispute forced the orchestra to disband. It was reorganized in 1909 under Leopold Stowkowski (1909–12), who was succeeded by Eugène Ysaÿe (1918–22), Fritz Reiner (1922–31), Eugene Goossens (1931–46), Thor Johnson (1947–58), Max Rudolf (1958–70), Thomas Schippers (1970–77), Walter Susskind (1978–80), and Michael Gielen (1980–86). Since 1986 the Spanish conductor Jesus López-Cobos has been musical director. Mrs. William Howard Taft, incidentally, was the first president of the Cincinnati Orchestra Association.

Cleveland Orchestra. The Cleveland Orchestra was founded in 1918 by a public Musical Arts Association. From the earliest days its program of touring, particularly in the Midwest, has had important consequences for the spread of serious orchestral music in the United States. The orchestra occupies Severance Hall, opened in 1931 as a memorial to the wife of the donor, John L. Severance.

The Cleveland Orchestra was conducted from 1933 to 1943 by Artur Rodzinski and the following season, until he was drafted, by Erich Leinsdorf (1943–44). Under George Szell (1946–70) it became arguably the best of the American orchestras, recording, on the Columbia Label, breathtaking performances of the complete symphonies of Beethoven, Brahms, Dvořák, and others. No conductor has outdone Szell in the studied precision of the recorded performances, in doggedly intellectual control of the greatest symphonic music, and in tasteful grandeur of orchestral sound.

Szell was succeeded by Lorin Maazel (1972–82) and Christoph von Dohnányi (since 1982). James Levine, as assistant conductor (1964–70), mastered his symphonic repertoire in Cleveland.

The Cleveland Orchestra gives summer concerts at the Blossom Music Center in Northampton Township.

Dallas Symphony Orchestra. Hans Kreissig established a Dallas Symphony Club in 1900 and conducted the first concert of the Dallas Symphony the following year. His small band of players was expanded into a fully professional orchestra by Antal Doráti (1945–49), whose successors were Walter Hendl (1949–58) and Paul Kletzki (1958–61). Solti was appointed music director in 1961 but never took residence there; a period of financial uncertainty followed, and so distinguished a conductor as Max Rudolf (1973–74) was unable to prevent a fiscal collapse in the spring of 1974. The orchestra was reconstituted in 1975 under Louis Lane (1975–76), and then Eduardo Mata (1977–90). In 1991 the search for Mata's successor was underway.

The original home of the Dallas Symphony was MacFarlin Memorial Auditorium on the Southern Methodist University campus; from 1956 it played at State Fair Auditorium, remodeled in 1973 as State Fair Park Music Hall. In 1990 it moved to its new home downtown, the Morton H. Meyerson Symphony Center, designed by I. M. Pei.

Detroit Symphony Orchestra. The founding conductor of the Detroit Symphony was Weston Gales (1914–18), but the more colorful character of the early years was his successor Ossip Gabrilowitsch (1919–35), husband of Mark Twain's daughter Clara Clemens, who greatly extended the scope of the ensemble's activities. After Gabrilowitsch, inevitable financial verities led to two failures of the orchestra, but both times it was sucessfully reconstituted (1943, when it first occupied Detroit Music Hall, and 1951). Conductors since then have been Paul Paray (1951–63); Sixten Ehrling (1963–73), who had come from the Royal Swedish Opera and went on to become director of the conducting program at the Juilliard School of Music; Aldo Ceccato (1973–77); Antal Doráti (1977–81); Gary Bertini (1981–84); and Günther Herbig (1984–89). Since 1990, the music director has been Neeme Jarvi. In 1989 the Detroit Symphony moved into its new auditorium, Orchestra Hall, on the shores of Lake Erie.

Dresdner Staatskapelle (Dresden State Orchestra). This august institution is, arguably, the oldest of them all, tracing its lineage to 1548 when an orchestra was established for the concerts at the Saxon Imperial Chapel. In assuring both stage and concert performances, it has had several organizational schemes and operated under various names, with the conductors given titles according to their range of duties. The concerts this century flourished under Fritz Reiner (1914–21), Fritz Busch (1922–33) and Karl Böhm (1934–42). Among the post-War conductors have been Rudolf Kempe (1949–52), Lovro von Matacic (1956–58), Kurt Sanderling (1964–67), Herbert Blomstedt (1975–85), and Hans Vonk (since 1985). Before the Staatskapelle's 1979 American tour under Blomstedt, its work was known in the West principally from its excellent recordings on the Philips and Angel labels.

Houston Symphony Orchestra. The Houston Symphony was established in 1913 and achieved its national prominence under the venerable Leopold Stowkowski (1955–61; he was 73 when he took the post). Stowkowski's successors were John Barbirolli (1961–67), André Previn (1967–69), Lawrence Foster (1971–78), and Sergiu Commissiona (1980–87). Christoph Eschenbach, before becoming its director in 1988, had been known primarily as a concert pianist; in Houston, particularly with the late Romantic repertoire, he has demonstrated unquestionably superb qualifications in his new role. In 1989 the Houston Symphony moved to the lavish new Jones Hall for the Performing Arts.

Indianapolis Symphony Orchestra. The modern Indianapolis Symphony was established in 1930, though earlier there had been a sixty-piece municipal orchestra (1896–1906, under Karl Schneider) as well as several short-lived ensembles. The founding conductor was the German violinist Ferdinand Schaeffer (1930–36); his successors were Fabien Sevitzky (1937–55), Izler Solomon (1956–77), John Nelson (1976–87), and Raymond Leppard (since 1988). The Indianapolis Symphony's longtime home was Clowes Memorial Hall on the Butler University Campus; in 1984, it moved to the renovated Circle Theatre downtown.

Israel Philharmonic. Founded in 1936 as the Palestine Symphony by the Polish violinist Bronislaw Huberman, the Israel Philharmonic is today one of the most active touring ensembles in the trade, performing over two hundred concerts a year throughout the world. During its brief but impressive history, the orchestra has collaborated with many of the greatest conductors of this century, including Arturo Toscanini, Sir John Barbirolli, Leonard Bernstein, Serge Koussevitzky, and Eugene Ormandy. In 1981, Zubin Mehta was elected by the orchestra to be its Music Director for Life, in appreciation for their long and prosperous relationship.

Leipzig Gewandhaus Orchestra. The Gewandhaus concerts presented by this famous organization lost some of their international celebrity after Leipzig became part of East Germany but in the 1970s the orchestra re-emerged as a modern powerhouse. The concert series took its name from the place where it was first offered, the guildhall of cloth merchants. This *Grosse Concert* Society began in 1743 during Bach's tenure as cantor at the Leipzig St.-Thomaskirche, with the series assuming more or less its modern form in 1781, the year it occupied the Gewandhaus. In 1884 a larger building was erected for the society, including both large and small concert halls.

The most influential conductor of the Gewandhaus Orchestra was Felix Mendelssohn (1825–43), who among other things helped reintroduce the music of Bach to the public, programed Schumann's symphonies, premiered the Great C-Major Symphony of Schubert, and offered many of his own works. Among his successors were Arthur Nikisch (1895–1922), Wilhelm Furtwängler (1922–29), Bruno Walter (1929–33), and Hermann Abendroth (1934–42). Since the war, the conductors have been Franz Konwitschny (1949–62), Václav Neumann (1964–68), and Kurt Masur (1970–91).

London: BBC Symphony Orchestra. The BBC first established a radio orchestra in 1930 under the direction of Adrian Boult (1930–50). It has had a notable roster of conductors, including Malcolm Sargent (1950–57), Rudolf Schwarz (1957–63), Antal Doráti (1963–67), Colin Davis (1967–71), Pierre

Boulez (1971–75), Rudolf Kempe (1975–76), Gennadi Rozhdestvensky (1978–81), John Pritchard (1982–88), and Andrew Davis (since 1989). In addition to its radio services, the BBC supports the London Proms concerts and has standing orchestras in Manchester, Wales, and Scotland; it is the largest single employer of musicians in Great Britian.

London: Philharmonia Orchestra. This was established in 1945 primarily to make phonograph recordings. For a time it was known as the New Philharmonia Orchestra, then returned, in 1977, to its original name. Its recent conductors have been Herbert von Karajan (1950–59), Otto Klemperer (1955–73), Riccardo Muti (1977–82), and Giuseppe Sinopoli (since 1988).

London Philharmonic Orchestra (not the same as the much older Royal Philharmonic Society of London). The London Philharmonic was founded by Thomas Beecham in 1932, when he lost control of the Royal Philharmonic Society. After World War II it became a self-managing society, electing its own conductors. These were Eduard van Beinum (1949–51), Adrian Boult (1950–57; Boult led the historic tour of the London Philharmonic to the Soviet Union in 1956), William Steinberg (1958–60), John Pritchard (1962–66), Bernard Haitink (1967–79), Georg Solti (1979–83), and Klaus Tennstedt (since 1983).

London Symphony Orchestra. The London Symphony Orchestra was established in 1904 as a self-governing ensemble. Hans Richter conducted the first concerts and became principal conductor (1904–11); he was succeeded by Arthur Nikisch, Sir Hamilton Harty, Josef Krips (1950–54), Pierre Monteux (1961–64; he was 86 when named conductor for life), István Kertesz (1965–68; his career was cut short when he drowned in Israel, 1973), André Previn (1968–79), Claudio Abbado (1979–87), and Michael Tilson Thomas (since 1988). In 1966 the LSO moved to its first permanent home, the Barbican Arts Centre.

Los Angeles Philharmonic Orchestra. The "LA Phil," as everybody calls it, was founded in 1919 by William Andrews Clarke and first conducted by Walter Henry Rothwell (1919–27). Among Rothwell's successors were Artur Rodzinski (1929–33), Otto Klemperer (1933–39), Alfred Wallenstein (1943–56), Eduard van Beinum (1957–59), Zubin Mehta (1962–78), Carlo Maria Giulini (1978–84), and André Previn (1986–89; he resigned in a dispute with the general manager). The Finnish conductor Esa-Pekka Salonen has been named music director beginning in 1992.

The Los Angeles Philharmonic gives very popular summer concerts at the Hollywood Bowl; in 1964 it occupied the newly built Dorothy Chandler Pavilion in downtown Los Angeles for its main series.

Louisville Orchestra. From its founding in 1937 by Robert Whitney, the Louisville Orchestra has had a significant place in American music for its first performances of new orchestral compositions. In its second decade it offered nearly 130 world premieres; a major grant from the Rockefeller Foundation supported the commissions and first performances of new works by living composers, as well as a very fine series of recordings (First Edition Records) of these works. Whitney remained its conductor until 1967; his successors were Jorge Mester (1967–79), Akira Endo (1980–82), and Lawrence Leighton Smith (since 1983).

Milwaukee Symphony Orchestra. Founded in 1958 (though the Milwaukee Pops Orchestra dates from 1954), its musical directors have been Harry John Brown (1958–68), Kenneth Schermerhorn (1968–80). Lukas Foss (1981–86), and Zdenek Mócal (since 1985). It occupies Uihlein Hall in the Milwaukee Arts Center (built 1969).

Minnesota Orchestra. As the Minneapolis Orchestra it was founded by Emil Oberhoffer and gave its first concert on 5 November 1903. Oberhoffer (1903–21) was followed by Bruno Walter (1922–23), Henry Verbrugghen (1923–31), Eugene Ormandy (1931–35), José Iturbi (1935–36), Dmitri Mitropoulos (1937–49), Antal Doráti (1949–60), Stanislaw Skrowaczewski (1960–79), Neville Marriner (1979–86), and Edo De Waart (since 1986). Doráti was architect of the orchestra's present spectrum of activities, leading it for example on its first international tour, to the Near East in 1957.

The longtime home of the Minneapolis Orchestra had been the Northrup Memorial Auditorium on the University of Minnesota campus, halfway between Minneapolis and St. Paul. In 1968, the orchestra took its present name and from October 1970 began to offer its concert series in St. Paul as well. From 1974 its Minneapolis home has been Orchestra Hall, designed by Cyril M. Harris; its St. Paul home, since 1985, has been the Ordway Music Theatre.

Montreal Symphony Orchestra / Orchestre Symphonique de Montréal. The Montreal Symphony is descended from two rival enterprises: a Montreal Orchestra founded by Douglas Clarke, dean of music at McGill University (1930–41), and an Orchestre des Concerts Symphoniques, conducted most notably by Wilfrid Pelletier (1936–40; his wife was the opera soprano Rose Bampton), Désiré DeFauw (1941–48), and Otto Klemperer (1950–53). The present Montreal Symphony was constituted in 1954, led by Igor Markevitch (1958–61), Zubin Mehta (1961–67), Franz-Paul Decker (1967–75), and Rafael Frühbeck de Burgos (1975–77). With Charles Dutoit (since 1977) an unusually warm match of conductor and orchestra was found, and the Montreal Symphony Orchestra has attained a wide new following by virtue of its recordings on the London label.

National Symphony Orchestra (Washington, D.C.) Established in 1931 by its first conductor, Hans Kindler (1931–48), it offered concerts in Constitution Hall. Among Kinder's successors were Howard Mitchell (1949–60), Antal Doráti (1970–76), and Mstislav Rostrapovich (since 1977). In 1971 the National

Symphony moved to the new John F. Kennedy Center for the Performing Arts, on the banks of the Potomac River. Principal guest conductor is Rafael Frühbeck de Burgos.

New Jersey Symphony Orchestra. Incorporated in 1928, the Orchestra's roots go back to 1846. But it was not until the tenure of Kenneth Schermerhorn (1962–68) that the orchestra became fully professional. Henry Lewis (1968–76) brought the NJSO into the first rank of American orchestras; Max Rudolf was appointed Music Advisor in 1976, and Thomas Michalak served as Music Director from 1977 to 1983. The arrival in 1985 of the present music director, Hugh Wolff, generally acknowledged as one of the rising stars in the conducting field, has brought new artistic vitality and national prominence to the orchestra.

New York Philharmonic. The orchestra traces its ancestry to the founding of a New York Philharmonic Society in 1842. (From that point of view, the Philharmonic is probably the third oldest professional orchestra in the world.) Short-term engagements for principal conductors (Carl Bergmann, Leopold Damrosch, Theodore Thomas, and especially Anton Seidl, 1891–98, and Gustav Mahler, 1909–11) during the first decades were supplemented by appearances of famous visiting conductors. Among these were Felix Weingartner, Richard Strauss, Henry Wood, and Willem Mengelberg.

The Society absorbed the excellent New Symphony Orchestra (first conducted by Edgard Varèse; later called the National Symphony) and in 1928 embraced the rival New York Symphony Society (founded by Leopold Damrosch in 1878). At this point Arturo Toscanini moved to New York and for over five years was the principal conductor (1930–36). Subsequent conductors included John Barbirolli (1937–42), Artur Rodzinski (1943–47), Bruno Walter (1947–49; his influence as adviser extended far beyond those years, though he was never principal conductor), Leopold Stokowski and Dmitri Mitropoulos (1949–58), and of course Leonard Bernstein, the orchestra's first American-born conductor (1958–69). Bernstein's stellar tenure in New York—he remained conductor emeritus—was succeeded by those of Pierre Boulez (1971–77) and Zubin Mehta (1978–91). Kurt Masur became music director in 1991.

The Philharmonic has offered Young People's Concerts since the nineteenth century, and it has broadcast its Sunday afternoon concerts over CBS from the earliest days of radio. In 1962, the Philharmonic moved from Carnegie Hall to elegant new quarters in the new Lincoln Center for the Performing Arts, later renamed Avery Fisher Hall, and still later rebuilt to improve the acoustics (1976).

North Carolina Symphony Orchestra. The first American orchestra to enjoy official legislative patronage, the North Carolina Symphony was founded by the composer / conductor Lamar Stringfield (1937–43); it earned the enduring affection of North Carolinians across the state through the efforts of Benjamin Swalin (1944–72) and his wife, Maxine, who served as keyboard player and much beloved commentator for the public school concerts. (I speak from personal experience.)

Swalin's successors were John Gosling (1972–80) and Gerhardt Zimmermann (since 1982). The North Carolina Symphony's home is the Raleigh Memorial Auditorium at the opposite end of historic Fayetteville Street from the State Capitol.

Orchestre de Paris. The Orchestre de Paris was formed in 1828 as the Société des Concerts du Conservatoire. The bylaws required that all members of the society be former students or present staff members of the Conservatoire National de Paris. In 1967, during the civil and cultural unrest in France, the Conservatoire orchestra was disbanded and reconstituted as the Orchestre de Paris. Its conductors have been Charles Münch (1967–68), Serge Baudo (1969–71, with Karajan as artistic adviser), Georg Solti (1972–75), and Daniel Barenboim (1975–90). Their new conductor is Semyon Bychkov, born in the USSR in 1952 and a naturalized American citizen; he came to Paris from the Buffalo Philharmonic Orchestra.

The Orchestre de Paris now gives concerts at the Palais des Congrès (Porte Maillot), the Théâtre des Champs-Élysées, and its home venue, the "new" Salle Pleyel—actually a remodeled version of a hall that goes back to Chopin's day.

Oregon Symphony Orchestra. Renamed in 1967, it was formerly the Portland Symphony, tracing its roots to 1896 and thus among the earliest American symphony orchestras and the very first in the far west. Its recent conductors include Piero Bellugi (1959–61), Jacques Singer (1962–72), Lawerence Leighton Smith (1973–80), and James DePriest (since 1980). The orchestra offers its concerts in the remodeled Paramount Theater, now called the Arlene Schnitzer Concert Hall of the Portland Center for the Performing Arts.

Philadelphia Orchestra. Nineteenth-century musical life in Philadelphia rivaled that of New York in its enterprise, featuring concerts by Theodore Thomas's orchestra and by the Boston Symphony. Locally produced concerts were sponsored by the historic Musical Fund Society (patron of The Free Library of Philadelphia) and by the Germania Orchestra, which introduced many European masterworks to American audiences. In 1900 a new orchestra was formed, sponsored by the Symphony Society of Philadelphia and conducted by Fritz Scheel. On 17 May 1901 this became the Philadelphia Orchestra Association. Scheel, a student of Hans von Bülow, was succeeded by Leopold Stokowski, who molded the ensemble and tone quality for which the Philadelphia Orchestra remains justly famous. Stokowski conducted the orchestra for twenty-six years (1912–38), after which Eugene Ormandy, who had been Stokowski's assistant, became musical director. Ormandy's tenure of more than four decades (1938–80) is probably without parallel in the history of music. He was succeeded by Riccardo Muti (1980–92). Wolfgang Sawallisch has been named music director beginning in 1992.

The Philadelphia Orchestra gives its concerts in the Academy of Music and offers seasons of youth concerts and children's concerts in addition to its regular subscription series. The orchestra pioneered in recording the virtuoso orchestral works on the Columbia label. It has made numerous national and international tours, including a historic visit to the People's Republic of China in 1973.

Pittsburgh Symphony Orchestra. The Pittsburgh Symphony was founded in 1895 and offered its first concert in February of the following year. The most notable conductor of the early years was the American cellist-composer-conductor Victor Herbert (1904–10). The orchestra disbanded afterward, to be reconstituted in 1926 and again in 1937; conductors of the modern era have been Fritz Reiner (1938–48), William Steinberg (1952–76), André Previn (1976–84), and Lorin Maazel (since 1984). The longtime home of the Pittsburgh Symphony concerts was the Syria Mosque; since 1985 it has given its series in the Heinz Hall for the Performing Arts.

St. Louis Symphony Orchestra. Tracing its roots back to the founding of the St. Louis Choral Society in 1880, the St. Louis Symphony claims with some justification to be the second oldest orchestra (after the New York Philharmonic) in the United States; in 1900 it assumed more or less its present configuration. Among its prominent conductors have been Vladimir Golschmann (1931–58), noted for his work in modern ballet (including the first performance of, for example, Milhaud's *Le Bœuf sur le toit;* see p. 368); the Polish conductor Jerzy Semkow (1959–62); Walter Susskind (1968–75); and Leonard Slatkin (since 1979). The St. Louis Symphony moved from the Kiel Auditorium to the new Powell Symphony Hall in 1968. Since 1969 it has taken summer residence on the campus of Southern Illinois University, Edwardsville, for the Mississippi River Festival.

St. Paul Chamber Orchestra. This 34-piece ensemble, one of the very few professional chamber orchestras in the United States, was founded in 1959 by Leopold Sipe. His successors were Dennis Russell Davies (1972–79), who fostered the orchestra's strong commitment to the contemporary American repertoire; and Pinchus Zukerman (1980–85), who returned to the old-fashioned habit of conducting "from the violin." The present music director is Christopher Hogwood, whose reputation was established in the early music field. The Orchestra presents an extended and varied series in the Ordway Music Theatre.

San Francisco Symphony Orchestra. The San Francisco Symphony was founded in 1911 and presented its first concert on 29 December of that year, Henry Hadley conducting. Among Hadley's successors were Alfred Hertz (1915–30), who did much to establish a prosperous musical climate in the Bay Area, Pierre Monteux (1935–52), Enrique Jorda (1954–63), Josef Krips (1963–70), Seiji Oszawa (1971–76), Edo De Waart (1977–85), and Herbert Blomstedt (since 1985). Until 1980 the San Francisco Symphony was also the orchestra of the renowned San Francisco Opera, and both opera and concerts were given in the War Memorial Theatre across from City Hall. That year the orchestra separared into two, and the San Francisco Symphony moved into its elegant new home next door, the Louise M. Davies Symphony Hall.

Seattle Symphony Orchestra. The modern orchestra was a 1926 project of Karl Krueger and the local branch of the American Federation of Musicians, though its antecedents extend back to 1903. Since Thomas Beecham's tenure (1941–44), the conductors have been Manuel Rosenthal (1949–51), Milton Katims (1954–75), and Gerard Schwarz (since 1984). The orchestra plays in the Seattle Center Opera House, refashioned for the international exposition of 1962.

Toronto Symphony Orchestra. The Toronto Symphony grew out of a municipal concert series begun in 1926, its first quarter century dominated by the gifted Canadian conductor Ernest Macmillan (1931–56). Since then it has been able to attract and prosper under conductors of international repute: Walter Susskind (1956–65), Seiji Ozawa (1965–69), Karel Ancerl (1969–73), Andrew Davis (1975–89), and Günther Herbig (since 1990).

Utah Symphony Orchestra. Formed from the amalgamation of two theater orchestras in 1892, it had an irregular history until the foundation of the Utah State Symphony Orchestra in 1940. As the fully professional Utah Symphony, it flourished during the long tenure of Maurice Abravanel (1947–79); Abravanel was succeeded by Varujan Kojian (1979–83) and Joseph Silverstein (since 1983), with Grant Johannsen acting as artistic advisor. Concerts take place in Salt Lake City's Symphony Hall, opened in 1979.

Vienna: Wiener Philharmoniker. Of the dozens of important performing groups and societies in this most hallowed capital of classical music, the pre-eminent orchestra is the Vienna Philharmonic. It has offered subscription concerts without interruption since 1860, and traces its origin back to the Redoutensaal concerts of the Imperial Court Opera Orchestra begun by Otto Nicolai in 1842. The orchestra was (and is) made up of members of the Staatsoper orchestra; it was among the first societies to govern itself and to elect its own conductor. Its most famous music directors have been Hans Richter (1875–98), Gustav Mahler (1898–1901), Felix Weingartner (1908–27), Wilhelm Furtwängler (1927–30, 1938–45), and Bruno Walter (1933–38). Since World War II, the Vienna Philharmonic has had no chief conductor, but rather sojourns with the superstars: Karl Böhm and, more recently, Claudio Abbado, Leonard Bernstein, Lorin Maazel, and James Levine—in short, many of the greats of our time.

The season originally consisted of eight Sunday morning concerts in the hall of the Musikverein. There the Philharmonic canonized the Beethoven symphonies and presented the new work of Wagner, Bruckner, Brahms, Mahler, and Richard Strauss, and later Ravel, Stravinsky, and Hindemith.

The Vienna Philharmonic has from 1925 been the principal orchestra of the summer Salzburg Festival, where it has appeared since 1879.

Some

Great

Conductors

The profession of conducting was created in large measure by the great composer-conductors of the nineteenth century, about whom you may read above: Weber, Berlioz, Mendelssohn, Liszt, Wagner, Mahler, and Richard Strauss. What follows are summaries of the careers of some prominent conductors of the present and of the recent past.

Abbado, Claudio (b. 1933). He studied conducting from the noted teacher Hans Swarowsky of Vienna (1956–58) and in the famous master classes in Siena. Subsequently he won the Koussevitzky Prize at Tanglewood (1958), then was one of the three 1963 winners of the Mitropolous Competition in New York; this led to his debut with the New York Philharmonic in 1963. He became, in short succession, principal conductor at La Scala in Milan (1967, the year of his debuts at Covent Garden and the Metropolitan Opera), then La Scala's music director (1972), and finally artistic director (1972–86). From 1971 he was principal conductor of the Vienna Philharmonic, leading its tours to Japan and China (1972–73). In 1974 he took the La Scala company to Russia; in 1976, in conjunction with the American bicentennial, Abbado conducted both La Scala and the Vienna Philharmonic in the United States. His ascent has continued without interruption through the 1980s, as music director of the London Symphony Orchestra (1979–87), principal guest conductor of the Chicago Symphony (1982–85), and music director of the Vienna Staatsoper (from 1986). In 1989 he succeeded Karajan at the Berlin Philharmonic. He is one of the great masters of our time, a conductor of consummate grace, lyricism, and power.

Abravanel, Maurice (b. 1903). Born in Greece of Spanish-Portuguese Sephardic parents, he went to the University of Lausanne to study medicine, but gave that up to study with Kurt Weill in Berlin. His conducting career began at that time in various Berlin theaters, but Hitler's ascent to power made it necessary for Abravanel to leave Germany precipitously. He went to Paris, where he conducted ballet and toured Australia with the British National Opera Company. In 1936, on the recommendation of Bruno Walter, he was engaged by the Metropolitan Opera, but internal politics forced him to move to Broadway, where he conducted Weill's *Knickerbocker Holiday,* the composer's first popular musical. During the decade that followed, he became intimately associated with his former teacher's productions. In 1947, he was engaged as conductor of the newly formed Utah Symphony Orchestra, a group he brought to a very high level of professional excellence until his retirement in 1979, when he was named conductor emeritus.

Ansermet, Ernest (1883–1969). Ansermet was associated with Diaghilev's Ballets Russes from 1915 and founded the Orchestre de la Suisse Romande of Geneva (1918). Though comfortable in all styles, he was most admired for his performances of new music. Ansermet conducted the premiere of Stravinsky's *L'Histoire du soldat* (1918).

Barenboim, Daniel (b. 1942). Born in Buenos Aires, Argentina, Barenboim moved with his family in 1952 to Israel, by which time his promise as a concert pianist was already clear. He studied piano with Edwin Fischer and conducting with Igor Markevitch, then worked with Nadia Boulanger at Fontainebleau (1954–56), earned a diploma from the Santa Cecilia Conservatory in Rome (1956), and took the Siena conducting classes. In the late 1950s he secured his international celebrity as a pianist with debuts in Paris (1955), London (1956), and New York (1957). His very popular appearances in the late 1960s and early 1970s with his wife, the brilliant cellist Jacqueline Dupré (1945–87), ended when she fell victim to multiple sclerosis. He had made his conducting debut in 1957 in Haifa, and in the next decade was a frequent guest conductor of the Israel Philharmonic, the New York Philharmonic, and the London Symphony Orchestra. As music director of the Orchestre de Paris (1975–90), he brought the new ensemble to the level of excellence its organizers had optimistically envisaged. Barenboim was named first musical director of the new Paris Opéra-Bastille, then dismissed before it opened in an internationally publicized dispute over salary and working conditions. In 1991 he became Solti's successor as music director of the Chicago Symphony Orchestra.

Beecham, Thomas (Sir) (1879–1961). An affable Englishman of pronounced genius though little formal musical training, Beecham began conducting in 1906. For the next half century, he was the unrivaled master of London music, bringing the Ballets Russes to town, organizing opera companies and orchestras, welcoming the dawn of recorded sound and broadcasting. His working repertoire was enormous, including virtually all the operas then in vogue, and he nearly always conducted from memory. Aside from his recordings, Beecham's most significant legacy is the London Philharmonic Orchestra, which he founded in 1932. No conductor had a more pronounced sense of humor; Beecham anecdotes (for example, "Bring the *Ring*," when the podium was not high enough) have filled a book.

Bernstein, Leonard (see pp. 118–22).

Blomstedt, Herbert (b. 1927). Born in Springfield, Massachusetts of Swedish parents, Blomstedt was educated at the Royal Academy of Music in Stockholm and the University of Uppsala; he then studied conducting with Igor Markevitch in Paris and with Leonard Bernstein. Subsequently he became music director of the Norrköping Symphony Orchestra (1954–61), Oslo Philharmonic (1962–68), Danish Radio Symphony Orchestra in Copenhagen (1967–77), and the Dresden Staatskapelle (1975–85), which he led on a very successful American tour in 1979. In 1985 Blomstedt became musical director of the San Francisco Symphony.

Böhm, Karl (1894–1981). Master of the late nineteenth-century mega-repertoire, notably that of Mahler and Richard Strauss—he premiered two of Strauss's operas—Böhm began his career at the Bavarian State Opera in Munich (1921–27). Subsequently, he conducted at the theaters in Darmstadt (1927–31), Hamburg (1931–33), Dresden (1923–43), and Vienna (1944–45), returning to the Vienna State Opera in 1954 after a time in Buenos Aires (1950–54). In the last majestic decades of his long career, he was a much-admired guest conductor of the Berlin and Vienna Philharmonics and the New York Metropolitan Opera, and was president of the London Symphony Orchestra from 1977 until his death.

Boulez, Pierre (see pp. 135–39).

Boult, Adrian (Sir) (1889–1983). A student of Arthur Nikisch, he began his career with the City of Birmingham Symphony (1924–30), and then went to the BBC Symphony (1931–50) and the London Philharmonic (1951–57). Among his premieres were three of Vaughan Williams's symphonies and Holst's *The Planets.*

Chailly, Riccardo (b. 1953). Son of the Italian composer Luciano Chailly, he studied conducting with Franco Ferrara in Venice. In 1972, at the age of 19, he became assistant conductor (under Abbado) at La Scala. Two years later he conducted a successful *Madame Butterfly* with the Chicago Lyric Opera and the following season made his Metropolitan Opera debut with *Tales of Hoffmann*. In 1982 he became conductor of the West Berlin Radio Symphony Orchestra and principal guest conductor of the London Philharmonic, then succeeded Haitink at the Amsterdam Concertgebouw in 1988.

Chung, Myung-Whun (b. 1953). Born in Korea, he established his reputation as pianist in a trio with his sisters, the violinist Kyung-Wha Chung (b. 1948) and the cellist Myung-Wha Chung (b. 1944). His conducting debut in Seoul was followed by advanced study at Mannes and Juilliard (1974). That year he won second prize in piano at the Tchaikovsky Competition; subsequently he was assistant conductor of the Los Angeles Philharmonic (1978–81) and made his Metropolitan Opera debut (1986). In late 1989 he was named music director of the new Paris Opéra-Bastille after months of a flamboyant disagreement between Daniel Barenboim and the company's general manager; there, in March 1990, Chung inaugurated the new house with the first complete Paris performance, ever, of Berlioz's *Les Troyens* (The Trojans).

Davis, Colin (Sir) (b. 1927). He studied liberal arts at Cambridge and clarinet at the Royal Conservatory of Music. His training ground for conducting was the semiprofessional Chelsea Opera Group, where all sorts of fascinating projects blossomed. His debuts at the Edinburgh Festival (1958), in Minneapolis (1960), and as a last-minute substitution for Klemperer in 1959 led to a brilliant career on both sides of the Atlantic: as music director of the Sadler's Wells Opera (1961–65), chief conductor of the BBC Symphony Orchestra (1967–71), principal guest conductor of the Boston Symphony (1972–83), music director of the Royal Philharmonic (1974–76), and chief conductor of the Bavarian Radio Symphony Orchestra, Munich (since 1983). In 1971 he succeeded George Solti as music director of Covent Garden; in 1977 he became the first Englishman to conduct at Bayreuth. Davis recorded the prize-winning "Colin Davis Berlioz Cycle" with Philips and conducted premieres of Tippett's Second Symphony (1972) and operas *The Knot Garden* (1970) and *Ice Break* (1974). He was named a Commander of the Britsh Empire in 1965 and knighted in 1980; in 1988 he was named to an international chair at the Royal Academy of Music.

De Waart, Edo (b. 1941). Originally an oboist, he studied conducting with the American Dean Dixon in Salzburg and with Franco Ferrara in Hilversum. He won the 1964 Mitropoulos Competition in New York and thus became assistant to Leonard Bernstein (1965–66). On his return to the Netherlands, he was an assistant conductor of the Concertgebouw and founded the Netherlands Wind Ensemble. Since then he has conducted the Rotterdam Philharmonic (1973–

79), Santa Fe and Houston opera companies (early and mid-1970s), San Francisco Symphony (1977–85; in 1980 he conducted the gala inaugural concerts of Louise M. Davies Symphony Hall), and Minnesota Orchestra (since 1986).

Dohnányi, Christoph von (b. 1929). Born in Berlin, he was raised by his grandfather, the Hungarian composer Ernst von Dohnányi (1877–1960), after his father was executed for his presumed role in the July 1944 plot to assassinate Hitler. He studied law at the University of Munich (1948) and conducting at the Hochschule für Musik there (1949–51), where he won the Richard Strauss Prize in composition and conducting. He moved to the United States after his grandfather became a professor of composition at Florida State University in Tallahassee. At Tanglewood he studied with Leonard Bernstein and became a protégé of Georg Solti, who urged his appointment as chorusmaster and then conductor at the Frankfurt Opera (1952–57). His other posts have been as music director in Lübeck (1957–63), Kassel (1963–66), with the West German Radio Orchestra of Cologne (1964–70), director of the Frankfurt Opera (1968–77), and intendant of the Hamburg Staatsoper (1975–84). In 1984 he succeeded Szell as music director of the Cleveland Orchestra, where he had been named conductor designate in 1982. He is a particularly strong proponent of the work of Schoenberg, Berg, and Webern.

Doráti, Antal (1906–88). Born in Hungary, he became an American citizen in 1947 and greatly influenced the growth of a half dozen of what are now major orchestras. Doráti began as a conductor of ballet, in the last days of the Ballets Russes (1933–41) and the first of the American Ballet Theatre (1937–41). Subsequently he conducted the Dallas Symphony (1945–46), Minneapolis Orchestra (1949–60, where he led the first performance of Bartók's Viola Concerto), Stockholm Philharmonic (1962–74), BBC Symphony (1963–67), National Symphony Orchestra (1970–76), and Detroit Symphony (1977–81). He was the first conductor to record the complete Haydn symphonies, a project of the late 1960s.

Dutoit, Charles (b. 1936). A Swiss citizen by birth, Dutoit was educated at the conservatories in Lausanne and Geneva. He absorbed his conducting technique, he says, by watching Ansermet lead the Orchestre de la Suisse Romande and thereafter in conducting classes in Siena, Venice, and Tanglewood. He began his professional career as an orchestral violist in Lausanne, then as conductor of the Berne Symphony Orchestra (1963–67) and Zurich Radio Orchestra (1967–75). Also in the mid-1970s he appeared with the National Orchestra of Mexico and the Göteborg Symphony and conducted an important series of ballets at the Vienna Staatsoper. As music director of the Montreal Symphony Orchestra from 1977, he has been conspicuously prominent for his recordings of the French repertoire and Stravinsky's Paris ballets. In 1983 he was principal guest conductor of the Minnesota Orchestra; in 1991 he became conductor of the Orchestre National of France, founded in 1934 and rival of the Orchestre de Paris.

Eschenbach, Christoph (b. 1940). As a pianist, Eschenbach won the Clara Haskil Competition in Lucerne in 1965, then made his debuts in the late 1960s in Europe and the United States. His first performance of Hans Werner Henze's Piano Concerto (1968) earned him an additional measure of critical acclaim. In the 1970s he began to accept conducting engagements, eventually becoming principal conductor of the Zurich Tonhalle Orchestra (1982–86) and music director of the Houston Symphony (since 1988).

Furtwängler, Wilhelm (1886–1954). He succeeded Arthur Nikisch as conductor of the Leipzig Gewandhaus (1922–29) and Berlin orchestras (1922–54, with an interruption during the war). The exact nature of his relationship with the Nazis has never been made entirely clear, though it is certain they highly valued his international prestige. After the war he successfully reassembled his career. Furtwängler's posthumous reputation, however, remains mixed: in some quarters he is remembered for his uncommon understanding of how an orchestra works and his assurance on the podium, while others assert that his repertoire was parochial and his technique so quirky as to make orchestras habitually nervous.

Giulini, Carlo Maria (b. 1914). He entered the Santa Cecilia Conservatory in Rome at the age of sixteen and studied conducting with Bernardino Molinari in Siena. Having evaded service to Mussolini's army, he was chosen by the Allied forces to conduct the Augusteo Orchestra in the liberation concerts of 1944. Thereafter he conducted the RAI (Radio-Television of Italy) orchestras of Rome and Milan and became assistant (1952), then principal conductor at La Scala (1953–56). He was a frequent guest conductor of the Chicago Symphony Orchestra, and by the late 1960s had begun to be numbered among the distinguished masters of the symphonic repertoire. In 1973 he was named principal conductor of the Vienna Symphony Orchestra; in 1978 Giulini succeeded Zubin Mehta in Los Angeles (1978–84). His was as distinguished a tenure as Mehta's had been, culminating in a tour of Japan in 1983. Giulini's favored orchestral repertoire was that of the high Romantics, notably Bruckner, Brahms, and Mahler, and in those works his performances were unexcelled.

Haitink, Bernard (b. 1929). Born in Amsterdam, he studied violin and conducting at the Amsterdam Conservatory, then was a violinist in the Dutch Radio Philharmonic Orchestra of Hilversum, of which he became assistant conductor in 1955 and principal conductor in 1957. His debut with the Concertgebouw was in 1956; he succeeded van Beinum as music director there, jointly from 1961 with Eugen Jochum, then on his own from 1964. In 1958 he made his American debut with the Los Angeles Philharmonic. In 1967 he was appointed principal conductor and adviser to the London Philharmonic Orchestra and eventually its artistic director (1969–78), then chief conductor of the Glyndebourne Festival (1972) and its music director (1977–87). From 1987 he has been music director of the Royal Opera House, Covent Garden. Haitink is particularly noted for his recordings on the Philips label, especially his stunning interpretations of the Mahler symphonies.

Hogwood, Christopher (b. 1941). Educated at Cambridge University and the Charles University of Prague, he and David Munrow established the Early Music Consort in 1967, producing sensational recordings of medieval music that announced a new chapter in the early music movement. After Munrow's premature death Hogwood founded the Academy of Ancient Music (London) in 1973. This is an ensemble dedicated to the performance of early orchestral repertoire on period instruments. (And the name, in my view, is not especially apt: there's nothing ancient about such music, least of all in Hogwood's performances.) Their recording of all the Mozart symphonies on original instruments is highly prized, as is the set of *Brandenburg Concertos* with Hogwood as soloist. In the mid-1980s he began to appear throughout the United States; in 1986 he was named artistic director of the Boston Handel and Haydn Society (founded 1815, the oldest such organization in the country) and in 1988 became musical director of the St. Paul Chamber Orchestra.

Karajan, Herbert von (1908–89). Headstrong superstar of the Berlin Philharmonic for nearly as long as anybody could remember, Karajan was probably the last of the old-style imperial conductors in the lineage of Furtwängler, Strauss, and Toscanini. He studied at the Mozarteum in Salzburg and the Music Academy in Vienna, then conducted the Berlin State Opera (1938–42). After the war he was engaged by the Vienna Philharmonic (1946–52) and the Philharmonia of London (1947–55); Furtwängler's death in 1954 led to his accession in Berlin. Simultaneously he served long tenures with the Vienna Staatsoper (1956–64 as successor to Böhm) and as music director of the Salzburg Festival (1956–60), later as artistic adviser to the new Orchestre de Paris (1969–71). He was a champion of recorded sound, with eight hundred recordings that stretch from 78s in the 1940s to digital CDs—among them four complete Beethoven cycles. Beneath the ego lay a perfectionist and workaholic, and under his baton the Berlin Philharmonic became legendary in its phrasing, tone, and power. Some complained that his work was too much glamor and too little substance, but there was no denying the luster of its surface.

Kleiber, Carlos (b. 1930). He was born in Berlin, son of the eminent conductor Erich Kleiber (1890–1956). Opposing Nazi rule, the family emigrated to Argentina in 1935, thus the Spanishizing of the young Kleiber's name. After musical education in Buenos Aires and studies in chemistry at the University of Zurich, he conducted opera in Europe: Düsseldorf (1956–64), Zurich (1964–66), Stuttgart (1966–68), Munich (1968–73), and Vienna (since 1973), with debuts at Covent Garden and Bayreuth in 1974 and the San Francisco Opera in 1977. As a symphonic conductor he has had notable success with the Berlin and Vienna Philharmonics and, since 1979, as guest conductor of the Chicago Symphony. He has the additional distinction of having refused innumerable permanent posts, preferring an independant musical existence.

Klemperer, Otto (1885–1973). He began his career as Mahler's apprentice and assisted in the first performance of the Eighth Symphony (Munich, 1910); and it was on Mahler's recommendation that he was appointed to his first posts in Prague (1908–10) and Hamburg (1910–12). He then conducted the Cologne Opera (1917–23), the Berlin Volksoper (1924–26), the Berlin Staatsoper (1927–33), making his American debut with the New York Symphony Society in January of 1926. As a Jew he was forced from Germany in 1933, and was thereupon appointed music director of the Los Angeles Philharmonic (1933–39). After substantially recovering from the removal of a brain tumor, he led the Budapest Opera (1947–50), made wonderful recordings with the Philharmonia Orchestra of London in the mid-1950s (by then partially paralyzed), and in the 1960s conducted at Covent Garden. He became an Israeli citizen in 1970.

Though his early career was spent in the opera house, he was adept with the symphonic literature from the beginning, and had done much in his German years to forward the cause of Schoenberg, Stravinsky, and Hindemith. His leisurely accounts with the Philharmonia Orchestra of the Brahms symphonies (on Angel records) are among their most powerful interpretations.

Koussevitzky, Serge (1874–1951). Koussevitzky studied in Moscow, where he became a virtuoso double bass player and established his credentials as a conductor. He left Russia in the wake of the Revolution, arriving in the United States after a spectacularly successful series of concerts in Paris in the early 1920s. His quarter century as conductor of the Boston Symphony Orchestra (1924–49) remains the longest tenure of any of its leaders. He offered the first performances of the Mussorgsky / Ravel *Pictures at an Exhibition* (Paris, 1922), a number of Stravinsky's works, and compositions by nearly every significant American composer of his time; his Tchaikovsky was considered the best of its era. He was the guiding spirit behind the formation of the Berkshire Music Center in Tanglewood. Moreover the publishing house he and his wife founded, Éditions Russes de Musique, was a major force in the dissemination of the music of Rachmaninov, Prokofiev, Stravinsky, and the other Russians; later the foundation he established commissioned dozens of important works in memory of his wife, Natalie Koussevitzky.

Kubelík, Rafael (b. 1914). Son of the Czech violinist-composer Jan Kubelík (1880–1940), he attended the Prague Conservatory, then made his debut with the Czech Philharmonic in 1934. He conducted the National Theatre orchestra in Brno (1939–41) and the Czech Philharmonic (1942–48), but left his homeland following the communist takeover after World War II. As music director of the Chicago Symphony (1950–53) he gave significant first performances, including Roy Harris's Seventh Symphony (1952), but his promotion of new music and his stern manner were ultimately too controversial for Chicago. In a brilliant tenure at Covent Garden (1955–58), he led historic performances of erlioz's *Les Troyens*, Janáček's *Jenůfa*, and the original version of Mussorgsky's *Boris Godunov;* his appointment as musical director of the Metropolitan Opera (1973–74) was not, however, a success. Kubelík was also the very popular conductor of the Bavarian Radio Symphony Orchestra, Munich (1961–85). His cycle of Beethoven symphonies on the Deutsche Grammophon label is a curiosity in its use of nine different orchestras. Kubelík returned to his native land to conduct the Czech Philharmonic at the Prague Spring Festival in May 1990.

Leinsdorf, Erich (b. 1912). After master classes in conducting at the Mozarteum in Salzburg along with studies at the University of Vienna and Vienna Academy of Music (1931–33), he began his conducting career when he assisted Bruno Walter and Arturo Toscanini at the Salzburg Festival in 1934; shortly thereafter, however, he was compelled as a Jew to leave Austria. Leinsdorf made his Metropolitan Opera debut in 1937, was regularly engaged there from 1938, and in 1939 was appointed head conductor of the German repertoire; he became an American citizen in 1942. He was named music director of the Cleveland Orchestra in 1943, but in his first season was drafted for service in World War II. Subsequently he served with the Rochester Philharmonic (1947–55), the New York City Opera (1956–57), as adviser to the Met, and as music director of the Boston Symphony Orchestra (1962–69). After leaving Boston he conducted the Berlin Radio Symphony Orchestra (1977–80).

Levine, James (b. 1943). American pianist and conductor, he grew up in a family that encouraged serious music making (his grandfather, for example, was a cantor) and by age 10 made his concerto debut at a youth concert of the Cincinnati Orchestra. His advanced studies in piano were with Rudolf Serkin at Marlboro (1956) and Rosina Lhévinne, *grande dame* of the Juilliard School (1961); he studied conducting at the Juilliard with Jean Morel. In 1964, through the American Conductors Project, he became assistant to Szell in Cleveland, where he remained for six years. In the summer of 1970 he made his debut with the Philadelphia Orchestra at a Robin Hood Dell concert, and in the fall appeared with the Welsh National Opera and the San Franciso Opera. These successes led to his meteoric career at the Metropolitan Opera, where he first conducted in June 1971 and was named in short succession its principal conductor (1973) and musical director (1975). Meanwhile he continued his symphonic conducting, notably at the Ravinia Festivals of the Chicago Symphony (from 1973) and the May Festivals in Cincinnati, his hometown (1974–78). Of late he has made excellent recordings with the Chicago Symphony and the Berlin Philharmonic.

Maazel, Lorin (b. 1930). He was born in Paris of American parents who moved to Los Angeles when he was an infant. The indications of his musical precocity were soon clear, and as a very young child he found himself a protégé of Vladimir Bakaleinikov, associate conductor of the Los Angeles Philharmonic at the time (and author of a book of conducting exercises I can still hum). In 1938 the family followed Bakaleinikov to Pittsburgh; the next summer Maazel conducted the

Interlochen (i.e. National Music Camp) Orchestra at the 1939 New York World's Fair. At age 11 he appeared with the NBC Symphony and at age 12 conducted a concert of the New York Philharmonic. This is the sort of childhood that can too readily warp the adult; instead Maazel earned a degree at the University of Pittsburgh and dutifully spent time as a violinist in the Pittsburgh Symphony. As a Fulbright Fellow in Italy (1952) he began to make his European debuts and shortly thereafter was making the rounds of the famous music festivals (Florence, Vienna, Edinburgh, 1955–57). In 1960, with *Lohengrin,* he became the first American to conduct at Bayreuth; in 1962 he made his Metropolitan Opera debut with *Don Giovanni.* Subsequently, he was music director of the Deutsche Oper, West Berlin (1965–71) and West Berlin Radio Symphony Orchestra (1965–75), associate principal conductor of the [New] Philharmonia Orchestra London (1971–72), and eventually its principal guest conductor (1978–80). He succeeded George Szell in Cleveland (1972–82); this daunting task he accomplished with good-natured dexterity, and his tenure in Cleveland was a happy one with fine musical results and several significant tours, including to Australia and Japan. He took the prestigious post of artistic director at the Vienna Staatsoper (1982–84), and in 1988 was appointed music director of the Pittsburgh Symphony.

Marriner, Neville (Sir) (b. 1924). After studies at the Royal College of Music and Paris Conservatory and Monteux's conducting classes in Maine, he taught at Eton (1947–48) and the Royal College of Music (1949–59) and played as assistant concertmaster of the London Symphony Orchestra under Monteux and Kertesz. In 1959 he founded the Academy of St.-Martin-in-the-Fields (see p. 652), of which he remains artistic director. Since then he has been the musical director of the Los Angeles Chamber Orchestra, which he organized (1969–71), the Northern Sinfonia of Newcastle, England (1971–73), and the Minnesota Orchestra (1978–86). In 1980 Marriner became principal conductor of the South German Radio (Süddeutchen Rundfunk) Orchestra, Stuttgart, after two years as principal guest conductor. He was made C.B.E. in 1979 and knighted in 1985.

Masur, Kurt (b. 1927). He studied in Breslau and Leipzig, then conducted opera companies in Halle, Erfurt, Leipzig (1948–55), Schwerin (1958–60), and East Berlin (1960–64). His impressive work as orchestral conductor of the Dresden Philharmonic (1955–58, 1967–72) and Leipzig Gewandhaus Orchestra (1970–90) was admired in professional circles long before the average American concertgoer had heard his name. Following his British and American debuts (1973–74), he became the principal guest conductor of the Dallas Symphony (from 1976). In 1991 he succeeded Zubin Mehta as conductor of the New York Philharmonic.

Mehta, Zubin (b. 1936). Mehta (widely characterized as "exuberant, effulgent, and eloquent") was born in Bombay, the son of the Indian violinist Mehli Mehta, later conductor of the orchestra at UCLA. He abandoned his medical studies in Bombay after conducting lessons with Hans Swarowsky in Vienna and at the

Siena master classes (1956–57), eventually earning a diploma from the Vienna Conservatory (1957). After winning several conducting competititons, he appeared, in 1959, with the Vienna Symphony Orchestra and at a Lewisohn Stadium Concert of the New York Philharmonic. He was named music director of the Montreal Symphony Orchestra (1960–62). One of the first and probably the most glamorous of the jet-set conductors in the 1960s and '70s, he was able to manage with unfailing gusto his simultaneous directorships in Los Angeles (1962–78), and with the Israel Philharmonic (1962–77). In 1978, he succeeded Leonard Bernstein at the New York Philharmonic, resigning that post in 1990 to devote more time to the Israel Philharmonic, of which he had been named conductor for life and for which he has had a long affection (though he is not Jewish, but rather a Zoroastrian). He conducted in Israel during the Six-Day War in 1973, for the anniversary of the state of Israel in 1975, and in general whenever his presence would lend gravity to a ceremonial or historic occasion. In 1974 he was given an honorary doctorate from the University of Tel Aviv; in 1991, when guided missles were sent from Iraq toward Israel, he hurried there to be among the Israeli musicians.

Monteux, Pierre (1875–1964). Monteux attended the Paris Conservatoire and in his nineteenth year (1894) became choirmaster and assistant conductor of the famous Concerts Colonne, moving from there to conduct the chic summer concerts of the casino orchestra in Dieppe (1908–14). His earned his stardom with the Ballets Russes, conducting the first performances of *Daphnis and Chloe* (1912), *Petrushka* and *The Rite of Spring* (1911, 1913), and Debussy's *Jeux* (1913), among others. In 1917 he came to New York to conduct at the Metropolitan Opera, then was principal conductor of the Boston Symphony Orchestra (1919–24). He returned to Europe to conduct the Amsterdam Concertgebouw and to establish in Paris an École Monteux (from 1932); this marked the beginning of his quite substantial influence as teacher of a new generation of conductors, among whom are Neville Marriner and André Previn. During his long tenure as music director of San Francisco Symphony (1936–52), Monteux became an American citizen (1942). In his later years he organized an important conducting seminar at his home in Hancock, Maine.

Münch, Charles (1891–1968). Born in Strasbourg, Münch became a conductor after some time as concertmaster of the Gewandhaus orchestra in Leipzig. He guided the prestigious Société des Concerts du Conservatoire in Paris through the difficult war years (1938–46); then he abandoned it during a highly publicized quarrel with the general manager to accept the chief conductorship of the Boston Symphony Orchestra (1949–62). In Paris it was always hoped that he would return, such that it was a great triumph for all concerned when he was named the first music director of the new Orchestre de Paris, successor to the Société des Concerts organized along the very lines he had urged two decades before. This was the orchestra he was leading on tour when he died in Richmond, Virginia, following a concert in Raleigh, North Carolina. I was present in the audience that night, flush with my own discovery of conducting, and ca never forget the rafters resounding with the *Dies irae* as the venerable old man conducted Berlioz's *Symphonie fantastique* with the tiniest gestures I had ever seen.

Muti, Riccardo (b. 1941). He studied at the Conservatory of Naples, where he was born, and in Milan and Venice (with Franco Ferrara). As winner of the 1967 Guido Cantelli Competition, he was invited to conduct the RAI (Radio-Television of Italy) Orchestra of Milan and the Maggio Musicale ("May Music Festival"), the major orchestral concerts of Florence (1969–80). In 1970 he became principal conductor of the Florence Opera (Teatro Communale), meanwhile establishing growing prestige at the European summer festivals. While conductor of the Philharmonia Orchestra of London (1972–82, following Klemperer), he appeared frequently as principal guest conductor of the Philadelphia Orchestra (from 1975), then followed Eugene Ormandy as its music director (1980). In 1986 he succeeded Claudio Abbado as music director of La Scala. Muti's appearance on the podium is one of the most striking of the era, with his athletic build, shock of black hair, and look of intense concentration; the sounds that come out are competitive with the best anywhere, and his amicable rivalry with Abbado for dominion over the Verdi repertoire is one to watch.

Norrington, Roger (b. 1934). He was educated at Cambridge and studied conducting under Boult at the Royal Conservatory of Music. In 1962 he established the Heinrich Schütz Choir, a group which has made numerous important recordings of the Renaissance and Baroque choral repertoire. In 1978 he founded the London Classical Players, an ensemble that plays the Classical repertoire on period instruments and with what it understands to be authentic performance practice for the composer under scrutiny. The festivals of the London Classical Players ("The Mozart Experience," etc.) include scholarly lectures, seminars, and theatric presentations; their recordings, particularly those of the Beethoven symphonies (since 1987), have attracted intense international admiration and challenged some of our fundamental notions of how this music was meant to sound. Since 1990 the Norrington festivals have been repeated in Saratoga, New York, sponsored by the Pepsi-Cola corporation.

Ormandy, Eugene (1899–1985). Born in Budapest, he studied at the Royal Academy of Music there, emigrating to the United States in 1921. In New York he conducted the Capitol Theatre Orchestra from 1925, became a citizen in 1927, and in the summer of 1929 made his debut with the New York Philharmonic at a Lewisohn Stadium Concert. He served as music director of the Minneapolis Orchestra (1931–35), then began his astonishingly long association with the Philadelphia Orchestra, first as Leopold Stokowski's assistant (1936–38), then as his successor (1938–80). Under Ormandy the celebrated "Philadelphia sound" prospered and became legendary, and the orchestra gave many first performances (Rachmaninov's Symphonic Dances in 1941, for example, and Bartók's Third Piano Concerto in 1946). Ormandy was awarded the French Legion

Honor (1952, commander 1958), the Presidential Medal of Freedom (1970), and an honorary knighthood of the British Empire (1976, on the occasion of the American bicentennial); on his retirement he was named conductor laureate of the Philadelphia Orchestra.

Ozawa, Seiji (b. 1935). Born in Manchuria of Japanese parents, he had appeared with the NHK (Japanese Broadcasting) Symphony and the Japan Philharmonic by the time he graduated from the Toho School of Music in Tokyo (1959). He then moved to Europe, studying conducting with Charles Bigot in Paris, and attracted the attention of Charles Münch. The latter arranged for his further study at Tanglewood, where Ozawa won the Koussevitzky Prize in 1960 and an apprenticeship with Karajan and the Berlin Philharmonic. So it was that Leonard Bernstein heard Ozawa conduct in Berlin and, with the forthcoming Japanese tour of the New York Philharmonic in mind, engaged him as assistant conductor. He was music director of the Chicago Symphony's Ravinia Festivals (1964–68; also principal guest conductor of the Chicago Symphony), Toronto Symphony (1965–69), and San Francisco Symphony (1970–76). In 1970 he became artistic director of the Berkshire Music Center at Tanglewood; this led to his appointment in 1972 as advisor to the Boston Symphony, and in 1973 as its music director. Ozawa's tenure in Boston has been splendid indeed, featuring several international tours, including to China and Japan, and the glamorous centenary of the Boston Symphony in 1981.

Among his many first performances have been Toru Takemitsu's *Autumn* (Tokyo, 1973), György Ligeti's *San Francisco Polyphony* (1975), Peter Maxwell Davies's Second Symphony (1981), and Olivier Messiaen's opera *St. François d'Assise* (Paris, 1983). Ozawa is the most visible symbol of the remarkable contribution Asian musicians have made to concert music in recent decades; his gifts are virtually unrivaled, his technique one of consummate precision, and his interpretations knowledgeable, inspired, and loving. The atmosphere of an Ozawa performance is about as thrilling as they come.

Previn, André (b. 1929). Born in Germany of Russian-Jewish parents, he came to the United States with his family in 1939 after early studies at the Berlin Hochschule für Musik and the Paris Conservatoire. Family connections led to his engagement by MGM Studios in Hollywood, where Previn enjoyed considerable success as a composer-arranger-conductor of film and popular music. (He won, for example, four academy awards for his film scores: *Gigi,* 1958; *Porgy and Bess,* 1959; *Irma La Douce,* 1963; and *My Fair Lady,* 1964.) In 1951, while stationed with the Army in San Francisco, he studied orchestral conducting with Pierre Monteux. He made his debut on the podium with the St. Louis Symphony Orchestra (1962), then became conductor-in-chief of the Houston Symphony Orchestra (1967–69). He then served as principal conductor of the London Symphony Orchestra (1968–79, where he recorded the Vaughan Williams symphonies and became a popular television personality), music director of the Pittsburgh

Symphony (1976–86), and of the Los Angeles Philharmonic (1986–89). Si. 1985 he has also been principal conductor of the Royal Philarmonic, London.

Reiner, Fritz (1888–1963). A Hungarian, Reiner led the Chicago Symphony into the front ranks of American orchestras (1953–62). Before that he had con- ducted in Budapest, Dresden, Cincinnati (1922–31), and Pittsburgh (1938– 48); additionally, he was professor of conducting at the Curtis Institute of Music in Philadelphia, where among his students were the composer-conductors Leonard Bernstein and Lukas Foss. Reiner's reputation was as a stern and ruthless taskmaster, but his musicians took it in stride and now enjoy circulating a Reiner story for every Beecham anecdote that makes the rounds. His contribution to twentieth-century music, particularly for Cincinnati and Pittsburgh in those years, has been substantial; in 1984, a Fritz Reiner Center for Contemporary Music was established at Columbia University.

Salonen, Esa-Pekka (b. 1958). After studying French horn at the Sibelius Academy in Helsinki (1973–77), he went to Italy to study conducting and composition in Milan and Siena (1979–81). He soon established himself in Finland as an important composer; his conducting career was launched in 1983 when he replaced Michael Tilson Thomas in London on very short notice. In 1985 he was named conductor of the Swedish Radio Orchestra, where his repertoire has been adventurous in the extreme. His 1986 recording of Witold Lutosławski's Symphony No. 3 (for CBS) attracted international admiration. Salonen has been named music director of the Los Angeles Philharmonic, effective 1992.

Sawallisch, Wolfgang (b. 1923). He earned a degree from the Munich Conservatory in 1946, then was music director in Aachen (1953–57), Wiesbaden (1957–59), and Cologne (1959–63); he was the youngest conductor ever to appear at Bayreuth (1957, for *Tristan und Isolde*). Subsequently Sawallisch was music director of the Hamburg Philharmonic (1961–73) and chief conductor of the Vienna Symphony Orchestra (1960–70), which he brought to the United States in 1964. Thereafter he has been conductor of the Orchestre de la Suisse Romande (1970–80) and general music director of the Bavarian State Opera, Munich (1971–92). Sawallisch was named music director of the Philadelphia Orchestra, beginning in 1992.

Shaw, Robert (b. 1916). He attended Pomona College (1934–38), where he directed the glee club, then helped organize and conduct Fred Waring's Glee Club (through 1945). Meanwhile he became one of the nation's most influential teachers of choral conducting (including at Tanglewood, 1942–45; and Juilliard, 1946–49). In 1948 he founded the Robert Shaw Chorale, probably the most important vocal ensemble of its era, conducting it for two decades across the nation and on several international tours. The expansion of his career into orchestral conducting began when he studied with Monteux and Rodzinski in

. early 1950s; this led to his summer concerts with the San Diego Symphony ●rchestra (1953–58) and in turn to his appointment as choral associate to Szell in Cleveland (1956–67). Shaw thereupon became music director of the Atlanta Symphony Orchestra (1967–88), bringing that group to national prominence through fine recordings and, at the close of his tenure, a successful tour of Europe (1988).

Silverstein, Joseph (b. 1932). Born in Detroit, he joined the Boston Symphony Orchestra in 1955 and was its longtime concertmaster (1962–83) and assistant conductor (from 1971). He made increasingly frequent appearances as guest conductor, leading to his appointment as music director of the Toledo Orchestra (1979–80) and principal guest conductor of the Baltimore Symphony (1981–83). He left Boston to become musical director of the Utah Symphony Orchestra (since 1983), as successor to the legendary Maurice Abravanel, who had reigned over that orchestra for 32 years (1947–79).

Sinopoli, Giuseppe (b. 1946). Sinopoli studied medicine and music in Venice, his native city, before he began advanced studies in composition at Darmstadt (1968) and in conducting with Swarowsky in Vienna (1972). He was then appointed a professor of music at the Benedetto Marcello Conservatory in Venice (1972) and in 1975 founded the Bruno Maderna Ensemble, devoted to the performance of new music. From 1979 he conducted the contemporary music concerts of the Berlin Philharmonic as well. In 1983 he became permanent conductor of the Santa Cecilia Orchestra of Rome, made his New York Philharmonic debut, and was named principal conductor of the Philharmonia Orchestra of London; his Bayreuth debut followed in 1985. In 1990 Sinopoli became music director of the Berlin Opera.

Slatkin, Leonard (b. 1944). His parents were both noted professional musicians (and his brother is an excellent cellist). Slatkin studied conducting with his father, with Jean Morel at Juilliard (earning a degree in 1968), and Walter Susskind at Aspen. He made his conducting debut in Aspen at age nineteen; at twenty-two he led the Youth Symphony Orchestra of New York at Carnegie Hall. In 1968 he became assistant conductor in St. Louis, associate principal conductor in 1974, and music director in 1979. He appeared with most of the major American orchestras as well as the Concertgebouw and London Symphony Orchestra. Under Slatkin the St. Louis Orchestra has prospered at a time when many of its counterparts (Denver and Oakland, for example) had to fold. Slatkin also conducts the Grant Park Concerts in Chicago.

Solti, Georg (Sir) (b. 1912). Fleeing the German invasion, he arrived in Switzerland from Hungary in 1939. After World War II his career centered for a quarter century on opera, as he conducted the Bavarian State Opera, Munich (1946–52), the Frankfurt Opera (1952–61), and at Covent Garden (1961–71). In 1969 he began his stellar tenure as music director of the Chicago Symphony, where he remained until 1991. Solti was chosen to conduct the 1983 Salzburg

Ring on the hundredth anniversary of Wagner's death. He was made hon. Commander of the Order of the British Empire and in 1971 an honorary kni£ when he elected British citizenship in 1972 he thus became Sir Georg Solti. f succeeded von Karajan as artistic director of the Salzburg Easter Festival.

Stokowski, Leopold (1882–1977). Born in London of a Polish father and an Irish mother, Stokowski was an organist in England before coming to the United States to lead the Cincinnati Orchestra (1909–12). Afterward he conducted the Philadelphia Orchestra (1912–38), where he literally created the famed "Philadelphia sound," and the New York Philharmonic (1949–50). A great showman, he appeared in films (clowning, in *Fantasia*, with Mickey Mouse), admonished audiences from the podium, courted glamorous women (including Greta Garbo and Gloria Vanderbilt, whom he married), and assiduously cultivated stardom. He conducted without a baton, finding the hands alone to be more expressive. Stokowski often exercised questionable judgment and disregarded matters of historical authenticity altogether. None of this detracts from his accomplishment in the realm of orchestral sound: in this, he was a consummate master. In his later years he conducted the Houston Symphony (1955–61) and founded the American Symphony Orchestra (1962).

Szell, George (1897–1970). Szell, another Hungarian, first earned his reputation as a composer and pianist. He turned to conducting when, in 1917, Richard Strauss recommended him as principal conductor of the Strasbourg Opera. Subsequently he was conductor of the Berlin State Opera, a conductor and professor in Prague, and frequent guest conductor in England and the United States. His great achievement was the modern Cleveland Orchestra (see p. 655), which he conducted from 1946 until his death.

Tennstedt, Klaus (b. 1926). After studies in piano and violin at the Leipzig Conservatory, he was principal conductor at Halle (1948–57), the Dresden Opera (1958–60), the Mecklenberg State Theatre in Schwerin (1960–69), and the Kiel Opera (1970–75). Tennstedt's North American exposure began in 1974 with successful appearances in Toronto and Boston orchestras and an acclaimed debut with the New York Philharmonic in 1977. Thereafter he was principal guest conductor of the Minnesota Orchestra (1979–82) and conductor of the North German Radio Symphony Orchestra, Hamburg (1979 82). Tennstedt succeeded Solti as principal conductor and music director of the London Philharmonic Orchestra in 1983, the year he made a highly successful debut at the Metropolitan Opera with *Fidelio*.

Thomas, Michael Tilson (b. 1944). Born in Los Angeles and demonstrating his exceptional gifts in childhood, Thomas went to the University of Southern California; from age nineteen he conducted the Young Musicians Foundation Debut Orchestra (1963–67) and the Monday Evening Concerts of new music in Los Angeles. He was assistant to Boulez at the Ojai Festival of 1967 and subsequently had an ongoing affiliation there. In 1968 he won the Koussevitzky Prize

.nglewood, which led to his engagement as assistant conductor of the Boston
..phony at age twenty-four; after taking over at intermission from the ailing
√illiam Steinberg in October 1969, he was named associate conductor in Boston. He served as principal guest conductor with that orchestra (1972–74), was
music director of the Buffalo Philharmonic (1971–79), and music director of the
New York Philharmonic Young People's Concerts (1971–76). Thomas conducted the first complete American performance of Berg's *Lulu* at the Santa Fe
Opera in 1979, and from 1981 was principal guest conductor with Simon Rattle
of the Los Angeles Philharmonic. He was elected music director of the London
Symphony Orchestra in 1988. Michael Tilson Thomas is an engaging personality
and a *bon vivant* of markedly good humor—as keen for his Gershwin (he is a fine
pianist) as for his Schoenberg.

Toscanini, Arturo (1867–1957). After cello studies at the conservatories in
Parma and Milan, Toscanini became a member of the opera orchestra in Rio de
Janeiro. There, in 1886, he rescued a performance of *Aïda* by conducting it from
memory after two other conductors had failed to complete the work. He was
soon engaged to conduct at the famous La Scala opera house in Milan, and later
at the Metropolitan Opera in New York. For the rest of his life, these two cities
were his primary spheres of activity, though his successes at Bayreuth, the Salzburg Festival, and elsewhere in Europe were notable. But his most lasting fame
was as director of the NBC Symphony Orchestra (1937–54), which was founded
primarily to give him a prestigious American forum. (Rodzinski trained the new
group, and Monteux conducted the first performance in November 1937; Toscanini first conducted on Christmas Day that year. In 1954 NBC withdrew its
support and the orchestra's successor, which called itself the Symphony of the
Air, was short-lived.) Recordings of many of the NBC Symphony concerts survive and have been re-released; there is also some memorable film.

Toscanini's repertoire revolved around the greatest masterworks of Beethoven,
Verdi, Brahms, Wagner, and Debussy. For these he was able to create performances that stood for more than a generation as definitive. His hallmarks are
electric excitement in tempo and volume, crisp and vigorous attacks, fanatic
devotion to the letter of the score, and perhaps most of all, careful attention to
lyricism of phrase. (His favorite remark to his orchestras was "Cantare, cantare,
cantare" ["sing, sing, sing"].) It is said that his fiery temperament brought new
intensity and meaning to Verdi's works, while his innate Italian lyricism added
new warmth and richness to the work of the German masters. It was Toscanini
and Ormandy, I believe, who popularized the conducting of symphonic concerts
from memory, though in Toscanini's case the practice had more to do with
myopia than principle.

For all his bombast, Toscanini was personally insecure, embarrassed by applause,
and prone to decline honorary degrees and other forms of public recognition.
During the War, he refused to conduct in Germany or the occupied territories
and made a point of conducting the Jewish Orchestra both in Palestine and

Egypt; afterward he was an important voice in the reconstruction of Italian m
cal institutions.

Zinman, David (b. 1936). He earned a bachelor's degree from Oberlin (1958,
and an M.A. from the University of Minnesota (1963) simultaneous with conducting studies at Tanglewood and an assistantship with Pierre Monteux in Maine
(1961–64). After a long and impressive tenure as conductor of the Netherlands
Chamber Orchestra (1964–77), he became music director of the Rochester Philharmonic (1974–85) and the Rotterdam Philharmonic (1979–82). He was named
music director of the Baltimore Symphony Orchestra in 1984. He has brought
that orchestra to the forefront of American musical life through imaginative
programing, recordings, and tours, among the latter a visit to the Soviet Union
in 1987.

Glossary

—⟨∞⟩—

A CAPPELLA: For voices alone, without instrumental accompaniment.

ACCELERANDO: Speeding up.

ADAGIETTO: A short, slow movement in a tempo somewhat faster than adagio.

ADAGIO: A slow tempo—between andante and largo.

AD LIBITUM: Optional.

ALBERTI BASS: Rapid and repeated broken triads comprising a left-hand accompaniment figure in the manner of eighteenth-century keyboard compositions; named for the Italian composer Domenico Alberti (c. 1710–40).

ALLARGANDO: Broadening (and, often, swelling).

ALLEGRETTO: Moderately fast, but not as fast as allegro.

ALLEGRO: Fast. Often used with the following modifiers (as in *Allegro con brio*), all of which are defined in this glossary: *assai, cantabile, con brio, ma non troppo, maestoso, moderato, molto, spirioso, vivace.*

ALLEMANDE (Ital. *allemanda*): A Baroque dance in moderate duple meter, usually the first in a suite of dances.

ANTE: Literally, "walking," i.e., moving along.

ANDANTINO: Somewhat faster than andante.

ANIMATO: Animated, lively.

ANSWER: In a fugue, the entry of the theme at a different pitch level from the subject.

ANTECEDENT: The initial four measures of an eight-measure phrase (followed by the **consequent**).

ANTIPHONAL: Performing in alternation, as in the case of brass choirs exchanging material from two separate lofts in a cathedral.

ARIA: An accompanied composition for vocal soloists within the context of a larger work.

ARIOSO: A freely lyrical passage, in style somewhere between an aria and a recitative.

ARPEGGIO: A broken chord, with the notes sounded one after the other rather than all at once. Literally "harplike" (as a harp might play).

ASSAI: Quite, as in *Allegro assai.*

A TEMPO: Back to the main or first speed.

ATONAL: Lacking a key center.

AUGMENTATION: Increasing the note values of a theme, thus making it slower; opposite of **diminution**.

BAR: see **measure**

BEL CANTO: Literally, "beautiful singing," the florid style of early nineteenth-century Italian opera.

BITONAL: Implying two keys at once, typically when one voice or choir of instruments is playing in one key as a second voice or choir goes on in another.

BOURRÉE: A French dance in fast duple meter in a Baroque suite, it usually follows the **sarabande**.

CADENCE: Harmonic formula bringing a phrase, section, or movement to its end.

CADENZA: Originally, an improvised passage in a concerto designed to show the soloist's virtuosity and understanding of the composition.

CANON: Literally, "according to rule." A composition for two or more parts in which the leader is imitated exactly by the follower(s), though not always at the same pitch level.

CANTABILE: Singingly; like a song.

CANTUS FIRMUS: A voice part based on a pre-existing melody, often heard in long notes. In any number of eighteenth- and nineteenth-century compositions a medieval chant is the cantus firmus.

CAPRICCIO: A free, lively work, often an orchestral showpiece.

CELESTA: A keyboard instrument in which metal plates are struck by hammers; the name characterizes the sound, which is much gentler than that of the glockenspiel or xylophone.

CHACONNE: A composition built over a repeating bass pattern; for all inten[s] and purposes equivalent to a **passacaglia.**

CHANSON: French for "song," implying a light or theatrical song.

CHORALE: Originally, a Lutheran congregational hymn; in orchestral writing, a hymn-like passage, usually homophonic.

CHORD: The simultaneous sounding of three or more notes.

CHROMATIC: A scale resulting from the division of the octave into twelve semitones or half-steps; an instrument is said to be chromatic when it can produce all the semitones within its range; a passage in which these semitones occur is called chromatic.

CIRCLE OF FIFTHS: The arrangement of the twelve major or minor keys in which adjacent keys are five scale-steps apart (a "fifth"); going up increases the number of sharps and decreases the number of flats; going down has the reverse effect. In either direction, equivalent keys are eventually reached (G$\flat$ = F$\sharp$)—thus it is called a "circle."

CLEF: The sign found at the beginning of a staff indicating the position of a specific pitch.

CODA: The concluding section of a piece.

CODETTA: A short, conclusive section, like the one at the end of a sonata exposition.

COL LEGNO: Striking the strings with the wood of the bow.

COLLEGIUM MUSICUM: A musical association for the performance of serious music; nowadays usually affiliated with an academic institution.

COLORATURA: Highly florid and embellished ornamentation; also the kind of high soprano who specializes in such music.

CON BRIO: With brightness and spirit.

CONCERTANTE: Describing a work in which two or more players have virtuosic solo parts, as in a *sinfonia concertante.*

CONCERTINO: The group of soloists in a Baroque concerto grosso, as opposed to the orchestral ensemble, or **ripieno.**

CONCERTO: Multi-movement work for solo instrument(s) and orchestra.

CONCERTO GROSSO: Baroque concerto type based on the opposition between a small group of soloists (the **concertino**) and the orchestra (the **ripieno**).

CON FUOCO: Furiously.

CON MOTO: With motion.

CONSEQUENT: The second half of an eight-measure phrase (preceded by the **antecedent**).

CONTINUO: Short for "basso continuo," the bass line and the chords improvised above it by the keyboard player in Baroque music; the continuo force includes any or all of the bass instruments and a harpsichord or organ.

CONTRALTO: The lowest female voice; also called alto.

CONTRAPUNTAL: Describing music consisting of two or more strands heard simultaneously; in the style of counterpoint.

CONTREDANSE: A country dance, often of rustic melody and instrumentation.

CORRENTE; COURANTE: Italian and French versions, respectively of a Baroque dance in triple meter, often the second dance in a suite following the **allemande.** The Italian variety is typically rapid, the French rather slower and given to metric ambiguity.

COUNTERPOINT: The combining of individual melodic lines in pleasing, and correct, polyphony.

COUNTERSUBJECT: In fugal writing, a theme played simultaneously with the fugue subject or answer.

CRESCENDO: ———————— Growing louder.

DA CAMERA: For the chamber, as opposed to the church (*da chiesa*). Sonatas and concertos *da camera* typically include movements in dance forms.

DA CAPO: "From the head": a direction to the performers to go back to the beginning of the movement.

DA CHIESA: For the church, as opposed to the chamber (*da camera*). Sonatas and concertos *da chiesa* typically include fugal movements.

DECRESCENDO: ———————— Growing softer.

DIATONIC: A scale consisting of five whole tones and two semitones in prescribed order, such as the major or minor scales; an interval found in the diatonic scale.

DIES IRAE: Medieval chant for the dead, the longest movement in a Requiem mass.

DIMINUENDO: Growing softer.

DIMINUTION: Decreasing the note values of a theme, thus making it faster; opposite of **augmentation.**

DIVERTIMENTO, DIVERTISSEMENT: A light composition, a "diversion"; used in the eighteenth century to describe the sort of works written for the amusement of the players or the entertainment of guests.

DOLCE: Sweetly.

DOMINANT: The fifth degree of the major or minor scale, or the chord built on it, having the strongest pull toward tonic resolution.

DOUBLE FUGUE: A fugue having two equally prominent subjects, or one where the subject and its countersubject are equally important at all times.

DOUBLE-STOP: A sonority produced by playing two strings simultaneously.

DOWNBEAT: The accented beat at the beginning of a measure.

FANTASIA: A free composition. Used to describe many Romantic character pieces by composers like Schubert, Liszt, and Brahms. Twentieth-century composers, such as Schoenberg, Tippett, and Vaughan Williams, have used the title for extended instrumental pieces.

FARANDOLE: A dance from southern France usually in a moderate, $\frac{6}{8}$ tempo.

FEIERLICH: Solemn, festive.

FERMATA: ⌢ A sign instructing the performer to sustain a pitch or chord at will or until instructed by the conductor to continue.

FIGURED BASS: A Baroque practice wherein numerical figures are placed below the bass line indicating the chords to be played by the performer at the keyboard in the continuo ensemble.

FLUTTER-TONGUING: Articulation of wind instrument pitches by rolling the tongue against the palate.

FORTE (*f*): Loud.

FORTISSIMO (*ff*): Very loud.

FROG: The base of the bow, where the hairs are attached.

FUGATO: A passage in fugal style in a primarily noncontrapuntal work.

FUGUE: see page 35.

GALOP: A lively ballroom dance in $\frac{2}{4}$ time.

GAVOTTE (Ital. *gavotta*): A Baroque dance of moderate duple meter and prominent upbeat, favored by Bach in his dance suites.

GIGUE (Ital. *giga*): A dance movement in triple time, usually the last in a suite of dances; it evolved from the Irish and English jig.

GIOCOSO: Merrily, playfully.

GLISSANDO: An effect achieved by sliding rapidly through the pitches of a scale.

GRACE NOTE: A decorative, neighboring pitch, played quickly and without fixed rhythmic value.

GRAVE: Slow, solemn; an instruction often found at the opening of a Baroque overture.

GRAZIOSO: Gracefully.

GROUND BASS (Ital. *basso ostinato*): A short melody recurring many times with continuous variation in the upper parts.

HARMONIC: A very high pitch, usually of eerie sound, artificially produced by forcing a string or wind column to vibrate at one of its high subdivisions.

HOMOPHONIC: Describing musical texture in which all the parts move in the same rhythm, resulting in a conventional chord progression; the typical sound of hymns and chorales.

IMPROVISATION: Creation of a musical work as it is being performed and without the aid of notated music.

INTERMEZZO: Originally a light dramatic entertainment to go between the acts of a more serious opera; later used to describe short nineteenth-century piano works (particulary by Brahms) of a somewhat casual nature.

INTERVAL: The distance separating two pitches; also the simultaneous sounding of two tones.

INVERSION: Reversing the nature of a musical relationship: one can invert two voices by putting the lower of a pair on top, or invert a theme by turning each interval in the opposite direction.

APELLMEISTER: Literally, chapel-master: a court composer-conductor who wrote music for and led the palace opera and orchestra. The Kapellmeister and his musicians also provided the music for religious services. Same as *maestro di cappella*.

KEY: The main note or tonal center to which all the notes in a piece gravitate.

LÄNDLER: A slow, waltz-like dance of Austrian origin.

LANGSAM: Slow.

LARGAMENTE: Grandly; broadly.

LARGHETTO: Less slow and dignified than largo.

LARGO: Quite slow; broad.

LEBHAFT: Lively; brisk.

LEGATO: Connected; smooth; the opposite of **staccato**.

LENTO: Slow.

LIBRETTO: The text of an opera, generally distributed as a small booklet.

LIED(ER): Term generally used for the Romantic art song(s), especially in German.

MA: But, as in *Allegro ma non troppo*.

MAESTOSO: Majestic.

MAESTRO DI CAPPELLA: Same as *Kapellmeister*.

MASS: See p. 36.

MÄSSIG: Moderately.

MAZURKA: Polish dance in fast triple meter, often accenting the "weak" beat in the measure. One of Chopin's favorite forms.

MEASURE (also **bar**): A metrical unit indicated in written music by vertical lines (barlines) on the staff.

MELISMATIC: Characterized by florid melodic work, generally on a single syllable of text.

MENO: Less, as in *meno mosso*.

MEZZO: Half; medium, as in *mezzo piano* and *mezzo forte* (**mp, mf**). Also short for mezzo-soprano, the female voice lower than soprano and higher than contralto.

MINUET: A dance of French origin in moderate triple meter. Often the third movement in a classical sonata cycle.

MODAL: Based on scalar patterns derived from the medieval and Renaissance church modes, therefore neither major nor minor.

MODERATO: Moderately.

MODULATION: Moving from one key to another, as in a modulation from C major to G major.

MOLL: Minor, as in Bach's Messe in H Moll (B-Minor Mass).

MOLTO: Very, as in *Molto adagio*.

MONOPHONIC: For a single voice or instrumental part, as in plainchant or other unaccompanied song.

MONOTHEMATIC: Having a single predominant theme.

MORENDO: Dying away.

MOSSO: Motion; speed.

MOTET: An unaccompanied choral composition, sometimes with sacred L.
text. Actually the meaning mutated over the years from its first use ("piec
with texted parts") in the thirteenth century; eventually it was used for almost
any sacred choral work that is not a mass.

NON TROPPO: Not too much, as in *Allegro non troppo*.

NOTTURNO: Nocturne: a piece of night music, often quiet and lyrical.

OBBLIGATO: Required; a part that must not be omitted.

OPUS: Latin for "work"; the number assigned to a composition that suggests its
order within the composer's output.

ORATORIO: A large dramatic work for soloists, chorus, and orchestra to biblical
texts; performed without scenery or costumes.

ORDINARY: That part of a Catholic mass common to every feastday (see p. 36).

OSTINATO: A persistent (i.e., obstinate) repeated figure, either rhythmic, harmonic, or melodic.

PASSACAGLIA: See p. 35.

PASSEPIED: A French court dance and instrumental form of the seventeenth
and eighteenth centuries; gay and spirited in quick $\frac{3}{8}$ or $\frac{6}{8}$ meter.

PASTORALE: A work of bucolic character, usually in $\frac{6}{8}$ and often with drones
and piped melody.

PEDAL: A lever operated by the foot which can alter pitch or produce expressive
effects.

PEDAL POINT: A sustained or repeated note, usually in the bass, around which
other harmonic activity is carried on.

PERPETUUM MOBILE: Perpetual motion, usually a movement or passage of great
speed and uninterrupted passagework.

PESANTE: Heavily.

PIANISSIMO (*pp*): Very soft.

PIANO (*p*): Soft

PIÙ: More, as in *più mosso*.

PIZZICATO: Plucking the string (rather than bowing it).

POCO: A little; somewhat, as in *poco forte*.

POLKA: A lively couple dance of Bohemian origin in duple meter.

POLONAISE: A stately Polish dance, with the character of a grand march.

POLYPHONIC: Musical texture consisting of multiple parts moving in independent lines of equal importance, i.e., contrapuntally.

POLYRHYTHM: Simultaneous use of contrasting rhythms.

POLYTONAL: Simultaneous use of more than two different keys.

PONTICELLO: The bridge of a string instrument (see also, **sul ponticello**).

MENTO: A smooth and rapid sliding between two pitches.

ISSIMO: Extremely fast (generally speaking, as fast as possible).

TO: Fast.

OGRAM MUSIC: Instrumental music with literary or pictorial associations; especially popular in the nineteenth century.

QUARTER-TONE: A pitch that falls between two notes a half-step or semitone apart.

RALLENTANDO: Slowing down.

RECITATIVE (RECITATIVO): A type of vocal setting that is imitative of speech.

REQUIEM: The Mass for the dead of the Roman Catholic Church.

RETROGRADE: Backwards; a refashioning of a theme to begin at the end and continue back to the beginning.

RHAPSODY: An instrumental piece of loose, episodic form.

RIPIENO: The orchestral ensemble in a Baroque concerto grosso, as opposed to the group of soloists, or **concertino.**

RITARDANDO (RITARD): A gradual slowing down.

RITENUTO: Held back; more sudden than ritardando.

RITORNELLO: A short, recurring passage in a composition; a primary compositional practice in Baroque music; also used to describe repeated tutti passages in concertos from later periods. (See pp. 34–35.)

ROMANZA: A ballad-like lyric movement, often the second movement of a solo concerto.

RONDO: A musical form in which the main section recurs, usually in the tonic, between subsequent sections. (See p. 34.)

RUBATO: Manner of playing in which time is "borrowed" from one portion of the measure to allow hesitation or haste in another; it imparts flexibility to written note values.

SARABANDE (Ital. *sarabanda*): A Baroque dance in triple meter, often the third in a suite. The French and German varieties are slow and stately, characterized by short-long (quarter, half) patterns; the Italian variety is rather faster.

SCENA: In Italian opera and its imitators, a dramatic scene for one character embracing a sequence of diverse episodes, typically recitative, aria, and rapid close.

SCHERZANDO: Playfully; jokingly.

SCHERZETTO: A short, usually brisk piece of scherzo character.

SCHERZO: A dance form widely used by Beethoven as an alternative to the minuet in multimovement works; A–B–A form in triple meter.

SCHNELL: Fast.

SCORDATURA: An unconventional tuning of a stringed instrument in order to increase its range or achieve a special effect.

SECCO: Short for *recitativo secco* (dry recitative).

SEMITONE: Also called half-step, the distance between two adjacent notes on keyboard.

SEMPLICE: Simply.

SEMPRE: Always.

SEQUENCE: Restatement of a motive at different pitch levels.

SERIAL: Describing compositional method in which the elements (e.g. pitch, rhythm, attack, dynamic) are organized in a fixed series.

SFORZANDO, SFORZATO: Sudden sharp accent on a single note or chord.

SICILIANA (Fr. *sicilienne*): Instrumental movement of pastoral nature, typically in $\frac{12}{8}$.

SONATA: See pp. 29–34.

SORDINO: Mute (*con sordino*, with mutes; *senza sordino,* without).

SOSTENUTO: Sustained in duration, sometimes with the implication of a slower than usual tempo, as in *Andante sostenuto.*

SOTTO VOCE: In an undertone.

SPIRITOSO: Spirited.

STACCATO: Short, detached; the opposite of **legato.**

STRETTO: In a fugue, overlapping imitation at close distance, usually near the end of a work.

STRINGENDO: Accelerating.

STURM UND DRANG: "Storm and stress," a literary movement in eighteenth-century Germany. The term is also applied to pre-Classical and Classical symphonies displaying fervent emotionalism.

SUBITO: Suddenly; abruptly; as in *subito forte.*

SUBJECT: A theme on which a composition is based.

SUL PONTICELLO: Played at the bridge of a stringed instrument for muted effect.

SUSPENSION: A pitch held over from a previous chord, becoming thereby dissonant before resolving downward to consonance.

SYMPHONIC POEM: One-movement orchestral form in which a poetic or narrative idea is developed.

SYMPHONY: An extended work for orchestra, usually in three or four movements.

SYNCOPATION: Shifting the accent to the weak beats of a measure.

TEMPO: The rate of speed in a piece of music.

TESSITURA: The prevailing range in which a piece of music lies.

TIMBRE: Tone color, the distinguishing character of an instrumental or vocal sound.

THEME: Melodic idea used as a basic element in the construction of a piece of music.

TONIC: The first scale degree, or the chord built on it; it defines the key of the work.

TRANQUILLO: Quiet.

TRANSPOSITION: The notation or performance of music at a pitch other than the original one.

TREMOLANDO: With tremolo; tremolo-like.

TREMOLO: The rapid repetition of a tone, most often heard in the strings, achieved by very rapid alternation of bowing

TRIAD: Chord consisting of three pitches built on alternate tones of the scale.

TUTTI: Everybody; the entire performing force.

UNISON: The interval between two notes identical in pitch.

UPBEAT: The weak beat at the end of a measure that anticipates the downbeat.

VALSE: Waltz.

VIBRATO: Fluctuation of pitch by alternating just above and below it; used by vocalists and woodwind and string players to enrich the sound.

VIVACE: Lively, bright, vivacious.

VIVO: Alive, vigorous.

ZU: Too, as in *nicht zu schnell.*

Suggestions
for
Further
Reading

————◦⟨∞⟩◦————

I. REFERENCE

Nearly everything a concertgoer might need to know can be found, in English, in one of the following four reference works:

The New Grove Dictionary of Music and Musicians, ed. Stanley Sadie (London: Macmillan, 1980). This is an expensive twenty-volume set summarizing virtually the whole of recent musicological scholarship. Among its many treasures are to be found articles on individual composers with worklists and bibliography, on genres and styles, on musical instruments, and on the musical life of individual cities and nations.

Baker's Biographical Dictionary of Musicians, 7th edition, ed. Nicolas Slonimsky (New York: Schirmer Books, 1984). Articles on composers, performers, and others of importance to the history of music, with summary worklists and good bibliography.

The New Harvard Dictionary of Music, ed. Don Michael Randel (Cambridge, Mass.: Harvard University Press, 1986). A one-volume dictionary of terms, foreign words,

ِbjects as acoustics, musical instruments, and harmonic practice. It does
ٰe biographies of composers.

ٰrton / Grove Concise Encyclopedia of Music, ed. Stanley Sadie with Alison Latham
ٰ York: Norton, 1988). A one-volume distillation of the twenty-volume set
ِ.cribed above, considerably updated, and more likely to be in your price range.

In paperback there are, among others, the Harvard Concise Dictionary of Music, ed.
Don M. Randel (Cambridge, Mass.: Belknap Press); the Concise Oxford Dictionary of
Music, 4th edition, ed. Michael Kennedy (London: Oxford University Press, 1991);
and a Dictionary of Music by Theodore Karp (New York: Dell, 1973).

II. RECORDINGS AND SCORES

The old Schwann Catalogue of recordings in print is now entitled Opus, and subtitled America's Guide to Classical Music. It is published quarterly and is available at
most record stores, some newstands, and by individual subscription. There is also a
fancy new electronic listing called the CD Guide which you may consult in some
libraries and record shops.

Scores for the music of nearly every major composer are available in complete editions,
encyclopedia-like reference works which try to assemble the most critical texts for a
composer's works. Complete editions of the major composers are found in university
libraries and sometimes circulate to holders of library cards. Inexpensive editions of
many musical masterpieces are also available in reprints from Dover Publications of
New York.

III. INDIVIDUAL COMPOSERS

Works available in paperback are prefaced with an asterisk (*).

BACH
*David, Hans T., and Arthur Mendel, eds. The Bach Reader, rev. (New York: Nor-
    ton, 1966)
Geiringer, Karl, with Irene Geiringer. Johann Sebastian Bach: The Culmination of an
    Era (New York: Oxford University Press, 1966)
*Wolff, Christoph, et al. The New Grove Bach Family (New York: Norton, 1983)

BARBER
Broder, Nathan. Samuel Barber (New York: Schirmer, 1954)
*Jackson, Richard with Barbara Heyman. "Samuel Barber." In The New Grove Twen-
    tieth-Century American Masters (New York: Norton, 1988)

BARTÓK
*Lampert, Vera, and László Somfai. "Béla Bartók." In The New Grove Modern Masters
    (New York: Norton, 1984)
Stevens, Halsey. The Life and Music of Béla Bartók, rev. (New York: Oxford Univer-
    sity Press, 1967)

BEETHOVEN
Arnold, Denis, and Nigel Fortune, eds. The Beethoven Reader (New York: Norton,
    1971)

*Forbes, Elliot, ed. *Thayer's Life of Beethoven,* rev. ed. (Princeton, N.J.: Prince University Press, 1964)

*Solomon, Maynard. *Beethoven* (New York: Schirmer, 1977)

*Tyson, Alan, and Joseph Kerman. *The New Grove Beethoven* (New York: Norton, 1983)

BERG

Jarman, Douglas. *The Music of Alban Berg* (Berkeley and Los Angeles: University of California Press, 1978)

*Peile, George. "Alban Berg." In *The New Grove Second Viennese School* (New York: Norton, 1983)

Reich, Willi. *The Life and Works of Alban Berg* (New York: Da Capo, 1982)

BERLIOZ

Berlioz, Hector. *Memoirs,* trans. and ed. David Cairns (Chicago: University of Chicago Press, 1987)

Holoman, D. Kern. *Berlioz* (Cambridge, Mass.: Harvard University Press, 1989)

*Macdonald, Hugh. "Hector Berlioz." In *The New Grove Early Romantic Masters 2* (New York: Norton, 1985)

BERNSTEIN

Gradenwitz, Peter. *Leonard Bernstein* (New York: St. Martin's, 1987)

*Peyser, Joan. "Leonard Bernstein." In *The New Grove Twentieth-Century American Masters* (New York: Norton, 1988)

BIZET

Curtiss, Mina. *Bizet and His World* (Westport, Conn.: Greenwood Press, 1977)

Dean, Winton. *Georges Bizet: His Life and Work,* 3rd ed. (London: Dent, 1975)

BLOCH

Strassburg, R. *Ernest Bloch: Voice in the Wilderness* (Los Angeles: Trident, 1977)

BORODIN

*Abraham, Gerald, with David Lloyd-Jones. "Alexander Borodin." In *The New Grove Russian Masters 1* (New York: Norton, 1986)

Dianin, Sergei A. *Borodin,* tr. and ed. Robert Lord (New York and London: Oxford University Press, 1963)

BOULEZ

Griffiths, Paul. *Boulez* (London: New York Press, 1978)

*Hopkins, G.W. "Pierre Boulez." In *The New Grove Twentieth-Century French Masters* (New York: Norton, 1986)

BRAHMS

*Becker, Heinz. "Johannes Brahms." In *The New Grove Late Romantic Masters* (New York: Norton, 1985)

Geiringer, Karl. *Brahms: His Life and Works,* 3rd ed. (New York: Da Capo, 1981)

BRITTEN

*Evans, Peter. "Benjamin Britten." In *The New Grove Twentieth-Century English Masters* (New York: Norton, 1986)

..ddington, Christopher. *Britten* (London: Methuen, 1981)

Palmer, Christopher, ed. *The Britten Companion* (London: Faber & Faber, 1984)

BRUCKNER

Schönzeler, Hans Hubert. *Bruckner* (London: Grossman, 1970)

Simpson, Robert. *The Essence of Bruckner* (London: Gollancz, 1967)

CARTER

Edwards, Allen. *Flawed Words and Stubborn Sounds: A Conversation with Elliott Carter* (New York: Norton, 1972)

*Northcott, Bayan. "Elliott Carter." In *The New Grove Twentieth-Century American Masters* (New York: Norton, 1988)

Schiff, Elliott. *The Music of Elliott Carter* (New York: Da Capo, 1983)

CHABRIER

Myers, Rollo. *Emmanuel Chabrier and His Circle* (London: Dent, 1965)

CHAUSSON

Grover, R. Scott. *Ernest Chausson: The Man and His Music* (Lewisburg, Pa.: Bucknell University Press, 1980)

CHOPIN

*Temperley, Nicholas. "Fryderyk Chopin." In *The New Grove Early Romantic Masters 1* (New York: Norton, 1985)

*Walker, Alan. *The Chopin Companion: Profiles of the Man and the Musician* (New York: Norton, 1973)

COPLAND

*Austin, William W., with Vivian Perlis. "Aaron Copland." In *The New Grove Twentieth-Century American Masters* (New York: Norton, 1988)

Copland, Aaron, and Vivian Perlis. *Copland: 1900 through 1942* (New York: St. Martin's, 1984)

————. *Copland: Since 1943* (New York: St. Martin's, 1989)

CORELLI

Pincherle, Marc. *Corelli* (New York: Da Capo, 1971)

DEBUSSY

Lockspeiser, Edward. *Debussy: His Life and Mind,* 2 vols. (New York: Macmillan, 1965)

*Nichols, Roger. "Claude Debussy." In *The New Grove Twentieth-Century French Masters* (New York: Norton, 1986)

Vallas, Léon. *Claude Debussy: His Life and Works* (New York: Dover, 1973)

DVOŘÁK

Clapham, John. *Dvořák* (New York: Norton, 1979)

ELGAR

Kennedy, Michael, *Elgar: Orchestral Music* (London: BBC, 1970)

*McVeagh, Diana. "Edward Elgar." In *The New Grove Twentieth-Century English Masters* (New York: Norton, 1986)

Parrott, Ian. *Elgar* (London: Dent, 1971)

FALLA

Burnett, Manes. *Manuel de Falla and the Spanish Musical Renaissance* (Londc
   lancz, 1979)

Crichton, Ronald. *Falla* (London: BBC, 1982)

FAURÉ

Orledge, Robert. *Gabriel Fauré,* rev. ed. (London: Eulenburg, 1983)

*Nectoux, Jean-Michel. "Gabriel Fauré." In *The New Grove Twentieth-Century French
   Masters* (New York: Norton, 1986)

FRANCK

Davies, Laurence. *Franck* (London: Dent, 1973)

GERSHWIN

*Crawford, Richard, with Wayne Schneider. "George Gershwin." In *The New Grove
   Twentieth-Century American Masters* (New York: Norton, 1988)

Jablonski, Edward, and Lawrence D. Stewart. *The Gershwin Years,* 2nd ed. (New
   York: Doubleday, 1973)

Kimball, Robert, and Alfred Simon. *The Gershwins* (New York: Athaneum, 1973)

GLINKA

*Brown, David. "Mikhail Glinka." In *The New Grove Russian Masters 1* (New York:
   Norton, 1986)

GRIEG

Horton, John, *Grieg* (London: Dent, 1974)

HANDEL

*Dean, Winton, with Anthony Hicks. *The New Grove Handel* (New York: Norton,
   1983)

Hogwood, Christopher. *Handel* (London: Thames and Hudson, 1984)

*Lang, Paul Henry. *George Frideric Handel* (New York: Norton, 1966)

HAYDN

Geiringer, Karl. *Haydn: A Creative Life in Music,* rev. (Berkeley and Los Angeles:
   University of California Press, 1982)

Landon, H. C. Robbins, and David Wyn Jones. *Haydn: His Life and Music* (Bloom-
   ington, Ind.: Indiana University Press, 1988)

*Larsen, Jens Peter, with Georg Feder. *The New Grove Haydn* (New York: Norton,
   1983)

HINDEMITH

*Kemp, Ian. "Paul Hindemith." In *The New Grove Modern Masters* (New York: Norton, 1984)

Skelton, Gregory. *Paul Hindemith: The Man Behind the Music* (London: Gollancz,
   1975)

HOLST

Holst, Imogen, *The Music of Gustave Holst,* 3rd ed. (London: Oxford University Press,
   1985)

Short, Michael, *Gustave Holst: A Centenary Documentation* (London: White Lion, 1974)

...der, J. Peter. *Charles Ives: The Ideas Behind the Music* (New Haven: Yale University Press, 1985)

...rkpatrick, John, ed. *Charles E. Ives: Memos* (New York: Norton, 1991)

Kirkpatrick, John, with Paul Echols. "Charles Ives." In *The New Grove Twentieth-Century American Masters* (New York: Norton, 1988)

* Perlis, Vivian. *Charles Ives Remembered: An Oral History* (New York: Norton, 1976)

JANÁČEK

* Tyrell, John. "Leos Janáček." In *The New Grove Turn-of-the-Century Masters* (New York: Norton, 1985)

KODÁLY

Young, Percy M. *Zoltán Kodály: A Hungarian Musician* (London: Benn, 1985)

LISZT

* Searle, Humphrey. "Franz Liszt." In *The New Grove Early Romantic Masters 1* (New York: Norton, 1985)

Walker, Alan. *Franz Liszt: The Virtuoso Years, 1811–47* (Ithaca, N.Y., Cornell University Press, 1987)

———. *Franz Lizst: The Weimar Years, 1848–61* (New York: Knopf, 1989)

MAHLER

* Banks, Paul, and Donald Mitchell. "Gustav Mahler." In *The New Grove Turn of the Century Masters* (New York: Norton, 1985)

* Cooke, Deryck. *Gustav Mahler: An Introduction to His Music* (Cambridge: Cambridge University Press, 1985)

* Lebrecht, Norman, ed. *Mahler Remembered* (New York: Norton, 1990)

Mitchell, Donald. *Gustav Mahler: The Early Years,* rev. ed. with Paul Banks and David Matthews (Berkeley and Los Angeles: University of California Press, 1980)

———. *Gustav Mahler: The Wunderhorn Years* (Berkeley and Los Angeles: University of California Press, 1980)

———. *Gustav Mahler: Songs and Symphonies of Life and Death* (Berkeley and Los Angeles: University of California Press, 1985)

MENDELSSOHN

* Köhler, Karl-Heinz. "Felix Mendelssohn." In *The New Grove Early Romantic Masters 1* (New York: Norton, 1985)

Werner, Eric. *Mendelssohn: A New Image of the Composer and His Age* (New York: Free Press, 1963)

MILHAUD

Collaer, Paul, *Darius Milhaud* (San Francisco: San Francisco Press, 1988)

Milhaud, Darius. *Notes without Music,* tr. Donald Evans; ed. Rollo Myers (London: Calder & Boyars, 1967)

MOZART

Anderson, Emily, ed. *The Letters of Mozart and His Family* (New York: Norton, 1985)

* Blom, Eric. *Mozart* (New York: Macmillan, 1966)

*Lang, Paul Henry, ed. *The Creative World of Mozart* (New York: Norton, 1963)

*Sadie, Stanley. *The New Grove Mozart* (New York: Norton, 1983)

Zaslaw, Neal, with William Cowdery. *The Compleat Mozart* (New York: Norton, 1991)

MUSSORGSKY

*Abraham, Gerald. "Modest Musorgsky." In *The New Grove Russian Masters 1* (New York: Norton, 1986)

Seroff, Victor. *Modeste Mussorgsky* (New York: Funk and Wagnalls, 1968)

PAGANINI

Day, Lillian. *Paganini of Genoa* (London: Gollancz, 1966)

PENDERECKI

Robinson, Ray. *Krysztof Penderecki: A Guide to his Works* (Princeton, N.J.: Prestige, 1983)

PISTON

Pollack, Howard. *Walter Piston* (Ann Arbor, Mich.: UMI, 1982)

POULENC

*Daniel, Keith W. *Francis Poulenc: His Artistic Development and Musical Style* (Ann Arbor, Mich.: UMI, 1982)

*Nichols, Roger. "Francis Poulenc." In *The New Grove Twentieth-Century French Masters* (New York: Norton, 1986)

PROKOFIEV

*McAllister, Rita. "Sergey Prokofiev." In *The New Grove Russian Masters 2* (New York: Norton, 1986)

Robinson, Harlow. *Prokofiev* (New York: Viking, 1987)

RACHMANINOV

*Norris, Geoffrey. "Sergey Rakhmaninov." In *The New Grove Russian Masters 2* (New York: Norton, 1986)

*Piggot, Patrick. *Rachmaninov: Orchestral Music* (London: BBC, 1974)

RAVEL

*Hopkins, G.W. "Maurice Ravel." In *The New Grove Twentieth-Century French Masters* (New York: Norton, 1986)

Nichols, Roger, ed. *Ravel Remembered* (New York: Norton, 1988)

Orenstein, Arbie. *Ravel: Man and Musician* (New York: Columbia University Press, 1975).

RESPIGHI

Respighi, Elsa. *Ottorino Respighi: His Life Story* (New York: Ricordi, 1971)

RIMSKY-KORSAKOV

*Abraham, Gerald. "Nikolay Rimsky-Korsakov." In *The New Grove Russian Masters 2* (New York: Norton, 1986)

———. *Rimsky-Korsakov: A Short Biography* (London: Duckworth, 1949)

Rimsky-Korsakov, Nicolai. *My Musical Life,* tr. Judah A. Joffe, rev. ed. (New York: Knopf, 1942)

ROSSINI

*Gossett, Philip. "Gioachino Rossini." In *The New Grove Masters of Italian Opera* (New York: Norton, 1983)

Weinstock, Herbert. *Rossini, A Biography* (New York: Knopf, 1968)

SAINT-SAËNS

Harding, James. *Saint-Saëns and His Circle* (London: Chapman and Hall, 1965).

SATIE

*Gillmor, Alan M. *Erik Satie* (New York: Norton, 1992)

*Gowers, Patrick, with Nigel Wilkins. "Erik Satie." In *The New Grove Twentieth-Century French Masters* (New York: Norton, 1986)

Wilkins, Nigel, tr. and ed. *The Writings of Erik Satie* (London: Eulenberg, 1980)

SCHOENBERG

*Neighbour, Oliver W. "Arnold Schoenberg." In *The New Grove Second Viennese School* (New York: Norton, 1983)

*Rosen, Charles. *Arnold Schoenberg* (Princeton, N.J.: Princeton University Press, 1981)

Stuckenschmidt, Hans H. *Arnold Schoneberg: His Life, World, and Work,* tr. Humphrey Searle (London: Calder, 1977)

SCHUBERT

*Brown, Maurice J. E., with Eric Sams. *The New Grove Schubert* (New York: Norton, 1983)

Deutsch, Otto Erich. *Schubert: Memoirs by His Friends* (New York: Humanities, 1958)

Hilmar, Ernst. *Franz Schubert in His Time* (Portland: Amadeus, 1989)

SCHUMANN

*Abraham, Gerald. "Robert Schumann." In *The New Grove Early Romantic Masters 1* (New York: Norton, 1985)

*Walker, Alan, ed. *Robert Schumann: The Man and His Music* (London: Barrie and Jenkins, 1976)

SESSIONS

*Harbison, John, with Andrea Olmstead. "Roger Sessions. " In *The New Grove Twentieth-Century American Masters* (New York: Norton, 1988)

SHOSTAKOVICH

Norris, Christopher, ed. *Shostakovich: The Man and His Music* (London: Laurence & Wishart, 1982)

*Schwarz, Boris. "Dimitry Shostakovich." In *The New Grove Russian Masters 2* (New York: Norton, 1986)

SIBELIUS

*Layton, Robert. "Jean Sibelius." In *The New Grove Turn of the Century Masters* (New York: Norton, 1985)

Tawaststjerna, Erik. *Sibelius* (Berkeley and Los Angeles: University of California Press, 2 vols. 1976, 1986)

SMETANA
Large, Brian. *Smetana* (New York: Praeger, 1970)

STRAUSS, J.
Gartenberg, Egon. *Johann Strauss: The End of an Era* (University Park, Pa., Penn. State University Press, 1974)

STRAUSS, R.
Del Mar, Norman. *Richard Strauss: A Critical Comentary on His Life and Work,* 3 vols. (Ithaca: Cornell University Press, 1986)
*Kennedy, Michael. "Richard Strauss." In *The New Grove Turn of the Century Masters* (New York: Norton, 1985)

STRAVINSKY
*Stravinsky, Igor. *An Autobiography* (New York, Norton, 1962)
*White, Eric Walter. *Stravinsky: The Composer and His Works,* 2nd ed. (Berkeley and Los Angeles: University of California Press, 1979)
*White, Eric Walter, and Jeremy Noble. "Igor Stravinsky." In *The New Grove Modern Masters* (New York: Norton, 1984)

TCHAIKOVSKY
Abraham, Gerald. *The Music of Tchaikovsky* (New York: Norton, 1974)
*Brown, David. "Pyotr Il'yich Tchaikovsky." In *The New Grove Russian Masters 1* (New York: Norton, 1986)
————. *Tchaikovsky: The Early Years, 1840–74;* id., *Tchaikovsky: The Crisis Years, 1874–78;* id., *Tchaikovsky: The Years of Wandering, 1878–85;* id., *Tchaikovsky: The Final Years, 1885–93* (New York: Norton, 1978, 1983, 1986, 1992)
Warrack, John. *Tchaikovsky* (New York: Scribner, 1973)

TIPPETT
*Kemp, Ian. "Michael Tippett." In *The New Grove Twentieth-Century English Masters* (New York: Norton, 1986)
————. *Tippett : The Composer and His Music* (London: Eulenberg, 1984)

VARÈSE
Ouellette, Fernand. *A Biography of Edgard Varèse* (London: Calder & Boyars, 1973)
Varèse, Louise, *Varèse: A Looking Glass Diary* (New York: Norton, 1972)

VAUGHAN WILLIAMS
Hurd, Michael. *Vaughan Williams* (London: Faber & Faber, 1970)
*Ottaway. Hugh. "Vaughan Williams." In *The New Grove Twentieth-Century English Masters* (New York: Norton, 1986)

VERDI
*Budden, Julian. *The Operas of Verdi,* 3 vols. (New York: Oxford, 1984)
*Porter, Andrew. "Giuseppe Verdi." In *The New Grove Masters of Italian Opera* (New York: Norton, 1983)
Walker, Frank. *The Man Verdi* (Chicago: University of Chicago Press, 1982)

VIVALDI
*Pincherle, Marc. *Vivaldi* (New York: Norton, 1962)

ER

chridge, John, and Carl Dahlhaus. *The New Grove Wagner* (New York: Norton, 1983)

Gutman, Robert. *Richard Wagner: The Man, His Mind, and His Music* (New York: Harcourt Brace Jovanovich, 1974)

*Millington, Barry. *Wagner* (New York: Vintage, 1987)

WEBERN

*Griffiths, Paul. "Anton Webern." In *The New Grove Second Viennese School* (New York: Norton, 1983)

Kolneder, Walter. *Anton Webern: An Introduction to His Works,* tr. Humphrey Searle (Berkeley and Los Angeles: University of California Press, 1968)

Index